TAKING SIDES

Clashing Views in

Educational Psychology

TAKING SIDES

Clashing Views in

Educational Psychology

FOURTH EDITION

Selected, Edited, and with Introductions and Postscripts by

Leonard Abbeduto
University of Wisconsin–Madison

McGraw-Hill **Contemporary Learning Series**

To Sheldon Rosenberg—my mentor, colleague, and friend

Photo Acknowledgment
Cover image by D. Berry/PhotoLink/Getty Images
and PhotoDisc Collection/Getty Images

Cover Acknowledgment
Maggie Lytle

Copyright © 2006 by McGraw-Hill Contemporary Learning Series
A Division of The McGraw-Hill Companies, Inc., Dubuque, Iowa 52001

Manufactured in the United States of America

Fourth Edition

123456789DOCDOC98765

Library of Congress Cataloging-in-Publication Data
Main entry under title:
Taking sides: clashing views on controversial issues in educational psychology/selected, edited,
and with introductions by Leonard Abbeduto. -4th ed.
Includes bibliographical references and index.
1. Multicultural education. I. Abbeduto, Leonard,comp
370.19
0-07-319510-3
ISSN: 1091-8787

Printed on Recycled Paper

Preface

The field of educational psychology seems to be constantly enmeshed in controversy. Some of the controversies are ongoing; occasionally, the debate may die down a bit only to return in full force again, perhaps in a slightly different form. Other controversies are more short-lived; either they are resolved or they are abandoned as intractable. From the outside it may seem that these controversies reflect inefficiency and a lack of progress in the field of educational psychology. But are these controversies really as counterproductive as they appear?

In fact, controversies provide the foundation for deeper understanding of the educational issues involved, thereby leading to progress. This is not merely my personal belief. There is considerable empirical evidence from research in educational psychology and cognitive science to support the contention. It is not too difficult to see why this is the case. When we engage in discussion of a controversy, we are forced to muster evidence to support our position and to fully develop in a systematic fashion all of its implications. This can lead us to see gaps in our evidence and fallacies in our reasoning, or to recognize previously unrealized implications. As a result, we may decide to gather additional evidence, modify our position, or even abandon it entirely. It is this spirit of controversy and argumentation that is the basis of this textbook.

This book contains 18 issues in educational psychology, each of which has elicited sharply divergent responses from scholars and practitioners. I have organized these issues into three parts. In the first part are issues that concern the impact of the diverse needs and characteristics of the students found in most classrooms in U.S. schools today: gender equity, ability-level tracking, bilingual education, inclusion of students with special educational needs, the achievement gap between ethnic and racial majority and minority students, and affective and moral education. In the second part are issues that concern the theoretical foundations of teaching and learning in the classroom: the value of constructivism, the effectiveness of rewards for enhancing student learning, the educational implication of Howard Gardner's theory of multiple intelligences, the impact of standards on student motivation, and the pedagogical implications of recent work on brain development. The final part of the book features issues surrounding the effectiveness of teaching and assessment in the classroom: the whole language approach to teaching reading, the impact of parental involvement on student outcomes, the role of new technologies in education, the educational value of performance assessments, methods for dealing with violent and disruptive students, and comparisons of U.S. schools with schools in other industrialized nations.

Each issue is stated as a question and is represented by two previously published articles, the first supporting a yes answer to the question and the second arguing a no response. Each issue is accompanied by an introduction, which provides background and a context for evaluating the articles. Each issue ends with a *postscript*, which points out additional dimensions on which the issue might be analyzed as well as suggesting some further reading. I have also provided a brief introduction to each part of the book as well as relevant Internet site addresses (URLs) on the *On the Internet* page accompanying the introduction to each part.

Changes to this edition   To bring this edition of *Taking Sides: Clashing Views in Educational Psychology* up to date, two issues have been added: "Can Schools Close the Achievement Gap Between Students from Different Ethnic and Racial Backgrounds?" (Issue 5) and "Is Greater Parental Involvement at Schools Always Beneficial?" (Issue 14). In addition, for one of the issues retained from the third edition—Issue 1 on the value of single-gender classes— has been replaced to bring a fresh perspective to the debate. In all, there are five new selections. Also, many of the postscripts have been revised to include more recent suggestions for further reading.

A word to the instructor   An Instructor's Manual With Test Questions (multiple choice and essay) is available for use with Taking Sides. Also available is a general guidebook, *Using Taking Sides in the Classroom*, which includes a discussion of techniques for integrating the pro–con format into an existing course. Instructors adopting this text also have access to an online version of *Using Taking Sides in the Classroom* as well as a correspondence service at http://www.mhcls.com/usingts/.

Taking Sides: Clashing Views in Educational Psychology* is only one of many titles in the Taking Sides series. Users of this text may find *Taking Sides: Clashing Views on Controversial Educational Issues* and *Taking Sides: Clashing Views on Controversial Psychological Issues* to be particularly relevant to some of the issues considered in the present text. For a complete table of contents for these or any other title in the Taking Sides series, visit the Taking Sides Web site at http://www.mhcls.com/takingsides/.

Acknowledgments   I am indebted to Terry McMenamin for her many hours of painstaking library work and for her thoughtful comments on many of the introductions and postscripts in this volume. Thanks also to my colleagues at the University of Wisconsin–Madison for their support and for teaching me so much about educational psychology. Thanks must also go to Jackson and Mark Abbeduto for their editorial and clerical assistance. Finally, this book would not have been possible without the encouragement, boundless understanding, and good humor of my wife, Terry, and my sons, Jackson and Mack, and my mother, Dorothy—I am forever in their debt.

Leonard Abbeduto
University of Wisconsin–Madison

Contents In Brief

Contents

Janice Streitmatter, a professor of educational psychology, found that the behavior and attitudes of girls in gender-segregated classes are dramatically different from, and more success-oriented than, those of girls in coeducational classes. She argues that the culture and practices of the coeducational classroom limit educational opportunities for girls in a way that can now be overcome most easily (or perhaps only) through gender segregation. Jo Sanders and Sarah Cotton Nelson argue that gender differences in achievement in physics, chemisty, and computer sciences are caused by inequities in classroom practices that deny young girls full participation in the activities required for success in these acedemic domains. They also describe a program initiated in the Dallas school system in which the classroom behavior of teachers and students in coeducational classrooms is targeted for change so as to provide more gender-equitable pedagogical experiences.

Jeannie Oakes and Amy Stuart Wells, both professors in the Graduate School of Education and Information Studies at the University of California, Los Angeles, argue that tracking ensures that low-achieving students will be exposed to a watered-down curriculum, have access to fewer educational resources, and experience a less-than-stimulating school environment, all of which will prevent them from ever escaping their low-achieving track. They argue that all students should be expected to master the same curriculum. Professor of educational psychology Sally M. Reis and her colleagues argue that detracking leads teachers to adopt a middle-of-the-road curriculum that fails to challenge the best and brightest students in the class. They argue that teachers do not know how to meet the needs of gifted children within the context of a heterogeneous classroom; thus, tracking is critical for the success of the best and brightest students.

Educational consultant Keith Baker argues that empirical evidence indicates that Structured English Immersion, which provides academic instruction in English, leads to larger gains in academic achievement and English mastery than bilingual education, which provides academic instruction in the students' native language. Josephine Arce, assistant professor of elementary education, College of Education, at San Francisco State University, argues that the anti-bilingual-education movement sweeping the country has resulted from a conservative political agenda designed to oppress racial and ethnic minorities. She asserts that the empirical evidence supports the superiority of bilingual education over Structured English Immersion.

Mara Sapon-Shevin, a professor of education at Syracuse University, argues that all students, whatever the nature of their disability, are best served within the "regular" classroom alongside their typically developing peers. Naomi Zigmond, chair of the department of instruction and learning at the University of Pittsburgh, and Janice M. Baker, assistant professor of special education and clinical services at Indiana University of Pennsylvania, argue that the accommodations that teachers make are seldom tailored to the needs of the particular students with disabilities enrolled in their classes. They maintain that meaningful remediation requires some form of "pull out" from the regular classroom.

Carol Corbett Burris and Kevin G. Welner argue that the achievement gap between white students and African-American and Hispanic students is a consequence of the over-representation of students from ethnic and racial minorities in low ability-track classes. They argue that the watered-down curriculum and low expectations associated with low ability-track classes prevent ethnic and racial minority students from achieving the same levels of academic success as white students. William J. Mathis argues that the achievement gap between white and African-American and Hispanic students has been created by discriminatory social and political pressures that pervade all facets of life. He argues that it is, therefore, unreasonable to expect to eliminate the gap through curricular or other innovations in the schools. Mathis cites school vouchers as an example of a failed attempt to use schooling as a means of undoing the achievement gap.

Robert Sylwester, an emeritus professor of education at the University of Oregon, argues that self-esteem is rooted in brain biology and that low self-esteem can result in impulsive and violent actions. He sees schools as a particularly important mechanism for delivering the positive feedback and successes that are required for the development of high self-esteem. Carol S. Dweck, a professor in the department of psychology at Columbia University, argues that programs to boost self-esteem have not had the hoped-for positive effects on student achievement. She argues that the indiscriminate use of praise makes students passive and fearful of losing the favorable opinion of others.

Thomas Lickona, a professor of education at the State University of New York College at Cortland, argues that U.S. schools must return to the teaching of character, or morality. He also proposes a set of core values that should be the basis of such teaching and outlines a plan for implementation. Alfie Kohn is a professional writer and lecturer who frequently addresses psychological and educational issues and controversies. Kohn questions whether current programs of moral education can have a lasting impact and, if they do, whether they have the outcome that is best for a democratic society.

Mark Windschitl, an assistant professor in the department of curriculum and instruction at the University of Washington, argues in favor of constructivism, a child-centered approach to education that is defined by student participation in hands-on activities and extended projects that are allowed to "evolve" in accordance with the students' interests and initial beliefs. E.D.Hirsch, Jr., a professor in the School of Education at the University of Virginia, Charlottesville, argues that child-centered approaches have failed and points to research demonstrating the superiority of fact-based, teacher-centered approaches.

Tashawna K. Duncan, Kristen M. Kemple, and Tina M. Smith from the School of Teaching and Learning at the University of Florida, argue that reinforcement has a long history of successful application in the classroom. They dismiss concerns that it lowers intrinsic motivation or that it is ethically equivalent to paying children to learn. They do acknowledge, however, that reinforcement must be integrated with a consideration of the developmental and unique needs of each child. Charles H. Wolfgang, a professor of early childhood education, admits that reinforcement and other techniques derived from behaviorist theory do control children's behavior in the short term. He asserts, however, that such techniques do little to encourage internalization of the types of standards that will ultimately lead children to behave effectively and appropriately in a range of situations in the future.

Howard Gardner, a professor in the Graduate School of Education at Harvard University, discusses what he considers to be seven misunderstandings, or myths, that have surrounded his theory of multiple intelligences. He also discusses the implications of the theory for educational practice. Perry D. Klein, a member of the Faculty of Education at the University of Western Ontario, argues that although a number of diverse pedagogical practices have been inspired by Gardner's theory, the theory is really too broad to be particularly informative about education.

Lauren B. Resnick, a professor of psychology at the University of Pittsburgh, argues that setting clear achievement standards for *all* students, not just those who are assumed to have the highest academic aptitude, will motivate students to work harder and, thus, increase achievement by all students. Kennon M. Sheldon and Bruce J. Biddle, both members of the faculty of the department of psychology at the University of Missouri, argue that an emphasis on standards is inconsistent with the mission of schooling because it rewards (and punishes) students and teachers for achieving a narrowly defined set of outcomes.

Mariale M. Hardiman, principal of a combined elementary and middle school in Baltimore, Maryland, argues that the pedagogical techniques that are employed in her school are successful because they fit with what is known about how the human brain works. John T. Bruer, president of the James S. McDonnell Foundation, an organization that provides financial support to researchers investigating basic and applied problems in the behavioral and biomedical sciences, argues that although scientists have recently learned many interesting things about the developing human brain, this research currently has little direct application to education.

Steve Zemelman, Harvey Daniels, and Marilyn Bizar, faculty in the Center for City Schools at National-Louis University, argue that there is substantial empirical evidence supporting the effectiveness of a whole language approach to teaching reading. G. Reid Lyon, chief of the Child Development and Behavior Branch of the National Institute of Child Health and Human Development (NICHD), argues that becoming a skilled reader requires explicit, systematic, and direct instruction and practice.

Laura Van Zandt Allen and Eleanor T. Migliore point to evidence that parental involvement in children's schooling is associated with improvements in children's academic performance and social-emotional development. Van Zandt Allen and Migliore also describe a program to help teachers solicit and use parental input, something the authors argue few teachers are normally prepared to do. Although Rodney T. Ogawa acknowledges that there is evidence that parental involvement has a positive impact on student outcomes, he questions the assumption that if some parental involvement is good, more must be even better. Ogawa argues, instead, that schools must build "buffers" as well as bridges between themselves and parents.

Marcia C. Linn, a professor of cognition and development, and James D. Slotta, director of the Web-based Integrated Science Environment (WISE) project library at the University of California, Berkeley, present an overview of the WISE project, which is designed to teach science and technological literacy through Web-based activities. They contend that this project will make teachers more effective and increase their flexibility in the classroom. R. W. Burniske, of the Computer Writing and Research Lab at the University of Texas, Austin, argues that schools have been too uncritical in their acceptance of technology and that computer-based education, in many instances, may actually contribute to the very problems it is intended to correct.

D. Monty Neill, executive director of the National Center for Fair and Open Testing, argues that performance assessment is consistent with the emphasis on standards and accountability of the high-stakes testing reform movement but avoids many of the pitfalls of traditional approaches to testing. Edward H. Haertel, a professor in the School of Education at Stanford University, argues against the philosophy of "high-stakes testing and accountability" and contends that performance assessment does not make this philosophy any more palatable or successful than does the use of traditional standardized tests.

The late Albert Shanker, long-time president of the American Federation of Teachers (AFT), advocates a policy of zero tolerance for violence and other disruptive behavior in school. He argues that such a policy is necessary because disruptive and violent behavior denies equal access to educational opportunities for the nonoffending students in a class or school. Russ Skiba, director of the Institute for Child Study at Indiana University, and Reece Peterson, a member of the faculty in the Department of Special Education at the University of Nebraska, argue that despite several recent, highly publicized incidents of violence, there are no data to support the contention that there has been an increase in school-based violence, nor are there data demonstrating the effectiveness of zero-tolerance policies in deterring violence and crime.

Richard M. Haynes and Donald M. Chalker, professors of administration, curriculum, and instruction, summarize the results of their analysis of the educational systems in 10 countries, including the United States and several countries considered by many to have successful, or "world-class," schools. They identify eight dimensions of difference between U.S. and world-class educational systems—dimensions that they feel explain the relative lack of success of U.S. schooling. Ernest G. Noack, a faculty member in education, argues that comparisons between the U.S. educational system and the educational systems of other countries are not useful because schooling serves a role in the United States that is different from that in other countries.

Introduction

Leonard Abbeduto

What Is Educational Psychology?

Educational psychology has traditionally been defined as the application of psychological theories, methods, and findings to the study of learning and teaching. This has led educational psychologists to study such topics as the development of particular academic skills (e.g., reading); the ways in which children acquire and represent knowledge in particular substantive domains (e.g., mathematics), and how those representations are supported or hindered by classroom instruction; individual differences in intelligence and achievement, and their relation to classroom instruction; how student motivation is related to learning and to different pedagogical practices; the relations between different domains of ability and functioning in students, including the relation between the cognitive and social domains; how best to assess ability, achievement, and teaching effectiveness; and how to effect change in the beliefs and practices of teachers.

Such a diverse range of interests has always required an eclectic approach. Thus, educational psychologists have traditionally drawn on the concepts and tools of many of the subdisciplines of psychology: developmental psychology, psychometrics, cognitive psychology, clinical psychology, learning science, and social psychology, to name but a few. In recent years, moreover, educational psychologists have begun to more fully understand the complexity of the factors and systems at play in teaching and learning. This has led them to cross disciplinary boundaries and draw on the theories, methods, and findings from other disciplines, including cultural anthropology, linguistics, philosophy, educational administration, political science, sociology, and social work. In turn, they have begun to ask questions and examine variables that have not previously been seen as within their purview, such as the relation between family variables and academic performance, the role of cultural identity in student achievement, the relation between economic conditions and pedagogical practices, the impact of changing societal conceptions of juvenile crime on the educational process, the role of the school in the life of a community, and the interaction between experience and the biological processes underlying brain function and development.

Educational psychologists have also begun to see the need to more fully understand the domains that form the subject matter of schools, which has led them to questions about the nature of expertise in domains such as mathematics and science. And finally, educational psychologists have come to view themselves as the agents of educational reform. In short, traditional boundaries between educational psychology and other disciplines concerned with children, families, learning education, and social change have begun to blur. This expansion of scope and crossing of disciplinary boundaries, however, have meant that educational psychologists have become enmeshed in an increasing number of controversies.

Controversies in Educational Psychology: Where They Come From and How They Can Be Resolved

In this text, each of 18 controversies has been framed as a question, such as *Should ability-level tracking be abandoned? Should English immersion replace bilingual education?* and *Is full inclusional ways the best option for children with disabilities?* This approach is useful because, at its most basic level, educational psychology is the science of providing answers to questions about teaching and learning. Sometimes these questions arise from outside the field of educational psychology or even from outside the field of education, as when business leaders turn to educators with questions about how to prepare children for the technological workplace they will face as adults, or when political leaders ask educational psychologists whether or not the inclusion of students with disabilities within the regular classroom is "working." At other times, the questions come from within the field of educational psychology itself, as in the case of questions about the best way to measure student achievement. Whatever the sources of these questions, it often happens that educational psychologists and other stakeholders in the educational process end up holding sharply different views about the answers. What creates these controversies? Why do experts in the field hold contrasting theories and beliefs? Analyzing some of the causes of controversies in educational psychology may allow us to understand the paths that must be taken to resolve them.

Empirical Data

Many questions become controversial because the empirical data needed to supply the answer are lacking. In some cases, the lack of data simply reflects the fact that the question has been asked only recently and, thus, there has not been sufficient time to conduct the necessary research. In other cases, however, the question has become controversial *because* of thedatathathave been collected. That is, the data generated have been inconsistent across studies or can be interpreted as providing support for conflicting theories. Such ambiguity often occurs when the question has been addressed through a *correlational* approach rather than through an *experimental* approach.

In a correlational study, an investigator examines the relationship that exists naturally between two or more variables. In this approach, the scientist does not control or manipulate nature but, rather, measures it, or at least parts of it. Consider, for example, the controversy surrounding the implementation of explicit uniform educational standards and procedures for ensuring the accountability of students, teachers, and schools for failing to achieve those standards (Issue 11). One way to address this "standards" question would be to find schools that have adopted the approach for some length of time and compare the achievement of the students in those schools to the achievement of students from schools that have not adopted such an approach. The interpretative problems for such a study, as for any correlational study, are that there may be other differences between the two types of schools—differences that have nothing to do with standards—and that these unmeasured differences may really be responsible for any differences in student achievement that are observed. These differences might include differences in family demographics (e.g., socioeconomic status, race, and ethnicity), resources available to the schools, level of parental commitment, and so on.

Such alternative interpretations could be ruled out by adopting an experimental approach. In an experiment, the researcher exerts control over the variables. In a true experiment, participants (e.g., students, classes, or schools) are assigned at random to the various *conditions* of interest (e.g., the standards and nonstandards approaches in our example). The value of such random assignment is that—given a large enough sample of participants—it ensures that the conditions being compared are similar on all variables except those being studied. So, for example, if we have a large number of schools in our sample and we assign them randomly to the standards and the nonstandards conditions, we will end up, on average, with about the same number of affluent and economically disadvantaged schools in each condition, the same number of ethnically diverse and ethnically homogeneous schools in each condition, the same number of initially high-achieving and low-achieving schools in each condition, and so on. Such similarity across conditions makes for unambiguous results. In this example, an experimental approach would entitle us to conclude unambiguously that any differences in student achievement observed between the two types of schools had been caused by the difference in their adoption of the standards approach.

If the experimental approach allows for unambiguous interpretation and the correlational approach does not, it would seem sensible to always opt for the former and thereby avoid any controversy about what the data say. Unfortunately, it is not that simple. For many questions about teaching and learning, it is not possible to do an experiment. Either the situation does not allow the researcher to control the relevant variables or control can be achieved only by creating such an artificial version of the phenomenon to be studied that the possibility of generalizing from the results of the experiment to the "real world" seems remote. Examining the relative effectiveness of gender-segregated and coeducational classes (Issue 1) provides an example of a question that does not easily lend itself to an experimental approach. In particular, it is likely that many students, parents, teachers, and school administrators will feel strongly about whether gender segregation is a good idea or not. This means that it is highly unlikely that they will submit to being randomly assigned to a gender-segregated or coeducational class. And if random assignment is not possible, neither is the experimental approach. In this case, we might need to be content with comparisons among naturally formed classes (i.e., the correlational approach), trying to rule out some of the alternative interpretations by recourse to other statistical or logical means.

In the *postscript* to each of the 18 issues in this volume, I have briefly summarized the empirical data that are available and discussed whether or not these data have helped to fuel the controversy. Much of what I have had to say in this regard hinges on the distinction between the correlational and experimental approaches. I also have made suggestions, when possible, about the studies needed to resolve the controversies, as well as pointing out the difficulties that might be encountered in such studies.

Theoretical Perspectives

Questions can also become controversial because different theories provide different answers. The role of theory in advancing scientific understanding is frequently misunderstood. This misunderstanding most often takes the form of a statement (or an attitude) such as "It's only a theory" (meaning "as opposed to a fact or objective truth"). But it would be impossible for any science—including the science of educational psychology—to advance very far without theories. Theories serve three purposes:

1. Theories specify which observations arerelevant and which are irrelevant to understanding the phenomena of interest. By way of illustration, consider the task of understanding children's cognitive development. Think of all the things that a child does in his or her very busy day. Although the child engages in many behaviors, not all will be relevant to understanding how his or her cognitive skills develop. We might easily dismiss behaviors such as sneezing, blinking, coughing, giggling, and a host of other seemingly irrelevant behaviors. But what about cases in which the child talks to himself or herself while trying to figure out how a toy works? Or how about the length of time he or she stares at a math problem before beginning to work on it with pencil and paper? For these and a host of other behaviors, theories tell us whether these behaviors are relevant or irrelevant to understanding cognitive development.

2. Theorieshelp to explain the observations that have been collected about the phenomena of interest. They tell us why the observations are relevant. In the theory of Jean Piaget, for example, children's self-talk (i.e., talking aloud to the self) is relevant to understanding cognitive development because it reflects the child's egocentrism, or self-centeredness—a characteristic that prevents the child from recognizing flaws in his or her reasoning about other people and about problems in the physical world. In Piaget's theory, self-talk is a behavior to be overcome by development.

3. Theories generate predictions that can then be tested by collecting new observations. If the predictions are supported, then we can have more confidence in the theory. If the predictions are not supported, then we must either revise the theory or abandon it. Consider, for example, the explanation of the infant's formation of an attachment to its parent. Behaviorist theories traditionally proposed that the infant "learns" to become attached to its mother not because of any quality of the mother or infant but

because the mother typically provides food and, thus, comes to have reinforcing properties. One of the predictions of such a theory is that the failure of a mother to provide food should preclude the infant's attachment to her. In fact, this prediction was not supported either by experimental work with nonhuman primates or by correlational studies involving humans. Hence, behaviorist theories have been largely abandoned by researchers seeking to understand attachment.

Although theories serve valuable roles, typically the process of theory testing is a protracted one. Seldom do the results of a single empirical study lead to the rise of one theory and the downfall of another. In part, this is because theories often can be revised to accommodate inconsistent results—although at some point the revisions may become so extensive as to render the theory useless. In addition, different theories often lead their proponents to examine very different sorts of observations (i.e., those depicted as relevant by the theory), which means that direct comparison of the predictions of contrasting theories is sometimes difficult or impossible. Whatever the reasons, the fact is that different theories, each of which attempts to explain the same phenomena (e.g., classroom learning), can coexist and enjoy support, which, of course, ensures controversy. Eventually, however, these controversies will be resolved as evidence accumulates in favor of one theory and against the others.

The role of theory in generating (and resolving) controversy is an important theme throughout this book. In fact, the controversies in Part 2 of this book are motivated almost entirely by theoretical disputes. The reader will see that often the controversies emerge from the clash of formal theories—theories built within, and explicitly recognized by, a particular academic discipline, such as educational psychology. In some instances, however, the reader will see that the controversy is fueled by informal theories that are held tacitly by the people involved and that are the product of the contexts in which they themselves have lived and grown.

Contextual Influences on the Stakeholders in the Educational Process

Many of the controversies that arise in educational psychology are not the product of vagaries in empirical data or of the existence of competing theories. Instead, many controversies result from contextual influences on the various stakeholders in the educational process—students, teachers, administrators, parents, civic leaders, and politicians. The late William Kessen, a professor at Yale University, was among the first to draw attention to the influence of context on children and on those who care for and study children. He outlined these influences in the provocatively entitled article "The American Child and Other Cultural Inventions," AmericanPsychologist(October 1979). Three of Kessen's points are particularly important for understanding the source (and the potential resolution) of many of the 18 controversies considered in this text.

1. Children's lives and development are shaped by the contexts in which they live.   These contexts are multidimensional and can be defined by, among other things, physical variables (e.g., whether or not children are exposed to lead paint through living in an older home), family variables (e.g., whether they live in a two-parent or single-parent home), economic variables (e.g., whether their families are impoverished or affluent), social variables (e.g., whether they live in a safe or high-crime neighborhood), institutional variables (e.g., whether they are required to attend school or to hold down a job), cultural variables (e.g., beliefs and practices related to disciplining children), and historical variables (e.g., whether they happen to live during a time of war or peace). When we think about children attending schools in the United States today, for example, we need to remember that those children are living in very different contexts than were children living during, for example, the early part of the twentieth century. We should also remember—especially as we compare today's students in the United States to those attending schools in other countries—that the contexts for children in the United States may differ in important respects from those of children in Japan or in South Africa. And finally, we should remember that not all children attending U.S. schools today are growing up in precisely the same contexts. Unfortunately, far too many children come to school carrying the scars of homelessness, abuse, and racial discrimination— scars that may interfere with their ability to derive maximum benefit from the educational opportunities afforded them. In other words, Kessen argued that the diverse circumstances of children's lives—diversity across historical time, across cultures or nations, and even within a culture or nation—can lead to a diversity of outcomes.

Many of the questions considered in this text have arisen in part because of such contextually determined diversity. Concerns about the decline in student achievement in the United States in recent years have led to the question of whether or not schools should return to a curriculum that emphasizes "basic" academic skills and drill-and-practice (Issue 8). Concerns about lower levels of achievement, particularly in mathematics and science, among students in the United States compared to students in industrialized nations in Europe and Asia have led to a variety of questions about whether and how U.S. education should be reformed (Issue 18). Concerns about the diversity within any classroom with regard to student background, preparation, and needs have led to a host of questions about whether and how to accommodate such diversity in the classroom. In fact, it is questions of the latter sort that form Part 1 of this book. Questions about contextually determined diversity have become controversial in part because of empirical data. They also have become controversial, however, because of two other types of contextual influences identified by Kessen.

2. The views and behaviors of those who care for children are also shaped by the contexts in which they have lived.   By this, Kessen meant that the parents, teachers, community leaders, politicians, and other adults who directly or indirectly influence children's lives are themselves the product of the contexts in which they have lived. As a result, the attitudes they have about the nature of children (e.g., whether children are born inherently willful or inherently loving), about appropriate child-rearing practices (e.g., whether or not children should be spanked), about the developmental outcomes that are optimal (e.g., whether it is better for children to grow into compliant and conforming adults or into autonomous and critical adults), and, of course, about education will differ depending on the contexts of their lives. In short, the answers that teachers, administrators, civic leaders, and politicians arrive at when faced with questions about education—and, thus, the controversies surrounding these questions—are sometimes determined more by the contexts of their lives than by any formal theory or the results of any empirical investigations.

Many of the questions considered in this text have become controversial precisely because of this type of contextual influence. Consider, for example, the rise of Japan as an industrial and economic power over the last decades of the twentieth century. This has incited a competitive spirit within the United States that has spilled over into the educational arena. In particular, the educational achievement of students in the United States is now compared on a regular basis with that of students in Japan, with unsettling results from the U.S. viewpoint (Issue 18). This has led to calls for the reform of United States schools, many of which have involved plans for the adoption of pedagogical practices exemplified in Japanese schools. It also has led, on occasion, to a denigration of Japanese educational achievements as "superficial" or as not worth the costs in the purportedly stressed lives of Japanese children. As another example, consider the controversy surrounding bilingual education (Issue 3). In large part, the positions of various groups of stakeholders in this issue have been shaped by their views about whether or not everyone in the United States should speak English. Some critics would also say that stakeholders' positions reflect their views on the rights and inherent worth of individuals from various ethnic groups.

3 The views and behaviors of scholars who study children, development, and education are also shaped by the contexts in which they have lived. Kessen was among the first to chastise education researchers and theorists for their rather "superior attitude"—the assumption that somehow they were immune from the same influences that affect parents, teachers, and the rest of the public, and the assumption that somehow their scientific objectivity transcended historical time and place. Kessen was not simply arguing that scholars have incomplete knowledge and that somehow, as they learn more, they get closer to the truth and less susceptible to contextual influence. Instead, he argued that scholars are people too and that they can never escape the influence of the contexts in which they have lived. Some of the controversies considered in this text have arisen from these types of contextual influence. We see this, for example, in a tendency of researchers to have an almost blind devotion to a particular investigative approach or method of measurement, one in which they see only the advantages and none of the disadvantages. This is illustrated, for example, in the controversy about the effectiveness of ability-level tracking (Issue 2).

Throughout this book, I have endeavored to point out various contextual influences on the controversies considered. It is my hope that by doing so, we take a step toward clarifying these influences and thereby move closer to resolving the controversies. Identifying these contextual influences, however, is a difficult and ad hoc process. It is also, of course, a subjective process, shaped by my own context. I urge the reader to look critically at the ways in which context shapes the views of the writers of these selections. I urge the reader also to examine how his or her own context may be affecting how he or she regards the data and theories presented in these selections.

Association for Supervision and Curriculum Development

The Association for Supervision and Curriculum Development (ASCD) is an international, nonprofit educational association that promotes professional development in curriculum and supervision through a variety of activities, including conferences and publications. In recent years, the organization has considered the issues of ability-level tracking, gender equity in education, learning style differences, and inclusion.

http://www.ascd.org

Office of English Language Acquisition, Language Enhancement, and Academic Achievement for Limited English Proficient Students

The purpose of the Office of English Language Acquisition, Language Enhancement, and Academic Achievement for Limited English Proficient Students (OELA) is to ensure that schools are able to meet their responsibility to provide equal access to education for children with limited proficiency in English.

http://www.ed.gov/offices/OBEMLA

Inclusion in Science Education for Students With Disabilities

This site, which is housed at West Virginia University, is designed to share information about science education as it relates to the inclusion of students with disabilities. The site lists more than 800 strategies that can be implemented in the classroom to ensure the full participation of these students.

http://www.as.wvu.edu/~scidis/

National Association for Self-Esteem

The National Association for Self-Esteem (NASE) is devoted to promoting the wide-scale adoption of self-esteem concepts in educational and other contexts in the lives of children and adults. This site includes bibliographies and "think pieces" by scholars and laypeople alike.

http://www.self-esteem-nase.org

Center for the Fourth and Fifth Rs

The Center for the Fourth and Fifth Rs, which is designed to serve as are source on character education, is directed by developmental psychologist Thomas Lickona. The center disseminates articles on character education, publishes a news letter, and works with schools that are interested in implementing curricula that focus on teaching respect, responsibility, and other ethical values that are considered the bases of good character.

http://www.cortland.edu/www/c4n5rs/

PART 1

Meeting the Diverse Needs of a Diverse Classroom

*A*s we reflect on the decade of the 1990s, it seems that schools in the United States are now being asked to do more and more. On the one hand, the scope of education for any individual student is more inclusive than ever before. Schools must now meet not only the needs of students in traditional academic domains, such as mathematics and science, but also the needs they have (or are perceived to have) in the social and emotional domains. So, for example, educators now pledge to educate the "whole" child. On the other hand, there has been an increased recognition of the diversity that characterizes the student population and an increased effort to tailor the curriculum to the unique needs of various subgroups. This has led, for example, to separate science and math classes for male and female students, separate tracks for higher- and lower-achieving students, and calls for greater attention to the disparate academic outcomes often seen for students of different ethnicities and races. Some of these attempts to expand the educational agenda have been legislated, as in the case of the inclusion of students with disabilities in regular classrooms. Other attempt shave emerged from particular ideological positions, as in the case of the self-esteem and moral education "movements." These changes in the educational agenda, however, have not gone unchallenged. In this section, we consider the controversies that have arisen as schools have tried to meet the diverse needs of a diverse classroom.

- Are Single-Gender Classes the Only Way to Ensure Equal Educational Opportunities for Boys and Girls?
- Should Ability-Level Tracking Be Abandoned?
- Should English Immersion Replace Bilingual Education?
- Is Full Inclusion Always the Best Option for Children With Disabilities?
- Can Schools Close the Achievement Gap Between Students from Different Ethnic and Racial Backgounds?
- Should Schools Try to Increase Students' Self-Esteem?
- Should Moral Education Be Part of the School Curriculum?

ISSUE 1

Are Single-Gender Classes the Only Way to Ensure Equal Educational Opportunities for Boys and Girls?

YES: Janice Streitmatter, from "An Exploratory Study of Risk-Taking and Attitudes in a Girls-Only Middle School Math Class," *The Elementary School Journal* (September 1997)

NO: Jo Sanders and Sarah Cotton Nelson, from "Closing Gender Gaps in Science" *Educational Leadership* (November 2004)

ISSUE SUMMARY

YES: Janice Streitmatter, a professor of educational psychology, found that the behavior and attitudes of girls in gender-segregated classes are dramatically different from, and more success-oriented than, those of girls in coeducational classes. She argues that the culture and practices of the coeducational classroom limit educational opportunities for girls in a way that can now be overcome most easily (or perhaps only) through gender segregation.

NO: Jo Sanders and Sarah Cotton Nelson argue that gender differences in achievement in physics, chemisty, and computer sciences are caused by inequities in classroom practices that deny young girls full participation in the activities required for success in these acedemic domains. They also describe a program initiated in the Dallas school system in which the classroom behavior of teachers and students in coeducational classrooms is targeted for change so as to provide more gender-equitable pedagogical experiences.

Despite changing attitudes and the enactment of laws designed to ensure that males and females are afforded equal educational opportunities, gender related differences in academic achievement still exist. In reading and language arts, girls score higher on achievement tests and are less likely to be referred for remedial programs than are boys. In math and science, boys maintain an advantage. Although gender differences in academic achievement are relatively small, and certainly less than the differences observed among males or among females, they are important because of their influence on the career paths available to men and women.

Gender-related differences in academic achievement are due, in part, to the beliefs that children bring to school and to their behavior in the classroom. Importantly, there is considerable evidence that differences in academic preparation and behavior are largely the result of the environment rather than of direct biological influences on development.

Parents are an important part of the environment that serves to push boys and girls down different academic paths. The role of the media has also been much debated. Unfortunately, teachers and the culture of most U.S. schools are at fault as well. Consider the following:

1. In preschool and early elementary school years, the physical arrangement of the classroom often segregates boys and girls and reinforces the differences between them. For example, a pretend kitchen and associated role-playing materials are typically housed in a different location than are blocks and other building materials.
2. Teachers attend more to boys than to girls, are more likely to ask boys questions (especially open-ended, thought-provoking questions), and give boys more constructive criticism. Such behaviors are especially evident in traditionally male domains, such as science.
3. Teachers are more tolerant of interruptions from boys than from girls and encourage the latter to wait their turn.
4. Teachers are more likely to provide help to girls during difficult academic tasks, including during experiments and other hands-on science activities, while encouraging boys to resolve difficulties on their own.
5. Teachers spend more time with girls during reading and language arts classes but more time with boys during math classes.
6. Teachers are less likely to assign girls than similarly achieving boys to high-math-ability groups. In general, girls are less likely than boys to be identified for inclusion in programs for gifted students.

How can schools be reformed to ensure that they help children to break free of gender stereotypes rather than maintain and even exacerbate achievement differences between boys and girls? Much of the debate surrounding the question of reform has focused on the achievement gaps in math and science, which appear to have the greatest potential for limiting career options. Two approaches to reform have been advocated. In the first, and certainly more popular approach, scholars and policymakers, assuming that coeducational classrooms are a fact of life, have made suggestions for changing the culture and practices of these classrooms. Proponents of the second, more controversial, approach argue that gender-segregated classes are necessary to allow girls the opportunity to learn in a climate that is suited to their characteristics and needs.

The following two selections weigh in on this issue of gender-segregated classes. In the first, Janice Streitmatter argues that the behavior and attitudes of girls in gender-segregated classes are dramatically different from, and more success-oriented than, girls in coeducational classes. In the second selection, Jo Sanders and Sarah Cotton Nelson maintain that gender equity is possible within the context of the coeducational classroom provided that teachers and student behavior are the focus of chance.

Janice Streitmatter  **YES**

An Exploratory Study of Risk-Taking and Attitudes in a Girls-Only Middle School Math Class

Literature Review

Gender equity in schools has been the focus of intense research over the past several years. Works such as *How Schools Shortchange Girls* (American Association of University Women, 1992), Orenstein's (1994) *SchoolGirls*, and Sadker and Sadker's (1994) *Failing at Fairness* supported the contention, cast into debate most recently in 1972 via Title IX, that females and males do not receive the same opportunities in schools.

Research has demonstrated that, in comparison to males, females tend to be disadvantaged systematically in important ways in schools. For example, in some coeducational classrooms females receive less attention, both positive and negative, from teachers than do males (e.g., Fennema & Peterson, 1987; Irvine, 1986). In addition, girls tend to receive qualitatively different instruction than do boys (e.g., Sadker & Sadker, 1994). Questioning methods and praise differ substantially for girls and boys. Girls tend to be praised simply for trying, whereas teachers tend to withhold praise for boys until they produce a correct answer. Finally, boys are much more likely to engage in classroom behaviors such as asking and answering questions than are girls (Sadker & Sadker, 1994)....

The American Association of University Women (1992, 1993) findings offered a bleak picture of female students in coeducational public schools. Girls spoke of sexual harassment ignored by adults in schools and a sense of invisibility in classrooms that were dominated by boys. In general, girls described receiving far less than an equal share of the public schooling experience (American Association of University Women, 1992).

Orenstein (1994) reported her classroom and home observation and interview data of over 150 middle school girls in California during 1992–1993. Orenstein was particularly interested in understanding factors that affected the girls' self-confidence and how schools were working to counter gender bias. The research focused on girls in two middle schools, a suburban school with mostly white students, and an urban school with poor and ethnic minority students. The girls in this study expressed their lack of self-confidence in the face of overwhelming dominance by boys in their classes. One girl talked about participating in classes that included boys: "I don't raise my hand in my classes because I'm afraid I have the wrong answer and I'll be embarrassed. My self-confidence will be taken away, so I don't want to raise my hand even if I really do know" (pp. 11–12). Another girl commented, "Boys never care if they're wrong.... I'm not shy. But it's like, when I get into class, I just ...I just can't talk" (p. 12).

Even some of the teachers who participated in Orenstein's study, which uncovered gross gender differentiation in schools, described being troubled by girls' acceptance of the status quo in coeducational classes. One teacher discussed how the girls and boys in her class viewed math: "The boys see math as something that shows they're brainy, and they like being able to show off that way. They're more risk-taking than the girls, so they'll do better on tests every time, even if the girls turn in all their work and the boys don't" (Orenstein, 1994, p. 20).

There are several clear issues regarding girls in public, coeducational education. Girls tend to receive higher grades than boys in all subjects, even those historically considered to be "masculine" such as math and science, although girls generally score lower than boys on standardized measures of math and science (Hyde & Linn, 1986). During the middle school years girls' attitudes toward some subjects, particularly math, change (Fennema & Meyer, 1989). Girls in elementary school describe themselves as confident in doing math. However, as they go through middle school, this confidence, and the degree to which girls consider math a subject in which it is appropriate for girls to achieve, decline.

McSheffrey (1992) interviewed seven women and 15 eighth-grade girls in an attempt to determine why females tend to avoid mathematics. Four themes emerged from the data: the influence of teachers' behavior on female students, the influence of parents' support for students, students' personal decisions about mathematics and how they affected attitudes toward mathematics, and students' perceptions of boys' attitudes toward girls. According to the women and girls in this study, the best teachers taught math by making authentic connections between the subjects and real life. Participants also spoke of their sense that boys in classrooms valued girls and their contributions less than boys'. A math teacher bound to traditional teaching methods, and male classmates who the females perceived as hostile to them, discouraged the female students from taking math classes.

Collectively, the research examining girls' experiences in U.S. public schools, as well as Guinier et al.'s (1994) study of women law school students, suggest that the goal of providing equivalent educational experiences and opportunities for female and male students has not been achieved.

Single-Gender Schooling

One response to differences in the education girls and boys receive is the creation of schooling for girls only. Single-gender education is not new; such schools have existed in the United States since the establishment of formal schooling (Clabaugh & Rozycki, 1990). Prior to the late 1960s, single-gender preparatory and higher education, nearly always within the private sector, was an option for both males and females. However, in the late 1960s, two trends developed. First, an increasingly widely held view—that only through mixing groups of people could prejudice be diminished, was implemented through school desegregation. Similarly, as a means of ending gender discrimination, Congress passed legislation known as Title IX (1972), which granted access and opportunity to females (and in some situations to males) in educational contexts where they previously had been excluded or only marginally included. Single-gender schools conflicted with this mandate.

The second trend to affect single-gender education involved the economic difficulties of these schools. As the school-age population decreased and the notion of separation became increasingly unpopular, most single-gender schools desegregated either by merging with other single-gender schools or simply by accepting students of the other gender. By 1990, few such schools remained in the United States (Clabaugh & Rozycki, 1990).

It is ironic that in 1995, when single-gender schools had virtually disappeared, a trend toward girls-only classes in public coeducational schools began (Hollinger, 1993). These classes appeared to be a response to broadly publicized research regarding the failure of schools to provide girls the same number and types of experiences that boys receive.

Research over the last 20 years on the effects of single-gender education, however, has suggested that little is gained from separating males and females, either in achievement or attitude toward schooling, particularly when personal characteristics of students are controlled for statistically (e.g., Dale, 1974; Marsh, 1989; Riordan, 1985). However, this research, nearly all quantitative, has failed to examine variables such as girls' sense of confidence, their career aspirations in various academic subjects, and their sense of being invisible in mixed-gender classrooms. There is a clear need for more systematic study of what takes place in girls-only classes and how participants feel about such settings....

Two aspects of girls' schooling and well-being appear to coincide. During early adolescence, girls must begin to take risks in order eventually to fully understand their identity. At the same time, recent research (e.g., Sadker & Sadker, 1994) has shown that many girls are reluctant to take risks in coeducational classrooms in part due to boys' domination. Girls-only middle school classes may be a means of addressing both the issue of psychosocial development as well as educational opportunity and achievement.

The Girls-Only Math Class

The purpose of this initial, exploratory study was to examine over 2 years the dynamics of a girls-only math class in a public coeducational middle school. My major research question was whether and how this class might affect girls' academic risk-taking. I conducted classroom observations of the 24 girls that focused on the behaviors of raising questions with the teacher, answering questions posed by the teacher, and behavior toward one another in one pre-algebra and one algebra class when the students were in seventh and eighth grades, respectively.

During the summer of 1992, the principal of the middle school read a newspaper article that described the establishment of a girls-only math program in a public high school.... He thought the idea was worth trying in his middle school. After reviewing the achievement test scores and grades of incoming seventh-grade girls, he selected 24 girls to be enrolled in an experimental all-girls class. To promote the success of the class he chose girls he considered the strongest female math students (those with the highest test scores, grades, and teacher recommendations).

Two weeks before the beginning of school, he contacted one of the four math teachers and told her of this class and that she would be the teacher.... Shortly after the school year began, the teacher (a former teacher education student I had taught at the university) contacted me about her new girls-only class....

Participation by the girls and the teacher was not voluntary in the beginning; in fact, the principal worked at keeping the existence of the class secret from other district administrators for most of the program's first year....

During a conversation I had with the teacher toward the end of the girls' seventh-grade year, she recalled that on the first day of class, one student raised her hand and asked, "Where are the boys?" The teacher had been told by the principal not to make public the gender-based nature of the class in order to avoid lawsuits. She replied, "I guess you're right. There aren't any boys. Is that all right with you?" The girl's prompt reply was "Oh yes!" and was accompanied by a chorus of "All right!" from the other girls. By the end of the first quarter, all of the girls' parents had become aware that their daughters were in an experimental course....

Method

Either I or a doctoral student working with me observed the class approximately every 10 school days from the last quarter of the seventh-grade year through the end of the eighth-grade year (approximately 30 hours total). I held a group discussion with the students and teacher toward the end of the seventh-grade class. During this conversation, I asked the 24 girls what they thought about being in the class. At the beginning of the eighth-grade year, we interviewed each of 14 girls individually who were representative of the class and whose parents had given permission for their daughters to be interviewed. Two were African-American, and two were Latina; one from each of these categories lived in a low-socioeconomic area and was attending the school through the magnet transfer program. Two of the interviewees were Asian-American, and the remainder represented the majority population at the school, which is European-American and middle class. At the end of the eighth-grade year, we interviewed four students again—one Asian and the rest European-American. I intended to reinterview as many of the 14 girls as time allowed; I selected the latter four students at random.

At the suggestion of the teacher, the initial interviews took place during math class. Each interview lasted approximately 50 minutes, the length of the class. All students were asked the same questions, which focused on the girls' reflections about the girls-only format compared with their other coeducational classes, their sense of achievement in mathematics in this class compared with their previous math classes, their aspirations for their future, their parents' aspirations for them, and their family composition. The final interviews also took place during the math class and included many of the questions asked in the initial interview. In addition, we asked the four girls to summarize their feelings about the girls-only experience and whether they would take the class again given that choice....

Analyses

The design and data analysis for this study were qualitative. Through analysis of field notes taken during numerous observations of the girls-only and mixed-gender classes, I developed categories of teacher behaviors and also student behaviors that appeared to involve taking academic risks, specifically, asking and answering questions in class. Because only girls were in the class, I divided the latter two categories into several more narrow categories, for example, frequency of students asking or answering teacher-initiated questions, whether the questions and answers were in response to a teacher question and on-task, and whether students' answers were correct or not. Among these categories, the last became increasingly intriguing.

Results

Observations

In the all-girls classroom it soon became clear to me that the students were comfortable volunteering their thoughts—through questions, answers, and speculations—whether or not they were sure of being "right." This behavior was at odds both with research as well as the girls' reports of their own behaviors in other classes. The students in the girls-only math program took academic risks repeatedly during their work with the teacher and each other.

In most lessons, the teacher introduced an idea or reviewed a problem and then immediately engaged one of the girls in gaining an understanding of the concept or solving for the answer. Especially if the material was new, it was not unusual for the student responding to have some or all of the answer wrong initially. When this occurred, the teacher usually pressed the girl to carry on as the student verbally worked her way through the question. The teacher frequently instructed the student to collaborate with another student to obtain the answer. The following incident is one of many that illustrate the teacher's and girls' behavior (all names are pseudonyms): "The teacher wrote an equation on the board and said, 'Melissa, tell me what to do next.' Melissa responded, 'Take the first number and make it positive.' Two girls groaned. 'I guess we need to do something else, Melissa. What should it be?' Several girls raised their hands and waved them wildly. 'No, Melissa needs to keep thinking,' the teacher directed. After one more attempt, Melissa got the answer right, and the teacher moved on quickly. Melissa smiled."

The following is an example of other means the teacher used to engage the girls in working through solutions verbally: "The teacher asked students to take out their homework. 'Okay, Allysa, what did you get for number one, and how did you do it?' 'Well, I really didn't understand it.' 'All right, let's get Maria to help you.' Allysa leaned over to Maria's desk across the aisle, and they whispered for a moment. Allysa straightened and said, 'Okay, now I get some of it anyway. You just add the three to both sides, then divide both by two.' 'Right. Now, Maria, tell us how you got it,' the teacher directed."

Here two students collaborated on an answer, each receiving acknowledgment from the teacher. Later in the class session, both Allysa and Maria answered questions incorrectly, but they did so without hesitation. At no time during the observations did we see any girl act as if she were reluctant to answer a question. The girls showed a similar lack of hesitation in asking questions.

In the girls-only class, there was rarely a moment when, unless the teacher was talking or a student was responding to the teacher, a student was not asking a question. Some questions were relevant to the situation at hand; others involved joking or bantering: "What would happen if you did ...?" "How come the answer is negative?" "Why do we have homework this weekend?" "Can you come to us and check what we got for this problem?"

One of the most striking characteristics of this class was the noise; although most talking was math-related, there was constant noise. The teacher did not use a teacher's edition of the text with answers but instead worked the problems with the girls during class. The teacher often thought out loud, and most of the girls did the same. When the students did not understand something, wanted the teacher to see their good work, or simply wanted to be noticed, they did not hesitate to speak out or raise their hands.

The outgoing behavior of the girls, their sense of freedom to make their presence known in the girls-only class, and their willingness to take academic risks stood in sharp contrast to the behavior of most of the girls in the same teacher's mixed-gender pre-algebra class, which had 26 students.

The following description of several minutes in the mixed-gender class represents a typical day:

> After the bell rang, the students were seated, alternating by gender. The teacher put the problem on the board and called on a girl to give the answer. "Susan, what did you get and how did you get it?" The teacher waited for Susan to answer. After a number of seconds, Susan spoke hesitantly and quietly. The students responded to Susan's answer quickly, some by laughing at how long it took her to answer. One student shook his head and muttered, one boy swore under his breath, one boy clapped, and several boys and girls sighed. That was the only contribution Susan made during the class, but later the teacher sat with her as she worked on

some seat work. During the remainder of the class, no girl spoke out without raising her hand or behaved inappropriately, and few girls initiated questions. The mixed-gender class was not characterized by the constant chatter of the girls-only class. Some of the boys were not as quiet as the girls. Several times during the class, one boy slid from his seat to the floor, boys often called out answers, and one spent most of his time with his head on the desk. Another boy made a number of trips to the pencil sharpener, taking side trips to his seat, whispering to some of the girls. Throughout this, the teacher as well as the girls attempted to ignore the boys' behavior.

It is problematic to compare and contrast these two classes for a number of reasons. The classes contained different students, and the overall achievement and motivation of the classes were likely different, given the care with which the principal selected students for the girls-only class. However, in one interview, the teacher described her attempts to teach both classes similarly. Despite this, she found that she reacted to the boys' more aggressive behavior. Although the teacher did not always acknowledge the boys' behavior, for example, when she ignored the boy who was sliding in his seat, or the boy who spoke to the girls on his way back to his chair, she had to adjust to the misbehavior through ignoring it....

Interviews

Analysis of the interview responses of 14 students (among whom four were reinterviewed at the end of eighth grade) in the girls-only class suggested that several issues were important to the girls' understanding about taking risks in classes, especially as the students compared their experiences in the girls-only class to those in their other classes. As I developed categories, three emerged as primary: the girls' sense of freedom to ask questions and to answer questions without having to be certain that their answers were correct, their greater confidence in their abilities in math than in earlier math classes, and a classroom climate that created a place of greater personal freedom.

Moreover, the interview data converged. All 14 girls' responses to my questions were essentially the same. When this occurred, I asked the teacher to identify students who might hold other views. The three students she thought might fall into that category, however, were already in the interview sample. The fact that only one student left the class to return to a coeducational class at the end of the first year, and that none transferred during the second year, supports my conclusion from the interview data that the girls were nearly unanimous in their positive view of the program.

The 14 girls who we interviewed initially all spoke indirectly about risk taking through answering and asking questions in the classroom, both of the teacher as well as peers. One student, Susan, said she had not liked math before being in this class. She described one difference between mixed- and single gender classes: "It's real different. It's easier to learn when you can just turn around, and you don't have to worry that there's this boy who's going to turn around and say, 'You don't know that?' You can just turn around to the girl in back of you and say, 'What do you mean by this?' Or if you find some-one [a girl] who has the same problem, it's just different from finding some guy who has the same problem." Andrea described similar feelings: "It's better with just girls in the math class. There aren't any guys. So ... if you mess up on a problem, they [the boys] won't just sit there and laugh at you because it's all girls." Kendall mentioned that, "We don't have to worry about asking ques-tions or feeling stupid. We can ask questions about anything we want." She also compared how she felt in one of her mixed-gender classes with the girls-only class when the teacher handed back graded papers: "Yesterday I got a paper back in my language arts class. Nobody really wanted to show each other their grades if they did bad. But it's different in this class. Nobody really cares. Someone will just say, 'Everybody makes mistakes sometimes.' But in those other classes, a boy will say, 'You got an F? Wow, you must be stupid or something!' In this class, it's just like, 'Well, ya know, the test was hard.' And there's usually somebody else who got the same grade as you for the same rea-son." Jessie's comment about how mistakes are viewed echoed the feelings of the other girls: "In my other classes, if someone makes a mistake other people see something that they think is not right. And it's not really that, but they'll go around and spread it around, and they don't really care if anybody gets hurt. Girls and guys do that in mixed classes, but in this class none of the girls do that." When I asked Jessie why she thought girls behaved differently about mistakes in mixed classes than in the girls-only class, she responded: "I think we feel special together, and nobody would do that in here, even if they might in another class. We work together."

The second important issue to emerge from the interview data was the 14 girls' confidence in their capabilities in math in the girls-only class. Although there were several self-proclaimed math experts in the teacher's mixed-gender class, all were male. (Comments from Darren and Michael to the girls seated close to them are representative: "I'm smart in math. I'll tell you the answers" and "I can do this stuff. You're not good like me.") Our observations revealed that the "experts" were not quite as good in math as they pretended and that they often provided wrong answers. The girls did not question the boys' expert status, even when one boy told a girl that she was stupid. In the girls-only class, there were no self-proclaimed experts. During the interviews, no girl indicated that the teacher favored anyone in the class or that any student performed better than any other or dominated the class in any way.

In the interviews, the 14 girls spoke primarily of feeling good about doing math. Kendall described how her confidence about the willingness to display her competence in math had been affected by her 2 years in the pro-gram: "I consider myself a good student, but sometimes I've been afraid to show it. In here it's okay to do well. I guess when I don't feel like I can answer questions in class and show people that I can do it, I start not liking the class and the things we're supposed to learn. But in here I can be myself, feel smart, and get good grades. I'm going to take geometry next year in high school. I just wish that there were a girls-only class for that. But at least I feel like I can do the math. I know I can."

Unlike Kendall, Nona did not consider herself a strong student when she entered the girls-only class. By the end of the eighth-grade year, however, she described her feelings about herself in math class this way:

> Since this class, I've liked math a lot more than before. I see the usefulness of math in a lot of other things, like I'm into astronomy now, and you need math for that. If I had to start all over, I would take this class instead of the regular ones. There was still some stuff in it that I'm not sure I understand, so I'm going to take algebra I next year in high school. And then I'll take geometry during the summer so I can catch up. That way I can be ready for calculus. I never thought I'd go on in math. In fact, a lot of my friends in the neighborhood talk about dropping out altogether. But I'm not going to do that, and I'm going to take more math. I do wish that there were more girls-only classes, some in high school. I feel better in them. I'm not afraid to ask questions and get things wrong. I'll miss being with just girls, but I think I'll be okay now.

At the end of the eighth grade, other girls like Nona did not pass the algebra I competency test required by the school district in order to receive high school credit for the eighth-grade course. Seven of them would have to retake the course in ninth grade....

During the last week of the eighth-grade year, we met with all of the girls together in their class. The girls responded to some final questions about their time in the girls-only class. In addition to groans about moving on to mixed-gender math classes in high school, they offered some thoughtful responses to the question, "How has it been for you in this class?", responses that alluded to the issue of risk-taking in class. Cristina said: "I feel good about math now. I know that I'm not stupid in it, and I can ask any question I want to. In here nobody worried about anyone, especially a boy, telling us we couldn't do it, or telling us to shut up when we wanted to ask a question. And there was nobody in here but us, so we were the ones to answer all the questions."...

Discussion

The girls' interview responses indicate that the girls-only math class provided a setting that, compared to their earlier math classes, promoted the girls' freedom to risk asking and answering questions (even if doing so entailed being wrong) and their confidence in their math abilities. The willingness to speak out in class both reported and demonstrated by the girls may indicate that they are developing greater insight into who they are and can be, at least in this class (Erickson, 1968). Follow-up data will be necessary in order to determine any long-range effects of the class on the girls' classroom behavior and attitudes in high school and beyond....

Despite the questions remaining about the benefits of single-gender classes, the testimony of the 14 girls interviewed in this study about their own feelings and our classroom observations suggest that being in the girls-only class increased their confidence in their mathematics ability and their willingness to ask and answer questions during class. In a sense, this class provided a respite. Without having to force a space for themselves within a mixed-gender group first or work to "push themselves to the front," as Kendall called it, they were freer to concentrate on learning math and to offer their ideas and questions in a context where no one questioned their ability to do so based simply on their gender.

This study was limited in that, although it was conducted over 2 years, only one group of students and one teacher participated, that is, there was no control group; nor did I observe the girls' behavior in a mixed-gender class. The findings are not definitive regarding the benefits of a girls-only math program in a middle school. Other conditions in this class may have contributed to the girls' perceptions. For instance, the fact that all the girls were relatively high achievers and that all but a few were selected for enrollment in this class may have increased the students' sense of being part of something special, thus creating a Hawthorne effect [the effect upon behavior of the subject's knowing he or she is in an experiment]. However, the 14 girls' consistent reports of their enhanced math self-concepts and the power they credited to the experience of being in the class provide a foundation for future research in this area.

References

American Association of University Women. (1992). *How schools shortchange girls.* Washington, DC: American Association of University Women Educational Foundation.

American Association of University Women. (1993). *Hostile hallways: The American Association of University Women survey of sexual harassment in American schools.* Washington, DC: American Association of University Women Educational Foundation.

Clabaugh, G. K., & Rozycki, E. G. (1990). *Understanding schools: The foundations of education.* New York: Harper & Row.

Dale, R. R. (1974). *Mixed or single-sex schools? Vol. 3. Attainment, attitude and overview.* London: Routledge & Kegan Paul.

Erikson, E. (1968). *Identity, youth and crisis.* New York: Norton.

Fennema, E., & Meyers, M. R. (1989). Gender, equity, and mathematics. In W. G. Secada (Ed.), *Equity in education* (pp. 146–157). New York: Falmer.

Fennema, E., & Peterson, P. (1987). Effective teaching for girls and boys: The same or different? In D. Berliner & B. Rosenshine (Eds.), *Talks to teachers* (pp. 111–125). New York: Random House.

Guinier, L., Fine, M., Balin, J., Bartow, A., & Stachel, D. L. (1994). Becoming gentlemen: Women's experiences at one ivy league law school. *University of Pennsylvania Law Review, 143*(1), 1–110.

Hollinger, D. K. (1993). (Ed.). *Single-sex schooling: Perspectives from practice and research* (Vols. 1 & 2). Washington, DC: U. S. Department of Education, Office of Research.

Hyde, J. S., & Linn, M. C. (1986). (Eds.), *The psychology of gender: Advances through meta-analysis.* Baltimore: Johns Hopkins University Press.

Irvine, J. J. (1986). Teacher-student interactions: Effects of: Student race, sex, and grade level. *Journal of Educational Psychology, 78*(1), 14–21.

Marsh, H. W. (1989). Effects of attending single-sex and coeducational high schools on achievement, attitudes, behaviors, and sex differences. *Journal of Educational Psychology*, 81, 70–85.

McSheffrey, K. (1992). *Mathematics experience of women and girls: A narrative inquiry.* Unpublished master's thesis, Queen's University, Kingston, Ontario.

Orenstein, P. (1994). *SchoolGirls: Young women, self-esteem, and the confidence gap.* New York: Doubleday.

Riordan, C. (1985). Public and Catholic schooling: The effects of gender context policy. *American Journal of Education,* 5, 518–540.

Sadker, M., & Sadker, D. (1994), *Failing at fairness: How our schools cheat girls.* New York: Simon & Schuster.

**Jo Sanders and
Sarah Cotton Nelson**

Closing Gender Gaps in Science

High school students across the United States, hoping to get a head start on their college credits, took 1,700,000 advanced placement (AP) exams in 34 subjects in 2003. Students who take these exams tend to be the more ambitious ones. The presence of AP exams in a school's curriculum is a good indication of where tomorrow's academic high achievers will be coming from and what fields these students might enter.

An interesting aspect of the AP exams is how lopsided many of them are by gender. Girls constitute the majority of test takers of many of the exams—66 percent in art history, for example, and 64 percent in English literature and composition. These female-dominant imbalances can create serious gender issues for boys: It's not healthy for us as a society, or for boys individually, to think that excellence in reading and writing is "feminine."

As for the male-dominant imbalances, girls used to be a minority in AP exams on mathematics, biology, and chemistry, but these numbers have equalized in recent years to the point where girls make up roughly half the test takers in these subjects.

The AP exams of continuing concern for girls since the 1970s are the three physics exams (the AP Physics B exam, the AP Physics C exam on electricity and magnetism, and the AP Physics C exam on mechanics) and the two computer science exams (CS-A and the more advanced CS-AB). ...

In computer science, girls' track record has actually worsened. In 1992, girls represented 21 percent of the CS-A test takers and 13 percent of the CS-AB test takers, compared with 16 percent and 10 percent respectively in 2003. The 2003 numbers show an average of only 44 girls in each state taking the CS-A exam and a mere 14 girls in each state taking the CS-AB exam.

When many *Educational Leadership* readers went to high school, students were exhorted to take as much mathematics as possible because math, we were told, was the key to a whole raft of high-paying, high-status careers in technical areas. For the new generation, however, science and technology have replaced math as the gateways to a wide variety of technical careers in the sciences and in engineering. When high school girls represent only one-fourth to one-third of students enrolled in AP physics—and when they represent an even smaller portion of those enrolled in computer science—they are deprived of an important leg up to technology-related majors in college. Girls' under-representation in these fields must be taken seriously because society simply cannot afford to waste this much talent.

Data on Gender Disparity

In Dallas, Texas, enrollments in the AP mathematics and the AP biology courses are fairly equally balanced in terms of gender, but enrollments in AP physics and computer science remain primarily male. These patterns mirror the national situation. Further, the pass rates in Dallas on AP exams in physics and computer science were found to be substantially lower for girls than for boys.

We discovered that the problem went far beyond gender imbalances in AP course enrollment and test taking. To test a frequently heard argument—that boys are simply better suited to higher-level math and science—we correlated girls' and boys' PSAT math scores in the Dallas Independent School District with their pass rates on the AP exams in science and technology. It was a revelation: Girls who scored in the 70s in PSAT math (a score equivalent to a 700 in the SAT) scored considerably lower in the AP exams than equally qualified boys did.

For instance, all the boys who scored 70 or above in the PSAT math exam passed the AP chemistry exam; the same was true for only 50 percent of the high-scoring girls. In the Physics C exam on mechanics, the pass rate for boys who scored 70 or above in the PSAT math exam was 94 percent; for girls in the same category, the pass rate was 71 percent. Six of the nine boys who scored 70 or above in the math exam passed Physics B, but none of the four girls who took Physics B passed it. In Computer Science AB, the pass rates for boys and girls who scored 70 or above in the PSAT math exam were 44 percent and 25 percent respectively.

Therefore, not only do fewer girls in Dallas take the science and technology exams to begin with, but girls with high ability as measured by their PSAT math exams also score lower in their AP exams than comparably qualified boys do. What's going on that would lead to such gender disparities among students who sit in the same classrooms and learn from the same teachers?

Four interested parties decided to find out: the Dallas Independent School District; several women employees from Texas Instruments; the Dallas Women's Foundation; and AP Strategies, a not-for-profit agency in Texas that works to improve student pass rates in the state on AP exams. Together, these four parties created a program to advance girls' participation and performance in AP science and technology in Dallas high schools: the Dallas Gender Equity Project.

The Dallas Gender Equity Project

The Dallas Gender Equity Project began in October 2003 with a full-day workshop for 14 teachers of AP chemistry, physics, and technology courses in Dallas high schools. The workshop instructor presented the data on girls' underachievement in Dallas AP exams. Despite some initial skepticism about gender equity, the data-oriented science and technology teachers were curious about the causes of the imbalance. The teachers talked at length about the gender issues they were seeing in their classes and about the efforts they had made to deal with the disparity. Some pointed out their unsuccessful efforts to recruit girls for their classes; others noted the girls' reticence to speak up in class despite invitations to do so.

Every few months for the rest of the school year, participants met in half-day follow-up workshops held after school. Before each workshop, teachers completed mini-assignments that focused on gender issues surfacing in such venues as toy stores, Saturday morning television shows, or magazines and Web sites familiar to high school students. Other mini-assignments dealt more directly with school, requiring participants to look for gender bias in textbooks, in teacher-student interactions, and even in classroom wall displays.

Each workshop focused on a specific topic, such as teacher expectations and stereotype threat, interpersonal dynamics among minority and nonminority groups, and curriculum bias. The instructor also introduced interesting research studies on gender in science or technology. In fact, one of the program's strengths was that it addressed the gender issue with solid data. Physics teacher and workshop participant Rebecca McGowan Jensen explained,

> We were given real data from education journals, the context in which to understand [this information], and concrete methods to change our classroom instruction and get quantifiable results. We were treated as collaborators rather than people to be lectured at.

Reality Versus Perception

Teachers brought fascinating stories back to the group from classroom experimentation. Daniel Brown, an AP physics teacher, reported that he had initially been skeptical of any gender inequity in his classroom. "Maybe in other teachers' classrooms," he insisted, "but certainly not in mine." He set out to prove the statistics wrong for his classroom by conducting an experiment.

He asked a teacher to observe his class and time his responses to both his male and female students. This was a gender issue that one of the earlier workshops had tackled. Just knowing that someone was clocking him during that period made him extra aware; he was all the more certain that his time allocation would be fair. At the end of the class, his colleague showed him the results: Taking into account the class's gender representation, the teacher had spent 80 percent of his time responding to boys and 20 percent to girls. "It absolutely bowled me over," Brown said.

He worked hard the next month on implementing strategies presented in the workshops to make the classroom environment more gender-equitable. Making changes in his teaching practice meant becoming aware of a number of gender-based patterns that are below most teachers' level of conscious awareness. He paid attention to which students he called on, how much time he spent waiting for their responses, how much eye contact he maintained, which types of questions he asked specific students, and whether he accepted or refused called-out answers.

Once again, he asked his colleague to observe him in class. During that period of observation, he felt that he had gone overboard in his attention to the girls. He was sure that the observing teacher would tell him that he had swung the pendulum completely back the other way—that he was now spending 80 percent of his time responding to girls and 20 percent to boys. At the end of the period, the observing teacher told him the results: "Fifty-fifty, dead on."

Changes in the Classroom

Science teacher Chris Bruhn, a former aerospace engineer, appreciated the need for getting more girls into technical fields and had experienced similar gender imbalances in science classrooms. Said Bruhn,

> When I was in college, there were at least five boys for every girl in the engineering classes. My graduating class of 30 aerospace engineers included only one female, and I soon learned that the workforce was not much different. One of my missions when I became a physics teacher was to convince more girls to become engineers.

Bruhn experimented with two gender-related activities in his high school physics classes. The results were eye-opening. In the first experiment, he asked students to determine the tension in a string suspended from the ceiling. At the end of the string was a toy eagle that could "fly" around in a circle. He gave no instructions for getting the eagle to fly or suggestions about equipment to use, measurements to make, or equations to apply. Although there were several ways to determine the string's tension, solving the problem really only required a stopwatch, a meter stick, and a balance. He asked the girls to set up the equipment and the boys to record the data. This resulted, in his words, "in a meltdown in the classroom." According to Bruhn,

> The girls did not want to do it! "We don't know how to do it," they said. "Can the boys set it up?" Of course, the boys were all too eager to do it for them. This was an appalling surprise to me. Needless to say, I had a lot of work to do, but by the end of the year the girls were just as possessive of the lab equipment as the boys were.

In the second experiment, Bruhn videotaped a class period. When he watched the tape, he discovered that he was allowing boys to interrupt the girls. "This had the effect of rewarding the boys for being outspoken and rewarding the girls for being quiet," he said. "This was the exact opposite of what I wanted." Bruhn then explained to the students why he had videotaped the class and what he had found. The students were intrigued and a discussion followed of what the teacher had been learning in the Gender Equity Project. In subsequent classes, the boys began to apologize when they interrupted the girls or when they tried to take over; they eventually learned to wait their turn. Just as important, the girls learned to stand their ground during discussions in class, and they took on positions of leadership.

Daniel Brown noticed similar changes when he began to focus on the girls in his class. The girls became more confident that they could do physics, they participated more in class, and they learned to deal more effectively with some of the disruptive male behaviors. Brown revised his teaching style in all six of his classes; in three of them, he specifically announced the changes he was making and his reasons for making them because the subject happened to come up in class. The girls pointed out that they had not even noticed anything wrong with his teaching style because they were so used to it.

Changes entailed making sure to ask both girls and boys deeper follow-up questions, calling on girls as often as on boys, and refusing to permit the boys to interrupt the girls. In the classes in which he made the announcement, the girls became even bolder and more confident than the girls in the other three classes. According to Brown, making this conscious effort every period of every day prevented him from "slipping back into his old ways."

Changes in Brown's teaching practices have resulted in enrollments in AP physics jumping from four girls out of 13 students in the 2003-2004 school year to 10 out of 20 for the 2004-2005 school year, or from 31 percent to 50 percent female. He has seen a dramatic increase in minority enrollment as well.

What's Next?

Gender-equitable teaching practices have started flowing into mainstream Dallas schools. The Gender Equity Institute, supported by the Women of TI Fund, was initiated this year at the University of Texas at Arlington to serve both teacher education students and classroom teachers seeking continuing education credits. A gender equity component will be included in a math training program for teachers. In addition, other local school districts are becoming interested in adopting the Gender Equity Project approach.

Gender equity activities continue to thrive in Dallas high schools. Several "booster shot" workshops will take place during the 2004-2005 school year, with a whole new round of workshops scheduled for teachers who teach pre-AP classes. High school principals and counselors have already attended an evening workshop on gender equity. Female students of science, technology, and engineering from Southern Methodist University in Dallas and women from Texas Instruments who are involved in technical careers have volunteered to attend the sessions.

Commenting on the program, one physics teacher said,

> The most important lesson I took away for my female students was this: Each student needs to feel that she is competent, important, and talented. The number one thing we can do for a student is to sit her down, look her in the eye, and tell her that she's good at this subject.

And this is what we did. No one can change the world entirely, but we found that focusing on gender equity in our classrooms helped us change a bit of it.

POSTSCRIPT

Are Single-Gender Classes the Only Way to Ensure Equal Educational Opportunities for Boys and Girls?

Can we rely on empirical research to decide whether or not single-gender classes ensure that boys and girls have equal chances to succeed in all academic fields? In principle, the answer is yes. It should be possible, for example, to compare the math or science achievement of girls enrolled in girls-only classes to that of girls enrolled in coeducational classes. Do the former have higher achievement than the latter? Does their achievement equal that of boys? In fact, several studies, suggest that achievement is higher for girls in single-gender classes than in coeducational classes. See "The Effects of Sex-Grouped Schooling on Achievement: The Role of National Context," by David P. Baker, Cornelius Riordan, and Maryellen Schaub, *Comparative Education Review* (November 1995). Unfortunately, interpreting such comparisons is often not a straightforward matter because researchers have been content largely with comparisons of "naturally occurring" classes; that is, classes over which they had little or no control in terms of the assignment of students and teachers to classes or the curriculum. As a result, the classes that were compared may have differed in many ways, including in parental beliefs about innate differences between boys and girls, the motivation of the students to master the subject in question, the intensity and content of the instruction, and the extent to which single-gender classes are perceived to have high status or prestige by the community. This makes it difficult to determine whether differences in achievement between girls in girls-only classes and girls in coeducational classes are due to the gender composition of the classes (and the associated differences in climate) or to one or more of these "confounding" factors. Controlled experiments are needed to show the full impact of singlegender classes on the achievement of girls.

Few would deny that schools are a powerful source of change in our society and that we must do all we can to ensure that they are settings in which all children can reach their fullest potential. Valuable insights about schooling and gender-related differences in academic achievement can be found in Deborah A. Garrahy, "Three Third-Grade Teachers' Gender-Related Beliefs and Behavior," *The Elementary School Journal* (vol. 102, 2001), pp. 81–94, and David M. Sadker and Myra P. Sadker, *Failing at Fairness: How America's Schools Cheat Girls* (Simon & Schuster, 1994).

ISSUE 2

Should Ability-Level Tracking Be Abandoned?

YES: Jeannie Oakes and Amy Stuart Wells, from "Detracking for High Student Achievement," *Educational Leadership* (March 1998)

NO: Sally M. Reis et al., from "Equal Does Not Mean Identical," *Educational Leadership* (November 1998)

ISSUE SUMMARY

YES: Jeannie Oakes and Amy Stuart Wells, both professors in the Graduate School of Education and Information Studies at the University of California, Los Angeles, argue that tracking ensures that low-achieving students will be exposed to a watered-down curriculum, have access to fewer educational resources, and experience a less-than-stimulating school environment, all of which will prevent them from ever escaping their low-achieving track. They argue that all students should be expected to master the same curriculum.

NO: Professor of educational psychology Sally M. Reis and her colleagues argue that detracking leads teachers to adopt a middle-of-the-road curriculum that fails to challenge the best and brightest students in the class. They argue that teachers do not know how to meet the needs of gifted children within the context of a heterogeneous classroom; thus, tracking is critical for the success of the best and brightest students.

Historically, public schooling has been seen as the mechanism by which all children are afforded an equal opportunity to reach their fullest potential. In practice, however, it has been difficult to ensure the equitable treatment of all children within the classroom. One reason for this is that children come to school with different experiences and different academic strengths. This means that different children may need different educational experiences to reach their full potential. However, providing individualized instruction has proven difficult to do, especially since the resources devoted to education have dwindled in recent years. Many educational critics have argued that teachers cope by offering a middle-of-the-road curriculum that fails to meet the needs of the students at the extremes—exceeding the capabilities of many low-achieving students and failing to challenge the most gifted students. Educators and policymakers have offered a number of solutions to deal with the dilemma created by student heterogeneity. One of the most controversial of these solutions has been *ability grouping*, or *tracking*.

Ability grouping is designed to decrease the heterogeneity that teachers face by forming groups of students who are similar in terms of academic achievement and preparation. Supporters of ability grouping argue that by constituting homogenous groups, the teacher of a group can devise a curriculum that meets the needs of all students in the group. Ability grouping typically has been implemented in one of two ways. In *between-class* ability grouping, students at a particular grade level—say, fourth grade—are assigned to classrooms according to ability. So, for example, a distinction might be drawn between high-achieving and low-achieving fourth graders. The former might be assigned to the classroom taught by Mr. Jones and the latter to the classroom taught by Mr. Smith. Presumably, each class would receive a different curriculum, tailored to their current level of academic achievement and readiness. Between-class ability grouping can be found at all grade levels, but it is seen in perhaps its most extreme form in the college preparatory and vocational tracks in many of U.S. high schools.

In *within-class* ability grouping, a teacher organizes the students in his or her class into groups—again according to academic ability—but only for a particular subject. So, for example, the teacher may form three reading groups, with the groups distinguished by their performance on various assessments of reading skill. The three groups might remain in class for reading, with the teacher working with each group at different times. Alternatively, one or more groups might spend part of the day in another classroom where they would receive instruction in reading with other students of like ability from other classrooms around the school. In either case, students in the different groups would receive different curricula in reading but the same curriculum for other subjects. Within-class ability grouping is quite common at the elementary school level.

In recent years, the voices of the critics of ability grouping have been louder than those of the supporters. In part, this has been fueled by various critiques of the data generated by studies comparing the academic achievement of high- and low-ability-track students. However, it has also been fueled by concerns about social justice. For example, there is some evidence that students who are members of racial and ethnic minorities are more likely to be placed in low-ability tracks than are students from the mainstream culture. This has led some to argue that ability grouping is yet another institutional mechanism for oppressing ethnic and racial minorities.

The following selections address the question, Should schools abandon ability-level tracking? In the first selection, Jeannie Oakes and Amy Stuart Wells contend that all students should be expected to master the same curriculum. In the second selection, Sally M. Reis et al. argue that tracking is critical for the success of the best and brightest students.

**Jeannie Oakes and
Amy Stuart Wells**

 **YES**

Detracking for High Student Achievement

Standards reform in the United States aims at providing all children with a more challenging curriculum and holding schools accountable for their achievement. High academic standards, proponents argue, will alleviate inequalities in curriculum, instruction, and expectations for students. Purportedly, standards will also bring excellence by requiring all students to demonstrate higher levels of achievement and by providing all students with equal educational opportunities while preparing a more informed citizenry and a better trained work force.

But what about the firmly entrenched system of tracking that exposes students to dramatically different and unequal levels of curriculum? Consider the daily experiences of many lower-track students—particularly low-income students of color—whose classrooms offer fewer resources, low-level curriculum, and less powerful learning environments. How can these students reach higher standards?

The Reform Possibilities

For three years, we have followed the progress of 10 U.S. secondary schools where administrators and teachers have worked to restructure their schools in ways that could bring all students to high academic standards. The schools, which vary in size from 500 to 3,000 students, have racially and socioeconomically mixed student populations. They are widely dispersed across the country, with one in the Northeast, three in the Midwest, one in the South, two in the Northwest, and three in various regions of California.

Faculties at these schools became disenchanted with their tracking systems, which had created academic, racial, and socioeconomic divisions among students. White and middle-class students were overrepresented in honors and advanced classes, while lower-income African American and Latino students were disproportionately represented in general and remedial classes. These educators saw detracking as a way to pursue both excellence and equity. In addition to reducing or eliminating tracks, the schools created new schedules, reorganized teachers into teams, provided all students access to honors programs, instituted integrated curriculums, and created opportunities for students to get extra academic support—all in an effort to make standards-based education possible.

Toward Detracked Courses

For most schools, the first step was to do away with low-level classes. Union High School (all school names are pseudonyms) eliminated remedial tracks, leaving only one regular and one advanced track. Grant High School's English department eliminated its low-level 12th grade electives; all current electives are of equal rigor and offer an honors option.

Other schools required students to take a core of heterogeneous courses. Two middle schools, King and Explorer, developed a common curriculum for all students. Some of the high schools required all students to pass bench-mark classes—English I at Green Valley, biology at Grant, and algebra at Union. At Central High, all students begin 9th grade on a college-prep trajectory in English, science, and math.

Many schools simultaneously opened the top levels by allowing almost everyone access to honors programs. Others provided honors activities within heterogeneous classes. Teams at Explorer Middle School offer either multi-level activities or pullout challenge classes, available to all students, several times a week. Traditionally low-achieving students and mainstreamed special education students frequently participate.

Green Valley also offers challenge projects within heterogeneous English classes. Students must complete at least one challenge class per quarter to receive an A in the class. Grant High's honors-option language arts classes allow any student who completes the work to receive an honors designation on his or her transcript. Plainview started a "Jaime Escalante" campaign that encourages minority students to enroll in advanced placement classes.

Double Doses of Curriculum

Many schools created opportunities for students to get extra help to master more challenging curriculum. Central High's faculty designed a customized calendar to provide a "double dose" of instruction for students having diffi-culty.[1] The intercessions allow low-achieving students a chance to repeat classes they had previously failed, without affecting their course load during the normal sessions. Several schools offer resource classes for low-achieving students; students enroll in these classes in place of an elective. Union High encourages capable students to double up in math courses and offers a sup-port class, Transitions to College Math, for students who need a review of algebra concepts while enrolled in Algebra II or geometry. Bearfield Middle's math teachers offer tutoring sessions before or after school.

Grant High operates a math homework center one day a week in which teachers, community volunteers, and upper-level students tutor students who need help. In addition, two math teachers offer a summer challenge program in which minority students can complete a year's worth of math in an eight-week course. Students who complete the summer challenge may then skip to a higher-level math class in the fall. The class has already produced increased enrollments in calculus among formerly underrepresented minority groups.

Accommodating Diversity

Many teachers adopted classroom strategies that allow students to demonstrate their ability in previously unrecognized ways. Teachers at Explorer Middle School use Socratic Seminars, where students discuss open-ended questions in a format described by one teacher as "analogous to a conversation around the dinner table. ... It allows those kids who don't feel comfortable in other settings a chance to speak their minds ... because they know they can't be wrong."

Grant High School developed a Marine Science curriculum that relies very little on textbooks; instead, students take frequent field trips and complete small-group projects. Students might make anatomical models of fish out of play dough, or collect and identify various forms of ocean plant and animal life. All Marine Science students are required to design and teach a week of science classes at a local elementary school and guide a group of children on a beach walk.

Several high schools adopted programs that provide low-achieving students access to a broad span of math concepts. Interactive Math at Central and Liberty and Integrated Math at Grant interweave concepts from algebra, statistics, geometry, probability, and logic, with the conceptual demands increasing each year. Bob Jackson, math chair at Grant, credited the Integrated Math program for enabling a diverse group of students to learn math well:

> They're the kind of kids who probably would have been doomed to spending two years in arithmetic and not doing anything substantive. And with the new mathematics, I can't believe the type of things and level they've achieved right now.

The math chair at Central High, Faith Jacobs, told us that you can't detrack in a traditional curriculum. Her colleague Christie Jeffries summed up their new curriculum: "We teach problem solving, writing, and communicating your mathematical thoughts." She also emphasized problem finding as an important dimension of mathematics: "They have to figure out what problems to do before they can even do the problems."

A Green Valley team of teachers piloting an integrated math and engineering program were excited about the content of combined mathematics and vocational studies. Math teacher Gloria Pedroza said,

> It is really good math. It isn't watered down, and it is very much applied. You won't ever get this question from a kid: "When will I ever use this?"

Many schools developed multicultural curriculums, such as Grant's required 9th grade World Cultures course and Liberty's Ethnic Studies class, which engage students who show little interest in traditional curriculum and allow low-achieving minority students to display their culturally specific knowledge. Many schools offer African American or Mexican American History, African American or Latin American Literature, Ethnic Literature, and

Women's Literature. As an English teacher at Green Valley stated, "We have got to find ways for all kids to find entry and go as far as they can."

King Middle School's Project Equal incorporates multicultural literature into the curriculum and the library. Last year, several 8th grade teachers attended a course on how to teach a unit on the Holocaust. Teachers at other schools studied culturally related learning styles.

We also found teachers who based their curriculum and pedagogy on theories of the multidimensional nature of intelligence and giftedness. Plainview English teacher Olivia Jeffers developed an interdisciplinary, individualized course that a multiracial group of both high- and low-track students take to help satisfy college-entrance English requirements. Students choose much of their own reading and work on research projects at their own pace. Jeffers does not feel that she is holding the high-achieving students back by having them in the same room with low-achieving students. In fact, she sees it as quite the opposite. She described the benefit of the detracked classroom for a high-achieving white student from a wealthy suburban family:

> In class discussions, this girl not only contributes her ideas, but she also gets insight from somebody else who hasn't had her experience, or doesn't own a horse, or a place out in the country—a kid who gets on the bus every day and lives in two rooms. She listens to kids who've had to struggle just to survive.

Jeffers says she has constructed a learning environment for students where she can find "the genius within them." She finds that when students develop insight into their own ways of knowing and learning, they become highly motivated *students* in the broader sense of the word, thirsty for a greater understanding of the world around them.

Like Jeffers, other teachers changed their conceptions of ability after creating environments in which all students could be smart. One teacher told us, "Heterogeneous grouping has made teachers think differently about all kids; they seemorepotential."

Another teacher stated, "The program has done amazing things for standard-track kids. All of a sudden, somebody says, 'You can do this!' "

A Cautionary Note

Most of the educators we studied changed their practices in the belief that colleagues, families, and students would happily support reform that enhanced the achievement of students previously in the low track, without harming—and perhaps even enriching—the experiences of students who would otherwise be in high tracks. Yet they quickly learned that their challenges were compounded by formidable cultural and political obstacles. They ran headlong into deeply held beliefs and ideologies about intelligence, racial differences, social stratification, and privilege. Conventional conceptions of intelligence, ability, and giftedness combined with the local community culture and politics around race and social class to fuel enormous resistance.

In the end, none of the schools achieved the extent of detracking and curriculum reform hoped for. Their promising efforts toward high standards for all students were cut short by fears that the advantages of high-achieving students would be compromised.

The experience of the gifted education specialist at Explorer Middle School, which offered challenge courses to *all* students, captures the essence of the battles. Parents of identified gifted students severely criticized her for not offering their children separate enrichment classes. What upset the parents most was not the quality of the curriculum. It was that their children were no longer being singled out and treated differently:

> They didn't ask, "Well, what are our kids learning in your classes?" I found that really dismaying, because I was prepared to tell them what we do in class. I had course outlines. I send objectives, goals, and work requirements home with every class, and nobody asked me anything about that. ... I'm dealing with their egos, more than what their kids really need educationally.

This political battle was ostensibly fought over which kids—gifted or not gifted, and according to which definition—would have access to which curriculum and which teacher. The cultural underpinnings of such battles, however, are far more profound. At risk for the families of high-track students is the entire system of meritocracy on which they base their privileged positions in society. As this system begins to crack, these parents often employ tactics that make reform politically impossible. Given that detracking is basic to standards-based reform, policymakers and educators stand forewarned.

Note

1. MacIver uses the term *double dose* to describe strategies that provide low-achieving students with extra time and instruction on the regular curriculum, rather than a separate remedial curriculum. See *Helping Students Who Fall Behind*, by Douglas MacIver (Baltimore: Center for Research on Students Placed at Risk, Johns Hopkins University 1991).

Equal Does Not Mean Identical

Latoya was already an advanced reader when she entered 1st grade in a large, urban school district. Her teacher noticed the challenging chapter books Latoya brought to school and read with little effort. After administering a reading assessment, the school's reading consultant confirmed that Latoya was reading at the 5th grade level. Latoya's parents reported with pride that she had started to read independently when she was 3 years old and "had read every book she could get her hands on."

In the March 1998 issue of *Educationa Leadership* Jeannie Oakes and Amy Stuart Wells argue in their article "Detracking for High Student Achievement" that high academic standards "will also bring excellence by requiring all students to demonstrate higher levels of achievement and by providing all students with *equal* [emphasis added] educational opportunities while preparing a more informed citizenry and a better trained work force" (p. 38). But what about Latoya? If, as it sounds, *equal* means *identical*, will equal educational opportunities sufficiently challenge Latoya in reading?

Equal and Identical Are Not the Same

Providing identical educational opportunities for all students will not enable Latoya to increase her reading level, nor will they help her attain more advanced and more sophisticated levels of accomplishments in reading. Rather, if appropriate curriculum and instruction are not supplied, she will systematically be held back and will stagnate in a system that offers identical opportunities for all students. What she needs is different content, resources, and support! It is clear that in Latoya's class *all children should not be reading at the 1st grade level just because they are 1st graders*. If Latoya has not made any further progress in reading by the end of the school year, she will have wasted valuable opportunities. To achieve at increasingly higher levels in reading and to continue to develop her talents, she will require different, not equal, resources, teaching strategies, and content. How can equal curriculum, instruction, and expectations address the diverse learning needs in Latoya's classroom?

Why Is Differentiation Difficult?

Latoya is now a 5th grader. When Latoya was in 1st grade, her teacher had to simultaneously meet Latoya's educational needs and address the needs of her classmates, many of whom neither recognized initial consonant sounds nor had begun to read. Four years later, Latoya's 5th grade teacher, looking for information in Latoya's permanent file, noticed the reading assessment completed in 1st grade and read with amazement about her early, advanced reading. As a 5th grader, Latoya is still reading only slightly above the 5th grade level. Her teacher could find no evidence that any curricular or instructional adjustments had been made in previous years to meet Latoya's learning needs. Discouraged about what she perceived as the school system's inability to develop Latoya's talents in reading, the 5th grade teacher contacted the special education coordinator and asked about provisions to challenge advanced students in reading. The special education coordinator responded with amazement, "We don't need any services for gifted students. We expect high levels of achievement from all students. And anyway, we don't have any gifted kids in this school." The classroom teacher was left wondering what she could do to motivate Latoya, who still seems to have a talent in reading but is achieving only slightly above grade level. Latoya's story is true.

The needs of students like Latoya are often unmet in their classrooms. All children need to learn and to increase their current levels of achievement, yet whole-group, single-size-fits-all instruction rarely offers the kinds of adaptation required to meet the needs of a diverse group of learners. Differentiation is defined in various ways, but it is usually regarded as accommodating learning differences in children by identifying students' strengths and using appropriate strategies to address a variety of abilities, preferences, and styles. Then, whole groups, small groups, and individual students can equally engage in a variety of curriculum enrichment and acceleration experiences.

Teachers who offer differentiated curriculum and instruction view students as individuals with their own skills, interests, styles, and talents. They tailor their curriculum and instruction to meet the needs of advanced learners by using such strategies as curriculum compacting. This technique eliminates or streamlines content that students already know and replaces it with more challenging material, often based on students' interests (Reis & Renzulli, 1992; Renzulli, 1978). Other strategies include tiered instruction and assignments, which provide different learning opportunities for students at different achievement levels. Independent study and opportunities for individually prescribed levels of content and instruction are also important differentiation strategies (Renzulli, 1977; Tomlinson, 1996, 1997).

Unfortunately, recent research indicates that only a small number of teachers offer differentiation in their classrooms (Archambault et al., 1993; Tomlinson et al., 1995). Similar research about high-achieving learners in heterogeneous classrooms indicates that many children are unchallenged and are not given appropriate levels of curriculum and instruction (Cohen, 1997). In one study, observers in 46 classrooms found that high-achieving students were asked to do exactly what students who achieved at average levels were doing in

84 percent of the activities. Very little differentiation of content or instruction was provided (Westberg, Archambault, Dobyns, & Salvin, 1993).

We have also investigated why many teachers do not offer differentiation. In a survey of randomly selected 3rd and 4th grade teachers in public schools, 61 percent indicated that they had no training in meeting the needs of high-achieving students in heterogeneous classrooms. Fifty-four percent of the responding teachers in private or independent schools indicated that they had no background or training in meeting the needs of such students (Archambault et al., 1993). We also know that preservice and novice teachers understand, but do not have the background and skills to assess or address, the diversity in levels of achievement and aptitude for learning in the classroom (Tomlinson et al., 1995). The good news is that when trained in differentiation, 90 percent of classroom teachers were able to compact curriculum for students who had already mastered the content (Reis et al., 1993). In the same study, we also learned that more training time and differing types of professional development experiences, such as peer coaching, resulted in higher levels of success in implementing curriculum compacting. In another study, we found that when training and support are provided, many classroom teachers can and do furnish differentiation to above-average and advanced students in both heterogeneous and homogeneous groups (Westberg & Archambault, 1995).

It's Not the Grouping That Matters, It's What Happens in the Group

Does providing differentiated curriculum and instruction mean that we create inequalities, even if it occurs within various grouping options? If one reads the article "Detracking for High Student Achievement" by Oakes and Wells (1998), it would certainly appear so. "But what about the firmly entrenched system of tracking that exposes students to dramatically different and unequal levels of curriculum?" they ask (p. 38). What does tracking have to do with Latoya? The issue is not grouping or tracking, which we regard as two quite different concepts. Tracking is the general, and usually permanent, assignment of students to classes that are taught at a certain level and with whole-group instruction. Grouping is a more flexible, less permanent arrangement of students that takes into account factors in addition to ability, such as motivation, interests, instructional levels, and student effort (Renzulli & Reis, 1991). What is important, in our belief, is what happens within the different types of grouping arrangements used in schools—age groups, instructional groups, or interest groups. We believe that assigning children to predetermined tracks on the basis of ability or achievement is wrong, but so is whole-class instruction with no instructional modification that systematically holds back children like Latoya. All learners in our schools, including those who are advanced, should be challenged academically. The context in which that learning takes place is negotiable, but whether it takes place is not negotiable.

All Parents Want Their Children Challenged

To argue that parents of high-achieving or gifted students want to create or continue a system of "meritocracy on which they base their privileged positions in society" (Oakes & Wells, 1998, p. 41) seems to perpetuate a false belief that pits parents of high-achieving students against all others, a condition simply not backed up either by data presented in the article or by our experiences. Some parents of students identified as gifted may have separate classes as their goals, but in our collective years of experience working with these parents, they have not been the majority.

The thousands of parents with whom we speak each year are more interested in finding the best possible education for their children. In a small manufacturing city in Connecticut, a city where over 55 percent of the population is Hispanic, parents of high-achieving Hispanic students argued for a return to some form of grouping for their children. Their middle school had eliminated all forms of grouping in all classes. With no appropriate differentiation in the classroom, parents saw that their children were not being academically challenged. Many teachers told the parents that they simply could not meet the needs of students representing a seven- or eight-year range of achievement in some of their classes. The teachers themselves asked for help in flexibly grouping students into clusters within specified classes so that they could better address students' differing instructional needs.

In a magnet school for high-achieving Hispanic students in Los Angeles, talented students are flexibly grouped for instruction in all content areas. Providing for the academic readiness of learners happens in all sorts of forms in all sorts of schools where educators strive for the maximum development of student potential.

All parents want their children to achieve at high levels and to learn at an appropriate pace, depth, and level of complexity. To blame parents for wanting challenge for their children or to accuse them of creating a meritocracy ignores the very real evidence that some students are not being challenged in school. Instead of attacking the parents of these students, we invite them to participate in the dialogue on school improvement by encouraging open discussion about how schools can address the needs of all children and, indeed, how parents can be active partners in achieving this goal.

References

Archambault, F. X., Jr., Westberg, K. L., Brown, S., Hallmark, B. W., Zhang, W., & Emmons, C. (1993). Classroom practices used with gifted third and fourth grade students. *Journal for the Education of the Gifted, 16*(2), 103–119.

Cohen, C. S. (1997). *The effectiveness of peer-coaching on classroom teachers' use of dif-ferentiation for gifted middle school students.* Unpublished doctoral dissertation, University of Connecticut.

Oakes, J., & Wells, A. S.(1998). Detracking for highstudent achievement. Educational Leadership, 55(6), 38–41.

Reis, S. M., & Renzulli, J. S. (1992). Using curriculum compacting to challenge the above-average. *Educational Leadership, 50*(2), 51–57.

Reis, S. M., Westberg, K. L., Kulikowich, J., Caillard, F., Hébert, T., Plucker, J., Purcell, J. H., Rogers, J. B., & Smist, J. M. (1993). *Why not let high ability students start school in January? The curriculum compacting study.* (Research Monograph 93106). Storrs, CT: University of Connecticut, The National Research Center on the Gifted and Talented.

Renzulli, J. S. (1977). *The enrichment triad model.* Mansfield Center, CT: Creative Learning Press.

Renzulli, J. S. (1978). What makes giftedness? Re-examining a definition. *Phi Delta Kappan, 60,* 180–184, 261.

Renzulli, J. S., & Reis, S. M. (1991). The reform movement and the quiet crisis in gifted education. *Gifted Child Quarterly, 35*(1), 26–35.

Tomlinson, C. A. (Developer). (1996). Differentiating instruction for mixed-ability classrooms. [Professional Inquiry Kit]. (Available from ASCD)

Tomlinson, C. A. (Developer). (1997). Differentiating instruction. [Facilitator's Guide and Videos]. (Available from ASCD)

Tomlinson, C. A., Callahan, C. M., Moon, T. R., Tomchin, E. M., Landrum, M., Imbeau, M., Hunsaker, S. L., & Eiss, N. (1995). *Preservice teacher preparation in meeting the needs of gifted and other academically diverse students.* (Research Monograph 94134). Charlottesville, VA: University of Virginia, The National Research Center on the Gifted and Talented.

Westberg, K. L., & Archambault, F. X., Jr. (Eds.) (1995). *Profiles of successful practices for high ability students in elementary classrooms.* (Research Monograph 95122). Storrs, CT: University of Connecticut, The National Research Center on the Gifted and Talented.

Westberg, K. L., Archambault, F. X., Dodyns, S. M., & Salvin, T. J. (1993). The classroom practices observation study. *Journal for the Education of the Gifted, 16*(2), 120–146.

POSTSCRIPT

Should Ability-Level Tracking Be Abandoned?

Despite numerous studies designed to determine whether ability-level tracking is beneficial or detrimental to the academic achievement of students, a consensus has yet to emerge among either researchers or policymakers about whether or not the practice should be abandoned. In large measure, consensus has been difficult because of the variable results that have been obtained across studies. In part, this variability is due to differences in the ways in which studies have been designed. Correlational studies have involved comparisons between existing classrooms—that is, classrooms over which the researchers have had no control in terms of assignment of students, design of curriculum, or implementation. Many of these studies have found that tracking affects student achievement in comparison to the heterogeneous grouping of students. See "The Stratification of High School Learning Opportunities," by Adam Gamoran, *Sociology of Education* (vol. 60, no. 3, 1987). These studies have been criticized, however, because it is often not clear whether differences in student achievement have arisen because of tracking per se or because of some other preexisting difference between students, classes, or schools. See "Detracking America's Schools: Should We Really Care?" by Richard M. Jaeger and John A. Hattie, and "Detracking and Its Detractors: Flawed Evidence, Flawed Values," by Robert E. Slavin, *Phi Delta Kappan* (November 1995). Controlled experiments, which avoid this interpretive problem, have generally demonstrated that tracking has rather minimal effects on student achievement. These controlled experiments, however, have been criticized because they often exclude intellectually gifted students (see "Comments on 'The Reform Without Cost?'" by James J. Gallagher, *Phi Delta Kappan*, November 1995) or involve very few students and sometimes only a single school, all of which raise questions about whether or not the experiments could detect the effects of tracking if they existed and about the generalizability of their results. Faced with such variability, some scholars and policymakers have focused on the studies that support their position and ignored the remainder, whereas others have tallied the studies showing beneficial, detrimental, and no effects, and argued in favor of the position with the most tally marks. See "Will Tracking Reform Promote Social Equity?" by Tom Loveless, *Educational Leadership* (April 1999).

Ultimately, decisions about abandoning tracking may depend more on political and ideological factors than on empirical data. On the one hand, some have argued against ability-level tracking based not only on results from controlled experiments but also on the grounds that it is inconsistent with the concept of equal opportunity—the ideal on which public schools were initially founded. On the other hand, there are scholars who point to data, albeit from correlationalstudies, indicating that high-achieving students benefit from ability-level tracking whereas low-achieving students are hurt by it. These latter scholars argue that such data create an ideological dilemma: Should we institute educational practices that favor gifted students, who are more likely to be from the mainstream culture, or lower-achieving students, who are more likely to be members of ethnic and racial minorities and be economically disadvantaged? As James Gallagher puts it, Should we choose excellence or equity? In fact, some writers favor excellence, while others favor equity (see "Untracking and Students' Futures: Closing the Gap Between Aspirations and Expectations," by Renee Smith Maddox and Anne Wheelock, *Phi Delta Kappan,* November 1995).

Comprehensive summaries of the empirical studies of ability-level tracking can be found in "Ability Grouping and Student Achievement in Elementary Schools: A Best-Evidence Synthesis," by Robert E. Slavin, *Review of Educational Research* (vol. 57, 1987), pp. 293–336, and in "Achievement Effects of Ability Grouping in Secondary Schools: A Best-Evidence Synthesis," by Robert E. Slavin, *Review of Educational Research* (vol. 60, 1990), pp. 471–499. A paper focusing on the impact of tracking on self-esteem and other dimensions of student functioning besides academic achievement is "Do Students Learn More in Heterogeneous or Homogeneous Groupings?" by T. Good and S. Marshall, in P. Peterson, L. Wilkinson, and M. Hallinan, eds., *The Social Context of Instruction: Group Organization and Group Processes* (Academic Press, 1991). The paper by Jaeger and Hattie in the November 1995 issue of *Phi Delta Kappan* may help to place the controversies about ability-level tracking into perspective. These authors suggest that teacher practices are likely to be a far more important determinant of student achievement than whether or not students are grouped by ability. Finally, a provocative paper by James E. Rosenbaum entitled "If Tracking Is Bad, Is Detracking Better?" *American Educator* (Winter 1999–2000) examines the political and logistical problems that might arise from abandoning ability-level tracking.

ISSUE 3

Should English Immersion Replace Bilingual Education?

YES: Keith Baker, from "Structured English Immersion: Breakthrough in Teaching Limited-English-Proficient Students," *Phi Delta Kappan* (November 1998)

NO: Josephine Arce, from "Cultural Hegemony: The Politics of Bilingual Education," *Multicultural Education* (Winter 1998)

ISSUE SUMMARY

YES: Educational consultant Keith Baker argues that empirical evidence indicates that Structured English Immersion, which provides academic instruction in English, leads to larger gains in academic achievement and English mastery than bilingual education, which provides academic instruction in the students' native language.

NO: Josephine Arce, assistant professor of elementary eduction, College of Education, at San Francisco State University, argues that the anti-bilingual-education movement sweeping the country has resulted from a conservative political agenda designed to oppress racial and ethnic minorities. She asserts that the empirical evidence supports the superiority of bilingual education over Structured English Immersion.

U.S. schools face the challenge of educating an ever-increasing number of children whose native language is not English. In the 1980s, for example, the number of Hispanic students in U.S. schools increased by 50 percent. The number of Asian American students increased by 100 percent during this same period. This trend continued throughout the 1990s, with the number of non-English-language-background (NELB) children in the United States now exceeding 5 million.

How can the educational needs of NELB children best be met, thereby ensuring their full participation in society? To date, educational programs for NELB children have typically reflected either a subtractive or an additive approach. In the subtractive approach, the goal is to replace—at least within the context of the school—the child's native language with English as quickly as possible. In the subtractive approach, NELB students participate—sometimes outside of the regular classroom—in programs designed to increase their facility with English. Instruction in academic content areas (e.g., science) may be delayed until the NELB student gains some minimal facility with English, or it may be conducted in parallel with the teaching of English language skills. In either case, in the subtractive approach content-area instruction occurs largely (if not exclusively) in English and in the regular classroom. Ideally, the regular classroom teacher uses English that is adapted in various ways (e.g., through simplification, repetition, and the use of supporting visual material) to the skills of the NELB students so as to make content-area instruction as comprehensible as possible.

Critics of the subtractive approach argue that it limits NELB students' access to academic content because of the time spent targeting their English language skills rather than academics, or because the students' limited proficiency in English prevents them from assimilating much of the content of the academic instruction.

In the additive approach to the education of NELB children, English is seen as a supplement rather than as a replacement for the child's native language. In the additive approach, much (if not all) content-area instruction is provided in the NELB student's native language. Many argue that NELB students should receive such non-English instruction for a minimum of five to seven years. English is targeted as well in this approach but less intensely than in the subtractive approach. Critics argue that this approach is based on the assumption that academic content mastered in the native language will become accessible to the student in English more or less automatically—an assumption for which there is little empirical support. Programs labeled as bilingual education typically reflect the additive approach.

In the past few years, the voices championing the subtractive approach have grown stronger and have had greater influence on public policy. School districts from around the United States have begun to place NELB students into English-based content-area instruction more quickly and at ever younger ages. In California, additive bilingual education, the state-mandated approach for many years, was voted out by the electorate in 1998 and replaced with Structured (or Sheltered) English Immersion (SEI), a program that clearly reflects a subtractive approach.

The two readings that follow use the California adoption of SEI as a starting point for a broader consideration of whether or not SEI should replace additive bilingual education. In the first selection, Keith Baker describes SEI and argues that there is empirical support for its superiority over bilingual education, as evidenced by differences in achievement test scores in academic content areas and in English as well as by teacher judgments of NELB students' proficiency in English. In the second selection, Josephine Arce argues that there is ample empirical evidence that additive bilingual programs are superior to subtractive programs on variables such as achievement test scores and parent involvement.

Keith Baker    **YES**

Structured English Immersion

By popular referendum in June 1998, California's voters replaced the country's most extensive bilingual education program for limited-English-proficient (LEP) students with a program of "Structured English Immersion" (SEI). Adriana de Kanter and I were the first to name and describe such a program when we recommended that schools teaching English to students with limited proficiency try the impressive Canadian Immersion method of teaching second languages.[1]

In the nearly two decades since our suggestion, a few SEI programs have been developed and tested. The experience of these programs, especially Seattle's, can provide much-needed guidance to California's schools—and to others interested in the reform of bilingual education programs.

What Is SEI?

J. David Ramirez and his colleagues offer the most extensive discussion of the characteristics of SEI. As the first step in a longitudinal study comparing SEI to two types of bilingual education programs, Ramirez' group reviewed the literature to determine the theoretical and instructional differences among the three programs. Next they conducted extensive classroom observations over a period of four years to verify the presence of these hypothesized differences. But the differences posited by academic theorists were not apparent in actual practice. The *only* hypothesized difference found to occur in actual practice was the percentage of instructional time teachers taught in English as opposed to Spanish.[2]

In all likelihood, classroom teachers are exercising their good judgment by ignoring a lot of academic mumbo jumbo that has no practical application. It seems sufficient to define an SEI program as one in which 1) English is used and taught at a level appropriate to the class of English learners (that's different from the way English is used in the mainstream classroom), and 2) teachers are oriented toward maximizing instruction in English and use English for 70% to 90% of instructional time, averaged over the first three years of instruction.[3]

Ramirez also reviewed the literature on second-language learning in general to identify the properties of a good setting for such learning. He then looked for these properties in actual classroom practice. Again, there was no difference among the three programs: all were really bad places in which to learn a second language. The common problem seemed to be the instructional constraints imposed by large classes. The optimal setting for learning a second language is one that allows for extensive dialogue between teacher and learner, which is impossible in classes with more than eight students. Drastic reductions in class size may be the most productive step that could be taken to improve the instruction of LEP students.[4]

Is SEI Effective?

Over the last 18 years, I have identified the following programs as effective examples of SEI.[5]

The Canadian Immersion program, first detailed by Wallace Lambert and Richard Tucker, is the exemplar for SEI.[6] Advocates of bilingual education programs argue that this instructional method, although very successful in Canada, will not generalize to LEP students in the U.S. However, the program evaluations that I am about to discuss show that this fear is baseless.

Russell Gersten and his colleagues found SEI superior to bilingual education for Vietnamese immigrants in California and for Hispanics in Texas. An SEI program for Hispanics in Uvalde, Texas, was found to have improved high school graduation rates and lowered retention throughout the grades compared to a prior, ill-defined program.[7] The Uvalde program and the one Gersten and John Woodward studied in a California district were all-English direct instruction programs (Distar) used with LEP students. Distar provides a structured curriculum that can be adjusted to the level of the learner and clearly works well both with students learning English as a second language and with English-speaking at-risk students.

Ramirez and his colleagues compared SEI to two types of bilingual education programs that differed in the number of years Spanish was used and in the amount of Spanish used during the school day. (Early-exit programs aim to put their students in mainstream classes after about three years; late-exit programs aim for about seven years.) After four years of schooling in the respective programs, students in the early-exit and immersion programs had scores roughly one-third higher than the late-exit students in reading, language, and math. There was no difference between the immersion and early-exit students' test scores. ... Late-exit programs were previously required by the federal *Lau* remedies and by California state law; are currently required under state law in Massachusetts, New York, and Texas; and are the model stressed by advocates of bilingual education.[8] The superiority of SEI over bilingual education programs for teaching English [was] clear.

Kim Yap and Donald Enoki compared ESL (English as a Second Language) and bilingual education programs serving 4,000 students in 55 schools.[9] The authors concluded that there was no difference in English learning between ESL and bilingual education programs, but, of the 47 comparisons they conducted over several years of school and across several different measures, 31 favored ESL, a statistically significant advantage. ... Other examples of effective ESL programs are in Fairfax County, Virginia, and Prince George's County, Maryland.

Texas state law requires bilingual education, as California used to. The Texas law allows temporary experimental trials of alternatives. In the mid-1980s, seven local education agencies in Texas conducted a multi-year trial comparing SEI to bilingual education, which was evaluated by the state education agency. SEI was the clear winner.

El Paso created an SEI program in which Spanish instruction was reduced to 30 minutes a day. The district followed students from this program and from the state-mandated bilingual education program for 12 years.[10] The SEI students scored significantly higher on all tests for 11 straight years. In the 12th year, the SEI students still scored higher, but their advantage was no longer statistically significant, suggesting that, after a decade or so, the harm that bilingual education programs do to learning English is more or less wiped out by continued exposure to English outside the bilingual classroom.

Gersten and Woodward also surveyed teachers in El Paso.[11] The results indicate[d] that the teachers in the program using more English were more confident that their students would succeed when mainstreamed.

J. Webb, R. Clerc, and A. Gavito looked at 16 schools in Houston, eight with SEI programs and eight with bilingual education.[12] [They] found that SEI produced higher English achievement. ... In ... the Houston study, the superiority of SEI over bilingual education on learning was more than twice as great as the impact of nonverbal intelligence on learning.

In 1994 New York City issued a longitudinal study of 15,000 LEP students.[13] On every measure, those in ESL programs outperformed those in bilingual education. However, since the report did not control for ethnicity, which was confounded with program assignment, the results have been dismissed as invalid. Nevertheless, the report deserves to be taken seriously. There were five ethnic groups included. When these groups were rank ordered by the percentage of students in ESL programs, the rank order correlation between exposure to ESL and the percentage of the ethnic population mainstreamed within three years was $r = 1.0$. ...

I need hardly point out that correlations at these levels are unheard of in educational research. This is a remarkable relationship between program and effect. The correlations tell us we can pick any two ethnic groups and predict with perfect accuracy which one will have had the most success if we know the percentage of the population in ESL programs. Indeed, we can pick any three or any four or all five ethnicities and predict with perfection their success in learning English if we are told the percentage of each group in ESL programs. On the other hand, if all we know are the ethnic groups, these predictions cannot be made accurately. We might make some accurate predictions about outcomes—with Hispanics or Chinese perhaps—but what about Hispanics or Haitians, Koreans or Chinese, Russians or Chinese? What if we go to triples? What is the academic rank order of Chinese, Koreans, and Russians? Given only the ethnicity, we don't know, but once we know the percentage in ESL programs, we can answer all these questions accurately. The relationship between ethnicity, type of program, and outcome is beyond coincidence. It is not necessary to statistically control for ethnicity to see that there is a difference in effect between the programs.

California's Proposition 227 imposes the added constraint of requiring LEP students to be mainstreamed after one year. Although many of the SEI programs described so far mainstream their students in two to three years, compared to the five to eight years called for by a full bilingual education program, the only SEI program I know that can satisfy California's new law is Seattle's Newcomers Program. LEP students in Seattle are first placed in "Newcomer Centers" for half a year to one year, where they receive intense instruction in English. After no more than a year, they are mainstreamed. They get additional help in the mainstream classroom as needed through ESL instruction and native language support from bilingual teacher aides.

Madeline Ramey and I looked at test results over three years for three groups of students in Seattle: 1) LEP students in the ESL/native language support program, 2) LEP students whose parents opted them out of the program into the mainstream classroom, and 3) English-speaking students from the mainstream classroom scoring below the 35th percentile, the score used to classify language-minority children as LEP. LEP students in the program gained 7-8 NCEs (normal-curve equivalents) in reading, language, and math over three years while LEPs in the regular classroom gained only 0.5-4 NCEs. Non-LEPs initially scoring below the 35th percentile gained 1.5-5 NCEs.

The LEP students in the program gained about twice as much in terms of NCEs in a year as did LEP students whose parents opted them out of the program and into the mainstream classroom. This outcome shows that the Seattle program—a model for the requirements of Proposition 227—is remarkably effective in moving LEP students toward full participation in an English-speaking society.

How Does SEI Work?

Although SEI, which uses more English than bilingual education programs do, results in students' learning more English, it is not merely a matter of additional time on the task of learning English, as Rosalie Porter has simple-mindedly asserted.[14] The teachers of Ramirez' early-exit students used considerably more Spanish than did the SEI teachers, with equally good results. Adriana de Kanter and I identified a few bilingual education programs in which LEP students learned more English than did comparable students in an all-English setting.[15]

Some (minimal) use of a student's non-English language may help in any or all of several ways. It may make the student more comfortable in school. It may more quickly get through really difficult communication problems between teacher and student. It may boost student self-esteem.[16] It may help motivate learners. It may take advantage of the powerful effect of massed versus spaced trials on learning.

On the other hand, monolingual teachers can also do well in teaching LEP students. Gersten concludes that, "based on the two years of observational research and analysis, ... monolingual English speaking teachers can work productively with language minority students, and teachers need not radically alter their approaches to teaching to be successful."[17] Joan Fitzgerald notes that "teachers of ESL students could follow sound principles of reading instruction based on current cognitive research done with native English speakers. There was virtually no evidence that ESL learners need notably divergent forms of instruction."[18]

Adjusting instruction in English to the learner's level of English seems important, if not essential. Seattle did something with its ESL students that did not happen to fully mainstreamed LEP students. The two direct instruction programs that Gersten examined, which I mentioned earlier, used a structured approach in which teaching was adjusted to the level of the learner.

Although it apparently has not been addressed in the research literature, it seems that an important ingredient in teaching English is a teacher with a good command of standard English who can model English well. This point is indirectly supported by several studies showing that the more competent teachers are by the standards of bilingual education programs, which place a premium on speaking some other language, the less well their students learn English.[19]

Classroom aides who speak a non-English language contribute to an SEI program by providing instructional support to children having temporary difficulty following a lesson in English.

Why Use SEI?

California's schools have no choice. Others should consider SEI as an effective alternative to bilingual education programs for meeting the legal requirements of Laufor teaching LEP students. Another important reason to use SEI is that it solves a vexing problem in bilingual education programs. Assuming that bilingual education program theory is correct, there is no valid method of identifying which students will benefit from bilingual education. LEP identification procedures and the procedures used to determine when a student is ready to move from a bilingual education program to the mainstream classroom are psychometric nightmares of error and false assignments. One major error is assigning students who speak and use English better than they speak or use another language to bilingual education programs.

The only valid information known about LEP students is that they need help with English. Therefore, teaching and helping them in English is indisputably correct. The assumption that we can identify those students who need help in English because they depend on some other language is invalid; it can't be done at any acceptable level of accuracy. SEI, especially the direct instruction model, finesses the identification problem by using English to teach students having trouble with English—not some other language they may or may not know well enough for schooling.

Moreover, many local education agencies as well as the states of California and New York require a LEP student to pass both an English reading and an English language standardized achievement test at the 40th percentile. By definition, 40% of the monolingual English-speaking population could not pass a 40th-percentile cutoff. To make matters even worse, the joint requirement—the 40th percentile on two subtests—is about a 60th-percentile score on the total test battery. *The majority of monolingual English-speaking students could never pass the test to get out of these programs.*

California's new law solves this problem with heavy-handed finesse—everybody is mainstreamed after one year. Even if California continues its absurd 40th-percentile cutoff score, it is no longer a problem: 1) LEP students will be in the mainstream after no more than one year, and 2) schools will probably have to continue to give them extra help in English after they are mainstreamed until they meet the English cutoff score—performance higher than the typical native English speaker. California's new law seems to have inadvertently created a program of extensive help in English within the regular classroom setting until LEP students master English at a level well above that of the average English speaker. While this may be silly in some respects, it is an interesting civil rights program, in that it provides extra help to language-minority students until they surpass the majority. Since lack of English ability is the driving force behind the low socioeconomic status of language minorities in the U.S., the overdose of English instruction produced as a side effect of California's new law will be of great help to these children in an English-speaking country.

Conclusions

SEI is not necessarily an all-English program, but it does make considerably less use of the non-English language for instruction than does bilingual education.

Schools that decide, or are forced by law, to change to SEI do not face as formidable a task as many fear. Not only have others paved the way in developing effective SEI programs to serve as a model, but also the job seems easier to do than most believe. The schools discussed earlier created effective SEI programs without much trouble, and they did it in the face of considerable opposition from bilingual education program advocates, college professors, and state and federal educational bureaucracies.

Linguists and professors of second-language learning and bilingual education overdramatize the difficulty that LEP students face in learning English. Humans are remarkably good at language learning. There seem to be only two ways to screw up a LEP child's opportunity to learn English. The first is to use too much of the non-English language in the classroom, and this seems to be the problem in many bilingual education programs. The second is to fail to realize that LEP students face a more demanding task in school than do native English-speaking students. LEP students have to learn everything in the curriculum and then learn English on top of it.

Both bilingual education and SEI theory maintain that this extra learning load can be handled within the normal school day, although by different mechanisms. Bilingual education posits that it can be done by teaching non-language subjects in the non-English language while the student is learning English. There is very little research support for this contention, and considerable evidence to the contrary.[20] SEI argues that content and English can be taught together by teaching content through learner-appropriate English. Despite the demonstrated successes of SEI, this is asking a lot. Much can be said for extending the school day or the school year for LEP students as perhaps the best way to meet their special needs.

Finally, direct instruction is particularly interesting since it works well with both monolingual at-risk students and with LEP students. A program with this kind of record should not be ignored.

Notes

1. Keith Baker and Adriana de Kanter, "Federal Policy and the Effectiveness of Bilingual Education," in idem, eds., *Bilingual Education: A Reappraisal of Federal Policy* (Lexington, Mass.: Lexington Books, 1983), pp. 33-86.
2. Linda Schinke-Llano and J. David Ramirez, *Programmatic and Instructional Aspects of Language Immersion Programs* (Mountain View, Calif.: SRA Technologies, 1984); and J. David Ramirez et al., *Final Report: Longitudinal Study of Structured Immersion Strategy, Early-Exit, and Late-Exit Transitional Bilingual Education Programs for Language-Minority Children* (San Mateo, Calif.: Aguirre International, 1991).
3. Ramirez et al., op. cit.; and Tamara Lucas and Anne Katz, "Reframing the Debate: The Role of Native Language in English Only Programs for Language Minority Students," *TESOL Quarterly,* vol. 28, 1994, pp. 537-61.
4. J. David Ramirez and Keith Baker, "Becoming a More Frequent Speaker of a Second Language," paper presented at the annual meeting of the American Educational Research Association, Washington, D.C., 1987; and Ramirez et al., op. cit.
5. My criterion for effectiveness is that English and other subjects are tested in English. This is the legal requirement set forth in the Supreme Court's *Lau* decision. There is no doubt that bilingual education programs succeed in teaching more Spanish than does SEI, but legally that does not matter.
6. There is an extensive literature on the Canadian Immersion program. See especially Wallace E. Lambert and G. Richard Tucker, *Bilingual Education of Children: The St. Lambert Experiment* (Rowley, Mass.: Newbury House, 1972); and Fred Genesee et al., "Three Elementary School Alternatives for Learning Through a Second Language," *Modern Language Journal,* vol. 73, 1989, pp. 250-63.
7. Wesley Becker and Russell Gersten, "A Follow-Up of Follow Through: The Later Effects of the Direct Instruction Model on Children in Fifth and Sixth Grades," *American Educational Research Journal,* vol. 19, 1982, pp. 75-92; Russell Gersten, "Structured Immersion for Language Minority Students: Results of a Longitudinal Evaluation," *Educational Evaluation and Policy Analysis,* vol. 7, 1985, pp. 187-96; Russell Gersten and John Woodward, "A Longitudinal Study of Transitional and Immersion Bilingual Education Programs in One District," *Elementary School Journal,* vol. 95, 1995, pp. 223-39; and idem, "A Case for Structured Immersion," *Educational Leadership,* September 1985, pp. 75-79.
8. See Virginia Collier, *The Effect of Age on Acquisition of a Second Language for School* (Washington, D.C.: National Clearinghouse for

Bilingual Education, 1987); idem, "Age and Rate of Acquisition of Second Language for Academic Purposes," *TESOL Quarterly*, vol. 21, 1987, pp. 617-41; James Cummins, "Educational Implications of Mother Tongue Maintenance in Minority Language Groups," *Canadian Modern Language Review*, vol. 34, 1978, pp. 395-416; idem, "The Role of Primary Language Development in Promoting Educational Success for Language Minority Students," in California State Department of Education, *Schooling and Language Minority Students: A Theoretical Framework* (Los Angeles: Evaluation, Dissemination, and Assessment Center, UCLA, 1981); idem, "The Construct of Language Proficiency in Bilingual Education," in *Perspectives on Bilingualism and Bilingual Education* (Washington, D.C.: Georgetown University Press, 1985), pp. 209-31; and Stephen Krashen and Douglas Biber, *On Course: Bilingual Education's Success in California* (Sacramento: Association for Bilingual Education, 1988).

9. Kim Yap and Donald Y. Enoki, "SLEP Student Achievement," paper presented at the annual meeting of the American Educational Research Association, New Orleans, 1988.

10. El Paso Independent School District, *Interim Report of the Five-Year Bilingual Education Pilot, 1986-87 School Year* (El Paso: Office for Research and Evaluation, 1987); idem, *Bilingual Education Evaluation: The Sixth Year in a Longitudinal Study* (El Paso: Office for Research and Evaluation, 1990); and idem, *Bilingual Education Evaluation* (El Paso: Office for Research and Evaluation, 1992).

11. Gersten and Woodward, "A Longitudinal Study."

12. J. Webb, R. Clerc, and A. Gavito, "Comparison of Bilingual and Immersion Programs Using Structural Modeling," HISD, mimeograph, 1987.

13. *Educational Progress of Students in Bilingual and ESL Programs: A Longitudinal Study* (New York: New York City Public Schools, October 1994).

14. Rosalie Porter, Forked Tongue (New York: Basic Books, 1990); and idem, "Reflections on the Politics of Bilingual Education," *Journal of Law and Politics*, vol. 6, 1990, pp. 573-99.

15. Baker and de Kanter, op. cit.

16. Susan Alexander and Keith Baker, "Some Ethical Issues in Applied Social Psychology: The Case of Bilingual Education and Self-Esteem," *Journal of Applied Social Psychology*, vol. 22, 1992, pp. 1741-57.

17. Russell Gersten, "Literacy Instruction for Language Minority Children," *Elementary School Journal*, vol. 96, 1996, p. 239.

18. Jill Fitzgerald, "English as a Second Language Learners' Cognitive Processes: A Review of Research in the United States," *Review of Educational Research*, vol. 65, 1995, p. 184.

19. Christine Rossell and Keith Baker, *Bilingual Education in Massachusetts* (Boston: Pioneer, 1996).

20. Rossell and Baker, *Bilingual Education*, and Baker and de Kanter, op. cit.

Cultural Hegemony: The Politics of Bilingual Education

On June 2, 1998, California passed Proposition 227, an initiative to eliminate bilingual education from the state's public schools, by a 61-39 percent margin. Proposition 227, the Unz Initiative, mandates that all children in California's public schools be taught in English as rapidly and effectively as possible without using a child's primary personal resource: his or her native language (unless it is English). Successful and not so successful bilingual programs are being dismantled as a result.

Ron Unz, who co-authored and financially sponsored Proposition 227, along with other proponents of the initiative, made no reference to the current research on bilingual education in their campaign. ... Unz took two viable terms used in the field of bilingual education and coined them into a mythological technique which he calls "Sheltered English Immersion." ...

Given the provisions of Proposition 227, to be placed in a bilingual classroom a child's parents must first sign a waiver to request it. Even with the waiver signed, there must be at least 20 students with parental waivers at the given grade level before a school can provide such a class. If there are not enough students for one class at the child's school, then the child must transfer elsewhere. Parents must apply annually for such a waiver. ...

Perhaps the most outrageous provision of Proposition 227 is that it holds teachers, staff, and school administrators personally liable against lawsuits if they provide instruction to language-minority children in any other language than English. The new law clearly encourages parents to act as watchdogs and spies over teachers' instructional delivery. ...

This punitive measure was approved by two-thirds of California's voters [in] June. How do we explain this overwhelming support for Proposition 227? ...[H]ow do we explain why bilingual education has become such a high profile and negatively-perceived political issue? ...

The Concept of Cultural Hegemony

One possible explanation is that bilingual education is apparently the most recent casualty of a rather virulent form of cultural hegemony imposed on immigrants and language-minority communities. It is a hegemony of cultural and political forces (such as conservative ideologues, politicians, and media fig-

From Josephine Arce, "Cultural Hegemony: The Politics of Bilingual Education," *Multicultural Education* (Winter 1998). Copyright ©1998 by *Multicultural Education*. Reprinted by permission of *Multicultural Education*, Caddo Gap Press.

ures) inciting voters (working people, by and large) to guiltlessly vent their economic uncertainty and general unease with the conditions of the culture. ...

Antonia Darder defines the dominant culture as those who control the material and symbolic wealth in a society, and the subordinate class as those who exist in social and material subordination to the dominant culture (1991, p. 30). The culture of the dominant class permeates society at multiple levels, which creates ... cultural hegemony. ... Bilingual education is viewed in the dominant ideology as an accommodation by the dominant sociopolitical class to a subordinated class, i.e., immigrants and language-minority communities.

The dominant culture operates on the assumption that the subordinated group should accommodate by assimilating and rejecting its native cultures and languages. According to Darder, there is endemic to the perceptions and assumptions made about minority groups by the dominant culture a pervasive individualistic ideology supported by cultural hegemony that truncates the ability of Euroamericans to shift from an individual to an institutional context (1991, p. 38). Thus citizens vote based on socially constructed and rarely questioned images of the "others." These images, which become "truths," are reinforced by one of the most powerful hegemonic tools: the media.

What must be understood in this analysis of the apparent fate of bilingual education is the theme of power which permeates the social relationships between dominant and subordinate groups. Power relations are reflected in hierarchical social and economic structures between those who control economic, political, and ideological sources. Immigrant people and language-minority groups in the United States do not have access to these structures. Nor do language-minority groups have access to the resources (material, monetary, knowledge) that dominant groups possess. ...

A Reactionary Direction

The Unz Initiative's title, "English for the Children," was intended to play on these very sentiments as well as the resentments of taxpayers. People across ethnic, social, and economic classes want all children living in the United States to speak English, but at what cost to their self-identity and academic success. The apparently common sense notion that English must be the immediate goal of any "worthy" immigrant is powerfully reinforced in the media. ...

Advocates for bilingual education challenge the dominant-subordinate power relations that keep language minorities in a subordinate position. Language-minority groups are not willing to accept unequal educational opportunities for their children. In the face of this challenge it apparently becomes necessary for English-speaking Americans of all races to suppress bilingualism.

Early advocates of bilingual education, understandably, could not have anticipated the ferocity of the backlash. At the time, they were merely responding to research which suggested that bilingual teaching would be effective and a pedagogically sound notion that learning occurs best in a linguistically and culturally comfortable environment.

An historical precedent for instruction in one's own language also occurred from earlier periods of large-scale immigration to the United States. Unfortunately, those periods were also notable for the intolerance demonstrated by English-speaking Americans toward language-minority groups.

The Schooling of Language-Minority Children

... Education is a vulnerable target for political mischief because of its role as a potentially strong disseminator of values to the children of our society. Public schools are not isolated institutions; they were created to serve an ideological perspective as well as to be learning centers. Elected government officials and those with political aspirations (e.g., Unz ran for governor in 1994 in California's Republican primary) have greatly influenced public opinion about schools. Yet those same officials have done little to support or create conditions for public schools to flourish.

The result is that American schools must make difficult educational choices based on political trends which, at best, only have a rhetorical interest in how children learn and develop socially. The present structure of today's schools, driven by political and economic conditions, is unlikely to coherently address the needs of a diverse society.

Current liberal and conservative political perspectives have one major element in common. Both view the language-minority student as either having a problem or being the problem. When children are viewed as the creators of the problem, those in high decision-making positions relinquish their responsibility for providing alternative solutions. This perspective feeds into the backlash against bilingual education or any other alternative educational program design.

It is significant that among conservative intellectuals and politicians the realization has dawned that states such as California will soon have a Latino school-aged population that outnumbers any other group. Latino students are projected to form 50 percent of the California school population by the year 2030 (Cummins, 1996, p. 27). Conservative political groups have initiated a variety of campaigns, such as the well funded U.S. English Only, an anti-immigrant organization, to alert the general population of the threat of a growing language-minority population, particularly Latinos.

Bilingual Education

Bilingual education is at the heart of the matter because it represents the acceptance of diversity of cultures and recognition of other languages as having a significant or even an equal status in American mainstream institutions. As C.E. Walsh (1991) states, language is one of the principle ways people define themselves; through language we establish alliances with a community, undertake interactions with others, and communicate and receive information (p. 1). Bilingual communities have the potential to build unity, to demand equitable education, and to prepare their children to have the resources needed for better employment opportunities that will result in higher economic standards of living. The collective power of such groups of people can be immense; yet does the empowerment of a community represent a threat to others? Limiting the use of, and eventually doing away with, the native language of a community is just another step toward controlling and subordinating language-minority groups (Walsh, 1991, p. 3).

Minority communities view educational institutions in two ways: as vehicles to further economic opportunities, and as structures that reinforce negative stereotypes. Recent Latino and Asian immigrants, unlike disenfranchised African Americans or Chicanos who have lived a long history of inequity, strongly believe education in the United States is the path toward prosperity. As evidence of this situation, more than 40,000 newcomers were on a waiting list to take English-as-a-second-language classes in Los Angeles on the same day Proposition 63 passed, making English the only official language in government offices in California (Crawford, 1992, p. 17).

My personal experience confirms this fact; in 19 years as an educator, and as the daughter of immigrants, I have never met an immigrant who does not embrace the American dream for his or her children. If English is to be enforced as the language of all official social interaction, what, except chauvinism, explains the refusal to fund English-as-a-second-language programs and the drive to feed intense backlash against bilingual education?

Hope Through Critical Pedagogy?

Perhaps the dominant power structure fears that if the Latino community continues to insist on retaining elements of its culture and language, then this ever-growing population can challenge the hegemonic political control in state and national elections, thus influencing future legislation. Could Latinos become the strongest ethnic group in the United States? To do so, however, they will need to overcome many barriers, such as acquiring legal status, gaining access to quality education, and achieving entry through affirmative action programs at universities and in employment opportunities. These obstacles seem insurmountable at times.

The fact that a limited number of Latino children have been and still are in bilingual classrooms does not guarantee quality education per se. The nature of school structures reflects the values of mainstream culture, which do not allow for language-minority and poor children to flourish socially and academically. This dilemma further complicates our need for a unified comprehensive critical pedagogy which includes bilingual education.

Critical pedagogy, or a critical theory of education, has developed in the United States in the last 20 years (McLaren, 1989, p. 159). Critical pedagogues analyze schools in two modes: as sorting mechanisms in which a select group of students are favored on the basis of race, class, and gender, but also as potential agencies for self and social empowerment (McLaren, 1989, p. 160). The fundamental principles of critical pedagogy are a commitment to changing American schools which have traditionally reflected only the values of the dominant culture. Bilingual education represents the potential for guiding students to become active participants in challenging cultural hegemony. ...

An American History of Bilingualism

Since its founding, the United States has had a history of multilingualism as well as bilingual education. Throughout the 18th and 19th centuries, communities and schools functioned in the language of their residents. The Midwest was populated by immigrant Germans and Scandinavians, Hispanics lived and continue to live in New Mexico and the Southwest, Indians were relocated throughout the country, and in Louisiana and Northern New England French-speaking communities were vital (Padilla, Fairchild, & Valdez, 1990, p. 28).

These communities faced exploitation and were in subordinate positions with respect to the dominant culture. However, the government did not pay much attention to language policy, nor was there any debate on which language of instruction was more efficient. The primary goal of public schools was to guide immigrant students in becoming good Americans who could contribute to a better America (Crawford, 1989, p. 24).

By the late 19th century, when Catholic Southern Europeans immigrated in large numbers, the political arena was suddenly dominated by nativists who created an atmosphere of xenophobia (Padilla, Fairchild, & Valdez, 1990, p. 28). The new mandate to public schools was to assimilate immigrant children as quickly as possible. State legislatures began regulating the language of instruction. This antagonistic political atmosphere influenced how the dominant culture was to view future waves of immigrants as they arrived from southern and eastern Europe, Mexico, China, and more recently Southeast Asia and Central America.

The geopolitics of World War I were often reflected in xenophobic propaganda. For example, social pressures led to the dismantling of German bilingual programs. German was declared illegal for use in schools, public places, and churches. The state of Ohio, with a predominance of Germans, launched a major xenophobic campaign. German language teachers were fired, and German language books burned or disposed (Crawford, 1989, p. 28). Immigrants often responded to these pressures by voluntarily assimilating.

The Supreme Court intervened in 1923 in the now famous linguistic case, *Nebraska v. Meyer*, involving an elementary school teacher who read a chapter of the Bible in German to a ten-year-old child. The Court ruled that although it might not be in the best interest of this country, the protection of the Constitution extended to all including those who speak a language other than English (Crawford, 1989, p. 29; Padilla, Fairchild, & Valdez, 1990, pp. 29-30). While taking care to stress the need to assimilate to "American speech and ideals," the Court sought to stop constitutional violations. However, states interpreted the assimilationist aspects of the ruling as an opportunity to regulate schools, including specifying the mode of instruction as English.

This ideology became clearly established in the consciousness of Americans; it was unAmerican to speak a language other than English. Since then immigrants have joined the large numbers of African Americans and Chicanos who are regularly placed in educational environments which require children to "sink or swim." Specific attention to linguistic or cultural issues of language-minority students did not reappear until the end of the 1960s civil rights movement. Then, broadly-based social movement forced the dominant hegemony to respond to a new American sociopolitical paradigm.

Legislation for Bilingual Education

In 1968, President Lyndon Johnson signed into law the Bilingual Education Act (BEA) as an addendum to Title VII of the Elementary and Secondary Education Act (Padilla, Fairchild, & Valdez, 1990, pp. 29-30). The intent of the legislation was to redress historical evidence of discrimination against school-aged students whose language differed from English. In particular the BEA provided financial aid to school districts developing innovative programs which addressed the special needs of low income minority students.

The law allowed for a wide range of possibilities, everything from language instruction in the native language and English-as-a-second-language to building students' self-esteem. In 1968, 37 bilingual education bills were introduced to the House of Representatives, yet few of the congressional representatives understood the pedagogical and sociolinguistic implications of such measures (Crawford, 1989, p. 42). Most were content with knowing that bilingual education meant equal access to the curriculum and that students would transition into English.

Bilingual programs ranged from exemplary models such as Coral Way School in Florida, a Spanish two-way immersion program for Cuban immigrants and native English speakers, to inadequate programs whose sole interest was to obtain federal funds. The 1974 Supreme Court decision in *Lau v. Nichols* ruled that any school receiving federal funds under Title VII was obligated to follow both Title VII and the Housing, Education, and Welfare (HEW) guidelines. Furthermore, the Court held that if the California educational system required the knowledge of English in order to participate in the classroom and read its texts, then students who did not know or understand English were "effectively foreclosed from any meaningful education" (Malakoff & Hakuta, 1990, p. 34).

Even though no prescribed remedial program was issued by the Court, school districts did realize that they had to implement bilingual educational programs which followed Title VII and HEW guidelines. Subsequent lawsuits focused on the effect of discrimination on large numbers of students, not the intent. That same year Congress passed the Equal Education Opportunity Act to apply the *Lau* decision to all public schools whether they received federal funds or not (Malakoff & Hakuta, 1990, p. 35).

Then U.S. Commissioner of Education Terrel Bell announced the Lau Remedies in 1975. These guidelines clearly directed school districts how to identify and evaluate English second-language learners by suggesting the appropriate instructional methods, criteria to be used to transition children into mainstreamed English classes, and the professional standards for teachers (Crawford, 1989, p. 46). In addition, the Lau Remedies specifically stipulated that English-as-a-second-language (ESL) pull-out programs did not comply with the directives because they did not provide consistency with either the students' cognitive nor affective development. Unfortunately, the Lau Remedies were only guidelines, not regulations, and the document applied only to districts found to be out of compliance. From 1975 to 1980, nearly 500 school districts had to comply with the guidelines (Malakoff & Hakuta, 1990, p. 37).

On the surface, the federal government became the caretaker for language-minority students. However, during the "New Federalism" of the Reagan administration, government stewardship of programs for minorities of any type became easy for conservatives to characterize as big government enforcing its will on the public. It is a sad irony of the 1980s that shortly after disenfranchised minorities obtained the begrudging patronage of the federal government, conservative politicians cynically led the public against that government. Educational organizations, such as teachers' unions, resisted the mandates. At all levels of the educational structure resentment toward bilingual education arose. Unfortunately, the resentment was also turned against bilingual teachers, bilingual students, and immigrant parents as well.

On the local level, school districts had to meet evolving compliance requirements. They created bilingual departments staffed with administrators and bilingual resource teachers who hoped to develop quality programs only to find themselves enforcing federal and state compliance requirements. Bilingual department liaisons were resented and mistreated by non-bilingual teachers and site administrators. At that point, all hope of creating an alternative pedagogy had been sabotaged. Educational institutions from the elementary school to the university reflected more of the dominant hegemonic ideology than an inclusive collective multicultural ideology.

Vulnerability of Bilingual Education

After 30 years of bilingual education, initiated by liberals and begrudgingly adhered to by conservatives, how did the programs become so vulnerable? Why isn't the latest research which illustrates the success of bilingual education taken as seriously by the dominant culture as the specious claims of widespread failure? One likely explanation is that critics identify any language other than English as a problem to be solved or a condition to be remedied, contributing to a powerful sense of conflict between a community and its educational institutions.

In the present political climate, few government officials representing the dominant culture have acted to reduce the conflict between the communities' values and the educational values of the dominant culture which structure the relationships in schools (Darder, 1991, p. 3). This is partly due to the government's notion that schools are free from ideology or politics. Government representatives believe schools exist to educate students into mainstream society, which to a degree is necessary; however neither conservatives or liberals consider that a dominant ideology creates structures of inequities between socioeconomic classes which include language-minority groups.

Therefore, even reformist agendas supported by liberals do not change the structure of schools.

Much of the conflict stems from the inability of the hegemonic culture to view educational institutions as capable of accommodating alternative perspectives. As mentioned previously, bilingual education was legislated without much thought about its goals, much less its political dissent. As programs evolved, the education of bilingual children began to represent different ideas for different groups. Ruíz provides a conceptual three-part framework for defining language issues and language policies (as cited in Crawford, 1998, p. 3). By using Ruíz's framework and expanding on the categories, one can identify what bilingual education means to different interest groups.

(1) Language as a right   Bilingual education seeks to assert equal status of the minority language through the right of people to speak their native language in schools, official government agencies, and in their communities. Language is viewed as a primary way for groups to define their identity. Ethnic identity is directly linked to positive attitudes toward language. Identities become disempowered when the individual and a community are constantly imposed upon with the ways that the hegemonic culture delegitimizes the minority group's language and culture. Schools are viewed as potential centers for supporting students' sense of identity. Academic success and acquisition of English as a second language have a significant effect on the students' self-identity.

(2) Language as a problem   The minority language is considered an obstacle to students learning English rapidly. Schools are viewed as key places to teach English and mainstream immigrant students into the dominant culture. The support of many early advocates of bilingual education stemmed from the goal that bilingual programs would help to assimilate students into the American mainstream. Educators acquiesce to elements of the dominant hegemony by viewing bilingual education as a way of learning the established curriculum. Giroux refers to this perspective as legitimization of a "hidden curriculum" where hegemony is produced not simply through the diffusion of ideas, but also in the everyday routines and rituals of the classroom social encounter (1981, p.74).

(3) Language as a resource   This perspective holds that language is a valuable resource that allows dynamic social interactions, using language as a resource to empower self and community. Bilingual programs are seen as viable tools to support the empowerment of language-minority communities. The goal is to break the silence of students' voices and seek equity and access to the dominant infrastructure while at the same time creating a counterhegemony. Language-minority communities in partnership with the school can then view themselves as capable of taking action and defining their realities. These educators andadvocates support a major transformation in power relationships. Their aim isto challenge hegemony in the schools from a relationship of dominance andsubordination to collaborative relations of power.

A Creative Definition

If bilingual education is described creatively rather than allowed to be subsumed and dismissed by the dominant culture, we must look to the research. Current research on bilingual education has shown extensive evidence on its many benefits (Ada, 1997, 1990, 1988; California State Department of Education Office of Bilingual Education, 1991; Collier & Mann, 1997; Collier & Ovando, 1985; Colin, 1988; Cummins & Swain, 1986; Cummins, 1996; Genesee, 1987, 1994; González & Maez, 1995; Ramírez, Yuen, & Ramey, 1991; Skutnabb-Kangas, 1981). The most current longitudinal research studies (Ramírez, Yuen, & Ramey, 1991; Collier & Mann, 1997) have found that language-minority students who receive instruction in Spanish demonstrate higher transferability and sustain academic achievement in later years compared to students who are placed in total English immersion or even in early-exit bilingual programs.

The Ramírez et al. report involved 2,352 Latino elementary students in nine school districts, 51 schools, and 554 classrooms. Students' academic progress was compared in three program models: English immersion, early-exit bilingual, and late-exit bilingual. The English immersion program provided instruction almost exclusively in English throughout the students' elementary experience. In an early-exit bilingual program, students received Spanish instruction (usually in reading and language arts) in kindergarten and first grade. However, primary language instruction is phased out by the second grade. Students in the early-exit model are expected to depart from a bilingual program and be placed in general (mainstreamed) English classes by the end of first or second grade.

In the late-exit model students received instruction in their primary language throughout their elementary experience. Each grade level decreased the instructional time in Spanish, but it was never eliminated. For example, instruction in kindergarten was primarily in Spanish. Approximately three fourths of instruction was in Spanish for children in first and second grades. By the time students reached third grade, instruction was 50 percent in Spanish and English. In the following grades Spanish decreased to 40 percent or slightly less, and English increased to 60 percent or slightly more of the instructional time (1991, pp. 1-2, 5). Ramírez concluded that providing substantial instruction in the child's primary language does not impede the learning of the English language or reading skills (p. 40), and, as stated above academic achievement is extended.

Another finding of interest was that parent involvement appears to be the greatest in late-exit programs. The role parents play in their child's academic development is potentially a major indicator of the child's success. Traditionally Latino and other parents of color tend to stay away from the schools when the dominant cultural values do not allow for diversity, but this study found that Latino parents do get involved when they can speak their own language and are welcomed by the teacher.

Making Use of Research

Collier and Mann (1997) collected long-term data on student achievement in bilingual programs (including English Language Development Programs) from 1991-1996. Their research examined two-way immersion programs, arguing that this model may have the greatest potential for minority-language students' academic achievement. They present three overriding predictors to measure academic success (pp. 2-3).

The first predictor is providing cognitively complex academic instruction using the students' first language and in the second language throughout their educational experience from kindergarten to twelfth grade. The two-way model included children whose native language is not English, children who are losing their heritage language, and those who are beginning to learn English as a second language. In addition, the model includes English dominant children whose parents have chosen to place them in a two-waybilingual program. These parents want their children to learn a second language such as Spanish, Korean, or Chinese.

The second predictor is the use of instructional approaches based on cognitively complex learning strategies where interactive learning occurs among peers and between the teacher and the students. Students are involved in discovery learning using cooperative learning strategies and an interdisciplinary approach to education.

The third predictor is changes in the sociocultural context of the schooling. Bilingual education is viewed as the gifted and talented program for all students. The whole school is committed to support linguistic and cultural diversity, in order to foster a climate of multiculturalism. Two-way immersion models provide an opportunity to transform relations between the majority and the minority groups. Bilingual education is viewed as enrichment rather than as a remedial program to "fix some students."

These findings suggest that language-minority students in two-way immersion programs can benefit academically and socially by receiving instruction in their primary language throughout their elementary school years. Collier (1995, p. 236) states that a two-way immersion program lessens the distance between minority and majority language students by socially integrating the groups and providing high academic standards for all students. In a two-way immersion program, the language-minority students are not required to exit the program because they are in mainstream classes integrated with English-speaking students. Philosophically and politically the model is perceived as an additive bilingual program where both groups benefit.

Ramírez's (1991, p. 37) summary indicates that the instructional strategies used by teachers from all three types of programs analyzed (English immersion, early-exit, and late-exit) were based upon a transmission model (the teacher lectures while students listen passively). In the transmission model the teacher provides explanations, questions, commands, and feedback but the interaction with the students is passive. Students only respond when they are asked by the teacher. Ramírez reported that the late-exit bilingual teachers used more props and visuals to support learning and language structures that supported easier access to academic content. However, his concern was that the instructional strategies used by all teachers in all three programs produced a passive language learning environment (1991, p. 37). This is precisely the dilemma of a hegemonic educational structure, even for a well-designed program.

Counter-Hegemony

... [A] counter-hegemony exists within elements of bilingual and general education. This counter-hegemony supports a pedagogy that is based on theories and practices of liberation that empower students. An example of counter-hegemony is how some bilingual teachers use students' experiences as stepping stones to guide them in understanding their identity, their cultural strengths, and their potential for leadership within their community and on a broader sociopolitical level.

Critical pedagogy, also referred to as transformative or liberatory pedagogy (Ada, 1997; Cummins, 1997; Darder, 1991; Giroux, 1988; McLaren, 1989), represents a fundamental belief that all knowledge is socially constructed and rooted in power relationships that are always in transition. Its goal is to develop the critical consciousness of participants through dialogue, critical reflection and praxis.

Education, as it exists in the United States, imposes this hegemonic ideology through hierarchical structures, assumptions, practices, and curriculum which deny the realities of subordinate groups. It operates on the premise of transmitting knowledge, therefore it takes a form of social and intellectual control. Yet human beings are not passive, empty vessels waiting to be filled by those in positions of power. The critical educator supports and encourages students to examine and challenge the hidden curriculum by making links to their experiences. Those educators view themselves as facilitators who do not tell students what they should think or believe. Instead they provide an environment where the classroom community feels safe to raise challenging questions. Thus education becomes an authentic experience.

Applying critical pedagogy to the day-to-day classroom practices and the curriculum increases the potential for teachers, students, and their parents to view themselves as agents of change and advocates for a more equitable society. The classroom environment is one of an emancipatory nature where voices of the teachers and students speak from the depth of self. Bilingual education programs such as two-way immersion models have the potential for becoming liberating educational settings. As stated previously, even within a powerful dominant hegemony, there always exists some resistance. The passage of Proposition 227 has not extinguished the commitment of progressive educators. ...

Some Further News

Better late than never, the press is now beginning to provide some accurate coverage about the effects of bilingual education, although its members continue to share their cultural skepticism. On July 17, 1998, the *San Francisco*

Chronicle published a front page article entitled "Bilingual Surprise in State Testing." Two Northern California urban school districts, San Jose and San Francisco, reported that on recent achievement tests bilingual students outscored native English speakers. Results were from the newly administered Standardized Testing and Reporting (STAR) examination which examined the areas of reading, language arts, and mathematics. In reading, third graders in bilingual classes averaged 58 points while English native speakers averaged 49 points. However, third grade graduates of bilingual programs (those students who have transitioned to English) scored the highest, an average of 75 points. In all three areas the bilingual students scored higher than native English speakers. Third-grade bilingual graduates averaged 40 percentage points higher in mathematics than native English speakers. These higher scores are reflected throughout the elementary and middle schools in the San Francisco Unified School District and, to a lesser extent, in San Jose.

Collier and Mann (1997) reported that students who received strong cognitive and academic development in their primary language from kindergarten to at least grades five or six, and also received instruction in English as a second language were doing well in high school (pp. 1-2). Central to their argument is that only quality long-term, two-way immersion and late-exit bilingual programs using current teaching approaches (inquiry-based, discovery, child-centered, and language-rich) are the most beneficial. Bilingual programs designed to their full potential support the cognitive and academic development that language-minority students need to be academically successful in English as they reach high school (Collier & Mann, 1997, p. 2).

References

Ada, A. F. (1990). *A magical encounter.* Compton, CA: Santillana.

Ada, A. F. & Campoy, F. I. (1997). *Effective English acquisition for academic success.* San Francisco, CA: Transformative Education Materials.

Asimov, N. (1998, July 8). Bilingual surprise in state testing. *San Francisco Chronicle.* pp. 1, A11.

California State Department of Education. (1991). *Schooling and language minority students: A theoretical framework.* Los Angeles, CA: California State University.

Callaghan, A. (1997, August 15). Desperate to learn. *New York Times,* (n. vol.).

Collier, V. P. (1987-88 Winter). The effect of age on acquisition of a second language for school. *National Clearinghouse for Bilingual Education,* (2), 1-6.

Collier, V. P. (1995). A synthesis of studies examining long-term language minority student data on academic achievement. In Gustavo González, & Lento Maez (Eds.), *Compendium of research on bilingual education.* (pp. 231-243). Washington, DC: National Council for Bilingual Education.

Collier, V. P. (1996, August). What we've learned after 20 years of immersion education. In two-way bilingual immersion research institute. Symposium conducted at the Fourth Annual Two-Way Immersion Summer Conference, Long Beach, CA.

Collier, V. P. & Mann, T. (1997). A national study of school effectiveness for language-minority students' long term academic achievement. *National Clearinghouse for Bilingual Education.* Washington, DC: George Washington University.

Collier, V. P. & Ovando, C. (1985). *Bilingual and ESL classrooms: Teaching in multi-cultural context.* New York: McGraw-Hill.

Crawford, J. (1989). *Bilingual education: History, politics, theory and practice.* Los Angeles, CA: Bilingual Educational Services.

Crawford, J. (1992). *Hold your tongue: Bilingualism and the politics of "English Only."* Boston, MA: Addison-Wesley.

Crawford, J. (1998). Language politics in the U.S.A.: The paradox of bilingual education. [On-line]. Available: jwcrawford@compuserve.com.

Crawford, J. (1998). Surviving the English Only assault: Public attitudes and the future of language education. [On line]. Available: jwcrawford@compuserve.com.

Cummins, J. (1996). *Negotiating identities: Education for empowerment in a diverse society.* Ontario, CA: California Association for Bilingual Education.

Cummins, J. (1994). Knowledge, power, and identity in teaching ESL. In F. Genesee (Ed.), *Educating second language children* (pp. 33-58). New York: Cambridge University Press.

Darder, A.(1991). *Culture and power in the classroom.* Westport, CT: Bergin & Garvey.

Freire, P. (1985). *The politics of education.* (D. Macedo, Trans.). Boston, MA: Bergin & Garvey.

Freire, P. (1990). *Pedagogy of the oppressed.* (M.B. Ramos, Trans.). (Ed.). New York: Continuum.

Freire, P. (1994). *Education for critical consciousness.* (M. B. Ramos, Trans.). (Ed.). New York: Continuum.

Genesee, F. (1987). *Learning through two languages: Studies on immersion education.* Cambridge, MA: Newbury House.

Genesee, F. (Ed.). (1994). *Educating second language children.* New York: Cambridge University Press.

Giroux,H. A.(1988). *Schooling and the struggle for public life: Critical pedagogy in the modern age.* Minneapolis, MN: University of Minnesota Press.

Malakoff, M. & Hakuta, K. (1990). History of Language-minority Education in the United States. In A. M. Padilla, H. H. Fairchild, & C. M. Valdez (Eds.), *Bilingual education: Issues and strategies* (pp. 27-43). Newbury Park, CA: Corwin Press.

Mc Laren, P. (1989). *Life in schools.* New York: Longman.

Padilla, A. M., Fairchild, H. H., & Valdez, C. M. (Eds.). (1990). *Bilingual education: Issues and strategies.* Thousand Oaks, CA: Sage.

Ramírez, J. D., Yuen, S. D., & Ramey,D. R.(1991). Executive summary final report: Longitudinal study of structured English immersion strategy, early-exit and late-exit transitional bilingual education programs for language-minority children. Submitted to the United States Department of Education (Contract No. 300-870156). San Mateo, CA: Aguirre International.

Rodriguez, G. (1998, April 20). English lesson in California. *The Nation, 266,* (14), 15-19.

Walsh, C. E. (1991). *Pedagogy and the struggle for voice.* New York: Bergin & Garvey.

Will, G. (1997, October 26). Out of a linguistic ghetto. *Washington Post.* (n. vol.).

POSTSCRIPT

Should English Immersion Replace Bilingual Education?

Despite numerous studies of the effectiveness of various additive and subtractive programs, there is no consensus among researchers, educators, or policymakers as to which type of program leads to greater success—academic or otherwise—for NELB students. In part, this reflects limitations in the studies conducted. In most cases, researchers have compared existing programs, that is, programs over which they had no control in terms of design, implementation, or assignment of students or teachers. The programs compared have differed in many ways, including geographic location, the diversity of languages spoken by the students, the socioeconomic status of the students, the material and personnel resources available, and so on. This makes it difficult to discern whether differences in student achievement (or other "outcome" measures) have resulted from the different educational programs or from other variable factors. In addition, the measures of student performance selected are often focused narrowly on academic achievement or mastery of English. It may be, however, that the programs also influence factors such as student self-concept and attitudes toward school, as well as family harmony and vocational achievement. There is, therefore, a need for controlled experiments comparing additive and subtractive programs that include a comprehensive battery of outcome measures. A very readable scholarly review of older research on the education of NELB students is "Bilingualism and Education," by K. Hakuta and E. E. Garcia, *American Psychologist* (vol. 44, no. 2, 1989). A review of more recent research can be found in D. August and K. Hakuta, eds., *Improving Schooling for Language-Minority Children* (Prakken, 1997).

Both the design and the interpretation of the studies conducted have also been shaped by political and ideological agendas. For more about this, see "The Changing Face of Bilingual Education," by Russell Gersten, *Educational Leadership* (vol. 56, no. 7, 1999). Articles focusing on the benefits of additive programs are "Thought and Two Languages: The Impact of Bilingualism on Cognitive Development," by R. M. Diaz, *Review of Research in Education* (vol. 10, 1983), pp. 23-54, and "Understanding Bilingual/Bicultural Young Children," by L. D. Soto, *Young Children* (vol. 46, 1991), pp. 30-36. Those promoting the benefits of subtractive programs include "Americanization and the Schools," by E. D. Hirsch, *The Clearing House* (January/February 1999). An interesting paper that explores the need to embed second-language instruction in a broader cultural context is "Delving Deeper: Teaching Culture as an Integral Element of Second-Language Learning," by Sherry Rowan, *The Clearing House* (May/June 2001).

ISSUE 4

Is Full Inclusion Always the Best Option for Children With Disabilities?

YES: Mara Sapon-Shevin, from "Full Inclusion as Disclosing Tablet: Revealing the Flaws in Our Present System," *Theory Into Practice* (Winter 1996)

NO: Naomi Zigmond and Janice M. Baker, from "Full Inclusion for Students With Learning Disabilities: Too Much of a Good Thing?" *Theory Into Practice* (Winter 1996)

ISSUE SUMMARY

YES: Mara Sapon-Shevin, a professor of education at Syracuse University, argues that all students, whatever the nature of their disability, are best served within the "regular" classroom alongside their typically developing peers.

NO: Naomi Zigmond, chair of the department of instruction and learning at the University of Pittsburgh, and Janice M. Baker, an assistant professor of special education and clinical services at Indiana University of Pennsylvania, argue that the accommodations that teachers make are seldom tailored to the needs of the particular students with disabilities enrolled in their classes. They maintain that meaningful remediation requires some form of "pull out" from the regular classroom.

Public Law (P.L.) 94-142, the Education for All Handicapped Children Act (1975), required that all children with disabilities, whatever the nature or severity of their disability, be provided a free and appropriate education within the least restrictive environment possible. Later laws—P.L. 99-457, the 1986 Education of the Handicapped Act, and P.L. 101-476, the 1990 Individuals with Disabilities Education Act (IDEA)—clarified, strengthened, and expanded the 1975 legislation. Before the enactment of these laws, many children with disabilities, especially those with more severe or challenging disabilities, were segregated from their more typically developing peers. Students with disabilities attended special classes in their neighborhood schools, or they attended special schools for the disabled. In either case, they had minimal contact with their typically developing peers. Advocates for people with disabilities argued that a separate education denies children with disabilities the same opportunities afforded everyone else.

P.L. 94-142 and the subsequent laws brought about some fundamental changes in how children with disabilities are educated in the United States, as well as changes in the roles and responsibilities of teachers and other educational specialists. Rather than being segregated, many children with disabilities are now placed ("mainstreamed") into the regular classroom on at least a part-time basis. Mainstreaming ensures that students with disabilities have contact with their typically developing peers and the regular education curriculum. In recent years, advocates for people with disabilities have successfully argued that simple physical presence in the regular classroom may not lead to full participation in the classroom's intellectual or social life. Advocates, therefore, have argued that schools must move beyond mainstreaming to full inclusion. Full inclusion refers to placement in the regular classroom with appropriate supports and services—such as an interpreter who signs the teacher's talk for a student with impaired hearing—and includes active efforts to ensure participation of the student with disabilities in the life of the class. Moreover, it is argued that these supports and services must be tailored to the unique needs of each individual as set forth in the Individual Educational Plan (IEP). The IEP is prepared annually by a multidisciplinary team composed of, for example, the school psychologist, a special education teacher, the regular classroom teacher, and a speech-language clinician, all of whom assess the student's current level of functioning and set short-and long-term goals for his or her educational progress. Inclusion is intended to ensure that students with disabilities have the opportunity to develop to their fullest potential.

Although full inclusion may be the ideal, school districts have been granted considerable latitude by the courts to make educational placement. For example, the courts have allowed less than full inclusion if a student is unlikely to derive sufficient academic or nonacademic benefit from inclusion; if a student's placement in the regular classroom is likely to be disruptive, thereby "denying" his or her classmates the opportunity to gain full benefit from the curriculum; or if the cost of inclusion would be prohibitive for the district. As a result of these constraints, many students experience less than full inclusion—some may have "pull-out" classes, which segregate them from their more typically developing peers for part of the school day; others may be segregated for almost their entire school experience.

The authors of the following selections focus on students with learning disabilities, who arguably have the least severe and least pervasive impairments among the students who qualify for special education services. Nevertheless, this part of the controversy over full inclusion for children with disabilities is no less heated than in the case of students with mental retardation. In the first selection, Mara Sapon-Shevin acknowledges that inclusion will require dramatic changes in curriculum and teaching practices. She argues, however, that these changes are consistent with a child-centered philosophy and, thus, that all students will benefit. In the second selection, Naomi Zigmond and Janice M. Baker argue that meaningful remediation requires some form of "pull out" from the regular classroom.

Mara Sapon-Shevin  **YES**

Full Inclusion as Disclosing Tablet

If we include a student like Travis, we'll have to change our curriculum....

If we include students like Larissa, we'll have to change our teaching methods too—lecture just doesn't work with those kids....

If we include a student like Justin, the other kids will destroy him.... The kids in my class have no tolerance for kids who are different in any way....

And if we have to plan for a student like Marianna, our teachers will need time to meet and plan together....

The above statements are representative of the hue and cry that has been raised by the prospect of full inclusion in many school districts. Full inclusion, the movement to include students with disabilities as full-time members of general education classrooms, has come under sharp criticism of late, and has been blamed for a host of problems—overworked teachers, falling academic standards, lack of discipline, and poor teacher morale (Willis, 1994). Although some of these criticisms are consistent with the often inadequate and half-hearted ways in which inclusion has been implemented, negative responses to planning and implementing full inclusion tell us as much (or more) about the quality and responsiveness of the schools as it does about the challenges presented by the students themselves.

When children are being taught proper dental hygiene, the dentist sometimes gives them a little red pill to chew after they have brushed. The red dye sticks to any areas that have been inadequately brushed, thus making it obvious where problems remain. These pills are called "disclosing tablets" because they disclose the areas that require further attention.

It is possible to look at full inclusion as a disclosing tablet. Attempting to integrate students with significant educational and behavioral challenges tells us a lot about the ways in which our schools are unimaginative, underresourced, unresponsive, and simply inadequate. Full inclusion did not create these problems, but it shows us where the problems are. Children who stretch the limits of the system make it painfully clear how constricting and narrow those limits are. Full inclusion reveals the manner in which our educational system must grow and improve in order to meet the needs of all children.

Consider again the original set of complaints cited at the beginning.... What do these statements tell us about our schools?

From Mara Sapon-Shevin, "Full Inclusion as Disclosing Tablet: Revealing the Flaws in Our Present System," *Theory Into Practice*, vol. 35, no. 1 (Winter 1996). Copyright © 1996 by The College of Education, The Ohio State University. Reprinted by permission.

We'll have to change the curriculum....

Yes, we will need to change the curriculum if we want to include students with disabilities. But don't we believe that the curriculum already needs changing, is changing, and will be improved for all children by being reconceptualized more broadly and divergently?

We'll have to change the way we teach....

Yes, we will need to look at teaching structures and practices. Teachers whose teaching repertoires are limited to frontal, lecture style instruction will need to explore more interactive, engaging ways of teaching. Isn't that what the research tells us needs to happen anyway?

We'll have to pay close attention to the social dynamics....

Yes, including a child with a significant difference will mean that we need to pay closer attention to the social climate of the school. But, clearly, if children who are "different" in any way are routinely mocked, scorned, or excluded, this is not a productive learning environment. Why do we assume that a classroom in which a child with Down's syndrome would be teased is a comfortable classroom for children who are African-American, overweight, from single parent families, or non-English speaking? Wouldn't improvements in classroom climate have a salutary effect on all students?

We'll have to support teachers in their efforts at change....

It is true that including a student with a disability will require that teachers have time for collaborative planning and preparation. The kinds of creative, multi-level instruction and assessment necessitated by full inclusion make it imperative that teachers be given adequate time to think and plan together. But doesn't all good teaching require planning and preparation? And don't all teachers rise to higher expectations when they are treated as professionals who need thinking and planning time?

There is bad news and good news about full inclusion—and it is the same news. The "news" is that to do inclusion well will require changes in curriculum, pedagogy, staff development, school climate, and structures. This can be characterized as "bad news" because it means that mere tinkering on the edges of existing structures will not work; simply dumping children with disabilities into classrooms without adequate preparation, commitment, and support will certainly not work. But this same news—the need for wide-ranging change—is good news because there is considerable evidence that the kinds of changes necessitated by inclusion are consistent with and often can be a catalyst for broader, far-reaching school restructuring and reform efforts (Stainback & Stainback, 1992; Villa, Thousand, Stainback, & Stainback, 1992).

Like all reform efforts, the range of policies and practices implemented in the name of full inclusion has varied tremendously in quality and depth. Some school systems have simply eliminated costly special education services and teachers in the name of inclusion, dumping those students into inadequately prepared and supported classrooms. But in other schools, full inclusion has served as a spark, an organizing principle for wide-ranging change. In these schools, the inclusion of students with disabilities has been part of school reform and school restructuring that reaches far beyond the handful of labeled students identified as the purview of "special education" (Villa et al.,

1992). Like all reform movements that are clouded by misinformation, debated by experts, and shrouded by emotion, it can be difficult to discern what full inclusion really means.

This [selection] explores the vision and possibilities of full inclusion by addressing and responding to myths about full inclusion that block thoughtful and comprehensive implementation. Responding to these myths can help us to better understand the promise and the practice of full inclusion.

Myth: Inclusion is being imposed on schools by outside ideologues and unrealistic parents who do not accept their child's disability.

Inclusion did not spring, fully-formed, from any particular group. The evolution of the movement can be traced through changes in language and terminology. Twenty years ago, our efforts were directed toward "mainstreaming"—putting selected students with disabilities into general classrooms when a good "match" could be made. When those efforts proved inadequate to the task of changing classrooms so that students would fit in, we focused our efforts on "integration"—trying to mesh the systems of general and special education. Those efforts taught us about the need for unified services and collaboration and the importance of good communication and problem solving.

We have now articulated our task as inclusion—changing existing classrooms and structures so that all students can be served well within a unified system. Rather than merging two systems, we are trying to create a new, improved, more inclusive system for all students.

While parents have certainly played an important role in the inclusion movement, they have not acted alone. Teachers and administrators have shown great leadership in designing creative solutions to the problems inherent within pullout programs and remedial education. In the best case scenarios, parents and teachers have worked together to create programs that are effective and realistic. Inclusion is a product of many people's rethinking of the nature and quality of special education, as well as a by-product of new ways of thinking about teaching and curriculum.

Myth: Inclusionists only care about students with significant disabilities.

This is a complaint often raised by those whose primary concern is for students with mild disabilities, particularly learning disabilities. They fear that the educational needs of their students will get lost in the shuffle of full inclusion, while students with extensive challenges (of which there are fewer) will become the organizing focus of inclusion. These are valid concerns, and no inclusion advocate I know is callous to the very real learning needs of students with mild disabilities who are often abandoned without support in general education classrooms under the name of inclusion.

But, by definition, inclusion involves changing the nature and quality of the general education classroom. And there is no reason that the instructional strategies and modifications provided for students with learning disabilities in segregated settings cannot be provided in more typical classrooms if we are willing to reconceptualize those classrooms. Justine Maloney (1994/1995) of the Learning Disabilities Association of America argues against full inclusion and for a continuum of services; yet, she herself acknowledges that

> Students with learning disabilities would have a better chance of success in the general education setting if more of the strategies developed by special education, such as collaborative learning, cooperative teaching, peer tutoring and some of the innovative scheduling and planning developed in education reform models, became commonplace, rather than showpieces. (p. 25)

Myth: Inclusionists are driven only by values and philosophy—there is no research and no data.

The research in the field of inclusion is relatively recent, because it is difficult to collect data on programs and options until they exist. Advocates of full inclusion provide data indicating that students with disabilities educated in general education classrooms do better academically and socially than comparable students in noninclusive settings (Baker, Wang, & Walberg, 1994/ 1995). Those who do not support inclusion cite studies indicating that special education programs are superior to general education classrooms for some types of children (Fuchs & Fuchs, 1994/1995).

The controversy about the research and what it tells us is indicative of more fundamental disagreements about (a) what counts as research and (b) what research is of value and what it is of value for. Should inclusion programs have to prove they are better than segregated programs, or should the burden of proof be on those who would maintain students in more restrictive environments? What data are collected? Are reading scores the best indications of student success? Is growth in social and communicative skills considered of primary or secondary importance? And what about benefits to "typical" students? How should these be measured and valued? The lack of agreement on the quality and value of the research data gathered to this point is indicative of more basic conflicts about the value and purposes of inclusion.

Myth: Segregation is not inherently a problem—it is only bad segregation that is a problem.

Many anti-inclusionists have been angry about parallels drawn between racial segregation (Brown v. Board of Education's "segregation is inherently unequal") and the segregation of students with disabilities. Kauffman (quoted in O'Neil, 1994/1995) asserts:

> Certainly racial segregation is a great evil, and segregation that is forced and universal and unrelated to legitimate educational purposes certainly is wrong. But when separate programs are freely chosen and placement decisions are made on a case-by-case basis—not forced, not universal—I think it's inappropriate to call that segregation. (p. 9)

But most of the segregation that has been part of special education has been forced, has *not* been freely chosen, and has *not* been made on a case-bycase basis. Often parents have been forced to accept segregated special education services or nothing and have not been presented with a range of options. More importantly, it is not clear that segregating students with disabilities is directly related to a legitimate educational purpose! When all school districts offer parents and their children the choice of a well-developed, fully inclusive classroom, then we may be able to talk differently about the advisability and appropriateness of more segregated settings; until then, we cannot call segregation a legitimate choice.

Myth: The system isn't broken—why are we messing with it?

The eagerness with which educators embrace school reform in general and inclusion in particular is definitely related to the extent to which they believe that the existing system needs changing. Inclusion advocates do not believe the system (two systems, actually) is working. The disproportionate number of students of color in special education, the lack of mobility out of special education settings, the limited community connections for students with disabilities, and the human and financial costs of supporting two separate systems of teacher education, classroom programs, and curricular materials and resources have led many educators to welcome changes in the ways in which special education services are conceptualized and delivered.

Even those who recognize the need for change, however, do not necessarily agree on the nature or extent of that change. Some supporters of maintaining a continuum of services believe that we only need to do special education "better" to make it work. Inclusion advocates tend to look for more systemic, structural change; they do not see the problems as being linked to the quality or commitment of those who provide services but as more basic, requiring changes in more than just personnel.

Myth: Inclusionists think we need change because special educators are bad or incompetent.

This myth is closely related to the previous one. Those who promote inclusion in no way impugn the hard work, motives, or competence of special educators. Rather, they seek to find new ways to use those talents and skills so that all students can benefit from highly specialized teaching strategies and adaptations.

Myth: Inclusion advocates believe special educators are extinct (or should become that way).

Again, closely linked to the above two, inclusion will require that special educators reconceptualize their roles, acting more often as coteachers or resources than as primary sources of instruction or services. Conceiving of special education as a set of services rather than as a place allows us to conceive of special educators as educators with special skills, rather than as educators who work with "special" children.

Myth: It takes a special person to work with "those kids."

Idealizing the special educator as someone with unique personality characteristics (often patience) and a set of instructional tricks foreign to general education classroom teachers has served to deskill general education teachers, removing the motivation and the need to develop a wider repertoire of skills. "Those kids" need good teaching, as do all students. Our goal should be to have skilled (special education) teachers share what they know with others, rather than to isolate them in ways that minimize their breadth and long-term effectiveness.

Myth: Inclusion is beyond the reach of the already over burdened general education teacher.

There is no question that many general education teachers are overburdened and under-supported. Adding students with disabilities without committing the necessary resources and support is unethical as well as ineffective. We must make huge improvements in the kinds and quality of support we provide for teachers. Although many general education classroom teachers initially say, "If I take that kid, I'll need a full-time aide," more experienced inclusion teachers identify many kinds of support as important (sometimes eliminating the need for a full-time aide), including: planning and collaboration time with other teachers, modified curriculum and resources, administrative support, and ongoing emotional support.

Myth: We're talking about the same "regular classrooms" you and I grew up with.

This myth is a difficult one. It is true that many special education programs were developed because the "regular" classroom was inadequate for the learning needs of children with disabilities. So talk of "returning" such students seems illogical—if those classrooms were not good before, why should they be appropriate now? The answer is that inclusive classrooms are not and cannot be the same rigidly structured, everyone-on-the-same page, frontal teaching, individually staffed classrooms we all remember. Successful inclusion involves radical changes in the nature of the general education classroom.

Myth: The curriculum of the general education classroom will get watered down and distorted.

There is a fear that inclusion will force teachers to "dumb down" the curriculum, thus limiting the options for "typical students" and especially for "gifted and talented" students. The reality is that the curriculum in inclusive classrooms must be structured as multi-level, participatory and flexible.

For example, all the students might be working on the Civil War, but the range of books and projects undertaken and the ways in which learning is pursued can vary tremendously. Some students might be working on computer simulations, while others might write and perform skits or role plays. A wide range of books on the Civil War could allow students who read at a range of levels to find and share information. Inclusion invites, not a watered-down curriculum, but an enhanced one, full of options and creative possibilities (Thousand, Villa, & Nevin, 1994).

Myth: Special services must take place in special places.

Those who are fearful or antagonistic about full inclusion believe that we must maintain a *continuum of placements* in order to serve all children well. Inclusion advocates support the need for a *continuum of services* (e.g., occupational therapy, speech therapy, physical therapy) but propose that those services be provided in the most integrated way possible, sometimes in the general education classroom and sometimes with other nonhandicapped students participating.

Inclusion does not mean abandoning the special help and support that students with disabilities truly need. Rather, it means providing those services within more normalized settings and without the isolation and stigma often associated with special education services.

Myth: Without special education classes, children with disabilities will not learn functional life skills—the things they really need to know.

In many special education classes, students are still learning money skills by working with pretend coins and bills, doing workbook problems. In more inclusive settings, a student with a disability may be working at the school store, making change, and interacting with real customers using real money. Creative teachers (with adequate support) can find numerous ways to incorporate functional life skills into more typically "academic" settings, often benefiting all the students in the class.

Myth: The only way to keep "special children" safe is to keep them away from other children. If you include them you are setting them up to be victims; you are setting them up for failure. They can only feel good about themselves if they're with their "own kind."

No parent wants their child to be a victim of cruelty or violence, friendless and alone, abandoned and outcast in school. But when we think of the bigger picture—the future beyond school—it becomes evident that we cannot keep students with disabilities safe by sheltering them. They must learn repertoires of accommodation and adaptation (how to deal with teasing and rejection) and, more importantly, we must take active steps to shape the understanding, commitment, and active friendship of students without disabilities who will be the lifelong peers of people with disabilities.

When students grow up together, sharing school experiences and activities, they learn to see beyond superficial differences and disabilities and to connect as human beings. This applies to differences in race, religion, economic status, and skill and ability, as well as physical, emotional, and learning differences. It is vital that all students feel safe and welcome in the world, and inclusion provides us with an excellent way to model and insist on a set of beliefs about how people treat one another with respect and dignity.

Myth: Inclusion values "social goals" above "educational goals."

The accusation that inclusion advocates only care about "social" integration and that valuing social growth means that academic progress is not considered relevant or important has persisted for many years. In fact, all learning is social and all learning occurs in a social environment. Learning to talk, make friends, ask questions and respond, and work with others are all educational goals, important ones, and foundational ones for other learning.

There is little doubt that certain specific, concrete drill and practice skills can be better taught within intensified, one-on-one instructional settings; what is less clear is that those are the skills that matter or whether such learning will generalize to more "normal" environments. There is also little evidence that most special education settings are particularly effective at teaching academic skills. Some of the original motivation for mainstreaming, then integration, and then inclusion, was the recognition of the low expectations and distorted goals that were set for students with disabilities within more segregated settings.

Myth: Inclusion is a favor we are doing for children with disabilities at the cost of other children's education.

There is no evidence that the education of other students suffers in any way from the inclusion process. Al Shanker, president of the American Federation of Teachers (AFT) and a leading anti-inclusion force, commented on the students pictured in the Academy Award-winning film, *Educating Peter* (Wurtzberg & Goodwin, 1992), which detailed the classroom experience of Peter, a boy with Down's syndrome, during his third grade year:

> I wonder whether the youngsters in that class had spent a whole year in adjusting to how to live with Peter and whether they did any reading, whether they did any writing, whether they did any mathematics, whether they did any history, whether they did any geography.
>
> And it seems to me that it's a terrible shame that we don't ask that question. Is the only function of the schools to get kids to learn to live with each other? Would we be satisfied if that's what we did and if all the youngsters came out not knowing any of the things they're supposed to learn academically?
>
> Will any of them, disabled or non-disabled, be able to function as adults? (Shanker, 1994, p. 1)

The answer, Mr. Shanker, is that their teacher, Martha Stallings (1993, 1994) reports that the students in her class all had a wonderful year, learned their math and their history and their geography, did a great deal of writing and reading, and learned to be decent caring human beings as well. That seems like an incredibly successful year to me!

Will any of them be able to function as adults? Yes, they will function as adults who, in addition to knowing long division and the states and their capitals, also know how to actively support a classmate who is struggling and know not to jump to early conclusions about whether or not someone can be a friend.

Myth: It takes years of planning and preparation before you can start to do inclusion.

Planning and preparation certainly help inclusion to work well. And there is no denying that adequate lead time and thoughtful groundwork improve the quality of what can happen when students with disabilities are included. But it is also true that no teacher, school, and district ever feel truly ready to begin inclusion, and what is most necessary is ongoing support and commitment. Even schools that are well known for their inclusion programs acknowledge that there are always new issues and concerns. Although some aspects of the inclusion process become easier, they still require time and planning because every child and every situation is different.

The AFT has requested an inclusion moratorium, citing the many problems that schools experience when they attempt to implement inclusion. Shanker (1994/1995) cites lack of adequate preparation for teachers and lack of ongoing support as the two major barriers to successful inclusion. I would agree with his analysis completely. His conclusion, however, is quite different from mine. His solution to the lack of preparation and support is to call for a moratorium on inclusion. My solution is to commit the resources we know are required to do inclusion well.

Myth: If we just ignore inclusion long enough and hard enough, it will go away.

I cannot imagine that parents who fought so hard for the right to have their children included in general education classrooms will be willing to go back to segregated programming. And teachers who have experienced successful inclusive teaching are not likely to want to return to a segregated system. But is society willing to commit the funds and the human resources necessary to do inclusion well? That is a larger question that brings us to the very heart of our values and our priorities about children and their educational futures.

Conclusion

Examining these myths and the responses to them allows us to see how much is affected by our decision to include students with disabilities and how much change will be required for it to be successful. At stake is not just our special education programs, or even our educational system. What is at stake is our commitment as a democracy to educate all children to the best of their abilities and to teach them all to be responsible, caring citizens, cognizant of their inter-relationships and their mutual needs. A stirring song by Bernice Reagan, per-formed by the group "Sweet Honey in the Rock," says, "We who believe in freedom cannot rest until it comes." An appropriate paraphrase for thisstruggle might be: We who believe in inclusion cannot rest until it's done (well)!

References

Baker, E. T., Wang, M. C., & Walberg, H. J. (1994/1995). The effects of inclusion on learning. *Educational Leadership, 52*(4), 33-35.

Fuchs, D. & Fuchs, L. S. (1994/1995). Sometimes separate is better. *Educational Leadership, 52*(4), 22-26.

Maloney, J. (1994/1995). A call for placement options. *Educational Leadership, 52*(4), 25.

O'Neil, J. (1994). Can inclusion work? A conversation with Jim Kauffman and Mara Sapon-Shevin. *Educational Leadership, 52*(4), 7-11.

Shanker, A. (1994, Fall). A full circle? Inclusion: A 1994 view. In *The Circle*. Atlanta: Georgia Governor's Council on Developmental Disabilities.

Shanker, A. (1994/1995). Full inclusion is neither free nor appropriate. *Educational Leadership, 52*(4), 18-21.

Stainback, S., & Stainback, W. (1992). *Curriculum considerations in inclusive class-rooms: Facilitating learning for all students*. Baltimore: Paul H. Brookes.

Stallings, M. A. (1993, May). When Peter came to Mrs. Stallings' class. *NEA Today*, p. 22.

Stallings, M. A. (1994, December). *Educating Peter*. Presentation at the Association for Persons with Severe Handicaps Conference, Alliance for Action, Atlanta.

Thousand, J. S., Villa, R. A., & Nevin, A. I. (1994). *Creativity and collaborative learn-ing: A practical guide for empowering students and teachers*. Baltimore: Paul H. Brookes.

Villa, R. A., Thousand, J. S., Stainback, W., & Stainback, S. (1992). *Restructuring for caring and effective education*. Baltimore: Paul H. Brookes.

Willis, S. (1994, October). Making schools more inclusive. *ASCD curriculum update*, pp. 1-8.

Wurtzberg, G., & Goodwin, T. (1992). *Educating Peter*. Home Box Office Video.

NO

**Naomi Zigmond and
Janice M. Baker**

Full Inclusion for Students With Learning Disabilities

Inclusion is not a new concept for students with learning disabilities (LD); school personnel have been educating students with LD in general education classrooms for more than 2 decades. Ever since the passage of PL 94-142, the Education of Children with Disabilities Act, in 1975, and its reauthorization as the Individuals with Disabilities Education Act (IDEA) in 1990, public school systems have been obliged to provide special education and related services to students diagnosed as having LD and in need of specialized instruction or curricula. Consistent with the law, schools have organized special education services to allow eligible students to receive appropriate instruction from a special education teacher and also to participate, to the maximum extent possible, in the instruction being delivered to nondisabled peers in general education classrooms....

Historical Perspective

As early as 1970, Kephart was advocating for a full continuum of services. For some students with LD, "the so-called hard-core case[s] whose interferences are so extensive that [they] will probably need major alterations of educational presentations for the length of [their] educational career[s]" (p. 208), Kephart recommended a segregated classroom. But for those with somewhat less severe problems, "whose interference with learning is such that much of the activities of the [general education] classroom become meaningless ... [and who] need more intensive assistance than the classroom teacher can be expected to provide" (p. 208), Kephart suggested what would later be known as a resource room model:

> a clinical approach in which [the student] is removed from the classroom for a short time, a half-hour or an hour a day. During this short period, individually or in small groups of two or three, intensive attack is made on [the] learning problems—not upon curriculum matters, but upon the learning problem itself and the methods by which [the student] processes information. (p. 208)

The child with minor learning problems, Kephart believed, had much more to gain from interactions with peers in the general education classroom than from intensive activities in a segregated program. This child could be helped by the regular classroom teacher and would be fully included in the mainstream.

In the first edition of Lerner's classic textbook on LD (1971), she, too, called for a continuum of placements matched to the educational needs of the child with LD: special classes for students with severe problems, itinerant teaching services for children whose learning disability is not severe enough to warrant a special class, and resource rooms for most students with LD at both elementary and secondary school levels. By 1975, Hammill and Bartel were suggesting that special schools and special classes "should be used with considerable caution and viewed as a last resort" (p. 3). They also advocated a resource room model, which would permit the student

> to receive instruction individually or in groups in a special room ... [in which] the emphasis is on teaching specific skills that the pupil needs. At the end of [the] lesson, [the pupil] returns to the regular classroom. (p. 4)

Nearly 20 years later, this part-time model of service delivery, in which the student is included but also pulled out, is still preferred. The *Fifteenth Annual Report to Congress* (U.S. Department of Education, 1993) indicates that, across the nation, fewer than 25 percent of students with LD are placed in separate classes or separate schools; 54 percent of students with LD are based in general education classes and receive part-time special education services for 21-59 percent of the school day; but 22 percent of students with learning disabilities are in general education classrooms at least 80 percent of the school day.

Implicit in even the earliest descriptions of these service delivery options was a recognition that the prescribed educational intervention would be provided by a highly trained professional capable of diagnosing the child, planning a teaching program based on this diagnosis, and implementing the teaching plan (Lerner, 1971). That teaching plan would be "designed to support the students' accommodation in the mainstreamed curriculum.... Students [would] learn skills that will help them cope with the requirements of their mainstream classes" (Robinson & Deshler, 1988, p. 132). Furthermore, placement in the pullout setting would be *temporary*....

Instruction in the pullout setting would also be intensive. Indeed, "intensity of instruction" is what distinguished the special education that the students were to receive from the general education they were already getting (Meyen & Lehr, 1980). The goal was to have students acquire a significant number of skills and strategies in a relatively short period of time, so that they could more successfully benefit from the instruction being offered in their mainstream classes. "Regardless of what is being taught, it is imperative that it be taught with maximum effectiveness and efficiency" (Robinson & Deshler, 1988, p. 134).

Once students acquired the needed skills and strategies, they would no longer require direct, intensive, pullout instruction. A change of placement would then be initiated and, slowly, full reintegration would be accomplished. Students with LD assigned full time to a general education classroom were assumed to be capable of coping, on their own, with the ongoing mainstream curriculum so long as "the regular classroom teacher is trained in adapting materials and methods to the student's specific needs and has access to resource materials and consultation" (Meyen, 1988, p. 40).

Thus, inclusion for students with LD is not new; neither is full inclusion for those students with LD who have been taught successfully in a pullout program and are ready for full reintegration, or who have very mild disabilities. As early as 1969, a description of full inclusion services for students with LD appeared in the literature (see Serio & Todd, 1969). In Ohio, students with LD who had "graduated" from pullout programs and whose needs could now be met simply through adjustments within the regular classroom received no pull out services at all.

The Call for Full Inclusion

What *is* new is full inclusion for students with LD for whom, in the past, pullout services would have been deemed appropriate. The impetus to place these students with severe LD in general education classrooms *in lieu of* providing them with pullout special education services derives in large part from the call by Will (1986) for a greater sharing of responsibility for students with learning problems between general education and special education. The movement, dubbed the Regular Education Initiative (REI), received additional impetus from advocacy groups that consider access to the general education class setting as a right of all students, even those in need of a special education (Gartner & Lipsky, 1987; Snell, 1991; Stainback & Stainback, 1989).

REI was also spurred by the growing, national criticism of another large, pullout program, Chapter 1 (see Allington & McGill-Franzen, 1988; Allington, Steutzel, Shake, & Lamarche, 1986). The fact that there were data indicating that resource room programs for students with LD were actually beneficial (Carlberg & Kavale, 1980; Madden & Slavin, 1983) seemed to matter little. Full inclusion was advocated for all students, regardless of individual needs.

In response to the REI, practitioners and researchers implemented alternative service delivery models that virtually eliminated pullout services for students with LD. Now students who had been diagnosed, and for whom an Individualized Education Plan (IEP) had been written, were retained in the general education class full time, and special education resources were "pulled in," instead of the students being "pulled out." There were many variations on the theme (see Jenkins, Jewell, Leicester, Jenkins, & Troutner, 1990; Reynaud, Pfannenstiel, & Hudson, 1987; Stevens, Madden, Slavin, & Farnish, 1987; Wang, 1987; Zigmond & Baker, 1990), but in each of them, students who would otherwise have attended special education classrooms full or part time were returned full time to general education classes.

Lewis and Doorlag (1991) describe two components of instruction for mainstreamed students with LD.

> In the *remediation* approach, the teacher instructs the student in skills that are areas of need. For example, extra assistance might be provided to a fourth grader who spells at the second grade level. *Compensation*, on the other hand, attempts to bypass the student's weaknesses. For instance, to compensate for the reading and writing problems ... the teacher might administer class tests orally. (p. 240)

Wang (1989) describes these same two components (but in the reverse order) as *adaptive instruction,* which should be available to students in full inclusion models. It involves:

> modif[ication of] the learning environment to accommodate the unique learning characteristics and needs of individual students, and [provision of] direct or focused intervention to improve each student's capabilities to successfully acquire subject-matter knowledge and higher-order reasoning and problem-solving skills, to work independently and cooperatively with peers, and to meet the overall intellectual and social demands of schooling. (p. 183)

It is reasonable to question whether, in full-inclusion models judged to be successful by teachers, administrators, parents, and professional colleagues, students with LD are, in fact, experiencing both compensation (adapted learning environments) and remediation (direct or focused instruction in skills and strategies that would enable them to cope with the mainstream curriculum). If only the first were in place, students might be "managing the mainstream" but not learning fundamental skills and strategies that would allow them to become independent, self-directed learners. If only the second were going on, students might be spending a considerable portion of each day in failure experiences.

We have had the opportunity to explore this question in considerable depth in a qualitative study recently completed on full-inclusion elementary school models, described more completely in a special issue of *The Journal of Special Education* (Zigmond & Baker, 1995-b). In that research project, we studied five elementary school buildings that had, for several years, implemented a full inclusion service delivery model for students with LD. In two of the buildings, the full inclusion program was part of a continuum of services, and only students who no longer needed more intensive services were integrated full time. But in three of the buildings, full inclusion was the only special education service available, and students were reintegrated full time into general education, "ready or not." Observations and interviews in these three buildings illustrate what services are provided to students with LD in full inclusion models, and whether both features of adaptive education are addressed in meeting the needs of students with LD.

We searched our interview data from special and general education teachers and our observation notes from 2-day observations in a primary and an intermediate classroom in each building for evidence of the two kinds of services that students with LD could be receiving in these full inclusion models: (a) adaptations or accommodations that were designed to make the curriculum and instruction manageable for the student with LD by "bypassing" the student's deficits and (b) focused, remedial instruction that would increase the capacity of the student with LD to cope with curriculum and materials, however they were presented. We found a lot of the former, and disappointingly little of the latter.

The Schools

The three sites relevant to this discussion were located in Pennsylvania, Kansas, and Washington State (for a complete description of these sites and the educational experiences of students with LD in these sites, see Baker, 1995; Zigmond, 1995-a, 1995-b). The Pennsylvania school had an enrollment of about 460 students, K-6, and 16 students with LD on IEPs. The school was located in a small rural community. Full inclusion at this school was a school-wide effort, involving all of the teachers in the building. Two special education teachers (1.5 full-time equivalent) provided in-class support (coteaching), giving more time to teachers who had students with LD/IEPs in their classrooms (30 minutes, four times per week) and less time to teachers who did not (30 minutes, once or twice per week). Students with LD were distributed across teachers in the building so that no one teacher was particularly burdened by the inclusion.

The school in Kansas was urban, with an enrollment of about 315 students in grades K-5, two classes per grade level. The 45 students on IEPs were assigned in groups of seven or eight to one particular mainstream class at each grade level. At the primary level, one special education teacher formed a team with one first grade and one second grade teacher, and the special education teacher cotaught with each team member for 3 hours per day. At the intermediate level, one third, one fourth, and one fifth grade teacher collaborated with two special education teachers, each special education teacher spending 2 hours per day in each of the three classrooms.

The Washington school had over 400 students in grades K-6, and 42 students with LD, all placed full time in general education classrooms dispersed throughout the school. Special education services provided in the general education classroom replaced the more traditional resource room program in which students had been enrolled. One special education teacher and one paraprofessional provided support services on a flexible schedule, working in classrooms with small groups of students or with individuals, helping to modify academic assignments, and facilitating a cross-age peer tutoring program offered daily to any student who needed extra reading practice.

Adaptations and Accommodations

Accomodations for the Whole Class

Many of the teachers described how they altered an activity, an assignment, or a test based on their perceptions of the needs of the children with LD in their classes. But they invariably used the adaptation for the entire class, because it was easier to implement that way or because they wanted to avoid stigmatizing the specific target children. For example, after hearing from the special education teacher about the value of repeating instructions for students with LD, one fifth grade reading teacher informed us that she began "just more consciously going over it with everybody" (interview, 3/2/93). An intermediate math teacher began to make available to his whole class materials that he had not thought to use before.

> I have those product finders [for multiplication facts] that I allow those who are having difficulty to use and ... just a few will, and I can't recall if maybe two or three times that he [the student with LD] used the product finder when we did multiplication. (interview, 3/2/93)

Reading the textbook aloud was a frequently used accommodation in many of the classes we visited. "We'll talk about it [science, or health, or social studies] and I'll have them read it [the textbook] silently, then we'll read it together so even if he [the child with LD] doesn't read it silently he still hears it," said a second grade teacher (interview, 3/3/93). Reading tests aloud was also a common class-wide accommodation. A sixth grade general education teacher told us,

> If she [a student with LD in the sixth grade classroom] needs to have the test read, we just open it up to the whole group. We say, "I'm going to read the test; if you want to come with me that's fine." (interview, 5/3/93)

A fifth grade general education teacher also began to read her tests to the whole class after the special education teacher had advised her that it might help the students with LD.

> Another thing that I have found ... accommodation-wise for these kids,... it is just about as easy to read [the test] and do the whole thing with the whole class. Then there [are] no misinterpretations. I think that that has been one thing that I have put in my bag of tricks and it has helped everybody. I would say probably 90 percent of the time I do that now. (interview, 3/2/ 93)

An interesting extension of this idea of implementing something for the whole class because it might benefit the students with LD was seen in intermediate classes in one of the schools. Teachers in grades 3-5 routinely implemented peer tutoring (Greenwood, Delquadro, & Hall, 1989), in which all students in the class participated, to afford students with reading problems extra practice in reading fluency and comprehension.

In two of the schools, curricular changes for the whole school were spurred, in large part, by a concern for the students with LD who would be integrated into mainstream classes. A primary level special education teacher reported:

> Because of the thinking skills that we put into place and the way we use mediational questioning, the strategies we use, the graphic organizers we use, the way we set everything up, [the child with LD is] not getting any more than anybody else, but those things are from a special education background and do allow [the child] to function at a much higher level. (interview, 5/3/ 93)

Reducing Work Load

A second strategy that we found in these full inclusion classrooms was a conscious reduction of the work load for students with LD. These students were expected to do less of a specific assignment. As one second grade teacher put it,

> We may not expect an identified child, like in writing, to write pages and pages in their journal as I would someone else ... I mean if we feel like there are children that have done as much as they can do with an assignment, then that's fine. (interview, 5/3/93)

The same was true in another building. "We modify how much written work she [a student with LD] needs," the special education teacher told us (interview, 5/20/93).

The most common adjustment in work load came during spelling. In one school, students with LD were usually assigned a shorter list for the weekly spelling test, but in the other two schools, adjustments were also often made to the difficulty level of the words. According to one special education teacher, "Sometimes ... if there's a list that has pretty obscure words on it, [the sixth grade teacher will] delete some of those and put on some of the most frequently used words" (interview, 5/20/93). A second grade teacher said,

> I go ahead and choose four words of a skill I want to work on. Then they get to choose four or five words that they just want to learn to spell. They are usually on their level. The higher level kids choose words that are higher level. (interview, 5/3/93)

Accommodations for a Specific Student

Very few accommodations were focused on the needs of a particular child with LD. Those we did hear about were characterized as being easy to implement. For example, in one school, teachers highlighted key words on work sheets, homework assignments, and tests, specifically for the students who had serious reading problems. "I highlight things occasionally, like with the story problem ... just to focus him in, because he wouldn't know what the words were," the second grade general education teacher noted (interview, 3/3/93). Sometimes highlighting would be combined with oral reading, as reported by the mother of one of the children we observed. ... Another teacher reported, "Everything I give him I read to him" (interview, 3/3/93).

Focused Instruction on Skills or Strategies

Many of the teachers we talked to were surprised at how difficult it was for the students with LD integrated into their classes to learn what they were being asked to learn.

> The thing that is so amazing about these special ed kids is you always have to teach them: "Look at me, I'm talking; look at me; here I am, where's your eyes supposed to be?" Every day. Usually second grade, by the second week of school, you just say, "These are rules; here's the signal; I do this, you look." But

[these kids], you just have to keep [going over it again and again]. (second grade, general education teacher, interview, 5/19/93)

So, in addition to accommodations, these teachers attempted to find time and personnel to provide students with remedial instruction. To do so, they turned to the special education teacher who was coteaching with them, to the paraprofessionals available in the school, and, most often, to classroom peers.

Peer-Partners

The most available "personnel" for extra instruction were classroom peers. "I just go in and check on her [the student with LD], make sure that she has a very helpful partner," a second grade teacher said (interview, 5/19/93). In one of the schools, a second grader with LD was assigned to another second grader specifically for some extra drill on sight words in reading. In another school, very heavy use was made of study buddies, classmates paired together for up toa month at a time, so that the stronger could help the weaker complete classroom assignments.

"We try and pair usually a high child with an identified child just so they have someone else there, especially when I'm in the room by myself. They [the study buddies] are good teachers" (second grade, general education teacher, interview, 5/3/93). In no case did the partner receive training on what to teach or how to teach it.

Small Group Instruction

During coteaching periods, one special education teacher provided small group instruction to students with LD and other low achieving students in the class (often as many as one-third of the students). This was often a parallel lesson to the one being taught to more competent students by the general education teacher at the same time. The small group parallel lesson permitted more careful monitoring of the students' responses, more active student participation, and more feedback to the students on their answers and mistakes. The teacher did not focus the instruction on skills that might have been missed in earlier lessons, nor did she spend time teaching strategies for independent functioning.

We're not teaching them *how* to read. I think we're just doing total accommodation. Nobody has time to teach these kids [fifth graders] how to read back at their second grade level. In about two periods a week, I'm not going to teach kids how to read. (special education teacher, 3/3/93)

In another school, supplemental small group instruction was offered to any students who needed it, whether or not they were identified as in need of special education. Interestingly, for the convenience of both the general education teachers and the special education teacher and paraprofessional, this small group instruction was usually offered *outside* the classroom.

For example, each morning, the special education teacher or the aide provided 15-minute phonics lessons to small groups of primary grade students in the hall outside their classroom. There were three groups of first grade phonics students, three second grade groups, and one third grade group. Small group lessons were also offered before school or during lunch (by the special education teacher), and after school (by the paraprofessional) for primary and intermediate level students, respectively.

During these lessons, the teacher or the aide previewed the upcoming general education classroom work in reading, math, or language arts, "offering instruction that supports what they do in the classroom" (special education teacher, 5/20/93). There was no time for instruction on skills that might have been missed earlier or for explicit instruction in learning strategies. "It's all based on what the classroom is doing. I mean, I don't do a different curriculum," the special education teacher reported (interview, 5/20/93).

Individual Instruction

We saw a lot of individual attentionprovided to students—teachers stopping beside a student, looking over his or her shoulder, and giving feedback or on-the-spot tutoring. With two teachers in the room coteaching, there seemed to be more opportunities for this. In one building, the special education teacher reported:

> Sometimes I have pulled ... Gladys away from the group and we've worked in either skill groups or just one-on-one out in the hall where I've tried to show her some strategies on how to come up with the answer. With our program, oftentimes we don't have time to actually work one-to-one with that child. So I've tried to show her little strategies as we go around. (interview, 5/3/93)

Nevertheless, these one-to-one episodes were unplanned and infrequent.

We saw almost no other attempts to provide individual *instruction*,in which a student was explicitly taught skills or concepts that had been identified as outside her or his current repertoire yet needed for coping with the mainstream curriculum. No one had the time for it. The only way they could achieve one-to-one time was to use parent volunteers. "[When volunteers come on Fridays,] I have an adult that works with her," a second grade teacher told us (interview, 5/20/93).

There was one exception. In one second grade, the teachers had identified a student whose reading was very deficient. For this student, the special education teacher, the second grade teacher, and the Chapter 1 teacher had collaborated to offer 15-minutes per day of remedial instruction. On Monday through Thursday, this was provided before school officially started (Mondays, Wednesdays, and Thursdays by the second grade teacher, Tuesdays by the Chapter 1 teacher). When her schedule permitted, the special education teacher added a Friday session during the afternoon.

But for the fifth grader in that same school who needed more than was being provided in the full inclusion model, the parents arranged for privately funded, after-school tutoring, once a week. The fifth grade general education teacher recognized the need for this tutoring, and its utility, but made no attempt to find out about it or to influence what went on in it. In fact, the tutor and the teacher did not communicate even though they were both teachers in the same building.

Too Much of a Good Thing?

We have no doubt that full inclusion of students who in other schools would have been attending pullout programs carried with it many benefits. In all three schools, the planning for inclusion was quickly coopted into a total school improvement effort, involving all of the teachers in a reconsideration of curriculum, materials, pacing, and grading. The coteaching that accompanied inclusion of students with LD brought new educational opportunities to all students in general education. Adaptations that teachers implemented made the curriculum more accessible to a wider range of students than before and permitted the teachers to teach, more effectively, a far more diverse set of students.

Students with LD did not miss any instructional time or any of the non-instructional activities that occurred throughout the school day. They were fully integrated into the social fabric of their classes, participating in classroom and school events. The full inclusion programs eliminated whatever stigma results from the sorting that inevitably occurs when only a small number of students have access to special services. In-class services were available to everyone, and in the Washington school, new pull-aside services reached as many as one-third of the students in the school, because they were made available to any students referred by the teacher, whether or not they had been diagnosed as having disabilities.

These full inclusion models, with coteaching and often joint planning between general and special education teachers, achieved the first goal of adaptive education (Wang, 1989): "Teachers modified the learning environment to accommodate the unique learning characteristics and needs of the students" (p. 183). Teachers willingly changed assignments, activities, and tests. They learned new ways to teach through their collaborations with special education teachers and profited from the opportunities made available by having an extra teacher or paraprofessional in the classroom.

For the most part, however, the students with LD did not get the second feature of adaptive education—"direct or focused intervention to improve each student's capabilities" (Wang, 1989, p. 183). As we have described elsewhere (Zigmond & Baker, 1995-a), the special education we saw was superficial, impromptu, and hardly likely to have a lasting impact or to achieve long-term goals. It was seldom preplanned, and it lacked intensity. There was no sense of urgency over what needed to be taught and learned. It had none of the features of good special education practice outlined recently by Scruggs and Mastropieri (1995). And yet, the students with LD in these full inclusion models were clearly students who were still in need of focused, intensive, individualized instruction and would have been receiving pullout services if full inclusion had not been the prevailing social force.

We do not wish to imply that, had these students been in pullout special education settings, they would have received an appropriate (i.e., carefully planned, focused, intensive, goal-directed) special education. There is much legitimate criticism of current pullout special education practice (see Kauffman, 1993; Kauffman & Pullen, 1989; Leinhardt, Zigmond, & Cooley, 1981). Nor are we ruling out the possibility that this second feature of adaptive instruction, "direct or focused intervention" (Wang, 1989, p. 183), could be provided within a general education classroom. We must report, however, that it *was not* and *could not have been* provided in the general education classrooms we have seen. These classrooms were not organized or managed in ways that would have sustained direct and focused interventions for a select few students. That the phonics lessons in Washington were conducted in the hall outside the classroom indicates that the teachers themselves understood this, and believed that the opportunities for direct and focused instruction were limited within the four walls of the general education class. In general education classrooms, where the learning and social interactions of dozens of students must be orchestrated, the *how* of instruction (materials, instructions, structure) can be tinkered with, but the *what* of instruction (curriculum, pacing) is less amenable to change.

More than a decade ago, Meyen and Lehr (1980) described learning environments that were conducive to intense instruction. They are characterized by opportunities for consistent and sustained time on task; immediate, frequent, and appropriate feedback to the students; regular and frequent communication to each student that the teacher expects the student to accomplish the task and demonstrate continuous progress; and a pattern of interaction in which the teacher responds to student initiatives and uses consequences appropriate to the student's response. Like Meyen and Lehr, we believe that pullout settings are more likely to provide these opportunities. Furthermore, short-term, part-time, pullout programs should also afford a teacher and a student the opportunity to engage in intense instruction on material that a particular child must learn, that others have already learned, or that others will pick up on their own.

Based on our research, we cannot support elimination of a continuum of services for students with LD. Inclusion is good; full inclusion may be too much of a good thing. We do not mean to suggest that we return to business as usual in special education resource rooms. The hallway lessons in Washington worked well because only the students involved in the lessons were present for them; no other students were assigned to the special education teacher during those 15 minutes and thus no other students had to be put to work on something else while the directed phonics lesson was taking place. Also, the students assigned to the special education teacher did not have to be put to busy work while the teacher worked with another group. But the hallway was noisy, the students sat on the floor, and the teacher had no access to a chalkboard or supplemental materials.

Scheduling and excessive case loads have prevented special education teachers from accomplishing their intended purposes. Nevertheless, for students with LD, there are skills and strategies that need to be acquired if instruction in the mainstream is to be meaningful and productive, and these skills and strategies must be taught explicitly and intensively. Providing a venue and the resources for delivering this instruction is not only our moral obligation to students with LD, it is also our obligation under the law.

References

Allington, R., & McGill-Franzen, A. (1988). *Coherence or chaos? Qualitative dimensions of the literacy instruction provided low-achievement children.* Albany: State University of New York. (ERIC Document Reproductions Service No. ED 292 060)

Allington, R., Steutzel, H., Shake, M., & Lamarche, S. (1986). What is remedial reading? A descriptive study. *Reading Research and Instruction, 26,* 15-30.

Baker, J. M. (1995). Inclusion in Washington: Educational experiences of students with learning disabilities in one elementary school. *The Journal of Special Education, 29*(2), 155-162.

Carlberg, C., & Kavale, K. (1980). The efficacy of special versus regular class placement for exceptional children: A meta-analysis. *The Journal of Special Education, 14,* 295-309.

Gartner, A., & Lipsky, D. K. (1987). Beyond special education: Toward a quality system for all students. *Harvard Educational Review, 57,* 367-395.

Greenwood, C. R., Delquadro, J., & Hall, R. V. (1989). Longitudinal effects of class-wide peer tutoring. *Journal of Educational Psychology, 81,* 371-383.

Hammill, D. D., & Bartel, N. R. (1975). *Teaching children with learning and behavior problems.* Boston: Allyn & Bacon.

Individuals With Disabilities Education Act, 20 U.S.C. § 1400 et seq. (1990).

Jenkins, J. R., Jewell, M., Leicester, N., Jenkins, L., & Troutner, N. (1990, April). *Development of a school building model for educating handicapped and at-risk students in general education classrooms.* Paper presented at the annual meeting of the American Educational Research Association, Boston.

Kauffman, J. M. (1993). How we might achieve the radical reform of special education. *Exceptional Children, 60,* 6-16.

Kauffman, J. M., & Pullen, P. L. (1989). An historical perspective: A personal perspective on our history of service to mildly handicapped and at-risk students. *Remedial and Special Education, 10*(6), 12-14.

Kephart, N. C. (1970). Reflection on learning disabilities: Its contribution to education. In J. I. Arena (Ed.), *Meeting total needs of learning disabled children: A forward look* (pp. 206-208). Pittsburgh: Association for Children With Learning Disabilities.

Leinhardt, G., Zigmond, N., & Cooley, W. W. (1981). Reading instruction and its effects. *American Educational Research Journal 18*(3), 343-361.

Lerner, J. W. (1971). *Children with learning disabilities: Theories, diagnosis, and teaching strategies.* Boston: Houghton Mifflin.

Lewis, R. B., & Doorlag, D. H. (1991). *Teaching special students in the mainstream* (3rd ed.). New York: Merrill.

Madden, N. A., & Slavin, R. E. (1983). Mainstreaming students with mild handicaps: Academic and social outcomes. *Review of Educational Research, 53,* 519-569.

Meyen, E. L. (1988). A commentary on special education. In E. L. Meyen, & T. M. Skrtic (Eds.), *Exceptional children and youth: An introduction* (3rd ed.; pp. 3-48). Denver: Love Publishing.

Meyen, E. L., & Lehr, D. H. (1980). Evolving practices in assessment and intervention for mildly handicapped adolescents: The case for intensive instruction. *Exceptional Education Quarterly, 1*(2), 19-26.

Reynaud, G., Pfannenstiel, T., & Hudson, F. (1987). *Park Hill secondary learning disability program: An alternative service delivery model. Implementation Manual.* (ERIC Document Reproduction Service No. ED 289 321)

Robinson, S. M., & Deshler, D. D. (1988). Learning disabled. In E. L. Meyen & T. M. Skrtic (Eds.), *Exceptional children and youth: An introduction* (3rd ed.; pp. 109-138). Denver: Love Publishing.

Scruggs, T. E., & Mastropieri, M. A. (1995). What makes special education special: Evaluating inclusion programs with the PASS variables. *The Journal of Special Education, 29*(2), 224-233.

Serio, M., & Todd, J. H. (1969). Operations of programs in Ohio. In J. Arena (Ed.), *Successful programming: Many points of view* (pp. 377-379). San Rafael, CA: Academic Theory Publications.

Snell, M. E. (1991). Schools are for all kids: The importance of integration for students with severe disabilities and their peers. In J. W. Lloyd, N. N. Singh, & A. C. Repp (Eds.), *The regular education initiative: Alternative perspectives on concepts, issues, and models* (pp. 133-148). Sycamore, IL: Sycamore.

Stainback, W., & Stainback, S. (1989). Practical organizational strategies. In S. Stainback, W. Stainback, & M. Forest (Eds.), *Educating all students in the main stream of education* (pp. 71-87). Baltimore: Paul H. Brookes.

Stevens, R., Madden, N., Slavin, R., & Farnish, A. (1987). Cooperative integrated reading and composition: Two field experiments. *Reading Research Quarterly, 22,* 433-454.

U.S. Department of Education. (1993). *Fifteenth Annual Report to Congress on the Implementation of the Individual swith Disabilities Education Act.* Washington, DC: Author.

Wang, M. (1987). Toward achieving educational excellence for all students: Program design and student outcomes. *Remedial and Special Education, 8*(3), 25-34.

Wang, M. (1989). Accommodating student diversity through adaptive education. In S. Stainback, W. Stainback, & M. Forest (Eds.), *Educating all students in the main stream of education* (pp. 183-197), Baltimore: Paul H. Brookes.

Will, M. C. (1986). Educating children with learning problems: A shared responsibility. *Exceptional Children, 52,* 411-415.

Zigmond, N. (1995-a). Inclusion in Kansas: Educational experiences of students with learning disabilities in one elementary school. *The Journal of Special Education, 29*(2), 144-154.

Zigmond, N. (1995-b). Inclusion in Pennsylvania: Educational experiences of students with learning disabilities in one elementary school. *The Journal of Special Education, 29*(2), 124-132.

Zigmond, N., & Baker, J. (1990). Project MELD: A preliminary report. *Exceptional Children, 57,* 176-185.

Zigmond, N., & Baker, J. M. (1995-a) Concluding comments: Current and future practices in inclusive schooling. *The Journal of Special Education, 29*(2), 245-250.

Zigmond, N., & Baker, J. M. (Eds.) (1995-b). An exploration of the meaning and practice of special education in the context of full inclusion of students with learning disabilities [special issue]. *The Journal of Special Education, 29*(2).

POSTSCRIPT

Is Full Inclusion Always the Best Option for Children With Disabilities?

It is possible that research on inclusion to date has been inconclusive because researchers have focused on the wrong question. Much of the research in this area seems to have been designed to determine "once and for all" whether students with disabilities have better outcomes in segregated or inclusive educational programs. It is unlikely, however, that inclusion in all its forms will lead to better outcomes for all students and under all conditions. This has led some scholars to encourage researchers to ask more focused questions, such as, What types of students benefit from inclusion? What types of strategies are needed for inclusion to be effective? What types of training and belief systems do teachers need for inclusion to work? and, What resources are associated with effective inclusive programs? Addressing these questions may help educators to learn more about when and why inclusion is effective or ineffective.

Some scholars have argued that deciding whether or not inclusion is the best option for students with disabilities is an ethical question and, therefore, not answerable by research. See, for example, "Inclusion Paradigms in Conflict," by Peter V. Paul and Marjorie E. Ward, *Theory Into Practice* (vol. 35, no. 1, 1996). These scholars argue that segregated education is by its very nature discriminatory because it denies students with disabilities access to the same experiences and opportunities afforded everyone else. Although these scholars see a role for empirical research, that role is not to learn whether inclusion should occur but rather how it should occur.

Readers interested in pursuing this topic further can turn to edited volumes by Dorothy K. Lipsky and Alan Gartner, *Inclusion and School Reform: Transforming America's Classrooms* (Paul H. Brookes, 1997) and Susan Stainback and William Stainback, *Inclusion: A Guide for Educators* (Paul H. Brookes, 1996) for histories of educational practices and legislation relating to students with disabilities. Suggestions for implementing inclusive educational practices can be found in "School Change and Inclusive Schools: Lessons Learned From Practice," by James McLeskey and Nancy L. Waldron, *Phi Delta Kappan* (September 2002). Discussions of barriers to inclusion can be found in "Barriers and Facilitators to Inclusive Education," by Jayne Pivik, Joan McComas, and Marc Laflamme, *Exceptional Children* (Fall 2002) and "Attitudes of Elementary School Principals Toward the Inclusion of Students With Disabilities," by Cindy L. Praisner, *Exceptional Children* (Winter 2003). An argument against the proliferation of inclusive practices can be found in "The Oppression of Inclusion," by David A. Zera and Roy M. Seitsinger, *Educational Horizons* (Fall 2000).

ISSUE 5

Can Schools Close the Achievement Gap Between Students from Different Ethnic and Racial Backgrounds?

YES: Carol Corbett Burris and Kevin G. Welner, from "Closing the Achievement Gap by Detracking," *Phi Delta Kappan* (April 2005)

NO: William J. Mathis, from "Bridging the Achievement Gap: A Bridge Too Far?" *Phi Delta Kappan* (April 2005)

ISSUE SUMMARY

YES: Carol Corbett Burris and Kevin G. Welner argue that the achievement gap between white students and African-American and Hispanic students is a consequence of the over-representation of students from ethnic and racial minorities in low ability-track classes. They argue that the watered-down curriculum and low expectations associated with low ability-track classes prevent ethnic and racial minority students from achieving the same levels of academic success as white students.

NO: William J. Mathis argues that the achievement gap between white and African-American and Hispanic students has been created by discriminatory social and political pressures that pervade all facets of life. He argues that it is, therefore, unreasonable to expect to eliminate the gap through curricular or other innovations in the schools. Mathis cites school vouchers as an example of a failed attempt to use schooling as a means of undoing the achievement gap.

In 2004, the nation witnessed the fiftieth anniversary of the U.S. Supreme Court's decision in *Brown v. the Board of Education,* which declared that the segregation of public schools according to race denied African-American children the same educational opportunities as white children. Many educators and policy makers, however, did not view the anniversary as an occasion to celebrate, pointing to the continuing gap between the academic achievement of white students, on the one hand, and African-American and Hispanic students, on the other. Put simply, compared to white students, African-American and Hispanic students, on average, score lower on standardized achievement tests and tests of basic skills in mathematics and science, are more likely to leave school before graduating from high school, and are less likely to attend college. Although African-American and Hispanic students are overrepresented among lower-income families in this country, the achievement gap cannot be fully explained by economic differences. Racial and ethnic differences in academic achievement remain even in comparisons of families with similar annual incomes.

What role do schools play in creating or maintaining this achievement gap? And what role should schools play in reducing or preventing the gap? Some critics of public education suggest that schools have created the gap through discriminatory practices and subtle forms of racism perpetrated by teachers, administrators, and support staff, such as having lower expectations for African-American and Hispanic students and assigning them to low ability-track or special education classes at substantially higher rates than their white peers. These critics also point out that the achievement gap actually widens over the school years, with African-American and Hispanic students falling further and further behind their white peers as they move through the elementary to the middle and, eventually, the high school years. Critics suggest that this increasing gap is evidence that schools are causing, or at least contributing to, the problem. Indeed, President George W. Bush's controversial No Child Left Behind policy is based on the assumption that any student can succeed if given appropriate educational opportunities.

Many defenders of public education argue that it is not schools that are to blame for the existence of the achievement gap, but rather the broader social and economic conditions that create a wide array of disparities among different ethnic and racial groups. Years of discrimination, it is argued, have led to high rates of poverty among African-American and Hispanic families, and thereby to less adequate material resources in homes, including books and other materials that support academic growth; more limited access to the health care and nutrition necessary to ensure optimal development; and exposure to a variety of hazardous conditions, from exposure to lead in paints to crime and violence, all of which interfere with learning. These defenders of public education point out that children who live in poverty begin school less well prepared (e.g., with fewer pre-literacy skills, such as the recognition that print encodes language or of specific letters) than their more affluent peers and thus, wider social forces rather than schooling is to blame for the achievement gap. Thus, it is unreasonable, according to critics, to expect that schools can overcome the pervasive social and economic barriers that exist before an African-American or Hispanic child begins school and continue in his or her out-of-school hours.

In the first of the following selections, Carol Corbett Burris and Kevin G. Welner argue that the achievement gap between white students and African-American and Hispanic students is a consequence of the over-representation of minority students in low ability-track classes. Thus, for Burris and Welner, the desegregation ordered by the Supreme Court in *Brown v. the Board of Education* has not resulted in equal educational opportunities for all students. In the second selection, William J. Mathis argues that the discriminatory social and political pressures that have led to the achievement gap pervade all facets of life and thus, cannot be overcome by curricular or other innovations in public schooling. He argues that this is why the achievement gap has persisted despite good-faith efforts by educators to reform curricula and policy, and he cites the school voucher program as an example of the failure of such school-based reforms.

Carol Corbett Burris
and Kevin G. Welner

 **YES**

Closing the Achievement Gap
by Detracking

$\mathbf{T}$he most recent Phi Delta Kappa/Gallup Poll of the Public's Attitudes Toward the Public Schools found that 74% of Americans believe that the achievement gap between white students and African American and Hispanic students is primarily due to factors unrelated to the quality of schooling that children receive.[1] This assumption is supported by research dating back four decades to the Coleman Report and its conclusion that schools have little impact on the problem.[2] But is the pessimism of that report justified? Or is it possible for schools to change their practices and thereby have a strongly positive effect on student achievement? We have found that when all students—those at the bottom as well as the top of the "gap"—have access to first-class learning opportunities, all students' achievement can rise.

Because African American and Hispanic students are consistently overrepresented in low-track classes, the effects of tracking greatly concern educators who are interested in closing the achievement gap.[3] Detracking reforms are grounded in the established ideas that higher achievement follows from a more rigorous curriculum and that low-track classes with unchallenging curricula result in lower student achievement.[4] Yet, notwithstanding the wide acceptance of these ideas, we lack concrete case studies of mature detracking reforms and their effects. This article responds to that shortage, describing how the school district in which Carol Burris serves as a high school principal was able to close the gap by offering its high-track curriculum to all students, in detracked classes.

Tracking and the Achievement Gap

Despite overwhelming research demonstrating the ineffectiveness of low-track classes and of tracking in general, schools continue the practice.[5] Earlier studies have argued that this persistence stems from the fact that tracking is grounded in values, beliefs, and politics as much as it is in technical, structural, or organizational needs.[6] Further, despite inconsistent research findings,[7] many parents and educators assume that the practice benefits high achievers. This is partly because parents of high achievers fear that detracking and heterogeneous grouping will result in a "watered-down" curriculum and lowered learning standards for their children.

From *Phi Delta Kappan*, April 2005, pp. 594-598. Copyright © 2005 by The Liberty Partnership Program. Reprinted by permission of the author.

And so, despite the evidence that low-track classes cause harm, they continue to exist. Worse still, the negative achievement effects of such classes fall disproportionately on minority students, since, as noted above, African American and Hispanic students are overrepresented in low-track classes and underrepresented in high-track classes, even after controlling for prior measured achievement.[8] Socioeconomic status (SES) has been found to affect track assignment as well.[9] A highly proficient student from a low socioeconomic background has only a 50-50 chance of being placed in a high-track class.[10]

Researchers who study the relationship between tracking, race/ethnicity, and academic performance suggest different strategies for closing the achievement gap. Some believe that the solution is to encourage more minority students to take high-track classes.[11] Others believe that if all students are given the enriched curriculum that high-achieving students receive, achievement will rise.[12] They believe that no students—whatever their race, SES, or prior achievement—should be placed in classes that have a watered-down or remedial academic curriculum and that the tracking system should be dismantled entirely.[13] In this article, we provide evidence for the success of this latter approach. By dismantling tracking and providing the high-track curriculum to all, we can succeed in closing the achievement gap on important measures of learning.

Providing 'High-Track' Curriculum to All Students

The Rockville Centre School District is a diverse suburban school district located on Long Island. In the late 1990s, it embarked on a multiyear detracking reform that increased learning expectations for all students. The district began replacing its tracked classes with heterogeneously grouped classes in which the curriculum formerly reserved for the district's high-track students was taught.

This reform began as a response to an ambitious goal set by the district's superintendent, William Johnson, and the Rockville Centre Board of Education in 1993: *By the year 2000, 75% of all graduates will earn a New York State Regents diploma.* At that time, the district and state rates of earning Regents diplomas were 58% and 38% respectively.

To qualify for a New York State Regents diploma, students must pass, at a minimum, eight end-of-course Regents examinations, including two in mathematics, two in laboratory sciences, two in social studies, one in English language arts, and one in a foreign language. Rockville Centre's goal reflected the superintendent's strong belief in the external evaluation of student learning as well as the district's commitment to academic rigor.

Regents exams are linked with coursework; therefore, the district gradually eliminated low-track courses. The high school eased the transition by offering students instructional support classes and carefully monitoring the progress of struggling students.

While the overall number of Regents diplomas increased, a disturbing profile of students who were not earning the diploma emerged. These students were more likely to be African American or Hispanic, to receive free or reduced-price lunch, or to have a learning disability. At the district's high school, 20% of all students were African American or Hispanic, 13% received free and reduced-price lunch, and 10% were special education students. If these graduates were to earn the Regents diploma, systemic change would need to take place to close the gaps for each of these groups.

Accelerated Mathematics in Heterogeneous Classes

On closer inspection of the data, educators noticed that the second math Regents exam presented a stumbling block to earning the diploma. While high-track students enrolled in trigonometry and advanced algebra in the 10th grade, low-track students did not even begin first-year algebra until grade 10.

In order to provide all students with ample opportunity to pass the needed courses and to study calculus prior to graduation, Superintendent Johnson decided that all students would study the accelerated math curriculum formerly reserved for the district's highest achievers. Under the leadership of the assistant principal, Delia Garrity, middle school math teachers revised and condensed the curriculum. The new curriculum was taught to all students, in heterogeneously grouped classes. To support struggling learners, the school initiated support classes called math workshops and provided after-school help four afternoons a week.

The results were remarkable. Over 90% of incoming freshmen entered the high school having passed the first Regents math examination. The achievement gap dramatically narrowed. Between the years of 1995 and 1997, only 23% of regular education African American or Hispanic students had passed this algebra-based Regents exam before entering high school. After universally accelerating all students in heterogeneously grouped classes, the percentage more than tripled—up to 75%. The percentage of white or Asian American regular education students who passed the exam also greatly increased—from 54% to 98%.

Detracking the High School

The district approached universal acceleration with caution. Some special education students, while included in the accelerated classes, were graded using alternative assessments. This 1998 cohort of special education students would not take the first ("Sequential I") Regents math exam until they had completed ninth grade. (We use year of entry into ninth grade to determine cohort. So the 1998 cohort began ninth grade in the fall of 1998.) On entering high school, these students with special needs were placed in a double-period, low-track, "Sequential I" ninth-grade math class, along with low-achieving new entrants. Consistent with the recommendations of researchers who have defended tracking,[14] this class was rich in resources (a math teacher, special education inclusion teacher, and teaching assistant). Yet the low-track culture of the class remained unconducive to learning. Students were disruptive, and teachers spent considerable class time addressing behavior management issues. All students were acutely aware that the class carried the "low-track" label.

District and school leaders decided that this low-track class failed its purpose, and the district boldly moved forward with several new reforms the following year. All special education students in the 1999 cohort took the exam in the eighth grade. The entire 1999 cohort also studied science in heterogeneous classes throughout middle school, and it became the first cohort to be heterogeneously grouped in ninth-grade English and social studies classes.

Ninth-grade teachers were pleased with the results. The tone, activities, and discussions in the heterogeneously grouped classes were academic, focused, and enriched. Science teachers reported that the heterogeneously grouped middle school science program prepared students well for ninth-grade biology.

Detracking at the high school level continued, paralleling the introduction of revised New York State curricula. Students in the 2000 cohort studied the state's new biology curriculum, "The Living Environment," in heterogeneously grouped classes. This combination of new curriculum and heterogeneous grouping resulted in a dramatic increase in the passing rate on the first science Regents exam, especially for minority students who were previously overrepresented in the low-track biology class. After just one year of heterogeneous grouping, the passing rate for African American and Hispanic students increased from 48% to 77%, while the passing rate for white and Asian American students increased from 85% to 94%.

The following September, the 2001 cohort became the first class to be heterogeneously grouped in *all subjects* in the ninth grade. The state's new multiyear "Math A" curriculum was taught to this cohort in heterogeneously grouped classes in both the eighth and ninth grades.

In 2003, some 10th-grade classes detracked. Students in the 2002 cohort became the first to study a heterogeneously grouped pre-International Baccalaureate (IB) 10th-grade curriculum in English and social studies. To help all students meet the demands of an advanced curriculum, the district provides every-other-day support classes in math, science, and English language arts. These classes are linked to the curriculum and allow teachers to pre- and post-teach topics to students needing additional reinforcement.

Closing the Gap on Other Measures That Matter

New York's statewide achievement gap in the earning of Regents diplomas has persisted. In 2000, only 19.3% of all African American or Hispanic 12th-graders and 58.7% of all white or Asian American 12th-graders graduated with Regents diplomas. By 2003, while the percentage of students in both groups earning the Regents diploma increased (26.4% of African American or Hispanic students, 66.3% of white or Asian American students), the gap did not close.

In contrast, Rockville Centre has seen both an increase in students' rates of earning Regents diplomas and a decrease in the gap between groups. ... For those students who began South Side High School in 1996 (the graduating class of 2000), 32% of all African American or Hispanic and 88% of all white or Asian American graduates earned Regents diplomas. By the time the cohort of 1999 graduated in 2003, the gap had closed dramatically—82% of all African American or Hispanic and 97% of all white or Asian American graduates earned Regents diplomas. In fact,...for this 1999 cohort (the first to experience detracking in all middle school and most ninth-grade subjects), the Regents diploma rate for the district's minority students surpassed New York State's rate for white or Asian American students.

In order to ensure that the narrowing of the gap was not attributable to a changing population, we used binary logistic regression analyses to compare the probability of earning a Regents diploma before and after detracking. In addition to membership in a detracked cohort, the model included socioeconomic and special education status as covariates. Those students who were members of the 1996 and 1997 cohorts were compared with members of the 1998-2000 cohorts. We found that membership in a cohort subsequent to the detracking of middle school math was a significant contributor to earning a Regents diploma. ... In addition, low-SES students and special education students in the 2001 cohort also showed sharp improvement.

These same three cohorts (1998–2000) showed significant increases in the probability of minority students' studying advanced math courses. Controlling for prior achievement and SES, minority students' enrollment in trigonometry, precalculus, and Advanced Placement calculus all grew.[15] And as more students from those cohorts studied AP calculus, the enrollment gap decreased from 38% to 18% in five years, and the AP calculus scores significantly increased. ...

Finally, detracking in the 10th grade, combined with teaching all students the pre-IB curriculum, appears to be closing the gap in the study of the IB curriculum. This year 50% of all minority students will study IB English and "History of the Americas" in the 11th grade. In the fall of 2003, only 31% chose to do so.

·◦◉◦·

Achievement follows from opportunities—opportunities that tracking denies. The results of detracking in Rockville Centre are clear and compelling. When all students were taught the high-track curriculum, achievement rose for all groups of students—majority, minority, special education, low-SES, and high-SES. This evidence can now be added to the larger body of tracking research that has convinced the Carnegie Council for Adolescent Development, the National Governors' Association, and most recently the National Research Council to call for the reduction or elimination of tracking.[16] The Rockville Centre reform confirms common sense: closing the "curriculum gap" is an effective way to close the "achievement gap."

Notes

1. Lowell C. Rose and Alec M. Gallup, "The 36th Annual Phi Delta Kappa/Gallup Poll of the Public's Attitudes Toward the Public Schools," *Phi Delta Kappan*, September 2004, p. 49.
2. James Coleman et al., *Equality of Educational Opportunity* (Washington, D.C.: U.S. Government Printing Office, 1966).
3. Kevin G. Welner, *Legal Rights, Local Wrongs: When Community Control Collides with Educational Equity* (Albany: SUNY Press, 2001).
4. Clifford Adelman, *Answers in the Tool Box: Academic Intensity, Attendance Patterns, and Bachelor's Degree Attainment* (Washington, D.C.: Office of Educational Research, U.S. Department of Education, 1999), available on the Web at www.ed.gov/pubs/Toolbox; Henry Levin, *Accelerated Schools for At-Risk Students* (New Brunswick, N.J.: Rutgers University, Center for Policy Research in Education, Report No. 142, 1988); Mano Singham, "The Achievement Gap: Myths and Realities," *Phi Delta Kappan*, April 2003, pp. 586-91; and Jay P. Heubert and Robert M. Hauser, *High Stakes: Testing for Tracking, Promotion, and Graduation* (Washington, D.C.: National Research Council, 1999).
5. Jeannie Oakes, Adam Gamoran, and Reba Page, "Curriculum Differentiation: Opportunities, Outcomes, and Meanings," in Philip Jackson, ed., *Handbook of Research on Curriculum* (New York: Macmillan, 1992), pp. 570-608.
6. Welner, op. cit.
7. Frederick Mosteller, Richard Light, and Jason Sachs, "Sustained Inquiry in Education: Lessons from Skill Grouping and Class Size," *Harvard Educational Review*, vol. 66, 1996, pp. 797-843; Robert Slavin, "Achievement Effects of Ability Grouping in Secondary Schools: A Best-Evidence Synthesis," *Review of Educational Research*, vol. 60, 1990, pp. 471-500; and James Kulik, *An Analysis of the Research on Ability Grouping: Historical and Contemporary Perspectives* (Storrs, Conn.: National Research Center on the Gifted and Talented, University of Connecticut, 1992).
8. Roslyn Mickelson, "Subverting Swann: First- and Second-Generation Segregation in Charlotte-Mecklenburg Schools," *American Educational Research Journal*, vol. 38, 2001, pp. 215-52; Robert Slavin and Jomills Braddock II, "Ability Grouping: On the Wrong Track," *College Board Review*, Summer 1993, pp. 11-17; and Welner, op. cit.
9. Samuel Lucas, *Tracking Inequality: Stratification and Mobility in American High Schools* (New York: Teachers College Press, 1999).
10. Beth E. Vanfossen, James D. Jones, and Joan Z. Spade, "Curriculum Tracking and Status Maintenance," *Sociology of Education*, vol. 60, 1987, pp. 104-22.
11. John Ogbu, *Black American Students in an Affluent Suburb* (Mahwah, N.J.: Erlbaum, 2003).
12. Levin, op. cit.; and Slavin and Braddock, op. cit.
13. Jeannie Oakes and Amy Stuart Wells, "Detracking for High Student Achievement," *Educational Leadership*, March 1998, pp. 38-41; and Susan Yonezawa, Amy Stuart Wells, and Irene Sema, "Choosing

Tracks: 'Freedom of Choice' in Detracking Schools," *American Educational Research Journal*, vol. 39, 2002, pp. 37-67.

14. Maureen Hallinan, "Tracking: From Theory to Practice," *Sociology of Education*, vol. 67, 1994, pp. 79-91; and Tom Loveless, *The Tracking Wars: State Reform Meets School Policy* (Washington, D.C.: Brookings Institution Press, 1999).

15. Carol Corbett Burris, Jay P. Heubert, and Henry M. Levin, "Math Acceleration for All," *Educational Leadership*, February 2004, pp. 68-71.

16. Carnegie Council on Adolescent Development, *Turning Points: Preparing American Youth for the 21st Century* (New York: Carnegie Corporation, 1989); *Ability Grouping and Tracking: Current Issues and Concerns* (Washington, D.C.: National Governors Association, 1993); and National Research Council, *Engaging Schools: Fostering High School Students' Motivation to Learn* (Washington, D.C.: National Academies Press, 2004).

NO

William J. Mathis

Bridging the Achievement Gap: A Bridge Too Far?

Seeking to cut off German access to the Rhine, Allied commanders dropped a small force of lightly armed paratroopers deep behind enemy lines. They were to seize a key bridge in Holland. Due to poor planning, inadequate support, overextended lines, and dropping the paratroopers into the middle of two crack Panzer divisions, the Allied venture was doomed.

It was a bridge too far.

Of course, the moral imperative was right. And of course, it is the moral obligation of all educators to bridge the achievement gap between rich and poor, between boys and girls, and between brown, black, and white. Half a century after *Brown* v. *Board of Education*, we can mark the great progress we have made. But the gap remains.

Some federal and state political leaders have made gung-ho proclamations about leaving no child behind. Yet they send in too few troops, too lightly supported, and with too little planning. The vaunted "historic investments" actually increase total education spending by less than 1%. The mandates were air-dropped into inner cities without social, community, school, or occupational networks to overcome the effects of ingrained poverty. The law then says the troops will be punished if they don't succeed.

If we are to bridge the achievement gap, then we must view our social and educational obligations in a far richer and more expansive light.

Are We Bridging the Gap?

There is some good news about the achievement gap. While the National Assessment of Educational Progress scores in reading and math have increased between four and six points over the past five years for white students, the scores for minority groups have increased six to 13 points during this same time period.[1] Likewise, college entrance rates have increased by 5% for white students over the past decade, while the rates for black students have increased by 12%. Increases for Hispanic students match those for white students.[2]

The achievement gap cannot be completely closed, however, by simply carrying out more intensely some program that zealous adherents claim will close it. Certainly, some whole-school reforms have shown positive long-term effects when administered consistently over time. Nevertheless, to deal effec-

From *Phi Delta Kappan*, April 2005, pp. 590-593. Copyright © 2005 by William J. Mathis, Ph.D. Reprinted by permission of the author.

tively with the gap means that we must deal with the underlying problems of society.[3]

As any inner-city teacher can tell us (and many rural and suburban teachers as well), to pretend that schools can single-handedly overcome a lifetime of deprivation through a "whole-school action plan" or through rigorous and intensive adherence to a particular reading program is more an exercise in ritualistic magic than a realistic solution to social, economic, and personal problems.

Yet many politicians and educators contend—explicitly or implicitly and perhaps even complicitly—that the schools can and must go it alone. Four central fallacies are employed to argue that schools can do this job by themselves.

1. The fallacy of the successful example.

Countless profiles, filled with fine praise, have been written about successful schools. Typically, federal and state politicians stage a high-visibility media event to recognize a poor school that has registered high test scores despite the handicaps of poverty and inadequate facilities. ... The media message is that, because this school has achieved success through hard work, all similarly situated schools can do the same. Thus closing the achievement gap requires no additional resources. It is simply a matter of will and effort.

Certainly, there are thousands of teachers, aides, and principals across our land who are genuine heroes. They do miraculous work in impossible circumstances. However, more than likely, these photo ops are created by a statistical fluke.

As is well known, average test scores for schools tend to distribute themselves along a normal curve (even if they are from criterion-referenced or mastery tests). So it is simple for someone to look at the test scores of all low-income, high-minority schools, identify the school at the top of the test-score distribution, and use it as an example of how well the reforms are working.

The problem is that these improvements are most often merely random fluctuations. Walt Haney showed that "Medallion" schools identified in one year in Massachusetts actually fell backwards in the following cycle.[4] Likewise, scores between fourth-graders this year and fourth-graders next year, in the same school, represent 70% test and cohort error and not learning effects.[5]

Thus, while examples of success can always be found, they do not mean that the level of educational or social support is adequate. In fact, these successful examples hide disparities and offer false promise.

2. The fallacy of the educational panacea.

Any number of professional development groups and reform networks advertise workshops with names like "Bridging the Achievement Gap." They are featured at national conventions, and high-ticket three-day workshops are offered in desirable locations. (Andy Hargreaves refers to them as "training cults"[6]). It is strongly implied that, if we attend the workshop and implement the program faithfully, all children will achieve mastery. While these workshops may well provide good, solid, organized instructional approaches, there is scant independent and accepted research evidence that such programs can successfully—by themselves—bridge the achievement gap.[7]

Unfortunately, testimonies about these programs come from educators and provide a rationale for politicians to ignore social inequities. They become the basis for claiming that schools are inefficient and wasteful. From here, it is a simple step to conclude that public schools are "failing."

3. The fallacy that "adequate yearly progress" on test scores decreases the true education gap.

The federal No Child Left Behind Act places increasing pressure on schools to make adequate yearly progress (AYP), but it is well known that schools with high concentrations of poor and minority students will fail to make AYP in disproportionate numbers. Schools with more wealthy student populations can (at least temporarily) escape being classified as failing, even though their rate of improvement may be far lower than that of schools with more poor and minority students.[8]

The result is educational apartheid. The more affluent schools can continue to provide a rich variety of educational and cultural opportunities with field trips, advanced studies, arts programs, and the like. The poor schools, however, find themselves increasingly trapped into a dull and spiritless routine of drill and practice, with the narrow objective of passing the examinations.[9] The effect is to widen some truly significant gaps.

4. The fallacy that vouchers bridge achievement gaps.

Although some folks sincerely believe that voucher systems, whether state or federal, will narrow achievement gaps, 30 years of national and international research show that there is no initial or long-term pattern of improvement in test scores with such systems. On the other hand, there is a substantial body of evidence that shows that social gaps increase as a result of vouchers.[10]

It is well established that poverty explains more of the variation in test scores than does any educational reform.[11] However, parents with lower levels of education and income are less likely to choose vouchers. Likewise, choice schemes tend to skim more advantaged students from underperforming schools.[12] the overall effect is to segregate schools and society to a greater extent rather than to bridge the gap.

The pressure to make AYP also offers schools the perverse incentive to select those students closest to proficiency and work to push them over the bar. There is less incentive to help those who are woefully behind. The result is that some students are seen as "helpable" and others are seen as less worthy of attention.[13] Since poverty is the main divider, AYP, combined with vouchers, creates incentives to leave our poorest and neediest children behind. Truly, this is a perverse incentive for a democratic nation.

Bridging the Achievement Gap

To be clear, external social forces and political misdeeds in no way relieve us of our responsibility to provide equality in education, to engage students, to align instruction to standards, to improve pedagogy, to employ diverse methods, to use formative assessments, to disaggregate data, and to track every student's progress. Effective schools remain essential for educational achievement. Yet, by themselves, these approaches cannot be completely successful. Six hours of instruction a day for 180 days a year cannot overcome the effects of a deprived and impoverished home environment for 18 hours a day and 365 days per year.

If we desire is to see all children succeed, we must invest in programs that are well outside the conventionally ways of thinking about schools. We must address health, mobility, housing, nutrition, unemployment, family structure, medical and dental care, and a host of other factors.[14]

Within schools, early education programs, full day kindergarten, extensive summer programs, small class sizes, after-school programs, and adequate materials are essential. Furthermore, such support must continue throughout all the school years and not be confined solely to the early grades. Twenty-eight studies in 20 different states, conducted by a diverse group of sponsors and researchers, have shown an average increase of 30% in educational dollars will be needed if we are to provide an adequate education for all students.[15]

⌒◈⌒

If we are to bridge the achievement gap, educational leaders must adopt a broader vision of schooling and live that vision every day. They must take new leadership risks and engage the attention of state and federal legislators. They must expose the fallacies and advocate for comprehensive and democratic conceptions of education. Educational leadership is no longer just the safe (yet difficult) task of leading a faculty through a process of curriculum change.

Educational leaders must revise the definitions and solutions for leaving no child behind. They cannot passively let themselves be disempowered by simply accepting existing political formulations of the purpose of schools. They must be the public voice for the children who are left behind.

Educational leaders must therefore aggressively inform the public that narrow tests, adequate yearly progress targets, vouchers, and punishments will not—and cannot logically—constitute a system that will bridge the achievement gap. Instead, education must be seen as an integral part of the community and include a vast variety of human services and activities.

Bridging the achievement gap also means expanding our emphasis on civic virtues to equal that given to basic skills, and rejecting the fundamental premise that education is a business or commercial enterprise. It is an example of a "commons," owned and nourished by the citizenry, for the benefit and advancement of all groups. Its aim is to build a society that has no gaps.

Notes

1. Education Trust, "Education Watch: The Nation: Key Education Facts and Figures: Achievement, Attainment and Opportunity from Elementary School through College," Spring 2004, available at www2.edtrust.org/edtrust/summaries2004/USA.pdf.

2. Jack Jennings and Madlene Hamilton, "What's Good About Public Schools." available on the website of the Center on Education Policy, www.CEP-DC.org

3. Geoffrey D. Borman and Gina M. Hewes, "The Long-Term Effects and Cost-Effectiveness of Success for All." *Educational Evaluation and Policy Analysis,* Winter 2002, pp 243–66; and Richard Rothstein, *Class and Schools: Using Social, Economic, and Educational Reform to Close the Black-White Achievement Gap* (New York: Teachers College Press, 2004).

4. Walt Haney, "Lake Woebeguaranteed: Misuse of Test Scores in Massachusetts, Part I." *Educational Policy Analysis Archives,* 6 May 2002, available at http://epaa.asu.edu/epaa/v10n24.

5. Thomas J. Kane and Douglas O. Staiger, "Volatility in School Test Scores: Implications for School-Based Accountability Systems," unpublished paper, Hoover Institution, Stanford University, Stanford, Calif., 2001.

6. Andy Hargreaves, "Standardization and the End of the Knowledge Society," paper presented at the annual meeting of the American Educational Research Association, San Diego, April 2004.

7. Borman and Hewes, op. cit.

8. Robert L. Linn, "Accountability, Responsibility and Reasonable Expectations," *Educational Researcher,* October 2003, pp. 3-13.

9. Hargreaves, op. cit.

10. Henry Levin, "Educational Vouchers: Effectiveness, Choice and Costs," paper presented at the annual meeting of the American Economics Association, New Orleans, 1997.

11. Michael W. Apple, *Cultural Politics and Education* (New York: Teachers College Press, 1996).

12. Henry M. Levin, "Multiple 'Choice' Questions: The Road Ahead," in Noel Epstein, ed., *Who's in Charge Here? The Tangled Web of School Governance and Policy* (Washington, D.C.: Brookings Institution Press, 2004), pp. 246-47.

13. Michael W. Apple, "Creating Difference: Neo-Liberalism, Neo-Conservatism and the Politics of Education Reform," *Educational Policy,* January and March 2004, pp 12-45.

14. Rothstein, chap. 5.

15. William J. Mathis, "Two Very Different Questions: The Cost of Leaving No Child Behind? Or, the Cost of Implementing 'No Child Left Behind'?," *Education Week,* 21 April, 2004, pp 48, 33.

POSTSCRIPT

Can Schools Close the Achievement Gap Between Students from Different Ethnic and Racial Backgrounds?

It would appear from the results described by Burris and Welner that the answer to our question should be a resounding "yes." After all, Burris and Welner describe what seem to be substantial improvements in several indicators of the academic achievement of the participating youth. It is important to recognize, however, that before we fully understand the effects of any educational intervention or curricular change, we must evaluate both the long-term effects and their generalizability. Maintaining the momentum of these curricular changes may be especially difficult because so many of the students may still experience the pernicious effects of ethnic and racial discrimination outside of school. So, it will be important to continue to follow the achievement of the students experiencing the curricular change as well as cohorts of students who experience the curriculum in later years to determine the long-term effects of the change. Even if the effects last, we must still be concerned with whether the changes will lead to similar positive results if implemented in other school districts.

It is also important to point out that even if current school-based approaches turn out not to have lasting, transportable effects on the achievement gap, it is possible that more dramatic (i.e., far-reaching) changes could be successful. So, for example, perhaps extending the school year through the summer would help to reduce the achievement gap when coupled with the sorts of curricular changes described by Burris and Welner. In fact, there is considerable evidence that many of the benefits accrued during the school year by economically disadvantaged African-American and Hispanic students are "lost" during the summer, presumably because the pernicious effects of poverty overwhelm the benefits of schooling. Other changes might include having schools provide after-school care for students.

There are many interesting articles addressing the causes of, and the role of schools in reducing, the achievement gap, including "Education, Alone, Is a Weak treatment," by James Gallagher, *Education Weekly* (July 1998); "The Linkages Among Family Structure, Self-Concept, Effort, and Performance on Mathematics Achievement of American High School Students by Race," by Sharon A. O'Connor and Kathleen Miranda, *American Secondary Education* (2002); and "Class and the Classroom," by Richard Rothstein, *American School Board Journal* (October 2004). An excellent recent series of articles appeared in the *Phi Delta Kappan,* and included the present selections. Other articles in that series are "A Wider Lens on the Black-White Achievement Gap," by Richard Rothstein; "Reframing the Achievement Gap," by Robert Evans; and "Challenging Assumptions About the Achievement Gap," by Al Ramirez and Dick Carpenter. An interesting discussion of the decline in achievement during summer break is provided in "The Impact of Summer Setback on the Reading Achievement Gap," by Richard L. Allington and Anne McGill-Franzen, *Phi Delta Kappan* (September, 2003). And finally, highly recommended is *Savage Inequalities: Children in America's Schools,* by Jonathon Kozol (Crown, 1991), which eloquently describes the dramatically different school experiences of affluent and economically disadvantaged students and students of different races and ethnicities and the system of school funding that creates those differences.

ISSUE 6

Should Schools Try to Increase Students' Self-Esteem?

YES: **Robert Sylwester,** from "The Neurobiology of Self-Esteem and Aggression," *Educational Leadership* (February 1997)

NO: **Carol S. Dweck,** from "Caution—Praise Can Be Dangerous," *American Educator* (Spring 1999)

ISSUE SUMMARY

YES: Robert Sylwester, an emeritus professor of education at the University of Oregon, argues that self-esteem is rooted in brain biology and that low self-esteem can result in impulsive and violent actions. He sees schools as a particularly important mechanism for delivering the positive feedback and successes that are required for the development of high self-esteem.

NO: Carol S. Dweck, a professor in the department of psychology at Columbia University, argues that programs to boost self-esteem have not had the hoped-for positive effects on student achievement. She argues that the indiscriminate use of praise makes students passive and fearful of losing the favorable opinion of others.

Believers in the self-esteem movement argue that students who feel good about themselves—those who have high self-esteem—will tackle academic tasks with fervor and will strive for excellence. In contrast, students who view themselves in a negative light—those who have low self-esteem—are thought to be at risk for academic failure. Students with low self-esteem will not be enthusiastic in the pursuit of academic goals, which will lead to failure, thereby further damaging their already low self-esteem. The curriculum must be designed to enhance self-esteem or at least not to diminish it. Many in the self-esteem movement believe that children in today's society frequently bring low self-esteem with them to the classroom due to outside factors, like poverty, broken homes, and racial or class prejudice. Therefore, followers of the self-esteem movement argue, any effort at educational reform must include an affective component. This is often expressed with phrases such as

"We must educate the whole child" and "The emotional side of learning is important too."

What does such a self-esteem-enhancing curriculum look like? The following are a few of the strategies that have been suggested for such a curriculum:

1. Teachers should praise all products produced by students. In other words, teachers should reward effort, regardless of the quality of the work.
2. Teachers should encourage students to value any contributions to the discussion that their classmates make because "there are no bad ideas."
3. Students should be allowed choices about what to study and how to display the knowledge they have acquired because such choices allow them to tailor the tasks to their strengths and, most important, to avoid failure. In fact, *all* classroom activities should be engineered to ensure success (or, conversely, to avoid failure) for all students.
4. Students who are least successful academically are most at risk for low self-esteem and thus most in need of praise, which is the primary tool for boosting self-esteem.

What is common to all of these strategies is the belief that praise and other forms of positive feedback (e.g., displaying student-generated products for all to see) must be used in a way that is not contingent on the quality of the products that students generate. In a sense, self-esteem is more important than achievement.

Few would question that low self-esteem can have undesirable long-term effects. Low self-esteem has been found to be related to a variety of later adjustment problems, including depression and delinquency. Nevertheless, many scholars and educators have become highly critical of the self-esteem movement. They argue that the pursuit of high self-esteem is a foolish, wasteful, and self-destructive enterprise that may end up doing more harm than good.

The dispute between supporters and critics of the self-esteem movement is illustrated in the following selections. In the first selection, Robert Sylwester argues that positive feedback is essential for developing healthy self-esteem, and he sees schools as an important mechanism for delivering such feedback. Moreover, he sees low self-esteem as having serious negative consequences for the individual at both a behavioral and a biological level, including heightened aggression and lowered levels of necessary brain chemicals. In the second selection, Carol S. Dweck agrees that students should experience success. She argues, however, that they should receive realistic appraisals of their academic performance and earn praise by creating academic products that meet accepted standards. In short, the dispute between supporters and critics of the self-esteem movement revolves around whether or not praise and other forms of positive feedback should be contingent on academic performance.

Robert Sylwester 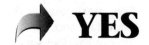 **YES**

The Neurobiology of Self-Esteem and Aggression

Violent acts like gang-related murders, playground shootings, riots, suicides, and assaults in school are prominently featured in the news, but they aren't the norm in social interactions. Young males commit most of the physically violent acts, and 7 percent of the population commits 80 percent of all the violent acts. Thus, violence is a limited social pathology, but one that evolutionary psychologists seek to explain because of its distressing, even tragic, results. Since impulsive behavior can lead to reckless or violently aggressive behavior, we also seek to understand impulsivity. Many personal and social problems begin with an impulsive act—triggered perhaps by the aggressor's low level of self-esteem. Impulsivity, recklessness, violence—all these behaviors can negatively affect educational processes. Some recent related research developments in brain chemistry—particularly the effects of the neurotransmitter serotonin—shed light on educational practices.

Self-Esteem in a Hierarchy

Consider the following scenario—from the point of view of a neurobiologist studying social hierarchies or an evolutionary psychologist studying human behavior.

> A young man joins an athletic team in his freshman year of high school. He's thrilled just to make the team, even thought he knows he's low in the hierarchy and won't get to play much in games. He's content for now because he also knows that the coaches and his teammates will note every successful act he makes in scrimmage, and so his playing time will come. He moves up the team hierarchy, substituting a few minutes here and there. His competition for most of this journey isn't the *alpha males* at the top of the hierarchy, but, rather, those who are competing with him for the next slot in the hierarchy.
>
> Over several years, his talent and that of his teammates will determine the level he achieves. He thus may settle for four years of comradeship, scrimmage, and limited game time because he realizes that's where he properly fits in the team hierarchy; or he may eventually bask in the celebrity afforded to him as one of the stars on the team. If the latter, he may seek to

begin the sequence anew in a college team, and then perhaps a pro team. If the former, his memories and friendships will have to suffice—and he will seek success in other social arenas.

But what if he believes that he rates very high compared to the others— but the coaches don't agree, and won't give him a chance to play? Perhaps it's because of something he can't control, such as his height (or by extension, gender or race or whatever defines the *glass ceiling*). Imagine his frustration and rage. His opportunities don't match his sense of self.

It is adaptive for a social species (like humans) to develop a system that arranges groups into reasonably compatible hierarchical arrangements to perform various group tasks. The entire group benefits if survival-related tasks are assigned to those who are generally recognized to be the most capable. But things often don't work the way we'd like them to.

The Roots of Violent Aggression

The cognitive drive to move into our expected slot in the hierarchy is so strong that many people will do whatever it takes to achieve success. To continue with our sports scenario, if the frustration becomes too intense, a person may act impulsively or recklessly for any possible chance of success—and such risk-taking may on occasion escalate into aggressive and violent acts, which we may witness in news accounts of various sports, from baseball to Olympic-level figure skating.

Evolutionary psychology argues that each success enhances the level of the neurotransmitter *serotonin* in the brain—and so also our motor coordination and self-esteem. Failure and negative social feedback inhibit the effects of serotonin and lead to lower self-esteem and possible violence.

When young people see no hope to rise within mainstream society, they may create their own hierarchical gang cultures that provide them with opportunities to succeed within their counterculture's mores. Those among successful people in mainstream society who decry gang symbols and exclusionary turf areas should look to the high-status symbols they use to flaunt their success and to their exclusionary golf courses and walled communities. People in both mainstream cultures and countercultures have the same biological need to succeed; they all need a positive self-concept and self-esteem. Wealthy financiers have ruined small communities by closing moderately profitable plants for even greater profits elsewhere. Are such exploitative acts any less psychologically violent to the victims than the physical violence that erupts later in such communities from those whose plummeting serotonin levels suggest no vocational hope?

Recent research on stress (Sapolsky 1994) shows that in primate groups with a developed, stable hierarchy, those at the bottom (who had little control over events) experienced far more stress and stress-related illness than those at the top. Conversely, during periods in which the hierarchical structure was unstable and shifting, those currently at the top (whose power position was threatened) experienced the most stress and stress-related illness. This finding suggests that it is in the interest of the power elite (in community and class-room) to maintain social stability, and it is in the interest of the currently dis-enfranchised to create as much social instability (and classroom disruption) as possible in a desperate search for respect and success.

The fewer opportunities young people have to succeed in mainstream society, the more social instability we can expect. It is in our best interest to support inclusionary policies that promote social goals and to enhance the powerful role that schools can play in helping students to seek their dreams.

Our Brain and Social Systems

Our brain's complex collections of neural networks process our cognitive activity. Several dozen neurotransmitter and hormonal systems provide the key chemical substrate of this marvelous information-processing system. Neu-rotransmitter molecules, which are produced within one neuron, are released from that neuron's axon terminal into the synaptic gap, where they attach to receptors on the dendrites or surface of the next neuron in the information sequence.

Recent studies with human and nonhuman primates suggest that fluctua-tions in the neurotransmitter serotonin play an important role in regulating our level of self-esteem and our place within the social hierarchy. Researchers associate high serotonin levels in the brain with high self-esteem and social sta-tus and low serotonin levels with low self-esteem and social status. High seroto-nin levels are associated with the calm assurance that leads to smoothly controlled movements, and low serotonin levels with the irritability that leads to impulsive, uncontrolled, reckless, aggressive, violent, or suicidal behavior.

Evolutionary psychologists focus on the biological underpinnings of such educationally significant concepts as self-esteem, impulsivity, and aggression and on the effects of drugs like Prozac. If genetics and fluctuations in biochemical systems combine to trigger aggression, for example, one could argue that chronically aggressive people have a reduced capacity for free will and thus are not (legally) responsible for their acts. Further, if courts mandate medical treatments for such people, the policy could be viewed as governmen-tal *mind control.* The social implications of this research are profound and wide ranging. For example, in determining responsibility for an aggressive act, how important are the negative effects of the aggressor's life experiences and the events that triggered the aggression?

Wright (1995) suggests that social feedback creates fluctuations from our basal serotonin levels, and these fluctuations help determine our current level of self-esteem. Thus, serotonin fluctuations are adaptive in that they help pri-mates to negotiate social hierarchies, to move up as far as circumstances per-mit, and to be reasonably content at each stage, as our earlier sports scenario suggests. Social success elevates our self-esteem (and serotonin levels), and each such elevation further raises our social expectations, perhaps to try for a promotion or leadership role we hadn't considered when we were lower on the hierarchy.

A biological system of variability in self-esteem prepares and encourages us to reach and maintain a realistic level of social status. A high or low level of self-esteem (and serotonin) isn't innate and permanent. Successful people may tumble percipitously in social status, self-esteem, and serotonin levels when they retire or are discharged and thereby may experience a rapid reduction in positive social feedback. This doesn't mean that the serotonin system developed to help low-status people endure their fate for the good of all. Evolutionary psychology argues that natural selection rarely designs things for the good of the group. But the serotonin system provides us with a way to cope in a bad social situation—to be content to play a group role that is consistent with our current limitations. The human serotonin system seems to function similarly in males and females in the important roles it plays in regulating self-esteem and impulse control.

The Role of Drugs and Nutrition

Is is possible to stimulate the serotonin system when conditions become so averse in a person's life that self-esteem and serotonin levels plummet into the depths of depression? Drugs such as Prozac (a fluoxetine antidepressant) can produce an elevation in the effects of serotonin that often enhances a person's self-esteem; this increased optimism and happier mood leads to the positive social feedback that allows the natural system to take over again in time and to function effectively. Think of jump-starting a dead car battery—a few miles of driving will reenergize the battery, and it can then function on its own.

People often use alcohol when they feel low, and alcohol does increase serotonin levels. Thus, it can temporarily help to raise our mood and self-esteem—but chronic alcohol use depletes a brain's store of serotonin, and so it makes matters even worse by further impairing the impulse control system.

Nutrition may provide another avenue to serotonin elevation. Prolonged period of stress increase our brain's need for serotonin. Nutrition researchers have discovered a connection between serotonin/carbohydrate levels and emotionally driven eating disorders that emerge out of family stress, premenstrual syndrome, shift work, seasonal mood changes, and the decision to stop smoking. Wurtman and Suffes (1996) propose nondrug diet adaptations that could solve some of these problems.

Prescription and other drugs can provide only a temporary chemical boost in self-esteem, and diets require a certain level of self-control. The best support for a serotonin deficiency is probably the natural system of positive social feedback that we have evolved over millennia.

Educational Implications

If positive social feedback is nature's way of regulating the serotonin system so that both an inexperienced substitute football player and the team's star can work together comfortably and effectively, then positive feedback in the classroom is a powerful social device for helping us to assess and define ourselves (self-concept) and to value ourselves (self-esteem). Serotonin research adds biological support to some educational practices that enhance self-esteem—and these practices don't require a prescription or an ID card that proves you are 21 years old.

- Portfolio assessments encourage self-examination in students and enhance student self-concept and self-esteem. Journals, creative artwork, and other forms of reflective thought can produce the same results.
- When students have many opportunities to work together in groups, they may experience success in both leading and supporting roles. Positive self-esteem can develop at any level in a work group, if the problem is challenging and the group values the contributions of all.
- Many school conflicts arise because an impulsive, reckless act escalates into aggression. We have tended to view these events only in negative terms—as misbehavior, as something to be squashed. But what if we used positive group strategies to help students study such behavior and discover how to reduce it? David and Roger Johnson (1995) provide practical cooperative learning strategies for conflict resolution that are consistent with neurobiological research.
- Emmy Werner's four-decade longitudinal study of seriously at-risk children who matured into resilient, successful adults found that they received unconditional love from family or nonfamily mentors, who encouraged their curiosity, interests, and dreams and assigned them responsibilities that helped them to discover their strengths and weaknesses (Werner and Smith 1992). We can also provide this support in the classroom—and parents, guardians, and other community members can help.

Cognitive science research is now providing some welcome biological support for practices that many educators have felt were simply right, even though these strategies take more instructional time and energy and result in less precise evaluations. Serotonin was identified as a neurotransmitter at about the time that Werner began her studies of resilient at-risk children in 1955—with no hint of the powerful biological substrate of her research. That kind of research is now becoming available to us. Let's use it.

References

Johnson, D., and R. Johnson. (1955). *Reducing School Violence Through Conflict Resolution*. Alexandria, Va.: ASCD.

Sapolsky, R. (1994). *Why Zebras Don't Get Ulcers: A Guide to Stress, Stress-Related Diseases, and Coping*. New York: Freeman.

Werner, E., and R. Smith. (1992). *Overcoming the Odds: High Risk Children from Birth to Adulthood*. Ithaca, N. Y.: Cornell University Press.

Wright, R. (March 13, 1995). "The Biology of Violence." *The New Yorker*: 68-77.

Wurtman, J., and S. Suffes. (1996). *The Serotonin Solution: The Potent Brain Chemical That Can Help You Stop Bingeing, Lose Weight, and Feel Great*. New York: Fawcett Columbine.

NO

Carol S. Dweck

Caution—Praise Can Be Dangerous

The self-esteem movement, which was flourishing just a few years ago, is in a state of decline. Although many educators believed that boosting students' self-esteem would boost their academic achievement, this did not happen. But the failure of the self-esteem movement does not mean that we should stop being concerned with what students think of themselves and just concentrate on improving their achievement. Every time teachers give feedback to students, they convey messages that affect students' opinion of themselves, their motivation, and their achievement. And I believe that teachers can and should help students become high achievers who also feel good about themselves. But how, exactly, should teachers go about doing this?

In fact, the self-esteem people were on to something extremely important. Praise, the chief weapon in their armory, is a powerful tool. Used correctly it can help students become adults who delight in intellectual challenge, understand the value of effort, and are able to deal with setbacks. Praise can help students make the most of the gifts they have. But if praise is not handled properly, it can become a negative force, a kind of drug that, rather than strengthening students, makes them passive and dependent on the opinion of others. What teachers—and parents—need is a framework that enables them to use praise wisely and well.

Where Did Things Go Wrong?

I believe the self-esteem movement faltered because of the way in which educators tried to instill self-esteem. Many people held an intuitively appealing theory of self-esteem, which went something like this: Giving students many opportunities to experience success and then praising them for their successes will indicate to them that they are intelligent. If they feel good about their intelligence, they will achieve. They will love learning and be confident and successful learners.

Much research now shows that this idea is wrong. Giving students easy tasks and praising their success tells students that you think they're dumb.[1] It's not hard to see why. Imagine being lavishly praised for something you think is pretty Mickey Mouse. Wouldn't you feel that the person thought you weren't capable of more and was trying to make you feel good about your limited ability?

But what about praising students' ability when they perform well on challenging tasks? In such cases, there would be no question of students' thinking you were just trying to make them feel good. Melissa Kamins, Claudia Mueller, and I decided to put this idea to the test.

Mueller and I had already found, in a study of the relationship between parents' beliefs and their children's expectations, that 85 percent of parents thought they needed to praise their children's intelligence in order to assure them that they were smart.[2] We also knew that many educators and psychologists thought that praising children for being intelligent was of great benefit. Yet in almost 30 years of research, I had seen over and over that children who had maladaptive achievement patterns were already obsessed with their intelligence—and with proving it to others. The children worried about how smart they looked and feared that failing at some task—even a relatively unimportant one—meant they were dumb. They also worried that having to work hard in order to succeed at a task showed they were dumb. Intelligence seemed to be a label to these kids, a feather in their caps, rather than a tool that, with effort, they could become more skillful in using.

In contrast, the more adaptive students focused on the process of learning and achieving. They weren't worried about their intelligence and didn't consider every task a measure of it. Instead, these students were more likely to concern themselves with the effort and strategies they needed in order to master the task. We wondered if praising children for being intelligent, though it seemed like a positive thing to do, could hook them into becoming dependent on praise.

Praise for Intelligence

Claudia Mueller and I conducted six studies, with more than 400 fifth-grade students, to examine the effects of praising children for being intelligent.[3] The students were from different parts of the country (a Midwestern town and a large Eastern city) and came from varied ethnic, racial, and socioeconomic backgrounds. Each of the studies involved several tasks, and all began with the students working, one at a time, on a puzzle task that was challenging but easy enough for all of them to do quite well. After this first set, we praised one-third of the children for their *intelligence*. They were told: "Wow, you got *x* number correct. That's a really good score. You must be smart at this." One-third of the children were also told that they got a very good score, but they were praised for their *effort*: "You must have worked really hard." The final third were simply praised for their *performance*, with no comment on why they were successful. Then, we looked to see the effects of these different types of praise across all six studies.

We found that after the first trial (in which all of the students were successful) the three groups responded similarly to questions we asked them. They enjoyed the task equally, were equally eager to take the problems home to practice, and were equally confident about their future performance.

In several of the studies, as a followup to the first trial, we gave students a choice of different tasks to work on next. We asked whether they wanted to try a challenging task from which they could learn a lot (but at which they might not succeed) or an easier task (on which they were sure to do well and look smart).

The majority of the students who had received praise for being intelligent the first time around went for the task that would allow them to keep on looking smart. Most of the students who had received praise for their effort (in some studies, as many as 90 percent) wanted the challenging learning task. (The third group, the students who had not been praised for intelligence or effort, were right in the middle and I will not focus on them.)

These findings suggest that when we praise children for their intelligence, we are telling them that this is the name of the game: Look smart; don't risk making mistakes. On the other hand, when we praise children for the effort and hard work that leads to achievement, they want to keep engaging in that process. They are not diverted from the task of learning by a concern with how smart they might—or might not—look.

The Impact of Difficulty

Next, we gave students a set of problems that were harder and on which they didn't do as well. Afterwards, we repeated the questions we had asked after the first task: How much had they enjoyed the task? Did they want to take the problems home to practice? And how smart did they feel? We found that the students who had been praised for being intelligent did not like this second task and were no longer interested in taking the problems home to practice. What's more, their difficulties led them to question their intelligence. In other words, the same students who had been told they were smart when they succeeded now felt dumb because they had encountered a setback. They had learned to measure themselves from what people said about their performance, and they were dependent on continuing praise in order to maintain their confidence.

In contrast, the students who had received praise for their effort on the easier task liked the more difficult task just as much even though they missed some of the problems. In fact, many of them said they liked the harder problems even more than the easier ones, and they were even more eager to take them home to practice. It was wonderful to see.

Moreover, these youngsters did not think that the difficulty of the task (and their relative lack of success) reflected on their intelligence. They thought, simply, that they had to make a greater effort in order to succeed. Their interest in taking problems home with them to practice on presumably reflected one way they planned to do this.

Thus, the students praised for effort were able to keep their intellectual self-esteem in the face of setbacks. They still thought they were smart; they still enjoyed the challenge; and they planned to work toward future success. The students who had been praised for their intelligence received an initial boost to their egos, but their view of themselves was quickly shaken when the going got rough.

As a final test, we gave students a third set of problems that were equal in difficulty to the first set—the one on which all the students had been successful. The results were striking. Although all three groups had performed equally well on the first trial, the students who had received praise for their intelligence (and who had been discouraged by their poor showing on the second trial) now registered the worst performance of the three groups. Indeed, they did significantly worse than they had on the first trial. In contrast, students who were praised for working hard performed the best of the three groups and significantly better than they had originally. So the different kinds of praise apparently affected not just what students thought and felt, but also how well they were able to perform.

Given what we had already seen, we reasoned that when students see their performance as a measure of their intelligence, they are likely to feel stigmatized when they perform poorly and may even try to hide the fact. If, however, students consider a poor performance a temporary setback, which merely reflects how much effort they have put in or their current level of skill, then it will not be a stigma. To test this idea, we gave students the opportunity to tell a student at another school about the task they had just completed by writing a brief description on a prepared form. The form also asked them to report their score on the second, more difficult trial.

More than 40 percent of the students who had been praised for their intelligence lied about their score (to improve it, of course). They did this even though they were reporting their performance to an anonymous peer whom they would never meet. Very few of the students in the other groups exaggerated their performance. This suggests that when we praise students for their intelligence, failure becomes more personal and therefore more of a disgrace. As a result, students become less able to face and therefore deal with their setbacks.

The Messages We Send

Finally, we found that following their experiences with the different kinds of praise, the students believed different things about their intelligence. Students who had received praise for being intelligent told us they thought of intelligence as something innate—a capacity that you just had or didn't have. Students who had been praised for effort told us they thought of intelligence more in terms of their skills, knowledge, and motivation—things over which they had some control and might be able to enhance.

And these negative effects of praising for intelligence were just as strong (and sometimes stronger) for the high-achieving students as for their less successful peers. Perhaps it is even easier to get these youngsters invested in looking smart to others. Maybe they are even more attuned to messages from us that tell them we value them for their intellects.

How can one sentence of praise have such powerful and pervasive effects? In my research, I have been amazed over and over again at how quickly students of all ages pick up on messages about themselves—at how sensitive they are to suggestions about their personal qualities or about the meaning of their actions and experiences. The kinds of praise (and criticism) students receive from their teachers and parents tell them how to think about what they do—and what they are.

This is why we cannot simply forget about students' feelings, their ideas about themselves and their motivation, and just teach them the "facts." No matter how objective we try to be, our feedback conveys messages about what we think is important, what we think of them, and how they should think of themselves. These messages, as we have seen, can have powerful effects on many things including performance. And it should surprise no one that this susceptibility starts very early.

Melissa Kamins and I found it in kindergarten children.[4] Praise or criticism that focused on children's personal traits (like being smart or good) created a real vulnerability when children hit setbacks. They saw setbacks as showing that they were bad or incompetent—and they were unable to respond constructively. In contrast, praise or criticism that focused on children's strategies or the efforts they made to succeed left them hardy, confident, and in control when they confronted setbacks. A setback did not mean anything bad about them or their personal qualities. It simply meant that something needed to be done, and they set about doing it. Again, a focus on process allowed these young children to maintain their self-esteem and to respond constructively when things went wrong.

Ways of Praising

There are many groups whose achievement is of particular interest to us: minorities, females, the gifted, the underachieving, to name a few. The findings of these studies will tell you why I am so concerned that we not try to encourage the achievement of our students by praising their intelligence. When we worry about low-achieving or vulnerable students, we may want to reassure them they're smart. When we want to motivate high-achieving students, we may want to spur them on by telling them they're gifted. Our research says: Don't do that. Don't get students so invested in these labels that they care more about keeping the label than about learning. Instead of empowering students, praise is likely to render students passive and dependent on something they believe they can't control. And it can hook them into a system in which setbacks signify incompetence and effort is recognized as a sign of weakness rather than a key to success.

This is not to say that we shouldn't praise students. We can praise as much as we please when they learn or do well, but we should wax enthusiastic about their strategies, not about how their performance reveals an attribute they are likely to view as innate and beyond their control. We can rave about their effort, their concentration, the effectiveness of their study strategies, the interesting ideas they came up with, the way they followed through. We can ask them questions that show an intelligent appreciation of their work and what they put into it. We can enthusiastically discuss with them what they learned. This, of course, requires more from us than simply telling them that they are smart, but it is much more appreciative of their work, much more constructive, and it does not carry with it the dangers I've been describing.

What about the times a student really impresses us by doing something quickly, easily—and perfectly? Isn't it appropriate to show our admiration for the child's ability? My honest opinion is that we should not. We should not be giving students the impression that we place a high value on their doing perfect work on tasks that are easy for them. A better approach would be to apologize for wasting their time with something that was too easy, and move them to something that is more challenging. When students make progress in or master that more challenging work, that's when our admiration—for their efforts—should come through.

A Challenging Academic Transition

The studies I have been talking about were carried out in a research setting. Two other studies[5] tracked students with these different viewpoints in a real-life situation, as they were making the transition to junior high school and during their first two years of junior high. This is a point at which academic work generally becomes more demanding than it was in elementary school, and many students stumble. The studies compared the attitudes and achievement of students who believed that intelligence is a fixed quantity with students who believed that they could develop their intellectual potential. We were especially interested in any changes in the degree of success students experienced in junior high school and how they dealt with these changes. For the sake of simplicity, I will combine the results from the two studies, for they showed basically the same thing.

First, the students who believed that intelligence is fixed did indeed feel that poor performance meant they were dumb. Furthermore, they reported, in significantly greater numbers than their peers, that if they did badly on a test, they would seriously consider cheating the next time. This was true even for students who were highly skilled and who had a past record of high achievement.

Perhaps even worse, these students believed that having to make an effort meant they were dumb—hardly an attitude to foster good work habits. In fact, these students reported that even though school achievement was very important to them, one of their prime goals in school was to exert as little effort as possible.

In contrast to the hopelessly counterproductive attitude of the first group, the second group of students, those who believed that intellectual potential can be developed, felt that poor performance was often due to a lack of effort, and it called for more studying. They saw effort as worthwhile and important—something necessary even for geniuses if they are to realize their potential.

So once again, for those who are focused on their fixed intelligence and its adequacy, setbacks and even effort bring a loss of face and self-esteem. But challenges, setbacks, and effort are not threatening to the self-esteem of those who are concerned with developing their potential; they represent opportunities to learn. In fact, many of these students told us that they felt smartest when things were difficult; they gained self-esteem when they applied themselves to meeting challenges.

What about the academic achievement of the two groups making the transition to junior high school? In both studies, we saw that students who believed that intelligence was fixed and was manifest in their performance did more poorly than they had in elementary school. Even many who had been high achievers did much less well. Included among them were many students who entered junior high with high intellectual self-esteem. On the other hand, the students who believed that intellectual potential could be developed showed, as a group, clear gains in their class standing, and many blossomed intellectually. The demands of their new environment, instead of causing them to wilt because they doubted themselves, encouraged them to roll up their sleeves and get to work.

These patterns seem to continue with students entering college. Research with students at highly selective universities found that, although they may enter a situation with equal self-esteem, optimism, and past achievement, students respond to the challenge of college differently: Students in one group by measuring themselves and losing confidence; the others by figuring out what it takes and doing it.[6]

Believing and Achieving

Some of the research my colleagues and I have carried out suggests that it is relatively easy to modify the views of young children in regard to intelligence and effort in a research setting. But is it possible to influence student attitudes in a real-life setting? And do students become set in their beliefs as they grow older? Some exciting new research shows that even college students' views about intelligence and effort can be modified—and that these changes will affect their level of academic achievement.[7] In their study, Aronson and Fried taught minority students at a prestigious university to view their intelligence as a potentiality that could be developed through hard work. For example, they created and showed a film that explained the neural changes that took place in the brain every time students confronted difficulty by exerting effort. The students who were instructed about the relationship between intelligence and effort went on to earn significantly higher grades than their peers who were not. This study, like our intelligence praise studies, shows that (1) students' ideas about their intelligence can be influenced by the messages they receive, and (2) when these ideas change, changes in performance can follow.

But simply getting back to basics and enforcing rigorous standards—which some students will meet and some will not—won't eliminate the pitfalls I have been describing. This approach may convey, even more forcefully, the idea that intelligence is a gift only certain students possess. And it will not, in itself, teach students to value learning and focus on the *process* of achievement or how to deal with obstacles. These students may, more than ever, fear failure because it takes the measure of their intelligence.

A Different Framework

Our research suggests another approach. Instead of trying to convince our students that they are smart or simply enforcing rigorous standards in the hopes that doing so will create high motivation and achievement, teachers should take the following steps: first, get students to focus on their potential to learn; second, teach them to value challenge and learning over looking smart; and third, teach them to concentrate on effort and learning processes in the face of obstacles.

This can be done while holding students to rigorous standards. Within the framework I have outlined, tasks are challenging and effort is highly valued, required, and rewarded. Moreover, we can (and must) give students frank evaluations of their work and their level of skill, but we must make clear that these are evaluations of their current level of performance and skill, not an assessment of their intelligence or their innate ability. In this framework, we do not arrange easy work or constant successes, thinking that we are doing students a favor. We do not lie to students who are doing poorly so they will feel smart: That would rob them of the information they need to work harder and improve. Nor do we just give students hard work that many can't do, thus making them into casualties of the system.

I am not encouraging high-effort situations in which students stay up studying until all hours every night, fearing they will displease their parents or disgrace themselves if they don't get the top test scores. Pushing students to do that is not about valuing learning or about orienting students toward developing their potential. It is about pressuring students to prove their worth through their test scores.

It is also not sufficient to give students piles of homework and say we are teaching them about the importance of effort. We are not talking about quantity here but about teaching students to seek challenging tasks and to engage in an active learning process.

However, we as educators must then be prepared to do our share. We must help students acquire the skills they need for learning, and we must be available as constant resources for learning. It is not enough to keep harping on and praising effort, for this may soon wear thin. And it will not be effective if students don't know *how* to apply their effort appropriately. It is necessary that we as educators understand and teach students how to engage in processes that foster learning, things like task analysis and study skills.[8]

When we focus students on their potential to learn and give them the message that effort is the key to learning, we give them responsibility for and control over their achievement—and over their self-esteem. We acknowledge that learning is not something that someone gives students; nor can they expect to feel good about themselves because teachers tell them they are smart. Both learning and self-esteem are things that students achieve as they tackle challenges and work to master new material.

Students who value learning and effort know how to make and sustain a commitment to valued goals. Unlike some of their peers, they are not afraid to work hard; they know that meaningful tasks involve setbacks; and they know how to bounce back from failure. These are lessons that cannot help but serve them well in life as well as in school.

These are lessons I have learned from my research on students' motivation and achievement, and they are things I wish I had known as a student. There is no reason that every student can't know them now.

Notes

1. Meyer, W. U. (1982). Indirect communications about perceived ability estimates. *Journal of Educational Psychology, 74*, 888-897.
2. Mueller, C. M., & Dweck, C. S. (1996). Implicit theories of intelligence: Relation of parental beliefs to children's expectations. Paper presented at the Third National Research Convention of Head Start, Washington, D.C.
3. Mueller, C. M., & Dweck, C. S. (1998). Intelligence praise can undermine motivation and performance. *Journal of Personality and Social Psychology, 75*, 33-52.
4. Kamins, M., & Dweck, C. S. (1999). Person vs. process praise and criticism: Implications for contingent self-worth and coping. *Developmental Psychology.*
5. Henderson, V., & Dweck, C. S. (1990). Achievement and motivation in adolescence: A new model and data. In S. Feldman and G. Elliott (Eds.), *At the threshold: The developing adolescent.* Cambridge, MA: Harvard University Press; *and* Dweck, C. S., & Sorich, L. (1999). Mastery-oriented thinking. In C. R. Snyder (Ed.). *Coping.* New York: Oxford University Press.
6. Robins, R. W., & Pals, J. (1998). Implicit self-theories of ability in the academic domain: A test of Dweck's model. Unpublished manuscript, University of California at Davis; *and* Zhao, W., Dweck, C. S., & Mueller, C. (1998). Implicit theories and depression-like responses to failure. Unpublished manuscript, Columbia University.
7. Aronson, J., & Fried, C. (1998). Reducing stereotype threat and boosting academic achievement of African Americans: The role of conceptions of intelligence. Unpublished manuscript, University of Texas.
8. Brown, A. L. (1997). Transforming schools into communities of thinking and learning about serious matters. *American Psychologist, 52*, 399-413.

POSTSCRIPT

Should Schools Try to Increase Students' Self-Esteem?

Critics of the self-esteem movement have amassed considerable evidence indicating that students who are rewarded for mediocre work or unduly praised for succeeding at trivial tasks not only fail to benefit but may actually be harmed. Dweck, for example, argues that the self-esteem movement has produced students who are afraid to take on challenging academic tasks because they fear failure and embarrassment. Other critics suggest that the self-esteem movement may produce students who are arrogant and egotistical. Roy Baumeister, a particularly vocal critic of the self-esteem movement, has suggested that in some instances inflated self-esteem may be associated with a penchant for bullying and violence. See "Should Schools Try to Boost Self-Esteem? Beware the Dark Side," *American Educator* (Summer 1996). In short, the critics' message is that academic standards must come first. Students should be praised, but only when they earn it—when they meet the expectations of teachers, school administrators, and the community. Only then, critics argue, will student self-evaluations be realistic and, thus, "healthy."

But should this message be extended to all students? Supporters of the self-esteem movement argue that many students are so ill-prepared for even the most basic academic tasks that they face constant failure and, thus, threats to self-esteem at every turn. These students include those with emotional and behavioral problems, those with learning disabilities or mental retardation, and those from severely economically disadvantaged backgrounds. Supporters also argue that many children leave school at the end of the day bound for impoverished homes and neighborhoods that have been "written off" by society and do nothing to help self-esteem. It is such "at-risk" students who supporters say benefit from the self-esteem movement. These students need a chance to succeed and to feel competent before they are required to tackle the challenge of a higher set of academic standards. Indeed, Sylwester implies that a failure to provide such opportunities will ensure that these students will continue to fail and might even lead them to resort to violence or other antisocial behaviors. Empirical studies of this claim, however, have yet to be conducted.

Readers interested in articles about the concept of self-esteem and its development should turn to "Processes Underlying the Construction, Maintenance, and Enhancement of the Self-Concept of Children," by Susan Harter, in Jerry Suls and G. Greenwald, eds., *Psychological Perspectives on the Self, Vol. 3* (Lawrence Erlbaum, 1986). To learn more about the negative consequences of self-esteem, see "Psychological Risk Factors Contributing to Adolescent Suicide

Ideation," by Susan Harter and D. B. Marold, in Gil G. Noam and Sophie Borst, eds., *Children, Youth, and Suicide: Developmental Perspectives* (Jossey-Bass, 1992). There are many readable critiques of the self-esteem movement in addition to the paper by Roy Baumeister cited above. These include "Praise That Doesn't Demean, Criticism That Doesn't Wound," by Adele Faber and Elaine Mazlish with Lisa Nyberg and Rosalyn Anstine Templeton, *American Educator* (Summer 1995) and "Self-Esteem and Excellence: The Choice and the Paradox," by Barbara Lerner, *American Educator* (Summer 1996). Finally, techniques for enhancing self-esteem in the classroom can be found in "Implementing a Successful Affective Curriculum," by Susan J. Wood, *Theory Into Practice* (November 1996); "Self-Esteem: Its Effect on the Development and Learning of Children With EBD," by Andrew Margerison, *Support for Learning* (vol. 11, no. 4, 1996); and *Guide to Human Development for Future Educators* by Leonard Abbeduto and Stephen N. Elliott (McGraw-Hill, 1998).

ISSUE 7

Should Moral Education Be Part of the School Curriculum?

YES: Thomas Lickona, from "Character Education: Seven Crucial Issues," *Action in Teacher Education* (Winter 1998)

NO: Alfie Kohn, from "How Not to Teach Values: A Critical Look at Character Education," *Phi Delta Kappan* (February 1997)

ISSUE SUMMARY

YES: Thomas Lickona, a professor of education at the State University of New York College at Cortland, argues that U.S. schools must return to the teaching of character, or morality. He also proposes a set of core values that should be the basis of such teaching and outlines a plan for implementation.

NO: Alfie Kohn is a professional writer and lecturer who frequently addresses psychological and educational issues and controversies. Kohn questions whether current programs of moral education can have a lasting impact and, if they do, whether they have the outcome that is best for a democratic society.

U.S. society is in a state of moral decay, or so say many government officials, politicians, and religious leaders. And, indeed, there are many alarming trends reflecting a tendency of citizens to harm or devalue themselves and others. Crime, violence, and high-risk behaviors (e.g., drug and alcohol abuse) are more common today than they were a few decades ago. In the past, concerns about the moral state of society typically led to a renewed interest in—and dedication to—society's children, who were seen as the hope for the future. What is unique about today's disintegration of the social order is that many of the crimes, acts of violence, and problem behaviors of greatest concern are those perpetrated by children and youth. Perhaps even more startling are the acts of violence committed by children against other children *at school*. In addition to the acts of violence, many social commentators point with concern and outrage to increases in teenage pregnancy, drug and alcohol abuse, gambling, and other problem activities. It often seems that every new report disseminated by the media suggests that children are engaging in risky or criminal behaviors at younger and younger ages.

Many social critics have argued that the solution to this problem is to teach morality, or character, in school. These critics suggest that schools rather than families must be the source of moral education because the American family is itself in disarray. As evidence that many families are poorly prepared to conduct the requisite moral education, critics point to the increasing divorce rate, the fact that the majority of American children live for at least some part of their lives in a single-parent home, and the decline in the amount of time that parents spend with their children. In fact, many believe that this so-called disintegration of the American family is largely responsible for what they see as the dismal moral state of today's youth.

Calls for the inclusion of a moral agenda in the school curriculum harken back to the early history of education in the United States. Prior to the twentieth century, moral education, which often took the form of inculcating a system of values and beliefs reflective of a particular religious ideology, was commonplace. In fact, the Bible was often the primary textbook not only for the curriculum of values but also for the more strictly academic curriculum. It was not until recently that the debate about the separation of church and state led to a more secular and, some would say, less moral curriculum. This movement away from explicit instruction in religiously derived morality was greatly hastened in the 1960s and 1970s by a rejection of "traditional" values and authority and an increased emphasis on personal freedom and autonomy. In more recent years, the increasing cultural diversity of U.S. schools has facilitated the adoption of moral relativism, a belief that there are differences across cultures (and perhaps even between individuals within a culture) with regard to the systems of values held and that all those systems should be seen as equally valid and moral.

Should schools once again incorporate morality into their agendas? What should this moral curriculum look like? Whose values should it reflect? Have American schools really stopped teaching moral values, or have they simply been teaching values that are at odds with the values held by those who call for a return to morality? These are some of the questions that shape the debate reflected in the following selections. In the first selection, Thomas Lickona implicitly rejects moral relativism and argues that, in fact, there are core values that are largely accepted as valid by all civilized people regardless of their culture of origin. These are the values that Lickona believes should be the goals of a moral education curriculum. He also outlines in broad form the shape that such a curriculum must take if it is to be successful as well as a program for teacher preparation. In the second selection, Alfie Kohn argues that most moral education programs that have been proposed to date employ a system of external rewards and indoctrination to encourage adoption of a particular set of values. He questions whether such programs can have a lasting impact and, if they do, whether they have the outcome that is best for a democratic society. In particular, he argues that these programs compel children to conform to the existing social order and to swear allegiance to a conservative political and religious ideology.

Thomas Lickona  **YES**

Character Education: Seven Crucial Issues

Defining character education as the cultivation of virtue, this article addresses seven questions:(1) What is the Relationship Between Character and Virtue? (2) What is the Nature of Character Education? (3) What are the Goals of Character Education? (4) What are the Psychological Components of Character? (5) What is the Content of Character? (6) What is the Comprehensive Approach to Character Development? (7) How Can Schools of Education Prepare Effective Character Educators?

One of the most important ethical developments of recent times has been a renewed concern for character. This is now here more ev-ident than in the national character education movement, arguably the most rapidly growing school reform initiative in the country today. To fulfill its potential, however, the character education movement must coherently address basic philosophical and pedagogical questions. In this article, I would like to address seven such issues.

What Is the Relationship Between Character and Virtue?

Good character consists of the virtues we possess. The more virtues we possess and the more fully we possess them, the stronger our character.

Virtues are objectively good human qualities such as wisdom, honesty, kindness, and self-discipline. Virtues are good for the individual in that they are needed to lead a fulfilling life, to be in harmony with ourselves. They are good for the whole human community in that they enable us to live together harmoniously and productively. Virtues provide a standard for defining good character.

Because they are intrinsically good, virtues don't change. Prudence, patience, perseverance, and courage always have been and always will be virtues. In this sense, virtues transcend time and culture, although their expression may vary culturally (with one culture giving move emphasis to respect for elders, for example, and another more emphasis to egalitarian relationships).

To speak of virtues and good character is to believe that there is an objective moral truth. Objective truth—whether it is scientific truth, historical truth, or moral truth—is truth that is independent of the knower (Kreeft & Tacelli, 1994). Although objective truth must always be grasped by a subjective knower, and therefore is often imperfectly known (a fact that should keep

From Thomas Lickona, "Character Education: Seven Crucial Issues," *Action in Teacher Education,* vol. 20, no. 4 (Winter 1998). Copyright © 1998 by The Association of Teacher Educators. Reprinted by permission of The Association of Teacher Educators and the author.

us humble), there is an objective reality outside of, and independent of, the mind. That Lincoln was president during the Civil War is objectively true, whether I know it or not.

In the moral realm, this philosophy of objective truth asserts that some things are truly right and others truly wrong. Some ways of behaving are truly better than others: It's better to be generous than selfish, better to be faithful than unfaithful, better to be self-controlled than reckless. Thus our life task in developing our personal character (and for all of us, our character is a work in progress) is to learn what is true and right and good, and then conform our conscience and conduct to that high standard.

It is a cultural cliche that we should each "follow our conscience," but that is a dangerous half-truth. Charles Manson, Adolf Hilter, and American slaveholders may have all been following their consciences. A malformed conscience has historically been the source of much evil. If following our conscience is to have any moral worth, we must first form our conscience correctly, in accord with what is truly right.

What Is the Nature of Character Education?

Character education is the deliberate effort to cultivate virtue. The school stands for virtues such as respect and responsibility and promotes them explicitly at every turn. Thinking and discussing are important, but the bottom line is behavior, taken to be the ultimate measure of character.

A core theoretical principle is Aristotle's: Virtues are not mere thoughts but habits we develop by performing virtuous actions. Acting on that principle, character educators seek to help students to perform kind, courteous, and self-disciplined acts repeatedly—until it becomes relatively easy for them to do so and relatively unnatural for them to do the opposite.

What Are the Goals of Character Education?

Character education has three goals: good people, good schools, and a good society.

The first goal asserts that we need good character to be fully human. We need strengths of mind, heart, and will to be capable of love and work, two of the hallmarks of human maturity.

The second goal asserts that we need character education in order to have good schools. Schools are much more conducive to teaching and learning when they are civil, caring, and purposeful communities.

The third goal asserts that character education is essential to the task of building a moral society. Societal problems—such as violence, dishonesty, greed, family disintegration, growing numbers of children living in poverty, and disrespect for life born and preborn—have deep roots and require systemic solutions. But it is not possible to build a virtuous society if virtue does not exist in the minds, hearts, and souls of individual human beings.

What Are the Psychological Components of Character?

Character must be broadly conceived to encompass the cognitive, affective, and behavioral aspects of morality: moral knowing, moral feeling, and moral action. Good character consists of knowing the good, desiring the good, and doing the good—habits of the mind, habits of the heart, and habits of behavior. We want young people to be able to judge what is right, care deeply about what is right, and then do what is right—even in the face of pressure from without and temptation from within.

The cognitive side of character includes at least six components: moral alertness (does the situation at hand involve a moral issue requiring moral judgment?), understanding the virtues and what they require of us in specific situations, perspective-taking, moral reasoning, thoughtful decision-making, and moral self-knowledge—all the powers of rational moral thought required for moral maturity.

The emotional side of character serves as the bridge between moral judgment and moral action. It includes at least five components: conscience (the felt obligation to do what one judges to be right), self-respect, empathy, loving the good, and humility (a willingness to both recognize and correct our moral failings).

There are times when we know what we should do, feel strongly that we should do it, and yet still fail to translate moral judgment and feeling into effective moral behavior. Moral action, the third part of character, involves three additional components: moral competence (including skills such as communicating, cooperating, and solving conflicts); moral will (which mobilizes our judgment and energy and is at the core of self-control and courage); and moral habit (a reliable inner disposition to respond to situations in a morally good way).

What Is the Content of Character?

Which virtues should a school use to define "the good"—the content of character?

The ancient Greeks named four "cardinal virtues": prudence (which enables us to judge what we ought to do), justice (which enables us to give other persons their due), fortitude (which enables us to do what is right in the face of difficulties), and temperance (which enables us to control our desires and avoid abuse of even legitimate pleasures). In his book *Character Building: A Guide for Parents and Teachers*, British psychologist David Isaacs (1976) offers a developmental scheme: 24 virtues, grouped according to developmental periods during which the different virtues should be given special emphasis: (1) Up to 7 years: obedience (respecting legitimate authority and rules), sincerity (truth-telling with charity and prudence), and orderliness (being organized and using time well); (2) From 8 to 12 years: fortitude, perseverance, industriousness, patience, responsibility, justice, and generosity; (3) From 13 to 15 years: modesty (respect for one's own privacy and dignity and that of others), moderation (self-control), simplicity (genuineness), sociability (ability to communicate with and get along with others), friendship, respect, patriotism (service to one's country and affirmation of what is noble in all countries); and (4) From 16 to 18 years: prudence, flexibility, understanding, loyalty, audacity (taking risks for good), humility (self-knowledge), and optimism (confidence). A recent book, *The Heart of Virtue* by Donald DeMarco (1996), recommends 28 virtues, from care and chastity through temperance and wisdom.

The choice of which virtues to teach is influenced by context. In democratic societies, for example, character education would logically include "democratic virtues" such as respect for individual rights, concern for the common good, reasoned dialogue, regard for due process, tolerance of dissent, and voluntary participation in public life—virtues that are important to the kind of character needed for democratic citizenship.

In a similar way, a religious context profoundly affects how the virtuous life is conceived. The proper aim of character education in a Catholic school, for example, is nothing less than to develop the character of Christ. That would include the natural moral virtues that can be taught in the public school, but it would also include spiritual virtues that public schools can't teach: faith in God, obedience to God's will, prayer, a sacrificial Christ-like love of others, sorrow for sin, and a humility that acknowledges our total dependence in God and is grateful for all our blessings. From this perspective, Jesus is both the example and the source of virtue; it is through our relationship with Him that we die to self and are transformed in Christ.

Public schools obviously can only study such world views, not teach them as truth. But even public schools do well to challenge students—drawing on their full intellectual and cultural resources, including their faith traditions if they have one—to develop a vision of the purpose of life that will guide them in the task of developing their personal character. Without this larger vision, the quest for character lacks a philosophical rudder.

What Is a Comprehensive Approach to Character Development?

In order to develop character in its cognitive, emotional, and behavioral dimensions, schools need a comprehensive approach. At the State University of New York at Cortland, our Center for the 4th and 5th Rs (Respect and Responsibility) defines a comprehensive approach in terms of twelve mutually supportive strategies, nine that are classroom-based and three that are school wide.

These twelve strategies are both direct and explicit (e.g., explaining the virtues, studying them, and intentionally practicing them) and indirect and implicit (e.g., setting a good example and providing a good moral environment that enables students to experience the virtues in their day-to-day relationships). A comprehensive approach regards adults' moral authority and leadership as an essential part of character education, but also values students' taking responsibility for constructing their own characters. There is an effort to transmit a moral heritage of tested virtues but also to equip students to think critically about how to apply the virtues to future moral challenges (e.g., combating the destruction of the environment and solving the problem of abortion in a way that both respects preborn life and supports women). Let me briefly explain and illustrate each of the twelve strategies in this comprehensive model....

Classroom Strategies

In classroom practice, a comprehensive approach to character-building calls upon the individual teacher to:

1. Act as caregiver, model, and mentor: Treat students with love and respect, setting a good example, supporting prosocial behavior, and correcting hurtful actions through one-on-one guidance and whole-class discussion.
2. Create a moral community: Help students know each other as persons, respect and care about each other, and feel valued membership in, and responsibility to, the group.
3. Practice moral discipline: Use the creation and enforcement of rules as opportunities to foster moral reasoning, voluntary compliance with rules, and a generalized respect for others.
4. Create a democratic classroom environment: Involve students in collaborative decision making and shared responsibility for making the classroom a good place to be and learn.
5. Teach character through the curriculum: Use the ethically rich content of academic subjects (such as literature, history, and science) as a vehicle for studying the virtues; ensure that the sex, drugs, and alcohol education programs promote self-control and other high character standards taught elsewhere in the curriculum (see, for example, Napier, 1996, and National Guidelines for Sexuality and Character Education, 1996).
6. Use cooperative learning: Through collaborative work, develop students' appreciation of others, perspective-taking, and ability to work toward common goals.
7. Develop the "conscience of craft": Foster students' valuing of learning, capacity for working hard, commitment to excellence, and public sense of work as affecting the lives of others.
8. Encourage moral reflection: Foster moral thinking and thoughtful decision-making through reading, research, essay writing, journaling, discussion, and debate.
9. Teach conflict resolution: Help students acquire the moral skills of solving conflicts fairly and without force.

Schoolwide Strategies

Besides making full use of the moral life of classrooms, a comprehensive approach calls upon the school as a whole to:

1. Foster service learning beyond the classroom: Use positive role models to inspire altruistic behavior and provide opportunities at every grade level for service learning.
2. Create a positive moral culture in the school: Develop a total moral environment (through the leadership of the principal, school wide discipline, a schoolwide sense of community, meaningful student government, a moral community among adults, and making time for discussing moral concerns) that supports and amplifies the virtues taught in classrooms.
3. Recruit parents and the community as partners in character education: Inform parents that the school considers them their child's first and most important moral teacher; give parents specific ways they can reinforce the character expectations the school is trying to promote; and seek the help of the community (including faith communities, businesses, local government, and the media) in promoting the core virtues.

How Can Schools of Education Prepare Effective Character Educators?

At the State University of New York at Cortland, we ... integrate character education into teacher preparation in the following ways:

1. An annual 4-day K-12 Summer Institute in Character Education (K12) ... [O]ur Summer Institute features national experts on character education and local practitioners—principals and teachers who describe their schools' character education initiatives.... [T]he Institute recruits school teams of 3-6 persons (e.g., a building administrator, several faculty, and, if possible, a parent leader) and teaches them our Center's comprehensive approach.... [T]hese teams develop an action plan that they later propose to their home school.
2. One-Day Character Education Conference. To stimulate and respond to broader interest in character education, we make Day 3 of our Summer Institute a one-day conference option. Each summer, more than 100 educators have taken advantage of that opinion; many have gone on to start character education efforts in their schools.
3. Two-Day High School Character Education Conference. Besides including sessions relevant to high school educators in our 4-day Institute, we also offer a two-day conference just for high school people. Seventy to 100 persons have attended that each year.
4. Follow-up Seminars. We invite all participants in our Summer Institutes and summer conferences to come back to campus for a day in the fall and a day in the spring to share what's working and to brainstorm solutions to problems in implementation.
5. Graduate course in character education. Each semester, for the past 12 years, I have taught an elective, 3-credit, Master's-level course in character education. This course examines contemporary approaches to character education, with an emphasis on a comprehensive approach.

6. Fourth and Fifth Rs Newsletter.... [O]ur Center publishes a quarterly newsletter that publishes practitioner-written articles recounting character education success stories. Many of these come from schools and teachers that have attended our summer programs. We distribute our newsletter to all Cortland College faculty and to ... schools of education around the country.

7. The integration of character education into undergraduate courses. Our undergraduate elementary education major includes a required course titled, Classroom Discipline. Education faculty who teach that course typically include character education as an important classroom and school wide approach to preventing and dealing with discipline problems. Methods courses in reading and social studies are other ready-made opportunities for incorporating character-relevant materials such as value-rich children's literature, and outstanding published curricula such as *Facing History and Ourselves* (Facing History and Ourselves National Foundation, 1994).

8. The informal dissemination of character education information to interested students and faculty. On the wall outside our Center, we have a nine-compartment "take-one" rack with assorted articles on the theory and practice of character education. Both undergraduate and graduate students regularly help themselves to this literature; we have probably reached more students in this way than in any other way. We also have a small library of books and other resources that students can borrow for a paper or project on character education they are doing for a course. We make videotapes on character education available to faculty, some of whom have begun to show them in their courses....

We have invited faculty teaching summer school to bring their classes to some of the keynote lectures in our Summer Institute. We have also asked faculty in our School of Professional Studies to offer workshops (e.g., "Fostering Virtue Through Children's Literature" and "Building Character Through Sports") for our Summer Institute—still another way to bring more people into the character education effort.

9. Collaboration with teacher in service programs. In New York State, most teacher professional development is carried out by Boards of Cooperative Educational Services [BOCES]. We have begun to work with two such groups in our region to co-sponsor breakfast meetings on character education for school administrators. We have also offered a free seat at our Summer Institute to several BOCES staff developers and have invited them to conduct Summer Institute workshops on aspects of character development such as cooperative learning and the Responsive Classroom. When people in schools of education notice that character education is beginning to appear on the menu of educational innovations offered by these leading-edge professional development agencies, character education will take on more importance in the minds of higher educators.

Not all of these approaches will work in all settings. But multiple approaches combining undergraduate, graduate, and in service education are needed if the character education movement hopes to be a major influence in forming the next generation of teachers.

[Adapted from a chapter in the ATE Commission on Character Education's report "Character Education: The Foundation for Teacher Education"(inpress)]

References

DeMarco, D. (1996). The heart of virtue. San Francisco: Ignatius Press. Facing History and Ourselves National Foundation. (1994).

Facing history and ourselves: The Holocaust and human behavior. Brookline, MA: Author.

Isaacs, D. (1976). Character-building: A guide for parents and teachers. Dublin, Ireland: Four Courts Press.

Kreeft, P., & Tacelli, R. K. (1994). Handbook of Christian apologetics. Downers Grove, IL: InterVarsity Press.

Lickona, T. (1991). Educating for character. New York: Bantam.

Napier, K. (1996). The power of abstinence. New York: Avon Books.

National guidelines for sexuality and character education. (1996). Austin, TX: Medical Institute (800/892-9484).

NO

Alfie Kohn

How Not to Teach Values

Were you to stand somewhere in the continental United States and announce, "I'm going to Hawaii," it would be understood that you were heading for those islands in the Pacific that collectively constitute the 50th state. Were you to stand in Honolulu and make the same statement, however, you would probably be talking about one specific island in the chain—namely, the big one to your southeast. The word *Hawaii* would seem to have two meanings, a broad one and a narrow one; we depend on context to tell them apart.

The phrase *character education* also has two meanings. In the broad sense, it refers to almost anything that schools might try to provide outside of academics, especially when the purpose is to help children grow into good people. In the narrow sense, it denotes a particular style of moral training, one that reflects particular values as well as particular assumptions about the nature of children and how they learn.

Unfortunately, the two meanings of the term have become blurred, with the narrow version of character education dominating the field to the point that it is frequently mistaken for the broader concept. Thus educators who are keen to support children's social and moral development may turn, by default, to a program with a certain set of methods and a specific agenda that, on reflection, they might very well find objectionable.

My purpose in this article is to subject these programs to careful scrutiny and, in so doing, to highlight the possibility that there are other ways to achieve our broader objectives. I address myself not so much to those readers who are avid proponents of character education (in the narrow sense) but to those who simply want to help children become decent human beings and may not have thought carefully about what they are being offered.

Let me get straight to the point. What goes by the name of character education nowadays is, for the most part, a collection of exhortations and extrinsic inducements designed to make children work harder and do what they're told. Even when other values are also promoted—caring or fairness, say—the preferred method of instruction is tantamount to indoctrination. The point is to drill students in specific behaviors rather than to engage them in deep, critical reflection about certain ways of being. This is the impression one gets from reading articles and books by contemporary proponents of character education as well as the curriculum materials sold by the leading national pro-

From Alfie Kohn, "How Not to Teach Values: A Critical Look at Character Education," *Phi Delta Kappan* (February 1997). Copyright © 1997 by Alfie Kohn. Reprinted by permission of the author.

128

grams. The impression is only strengthened by visiting schools that have been singled out for their commitment to character education. To wit:

> A huge, multiethnic elementary school in Southern California uses a framework created by the Jefferson Center for Character Education. Classes that the principal declares "well behaved" are awarded Bonus Bucks, which can eventually be redeemed for an ice cream party. On an enormous wall near the cafeteria, professionally painted Peanuts characters instruct children: "Never talk in line." A visitor is led to a fifth-grade classroom to observe an exemplary lesson on the current character education topic. The teacher is telling students to write down the name of the person they regard as the "toughest worker" in school. The teacher then asks them, "How many of you are going to be tough workers?" (Hands go up.) "Can you be a tough worker at home, too?" (Yes.)

> A small, almost entirely African American School in Chicago uses a framework created by the Character Education Institute. Periodic motivational assemblies are used to "give children a good pep talk," as the principal puts it, and to reinforce the values that determine who will be picked as Student of the Month. Rule number one posted on the wall of a kindergarten room is "We will obey the teachers." Today, students in this class are listening to the story of "Lazy Lion," who orders each of the other animals to build him a house, only to find each effort unacceptable. At the end, the teacher drives home the lesson: "Did you ever hear Lion say thank you?" (No.) "Did you ever hear Lion say please?" (No.) "It's good to always say ... what?" (Please.) The reason for using these words, she points out, is that by doing so we are more likely to get what we want.

> A charter school near Boston has been established specifically to offer an intensive, homegrown character education curriculum to its overwhelmingly white, middle-class student body. At weekly public ceremonies, certain children receive a leaf that will then be hung in the Forest of Virtue. The virtues themselves are "not open to debate," the headmaster insists, since moral precepts in his view enjoy the same status as mathematical truths. In a first-grade classroom, a teacher is observing that "it's very hard to be obedient when you want something. I want you to ask yourself, 'Can I have it— and why not?'" She proceeds to ask the students, "What kinds of things show obedience?" and, after collecting a few suggestions, announces that she's "not going to call on anyone else now. We could go on forever, but we have to have a moment of silence and then a spelling test."

Some of the most popular schoolwide strategies for improving students' character seem dubious on their face. When President Clinton mentioned the importance of character education in his 1996 State of the Union address, the only specific practice he recommended was requiring students to wear uniforms. The premises here are first, that children's character can be improved by forcing them to dress alike, and second, that if adults object to students' clothing, the best solution is not to invite them to reflect together about how this problem might be solved, but instead to compel them all to wear the same thing.

A second strategy, also consistent with the dominant philosophy of character education, is an exercise that might be called "If It's Tuesday, This Must Be Honesty." Here, one value after another is targeted, with each assigned its own day, week, or month. This seriatim approach is unlikely to result in a lasting commitment to any of these values, much less a feeling for how they may be related. Nevertheless, such programs are taken very seriously by some of the same people who are quick to dismiss other educational programs, such as those intended to promote self-esteem, as silly and ineffective.

Then there is the strategy of offering students rewards when they are "caught" being good, an approach favored by right-wing religious groups[1] and orthodox behaviorists but also by leaders of—and curriculum suppliers for—the character education movement.[2] Because of its popularity and because a sizable body of psychological evidence germane to the topic is available, it is worth lingering on this particular practice for a moment.

In general terms, what the evidence suggests is this: the more we reward people for doing something, the more likely they are to lose interest in whatever they had to do to get the reward. Extrinsic motivation, in other words, is not only quite different from intrinsic motivation but actually tends to erode it.[3] This effect has been demonstrated under many different circumstances and with respect to many different attitudes and behaviors. Most relevant to character education is a series of studies showing that individuals who have been rewarded for doing something nice become less likely to think of themselves as caring or helpful people and more likely to attribute their behavior to the reward.

"Extrinsic incentives can, by undermining self-perceived altruism, decrease intrinsic motivation to help others," one group of researchers concluded on the basis of several studies. "A person's kindness, it seems, cannot be bought."[4] The same applies to a person's sense of responsibility, fairness, perseverance, and so on. The lesson a child learns from Skinnerian tactics is that the point of being good is to get rewards. No wonder researchers have found that children who are frequently rewarded—or, in another study, children who receive positive reinforcement for caring, sharing, and helping—are less likely than other children to keep doing those things.[5]

In short, it makes no sense to dangle goodies in front of children for being virtuous. But even worse than rewards are awards—certificates, plaques, trophies, and other tokens of recognition whose numbers have been artificially limited so only a few can get them. When some children are singled out as "winners," the central message that every child learns is this: "Other people are potential obstacles to my success."[6] Thus the likely result of making students beat out their peers for the distinction of being the most virtuous is not only less intrinsic commitment to virtue but also a disruption of relationships and, ironically, of the experience of community that is so vital to the development of children's character.

Unhappily, the problems with character education (in the narrow sense, which is how I'll be using the term unless otherwise indicated) are not restricted to such strategies as enforcing sartorial uniformity, scheduling a value of the week, or offering students a "doggie biscuit" for being good.

More deeply troubling are the fundamental assumptions, both explicit and implicit, that inform character education programs. Let us consider five basic questions that might be asked of any such program: At what level are problems addressed? What is the underlying theory of human nature? What is the ultimate goal? Which values are promoted? And finally, How is learning thought to take place?

At What Level Are Problems Addressed?

One of the major purveyors of materials in this field, the Jefferson Center for Character Education in Pasadena, California, has produced a video that begins with some arresting images—quite literally. Young people are shown being led away in handcuffs, the point being that crime can be explained on the basis of an "erosion of American core values," as the narrator intones ominously. The idea that social problems can be explained by the fact that traditional virtues are no longer taken seriously is offered by many proponents of character education as though it were just plain common sense.

But if people steal or rape or kill solely because they possess bad values— that is, because of their personal characteristics—the implication is that political and economic realities are irrelevant and need not be addressed. Never mind staggering levels of unemployment in the inner cities or a system in whichmore and more of the nation's wealth is concentrated in fewer and fewer hands; just place the blame on individuals whose characters are deficient. A key tenet of the "Character Counts!" Coalition, which bills itself as a nonpartisan umbrella group devoid of any political agenda, is the highly debatable proposition that "negative social influences can [be] and usually are overcome by the exercise of free will and character."[7] What is presented as common sense is, in fact, conservative ideology.

Let's put politics aside, though. If a program proceeds by trying to "fix the kids"—as do almost all brands of character education—it ignores the accumulated evidence from the field of social psychology demonstrating that much of how we act and who we are reflects the situations in which we find ourselves. Virtually all the landmark studies in this discipline have been variations on this theme. Set up children in an extended team competition at summer camp and you will elicit unprecedented levels of aggression. Assign adults to the roles of prisoners or guards in a mock jail, and they will start to become their roles. Move people to a small town, and they will be more likely to rescue a stranger in need. In fact, so common is the tendency to attribute to an individual's personality or character what is actually a function of the social environment that social psychologists have dubbed this the "fundamental attribution error."

A similar lesson comes to us from the movement concerned with Total Quality Management associated with the ideas of the late W. Edwards Deming. At the heart of Deming's teaching is the notion that the "system" of an organization largely determines the results. The problems experienced in a corporation, therefore, are almost always due to systemic flaws rather than to a lack of effort or ability on the part of individuals in that organization. Thus, if we are troubled by the way students are acting, Deming, along with most social psychologists, would presumably have us transform the structure of the classroom rather than try to remake the students themselves—precisely the opposite of the character education approach.

What Is the View of Human Nature?

Character education's "fix-the-kids" orientation follows logically from the belief that kids need fixing. Indeed, the movement seems to be driven by a stunningly dark view of children—and, for that matter, of people in general. A "comprehensive approach [to character education] is based on a somewhat dim view of human nature," acknowledges William Kilpatrick, whose book *Why Johnny Can't Tell Right from Wrong* contains such assertions as: "Most behavior problems are the result of sheer 'willfulness' on the part of children."[8]

Despite—or more likely because of—statements like that, Kilpatrick has frequently been invited to speak at character education conferences.[9] But that shouldn't be surprising in light of how many prominent proponents of character education share his views. Edward Wynne says his own work is grounded in a tradition of thought that takes a "somewhat pessimistic view of human nature."[10] The idea of character development "sees children as self-centered," in the opinion of Kevin Ryan, who directs the Center for the Advancement of Ethics and Character at Boston University as well as heading up the character education network of the Association for Supervision and Curriculum Development.[11] Yet another writer approvingly traces the whole field back to the bleak world view of Thomas Hobbes: it is "an obvious assumption of character education," writes Louis Goldman, that people lack the instinct to work together. Without laws to compel us to get along, "our natural egoism would lead us into 'a condition of warre one against another.' "[12] This sentiment is echoed by F. Washington Jarvis, headmaster of the Roxbury Latin School in Boston, one of Ryan's favorite examples of what character education should look like in practice. Jarvis sees human nature as "mean, nasty, brutish, selfish, and capable of great cruelty and meanness. We have to hold a mirror up to the students and say, 'This is who you are. Stop it.' "[13]

Even when proponents of character education don't express such sentiments explicitly, they give themselves away by framing their mission as a campaign for self-control. Amitai Etzioni, for example, does not merely include this attribute on a list of good character traits; he *defines* character principally in terms of the capacity "to control impulses and defer gratification."[14] This is noteworthy because the virtue of self-restraint—or at least the decision to give special emphasis to it—has historically been preached by those, from St. Augustine to the present, who see people as basically sinful.

In fact, at least three assumptions seem to be at work when the need for self-control is stressed: first, that we are all at war not only with others but with ourselves, torn between our desires and our reason (or social norms); second, that these desires are fundamentally selfish, aggressive, or otherwise unpleasant; and third, that these desires are very strong, constantly threatening to overpower us if we don't rein them in. Collectively, these statements describe religious dogma, not scientific fact. Indeed, the evidence from several disciplines converges to cast doubt on this sour view of human beings and, instead, supports the idea that it is as "natural" for children to help as to hurt. I will not rehearse that evidence here, partly because I have done so elsewhere at some length.[15] Suffice it to say that even the most hard-headed empiricist might well conclude that the promotion of prosocial values consists to some extent of supporting (rather than restraining or controlling) many facets of the self. Any educator who adopts this more balanced position might think twice before joining an educational movement that is finally inseparable from the doctrine of original sin.

What Is the Ultimate Goal?

It may seem odd even to inquire about someone's reasons for trying to improve children's character. But it is worth mentioning that the whole enterprise—not merely the particular values that are favored—is often animated by a profoundly conservative, if not reactionary, agenda. Character education based on "acculturating students to conventional norms of 'good' behavior ... resonates with neoconservative concerns for social stability," observed David Purpel.[16] The movement has been described by another critic as a "yearning for some halcyon days of moral niceties and social tranquillity."[17] But it is not merely a *social* order that some are anxious to preserve (or recover): character education is vital, according to one vocal proponent, because "the development of character is the backbone of the economic system" now in place.[18]

Character education, or any kind of education, would look very different if we began with other objectives—if, for example, we were principally concerned with helping children become active participants in a democratic society (or agents for transforming a society *into* one that is authentically democratic). It would look different if our top priority were to help students develop into principled and caring members of a community or advocates for social justice. To be sure, these objectives are not inconsistent with the desire to preserve certain traditions, but the point would then be to help children decide which traditions are worth preserving and why, based on these other considerations. That is not at all the same as endorsing anything that is traditional or making the preservation of tradition our primary concern. In short, we want to ask character education proponents what goals they emphasize—and ponder whether their broad vision is compatible with our own.

Which Values?

Should we allow values to be taught in school? The question is about as sensible as asking whether our bodies should be allowed to contain bacteria. Just as humans are teeming with microorganisms, so schools are teeming with values. We can't see the former because they're too small; we don't notice the latter because they're too similar to the values of the culture at large. Whether or not we deliberately adopt a character or moral education program, we are always teaching values. Even people who insist that they are opposed to values in school usually mean that they are opposed to values other than their own.[19]

And that raises the inevitable question: Which values, or whose, should we teach? It has already become a cliché to reply that this question should not trouble us because, while there may be disagreement on certain issues, such as abortion, all of us can agree on a list of basic values that children ought to have. Therefore, schools can vigorously and unapologetically set about teaching all of those values.

But not so fast. Look at the way character education programs have been designed and you will discover, alongside such unobjectionable items as "fairness" or "honesty," an emphasis on values that are, again, distinctly conservative—and, to that extent, potentially controversial. To begin with, the famous Protestant work ethic is prominent: children should learn to "work hard and complete their tasks well and promptly, even when they do not want to," says Ryan.[20] Here the Latin question *Cui bono?* comes to mind. Who benefits when people are trained not to question the value of what they have been told to do but simply to toil away at it—and to regard this as virtuous?[21] Similarly, when Wynne defines the moral individual as someone who is not only honest but also "diligent, obedient, and patriotic,"[22] readers may find themselves wondering whether these traits really qualify as *moral*—as well as reflecting on the virtues that are missing from this list.

Character education curricula also stress the importance of things like "respect," "responsibility," and "citizenship." But these are slippery terms, frequently used as euphemisms for uncritical deference to authority. Under the headline "The Return of the 'Fourth R' "—referring to "respect, responsibility, or rules"—a news magazine recently described the growing popularity of such practices as requiring uniforms, paddling disobedient students, rewarding those who are compliant, and "throwing disruptive kids out of the classroom."[23] Indeed, William Glasser observed some time ago that many educators "teach thoughtless conformity to school rules and call the conforming child 'responsible.' "[24] I once taught at a high school where the principal frequently exhorted students to "take responsibility." By this he meant specifically that they should turn in their friends who used drugs.

Exhorting students to be "respectful" or rewarding them if they are caught being "good" may likewise mean nothing more than getting them to do whatever the adults demand. Following a lengthy article about character education in the *New York Times Magazine*, a reader mused, "Do you suppose that if Germany had had character education at the time, it would have encouraged children to fight Nazism or to support it?"[25] The more time I spend in schools that are enthusiastically implementing character education programs, the more I am haunted by that question.

In place of the traditional attributes associated with character education, Deborah Meier and Paul Schwarz of the Central Park East Secondary School in New York nominated two core values that a school might try to promote: "empathy and skepticism: the ability to see a situation from the eyes of another and the tendency to wonder about the validity of what we encountered."[26] Anyone who brushes away the question "Which values should be taught?" might speculate on the concrete differences between a school dedicated to turning out students who are empathic and skeptical and a school dedicated to turning out students who are loyal, patriotic, obedient, and so on.

Meanwhile, in place of such personal qualities as punctuality or perseverance, we might emphasize the cultivation of autonomy so that children come to experience themselves as "origins" rather than "pawns," as one researcher put it.[27] We might, in other words, stress self-determination at least as much as self-control. With such an agenda, it would be crucial to give students the chance to participate in making decisions about their learning and about how they want their classroom to be.[28] This stands in sharp contrast to a philosophy of character education like Wynne's, which decrees that "it is specious to talk about student choices" and offers students no real power except for when we give "some students authority over other students (for example, hall guard, class monitor)."[29]

Even with values that are widely shared, a superficial consensus may dissolve when we take a closer look. Educators across the spectrum are concerned about excessive attention to self-interest and are committed to helping students transcend a preoccupation with their own needs. But how does this concern play out in practice? For some of us, it takes the form of an emphasis on *compassion*; for the dominant character education approach, the alternative value to be stressed is *loyalty*, which is, of course, altogether different.[30] Moreover, as John Dewey remarked at the turn of the century, anyone seriously troubled about rampant individualism among children would promptly target for extinction the "drill-and-skill" approach to instruction: "The mere absorbing of facts and truths is so exclusively individual an affair that it tends very naturally to pass into selfishness."[31] Yet conservative champions of character education are often among the most outspoken supporters of a model of teaching that emphasizes rote memorization and the sequential acquisition of decontextualized skills.

Or take another example: all of us may say we endorse the idea of "cooperation," but what do we make of the practice of setting groups against one another in a quest for triumph, such that cooperation becomes the means and victory is the end? On the one hand, we might find this even more objectionable than individual competition. (Indeed, we might regard a "We're Number One!" ethic as a reason for schools to undertake something like character education in the first place.) On the other hand, "school-to-school, class-to-class, or row-to-row academic competitions" actually have been endorsed as part of a character education program,[32] along with contests that lead to awards for things like good citizenship.

The point, once again, is that it is entirely appropriate to ask which values a character education program is attempting to foster, notwithstanding the ostensible lack of controversy about a list of core values. It is equally appropriate to put such a discussion in context—specifically, in the context of which values are *currently* promoted in schools. The fact is that schools are already powerful socializers of traditional values—although, as noted above, we may fail to appreciate the extent to which this is true because we have come to take these values for granted. In most schools, for example, students are taught—indeed, compelled—to follow the rules regardless of whether the rules are reasonable and to respect authority regardless of whether that respect has been earned. (This process isn't always successful, of course, but that is a different matter.) Students are led to accept competition as natural and desirable, and to see themselves more as discrete individuals than as members of a community. Children in American schools are even expected to begin each day by reciting a loyalty oath to the Fatherland, although we call it by a different name. In short, the question is not whether to adopt the conservative values offered by most character education programs, but whether we want to consolidate the conservative values that are already in place.

What Is the Theory of Learning?

We come now to what may be the most significant, and yet the least remarked on, feature of character education: the way values are taught and the way learning is thought to take place.

> The character education coordinator for the small Chicago elementary school also teaches second grade. In her classroom, where one boy has been forced to sit by himself for the last two weeks ("He's kind of pesty"), she is asking the children to define tolerance. When the teacher gets the specific answers she is fishing for, she exclaims, "Say that again," and writes down only those responses. Later comes the moral: "If somebody doesn't think the way you think, should you turn them off?" (No.)
>
> Down the hall, the first-grade teacher is fishing for answers on a different subject. "When we play games, we try to understand the—what?" (Rules.) A moment later, the children scramble to get into place so she will pick them to tell a visitor their carefully rehearsed stories about conflict resolution. Almost every child's account, narrated with considerable prompting by the teacher, concerns name-calling or some other unpleasant incident that was "correctly" resolved by finding an adult. The teacher never asks the children how they felt about what happened or invites them to reflect on what else might have been done. She wraps up the activity by telling the children, "What we need to do all the time is clarify—make it clear—to the adult what you did."

The schools with character education programs that I have visited are engaged largely in exhortation and directed recitation. At first one might assume this is due to poor implementation of the programs on the part of individual educators. But the programs themselves—and the theorists who promote them—really do seem to regard teaching as a matter of telling and compelling. For example, the broad-based "Character Counts!" Coalition offers a framework of six core character traits and then asserts that "young people should be specifically and repeatedly told what is expected of them." The leading providers of curriculum materials walk teachers through highly structured lessons in which character-related concepts are described and then students are drilled until they can produce the right answers.

Teachers are encouraged to praise children who respond correctly, and some programs actually include multiple-choice tests to ensure that students have learned their values. For example, here are two sample test questions prepared for teachers by the Character Education Institute, based in San Antonio, Texas: "Having to obey rules and regulations (a) gives everyone the same right to be an individual, (b) forces everyone to do the same thing at all times, (c) prevents persons from expressing their individually [sic]"; and "One reason why parents might not allow their children freedom of choice is (a) children are always happier when they are told what to do and when to do it, (b) parents aren't given a freedom of choice; therefore, children should not be given a choice either, (c) children do not always demonstrate that they are responsible enough to be given a choice." The correct answers, according to the answer key, are (a) and (c) respectively.

The Character Education Institute recommends "engaging the students in discussions," but only discussions of a particular sort: "Since the lessons have been designed to logically guide the students to the right answers, the teacher should allow the students to draw their own conclusions. However, if the students draw the wrong conclusion, the teacher is instructed to tell them why their conclusion is *wrong*."[33]

Students are told what to think and do, not only by their teachers but by highly didactic stories, such as those in the Character Education Institute's "Happy Life" series, which end with characters saying things like "I am glad that I did not cheat," or "Next time I will be helpful," or "I will never be selfish again." Most character education programs also deliver homilies by way of posters and banners and murals displayed throughout the school. Children who do as they are told are presented with all manner of rewards, typically in front of their peers.

Does all of this amount to indoctrination? Absolutely, says Wynne, who declares that "school is and should and must be inherently indoctrinative."[34] Even when character education proponents tiptoe around that word, their model of instruction is clear: good character and values are *instilled in* or *transmitted to* students. We are "planting the ideas of virtue, of good traits in the young," says William Bennett.[35] The virtues or values in question are fully formed, and, in the minds of many character education proponents, divinely ordained. The children are—pick your favorite metaphor—so many passive receptacles to be filled, lumps of clay to be molded, pets to be trained, or computers to be programmed.

Thus, when we see Citizen-of-the-Month certificates and "Be a good sport!" posters, when we find teachers assigning preachy stories and principals telling students what to wear, it is important that we understand what is going on. These techniques may appear merely innocuous or gimmicky; they may strike us as evidence of a scattershot, let's-try-anything approach. But the truth is that these are elements of a systematic pedagogical philosophy. They are manifestations of a model that sees children as objects to be manipulated rather than as learners to be engaged.

Ironically, some people who accept character education without a second thought are quite articulate about the bankruptcy of this model when it comes to teaching academic subjects. Plenty of teachers have abandoned the use of worksheets, textbooks, and lectures that fill children full of disconnected facts and skills. Plenty of administrators are working to create schools where students can actively construct meaning around scientific and historical and literary concepts. Plenty of educators, in short, realize that memorizing right answers and algorithms doesn't help anyone to arrive at a deep understanding of ideas.

And so we are left scratching our heads. Why would all these people, who know that the "transmission" model fails to facilitate intellectual development, uncritically accept the very same model to promote ethical development? How could they understand that mathematical truths cannot be shoved down students' throats but then participate in a program that essentially tries to shove moral truths down the same throats? In the case of individual educators, the simple answer may be that they missed the connection. Perhaps they just failed to recognize that "a classroom cannot foster the development of autonomy in the intellectual realm while suppressing it in the social and moral realms," as Constance Kamii and her colleagues put it not long ago.[36]

In the case of the proponents of character education, I believe the answer to this riddle is quite different. The reason they are promoting techniques that seem strikingly ineffective at fostering autonomy or ethical development is that, as a rule, they are not *trying* to foster autonomy or ethical development. The goal is not to support or facilitate children's social and moral growth, but simply to "demand good behavior from students," in Ryan's words.[37] The idea is to get compliance, to *make* children act the way we want them to.

Indeed, if these are the goals, then the methods make perfect sense—the lectures and pseudo-discussions, the slogans and the stories that conk students on the head with their morals. David Brooks, who heads the Jefferson Center for Character Education, frankly states, "We're in the advertising business." The way you get people to do something, whether it's buying Rice Krispies or becoming trustworthy, is to "encourage conformity through repeated messages."[38] The idea of selling virtues like cereal nearly reaches the point of self-parody in the Jefferson Center's curriculum, which includes the following activity: "There's a new product on the market! It's Considerate Cereal. Eating it can make a person more considerate. Design a label for the box. Tell why someone should buy and eat this cereal. Then list the ingredients."[39]

If "repeated messages" don't work, then you simply force students to conform: "Sometimes compulsion is what is needed to get a habit started," says William Kilpatrick.[40] We may recoil from the word "compulsion," but it is the premise of that sentence that really ought to give us pause. When education is construed as the process of inculcating *habits*—which is to say, unreflective actions—then it scarcely deserves to be called education at all. It is really, as Alan Lockwood saw, an attempt to get "mindless conformity to externally imposed standards of conduct."[41]

Notice how naturally this goal follows from a dark view of human nature. If you begin with the premise that "good conduct is not our natural first choice," then the best you can hope for is "the development of good habits"[42]—that is, a system that gets people to act unthinkingly in the manner that someone else has deemed appropriate. This connection recently became clear to Ann Medlock, whose Giraffe Project was designed to evoke "students' own courage and compassion" in thinking about altruism, but which, in some schools, was being turned into a traditional, authoritarian program in which students were simply told how to act and what to believe. Medlock recalls suddenly realizing what was going on with these educators: "Oh, *I* see where you're coming from. You believe kids are no damn good!"[43]

The character education movement's emphasis on habit, then, is consistent with its view of children. Likewise, its process matches its product. The transmission model, along with the use of rewards and punishments to secure compliance, seems entirely appropriate if the values you are trying to transmit are things like obedience and loyalty and respect for authority. But this approach overlooks an important distinction between product and process. When we argue about which traits to emphasize—compassion or loyalty, cooperation or competition, skepticism or obedience—we are trafficking in value judgments. When we talk about how best to teach these things, however, we are being descriptive rather than just prescriptive. Even if you like the sort of virtues that appear in character education programs, and even if you regard the need to implement those virtues as urgent, the attempt to transmit or instill them dooms the project because that is just not consistent with the best theory and research on how people learn. (Of course, if you have reservations about many of the values that the character educators wish to instill, you may be *relieved* that their favored method is unlikely to be successful.)

I don't wish to be misunderstood. The techniques of character education may succeed in temporarily buying a particular behavior. But they are unlikely to leave children with a *commitment* to that behavior, a reason to continue acting that way in the future. You can turn out automatons who utter the desired words or maybe even "emit" (to use the curious verb favored by behaviorists) the desired actions. But the words and actions are unlikely to continue—much less transfer to new situations—because the child has not been invited to integrate them into his or her value structure. As Dewey observed, "The required beliefs cannot be hammered in; the needed attitudes cannot be plastered on."[44] Yet watch a character education lesson in any part of the country and you will almost surely be observing a strenuous exercise in hammering and plastering.

For traditional moralists, the constructivist approach is a waste of time. If values and traditions and the stories that embody them already exist, then surely "we don't have to reinvent the wheel," remarks Bennett.[45] Likewise an exasperated Wynne: "Must each generation try to completely reinvent society?"[46] The answer is no—and yes. It is not as though everything that now exists must be discarded and entirely new values fashioned from scratch. But the process of learning does indeed require that meaning, ethical or otherwise, be actively invented and reinvented, from the inside out. It requires that children be given the opportunity to make sense of such concepts as fairness or courage, regardless of how long the concepts themselves have been around. Children must be invited to reflect on complex issues, to recast them in light of their own experiences and questions, to figure out for themselves—and with one another—what kind of person one ought to be, which traditions are worth keeping, and how to proceed when two basic values seem to be in conflict.[47]

In this sense, reinvention is necessary if we want to help children become moral people, as opposed to people who merely do what they are told—or reflexively rebel against what they are told.

Notes

1. See, for example, Linda Page, "A Conservative Christian View on Values," *School Administrator*, September 1995, p. 22.
2. See, for example, Kevin Ryan, "The Ten Commandments of Character Education," *School Administrator*, September 1995, p. 19; and program materials from the Character Education Institute and the Jefferson Center for Character Education.
3. See Alfie Kohn, *Punished by Rewards: The Trouble with Gold Stars, Incentive Plans, A's, Praise, and Other Bribes* (Boston: Houghton Mifflin, 1993); and Edward L. Deci and Richard M. Ryan, *Intrinsic Motivation and Self-Determination in Human Behavior* (New York: Plenum, 1985).
4. See C. Daniel Batson et al., "Buying Kindness: Effect on an Extrinsic Incentive for Helping on Perceived Altruism," *Personality and Social Psychology Bulletin*, vol. 4, 1978, p. 90; Cathleen L. Smith et al., "Children's Causal Attributions Regarding Help Giving," *Child Development*, vol. 59, 1979, pp. 203–10; and William Edward Upton III, "Altruism, Attribution, and Intrinsic Motivation in the Recruitment of Blood Donors," *Dissertation Abstracts International* 34B, vol 12, 1974, p. 6260.
5. Richard A. Fabes et al., "Effects of Rewards on Children's Prosocial Motivation: A Socialization Study," *Developmental Psychology*, vol. 25, 1989, pp. 509–15; and Joan Grusec, "Socializing Concern for Others in the Home," *Develomental Psychology*, vol. 27, 1991, pp. 338–42.
6. See Alfie Kohn, *No Contest: The Case Against Competition*, rev. ed. (Boston: Houghton Mifflin, 1992).
7. This statement is taken from an eight-page brochure produced by the "Character Counts!" Coalition, a project of the Josephson Institute of Ethics. Members of the coalition include the American Federation of Teachers, the National Association of Secondary School Principals, the American Red Cross, the YMCA, and many other organizations.
8. William Kilpatrick, *Why Johnny Can't Tell Right from Wrong* (New York: Simon & Schuster, 1992), pp. 96, 249.
9. For example, Kilpatrick was selected in 1995 to keynote the first in a series of summer institutes on character education sponsored by Thomas Lickona.
10. Edward Wynne, "Transmitting Traditional Values in Contemporary Schools," in Larry P. Nucci, ed., *Moral Development and Character Education: A Dialogue* (Berkeley, Calif.: McCutchan, 1989), p. 25.
11. Kevin Ryan, "In Defense of Character Education," in Nucci, p. 16.
12. Louis Goldman, "Mind, Character, and the Deferral of Gratification," *Educational Forum*, vol. 60, 1996, p. 136. As part of "educa-

tional reconstruction," he goes on to say, we must "connect the lower social classes to the middle classes who may provide role models for self-discipline" (p. 139).

13. Jarvis is quoted in Wray Herbert, "The Moral Child," *U.S. News & World Report*, 3 June 1996, p. 58.

14. Amitai Etzioni, *The Spirit of Community: The Reinvention of American Society* (New York: Simon & Schuster, 1993), p. 91.

15. See Alfie Kohn, *The Brighter Side of Human Nature: Altruism and Empathy in Everyday Life* (New York: Basic Books, 1990); and "Caring Kids: The Role of the Schools," *Phi Delta Kappan*, March 1991, pp. 496–506.

16. David E. Purpel, "Moral Education: An Idea Whose Time Has Gone," *The Clearing House*, vol. 64, 1991, p. 311.

17. This description of the character education movement is offered by Alan L. Lockwood in "Character Education: The Ten Percent Solution," *Social Education*, April/May 1991, p. 246. It is a particularly apt characterization of a book like *Why Johnny Can't Tell Right from Wrong*, which invokes an age of "chivalry" and sexual abstinence, a time when moral truths were uncomplicated and unchallenged. The author's tone, however, is not so much wistful about the past as angry about the present: he denounces everything from rock music (which occupies an entire chapter in a book about morality) and feminism to the "multiculturalists" who dare to remove "homosexuality from the universe of moral judgment" (p. 126).

18. Kevin Walsh of the University of Alabama is quoted in Eric N. Berg, "Argument Grows That Teaching of Values Should Rank with Lessons," *New York Times*, 1 January 1992, p. 32.

19. I am reminded of a woman in a Houston audience who heatedly informed me that she doesn't send her child to school "to learn to be nice." That, she declared, would be "social engineering." But a moment later this woman added that her child ought to be "taught to respect authority." Since this would seem to be at least as apposite an example of social engineering, one is led to conclude that the woman's real objection was to the teaching of *particular* topics or values.

20. Kevin Ryan, "Mining the Values in the Curriculum," *Educational Leadership*, November 1993, p. 16.

21. Telling students to "try hard" and "do their best" begs the important questions. *How*, exactly, do they do their best? Surely it is not just a matter of blind effort. And *why* should they do so, particularly if the task is not engaging or meaningful to them, or if it has simply been imposed on them? Research has found that the attitudes students take toward learning are heavily influenced by whether they have been led to attribute their success (or failure) to innate ability, to effort, or to other factors—and that traditional classroom practices such as grading and competition lead them to explain the results in terms of ability (or its absence) and to minimize effort whenever possible. What looks like "laziness" or insufficient perseverance, in other words, often turns out to be a rational decision to avoid challenge; it is rational because this route proves most expedient for performing well or maintaining an image of oneself as smart. These systemic factors, of course, are complex and often threatening for

educators to address; it is much easier just to impress on children the importance of doing their best and then blame them for lacking perseverance if they seem not to do so.

22. Edward A.Wynne, "The Great Tradition in Education: Transmitting-Moral Values," *Educational Leadership*, December 1985/January 1986, p. 6.

23. Mary Lord, "The Return of the 'Fourth R,' " *U.S. News &World Report*, 11 September 1995, p. 58.

24. William Glasser, *Schools Without Failure* (New York: Harper & Row, 1969), p. 22.

25. Mare Desmond's letter appeared in the *New York Times Magazine*, 21 May 1995, p. 14. The same point was made by Robert Primack, "No Substitute for Critical Thinking: A Response toWynne," *Educational Leadership*, December 1985/January 1986, p. 12.

26. Deborah Meier and Paul Schwarz, "Central Park East Secondary School," in Michael W. Apple and James A. Beane, eds., *Democratic Schools* (Alexandria, Va.: Association for Supervision and Curriculum Development, 1995), pp. 29–30.

27. See Richard de Charms, *Personal Causation: The Internal Affective Determinants of Behavior* (Hillsdale, N.J.: Erlbaum, 1983). See also the many publications of Edward Deci and Richard Ryan.

28. See, for example, Alfie Kohn, "Choices for Children: Why and How to Let Students Decide," *Phi Delta Kappan*, September 1993, pp. 8–20; and Child Development Project, *Ways We Want Our Class to Be: Class Meetings That Build Commitment to Kindness and Learning* (Oakland, Calif.: Developmental Studies Center, 1996).

29. The quotations are from Wynne, "The Great Tradition," p. 9; and Edward A. Wynne and Herbert J.Walberg, "The Complementary Goals of Character Development and Academic Excellence," *Educational Leadership*, December 1985/January 1986, p. 17. William Kilpatrick is equally averse to including students in decision making; he speaks longingly of the days when "schools were unapologetically authoritarian," declaring that "schools can learn a lot from the Army," which is a "hierarchial [sic], authoritarian, and undemocratic institution" (see *Why Johnny Can't*, p. 228).

30. The sort of compassion I have in mind is akin to what the psychologist Ervin Staub described as a "prosocial orientation" (see his *Positive Social Behavior and Morality*, vols. 1 and 2 [New York: Academic Press, 1978 and 1979])—a generalized inclination to care, share, and help across different situations and with different people, including those we don't know, don't like, and don't look like. Loyally lending a hand to a close friend is one thing; going out of one's way for a stranger is something else.

31. John Dewey, *The School and Society* (Chicago: University of Chicago Press, 1900; reprint, 1990), p. 15.

32. Wynne and Walberg, p. 17. For another endorsement of competition among students, see Kevin Ryan, "In Defense," p. 15.

33. This passage is taken from page 21 of an undated 28-page "Character Education Curriculum" produced by the Character Education Institute. Emphasis in original.

34. Wynne, "Great Tradition," p. 9. Wynne and other figures in the character education movement acknowledge their debt to the French social scientist Emile Durkheim, who believed that "all education is a continuous effort to impose on the child ways of seeing, feeling, and acting which he could not have arrived at spontaneously.... We exert pressure upon him in order that he may learn proper consideration for others, respect for customs and conventions, the need for work, etc." (See Durkheim, *The Rules of Sociological Method* [New York: Free Press, 1938], p. 6.)

35. This is from Bennett's introduction to *The Book of Virtues* (New York: Simon & Schuster, 1993), pp. 12–13.

36. Constance Kamii, Faye B. Clark, and Ann Dominick, "The Six National Goals: A Road to Disappointment," *Phi Delta Kappan*, May 1994, p. 677.

37. Kevin Ryan, "Character and Coffee Mugs," *Education Week*, 17 May 1995, p. 48.

38. The second quotation is a reporter's paraphrase of Brooks. Both it and the direct quotation preceding it appear in Philip Cohen, "The Content of Their Character: Educators Find New Ways to Tackle Values and Morality," *ASCD Curriculum Update*, Spring 1995, p. 4.

39. See B. David Brooks, *Young People's Lessons in Character: Student Activity Workbook* (San Diego: Young People's Press, 1996), p. 12.

40. Kilpatrick, p. 231.

41. To advocate this sort of enterprise, he adds, is to "caricature the moral life." See Alan L. Lockwood, "Keeping Them in the Courtyard: A Response to Wynne," *Educational Leadership*, December 1985/January 1986, p. 10.

42. Kilpatrick, p. 97.

43. Personal communication with Ann Medlock, May 1996.

44. John Dewey, *Democracy and Education* (New York: Free Press, 1916; reprint, 1966), p. 11.

45. Bennett, p. 11.

46. Wynne, "Character and Academics," p. 142.

47. For a discussion of how traditional character education fails to offer guidance when values come into conflict, see Lockwood, "Character Education."

POSTSCRIPT

Should Moral Education Be Part of the School Curriculum?

Can the effectiveness of a moral education program be measured with data gathered by empirical research? In one respect, the answer is yes. It certainly would be possible to compare the relative effectiveness of two curricula—one including a moral education component and the other a strictly academic one—in achieving the hoped-for moral qualities in students. In any such study, of course, care would need to be taken to ensure that the students, classes, or schools compared were identical in all respects save the moral component of the curricula.

In another respect, however, the question, Should moral education be part of the school curriculum? may not be answerable by empirical data. It simply may not be possible to reach consensus on what the objectives of a moral education should be. Ultimately, decisions about the content of any moral education curriculum will be decided not by recourse to empirical investigation or by considerations of universal acceptance but rather by the beliefs and values of those who have the power to make decisions about the schools; namely, government leaders, the educational establishment that trains teachers, and the people who develop and administer the curriculum. Because access to these positions of power has been limited until recently to those of the majority culture, it is likely that the moral values contained in most educational programs will reflect those of the majority culture.

There are several thought-provoking books on the issues surrounding moral education, including *The Nature of Human Values* by Milton Rokeach (Free Press, 1973) and *How to Raise a Moral Child: The Moral Intelligence of Children* by Robert Coles (NAL/Dutton, 1998). The November 1993 issue of the journal *Educational Leadership* is devoted to a consideration of these issues and contains articles from authors in a variety of disciplines. Other worthwhile articles on moral education include "The Death of Character Education," by Timothy Rusnak and Frank Ribich, *Educational Horizons* (Fall 1997); "A Comprehensive Model of Values Education and Moral Education," by Howard Kirschenbaum, *Phi Delta Kappan* (June 1992); and "Creating a Curriculum for Character Development: A Case Study," by Andrew J. Milson, *The Clearing House* (November/December 2000). Additional, provocative articles by Lickona include "Religion and Character Education," *Phi Delta Kappan* (September 1999) and "Character-Based Sexuality Education: Bringing Parents Into the Picture," *Educational Leadership* (October 2000). Psychological perspectives on the development of morality in children can be found in *Essays on Moral Development, Vol. 1,* by Lawrence Kohlberg (Harper & Row,

1981) and *Helping Clients Forgive* by Robert D. Enright and Richard Fitzgibbons (American Psychological Association, 2000). Also recommended is *In a Different Voice: Psychological Theory and Women's Development* by Carol Gilligan (Harvard University Press, 1982).

Association for Behavior Analysis

The Association for Behavior Analysis is an international organization that promotes scientific inquiry into and clinical applications of the concepts and theories of behaviorism. The organization publishes scientific journals and books, holds conferences, and promotes information exchange among its members.

http://www.abainternational.org

Jean Piaget Society

Established in 1970, the Jean Piaget Society (JPS) is an international organization of scholars and teachers who are interested in constructivist approaches to human development and the application of these approaches to education. The JPS holds symposia and publishes books that focus on research, theory, and education.

http://www.piaget.org

Accelerated Learning Network

This educational testing and resource company Webpage has an informative description of Howard Gardner's theory of multiple intelligences and its implications for learning across the lifespan. It even includes a multiple intelligences self-test.

http://www.accelerated-learning.net/multiple.htm

National Information Center for Children and Youth With Disabilities

This site includes numerous publications and comprehensive bibliographies related to, among other things, the assessment of intelligence.

http://www.nichcy.org

James S. McDonnell Foundation

The James S. McDonnell Foundation provides funding for research in the behavioral and biomedical sciences. This site includes articles of general interest about current research, including research in the neurosciences and its application to education.

http://www.jsmf.org

PART 2

Theories of Learning and Their Implications for Educational Practice

*S*ince the 1990s there has been increasing dissatisfaction among politicians, parents, and educators with the performance of students in U.S. schools. Rightly or wrongly, the blame for the shortcomings of students has been placed squarely on the shoulders of teachers (and on the shoulders of those who train and supervise them). This has led to an increasing number of calls for reform of how and what teachers should teach. The criticisms and resulting proposals for reform have revolved around various theoretical controversies about teaching and learning that have characterized the field of educational psychology. Some of these controversies have been ongoing in the field for many years, such as the dispute about whether intelligence is best viewed as aunitary ability or as a collection of separate abilities. Other controversies have emerged more recently, such as the dispute about the pedagogical implications of research on brain structures and processes, the dispute about the educational value of constructivist approaches to learning and development, and arguments about the potential impact of adopting explicit and uniform educational standards. In this section, we consider these controversies within the context of teaching and learning in the classroom.

- Should Schools Adopt a Constructivist Approach to Education?

- Does Reinforcement Facilitate Learning?

- Can Howard Gardner's Theory of Multiple Intelligences Transform Educational Practice?

- Will a Push for Standards and Accountability Lead to More Motivated Students?

- Do Recent Discoveries About the Brain and Its Development Have Implications for Classroom Practice?

ISSUE 8

Should Schools Adopt a Constructivist Approach to Education?

YES: Mark Windschitl, from "The Challenges of Sustaining a Constructivist Classroom Culture," *Phi Delta Kappan* (June 1999)

NO: E. D. Hirsch, Jr., from "Reality's Revenge: Research and Ideology," *American Educator* (Fall 1996)

ISSUE SUMMARY

YES: Mark Windschitl, a member of the faculty in the department of curriculum and instruction at the University of Washington, argues in favor of constructivism, a child-centered approach to education that is defined by student participation in hands-on activities and extended projects that are allowed to "evolve" in accordance with the students' interests and initial beliefs.

NO: E. D. Hirsch, Jr., a professor in the School of Education at the University of Virginia, Charlottesville, argues that child-centered approaches have failed and points to research demonstrating the superiority of fact-based, teacher-centered approaches.

Observation of any school classroom in the United States at any point in history would reveal, to no one's surprise, a teacher (or teachers) and a varying number of students. In fact, although many other people, including administrators, parents, and even politicians, participate directly or indirectly in the educational process, most people view the teacher-student relationship as the primary determinant of what students accomplish in school. But the relationship between teachers and students has changed dramatically over the past few decades. In the 1950s, for example, the relationship was very much dominated by the teacher. He or she exerted a high degree of control over what students did at nearly every point throughout the day. In this teacher-centered approach, the teacher disseminated the "facts" to be learned to the students, typically within the context of a lecture. The teacher ensured that students would learn the facts by requiring that they listen carefully and engage in various highly structured, drill-and-practice activities. In recent years, however, students have come to exert considerably more control over the educational process and the teacher-student relationship. In many classrooms today, students are much more likely to be "doing" rather than "listening." This doing is often in the form of participation in an extended project of some form, such as building a Civil War-era town or collecting and cataloging insects. The teacher may assign these projects, but it is the students who shape the projects to suit their own interests as well as the discoveries that they make along the way. Although labeled in different ways (e.g., project-based, discovery learning, hands-on learning), the hallmark of this child-centered approach is a high degree of self-directed student activity.

Concerns about student achievement, especially as compared to student achievement in other industrialized nations, have led some scholars and administrators to begin calling for a return to a more teacher-centered, fact-based approach to education. Critics have argued that the constructivist approach is inefficient; that is, because children "waste time" with incorrect "discoveries" before arriving at the correct one, there often is not enough time to teach them all of the content that should be mastered. Other critics assert that some children never make the correct discoveries on their own and thus require greater teacher control and a more systematic introduction of the skills to be mastered. Finally, critics argue that acquisition of higher-order modes of thought applicable to a broad range of problems will not emerge without mastery of the rich networks of facts that constitute the domains of mathematics, physics, chemistry, and the like.

Supporters of the constructivist approach, however, are not without responses to these criticisms. They counter that a fact-based, teacher-centered approach is itself inefficient because of the sheer number of facts that compose any meaningful domain and because the "facts" change with new discoveries. This means, they argue, that the only lasting education is one that promotes higher modes of thought and action rather than storage of facts. Supporters also suggest that many attempts to implement a constructivist approach fail only because they do not go far enough; they merely insert a few student-initiated projects into an otherwise teacher-centered system. Finally, supporters argue that the well-documented decline in student interest in academic tasks that occurs throughout the school years is the result of a teacher-centered orientation. They point to numerous examples of constructivist classrooms in which students appear to be highly engaged in the academic life of the classroom.

In the following selection, Mark Windschitl argues for constructivism over a fact-based, teacher-centered approach to education. He also argues that constructivism is not merely a set of instructional practices but a way of thinking about the nature of child development and schooling. Successfully implementing this approach, he says, requires a fundamental change in the "culture" of the school, a change that affects not only how children are taught but how they are assessed, how classrooms are physically organized, how activities are scheduled, and how teaching is evaluated. In the second selection, E. D. Hirsch, Jr., argues that supporters of constructivist and other child-centered approaches have ignored empirical research, which, he argues, favors the use of a fact-based, teacher-centered approach.

Mark Windschitl  **YES**

The Challenges of Sustaining
a Constructivist Classroom Culture

Ms. Hughes' sixth-grade classroom is a noisy place, and if you come to visit you may have a hard time finding her. Today, students are clustered in small groups, bent over note cards and diagrams they have assembled in order to determine whether they can design a habitat that can support Australian dingoes and marmosets.

The students have just participated in three days of discussion and reading about interrelationships among mammals. They are divided into four groups, each of which has negotiated with Ms. Hughes to devise a complex problem to work on that reflects their interests and abilities. One group chose a design problem: creating a habitat for a local zoo that will support at least three kinds of mammals naturally found in the same geographic area.

The students are now engaged for the next two weeks on this project. They find and share dozens of resources, many of which are spread out on tables and on the floor around the room. Allen brings to class a video he shot at the zoo last week so that everyone can see what different habitats look like. Michelle loads a CD-ROM on mammals that she brought from home, and James donates one of his mother's landscape architecture books for ideas on how to diagram spaces and buildings.

During the next two weeks, these students will develop an understanding of how mammal species interact with one another, cope with the environment, and follow the natural cycles of reproduction. Concepts such as "competition for resources" and "reproductive capacity"—whose definitions in other classes might have been memorized—arise instead from a meaningful and multifaceted context. These concepts are built on the experiences of the students and are essential, interconnected considerations in the success of the habitat design. This is one of the many faces of the constructivist classroom.

A growing number of teachers are embracing the fundamental ideas of constructivist learning—that their students' background knowledge profoundly affects how they interpret subject matter and that students learn best when they apply their knowledge to solve authentic problems, engage in "sense-making" dialogue with peers, and strive for deep understanding of core ideas rather than recall of a laundry list of facts. Unfortunately, much of the public conversation about constructivism has been stalled on its philosophical contrasts with more traditional approaches to instruction. Constructivists have offered varying descriptions of how classrooms can be transformed, usually framed in terms of these contrasts. And although these descriptions have prompted educators to reexamine the roles of teachers, the ways in which students learn best, and even what it means to learn, the image of what is possible in constructivist classrooms remains too idealized.

To all the talk about theory, educators must add layers of dialogue about real classroom experiences and concerns about those experiences. An essential part of this dialogue is the articulation of the pedagogical, logistical, and political challenges that face educators who are willing to integrate constructivism into their classroom practice. The new discourse shifts the emphasis from comparisons between constructivism and traditional instruction to the refinement of constructivist practices in real classrooms. This frank conversation about challenges is equally valuable for sympathetic administrators—being informed and reflective about these issues is a necessary prerequisite to offering support for the classroom teacher.

In this article, I characterize and categorize these challenges and describe the kinds of administrative support necessary to create and sustain a culture of constructivist teaching in schools. First, however, it is necessary to examine constructivism as a philosophy on which a systemic classroom culture can be based rather than to view it as a set of discrete instructional practices that may be inserted into the learning environment whenever necessary. The challenges I describe here are challenges precisely because they cause us to reconsider and dare us to change the comfortable (and often unstated) norms, beliefs, and practices of the classroom culture we are so familiar with. Constructivism is more than a set of teaching techniques; it is a coherent pattern of expectations that underlie new relationships between students, teachers, and the world of ideas.

Constructivism as Culture

Constructivism is premised on the belief that learners actively create, interpret, and reorganize knowledge in individual ways. These fluid intellectual transformations occur when students reconcile formal instructional experiences with their existing knowledge, with the cultural and social contexts in which ideas occur, and with a host of other influences that serve to mediate understanding. With respect to instruction, this belief suggests that students should participate in experiences that accommodate these ways of learning. Such experiences include problem-based learning, inquiry activities, dialogues with peers and teachers that encourage making sense of the subject matter, exposure to multiple sources of information, and opportunities for students to demonstrate their understanding in diverse ways.

However, before teachers and administrators adopt such practices, they should understand that constructivism cannot make its appearance in the classroom as a set of isolated instructional methods grafted on to otherwise traditional teaching techniques. Rather, it is a culture—a set of beliefs, norms, and practices that constitute the fabric of school life. This culture, like all other cultures, affects the way learners can interact with peers, relate to the teacher, and experience the subject matter. The children's relationships with teachers, their patterns of communication, how they are assessed, and even their notion of "what learning is good for" must all be connected, or the culture risks becoming a fragmented collection of practices that fail to reinforce one another. For example, the constructivist belief that learners are capable of intellectual autonomy must coincide with the belief that students possess a large knowledge base of life experiences and have made sense out of much of what they have experienced. These beliefs are linked with the practice of problem-based learning within relevant and authentic contexts and with the norm of showing mutual respect for one another's ideas in the classroom.

Portraying the constructivist classroom as a culture is important because many challenges for the teacher emerge when new rituals take root or when familiar norms of behavior are transformed into new patterns of teacher/student interaction.[1] By contrast, if discrete practices that have been associated with constructivism (cooperative learning, performance assessments, hands-on experiences) are simply inserted as special activities into the regular school day, then it remains business as usual for the students. Teachers and students do not question their vision of learning, no one takes risks, and hardly a ripple is felt.

Throughout this article then, challenges become apparent when we question the fundamental norms of the classroom—the images and beliefs we hold of teachers and students, the kinds of discourse encouraged in the classroom, the way authority and decision making are controlled, and even what "counts" as learning. I begin with a subtle but powerful influence on classroom instruction.

Images of Teaching: The Chains That Bind Us

Most of us are products of traditional instruction; as learners, we were exposed to teacher-centered instruction, fact-based subject matter, and a steady diet of drill and practice.[2] Our personal histories furnish us with mental models of teaching, and these models of how we were taught shape our behavior in powerful ways. Teachers use these models to imagine lessons in their classrooms, develop innovations, and plan for learning.[3] These images serve to organize sets of beliefs and guide curricular actions.[4] Teachers are more likely to be guided not by instructional theories but by the familiar images of what is "proper and possible" in classroom settings.[5]

Unfortunately, the signs and symbols of teacher-centered education and learning by transmission, which are likely to be a part of teachers' personal histories, persist in classrooms today.[6] In this environment, it is assumed that the more quiet and orderly the classrooms are, the more likely it is that learning is taking place. Individual desks face the front of the room, where the teacher occupies a privileged space of knowing authority; students work individually on identical, skill-based assignments to ensure uniformity of learning. Value statements are embedded everywhere in this environment.

Constructivist teachers envision themselves emerging boldly from the confines of this traditional classroom culture, but the vision first requires critical reflection. Teachers must ask themselves, "Is my role to dispense knowledge or to nurture independent thinkers? How do I show respect for the ideas of the students? Am I here to learn from the students?" Teachers must struggle to develop a new, well-articulated rationale for instructional decisions and cannot depend on their previous teaching or learning experiences for much help in shaping their choice of methods; shifting the centers of authority and activity in accordance with this rationale requires persistence. For example, teachers can be uncomfortable with their apparent lack of control as students engage with their peers during learning activities and may be unwilling to allow supervisors who visit the classroom to observe this kind of environment. Teachers may reconsider their ideas of student-centered learning in favor of conforming to the more traditional images of the teacher as the hub of classroom discourse and attention.[7]

New Demands on the Teacher

Constructivist instruction, especially that which is based on design tasks or problem solving, places high demands on the teacher's subject-matter understanding. The teacher must not only be familiar with the principles underlying a topic of study but must also be prepared for the variety of ways these principles can be explored.

For example, if students are studying density in science class, the teacher must support the understanding of one group of students who want to approach the concept from a purely abstract, mathematical perspective as they construct tables, equations, and graphs to develop their knowledge. In this case, the teacher must understand these different representations of information and how they are interrelated. Another group of students may plan to recount the story of the *Titanic*, emphasizing the role that density played in the visibility of the iceberg, the ballast of the ship, and the sinking itself. Here, the teacher must be intellectually agile, able to apply his or her mathematical understanding of density to a real-life, inevitably more complex situation.

Teachers in different subject areas may allow students varying degrees of latitude in exploring content and will differ in how they accept student "constructions" of core curricular ideas. Mathematics is characterized by rule-based propositions and skills that may be open to discovery via many experiential pathways. Most forms of mathematics problems, however, have only one right answer. And if students are allowed to explore problems by their own methods, teachers may find it difficult to see exactly how the students are making sense of the problem-solving process—not all constructions are created equal. Science and social studies present the same challenges, although science is less axiomatic than mathematics, and the issues explored in social studies are open to wider interpretation. Dealing with the "correctness" of student constructions is an ongoing concern, and the arguments have barely been introduced here, but reflection on these issues helps teachers develop a critical awareness of disciplinary "truths" and the viability of various ways of knowing the world.

In addition to the necessity for flexible subject-matter knowledge, constructivism places greater demands on teachers' pedagogical skill. Crafting instruction based on constructivism is not as straightforward as it seems. Educators struggle with how specific instructional techniques (e.g., lecture, discussion, cooperative learning, problem-based learning, inquiry learning) fit into the constructivist model of instruction. Regardless of the particular techniques used in instruction, students will always construct and reorganize knowledge rather than simply assimilate information from teachers or textbooks. The question is not whether to use lecture or discussion, but how to use these techniques to complement rather than dominate student thinking. For example, constructivist principles suggest that students should experience the ideas, phenomena, and artifacts of a discipline before being exposed to formal explanations of them. Students might begin units of instruction in science class by manipulating a pendulum, in math class by constructing polygons, or in social studies by reading letters from Civil War battlefields. Only after these experiences do teachers and students together suggest terminology, explanations, and conceptual organization.

Even though designing instruction is important, constructivist teaching is less about the sequencing of events and more about responding to the needs of a situation.[8] Teachers must employ a sophisticated range of strategies to support individual students' understandings as they engage in the problem-based activities that characterize constructivist classrooms. These strategies include scaffolding, in which the task required of the learner is strategically reduced in complexity; modeling, in which the teacher either thinks aloud about or acts out how she would approach a problem; and coaching, guiding, and advising, which are loosely defined as providing learners with suggestions of varying degrees of explicitness.[9] The teacher is challenged to select the proper strategy and implement it with skill.

Problem-based activities exemplify another core value of the constructivist culture—collaboration. Students are witness to and participate in one another's thinking. Learners are exposed to the clear, cogent thinking of some peers as well as to the inevitable meandering, unreflective thought of others. Students do require training to function effectively in these groups.[10] However, even with training, many capable students are simply not interested in helping their peers, and negative consequences of group work—such as bickering, exclusion, and academic freeloading—are common.[11] These consequences can be minimized if the teacher is familiar with the principles of cooperative learning. And so, having students work together requires that the teacher have additional competencies in cooperative learning strategies and management skills particular to decentralized learning environments.

A final pedagogical challenge involves independent student projects. Depending on the degree of structure the teacher imposes in a classroom, students will have some latitude in choosing problems or design projects that relate to the theme under study. Often, students determine with the teacher suitable criteria for problems and for evidence of learning. Negotiation about criteria prompts questions such as: Is the problem meaningful? Important to the discipline? Complex enough? Does it relate to the theme under study?

Does it require original thinking and interpretation, or is it simply fact finding? Will the resolution of this problem help us acquire the concepts and principles fundamental to the theme under study? Because curricular materials are often filled with prepared questions and tasks, teachers seldom have occasion to introduce their students to this idea of "problems about problems." Clearly, teachers must develop their own ability to analyze problems by reflecting on the nature of the discipline and refining their ideas through extended dialogue with colleagues and experiences with students.

Logistical and Political Challenges

Effective forms of constructivist instruction call for major changes in the curriculum, in scheduling, and in assessment.[12] When students are engaged in problem solving and are allowed to help guide their own learning, teachers quickly find that this approach outgrows the 50-minute class period. This situation often means that the teacher will have to negotiate with administrators and other teachers about the possibilities of block scheduling and integrating curricula. If teachers can team with partners from other subject areas, they can extend the length of their class periods and develop more comprehensive themes for study that bridge the worlds of science, social studies, math, and the arts.

The purpose of integrated curricula and extended class periods is to allow students to engage in learning activities that will help them develop deep and elaborate understandings of subject matter. These understandings may be quite different in nature from student to student. Thus there is a need for forms of assessment that allow students to demonstrate what they know and that connect with rigorous criteria of excellence. These are not the paper-and-pencil, objective tests in which learners recognize rather than generate answers or create brief responses to questions in which they have little personal investment. Rather, students are required to produce journals, research reports, physical models, or performances in the forms of plays, debates, dances, or other artistic representations. Assessing these products and performances requires well-designed, flexible rubrics to maintain a link between course objectives and student learning. Designing these rubrics (through negotiation with students) builds consensus about what "purpose" means in a learning activity, about the nature of meaningful criteria, and about how assessments reflect the efficacy of the teacher as a promoter of understanding.

The final and perhaps most politically sensitive issue confronting teachers is that the diversity of understandings emerging from constructivist instruction does not always seem compatible with state and local standards. For example, student groups engaged in science projects on photosynthesis may have radically different approaches to developing their understanding of this phenomenon. One group may choose to focus on chemical reactions at the molecular level while another group may examine how oxygen and carbon dioxide are exchanged between animals and plants on a global scale. These two groups will take disconcertingly divergent paths to understanding photosynthesis.

This kind of project-based learning must be skillfully orchestrated so that, however students choose to investigate and seek resolutions to problems, they will acquire an understanding of key principles and concepts as well as the critical thinking skills that are assessed on standardized tests. Proponents of project-based learning have demonstrated that these kinds of learning outcomes are entirely possible.[13] Artful guidance by the teacher notwithstanding, it can be unsettling for teachers to reconcile the language of "objectives, standards, and benchmarks" with the diversity of understandings that emerge in a constructivist classroom.

Conclusions and Recommendations

How does a school community support the instructional expertise, academic freedom, and professional collaboration necessary to sustain a constructivist culture? First, a core group of committed teachers must systematically investigate constructivism in order to understand its principles and its limitations. The ideas behind constructivism seem intuitive and sensible, but teachers and administrators must go beyond the hyperbole and the one-shot-workshop acquaintance with constructivism. Interested faculty members should conduct a thorough reading campaign, and at least one or two teachers should extend their experience by participating in advanced workshops, attending classes, and witnessing how constructivist cultures operate in other schools. Stipends and released time can be provided for a cadre of lead teachers to attend classes, do extra reading, adapt curriculum, and offer their own workshops to fellow teachers. Workshop topics could include the constructivist implementation of cooperative learning, scaffolding techniques, problem-based learning, or multifaceted assessment strategies.

The faculty members must openly discuss their beliefs about learners and about their roles as teachers. If these beliefs are left unexamined or unchallenged, then individuals have feeble grounding for their personal philosophies. Just as problematically then, everyone operates on different, untested assumptions. And all decisions about curriculum, instruction, and assessment are built on such assumptions.

Personal philosophies of education are particularly important when constructivism is used to furnish underlying principles—important because constructivism means risk taking and a divergence from business as usual. Sooner or later, teachers will be asked, "Why do you teach that way?" Whatever form that question takes, teachers must be able to justify the choices they make. This task will not be as intimidating if the teacher has mindfully linked the aspects of his or her constructivist philosophy to the various dimensions of classroom experience and to the larger goals of education.

The process of making these beliefs explicit can also strengthen teachers' resolve to move beyond the traditional images of what is proper and possible in the classroom. It can make clear to them the characteristics and limitations of the system that encouraged images of teachers as dispensers of information and students as passive recipients of knowledge. Accordingly, teachers must try to arrive at a new vision of their role. This vision must include serving as a facilitator of learning who responds to students' needs with a flexible under-standing of subject matter and a sensitivity to how the student is making sense of the world.

Teachers and their principals must be prepared to go on record with these beliefs in discussions with parent groups and the school board. Educa-tors should always have a rationale for what and how they teach; however, because constructivism is so contrary to historical norms, it is even more important in this case that the rationale be well founded, coherent, and appli-cable to the current school context. Community members will undoubtedly be suspicious of teaching methods that are so different from the ones they remember as students and that sound too much like a laissez-faire approach to learning.

Administrators must also take the lead in supporting a "less is more" approach. The compulsion to cover material is antithetical to the aim of con-structivist instruction—the deep and elaborate understanding of selected core ideas. Textbooks, which are often the de facto curriculum, have become ency-clopedic, and administrators should make teachers feel secure about using a variety of other resources. They should also provide funds to purchase alter-native classroom materials. Furthermore, administrators must be open to sug-gestions for block scheduling and for integrating curricula, perhaps even arranging for interested teachers to be placed together in team-teaching situa-tions that are premised on the constructivist approach.

To strengthen the school's position on accountability, assessment spe-cialists who understand constructivism can be brought in to connect local standards with instruction and with evidence that learning is taking place. Teachers will undoubtedly appreciate assistance in investigating and evaluat-ing a variety of assessment strategies.

The list of challenges I have described here is not exhaustive. There are certainly others, and the challenges outnumber the solutions at the moment. But articulating these challenges is a significant step in helping educators create and sustain a classroom culture that values diversity in learning and offers a new vision of the roles of teachers and learners—the culture of constructivism.

Notes

1. Pam Bolotin-Joseph, "Understanding Curriculum as Culture," in Pam Bolotin-Joseph, Stevie Bravman, Mark Windschitl, Edward Mikel, and Nancy Green, eds., *Cultures of Curriculum* (Mahwah, N.J.: Erlbaum, forthcoming).

2. Thomas Russell, "Learning to Teach Science: Constructivism, Reflec-tion, and Learning from Experience," in Kenneth Tobin, ed., *The Practice of Constructivism in Science Education* (Hillsdale, N.J.: Erlbaum, 1993), pp. 247–58.

3. Corby Kennison, "Enhancing Teachers' Professional Learning: Rela-tionships Between School Culture and Elementary School Teachers' Beliefs, Images, and Ways of Knowing" (Specialist's thesis, Florida State University, 1990).

4. Kenneth Tobin, "Constructivist Perspectives on Teacher Learning," in idem, ed., pp. 215–26; and Kenneth Tobin and Sarah Ulerick, "An Interpretation of High School Science Teaching Based on Metaphors and Beliefs for Specific Roles," paper presented at the annual meeting of the American Educational Research Association, San Francisco, 1989.

5. Kenneth Zeichner and Robert Tabachnick, "Are the Effects of University Teacher Education Washed Out by School Experience?," *Journal of Teacher Education*, vol. 32, 1981, pp. 7–11.

6. Adriana Groisman, Bonnie Shapiro, and John Willinsky, "The Potential of Semiotics to Inform Understanding of Events in Science Education," *International Journal of Science Education*, vol. 13, 1991, pp. 217–26.

7. James H. Mosenthal and Deborah Ball, "Constructing New Forms of Teaching: Subject Matter Knowledge in Inservice Teacher Education," *Journal of Teacher Education*, vol. 43, 1992, pp. 347–56.

8. David Lebow, "Constructivist Values for Instructional Systems Design: Five Principles Toward a New Mindset," *Educational Technology, Research, and Development*, vol. 41, no. 3, 1993, pp. 4–16.

9. Jeong-Im Choi and Michael Hannafin, "Situated Cognition and Learning Environments: Roles, Structures, and Implications for Design," *Educational Technology, Research, and Development*, vol. 43, no. 2, 1995, pp. 53–69.

10. David W. Johnson, Roger T. Johnson, and Karl A. Smith, *Active Learning: Cooperation in the College Classroom* (Edina, Minn.: Interaction Book Company, 1991).

11. Robert E. Slavin, *Cooperative Learning* (Boston: Allyn and Bacon, 1995).

12. Phyllis Blumenfeld et al., "Motivating Project-Based Learning: Sustaining the Doing, Supporting the Learning," *Educational Psychologist*, vol. 26, 1991, pp. 369–98.

13. Ibid.

Reality's Revenge: Research and Ideology

The first step in strengthening education in America is to avoid the premature polarizations that arise when educational policy is confused with political ideology. In the United States today, the hostile political split between liberals and conservatives has infected the public debate over education—to such an extent that straight thinking is made difficult.

... I would label myself a political liberal and an educational conservative, or perhaps more accurately, an educational pragmatist. Political liberals really ought to oppose progressive educational ideas because they have led to practical failure and greater social inequity. The only practical way to achieve liberalism's aim of greater social justice is to pursue conservative educational policies.

That is not a new idea. In 1932, the Communist intellectual Antonio Gramsci, writing from jail (having been imprisoned by Mussolini), was one of the first to detect the paradoxical consequences of the new "democratic" education, which stressed "life relevance" and other naturalistic approaches over hard work and the transmission of knowledge. Il Duce's educational minister, Giovanni Gentile, was, in contrast to Gramsci, an enthusiastic proponent of the new ideas emanating from Teachers College, Columbia University, in the United States.[1] ...

Gramsci saw that to denominate such methods as phonics and memorization of the multiplication table as "conservative," while associating them with the political right, amounted to a serious intellectual error. That was the nub of the standoff between the two most distinguished educational theorists of the political Left—Gramsci and Paulo Freire. Freire, like Gramsci a hero of humanity, devoted himself to the cause of educating the oppressed, particularly in his native Brazil, but his writings also have been influential in the United States. Like other educational progressivists, Freire rejected traditional teaching methods and subject matters, objecting to the "banking theory of schooling," whereby the teacher provides the child with a lot of "rote-learned" information. The consequence of the conservative approach, according to Freire, is to numb the critical faculties of students and to preserve the oppressor class. He called for a change of both methods and content—new content that would celebrate the culture of the oppressed, and new methods that would encourage intellectual independence and resistance. In short, Freire, like other educational writers since the 1920s, associated political and educational progressivism.

Gramsci took the opposite view. He held that political progressivism demanded educational conservatism. The oppressed class should be taught to master the tools of power and authority—the ability to read, write, and communicate—and to gain enough traditional knowledge to understand the worlds of nature and culture surrounding them. Children, particularly the children of the poor, should not be encouraged to flourish "naturally," which would keep them ignorant and make them slaves of emotion. They should learn the value of hard work, gain the knowledge that leads to understanding, and master the traditional culture in order to command its rhetoric, as Gramsci himself had learned to do.

In this debate, history has proved Gramsci to be the better theorist and prophet. Modern nations that have adopted Gramscian principles have bettered the condition and heightened the political, social, and economic power of oppressed classes of people. By contrast, nations (including our own) that have stuck to the principles of Freire have failed to change the social and economic status quo....

The educational standpoint from which this article is written may be accurately described as neither "traditional" nor "progressive." It is pragmatic. Both educational traditionalists and progressivists have tended to be far too dogmatic, polemical, and theory-ridden to be reliable beacons for public policy. The pragmatist tries to avoid simplifications and facile oppositions. Thus, this article will argue that the best guide to education on a large scale is observation of practices that have worked well on a large scale, coupled with as exact an understanding as possible of the reasons why those practices have succeeded in many different contexts....

What Is Higher-Order Thinking?

The goal of present-day educational reformers is to produce students with "higher-order skills" who are able to think independently about the unfamiliar problems they will encounter in the information age, who have become "problem solvers" and have "learned how to learn," and who are on their way to becoming "critical thinkers" and "lifelong learners." The method advocated for achieving these "higher-order skills" is "discovery learning," by which students solve problems and make decisions on their own through "inquiry" and "independent analysis" of "real-world" projects—what [William Heard] Kilpatrick in the 1920s called the "project method."

The oft-repeated goal of the educational community—to inculcate general thinking skills—is not, however, soundly based in research. And that is stating the point too mildly. The idea that school can inculcate abstract, generalized skills for thinking, "accessing," and problem solving, and that these skills can be readily applied to the real world is, bluntly, a mirage. So also is the hope that a thinking skill in one domain can be readily and reliably transferred to other domains.

Yet broad-gauged thinking abilities do exist. Most of us know well-educated people, even some not very bright ones, who have high general competence, can think critically about diverse subjects, can communicate well, can solve a diversity of problems, and are ready to tackle unfamiliar challenges. The belief that our schools should regularly produce such people appeals to both experience and common sense. If the goal didn't make apparent sense, it could hardly have retained its attractiveness to the educational community and the general public. Rightly understood, then, the goal of general competence does define one important aim of modern education. The task is not to change that goal but to interpret it accurately so that it corresponds to the nature of real-world competency and can actually be achieved.

Two traditions in cognitive psychology are useful for understanding the nature of the critical-thinking, problem-solving skills that we wish to develop in our students. One tradition has studied the characteristic differences between expert and novice thinking, sometimes with the practical goal of making novices think more like experts as fast as possible.[2] Another tradition has investigated the differences between accurate and inaccurate thinking of the everyday newspaper-reading, bargain-hunting sort that all of us must engage in as non-experts.[3] Both sorts of study converge on the conclusion that, once basic underlying skills have been automated, the almost universal feature of reliable higher-order thinking about any subject or problem is the possession of a broad, well-integrated base of background knowledge relevant to the subject. This sounds suspiciously like plain common sense (i.e., accurate everyday thinking), but the findings entail certain illuminating complexities and details that are worth contemplating. Moreover, since the findings run counter to the prevailing fact-disparaging slogans of educational reform, it will be strategically useful to sketch briefly what research has disclosed about the knowledge-based character of higher-order thinking.

The argument used by educators to disparage "merely" factual knowledge and to elevate abstract, formal principles of thought consists in the claim that knowledge is changing so rapidly that specific information is outmoded almost as soon as it has been learned. This claim goes back at least as far as Kilpatrick's *Foundations of Method* (1925). It gains its apparent plausibility from the observation that science and technology have advanced at a great rate in this century, making scientific and technological obsolescence a common feature of modern life. The argument assumes that there is an analogy between technological and intellectual obsolescence. Educators in this tradition shore up that analogy with the further claim that factual knowledge has become a futility because of the ever-growing quantity of new facts. The great cascade of information now flowing over the information highway makes it pointless to accumulate odd bits of data. How, after all, do you know which bits are going to endure? It is much more efficient for students to spend time acquiring techniques for organizing, analyzing, and accessing this perpetual Niagara of information.

Like the tool metaphor for education, the model of acquiring processing techniques that would be permanently useful—as contrasted with acquiring mere facts that are soon obsolete—would be highly attractive if it happened to be workable and true. But the picture of higher thinking skills as consisting of all-purpose processing and accessing techniques is not just a *partly* inadequate metaphor—it is a totally misleading model of the way higher-order thinking actually works. Higher thought does not apply formal techniques to looked-up data; rather, it deploys diverse relevant cues, estimates, and analyses from preexisting knowledge. The method of applying formal techniques to looked-up data is precisely the inept and unreliable problem-solving device used by novices. As a model of real-world higher-order thinking, the picture is not simply inaccurate—it reverses the realities. It describes the lower-order thinking of novices, not the higher-order thinking of experts.

A useful illustration of the point is presented by Jill Larkin and Ruth Chabay in a study of the ways in which novices and experts go about solving a simple physics problem.[4] The problem Larkin and Chabay set up is (in simple terms) to find out how much friction there is between a sled and the snow-covered ground when a girl is pulling her little brother through the snow at a constant rate. The brother and the sled together weigh 50 pounds. The sister is pulling with a force of 10 pounds, and she pulls the rope at an angle of 30 degrees from the horizontal. What is the coefficient of friction? The typical novice tries to solve the problem by applying formal equations that can be looked up in a book, thus dutifully following the tool principle of problem solving. The student finds that the applicable formula is $f = {}_u N$, where f is force, N is the "normal force" (which is usually equal to weight), and $_u$ is the coefficient of friction, which is the quantity to be solved. The novice sees that $f = {}_u \times 50$. The student assumes that $f = 10$, the force exerted by the girl. So $10 = {}_u \times 50$ and $_u = {}^{10}/_{50}$, which equals .2. The answer is wrong, not because the equation or the math is wrong but because the novice doesn't know enough about real-world physics to know how to connect the formula to the problem. The novice's procedure illustrates not just the inappropriateness of the for-malistic model but also the bankruptcy of the claim that students need only learn how to look things up—so-called "accessing skills." In this typical case, the skill of looking things up simply lends spurious exactitude to the student's misconceptions.

The expert physicist goes about the problem differently. He or she ana-lyzes the critical components of the situation before looking up equations and makes two critical observations before even bothering with numbers. The first observation is that the sled is going at a constant speed, so that, in effect, there is no net residue of forces acting on the sled; there is an exact balance between the force exerted horizontally by the girl's pull and the force exerted against that pull by friction. If there had been some difference in the two forces, then the sled would speed up or slow down. So the answer has got to be that the friction is exactly equal to the horizontal component of the force exerted by the girl. The physicist also sees that since the rope is pulled at 30 degrees, part of the girl's 10 pounds of force is vertical. The answer is going to be that the friction equals the *horizontal* force of the girl's pull, which is going to be the 10 pounds minus its vertical component. The structure of the answer is solved on the basis of multiple cues and relevant knowledge, before any formulas are looked up and applied. Larkin and Chabay make the follow-ing comment (which is much more to our purpose than the details of the physics involved):

Scientists' problem solving starts with redescribing the problem in terms of the powerful concepts of their discipline. *Because the concepts are richly connected with each other, the redescribed problem allows cross-checking among inferences to avoid errors* [author's emphasis].[5]

An important feature of higher-order thinking is this "cross-checking among inferences," based on a number of "richly connected" concepts. In higher-order thinking, we situate a problem in mental space on analogy with the way we situate ourselves in physical space—through a process of cross-checking or triangulation among relevant guideposts in our landscape of pre-existing knowledge. If we look at a problem from a couple of different angles, using a couple of different cues, and if our different estimates converge, we gain confidence in our analysis and can proceed with confidence. If, on the other hand, there is some dissonance or conflict between our cues, then warning signals go up, and we figure out which approach is more probable or fruitful. The procedure is clearly a very different and far more reliable mode of thinking than the error-prone method of applying formal techniques to looked-up data.

The example also illustrates the implausibility of the claim that school-based information quickly grows outdated. How outmoded will the knowledge used to solve the sled problem become? A philosopher of science, Nicholas Rescher, once observed that the latest science is in a sense the least reliable science, because, being on the frontier, it is always in dispute with other, rival theories—any of which may emerge victorious. Accordingly, reasoned Rescher, the most reliable physics is "stone-age-physics": If you throw the rock up, it is going to come down. For most problems that require critical thought by the ordinary person regarding ethics, politics, history, and even technology, the most needed knowledge is usually rather basic, long-lived, and slow to change. True, just as physics is under revision at the frontier, so American history before the Civil War is constantly under revision in certain details (e.g., did Abraham Lincoln have an affair with Ann Rutledge?). But behind the ever-changing front lines, there is a body of reliable knowledge that has not changed, and will not change very much, and that serves very well as a landscape to orient us in mental space. It is true that, over time, the content of the most significant and useful background knowledge for today's world does change. But I have never seen a carefully reasoned defense of the repeated assertion that, in the new age, factual knowledge is changing so fast as to make the learning of significant information useless. Probably, no carefully reasoned defense of this mindless claim could be mounted.

The physics example from Larkin and Chabay, if viewed in isolation, might be taken to show that higher-order thinking depends on abstract concepts rather than on factual details. But most research indicates that while the thinking activities through which we reach conclusions and solve problems are not crowded with literally remembered facts, neither are they made up of abstract concepts alone. The models, cues, and schemas through which we think critically are neither pure concepts nor a literal recall of data but a complex and varied combination of concepts, estimates, and factual examples. The key trait to remember about higher-order thinking is its mixed character, consisting of operational facility and domain-specific knowledge.

Some of the most useful studies of higher-order thinking have been concerned with improving our ability to make intelligent and accurate estimates on which to base decisions in our ethical, economic, and civic lives.[6] Since most of us cannot remember, and do not want to take the time to learn, all the details of the U.S. budget deficit and similar matters, we follow political and economic debates with a degree of impressionism that leaves many of us open to slogans and demagoguery. What kind of critical thinking can improve our ability to reach accurate conclusions on such issues? How can we protect ourselves and our students from oversimplifications, lies, and scapegoating conspiracy theories?

It is hard to see why a generalized skepticism, unsupported by accurate knowledge, is superior to a generalized credulity, similarly unsupported. Indeed, uninformed, generalized skepticism expresses itself as a form of credulity, despite our inclination to call I'm-from-Missouri postures "critical thinking." Our best hope for intelligent civic thought lies in our ability to make good ballpark estimates that are close enough to truth to make our decisions well informed and sound. But life is too short, and learning too arduous, for all citizens to memorize a lot of economic and demographic data. Our current yearly government budget deficit—is it around $30, $300, or $3,000 per American family? Sure, we could look it up, but few of us will. If we can't make an intelligent estimate from the knowledge we already have, we usually won't make an intelligent estimate at all. A lot of higher-order thinking involves our ability to make these sorts of estimates, and to make them well. How do some people manage to do it? And how can we all learn how to do it? From answers to those questions, what implications can be deduced for the K-12 curriculum?

The best research on this subject shows that neither fact-filled memorization nor large conceptual generalizations are effective modes of education for higher-order thinking about the complexities of the modern world. On the other hand, it has been shown that accurate factual estimates are necessary for understanding many issues....

The breadth-depth issue will always be with us and will always require compromises and common sense. The particular compromise one makes will depend upon subject matter and goals. In practice, an appropriate compromise has been reached by self-taught, well-informed people and by the fortunate students of particularly able teachers. One well-tested teaching method, already followed by many good books and teachers, provides students with a carefully chosen but generous sampling of factual data that are set forth in a meaningful web of inferences and generalizations about the larger domain. Researchers have shown that such generally selective factual instruction leads to accurate inferences not directly deducible from the literal facts that were taught. The mechanisms by which we are able to use these selective exemplifications in order to make remarkably accurate factual guesses about untaught domains are a subject of vigorous current research.

Whatever the underlying psychological mechanisms prove to be, research has demonstrated that the teaching of a generous number of carefully chosen exemplary facts within a meaningful explanatory context is a better method for inducing insightful thinking than is any proposed alternative. These alternatives include (1) the teaching of the whole factual domain, (2) the teaching of the general principles only, and (3) the teaching of a single example in great depth (the less-is-more theory). None of these methods is as effective for inducing effective real-world thinking as sampling well-selected and consistent facts in a carefully prepared explanatory context.[7] This careful-sampling method works well even when (as usually happens) the literal details of the taught facts are not memorized by students and cannot be retrieved accurately from memory after a period of several months. Nonetheless, a strong improvement in accurate thinking persists if students have once been taught a carefully chosen sample of the factual data.

This finding has strong implications for curriculum making. The conclusion from cognitive research shows that there is an unavoidable interdependence between relational and factual knowledge and that teaching a broad range of factual knowledge is essential to effective thinking both within domains and among domains. Despite the popularity of the anti-fact motif in our progressive education tradition, and despite its faith in the power of a few "real-world" projects to educate students "holistically" for the modern world, no state board or school district has yet abandoned the principle of requiring a broad range of different subject matters in elementary school. Across the land, there are still universal requirements for mathematics, science, language arts, and social studies.

Is this curricular conservatism a mere residue of traditional thinking, or does it indicate that common sense has not been defeated by Romantic theory? I favor the latter hypothesis. Despite the vagueness of state and district guidelines, their continued parceling out of schooling into different subject matters, against continued pleas for a more "integrated" and holistic approach, shows an implicit understanding that breadth of knowledge is an essential element of higher-order thinking. School boards have rightly assumed that the mental landscape needs to be broadly surveyed and mapped in order to enable future citizens to cope with a large variety of judgments. No effective system of schooling in the world has abandoned this principle of subject-matter breadth in early schooling.

For later schooling, however, a good deal of evidence—marshaled in the superb research of John Bishop of Cornell—shows that in the last two years of high school, and later on, the balance of utility shifts in favor of deeper and more narrowly specialized training as the best education for the modern world.[8] This finding means that breadth in earlier schooling is all the more essential to developing adequate higher-order thinking and living skills in our citizens-to-be. If schooling is going to become more and more specialized in later life, it is ever more important to map out the wider intellectual landscape accurately and well in the earlier years. Otherwise, we shall produce not critical thinkers but narrow, ignorant ones, subject to delusion and rhetoric. This danger was uppermost in Jefferson's mind when he advocated teaching of human history in early years. In our age, the same argument holds for the domains connected with mathematics, science, technology, and communication skills. A wide range of knowledge and a broad vocabulary supply entry wedges into unfamiliar domains, thus truly enabling "lifelong learning," as well as the attainment of new knowledge and greater depth as needed. The unmistakable implication for modern education is that, instead of constantly deferring the introduction of challenging and extensive knowledge, we need to be taking the opposite tack by increasing both the challenge and the breadth of early education.

Consensus Researchon Pedagogy

A consensus regarding the most effective teaching methods has emerged from three independent sources whose findings converge on the same pedagogical principles. This pattern of independent convergence (a kind of intellectual triangulation) is, along with accurate prediction, one of the most powerful, confidence-building patterns in scientific research. There are few or no examples in the history of science (none that I know of) when the same result, reached by three or more truly independent means, has been overturned....

The independent convergence on the fundamentals of effective pedagogy that exists today is less mathematical but nonetheless compelling. The same findings have been derived from three quite different and entirely independent sources: (1) small-scale pairings of different teaching methods; (2) basic research in cognition, learning, memory, psycholinguistics, and other areas of cognitive psychology; and (3) large-scale international comparative studies. The findings from all three sources are highly consistent with each other regarding the most effective pedagogical principles. Because real-world classroom observations are so completely affected by so many uncontrolled variables, the most persuasive aspect of the current picture is the congruence of the classroom-based observations with cognitive psychology—which is currently our best and most reliable source of insight into the processes of learning.

In presenting these findings, my strategy will be briefly to go through some of the classroom studies and summarize their points of agreement. Then, I will relate those points to findings in cognitive psychology. Finally, I will comment on their congruence with the results of international comparisons....

New Zealand studies   In a series of "process-outcome" studies between 1970 and 1973, researchers from the University of Canterbury in New Zealand found that time spent focused on content and the amount of content taught were more important factors than the teacher behaviors that were used to teach the content.[9] ...

"Follow through" studies   Jane Stallings and her colleagues observed and evaluated results from 108 first-grade classes and fifty-eight third-grade classes taught by different methods. Programs having strong academic focus rather than programs using the project-method approach produced the highest gains in reading and math. Brophy and Good summarize the Stallings findings as follows: "Almost anything connected with the classical recitation pattern of teacher questioning (particularly direct, factual questions rather than more open questions) followed by student response, followed by teacher feedback, correlated positively with achievement." As in the New Zealand studies, students who spent most of their time being instructed or guided by their teachers did much better than students who did projects or were expected to learn on their own.[10]

Brophy-Evertson studies   Between 1973 and 1979, Brophy and his colleagues conducted a series of studies in which they first determined that some teachers got consistently good results over the years, and others consistently bad ones. They made close observations of the teacher behaviors associated, respectively, with good and bad academic outcomes. Teachers who produced the most achievement were focused on academics. They were warm but businesslike. Teachers who produced the least achievement used a "heavily affective" approach and were more concerned with the child's self-esteem and psychic well-being than with academics. They emphasized warmth, used student ideas, employed a democratic style, and encouraged student-student interaction. The researchers further found that learning proceeded best when the material was somewhat new and challenging, but could also be assimilated relatively easily into what students already knew. The biggest contrast was not between modes of academic instruction but between all such instruction and "learner-centered" "discovery learning," which was ineffective. Paradoxically, the students were more motivated and engaged by academic-centered instruction than by student-centered instruction.

In 1982, Brophy and his colleagues summarized some of their later findings on the effective teaching of beginning reading. These were the most salient points:

1. Sustained focus on content.
2. All students involved (whole-class instruction dominates).
3. Brisk pace, with easy enough tasks for consistent student success.
4. Students reading aloud often and getting consistent feedback.
5. Decoding skills mastered to the point of over learning (automaticity).
6. In the course of time, each child asked to perform and getting immediate, nonjudgmental feedback.[11]

Good-Grouws studies   For over a decade, Good and Grouws pursued process-outcome studies that support the Brophy-Evertson findings. Their 1977 summary contained the following points:

1. The best teachers were clearer.
2. They introduced more new concepts, engaged in less review.
3. They asked fewer questions.
4. Their feedback to the students was quick and nonevaluative.
5. They used whole-class instruction most of the time.
6. They were demanding and conveyed high expectations.[12]

The Gage studies   N. L. Gage and his colleagues at Stanford University have produced a series of process-outcome studies from the 1960s to the 1980s. These results, consistent with the above, are summarized in the following points of advice to teachers:

1. Introduce material with an overview or analogy.
2. Use review and repetition.
3. Praise or repeat student answers.
4. Be patient in waiting for responses.
5. Integrate the responses into the lesson.
6. Give assignments that offer practice and variety.
7. Be sure questions and assignments are new and challenging, yet easy enough to allow success with reasonable effort.[13]

Other studies In 1986, Rosenshine and Stevens listed five other "particularly praiseworthy" studies of effective teaching modes, all of which came to similar conclusions. They summarize these conclusions as follows:

1. Review prerequisite learning.
2. Start with a brief statement of goals.
3. Introduce new material in small steps.
4. Maintain clarity and detail in presentation.
5. Achieve a high level of active practice.
6. Obtain response and check for understanding (CFU).
7. Guide student practice initially.
8. Give systematic, continual feedback.
9. Monitor and give specific advice during seatwork.[14]

The Brophy-Good summary In their final summation of research in this area, Brophy and Good make a comment worth quoting directly. They draw two chief conclusions from reviewing all of this research:

> One is that academic learning is influenced by the amount of time students spend in appropriate academic tasks. The second is that students learn more efficiently when their teachers first structure new information for them and help them relate it to what they already know, and then monitor their performance and provide corrective feedback during recitation, drill, practice, or application activities.... There are no shortcuts to successful attainment of higher-level learning objectives. Such success will not be achieved with relative ease through discovery learning by the student. Instead, it will require considerable instruction from the teacher, as well as thorough mastery of basic knowledge and skills that must be integrated and applied in the process of "higher-level" performance. Development of basic knowledge and skills to the level of automatic and errorless performance will require a great deal of drill and practice. Thus drill and practice activities should not be slighted as "low level." They appear to be just as essential to complex and creative intellectual performance as they are to the performance of a virtuoso violinist.[15]

Before I go on to discuss correlations between these findings and research in cognitive psychology, I will digress to make an observation connecting these results to student motivation. While common sense might have predicted the *academic* superiority of structured, whole-class instruction over less academically focused, learner-centered instruction, it was unexpected that these studies should have demonstrated the *motivational* superiority of instruction centered on content rather than on students. Why is academically focused instruction more engaging and motivating to young learners than learner-centered instruction?

I know of no research that explains this finding, but I shall hazard the guess that individualized, learner-centered instruction must be extremely boring to most students most of the time, since, by mathematical necessity, they are not receiving individualized attention most of the time. It may also be the case that the slow pace and progress of less structured teaching may fail to engage and motivate students. A teacher must be extraordinarily talented to know just how to interact engagingly with each individual child. Given the strong motivation of young children to learn about the adult world, the best way to engage them is by a dramatic, interactive, and clear presentation that incidentally brings out the inherent satisfaction in skill mastery and interest in subject matter.

There is also a basis in cognitive psychology for the finding that students should be taught procedural skills to the point of "over learning." "Over learning" is a rather unfortunate term of art, since intuitively it seems a bad idea to overdo anything. But the term simply means that students should become able to supply the right answer or to follow the right procedure very fast, without hesitation. Through practice, they become so habituated to a procedure that they no longer have to think or struggle to perform it. This leaves their highly limited working memory free to focus on other aspects of the task at hand. The classroom research cited above simply reported that teachers who followed the principle of over learning produced much better results. Cognitive psychology explains why....

The classroom studies also stressed the importance of teaching new content in small incremental steps. This is likewise explained by the limitations of working memory, since the mind can handle only a small number of new things at one time. A new thing has to become integrated with prior knowledge before the mind can give it meaning, store it in memory, and attend to something else. New learnings should not be introduced until feedback from students indicates that they have mastered the old learnings quite well, though not, as in the case of procedural skills, to the point of over learning. Research into long-term memory shows why this slow-but-sure method of feedback and review works best: "Once is not enough" should be the motto of long-term memory, though nonmeaningful review and boring repetition are not good techniques. The classroom research cited above indicated that the best teachers did not engage in incessant review. Memory studies suggest that the best approach to achieving retention in long-term memory is "distributed practice." Ideally, lessons should spread a topic over several days, with repetitions occurring at moderately distant intervals.... This feature of learning explains the importance of a deliberate pace of instruction, as all the classroom studies showed. Whatever practical arrangements are chosen for classroom learning, the principle of content rehearsal is absolutely essential for fixing content in long-term memory. Until that fixation occurs, content learning cannot be said to have happened.

That receiving continual feedback from the students is essential to good teaching is a robust finding in all the studies, and also gets support from research into both short-term and long-term memory. Feedback indicates whether the material has been learned well enough to free short-term (i.e., working) memory for new tasks. Moreover, the process of engaging in question-answer and other feedback practices constitutes content rehearsal, which also helps achieve secure learning in memory. Good teachers seem to be implicitly aware of this double function of question asking—that is, simultaneous monitoring and rehearsing.

Finally, research in cognitive psychology supports the finding that classes should often begin with a review or an analogy that connects the new topic with knowledge students already have. Psycholinguistic studies have shown that verbal comprehension powerfully depends on students' relevant background knowledge and particularly on their ability to apply that knowledge to something new.[16] Meaningful understanding seems to be equivalent to joining the new knowledge to something already known. Other psycholinguistic studies show that comprehension is enhanced when clues are offered at the beginning of a written passage indicating the overall character and direction of the passage. One needs to have a sense of the whole in order to predict the character of the parts and the way they fit with each other. Just as holistic, generic clues are important for the reader's comprehension of a written passage, such clues are similarly important for the student's understanding in the classroom. This psycholinguistic principle shows why a summary at the beginning of a class can give students the right "mindset" for assimilating the new material.[17]

These few principles concerning working memory, long-term memory, and the best prior conditions for meaningful learning explain the effectiveness of almost all the practices that were found to be effective in the classroom studies. Their congruence with mainstream psychology was well observed by Rosenshine and Stevens when they stated that research in cognitive psychology

> helps explain why students taught with structured curricula generally do better than those taught with either more individualized or discovery learning approaches. It also explains why young students who receive their instruction from a teacher usually achieve more than those who are expected to learn new materials and skills on their own or from each other. When young children are expected to learn on their own, particularly in the early stages, the students run the danger of not attending to the right cues, or not processing important points, and of proceeding on to later points before they have done sufficient elaboration and practice.[18]

Now I shall turn to some data from international studies on classroom practice. The fullest such research has been conducted by Harold Stevenson and his several colleagues in the United States, China, Japan, and Taiwan, who observed 324 Asian and American mathematics classrooms divided between first grade and fifth grade. Each classroom was studied for more than twenty hours by trained observers who took voluminous notes....

In light of the contrast in outcomes, it is no surprise that the activities that typically occur in Asian classrooms follow the effective pedagogical principles deduced from small-scale American studies and from cognitive psychology. By contrast, the activities that typically occur in American classrooms run counter to those research findings....

To illustrate the agreement between the small-scale intranational studies and the international studies, I shall first summarize the small-scale research findings in each category, then the corresponding findings from the international studies.

Social Atmosphere

Small-scale intranational studies   In the best classrooms, the social atmosphere was warm and supportive, but at the same time businesslike and focused on the job at hand. By contrast, the worst-performing classrooms were "heavily affective," with a lot of verbal praise and self-esteem talk. In the best classes, the teacher was respectful to students but demanded good discipline as well as hard work. In the worst, the atmosphere was less ordered and disciplined.

International studies   The most frequent form of evaluation used by American teachers was praise, a technique that is rarely used in either Taiwan or Japan. Praise cuts off discussion and highlights the teacher's role as the authority. It also encourages students to be satisfied with their performance rather than informing them about where they need improvement. Chinese and Japanese teachers have a low tolerance for errors, and when they occur, they seldom ignore them. Discussing errors helps to clarify misunderstandings, encourage argument and justification, and involve students in the exciting quest of assessing the strengths and weaknesses of the various alternative solutions that have been proposed.[19]

Initial Orientation

Small-scale intranational studies   The teacher first reviews the knowledge prerequisite to the new learning and orients the class to what is in store. One good way is to introduce the material with an overview or analogy connecting it with previous knowledge and to present a brief statement of goals for the day's class.

International studies   The Asian teacher stands in front of the class as a cue that the lesson will soon start. The room quiets. "Let us begin," says the teacher in Sendai. After brief reciprocal bows between pupils and teacher, the teacher opens the class with a description of what will be accomplished during the class period. From that point until the teacher summarizes the day's lesson and announces, "We are through," the Japanese elementary school class—like those in Taiwan and China—consists of teacher and students working together toward the goals described at the beginning of the class....

Pace

Small-scale intranational studies   The best teachers introduce new material in small, easily mastered steps setting a deliberate but brisk pace, not moving ahead until students show that they understand. Better results come from teachers who move forward with new concepts, have higher expectations, and provide review, but not "incessant review."

International studies   The pace is slow, but the outcome is impressive. Japanese teachers want their students to be reflective and to gain a deep understanding of mathematics. Each concept and skill is taught with great thoroughness, thereby eliminating the need to teach the concept again later. Covering only a few problems does not mean that the lesson turns out to be short on content. In the United States, curriculum planners, textbook publishers, and teachers themselves seem to believe that students learn more effectively if they solve a large number of problems rather than if they concentrate their attention on only a few.[20]

Clarity

Small-scale intranational studies   The most effective teachers were not just clearer but more focused on the content or skill goal, asked questions but fewer of them, and kept the focus by continually integrating student responses into the lesson. A useful tool for clarity in presentation: an end-of-class summary review indicating where the lesson went and what it did.

International studies   Irrelevant interruptions often add to children's difficulty in perceiving lessons as a coherent whole. In American observations, the teacher interrupted the flow of the lesson with irrelevant comments, or the class was interrupted by someone else in 20 percent of all first-grade lessons and 47 percent of all fifth-grade lessons. In Sendai, Taipei, and Beijing, interruptions occurred less than 10 percent of the time at both grade levels. Coherence is also disrupted by frequent shifting from one topic to another within a single lesson. Twenty-one percent of the shifts within American lessons were to different topics (rather than to different materials or activities), compared with only 5 percent in the Japanese lessons. Before ending the lesson, the Asian teacher reviews what has been learned and relates it to the problem she posed at the beginning of the lesson. American teachers are much less likely than Asian teachers to end lessons in this way....

Managing and Monitoring

Small-scale intranational studies   In the most effective teaching, whole-class instruction is used most of the time. The teacher obtains responses and checks for understanding for each student, ensuring that each child gets some feedback and that all students stay involved. While feedback to the students is frequent, it is not incessant. The teacher is patient in waiting for responses. Student answers are often repeated for the class. Many effective teachers make constructive, nonevaluative use of student errors, working through how they were made. Students are more engaged and motivated in these classrooms than in student-centered ones.

International studies   Chinese and Japanese teachers rely on students to generate ideas and evaluate the correctness of the ideas. The possibility that they will be called upon to state their own solution keeps Asian students alert, but this technique has two other important functions. First, it engages students in the lesson, increasing their motivation by making them feel they are participants in a group process. Second, it conveys a more realistic impression of how knowledge is acquired. American teachers are less likely to give students opportunities to respond at such length. Although a great deal of interaction appears to occur in American classrooms—with students and teachers posing questions and giving answers—American teachers generally ask questions that are answerable with a yes or a no or a short phrase. They seek a correct answer and continue calling on students until one produces it.[21]

Drill and Practice

Small-scale intranational studies   Two kinds of practice are needed, corresponding to two objects of learning—content and skills. For content, new concepts are discussed and reviewed until secure in the memory. Procedural skills are mastered to the point of overlearning (automaticity). Guided practice should be part of whole-class instruction before seatwork occurs. Small-group seatwork generally works better than individual seatwork, but seatwork per se is used rather sparingly for both content and skills. Supervision and feedback are provided during seatwork.

International studies   When children must work alone for long periods of time without guidance or reaction from the teacher, they begin to lose focus on the purpose of their activity. Asian teachers assign less seatwork than American teachers; furthermore, they use seatwork differently. Asian teachers tend to use short, frequent periods of seatwork, alternating between discussing problems and allowing children to work problems on their own. When seatwork is embedded within the lesson, instruction and practice are tightly woven into a coherent whole. Teachers can gauge children's understanding of the preceding part of the lesson by observing how they solve practice problems. Interspersing seatwork with instruction in this way helps the teacher assess how rapidly she can proceed through the lesson. American teachers, on the other hand, tend to relegate seatwork to one long period at the end of the class, where it becomes little more than a time for repetitious practice.... American teachers often do not discuss the work or its connection to the goal of the lesson, or publicly evaluate its accuracy.[22] ...

   ... [C]onsensus [research into teacher effectiveness] among present-day reformers is well summarized by Zemelman, Daniels, and Hyde in their 1993 book, *Best Practice*.

In virtually every school subject, we now have recent summary reports, meta-analyses of instructional research, bulletins from pilot classrooms, and landmark sets of professional recommendations. Today there is a strong consensus definition of Best Practice, of state-of-the-art teaching in every critical field.... Whether the recommendations come from the National Council of Teachers of Mathematics, the Center for the Study of Reading, the National Writing Project, the National Council for the Social Studies, the American Association for the Advancement of Science, the National Council of Teachers of English, the National Association for the Education of Young Children, or the International Reading Association, the fundamental insights into teaching and learning are remarkably congruent. Indeed on many key issues, the recommendations from these diverse organizations are unanimous.

Zemelman, Daniels, and Hyde then list twenty-five "LESS" and "MORE" admonitions on which all these organizations agree. Among them are the following:

- LESS whole-class teacher-directed instruction
- LESS student passivity, sitting, listening, receiving
- LESS attempts by teachers to cover large amounts of material LESS rote memorization of facts and details
- LESS stress on competition and grades
- MORE experiential, inductive, hands-on learning
- MORE active learning with all the attendant noise of students doing, talking, collaborating
- MORE deep study of a smaller number of topics
- MORE responsibility transferred to students for their work: goal-setting, record-keeping, monitoring, evaluation
- MORE choice for students, e.g., picking their own books, etc.
- MORE attention to affective needs and varying cognitive styles of students MORE cooperative, collaborative activity.[23]

The authors praise the current consensus on these "child-centered" principles for being "progressive, developmentally appropriate, research based, and eminently teachable." These claims are not, however, "research based" in the way the authors imply. Quite the contrary. No studies of children's learning in mainstream science support these generalizations. With respect to effective learning, the consensus in research is that their recommendations are worst practice, not "best practice."

This Alice in Wonderland reversal of reality has been accomplished largely by virtue of the rhetorical device that I have called "premature polarization." Discovery learning is labeled "progressive," and whole-class instruction "traditional."... It overlooks, for instance, the different pedagogical requirements for procedural learning and content learning and thus neglects the different pedagogical emphases needed at the different ages and stages of learning. Effective procedural learning requires "overlearning," and hence plenty of practice. Content learning is amenable to a diversity of methods that accommodate themselves to students' prior knowledge, habits, and interests.

What the international data show very clearly is that both procedural and content learning are best achieved in a focused environment that preponderantly emphasizes whole-class instruction but that is punctuated by small-group or individualized work. Within that focused context, however, there are many good roads to Rome. The classroom observations of Stevenson and his colleagues bring home the ancient wisdom of integrating both direct and indirect methods, including inquiry learning, which encourages students to think for themselves, and direct informing, which is sometimes the most effective and efficient mode of securing knowledge and skill. A combination of show and tell, omitting neither, is generally the most effective approach in teaching, as it is in writing and speaking.

The only truly general principle that seems to emerge from process-outcome research on pedagogy is that focused and guided instruction is far more effective than naturalistic, discovery, learn-at-your-own-pace instruction. But within the context of focused and guided instruction, almost anything goes, and what works best with one group of students may not work best with another group with similar backgrounds in the very same building. Methods must vary a good deal with different age groups. Within the general context of focused and guided instruction, my own general preference, and one followed by good teachers in many lands, is for what might be called "dramatized instruction." The class period can be formed into a little drama with a beginning, middle, and end, well directed but not rigidly scripted by the teacher. The beginning sets up the question to be answered, the knowledge to be mastered, or the skill to be gained; the middle consists of a lot of back-and-forth between student and student, student and teacher; and the end consists of a feeling of closure and accomplishment....

The focused narrative or drama lies midway between narrow drill and practice (which has its place) and the unguided activity of the project method (which may also occasionally have a place). Sir Philip Sidney argued (in 1583!) that stories are better teachers than philosophy or history, because philosophy teaches by dull precept (guided instruction) and history teaches by uncertain example (the project method).[24] The story, however, joins precept and example together, thus teaching and delighting at the same time....

Excellent classroom teaching has a narrative and dramatic feel even when there is a lot of interaction between the students and the teacher—it has a definite theme, and a beginning, middle, and end. This teaching principle holds even for mathematics and science. When every lesson has a well-developed plot in which the children themselves are participants, teaching is both focused and absorbing. The available research is consistent with this scheme, though it by no means says that thoughtful sequencing, plotting, and dramatizing of learning activities are the exclusive or whole key to good pedagogy. For many elementary learnings, repeated practice has to be an integral part of the plot.

That recent psychological research should yield insights that confirm what ... Sidney said about stories should probably make us more, not less, confident in the results of this recent research. Education is as old as humanity. The breathless claim that technology and the information age have radically changed the nature of the education of young children turns out to be, like most breathless claims in education, unsupported by scholarship. Nor should current studies surprise us when they show that a naturalistic approach, lacking a definite story line and a sharp focus, has the defect Sidney saw in history as a teacher of humankind: it "draweth no necessary consequence." There *is* a modest place for discovery learning, just as there is for drill and practice. But research indicates that, most of the time, clearly focused, well-plotted teaching is the best means for "[holding] children from play and old men from the chimney corner."

Notes

1. For comments on Gentile's views and for basic insights into Gramsci's ideas about education, I am grateful to Entwistle, *Antonio Gramsci*. Additional commentary may be found in Broccoli, *Antonio Gramsci e l'educazione come egemonia*; Scuderi, *Antonio Gramsci e il problema pedagogico*; and De Robbio, *Antonio Gramsci e la pedagogia dell'impegno*. For modern data showing that Gramsciisright in holding that traditional schooling greatly improves the academic competencies of low achievers, see K. R. Johnson, and Layng, "Breaking the Structuralist Barrier," 1475-90.

2. Larkin et al., "Models of Competence in Solving Physics Problems," 317-48. Schoenfeld and Hermann, "Problem Perception and Knowledge Structure in Expert and Novice Mathematical Problem Solvers, 484-94.

3. Some work in this tradition: Tversky and Kahneman, "Availability," 207-32; Collins, *Human Plausible Reasoning*; and Fischoff, "Judgment and Decision Making," 153-87.

4. Larkin and Chabay, "Research on Teaching Scientific Thinking," 158.

5. Ibid., 150-72.

6. Kunda and Nisbett, "The Psychometrics of Everyday Life," 195-224.

7. Brown and Siegler, "Metrics and Mappings," 531. But see also Scardamalia and Bereiter, "Computer Support for Knowledge-Building Communities," 265-83; and Scardamalia, Bereiter, and Lamon, "CSILE: Trying To Bring Students into World 3," 201-28.

8. Bishop, *Expertise and Excellence*.

9. The data from the New Zealand study and most other studies cited here are taken from the excellent review by Brophy and Good, who conducted some of the most significant research into effective teaching methods. See Brophy and Good, "Teacher Behavior and Student Achievement," 328-75. Some of the New Zealand work is described in Nuthall and Church, "Experimental Studies of Teaching Behaviour." The importance of this kind of research was well argued by Gilbert T. Sewall in his *Necessary Lessons*, especially pages 131-33. Sewall cites highly similar findings from the British researcher Neville Bennett in N. Bennett, *Teaching Styles and Pupil Progress*. For an explanation why progressive methods like discovery learning have not worked well in teaching science, see Walberg, "Improving School Science in Advanced and Developing Countries," 625-99.

10. Stallings and Kasowitz, *Follow Through Classroom Evaluation*, 1972-1973.

11. Brophy and Evertson, *Learning from Teaching*. Anderson, Evertson, and Brophy, *Principles of Small-Group Instruction in Elementary Reading*.

12. Good and Grouws, "Teacher Effects," 49-54.

13. Gage, *The Scientific Basis of the Art of Teaching*.

14.   Rosenshine and Stevens, "Teaching Functions," 376-91.

15.   Brophy and Good, "Teacher Behavior and Student Achievement," 338.

16.   Spiro, "Cognitive Processes in Prose Comprehension and Recall"; and Anderson and Shifrin, "The Meaning of Words in Context."

17.   Bransford and Johnson, "Contextual Prerequisites for Understanding," 717-26. Spiro, "Cognitive Processes in Prose Comprehension and Recall."

18.   Rosenshine and Stevens, "Teaching Functions," 379.

19.   Stevenson and Stigler, *The Learning Gap*, 191.

20.   Ibid., 194.

21.   Ibid., 190.

22.   Ibid., 183.

23.   Zemelman, Daniels, and Hyde, *Best Practice*, 4-5.

24.   Sidney, *An Apology for Poetry*.

POSTSCRIPT

Should Schools Adopt a Constructivist Approach to Education?

Hirsch points to dozens of studies that he believes demonstrate the superiority of a teacher-centered, fact-based approach. Why, then, do Windschitl and other constructivists adhere so firmly to their position? How can they ignore the empirical evidence amassed by Hirsch? In fact, interpreting the studies that Hirsch cites is not so straightforward. Many of these studies are correlational, involving comparisons between existing classrooms exemplifying the different approaches. In a correlational study, the researcher has no control over factors such as the assignment of students or teachers to one approach or the other or the ways in which the two approaches are implemented. This means that it is often difficult to discern whether differences in student achievement have been caused by differences in pedagogical approach or by preexisting differences that were beyond the control of the researchers. In addition, constructivists would argue that many of the so-called constructivist classrooms examined in these studies did little more than insert a few hands-on activities into an otherwise teacher-centered classroom. They would question whether the classrooms that were evaluated really provided a fair test of the impact constructivism has on student learning and achievement. An even more vexing problem in interpretation, however, is that the two approaches appear to value very different types of outcomes for students. The teacher-centered, fact-based approach values a large quantity of decontextualized skills and facts, whereas the constructivist approach values the acquisition of more particular forms of knowing and acting. In other words, the two approaches seem to be designed to teach very different things. This raises the possibility that deciding between them cannot be done solely by relying on empirical data. Instead, we must decide what outcomes are most valuable for students—large collections of facts and skills or the particular modes of thought and action described by the constructivists. Only when that is decided can empirical research be carried out to determine whether the teacher-centered approach, the constructivist approach, or some other approach is best suited to reaching those outcomes in a timely and cost-effective manner.

Complicating matters further is the fact that both the teacher-centered approach and the constructivist approach are composed of many elements, and it may turn out to be that some elements of each may be most effective. In fact, this possibility has been suggested by a number of cognitive scientists, including David Perkins, codirector of Harvard Project Zero. In an insightful paper, "Teaching for Understanding," *American Educator* (vol. 17, no. 3, 1993), Perkins criticizes the drill-and-practice strategy for not providing students the means of knowing how to apply the facts that they have memorized to solve meaningful problems. At the same time, he acknowledges that deep understanding of any domain of knowledge demands that certain critical facts be mastered, although he stresses that real understanding ultimately requires that students recognize the relationships among these facts. Perkins is also critical of the constructivist approach for underestimating the sophistication of the cognitive capabilities of even the youngest children. This underestimation, he argues, often leads constructivists to withhold material that children could and should master early in their schooling. Perkins further criticizes constructivists for focusing so completely on the concept of hands-on activities that they ignore the possibility that verbal discourse can also be used to actively engage students in the material to be mastered. At the same time, however, he acknowledges that deep understanding of a domain—in the sense of recognizing the relationships among critical facts and being able to apply those facts to solve a range of meaningful problems—requires the active, extended engagement with tasks and materials that is characteristic of the hands-on constructivist approach. Perkins maintains that the goal for students should be deep understanding of the domains of knowledge we value and that this will require an approach that blends elements of both the teacher-centered and the constructivist approach.

Readers interested in learning more about the psychological theories underlying constructivist education should see Leonard Abbeduto and Stephen N. Elliott, *Guide to Human Development for Future Educators* (McGraw-Hill, 1998); "Constructing Scientific Knowledge in the Classroom," by R. Driver et al., *Educational Researcher* (vol. 23, no. 7, 1994); *In Search of Understanding: The Case for Constructivist Classrooms* by Jacqueline G. Brooks and Martin G. Brooks (Association for Supervision & Curriculum Development, 1993); and "Piaget's Equilibration Theory and the Young Gifted Child: A Balancing Act," by Leonora M. Cohen and Younghee M. Kin, *Roeper Review* (1999). Readers interested in reading original papers by developmental psychologist Jean Piaget, from whose work the constructivist approach has grown most directly, can turn to the collection *The Essential Piaget: An Interpretive Reference and Guide* edited by Howard E. Gruber and Jacques J. Voneche (Jason Aronson, 1995). Articles that provide illustrations of constructivist classrooms are "How to Build a Better Mousetrap: Changing the Way Science Is Taught Through Constructivism," by Thomas R. Lord, *Contemporary Education* (Spring 1998); "Constructivist Theory in the Classroom," by Mary M. Bevevino, Joan Dengel, and Kenneth Adams, *The Clearing House* (May/June 1999); and "Constructivism: Science Education's 'Grand Unifying Theory,'" by Alan Colburn, *The Clearing House* (September/October 2000). See also "The Role of Assessment in a Learning Culture," by Lorrie A. Shepard, *Educational Researcher* (October 2000) for an interesting article on the place of assessment in the constructivist classroom.

ISSUE 9

Does Reinforcement Facilitate Learning?

YES: Tashawna K. Duncan, Kristen M. Kemple, and Tina M. Smith, from "Reinforcement in Developmentally Appropriate Early Childhood Classrooms," *Childhood Education* (Summer 2000)

NO: Charles H. Wolfgang, from "Another View on 'Reinforcement in Developmentally Appropriate Early Childhood Classrooms,'" *Childhood Education* (Winter 2000/2001)

ISSUE SUMMARY

YES: Tashawna K. Duncan, Kristen M. Kemple, and Tina M. Smith from the School of Teaching and Learning at the University of Florida, argue that reinforcement has a long history of successful application in the classroom. They dismiss concerns that it lowers intrinsic motivation or that it is ethically equivalent to paying children to learn. They do acknowledge, however, that reinforcement must be integrated with a consideration of the developmental and unique needs of each child.

NO: Charles H. Wolfgang, a professor of early childhood education, admits that reinforcement and other techniques derived from behaviorist theory do control children's behavior in the short term. He asserts, however, that such techniques do little to encourage internalization of the types of standards that will ultimately lead children to behave effectively and appropriately in a range of situations in the future.

During the first half of the twentieth century, American psychology was dominated by *behaviorism*. Although expressed in a number of seemingly distinct theories, the fundamental assumption of behaviorism—that the behavior of any organism is controlled by forces that are external to it—has remained constant across its many manifestations. In Ivan Pavlov's theory of *classical conditioning*, a dog reflexively salivates in response to the sound of a bell that was previously paired with the delivery of food. In B. F. Skinner's theory of *operant conditioning*, a thirsty rat presses a bar when a light flashes because this results in the delivery of a few drops of water. In these examples, the organism's behavior is controlled by some feature of the world around it—the sound of a bell, the flash of light, the delivery of food or water. Despite its apparent complexity and the addition of a conscious mind, behaviorists have traditionally argued that human behavior, like the behavior of animals, is also controlled by external forces.

The influence of behaviorism has extended far beyond academic psychology to include the American classroom. This influence can be traced most directly to the work of Skinner (1904-1990), who emphasized the role of *reinforcement* in his theory of operant conditioning. According to Skinner, an event serves as reinforcement if it is contingent on an organism's response to a stimulus and increases the future likelihood of that response. If, for example, a student who is praised consistently by his teacher for completing assignments on time begins to meet deadlines with increasing frequency over time, the teacher's praise would be a reinforcer. It is important to note that, according to Skinner, we cannot know in advance whether praise, a gold star, a good grade, or any other stimulus will be reinforcing. In fact, he argued that we can only know that something is reinforcing if we observe that it leads to an increase in the target behavior. This was a critical point for Skinner. He felt that all too often teachers, parents, and cognitive psychologists expend too much effort "guessing" about what is going on inside a student's head: Is the student motivated? Will the student see my overture as positive or negative? Because we can never know for sure what is going on in another person's mind, Skinner believed that it is far more productive to analyze the consequences of a student's behavior. In short, according to Skinner, we can control a student's behavior by changing its consequences—removing the reinforcement for behaviors we see as negative and providing reinforcement for behaviors we see as positive.

In recent decades, the dominance of behaviorism in psychology and education has been challenged by *constructivist* approaches. Constructivist approaches envision a more active role for the student in learning, with either his or her mental action on the world or participation in interactions with a more highly skilled partner being the catalyst for change. Perhaps most important, these approaches are based on the belief that the student has a natural curiosity and inclination to try and master the problems posed in and out of the classroom. In constructivist theories, there is no need to posit a role for external reinforcement.

In the following selections, the debate about reinforcement is played out in the context of a discussion about early childhood education. In the first selection, Tashawna K. Duncan, Kristen M. Kemple, and Tina M. Smith side with Skinner and argue that reinforcement is an effective technique for producing positive changes in young children's behavior. They also argue that it is ethically acceptable when integrated into an approach that is sensitive to each child's individual needs and developmental level. In the second selection, Charles H. Wolfgang argues that reinforcement controls children's behavior in the short term but can have long-term negative consequences for child outcomes, including a failure to develop the internal resources needed to inhibit maladaptive behaviors.

Tashawna K. Duncan, Kristen M.
Kemple, and Tina M. Smith

YES

Reinforcement in Developmentally Appropriate Early Childhood Classrooms

Each day from 10:30 to 11:00, the children in Mrs. Kitchens's 1st-grade class-room are expected to sit silently in their desks and copy words from the chalk-board into their notebooks. Children who finish early are required to remain silently in their seats. After five minutes has passed, Mrs. Kitchens assesses whether every child in the class has been behaving according to the rules. If they have been, she makes a check mark on the chalkboard and announces, "Good! There's a check." If even one child has violated the rules, she announces "no check." At the end of the week, if 20 or more checks have accrued on the board, the whole group is awarded an extra-long Friday recess period. This longed-for reward is rarely achieved, however.

Five-year-old Rodney has recently joined Mr. Romero's kindergarten class. On his first day in his new class, Rodney punched a classmate and usurped the tri-cycle the other boy was riding. On Rodney's second day in the class, he shoved a child off a swing and dumped another out of her chair at the snack table. In an effort to deal with Rodney's problematic behavior, Mr. Romero is taking a num-ber of steps, including making sure that Rodney knows the classroom rules and routines, helping Rodney learn language and skills to resolve conflicts, explor-ing ways to make Rodney feel welcome and a special part of the class, and arranging for a consultation with a special education specialist to see if sup-port services would be appropriate. Mr. Romero is concerned for the emotional and physical safety of the other children, and he believes that Rodney will have a hard time making friends if his reputation as an aggressor is allowed to solid-ify. He feels the need to act fast. Deciding that a system of reinforcement, along with other strategies, may help Rodney control his aggressive behavior, Mr. Romero implements a token reinforcement system. Rodney earns a ticket, accompanied by praise, for each 30-minute period during which he does not behave aggressively. At the end of the day, Rodney can trade a specified number of earned tickets for his choice of small toys.

The above examples illustrate two teachers' efforts to use the behavioral strategy of reinforcement—with varying degrees of appropriateness. In Mrs. Kitchens's class, reinforcement is being used as a means to get children to sit still and be quiet in the context of a developmentally inappropriate lesson. In an effort to keep children "on task," Mrs. Kitchens substitutes a control tactic for a meaningful and engaging curriculum. Mr. Romero, on the other hand, is making efforts to identify and address the reasons for Rodney's behavior. Furthermore, he believes that Rodney's behavior is so detrimental to himself and to the other children that additional measures must be used to achieve quick results and restore a sense of psychological safety in the classroom community. Mr. Romero utilizes a variety of strategies in the hopes of creating lasting change in Rodney's behavior.

Inclusion of Children With Special Needs

The trend toward including children with disabilities in early childhood education settings is growing (Wolery & Wilbers, 1994). As greater numbers of children with disabilities participate in early childhood programs, teachers are faced with the challenge of expanding their repertoire of teaching and guidance practices to accommodate the needs of children with diverse abilities and needs. To this end, teachers responsible for the care and education of diverse groups of young children are encouraged to examine their beliefs about their role in promoting children's development and learning, and to explore their understanding of developmentally appropriate practices as outlined by the National Association for the Education of Young Children (NAEYC) (Bredekamp & Copple, 1997).

Recent federal legislation requires that children be educated in the "least restrictive environment." This means that, to the maximum extent possible, the setting in which children with special needs are educated should be the same as that in which typically developing children are educated, and that specialized services should be provided within the regular classroom (Thomas & Russo, 1995).

Early Childhood Education and Early Childhood Special Education

Most early childhood teachers have little or no training in early childhood special education. Historically, differences have existed between teachers who work with young children with disabilities and teachers who work with typically developing children, including different educational preparation, separate professional organizations, and reliance on different bodies of research (Wolery & Wilbers, 1994). As both groups of children are increasingly cared for and educated in the same programs, early childhood educators and early childhood special educators are called upon to work in collaboration to ensure that children receive individually appropriate education. This collaborative effort requires that all teachers have familiarity with and respect for the philosophy and practices of both disciplines.

Historically, early childhood special education has had stronger roots in behavioral psychology and applied behavior analysis than has early childhood education. As Wolery and Bredekamp (1994) noted, developmentally appropriate practices (DAP) (as outlined by NAEYC) have their roots primarily in maturational and constructivist perspectives. While current early childhood special education practices also tend to be rooted in constructivist perspectives, the additional influence of cultural transmission perspectives (including behaviorist models of learning) is evident. Given their diverse origins, it should not be surprising that the two disciplines would advocate, on occasion, different practices (Wolery & Bredekamp, 1994). This potential tension is exemplified in an editor's note found in the recent NAEYC publication *Including Children With Special Needs in Early Childhood Programs* (Wolery & Wilbers, 1994). Carol Copple (the series' editor) stated,

> Certainly early childhood educators are well aware of the limits of behaviorism as the sole approach to children's learning and are wary of overreliance on rewards as a motivational technique. From this vantage point, some readers may have a negative first response to some of the techniques described in this chapter. Although we must be aware of the limitations and pitfalls of such methods, I urge readers to keep an open mind about them.... They are not for every situation, but when used appropriately, they often succeed where other methods fail. (Wolery & Wilbers, 1994, p. 119)

The current authors hope that readers will be open to considering the judicious use of methods of reinforcement described in this article. When included as part of a total developmentally appropriate program and used after careful assessment of individual needs, these methods can be important tools for implementing *individually* appropriate practice.

Developmentally Appropriate Practice

In 1987, NAEYC published *Developmentally Appropriate Practice in Early Childhood Programs Serving Children From Birth to Age 8* (Bredekamp, 1987), which was revised and published in 1997 as *Developmentally Appropriate Practice in Early Childhood Programs* (Bredekamp & Copple, 1997). Many have argued that DAP provides an appropriate educational context for the inclusion of young children with disabilities, assuming that the interpretations of DAP guidelines leave room for adaptations and extensions to meet the child's specific needs (Bredekamp, 1993; Carta, 1995; Carta, Atwater, Schwartz, & McConnell, 1993; Carta, Schwartz, Atwater, & McConnell, 1991; Wolery & Bredekamp, 1994; Wolery, Strain, & Bailey, 1992; Wolery, Werts, & Holcombe-Ligon, 1994). For some young children, this may mean the use of behavioral strategies, such as planned programs of systematic reinforcement. In fact, the current DAP guidelines do not identify reinforcement systems as inappropriate practice. Some early childhood educators, however, view many forms of reinforcement as completely unacceptable. If inclusion is to succeed, it may be necessary for teachers to consider using such strategies for particular children in particular circumstances.

While reinforcement through use of stickers, privileges, and praise is *not* identified as developmentally *inappropriate* practice, it does become inappropriate when used in exclusion of other means of promoting children's engagement and motivation, and when used indiscriminately (for the wrong children, and/or in the wrong situations). Children's active engagement is a guiding principle in both DAP and early childhood special education (Carta et al., 1993). As Carta et al. (1993) have pointed out, however, many young children with disabilities are less likely to engage spontaneously with materials in their environments (Peck, 1985; Weiner & Weiner, 1974). The teacher's active encouragement is needed to help such children become actively involved in learning opportunities. A principal goal of early intervention is to facilitate young children's active engagement with materials, activities, and the social environment through systematic instruction (Wolery et al., 1992). Such instruction may include use of reinforcement as incentives.

Behavioral Strategies in Early Childhood Education

Behavioral theory holds that behaviors acquired and displayed by young children can be attributed almost exclusively to their environment. Several behavioral strategies are employed by early childhood teachers to facilitate children's learning, including the use of praise and external rewards. However, practitioners often fail to identify these strategies in their repertoire and dismiss, out of hand, their use in the classroom. Misunderstandings may exist concerning the appropriate use and potential effectiveness of these strategies for young children. As a result, they are not always well accepted in the early childhood community (Henderick, 1998; Rodd, 1996; see also Strain et al., 1992).

A review of contemporary literature suggests that behavioral strategies are appropriate for creating and maintaining an environment conducive to growth and development (e.g., Peters, Neisworth, & Yawkey, 1985; Schloss & Smith, 1998). Research has demonstrated that behavioral strategies are successful in school settings with various diverse populations, including those with young children (Kazdin, 1994). Furthermore, while many such "best practices" are unrecognized by early childhood professionals, they are grounded in behavioral theory (Strain et al., 1992).

The Use of Positive Reinforcement

Positive reinforcement is perhaps the strategy most palatable to educators who are concerned about the misuse of behavioral strategies. A particular behavior is said to be positively reinforced when the behavior is followed by the presentation of a reward (e.g., praise, stickers) that results in increased frequency of the particular behavior (Schloss & Smith, 1998). For example, Stella has been reluctant to wash her hands before lunch. Mrs. Johnson begins consistently praising Stella when she washes her hands by saying, "Now your hands are nice and clean and ready for lunch!" Stella becomes more likely to wash her hands without protest. In this case, we can say that Stella's handwashing behavior has been positively reinforced.

Most frequently, positive reinforcement strategies are used to teach, maintain, or strengthen a variety of behaviors (Zirpoli, 1995). Although some early childhood teachers may be reluctant to endorse the use of reinforcement, they often unknowingly employ reinforcement strategies every day in their classroom (Henderick, 1998; Wolery, 1994).

Types of Reinforcers

Reinforcers frequently used by teachers generally fall within one of three categories: social, activity, or tangible. These three categories can be viewed along a continuum ranging from least to most intrusive. Social reinforcers are the least intrusive, in that they mimic the natural consequences of positive, prosocial behavior. At the other end of the continuum are tangible reinforcers. Tangible reinforcers involve the introduction of rewards that ordinarily may not be part of the routine. In selecting a reinforcer, the goal is to select the least intrusive reinforcer that is likely to be effective. If reinforcers other than social ones are necessary, teachers should develop a plan to move gradually toward social reinforcers. The following sections describe each category of reinforcers and how they can be used effectively within the context of developmentally appropriate practice.

Social reinforcers.   Teachers employ social reinforcers when they use interpersonal interactions to reinforce behaviors (Schloss & Smith, 1998). Some commonly used social reinforcers include positive nonverbal behaviors (e.g., smiling) and praise (Alberto & Troutman, 1990; Sulzer-Azaroff & Mayer, 1991). Because they are convenient, practical, and can be highly effective, social reinforcers are the most widely accepted and frequently used type of reinforcer in the early childhood classroom (Sulzer-Azaroff & Mayer, 1991). One means of effectively reinforcing a child's behavior via social reinforcement is by using a "positive personal message" (Gordon, 1974; Kostelnik, Stein, Whiren, & Soderman, 1998). For example, Ms. Tarrant says, "Sally, you put the caps back on the markers. I'm pleased. Now the markers won't get dried up. They'll be fresh and ready when someone else wants to use them." This positive personal message reminds Sally of the rule (put the caps on the markers) at a time when Sally has clear and immediate proof that she is able to follow the rule. The personal message pinpoints a specific desirable behavior, and lets the child know why the behavior is appropriate. When used appropriately, social reinforcers have been shown to enhance children's self-esteem (Sulzer-Azaroff & Mayer, 1991). When used in tandem with less natural (e.g., tangible) reinforcers, social reinforcers have been shown to enhance the power of those less natural reinforcers (Sulzer-Azaroff & Mayer, 1991).

Of the various types of social reinforcers, praise is used most frequently and deliberately by teachers (Alberto & Troutman, 1990). In recent years, several articles have been published on the topic of praise (Hitz & Driscoll, 1988; Marshall, 1995; Van der Wilt, 1996). While praise has the potential to enhance children's self-esteem, research has demonstrated that certain kinds of praise may actually lower children's self-confidence, inhibit achievement, and make children reliant on external (as opposed to internal) controls (Kamii, 1984; Stringer & Hurt, 1981, as cited in Hitz & Driscoll, 1988). These authors have drawn distinctions between "effective praise" (sometimes called "encouragement") and "ineffective praise." Effective praise is consistent with commonly held goals of early childhood education: promoting children's positive self-concept, autonomy, self-reliance, and motivation for learning (Hitz & Driscoll, 1988).

Effective praise is specific. Instead of saying, "Justin, what a lovely job you did cleaning up the blocks," Mrs. Constanz says, "Justin, you put each block in its place on the shelf." In this case, Mrs. Constanz leaves judgment about the *quality* of the effort to the child. By pinpointing specific aspects of the child's behavior or product (rather than using vague, general praise), Mrs. Constanz communicates that she has paid attention to, and is genuinely interested in, what the child has done (Hitz & Driscoll, 1988).

Effective praise generally is delivered privately. Public uses of praise, such as, "I like the way Carlos is sitting so quietly," have a variety of disadvantages. Such statements are typically intended to manipulate children into following another child's example. In the example, the message was, "Carlos is doing a better job of sitting than are the rest of you." With time, young children may come to resent this management, and resent a child who is the frequent recipient of such public praise (Chandler, 1981; Gordon, 1974). As an alternative, the teacher could whisper the statement quietly to Carlos, and/or say to the other children, "Think about what you need to do to be ready to listen." As individual children comply, the teacher may quickly acknowledge each child, "Caitlin is ready, Tyler is ready; thank you, Nicholas, Lakeesha, and Ali ..." (Marshall, 1995).

Another characteristic of effective praise is that it emphasizes improvement of process, rather than the finished product. As Daryl passes out individual placemats to his classmates, he states their names. Mrs. Thompson says, "Daryl, you are learning more names. You remembered Tom and Peg today." She could have said, "Daryl, you are a great rememberer," but she chose not to, because Daryl knows that he did not remember everyone's name, and tomorrow he may forget some that he knew today. In this example, Mrs. Thompson's praise is specific and is focused on the individual child's improvement.

Activity reinforcers.   Teachers employ activity reinforcers when they use access to a pleasurable activity as a reinforcer (Sulzer-Azaroff & Mayer, 1991). Some commonly used and effective activity reinforcers include doing a special project, being a classroom helper, and having extra free-choice time (Sulzer-Azaroff & Mayer, 1991). When using activity reinforcers, teachers create a schedule in which an enjoyable activity follows the behavior they are trying to change or modify (Sulzer-Azaroff & Mayer, 1991). Teachers often use such activity reinforcers unknowingly. Following social reinforcers, activity reinforcers are the most frequently used (Alberto & Troutman, 1990), probably because teachers view them as more convenient and less intrusive than tangible reinforcers (Sulzer-Azaroff & Mayer, 1991). When used appropriately, activity reinforcers can modify a wide variety of behaviors. The following examples illustrate the appropriate use of activity reinforcers.

> In Miss Annie's class, a brief playground period is scheduled to follow center clean-up time. Miss Annie reminds the children that the sooner they have the centers cleaned up, the sooner they will be able to enjoy the playground. It appears that the playground time is reinforcing children's quick clean-up behavior: They consistently get the job done with little dawdling.

As part of a total plan to reduce Christopher's habit of using his cupped hands to toss water out of the water table, Mrs. Jackson has told Christopher that each day he plays without throwing water out of the table, he may be table washer after snack time (which Christopher delights in doing). This strategy was implemented following efforts to help Christopher develop appropriate behavior through demonstrations and by redirecting him with water toys chosen specifically to match his interests.

Tangible reinforcers.   Teachers sometimes employ tangible reinforcers, such as stickers and prizes, to strengthen and modify behavior in the early childhood classroom. Tangible reinforcers are most often used to modify and maintain the behavior of children with severe behavior problems (Vaughn, Bos, & Schumm, 1997).

Stacey, who has mild mental retardation, is a member of Miss Hamrick's preschool class. She rarely participates during free-choice activities. Miss Hamrick has tried a variety of strategies to increase Stacey's engagement, including using effective praise, making sure a range of activity options are developmentally appropriate for Stacey, modeling appropriate behaviors, and implementing prompting strategies. None of these strategies appear to work. Aware of Stacey's love of the TV show "Barney," Miss Hamrick decides to award Barney stickers to Stacey when she actively participates. Stacey begins to participate more often in classroom activities.

One major advantage of tangible reinforcers is that they almost always guarantee quick behavioral change (Alberto & Troutman, 1990), even when other strategies (including other types of reinforcers) fail. Although the use of tangible reinforcers can be very effective, their use in early childhood classrooms has been highly controversial. Many early childhood teachers have concerns about the use of tangible reinforcers and believe that they cannot be used appropriately in the early childhood classroom. Such reinforcers often are intrusive, and their effective use requires large amounts of teacher time and commitment.

Given these disadvantages, when using tangible reinforcers teachers should gradually move toward using more intangible, less intrusive reinforcers (Henderick, 1998). Teachers can accomplish this goal by accompanying all tangible reinforcers with social reinforcers (e.g., praise). Later, as children begin to exhibit the desired behavior consistently, the teacher may begin to taper off the use of tangible reinforcers while maintaining the use of social reinforcers. Eventually, the teacher will no longer need to award tangible reinforcers after the desired behavior occurs. In time, the teacher also should be able to fade out the use of social reinforcers, and the children will begin to assume control over their own behaviors.

Questions Frequently Asked About Reinforcement Strategies

The following is a discussion of some of the most common concerns about reinforcement strategies, particularly tangible ones.

Are reinforcers bribes?   Some have described reinforcement strategies as bribery (Kohn, 1993). Kazdin (1975) argues that such characterizations misconstrue the concepts of reinforcement and bribery:

> Bribery refers to the illicit use of rewards, gifts, or favors to pervert judgment or corrupt the conduct of someone. With bribery, reward is used for the purpose of changing behavior, but the behavior is corrupt, illegal or immoral in some way. With reinforcement, as typically employed, events are delivered for behaviors which are generally agreed upon to benefit the client, society, or both. (p. 50)

Kazdin's arguments point to clear distinctions between bribery and giving reinforcement for appropriate behaviors. No one would doubt that receiving pay for work is reinforcing, but few would suggest it is bribery. The difference may lie in the fact that bribes usually are conducted in secret for an improper purpose.

Does the use of reinforcers lower intrinsic motivation?   Intrinsic motivation refers to motivation that comes from within the child or from the activity in which the child is involved. Thus, an intrinsically motivated child would engage in an activity for its own sake (Eisenberger & Cameron, 1996). For example, external rewards frequently are used to motivate children extrinsically.

Some researchers have suggested that the use of reinforcers undermines intrinsic motivation (Kohn, 1993; Lepper & Greene, 1975). Lepper & Greene (1975) conducted a series of experiments on the effects of offering a child a tangible reward to engage in an initially interesting task in the absence of any expectation of external rewards. The results of their experiments suggested that extrinsic rewards can lower intrinsic motivation (Lepper & Greene, 1975). Therefore, when reinforcement is withdrawn after increasing a particular behavior, an individual may engage in an activity less often than before the reinforcement was introduced (Eisenberger & Cameron, 1996). Recent research offers alternative conclusions. After conducting a meta-analysis of over 20 years of research, Cameron and Pierce (1994) concluded that a tangible reward system contingent on performance will not have a negative effect on children's intrinsic motivation. In fact, they propose that external rewards, when used appropriately, can play an invaluable role in increasing children's intrinsic motivation (Cameron & Pierce, 1994, 1996; seel also Eisenberger & Cameron, 1996, 1998).

Although the evidence is still inconclusive, the results do suggest that negative effects of rewards occur under limited conditions, such as giving tangible rewards without regard to performance level. For example, if a teacher rewards a child regardless of performance, the child's intrinsic motivation may diminish for the particular activity. When external rewards are contingent on a child's performance, however, they can be used to enhance the child's intrinsic motivation for the particular activity. This is true because the positive or negative experiences surrounding an activity or task are likely to influence whether the activity is perceived as intrinsically enjoyable or unpleasurable (Eisenberger & Cameron, 1996). Therefore, the authors advocate the use of external reinforcement for behaviors that, for a particular child, are not currently intrinsically reinforcing. For example, children who hit other children to obtain desired toys may find getting what they want to be more intrinsically reinforcing than positive social behavior. In this case, the introduction of external reinforcers for prosocial behavior is unlikely to diminish intrinsic motivation.

By using reinforcement, are teachers "paying" children to learn?   Some argue that rather than being "paid" to behave a certain way or complete certain tasks, children should do these things simply because they are the right thing to do (Harlen, 1996; Schloss & Smith, 1998; Sulzer-Azaroff & Mayer, 1991). Children's individual differences (e.g., ability levels) often require teachers to use a number of strategies to meet each child's individual needs. An important goal of early childhood education is to move children toward behaving appropriately for moral reasons; in other words, "because it is the right thing to do." Strong evidence exists, however, that the behavior of preschoolers and primary grade children is largely controlled by external factors (Bandura, 1986; Walker, deVries, & Trevarthen, 1989). The move from external control to internalized "self-discipline" is only gradually achieved during this age. Adults can help children learn to behave in appropriate ways for moral reasons by combining developmentally appropriate explanations with carefully chosen consequences (see Kostelnik et al., 1998).

Must teachers use reinforcement "equally"?   It is important that early childhood teachers recognize children's unique differences (Bredekamp & Copple, 1997) and structure the early childhood classroom environment so that it meets each child's individual needs. This does not mean, however, that all children will be treated the same or even equally. In fact, the premise that all children should be treated equally is incongruent with developmentally appropriate practices (Zirpoli, 1995; see also Bredekamp & Copple, 1997). Early childhood teachers must recognize that all children are unique and develop at different rates (Bredekamp & Copple, 1997); therefore, some children may require special accommodations.

Using Reinforcers Effectively

Sometimes, reinforcement strategies fail because they are implemented incorrectly. Early childhood teachers should consider general guidelines when using reinforcers in their classroom. Furthermore, the teacher must fully understand the behavior and the function it serves for the child before beginning a reinforcement program.

Once a decision has been made to use reinforcement strategies, teachers must carefully consider implementation to ensure that the strategies are effective and to minimize any potential effects on the child's intrinsic motivation. This process can be viewed as consisting of four states: 1) behavior identification, 2) selection of reinforcers, 3) implementation, 4) and evaluation and fading.

Behavior identification.   In identifying the behavior, it is important to be as clear and objective as possible about the exact nature of the behavior, as well as about the times and settings under which the plan will be implemented. For example, while running in the classroom setting is dangerous, it is an important developmental activity outside the classroom. In order for the strategy to be successful, the child must understand not only "what" is being targeted, but also "when" and "where."

Selection of reinforcers.   The selection of reinforcers is a crucial step, because a successful reinforcer must be more powerful than the intrinsic reward of engaging in the behavior. However, the reinforcement plan also must be as naturalistic as possible. Tangible reinforcers should be used only as a last resort, either because other classes of reinforcers have been unsuccessful or because it is necessary to eliminate a behavior immediately (e.g., ones that are dangerous to the child or others). Social reinforcers should be considered first, by following the guidelines for effective praise. If praise is unsuccessful, teachers may want to consider using an activity reinforcer. One way to select activity reinforcers is to think about the following question: If given complete free choice in the classroom, what would this child choose to do?

Another very important consideration in the selection of reinforcers involves understanding the function that the challenging behavior is serving. For example, many preschoolers engage in challenging behaviors in order to gain attention. If children are not given more appropriate ways to obtain needed attention, the program is unlikely ot be successful.

Implementation.   In the implementation stage, the child receives the reinforcer contingent upon the appropriate behavior. Intitially, the child may need to receive reinforcement very frequently if the challenging behavior occurs frequently. As the child's behavior improves, the time between rewards can be extended. Another strategy is to "shape" the child's behavior, which teachers can do by breaking down the desired behavior into small steps. Each step is then reinforced on each occurrence. Teachers move to the next step only when the previous one is mastered (Schloss & Smith, 1998). Activity or tangible reinforcers should be accompanied by social praise.

Evaluation and fading.   Before beginning the intervention, base line observations need to be made so that any improvement can be systematically evaluated. As the program is implemented, the teacher will want to continue keeping records. As the child's behavior improves, the reinforcement should be phased out. This can be done by reducing the frequency of the reinforcer and beginning to rely on social praise more often than on tangible or activity reinforcers. If the child begins to revert to "bad habits," the program can be adjusted.

When Are Reinforcers Appropriate?

Reinforcement strategies, when used appropriately, can have numerous benefits. They are not, however, a cure-all. In the introductory example, Mrs. Kitchens attempted to use reinforcement as a substitute for appropriate practice. Rather than attempting to rely on reinforcement as a primary means of motivation and management, teachers may incorporate such strategies within the context of a developmentally appropriate program. Use of reinforcement certainly cannot substitute for a teacher establishing a warm, nurturing, and enticing classroom with developmentally appropraite materials, activities, and interactions (Wolery, 1994). Within such developmentally appropriate contexts, reinforcement strategies provide teachers with an effective means to help those children who require additional assistance in meeting particular behavioral, cognitive, and social goals. In all cases, the reinforcement strategy must be ethically definsible, compliant with all relevant school policies (Wolery & Bredekamp, 1994), and consistent with the program's philosophy.

Decisions about individual appropriateness are not always easy to make. Teachers must take into consideration all relevant factors bearing on the appropriateness of the strategy selected. Teachers are better equipped to make these assessments when they have solid knowledge of typical and atypical child development; are well acquainted with the needs, capabilities, and personalities of the children in their care; and are familiar with a wide continuum of strategies. Furthermore, they also must consider the student's familial and cultural experiences, the expectations and experiences of the student's family, and the mores of the society in which the student interacts (Bredekamp & Copple, 1997). The DAP guidelines (Bredekamp & Copple, 1997) emphasize the importance of children's cultural backgrounds. Developmentally appropriate practices should not discriminate against children from diverse backgrounds; rather, they should level the playing field (see Bredekamp & Copple, 1997). Therefore, when considering the use of various reinforcement strategies, teachers must consider the whole child, including his or her abilities, special needs, personality, and cultural background.

When a teacher works with young children who present a broad range of abilities, challenges, and cultural values, it is particularly improtant that he or she be an adaptive and thoughtful problem-solver, while respecting children's individuality. A widened range of acceptable options from which to choose, coupled with a keen sense of individual and situational needs, can empower teachers to make good decisions for a diversity of young children.

References

Alberto, P. A., & Troutman, A.C. (1990). *Applied behavior analysis for teachers* (3rd ed.). Columbus, OH: Merrill.

Bandura, A. (1986). *Social foundations of thought and action: A social cognitive theory.* Englewood Cliffs, NJ: Prentice-Hall.

Bredekamp, S. (1987). *Developmentally appropriate practice in early childhood programs serving children from birth through age eight.* Washington, DC: National Association for the Education of Young Children.

Bredekamp, S. (1993). The relationship between early childhood education and early childhood special education: Healthy marriage or family feud? *Topics in Early Childhood Special Education, 13*(3), 258–273.

Bredekamp, S., & Copple, C. (1997). *Developmentally appropriate practice in early childhood programs* (Rev. ed.). Washington, DC: National Association for the Education of Young Children.

Cameron, J., & Pierce, W. D. (1994). Reinforcement, reward, and intrinsic motivation: A meta-analysis. *Review of Educational Research, 64,* 363–423.

Cameron, J., & Pierce, W. D. (1996). The debate about rewards and intrinsic motivation: A meta-analysis. *Review of Educational Research, 66,* 39–51.

Carta, J. (1995). Developmentally appropriate practice: A critical analysis as applied to young children with disabilities. *Focus on Exceptional Children, 27*(8), 1–14.

Carta, J. J., Atwater, J. B., Schwartz, I. S., & McConnell, S. R. (1993). Developmentally appropriate practices and early childhood special education: A reaction to Johnson & McChesney Johnson. *Topics in Special Education, 13,* 243–254.

Carta, J. J., Schwartz, I. S., Atwater, J. B., & McConnell, S. R. (1991). Developmentally appropriate practice: Appraising its usefulness for young children with disabilities. *Topics in Early Childhood Special Education, 11*(1), 1–20.

Chandler, T. A. (1981). What's wrong with success and praise? *Arithmetic Teacher, 29*(4), 10–12.

Eisenberger, R., & Cameron, J. (1996). Detrimental effects of reward: Reality or myth. *American Psychologist, 51*(11), 1153–1166.

Eisenberger, R., & Cameron, J. (1998). Reward, intrinsic interest, and creativity: New findings. *American Psychologist, 53*(6), 676–679.

Gordon, T. (1974). *Teacher effectiveness training.* New York: Wyden.

Harlen, J. C. (1996). *Behavior management strategies for teachers: Achieving instructional effectiveness, student success, and student motivation; every teacher and every student can!* Springfield, IL: C.C. Thomas.

Henderick, J. (1998). *Total learning: Development curriculum for the young child.* Columbus, OH: Merrill.

Hitz, R., & Driscoll, A. (1988). Praise or encouragement? *Young Children, 43*(5), 6–13.

Kamii, C. (1984). The aim of education envisioned by Piaget. *Phi Delta Kappan, 65*(6), 410–415.

Kazdin, A. E. (1975). *Behavior modification in applied settings.* Pacific Grove, CA: Brooks/Cole.

Kazdin, A. E. (1994). *Behavior modification in applied settings* (5th ed.). Pacific Grove, CA: Brooks/Cole.

Kohn, A. (1993). *Punished by rewards: The trouble with gold stars, incentive plans, A's, praise and other bribes.* New York: Houghton Mifflin.

Kostelnik, M. J., Stein, L. C., Whiren, A. P., & Soderman, A. K. (1998). *Guiding children's social development* (2nd ed.). New York: Delmar.

Lepper, M. R., & Greene, D. (1975). When two rewards are worse than one: Effects of extrinsic rewards on intrinsic motivation. *Phi Delta Kappan, 56*(8), 565–566.

Marshall, H. H. (1995). Beyond "I like the way ..." *Young Children, 50*(2), 26–28.

Peck, C. (1985). Increasing opportunities for social control by children with autism and severe handicaps: effects on student behavior and percieved classroom climate. *Journal of the Association for Persons With Severe Handicaps, 10*(4), 183–193.

Peters, D., Neisworth, J. T., & Yawkey, T. D. (1985). *Early childhood education: From theory to practice.* Monterey, CA: Brooks/Cole.

Rodd, J. (1996). *Understanding young children's behavior: A guide for early childhood professionals.* New York: Teachers College Press.

Schloss, P. J., & Smith, M. A. (1998). *Applied behavior analyses in the classroom* (Rev. ed.). Boston: Allyn and Bacon.

Strain, P. S., McConnell, S. R., Carta, J. J., Fowler, S. A., Neisworth, J. T., & Wolery, M. (1992). Behaviorism in early intervention. *Topics in Early Childhood Special Education, 12*(1), 121–141.

Sulzer-Azaroff, B., & Mayer, G. R. (1991). *Behavior analysis for lasting change.* New York: Harcourt Brace.

Thomas, S. B., & Russo, C. J. (1995). *Special education law: Issues and implications for the 90's.* Topeka, KS: National Organization on Legal Problems of Education.

Van der Wilt, J. (1996). Beyond stickers and popcorn parties. *Dimensions of Early Childhood, 24*(1), 17–20.

Vaughn, S., Bos, C. S., & Schumm, J. S. (1997). *Teaching mainstreamed, diverse, and at-risk students in the general education classroom.* Boston: Allyn and Bacon.

Walker, L. J., DeVries, B., & Trevarthen, S. D. (1989). Moral stages and moral orientations in real-life and hypothetical dilemmas. *Child Development, 58*(3), 842–858.

Weiner, E. A., & Weiner, B. J. (1974). Differentiation of retarded and normal children through toy-play analysis. *Multivariate Behavioral Research, 9*(2), 245–257.

Wolery, M. (1994). *Including children with special needs in early childhood programs.* Washington, DC: National Association for the Education of Young Children.

Wolery, M., & Bredekamp, S. (1994). Developmentally appropriate practices and young children with disabilities: Contextual issues in the discussion. *Journal of Early Intervention, 18,* 331–341.

Wolery, M., Strain, P. S., & Bailey, D. (1992). Reaching potentials of children with special needs. In S. Bredekamp & T. Rosegrant (Eds.), *Reaching potentials: Appropriate curriculum and assessment for young children. Vol. 1* (pp. 92–111). Washington, DC: National Association for the Education of Young Children.

Wolery, M., Werts, M. G., & Holcombe-Ligon, A. (1994). Current practices with young children who have disabilities: Issues in placement, assessment and instruction. *Focus on Exceptional Children, 26*(6), 1–12.

Wolery, M., & Wilbers, J. S. (1994). Introduction to the inclusion of young children with special needs in early childhood programs. In M. Wolery & J. S. Wilbers (Eds.), *Including children with special needs in early childhood programs* (pp. 1–22). Washington, DC: National Association for the Education of Young Children.

Zirpoli, T. J. (1995). *Understanding and affecting the behavior of young children.* Englewood Cliffs, NJ: Merrill.

NO

Charles H. Wolfgang

Another View on "Reinforcement in Developmentally Appropriate Early Childhood Classrooms"

In the Summer 2000 issue of *Childhood Education*, the article written by Tashawna Duncan, Kristen Kemple, and Tina Smith supports reinforcement as a developmentally appropriate practice (Bredekamp & Copple, 1997). In the present article, the author contrasts the Duncan-Kemple-Smith position with another view: How to use developmental theory to inform us of appropriate strategies for dealing with young children in the classroom. The use of behavioral techniques such as reinforcers often can produce desired behavior changes. Behavior modification through the use of reinforcers, however, is a superficial effort to lead the child down the road of development without using the road map of developmental theory, which views the child's actions with regard to developmental constructs.

Let's take the Duncan-Kemple-Smith example. *"Five-year-old Rodney has recently joined Mr. Romero's kindergarten class. On his first day in his new class, Rodney punched a classmate and usurped the tricycle the other boy was riding. On Rodney's second day in the class, he shoved a child on a swing and dumped another out of her chair at the snack table"* (Duncan, Kemple, & Smith, 2000, p. 194). In essence, the authors support behavioral theory and advocate addressing Rodney's negative actions through the use of social reinforcers (e.g., praise, and similar teacher attention), *activity reinforcers* (e.g., earning use of a toy such as a tricycle with "good" behavior), and *tangible reinforcers* (e.g., stickers). Unfortunately, applying reinforcers to extinguish Rodney's "aggression" overlooks the context of how children develop.

The developmentalist, by contrast, would attempt to change Rodney's antisocial behaviors by trying to understand his developmental needs—specifically, what may be causing such behaviors in the first place. As this is Rodney's first day in his new class, the first question for the developmentalist, knowing the literature on attachment and separation fears (Mahler, 1970, 1975; Speers, 1970a, 1970b), would be: Did the teacher help Rodney make a gradual transition from home to school, and allow time for him to bond with his new teacher and become comfortable in this strange new world of the kindergarten classroom? The developmentalists may use supportive actions to help the child make a successful transition (Jervis, 1999). In Rodney's case, the teacher could have made home visits, giving Rodney a chance to meet his teacher on his own "turf"; permitted Rodney to bring a "transitional object" (his cuddle toy or his "Linus" blanket) (Wolfgang & Wolfgang, 1999); and encouraged a parent to stay in the class the first day or two so that Rodney could "wean" himself from parental support.

Developmentalists may, in fact, view Rodney's aggressive actions as *heroic* attempts to get his needs met in a strange new world. The developmentalist might ask: Are there enough tricycles (or similar favorite items) that would permit him to play in parallel form as a developmental step into associative and cooperative play? (Parten, 1971). Or is the playground developmentally appropriate? Are back-and-forth swings, because of the preoperational child's inability to understand movement between states, or states vs. transformations (Piaget & Inhelder, 1958), appropriate at the kindergarten level? Is the organization of snacks and the arrangement of chairs done in such a manner that certain chairs (e.g., those that allow children to sit with the teacher) are favored, thus causing competition? In viewing Rodney's aggressive behaviors, a developmentalist also would ask: Are the environment, procedures, rules, and daily activities developmentally appropriate for this child, especially when we have children with special needs in our classroom?

The teacher who is armed with a repertoire of *social reinforcers, activity reinforcers*, and *tangible reinforcers*, and who uses them daily as the general mode of guidance for children, is missing an opportunity to understand how a child's actions may give us insight into his developmental needs. When we have a medical visit, the doctor says, "Where does it hurt?" We show where the pain is, and the doctor then considers each ailment suggested by pain in that location. Similarly, "punching, pushing, and taking others' possessions" should prompt us to learn about this child's developmental needs, to draw on our knowledge to give meaning to the child's "symptoms," and to use developmentally appropriate practices.

Rather than administering a reinforcer to change the child's behavior, the developmental teacher asks: How does that child separate and bond? Can he cuddle with supportive adults, such as the teacher? How does he eat and handle himself at snack or at rest time? Can he handle demanding activities such as finger painting, water play, or painting? Can he do socio-dramatic play? How do his social skills relate to typical developmental stages? Can he express his needs with words while under pressure in a social situation? (Wolfgang, 1977; Wolfgang & Wolfgang, 1999). These questions can be posed only from within an understanding of certain developmental theories—Mahler's theories of bonding and attachment (1970, 1975), Anna Freud's developmental lines (1968, 1971), play research and theory (Erikson, 1950; Freud, 1968; Peller, 1969; Smilansky, 1969), and Parten's social stages (1971).

Considering Rodney From a Developmentally Appropriate Perspective

Young children who do not feel empowered or do not believe they will get their needs met begin to deal with their world in an automatic, reflexive manner. They may respond through verbal aggression (swearing or using bathroom talk), physical aggression (punching, pushing, and taking others' possessions), or passivity (flat, expressionless behavior accompanied by excessive thumb sucking, masturbation, or even self-abusive activities, such as striking their own head) (Wolfgang, 1977).

Children slowly "learn to be the cause" of events in their world over the first three years of life. The young infant attaches to a significant person, then begins a gradual separation process: first learning causality as a baby by throwing a spoon in order to get others to pick it up, acting upon objects during toddlerhood by opening all the kitchen cabinet doors and banging on pots and pans, and using language to achieve a goal in late toddlerhood by asking mommy for something. Thus, the child becomes socially adaptive. If development went well during these first three years, children will enter kindergarten expecting the best, with the confidence that they can master what lies before them. If this development has not gone well, they may enter kindergarten as Rodney did—by "punching, pushing, and taking others' possessions."

In behavioral theory, we address children's inappropriate behavior by moving away when the child acts out; otherwise, we would be reinforcing the behavior by attending to them. For example, we may ignore a child when he cries, in an effort to eliminate the crying. Developmentalists take just the opposite approach. The kindergarten teacher's first goal should be to rebond with Rodney, then gradually teach him to channel his energy (aggression is simply misdirected energy) from the body to the toy, from the toy to play, and from play to work (Freud, 1968).

On the third day of school, the developmental teacher would direct Rodney into a host of activities that permit him to divert his aggression (energy) from his body into the toy (pounding at the carpentry table, pounding with clay, or pursuing aggressive play themes in the safe, make-believe world of small animal toys). At the same time, the teacher would attempt to bond with Rodney (even to the point of cuddling him), so that he would begin to realize that he can depend on this caring adult to help get what he needs (Wolfgang, 1977; Wolfgang & Wolfgang, 1999).

Instead of permitting Rodney to have the tricycle after he goes for a period of time without pushing or hitting as a reinforcement (*activity reinforcers*), the developmental teacher might allow Rodney to use a tricycle whenever he wants, because it is an excellent outlet for his energy. Thus, Rodney can transfer his aggression from other children to the toy. The teacher may tape his picture or name to a chair at snack time so that he will know that this seat will always be reserved for him, and thus know that he does not need to fight for one.

Next, after Rodney has aggressively used the carpentry equipment, clay, or the make-believe rubber animal toys (such as lions and tigers), the teacher would help him cross the bridge into "making something" with the clay, or "making a story" with the animals. He then will move from the toy to play. Once he learns isolated play (Parten, 1971), the teacher can encourage others to join him; he will then move from parallel to associative play, and then to cooperative play (Smilansky, 1968; Smilansky & Shefatya, 1990), whereby he becomes a role-player with others and practices the social skills of give-and-take.

Rodney pushes, shoves, and hits because he does not yet have the social skills to work with others and to get his needs met. Reinforcing "good" behavior does not teach him the developmental skills he needs to function. Through role-play (as in socio-dramatic play), the child moves from isolated play into cooperation with others, which requires sophisticated social and language skills. Rodney, through such play, would be empowered and, therefore, would not need the teacher reinforcements, or control. He can develop effective adaptive skills.

As part of their advice for Rodney's teacher, Duncan, Kemple, and Smith write, *"Mr. Romero is concerned for the emotional and physical safety of the other children, and he believes that Rodney will have a hard time making friends if his reputation as an aggressor is allowed to solidify. He feels the need to act fast. Deciding that a system of reinforcement, along with other strategies, may help Rodney control his aggressive behavior, Mr. Romero implements a token reinforcement system. Rodney earns a ticket, accompanied by praise, for each 30-minute period during which he does not behave aggressively. At the end of the day, Rodney can trade a specified number of earned tickets for his choice of small toys"* (p. 194).

While it is certainly necessary to protect the other children and ensure fairness, the authors' advice fails to incorporate developmentally appropriate practice. At circle time, and possibly even before Rodney has arrived, a teacher using a developmentalist approach would have discussed Rodney's arrival with the other kindergarten children to help them develop empathy for Rodney, who is, after all, getting accustomed to a new place. The teacher could ask the children to think about how Rodney might feel, why he might push and shove and take other children's toys, and why the teacher might need to do special things for this new person. Young children can understand these concepts, and as they watch the developmental teacher guiding the "misbehaving" child they will become secure in the knowledge that the teacher will not punish them for similar actions. Thus, they can learn to master their own aggressive impulses as they watch Rodney strive for self-control and social skills.

The Duncan-Kemple-Smith article includes a short review of studies (e.g., Schloss & Smith, 1998; Zirpoli, 1995) demonstrating that reinforcers are effective in eliminating unwanted behaviors in early childhood settings. It is often true that behavioral techniques are powerful and effective when they are used with the narrow goal of changing a particular behavior. These brief targeted studies, however, do not answer the following questions: Should this behavior be extinguished? What caused the behavior in the first place? What are the new behaviors that result when this behavior is extinguished? There is no doubt that an experienced behavioral teacher using reinforcers can extinguish Rodney's aggression.

What happens, however, if we return the next month to observe Rodney and find that new problem behaviors have developed? In short, targeting one behavior obscures the perspective on the dynamic aspect of human behavior and the interdependence of social, emotional, and cognitive development. When we narrow our view of children's growth to one observable behavior, we lose the holistic view of the child.

Another Look at Specific Behavioral Techniques

In light of recommended developmentally appropriate practices, behavioral constructs of reinforcement raise some concerns.

Social Reinforcers   (e.g., praise and similar teacher attention). The narrow behavioral nature of a social reinforcer, such as teacher praise and attention, boxes the teacher into scripted behavior when used with young children. Teacher attention toward the child should be based on the teacher's insights into, and empathy with, the child's real development needs, as well as on an understanding of the necessary steps for the child to gradually gain autonomy.

Activity Reinforcers   (e.g., earning use of a toy with "good" behavior). In a developmental classroom, there are no activities, materials, and toys that are considered "treats." Instead, these items and processes are basic to the educational developmental model itself. One example of activity reinforcers from the Duncan, Kemple, and Smith article shows the teacher reminding the children that they must first clean up before they are permitted to go out to the playground. No one can disagree with the need to teach young children to clean up; with a child like Rodney, however, cleaning up will only come after he has become a co-player and a worker with others. This will take time. He should never be barred from a play activity, especially during his first days of kindergarten. Following the developmental construct of Anna Freud (1968), activities on the playground, with the guidance of an informed developmental teacher, are exactly what Rodney needs to help him gain control of his own behavior and attain true maturity. The developmentally appropriate classroom does not use toys, materials, and activities as "activity treats" or *activity reinforcers*; all toys, materials, and activities are there to contribute to children's development.

Tangible Reinforcers   (e.g., stickers). One kindergarten teacher once stated, "My students would kill for a sticker." Because Rodney does not yet have the developmental social skills to function at an age-appropriate level, he will miss out on such tangible reinforcers as stickers and feel resentment and anger toward those who do receive them. In fact, Rodney may push and hit to get a sticker. The use of stickers as a tangible reinforcer may achieve short-term success, but bring about unintended, long-term consequences for the children who do not, as yet, have the social skills to merit the reward.

Conclusion

The behavioral constructs of social reinforcers, activity reinforcers, and tangible reinforcers can be learned quickly by beginning teachers of young children, provide them with feelings of empowerment and control, and may help, in the short term, to curb children's aggressive behavior. It may be helpful, however, to view aggression from a developmental point of view—as children's attempts to adapt to new situations. Behavioral techniques that shape and change children's surface behaviors without placing these behaviors within a developmental context may, in the long run, interfere with the child's developmental needs and cause much harm.

References

Bredekamp, S., & Copple, C. (1997). *Developmentally appropriate practice in early childhood programs* (Rev. ed.). Washington, DC: National Association for the Education of Young Children.

Duncan, T. K., Kemple, K. M., & Smith, T. M. (2000). Reinforcement in developmentally appropriate early childhood classrooms. *Childhood Education, 76,* 194–203.

Erikson, E. (1950). *Childhood and society.* New York: Norton Press.

Freud, A. (1968). *Normality and pathology in childhood: Assessments of development.* New York: International Universities Press.

Freud, A. (1971). *The ego and the mechanisms of defense.* New York: International Universities Press.

Jervis, K. (1999). *Separation: Strategies for helping two- to four-year-olds.* Washington, DC: National Association for the Education of Young Children.

Mahler, M. S. (1970). *On human symbiosis and the vicissitudes of individuation.* New York: International Universities Press.

Mahler, M. S. (1975). *The psychological birth of the human infant.* New York: Basic Books.

Parten, M. B. (1971). Social play among preschool children. In R. E. Herron & B. Sutton-Smith (Eds.), *Child's play* (pp. 83–95). New York: John Wiley & Sons.

Peller, L. E. (1969). Libidinal phases, ego development and play. In *Psychoanalytic study of the child, no. 9* (pp. 178–197). New York: International Universities Press.

Piaget, J., & Inhelder, B. (1958). *The growth of logical thinking: From childhood to adolescence.* New York: Basic Books.

Smilansky, S. (1969). *The effects of sociodramatic play on disadvantaged preschool children.* New York: John Wiley & Sons.

Smilansky, S. J., & Shefatya, L. (1990). *Facilitating play: Medium for promoting cognitive, social-emotional and academic development in young children.* Gaithersburg, MD: Psychosocial & Educational Publishing.

Speers, R. W. (1970a). Recapitulation of separation-individuation processes when the normal three-year-old enters nursery school. In J. McDevitt (Ed.), *Separation-individuation: Essays in honor of Margaret Mahler* (pp. 38–67). New York: International Universities Press.

Speers, R. W. (1970b). *Variations in Separation—Individuation and implications for play abilities and learning as studied in the three-year-old in nursery school.* Pittsburgh, PA: University of Pittsburgh Press.

Wolfgang, C. H. (1977). *Helping aggressive and passive preschoolers through play.* Columbus, OH: Charles E. Merrill Publishing.

Wolfgang, C. H., & Wolfgang, M. E. (1999). *School for young children: Developmentally appropriate practices.* Boston: Allyn and Bacon.

POSTSCRIPT

Does Reinforcement Facilitate Learning?

It is perhaps surprising to many readers that there is still controversy about the effectiveness of reinforcement. After all, haven't psychologists been studying reinforcement for nearly a century? And haven't parents, teachers, and other adults been using rewards (and punishments) in one form or another to control children's behavior for even longer? Why, then, have we failed to answer the question, Does reinforcement facilitate learning? In part, it has been difficult to answer this question because, when we carefully analyze the concept of reinforcement, it turns out to be a bit slippery. Recall that, according to B. F. Skinner, it cannot be known whether or not a stimulus or an event is a reinforcer prior to observing its effects on an individual's behavior. We may have hunches or educated guesses about what a child might find reinforcing—money, a gold star, candy, a special outing—but we cannot know for certain until we observe the desired changes in the child's behavior. If we do not observe those changes, we may have guessed wrong and need to try some other stimulus or event. At first glance, this seems reasonable. Suppose, however, that we test another potential reinforcer, and another, and another, and still do not observe the desired change in behavior. Should we search indefinitely for the reinforcer? Or might it be that the behavior in question is controlled less by factors that are external to the child and more by internal factors, such as the child's interests, motives, and inclinations? This is the dilemma that many parents, teachers, and researchers face at one time or another. Unfortunately, there is no empirical means of determining whether we should keep searching for a reinforcer or whether the behavior in question is controlled by internal factors. As a result, some scholars, practitioners, and even parents adhere almost religiously to a belief in the power of reinforcement, whereas others dismiss reinforcement as a useless and, perhaps, even morally offensive concept.

Readers interested in pursuing the topic of reinforcement can turn to a number of excellent summaries of behaviorist theories, including *An Introduction to Theories of Learning*, 6th ed., by B. R. Hergenhan and Matthew H. Olson (Prentice Hall, 2001). A critique of reinforcement and its many manifestations in the classroom can be found in Alfie Kohn's *Punished by Rewards: The Trouble With Gold Stars, Incentive Plans, A's, and Other Bribes* (Houghton Mifflin, 1993) and *Beyond Discipline: From Compliance to Community* (Association for Supervision and Curriculum Development, 1996). Interesting discussions on the issue of grades as reinforcement can be found in "Let's End the Grading Game," by Clifford Edwards and Laurie Edwards, *The Clearing House* (May-June 1999) and "Can Grades Be Helpful and Fair?" by Dennis Munk and William Bursuck, *Educational Leadership* (December 1997/January 1998).

ISSUE 10

Can Howard Gardner's Theory of Multiple Intelligences Transform Educational Practice?

YES: Howard Gardner, from "Reflections on Multiple Intelligences: Myths and Messages," *Phi Delta Kappan* (November 1995)

NO: Perry D. Klein, from "Multiplying the Problems of Intelligence by Eight: A Critique of Gardner's Theory," *Canadian Journal of Education* (vol. 22, no. 4, 1997)

ISSUE SUMMARY

YES: Howard Gardner, a professor in the Graduate School of Education at Harvard University, discusses what he considers to be seven misunderstandings, or myths, that have surrounded his theory of multiple intelligences. He also discusses the implications of the theory for educational practice.

NO: Perry D. Klein, a member of the Faculty of Education at the University of Western Ontario, argues that although a number of diverse pedagogical practices have been inspired by Gardner's theory, the theory is really too broad to be particularly informative about education.

For the better part of the twentieth century, scholars, policymakers, and laypeople have debated the nature of intelligence. This issue considers one theory of the nature of intelligence that has been embraced by educators around the United States; namely, the theory of multiple intelligences proposed by Howard Gardner.

The centerpiece of Gardner's theory is the idea of independent domains (components, or modules) of cognitive ability, which he refers to as frames of mind. Gardner has proposed that there are seven (possibly eight or more) intelligences. These are separate areas of ability in the sense that a person can do well in one area but not in another. In fact—although Gardner relies on other forms of evidence as well—the most compelling evidence supporting the existence of independent intelligences comes from cases of people with special talents (e.g., musical prodigies who are otherwise "average") or with a circumscribed loss or limitation of abilities (e.g., savants, who are highly skilled painters, musicians, etc., despite having autism, mental retardation, or another pervasive disability). The intelligences proposed by Gardner include the linguistic, spatial, and logical-mathematical. These are the forms of intelligence that are most directly assessed by IQ tests, such as the Stanford-Binet. Also included on Gardner's list, however, are less traditional intelligences: bodily-kinesthetic, musical, interpersonal, intrapersonal, and the recently proposed intelligence of the naturalist. These latter intelligences are unlikely to be measured in a meaningful way by current IQ tests.

Gardner's theory has inspired calls for dramatic changes in education. Here are but a few examples of the changes called for in the name of the theory of multiple intelligences:

1. Education has focused too narrowly on tasks that fall within the linguistic and logical-mathematic intelligences. The scope of education should be expanded to value and nurture the development of the other intelligences as well.
2. Recent calls for a return to "basic skills" will only lead to a further narrowing of the scope of education and will marginalize many children whose talents fall within Gardner's nontraditional intelligences.
3. Evaluations of each intelligence should be made regularly so as to measure the effectiveness of educational efforts. Traditional psychometric methods of assessment are likely to be inadequate and should be replaced by more product-oriented methods, such as student portfolios of their classroom work.
4. Education must extend beyond the classroom and include nontraditional experiences, such as apprenticeships, mentorships, and participation in community-based volunteer programs.
5. Education should be structured to allow students to make discoveries on their own and to construct their own knowledge. A teacher-centered, fact-based, drill-and-practice approach bypasses the discovery process and, thus, is to be avoided.
6. Students may differ in how they approach the same academic content. Those differences should be honored and even encouraged.

Although the response from educators has been largely positive, some have been critical of Gardner's claims and have wondered whether or not the theory really has any significant implications for educational practice. The two selections that follow take very different views about the educational importance of the theory. In the first selection, Gardner discusses the implications of his theory for educational practice, although he warns that considerable work remains to be done in translating the theory into a set of prescriptions for the classroom. In the second selection, Perry D. Klein argues that although a number of diverse pedagogical practices have been inspired by Gardner's theory, the theory is really too broad to be particularly informative about education.

Howard Gardner

 **YES**

Reflections on Multiple Intelligences: Myths and Messages

A silence of a decade's length is sometimes a good idea. I published *Frames of Mind*, an introduction to the theory of multiple intelligences (MI theory) in 1983.[1] Because I was critical of current views of intelligences within the discipline of psychology, I expected to stir controversy among my fellow psychologists. This expectation was not disappointed.

I was unprepared for the large and mostly positive reaction to the theory among educators. Naturally I was gratified by this response and was stimulated to undertake some projects exploring the implications of MI theory. I also took pleasure from—and was occasionally moved by—the many attempts to institute an MI approach to education in schools and classrooms. By and large, however, except for a few direct responses to criticisms,[2] I did not speak up about new thoughts concerning the theory itself.

In 1993 my self-imposed silence was broken in two ways. My publisher issued a 10th-anniversary edition of *Frames of Mind*, to which I contributed a short, reflective introductory essay. In tandem with that release, the publisher issued *Multiple Intelligences: The Theory in Practice*, a set of articles chronicling some of the experiments undertaken in the wake of MI theory—mostly projects pursued by colleagues at Harvard Project Zero, but also other MI initiatives.[3] This collection gave me the opportunity to answer some other criticisms leveled against MI theory and to respond publicly to some of the most frequently asked questions.

In the 12 years since *Frames of Mind* was published, I have heard, read, and seen several hundred different interpretations of what MI theory is and how it can be applied in the schools.[4] Until now, I have been content to let MI theory take on a life of its own. As I saw it, I had issued an "ensemble of ideas" (or "memes") to the outer world, and I was inclined to let those "memes" fend for themselves.[5] Yet, in light of my own reading and observations, I believe that the time has come for me to issue a set of new "memes" of my own.

In the next part of this article, I will discuss seven myths that have grown up about multiple intelligences and, by putting forth seven complementary "realities," I will attempt to set the record straight. Then, in the third part of the article, reflecting on my observations of MI experiments in the schools, I will describe three primary ways in which education can be enhanced by a multiple intelligences perspective.

In what follows, I make no attempt to isolate MI theory from MI practice. "Multiple intelligences" began as a theory but was almost immediately put to practical use. The commerce between theory and practice has been ready, continuous, and, for the most part, productive.

Myths of Multiple Intelligences

Myth 1. *Now that seven intelligences have been identified, one can—and perhaps should—create seven tests and secure seven scores.*

Reality 1. MI theory represents a critique of "psychometrics-as-usual." A battery of MI tests is inconsistent with the major tenets of the theory.

Comment. My concept of intelligences is an outgrowth of accumulating knowledge about the human brain and about human cultures, not the result of a priori definitions or of factor analyses of tests cores. As such, it becomes crucial that intelligences be assessed in ways that are "intelligent-fair," that is, in ways that examine the intelligence directly rather than through the lens of linguistic or logical intelligence (as ordinary paper-and-pencil tests do).

Thus, if one wants to look at spatial intelligence, one should allow an individual to explore a terrain for a while and see whether she can find her way around it reliably. Or if one wants to examine musical intelligence, one should expose an individual to a new melody in a reasonably familiar idiom and see how readily the person can learn to sing it, recognize it, transform it, and the like.

Assessing multiple intelligences is not a high priority in every setting. But when it is necessary or advisable to assess an individual's intelligences, it is best to do so in a comfortable setting with materials (and cultural roles) that are familiar to that individual. These conditions are at variance with our general conception of testing as a decontextualized exercise using materials that are unfamiliar by design, but there is no reason in principle why an "intelligence-fair" set of measures cannot be devised. The production of such useful tools has been our goal in such projects as Spectrum, Arts PROPEL, and Practical Intelligence for School.[6]

Myth 2. *An intelligence is the same as a domain or a discipline.*

Reality 2. An intelligence is a new kind of construct, and it should not be confused with a domain or a discipline.

Comment. I must shoulder a fair part of the blame for the propagation of the second myth. In writing *Frames of Mind*, I was not as careful as I should have been in distinguishing intelligences from other related concepts. As I have now come to understand, largely through my interactions with Mihaly Csikszentmihalyi and David Feldman,[7] an intelligence is a biological and psychological potential; that potential is capable of being realized to a greater or lesser extent as a consequence of the experiential, cultural, and motivational factors that affect a person.

In contrast, a *domain* is an organized set of activities within a culture, one typically characterized by a specific symbol system and its attendant operations. Any cultural activity in which individuals participate on more than a casual basis, and in which degrees of expertise can be identified and nurtured, should be considered a domain. Thus, physics, chess, gardening, and rap music are all domains in Western culture. Any domain can be realized through the use of several intelligences; thus the domain of musical performance involves bodily-kinesthetic and personal as well as musical intelligences. By the same token, a particular intelligence, like spatial intelligence, can be put to work in a myriad of domains, ranging from sculpture to sailing to neuroanatomical investigations.

Finally, a *field* is the set of individuals and institutions that judge the acceptability and creativity of products fashioned by individuals (with their characteristic intelligences) within established or new domains. Judgments of quality cannot be made apart from the operation of members of a field, though it is worth noting that both the members of a field and the criteria that they employ can and do change over time.

Myth 3. *An intelligence is the same as a "learning style," a "cognitive style," or a "working style."*

Reality 3. The concept of style designates a general approach that an individual can apply equally to every conceivable content. In contrast, an *intelligence* is a capacity, with its component processes, that is geared to a specific content in the world (such as musical sounds or spatial patterns).

Comment. To see the difference between an intelligence and a style, consider this contrast. If a person is said to have a "reflective" or an "intuitive" style, this designation assumes that the individual will be reflective or intuitive with all manner of content, ranging from language to music to social analysis. However, such an assertion reflects an empirical assumption that actually needs to be investigated. It might well be the case that an individual is reflective with music but fails to be reflective in a domain that requires mathematical thinking or that a person is highly intuitive in the social domain but not in the least intuitive when it comes to mathematics or mechanics.

In my view, the relation between my concept of intelligence and the various conceptions of style needs to be worked out empirically, on a style-by-style basis. We cannot assume that "style" means the same thing to Carl Jung, Jerome Kagan, Tony Gregoric, Bernice McCarthy, and other inventors of stylistic terminology.[8] There is little authority for assuming that an individual who evinces a style in one milieu or with one content will necessarily do so with other diverse contents—and even less authority for equating styles with intelligences.

Myth 4. *MI theory is not empirical. (A variant of Myth 4 alleges that MI theory is empirical but has been disproved.)*

Reality 4. MI theory is based wholly on empirical evidence and can be revised on the basis of new empirical findings.

Comment. Anyone who puts forth Myth 4 cannot have read *Frames of Mind.* Literally hundreds of empirical studies were reviewed in that book, and the actual intelligences were identified and delineated on the basis of empirical findings. The seven intelligences described in *Frames of Mind* represented my best-faith effort to identify mental abilities of a scale that could be readily discussed and critiqued.

No empirically based theory is ever established permanently. All claims are at risk in the light of new findings. In the last decade, I have collected and reflected on empirical evidence that is relevant to the claims of MI theory, 1983 version. Thus work on the development in children of a "theory of mind," as well as the study of pathologies in which an individual loses a sense of social judgment, has provided fresh evidence for the importance and independence of interpersonal intelligence.[9] In contrast, the finding of a possible link between musical and spatial thinking has caused me to reflect on the possible relations between faculties that had previously been thought to be independent.[10]

Many other lines of evidence could be mentioned here. The important point is that MI theory is constantly being reconceptualized in terms of new findings from the laboratory and from the field (see also Myth 7).

Myth 5. MI theory is incompatible with g (general intelligence),[11] with hereditarian accounts, or with environmental accounts of the nature and causes of intelligence.

Reality 5. MI theory questions not the existence but the province and explanatory power of *g.* By the same token, MI theory is neutral on the question of heritability of specific intelligences, instead underscoring the centrality of genetic/environmental interactions.

Comment. Interest in *g* comes chiefly from those who are probing scholastic intelligence and those who traffic in the correlations between test scores. (Recently people have become interested in the possible neurophysiological underpinnings of *g*[12] and, sparked by the publication of *The Bell Curve,*[13] in the possible social consequences of "low *g.*") While I have been critical of much of the research in the *g* tradition, I do not consider the study of *g* to be scientifically improper, and I am willing to accept the utility of g for certain theoretical purposes. My interest, obviously, centers on those intelligences and intellectual processes that are not covered by *g.*[14]

While a major animating force in psychology has been the study of the heritability of intelligence(s), my inquiries have not been oriented in this direction. I do not doubt that human abilities—and human differences—have a genetic base. Can any serious scientist question this at the end of the 20th century? And I believe that behavioral genetic studies, particularly of twins reared apart, can illuminate certain issues.[15] However, along with most biologically informed scientists, I reject the "inherited versus learned" dichotomy and instead stress the interaction, from the moment of conception, between genetic and environmental factors.

Myth 6. MI theory so broadens the notion of intelligence that it includes all psychological constructs and thus vitiates the usefulness, as well as the usual connotation, of the term.

Reality 6. This statement is simply wrong. I believe that it is the standard definition of intelligence that narrowly constricts our view, treating a certain form of scholastic performance as if it encompassed the range of human capacities and leading to disdain for those who happen not to be psychometrically bright. Moreover, I reject the distinction between talent and intelligence; in my view, what we call "intelligence" in the vernacular is simply a certain set of "talents" in the linguistic and/or logical-mathematical spheres.

Comment. MI theory is about the intellect, the human mind in its cognitive aspects. I believe that a treatment in terms of a number of semi-independent intelligences presents a more sustainable conception of human thought than one that posits a single "bell curve" of intellect.

Note, however, that MI theory makes no claims whatsoever to deal with issues beyond the intellect. MI theory is not, and does not pretend to be, about personality, will, morality, attention, motivation, and other psychological constructs. Note as well that MI theory is not connected to any set of morals or values. An intelligence can be put to an ethical or an antisocial use. Poet and playwright Johann Wolfgang von Goethe and Nazi propagandist Joseph Goebbels were both masters of the German language, but how different were the uses to which they put their talents!

Myth 7. *There is an eighth (or ninth or 10th) intelligence.*

Reality 7. Not in my writings so far. But I am working on it.

Comment. For the reasons suggested above, I thought it wise not to attempt to revise the principal claims of MI theory before the 1983 version of the theory had been debated. But recently, I have turned my attention to possible additions to the list. If I were to rewrite *Frames of Mind* today, I would probably add an eighth intelligence—the intelligence of the naturalist. It seems to me that the individual who is able readily to recognize flora and fauna, to make other consequential distinctions in the natural world, and to use this ability productively (in hunting, in farming, in biological science) is exercising an important intelligence and one that is not adequately encompassed in the current list. Individuals like Charles Darwin or E. O. Wilson embody the naturalist's intelligence, and, in our consuming culture, youngsters exploit their naturalist's intelligence as they make acute discriminations among cars, sneakers, or hairstyles.

I have read in several secondary sources that there is a spiritual intelligence and, indeed, that I have endorsed a spiritual intelligence. That statement is not true. It is true that I have become interested in understanding better what is meant by "spirituality" and by "spiritual individuals"; as my understanding improves, I expect to write about this topic. Whether or not it proves appropriate to add "spirituality" to the list of intelligences, this human capacity certainly deserves discussion and study in nonfringe psychological circles.

Messages About MI in the Classroom

If one were to continue adding myths to the list, a promising candidate would read: There is a single educational approach based on MI theory.

I trust that I have made it clear over the years that I do not subscribe to this myth.[16] On the contrary, MI theory is in no way an educational prescription. There is always a gulf between psychological claims about how the mind works and educational practices, and such a gulf is especially apparent in a theory that was developed without specific educational goals in mind. Thus, in educational discussions, I have always taken the position that educators are in the best position to determine the uses to which MI theory can and should be put.

Indeed, contrary to much that has been written, MI theory does not incorporate a "position" on tracking, gifted education, interdisciplinary curricula, the layout of the school day, the length of the school year, or many other "hot button" educational issues. I have tried to encourage certain "applied MI efforts," but in general my advice has echoed the traditional Chinese adage "Let a hundred flowers bloom." And I have often been surprised and delighted by the fragrance of some of these fledgling plants—for example, the use of a "multiple intelligences curriculum" in order to facilitate communication between youngsters drawn from different cultures or the conveying of pivotal principles in biology or social studies through a dramatic performance designed and staged by students.

I have become convinced, however, that while there is no "right way" to conduct a multiple intelligences education, some current efforts go against the spirit of my formulation and embody one or more of the myths sketched above. Let me mention a few applications that have jarred me.

- *The attempt to teach all concepts or subjects using all the intelligences.* As I indicate below, most topics can be powerfully approached in a number of ways. But there is no point in assuming that every topic can be effectively approached in at least seven ways, and it is a waste of effort and time to attempt to do this.
- *The belief that it suffices, in and of itself, just to go through the motions of exercising a certain intelligence.* I have seen classes in which children are encouraged simply to move their arms or to run around, on the assumption that exercising one's body represents in itself some kind of MI statement. Don't read me as saying that exercise is a bad thing; it is not. But random muscular movements have nothing to do with the cultivation of the mind ... or even of the body!
- *The use of materials associated with an intelligence as background.* In some classes, children are encouraged to read or to carry out math exercises while music is playing in the background. Now I myself like to work with music in the background. But unless I focus on the performance (in which case the composition is no longer serving as background), the music's function is unlikely to be different from that of a dripping faucet or a humming fan.
- *The use of intelligences primarily as mnemonic devices.* It may well be the case that it is easier to remember a list if one sings it or even if one dances while reciting it. I have nothing against such aids to memory. However, these uses of the materials of an intelligence are essentially trivial. What is not trivial—as I argue below—is to think musically or to

draw on some of the structural aspects of music in order to illuminate concepts like biological evolution or historical cycles.

- *The conflating of intelligences with other desiderata.* This practice is particularly notorious when it comes to the personal intelligences. Interpersonal intelligence has to do with understanding other people, but it is often distorted as a license for cooperative learning or applied to individuals who are extroverted. Intrapersonal intelligence has to do with understanding oneself, but it is often distorted as a rationale for self-esteem programs or applied to individuals who are loners or introverted. One receives the strong impression that individuals who use the terms in this promiscuous way have never read my writings on intelligence.

- *The direct evaluation (or even grading) of intelligences, without regard to context or content.* Intelligences ought to be seen at work when individuals are carrying out productive activities that are valued in a culture. And that is how reporting of learning and mastery in general should take place. I see little point in grading individuals in terms of how "linguistic" or how "bodily-kinesthetic" they are; such a practice is likely to introduce a new and unnecessary form of tracking and labeling. As a parent (or as a supporter of education living in the community), I am interested in the uses to which children's intelligences are put; reporting should have this focus.

Note that it is reasonable, for certain purposes, to indicate that a child seems to have a relative strength in one intelligence and a relative weakness in another. However, these descriptions should be mobilized in order to help students perform better in meaningful activities and perhaps even to show that a label was premature or erroneous.

Having illustrated some problematic applications of MI theory, let me now indicate three more positive ways in which MI can be—and has been—used in the schools.

1. The cultivation of desired capabilities. Schools should cultivate those skills and capacities that are valued in the community and in the broader society. Some of these desired roles are likely to highlight specific intelligences, including ones that have usually been given short shrift in the schools. If, say, the community believes that children should be able to perform on a musical instrument, then the cultivation of musical intelligence toward that end becomes a value of the school. Similarly, emphasis on such capacities as taking into account the feelings of others, being able to plan one's own life in a reflective manner, or being able to find one's way around an unfamiliar terrain are likely to result in an emphasis on the cultivation of interpersonal, intrapersonal, and spatial intelligences respectively.

2. Approaching a concept, subject matter, or discipline in a variety of ways. Along with many other school reformers, I am convinced that schools attempt to cover far too much material and that superficial understandings (or nonunderstandings) are the inevitable result. It makes far more sense to spend a significant amount of time on key concepts, generative ideas, and essential questions and to allow students to become thoroughly familiar with these notions and their implications.

Once the decision has been made to dedicate time to particular items, it then becomes possible to approach those topics or notions in a variety of ways. Not necessarily seven ways, but in a number of ways that prove pedagogically appropriate for the topic at hand. Here is where MI theory comes in. As I argue in *The Unschooled Mind*, nearly every topic can be approached in a variety of ways, ranging from the telling of a story, to a formal argument, to an artistic exploration, to some kind of "hands-on" experiment or simulation. Such pluralistic approaches should be encouraged.[17]

When a topic has been approached from a number of perspectives, three desirable outcomes ensue. First, because children do not all learn in the same way, more children will be reached. I term this desirable state of affairs "multiple windows leading into the same room." Second, students secure a sense of what it is like to be an expert when they behold that a teacher can represent knowledge in a number of different ways and discover that they themselves are also capable of more than a single representation of a specified content. Finally, since understanding can also be demonstrated in more than one way, a pluralistic approach opens up the possibility that students can display their new understandings—as well as their continuing difficulties—in ways that are comfortable for them and accessible to others. Performance-based examinations and exhibitions are tailor-made for the foregrounding of a student's multiple intelligences.

3. The personalization of education.   Without a doubt, one of the reasons that MI theory has attracted attention in the educational community is because of its ringing endorsement of an ensemble of propositions: we are not all the same; we do not all have the same kinds of minds; education works most effectively for most individuals if these differences in mentation and strengths are taken into account rather than denied or ignored. I have always believed that the heart of the MI perspective—in theory and in practice—inheres in taking human differences seriously. At the theoretical level, one acknowledges that all individuals cannot be profitably arrayed on a single intellectual dimension. At the practical level, one acknowledges that any uniform educational approach is likely to serve only a minority of children.

When I visit an "MI school," I look for signs of personalization: evidence that all involved in the educational encounter take such differences among human beings seriously; evidence that they construct curricula, pedagogy, and assessment insofar as possible in the light of these differences. All the MI posters, indeed all the references to me personally, prove to be of little avail if the youngsters continue to be treated in homogenized fashion. By the same token, whether or not members of the staff have even heard of MI theory, I would be happy to send my children to a school with the following characteristics: differences among youngsters are taken seriously, knowledge about differences is shared with children and parents, children gradually assume responsibility for their own learning, and materials that are worth knowing are presented in ways that afford each child the maximum opportunity to master those materials and to show others (and themselves) what they have learned and understood.

Closing Comments

I am often asked for my views about schools that are engaged in MI efforts. The implicit question may well be: "Aren't you upset by some of the applications that are carried out in your name?"

In truth, I do not expect that initial efforts to apply any new ideas are going to be stunning. Human experimentation is slow, difficult, and filled with zigs and zags. Attempts to apply any set of innovative ideas will sometimes be half-hearted, superficial, even wrongheaded.

For me the crucial question concerns what has happened in a school (or class) two, three, or four years after it has made a commitment to an MI approach. Often, the initiative will be long since forgotten—the fate, for better or worse, of most educational experiments. Sometimes, the school has gotten stuck in a rut, repeating the same procedures of the first days without having drawn any positive or negative lessons from this exercise. Needless to say, I am not happy with either of these outcomes.

I cherish an educational setting in which discussions and applications of MI have catalyzed a more fundamental consideration of schooling—its overarching purposes, its conceptions of what a productive life will be like in the future, its pedagogical methods, and its educational outcomes, particularly in the context of the values of that specific community. Such examination generally leads to more thoughtful schooling. Visits with other schools and more extended forms of networking among MI enthusiasts (and critics) constitute important parts of this building process. If, as a result of these discussions and experiments, a more personalized education is the outcome, I feel that the heart of MI theory has been embodied. And if this personalization is fused with a commitment to the achievement of worthwhile (and attainable) educational understandings for all children, then the basis for a powerful education has indeed been laid.

The MI endeavor is a continuing and changing one. There have emerged over the years new thoughts about the theory, new understandings and misunderstandings, and new applications, some very inspired, some less so. Especially gratifying to me has been the demonstration that this process is dynamic and interactive: no one, not even its creator, has a monopoly on MI wisdom or foolishness. Practice is enriched by theory, even as theory is transformed in the light of the fruits and frustrations of practice. The burgeoning of a community that takes MI issues seriously is not only a source of pride to me but also the best guarantor that the theory will continue to live in the years ahead.

Notes

1. Howard Gardner, *Frames of Mind: The Theory of Multiple Intelligences* (New York: Basic Books, 1983). A 10th-anniversary edition, with a new introduction, was published in 1993.
2. Howard Gardner, "On Discerning New Ideas in Psychology," *New Ideas in Psychology,* vol. 3, 1985, pp. 101-4; and idem, "Symposium on the Theory of Multiple Intelligences," in David N. Perkins, Jack Lochhead, and John C. Bishop, eds., *Thinking: The Second International Conference* (Hillsdale, N.J.: Erlbaum, 1983), pp. 77-101.
3. Howard Gardner, *Multiple Intelligences: The Theory in Practice* (New York: Basic Books, 1993).
4. For a bibliography through 1992, see the appendices to Gardner, *Multiple Intelligences.*
5. The term "memes" is taken from Richard Dawkins, *The Selfish Gene* (Oxford: Oxford University Press, 1976).
6. See Gardner, *Multiple Intelligences.*
7. Mihaly Csikszentmihalyi, "Society, Culture, and Person: A Systems View of Creativity," in Robert J. Sternberg, ed., *The Nature of Creativity* (New York: Cambridge University Press, 1988), pp. 325-39; idem, *Creativity* (New York: HarperCollins, forthcoming); David H. Feldman, "Creativity: Dreams, Insights, and Transformations," in Sternberg, op. cit., pp. 271-97; and David H. Feldman, Mihaly Csikszentmihalyi, and Howard Gardner, *Changing the World: A Framework for the Study of Creativity* (Westport, Conn.: Greenwood, 1994).
8. For a comprehensive discussion of the notion of cognitive style, see Nathan Kogan, "Stylistic Variation in Childhood and Adolescence," in Paul Mussen, ed., *Handbook of Child Psychology,* vol. 3 (New York: Wiley, 1983), pp, 630-706.
9. For writings pertinent to the personal intelligences, see Janet Astington, *The Child's Discovery of the Mind* (Cambridge, Mass.: Harvard University Press, 1993); and Antonio Damasio, *Descartes' Error* (New York: Grosset/Putnam, 1994).
10. On the possible relation between musical and spatial intelligence, see Frances Rauscher, G. L. Shaw, and X. N. Ky, "Music and Spatial Task Performance," *Nature,* 14 October 1993, p. 611.
11. The most thorough exposition of g can be found in the writings of Arthur Jensen. See, for example, *Bias in Mental Testing* (New York: Free Press, 1980). For a critique, see Stephen J. Gould, *The Mismeasure of Man* (New York: Norton, 1981).
12. Interest in the neurophysiological bases of g is found in Arthur Jensen, "Why Is Reaction Time Correlated with Psychometric 'G'?," *Current Directions of Psychological Science,* vol. 2, 1993, pp. 53-56.
13. Richard Herrnstein and Charles Murray, *The Bell Curve* (New York: Free Press, 1994).
14. For my view on intelligences not covered by g, see Howard Gardner, "Review of Richard Herrnstein and Charles Murray, *The Bell Curve,*" *The American Prospect,* Winter 1995, pp. 71-80.

15. On behavioral genetics and psychological research, see Thomas Bouchard and P. Propping, eds., *Twins as a Tool of Behavioral Genetics* (Chichester, England: Wiley, 1993).

16. On the many approaches that can be taken in implementing MI theory, see Mara Krechevsky, Thomas Hoerr, and Howard Gardner, "Complementary Energies: Implementing MI Theory from the Lab and from the Field," in Jeannie Oakes and Karen H. Quartz, eds., *Creating New Educational Communities: Schools and Classrooms Where All Children Can Be Smart: 94th NSSE Yearbook* (Chicago: National Society for the Study of Education, University of Chicago Press, 1995), pp. 166-86.

17. Howard Gardner, *The Unschooled Mind: How Children Learn and How Schools Should Teach* (New York: Basic Books, 1991).

Multiplying the Problems of Intelligence by Eight

Howard Gardner introduced the theory of multiple intelligences (MI) in his book *Frames of Mind* (1983). In place of the traditional view that there is one general intelligence, he contended that there are seven, each operating in a specific cultural domain: linguistic, logical-mathematical, spatial, bodily-kinesthetic, musical, interpersonal, and intrapersonal. Since then, Gardner (1995) has tentatively added "the intelligence of the naturalist," which includes the ability to understand living things and to use this knowledge productively, as in farming. Each intelligence has its own core set of operations and supports specific activities. Spatial intelligence, for example, mentally represents and transforms objects, and underpins navigation, mechanics, sculpture, and geometry. Because the intelligences are independent, most individuals show an uneven profile, with some intelligences greater than others (Gardner, 1983, 1993b; Gardner & Hatch, 1989).

MI has swept education in the 15 years since its inception. ERIC [Education Resource Information Clearinghouse] citations favourable to the theory run into the hundreds, including some in prestigious or widely circulating journals (e.g., Armstrong, 1994; Gardner, 1994, 1995; Gardner & Hatch, 1989; Nelson, 1995). Most authors cite MI theory as an egalitarian alternative both to the theory that there is one general intelligence, and also to the practice of teaching a curriculum that emphasizes language and mathematics. They recommend innovations ranging from planning units of study that span each intelligence (Wallach & Callahan, 1994), to enriching education for gifted or learning-disabled students in their areas of strength (Hearne & Stone, 1995; Smerechansky-Metzger, 1995), to using virtual reality to educate each intelligence (McLellan, 1994).

However, few authors have systematically evaluated MI theory. D. Matthews (1988) argued in favour of it, noting that gifted students usually excel in a single domain, such as mathematics or music. Other authors have suggested friendly revisions, such as the need for a "moral" intelligence, clarification of the theory or its implications, more evidence, or recognition of other educational concerns (Boss, 1994; Eisner, 1994; Levin, 1994). Some researchers in the psychometric tradition have rejected MI theory outright, claiming that Gardner's intelligences correlate positively with I.Q. and therefore are factors of general intelligence (Brand, 1996; Sternberg, 1983). Morgan (1992) noted the same positive correlations, and added that several of Gardner's intelligences cannot be conceptually distinguished from one another. Instead, Morgan interpreted these "intelligences" as cognitive styles. In the most sustained critique of MI, Ericsson and Charness (1994) suggested that expert performances are based on highly specific skills developed largely through extended deliberate practice, rather than on broad abilities.

Conceptual Problems

If someone were to ask, "Why is Michael a good dancer?," the MI answer would be "Because he has high bodily-kinesthetic intelligence." If the questioner then asked, "What is bodily-kinesthetic intelligence?," the answer would be "[It] is the ability to use one's body in highly differentiated and skilled ways, for expressive as well as goal-directed purposes ... [and] to work skillfully with objects" (Gardner, 1983, p. 206). This explanation, however, is circular: the definition of bodily-kinesthetic intelligence is virtually a definition of dance, so the explanation says, in effect, that Michael is a good dancer because he is a good dancer. In fact, the explanation is less informative than the original question, which at least identified the type of physical activity in which Michael excels. MI's reliance on this sort of explanation makes the theory tautological, and, therefore, necessarily true (Smedslund, 1979). It also makes it trivial.

On the other hand, ascribing an achievement to an "intelligence" has a series of far-from-trivial implications. It means that performances are expressions of moderately general abilities, such as bodily-kinesthetic intelligence, rather than either very general abilities, such as general intelligence, or very specific skills, such as knowing how to dance. It also implies that whereas Michael may be better at dance than at other physical activities, his high "bodily-kinesthetic intelligence" should give him an advantage in these areas as well. Conversely, he need not be good at non-physical tasks, such as writing poems or solving mathematics problems. Furthermore, ascribing some level of achievement to an ability such as an "intelligence," rather than to an acquisition, such as "knowledge," suggests that this level will be relatively stable over time, and that its origins may be innate (Gardner, 1995).

Gardner (1983) goes even further, claiming that the "intelligences" are modules (pp. 55-56, 280-285) in approximately the sense proposed by Fodor (1983) or Allport (1980). Modules are neural structures that quickly process particular kinds of content. Colour vision, speech perception, and facial recognition have all been ascribed to modules. Each module is "computationally autonomous," meaning that it carries out its operations independently, and, for the most part, does not share resources with other modules. This autonomy implies that the internal workings of one module are not available to others, although the "output" of one module can become the "input" of another. In short, the implication of modularity for MI theory is that the mind is made up of seven (or eight) innate mechanisms, each of which works largely independently to handle one kind of content.

However, this independence makes the theory insufficient to account for some familiar experiences. Most activities involve several intelligences (Gardner, 1983, p. 304). Dance is both musical and physical; conversation is both linguistic and interpersonal; and solving a physics problem is both spatial and logical-mathematical. Modularity per se is not the problem, because the output of one module can become the input of another. But Gardner has defined the intelligences of MI in terms of their differing content, which raises the question of how they could exchange information....

The phenomenon of intentionality drives this problem home. As Husserl (1962/1977) observed, our mental acts are *about* something, so they include two poles: the intending act ("noesis"), and the intended object ("noema"). Often, MI theory assigns the intending act and intended object to different "intelligences." Many intending acts express logical-mathematical intelligence: inferring, classifying, hypothesizing, counting, calculating, and so on. But the objects of these intentions are assigned to other intelligences. They include material things ("spatial intelligence"), other people ("interpersonal intelligence"), physical activities ("bodily-kinesthetic intelligence"), personal experience ("intrapersonal intelligence"), music ("musical intelligence") and living things ("naturalist's intelligence"). These other intelligences carry out their own operations. Consequently, MI theory makes it difficult to understand how people can use logic and mathematics to think *about* anything....

The "strong" claim that humans have several distinct intelligences is difficult to defend, and Gardner sometimes presents MI theory in a "weak" form. He has written that it is "less a set of hypotheses and predictions than it is an organized framework" (Gardner, 1994, p. 578). He has allowed that the components of each intelligence can dissociate or uncouple (Gardner, 1983, p. 173). He also acknowledges that pairs of intelligences may "overlap" or be correlated (Gardner & Walters, 1993a, pp. 41-42). Finally, he has suggested that "many people can evaluate their intelligences and plan to use them together in certain putatively successful ways" (p. 43), leaving some room for an executive that spans the intelligences.

These concessions risk, however, returning Gardner to the first problem of MI theory: triviality. If the intelligences extensively exchange information, cooperate in activities, or share a common executive, then there is little warrant for characterizing them as independent entities. Of course, Gardner could claim that although the intelligences are distinct, in practice they always work together. However, this concession makes the multiplicity of the intelligences a distinction without a difference, and invites the reply that the system as a whole is one single intelligence, and specific abilities, such as spatial reasoning, are mere components of this intelligence....

Empirical Problems

Exceptional Populations

Gardner views the existence of groups that he believes to be high or low in one specific intelligence as part of the evidence for MI. The first of these are the geniuses: Yehudi Menuhin illustrates exceptional musical intelligence;

Babe Ruth, outstanding bodily-kinesthetic intelligence; and Barbara McClintock, outstanding logical-mathematical intelligence (Gardner, 1993b). However, the abilities of Gardner's candidates do not appear to correspond to the categories of MI theory. Many excel in more than one domain: Barbara McClintock's work spanned the logical-mathematical and natural domains (pp. 19-20), Virginia Woolf's, the linguistic and intrapersonal domains (pp. 24-25), and Albert Einstein's, the spatial and the logical-mathematical domains (Gardner, 1993a, pp. 104-105). It is to be expected that if the intelligences are independent, then some individuals will excel in two or more domains, but if Gardner fails to show that most achieve excellence in one specific domain, then his claim that the intelligences are independent is threatened. Conversely, Gardner does not show that any of the geniuses excel throughout one of the domains defined by MI theory; instead, each seems to excel on some smaller subset of activities within a domain. Unless Gardner can show that most geniuses perform relatively well throughout a domain, then the notion that the intelligences are integrated structures is threatened. Generally, the difficulty with Gardner's discussion of genius is that many psychological theories imply some way of categorizing individuals of exceptional ability; he has not yet shown that MI theory fits the data better than other theories.

The argument from genius could be bolstered by a second special population: prodigies. Gardner acknowledges that an individual's level of each intelligence is the result of both "nature" and "nurture." Furthermore, if outstanding individuals were to show exceptional abilities at a very early age, and these abilities were specific to domains, then it could be inferred that the structures of MI theory are "biopsychological potential[s]" (Gardner & Walters, 1993a, p. 36). But a competing theory would hold that prodigies appear in various fields because societies divide activities in specific ways and enculturate individuals accordingly. Gardner never tells the reader enough about any one case to indicate which alternative is more plausible. For example, he implies that Pablo Picasso was genetically prepared for prodigy, but later adds that no work he did prior to age 9 has survived (Gardner, 1993a, pp. 138-146). This kind of fragmentary anecdotal evidence raises a "chicken-and-egg" question: Is early tutoring a response to early talent, or vice versa? Howe (1990) has noted that children with exceptional abilities intensely explore and practise in their area of interest, observe models, and receive tutoring from an early age. In one historical study, Fowler (1986) found that of 24 outstanding mathematicians, 21 received special stimulation in mathematics before the age of 5, and several before the age of 3. Another objection to Gardner's view is that the talents of many prodigies simply do not fit the categories of MI theory; instead, they reflect the importance of specific enculturation. Talent at chess is a prime example. Thus, although the achievements of these children are impressive and difficult to explain, they do not establish the eight discrete "biopsychological potentials" that MI theory requires. And given that prodigy is rare, even among the most accomplished members of a field (Bloom, 1985; Feldman, 1986), this phenomenon is probably not a useful touchstone for educational practice.

In any case, exceptional accomplishments may not be based on the domain-wide abilities Gardner proposes. For example, he claims that excellence in chess expresses spatial intelligence (Gardner, 1983, pp. 192-195). But chess is one of the most-researched human cognitive activities, and general abilities, spatial or otherwise, seem to contribute little to its mastery (Ericsson & Smith, 1991). Chess masters are no better than other persons at spatial tasks, except at recognizing strategically significant board arrangements (Chase & Simon, 1973; Pfau & Murphy, 1988). Highly ranked players are less likely to work in professions that involve solving spatial problems, such as engineering, than they are to work in professions in the humanities, such as writing (de Groot, 1978; Elo, 1978). A defender of MI might counter that there are many domains of spatial abilities, and an individual who excels in one need not excel in others. But as this rebuttal tacitly concedes, if this were the case, then there is no reason to speak of a general "spatial intelligence" in the first place.

The third exceptional population Gardner discusses are savants, individuals who do one thing exceptionally well, such as calculating large products mentally, stating the day of the week for any given calendar date, or playing a piano piece after a single hearing. These include "idiot savants," many of whom are autistic. Savantry could support the coherence and independence of the intelligences if it were shown to embody one high intelligence in an otherwise average or low profile. However, savants usually do not excel across an entire domain. For example, hyperlexic autistic readers decode print better than other children their age, but because their comprehension is poor (Snowling & Frith, 1986), they could not be said to show high linguistic intelligence.

Gardner interprets autism as a limitation on intrapersonal intelligence (Gardner & Walters, 1993b, p. 25). However, its effects are not limited to this domain. Sloboda, Hermelin, and O'Connor (1985) described NP, a musical autistic savant, who could accurately play a piece on the piano after one hearing. Interestingly, 24 hours later, NP played the same piece in a way that sounded "metronomic in the extreme" (p. 165). Most autistic savants have difficulty planning and monitoring the use of their exceptional skills, which may explain why many cannot find employment in their areas of special interest (Frith, 1989). It appears that autism, primarily an impairment in intrapersonal understanding, affects other "intelligences," showing that these are not independent, but affects only some aspects of each intelligence, suggesting that they are not coherent entities.

Like the achievements of geniuses, those of savants are probably not based on the general operations that Gardner posits. Instead, these achievements rely on knowledge and skills specific to particular activities. When autistic savants replay a piece of music after one hearing, the errors they make are reversions to forms typical of the piece's genre, which indicates that they rely on matching the new tune to the repertoire of melodic forms they already know (Sloboda et al., 1985). Similarly, a case study of a non-autistic mathematical savant showed that through thousands of hours of practice she had learned the characteristics of a huge repertoire of numbers, recognizing at a glance, for instance that 720 equals 6 factorial (i.e., $6 \times 5 \times 4 \times 3 \times 2 \times 1$). She had also learned a collection of computational algorithms. This knowledge allowed her quickly to fit a routine to the numbers in most questions, and to solve those questions efficiently. In contrast, her basic cognitive processes did not differ from those of other adults (Jensen, 1990).

MI researchers also cite learning disabilities as evidence for their theory (Gardner & Hatch, 1989). The most common of these disabilities is dyslexia. Most dyslexic students have difficulty discriminating sounds in language, matching them to letters, and combining them to form words; some appear to have difficulty recalling word images (Patterson, Marshall, & Coltheart, 1985). However, because many dyslexic students equal their normal classmates in aspects of language other than reading, such as listening comprehension (Mosberg & Johns, 1994; Torgesen, 1988), dyslexia affects a range of abilities too narrow to comprise "linguistic intelligence." Another learning disability, Gerstmann syndrome, initially seems to represent difficulties in spatial reasoning (Gardner, 1983, p. 156). But its symptoms include problems in distinguishing left from right, making mathematical computations, and recognizing and remembering finger contact. Because these difficulties involve logical-mathematical and bodily-kinesthetic intelligence, Gerstmann syndrome corresponds to a broader set of abilities than does spatial intelligence. Indeed, I was not able to identify a single learning disability that maps onto an intelligence of MI theory....

Studies Concerning Transfer of Learning

If, as Gardner suggests, the core of each "intelligence" consists of knowledge and procedures that operate across a wide domain, then it would make sense to build school curricula around these cores. The "Right start" program illustrates this approach in mathematics. Griffin, Case, and Siegler (1994) researched the concepts central to understanding Grade 1 arithmetic. Then they created a set of mathematical games and activities, and engaged students in discussions that highlighted these concepts. As a result, the children's understanding of number improved dramatically compared with a control group, and transferred to a variety of new quantitative activities, such as telling time and predicting the behaviour of a balance scale. The Right start results are impressive. However, to support MI theory, it is necessary to show that students' gains transferred across the logical-mathematical domain, but not further (e.g., to spatial tasks).

Moreover, other kinds of transfer research bears on MI theory quite differently. When students articulate and elaborate on a concept, this helps them to apply it to new problems, a phenomenon called "high road transfer" (Brown & Kane, 1988; Chi & Bassok, 1989). Similarly, when teachers explicitly state the rules for solving a problem, this articulation adds significantly to the value of examples alone in helping students to transfer these rules to new content (Cheng, Holyoak, Nisbett, & Oliver, 1986; Fong, Krantz, & Nisbett, 1986). This transfer of strategies across domains is difficult to explain within MI theory. Even more problematic is the role of language in moving information within and among other "intelligences." Gardner (1983) is aware of transfer across domains, and notes that it is problematic, but does not attempt to reconcile this transfer with the notion of autonomous intelligences, except by alluding to "waves of symbolization" (pp. 306-309). In this sense, research on transfer is a double-edged sword for MI theory.

Psychometric Research

Gardner also relies on statistical research. Factor analysis is a procedure that can be used to tease out themes appearing within, or across, tests. Several factors similar to Gardner's intelligences have emerged in such analyses, including linguistic (Wiebe & Watkins, 1980), spatial (Gustafsson, 1984), and social factors (Rosnow, Skleder, Jaeger, & Rind, 1994). But this kind of research provides shaky support for MI. First, the factors in these studies typically are not independent, but instead correlate positively with one another, a fact that has been used to argue both for the existence of general intelligence and against MI (Brand, 1996; Sternberg, 1983). Although Gardner has replied that this evidence comes almost entirely from tests of logical-mathematical or linguistic intelligence (Gardner & Walters, 1993a, p. 39), it is important to note that spatial tasks correlate substantially with verbal tasks even when performance measures are used (Wechsler, 1974). Second, each factor splits into several smaller factors, each of these narrower than the intelligences of MI theory. For instance, in a review of "visual perception" abilities (similar to Gardner's "spatial intelligence"), Carroll (1993) examined 230 data sets. The factors of visual perception found in each study varied in number from one to six, which Carroll grouped into five categories "despite much difficulty" (p. 309). These results can be accommodated by theories of intelligence that recognize both general and specific components, but they present difficulties for MI theory, which recognizes only one level of structure.

Surprisingly, a re-examination of Gardner's own assessment research also challenges MI theory. He and his colleagues have developed assessment tasks based on authentic activities in several different domains. According to MI theory, students' performances on activities derived from the same intelligences should show high correlations, and activities derived from different intelligences should show low correlations, or none at all. However, in two studies with primary school children, several pairs of tasks that were supposed to represent independent intelligences correlated strongly, and those that were supposed to represent the same intelligences failed to correlate significantly, except for two number tasks (Gardner & Hatch, 1989; Gardner & Krechevsky, 1993). In both studies, the researchers interpreted these patterns as evidence against the existence of a single general intelligence. However, they failed to acknowledge that these same findings also weigh crucially against MI theory.

Experimental Studies

If the mind is composed of independent modules, as MI theory claims, then individuals should be able to carry out two activities that call on different intelligences at the same time, without one interfering with the other. Conversely, if two activities call on the same intelligence, then the speed or accuracy of at least one activity should suffer. Several studies have explored these possibilities using spatial and verbal tasks, and have shown that these predictions are largely true (e.g., Barton, Matthews, Farmer, & Belyavin, 1995; Liu & Wickens, 1992).

The picture is more complex, however, than MI theory would predict. First, verbal and visual tasks disrupt one another somewhat, indicating that they share some kind of resource, possibly an executive that switches attention between them (Logie, Zucco, & Baddeley, 1990). Second, experimental research indicates that people can translate information from verbal to visual form, or vice versa (Conrad, 1964; Holding, 1992, 1993; N. N. Matthews, Hunt, & MacLeod, 1980), which limits the notion that various kinds of knowledge are handled by separate intelligences. Most importantly, other "intelligences" seem to rely on linguistic or spatial resources: mathematical tasks interfere with verbal tasks (Logie & Baddeley, 1987; Logie et al., 1990), and verbal tasks interfere with musical tasks for novices (Pechmann & Mohr, 1992). Similarly, switching attention among sounds originating from different locations interferes with spatial tasks (Smyth & Scholey, 1994)....

Pedagogical Problems

One response to these criticisms could be to claim that even though MI theory is conceptually and empirically weak, it remains a useful framework for teaching. But this is far from clear. Interpretations have been so diverse that Kornhaber has noted that "one reason for the success of MI is that educators can cite it without having to do anything differently" (cited in Gardner, 1994, p. 580). Some practices based on the theory are no doubt misinterpretations. Reiff (1996), for example, has suggested that if a child is weak in one intelligence, he or she can be taught "through" another. Because this view assumes that the same material can be learned using a variety of modes, it could be called the "learning styles" interpretation. Whether this view is true or false, it is essentially the opposite of Gardner's (1995) theory. If each intelligence operates on a different domain, and represents a specific kind of content, then only rarely can a given piece of knowledge be presented in different ways for different intelligences.

A second common interpretation of MI theory claims that schools currently overemphasize linguistic and logical-mathematical knowledge, so curricula ought to be changed to balance the intelligences more equally. Educators could plan units of study that include activities to engage each intelligence (Hoerr, 1994; Wallach & Callahan, 1994), or that give a more prominent place to the arts (Deluca, 1993). Balanced programming and MI theory are obviously compatible, but one does not entail the other. The notion that there are eight intelligences does not imply that school should be the institution responsible for developing all of them. Conversely, if educators choose to offer balanced programming, they do not require Gardner's theory for justification, which is why such alternative systems as Waldorf schools long predated MI theory.

A more elaborate version of the balanced programming proposal suggests educators should assess children's intelligences, then provide programs that include remediation in their areas of weakness, and enrichment in their areas of strength (Gardner & Walters, 1993b, p. 31; Hearne & Stone, 1995; Hoerr, 1994). This approach is appealing, but presents practical problems. The first, already noted, is that despite several years of effort, MI researchers have not yet developed reliable methods for assessing the intelligences. The second problem is that growing class sizes in many jurisdictions, multiplied by the supposed existence of eight intelligences, and the many levels at which children could operate in each of these intelligences, would yield an explosion in the workload of the teachers who would have to plan and deliver these programs.

Gardner favours a general education in primary school. His preferences for the middle elementary years are less clear, in that he mentions "mastering the crucial literacies," but stresses "early specialization" in areas chosen by each child and family, and informed by an assessment of his or her intelligences (Gardner, 1993b, pp. 194-196). Later, students would pursue a broader education during adolescence. This preference for specialization in middle childhood may contradict the political goals of MI theory. Gardner (1993b) has criticized conventional education, particularly in its use of intelligence testing, as ethnocentric and elitist, or " 'Westist,' 'Testist,' and 'Bestist' " (p. 12). But, arguably, specialization represents a subtle kind of streaming. Opportunities for activities of various kinds are not allocated to all preschool children equally. Choosing specialties on the basis of the "intelligences" they have acquired by age 7 could potentially exacerbate these inequalities. And although Gardner wishes that society valued all intelligences equally, it does not. Mathematics, particularly, serves as a "gate-keeping" subject for admission to advanced study in many highly paid professions (Gainen, 1995). Therefore, contrary to Gardner's good intentions, his suggestions could lead to a hardening of traditional categories of privilege.

Some educators have claimed that a benefit of the MI framework is that children learn to identify their own "areas of strength," and some schools now issue report cards based on the theory (see Hanson, 1995; Hoerr, 1994; Wallach & Callahan, 1994). However, there is good reason to predict that these practices will backfire. The converse of being "high" in some intelligences is being "mediocre" or "low"in others. Students who believe that they are low in an ability often avoid activities that call on it, even when they might learn from the effort (Covington, 1992; Palmquist & Young, 1992). Paradoxically, students' beliefs that they are high in an ability can lead to the same result in the long run. Those who attribute their achievements to such ability approach tasks with confidence. But, when they encounter a problem that they cannot solve easily, they often quit. Apparently, their theory that achievement reflects ability leads them to interpret failure as a lack of this ability. In contrast, students who attribute achievement to effort, learning, and the application of appropriate strategies are more likely to persist when "the going gets tough," and to recover after initial failure (Dweck & Leggett, 1988).

These objections invite the fundamental pedagogical question: Is MI the right *kind* of theory for education? Although Gardner stresses the differences between general intelligence and multiple intelligences, the two frameworks nevertheless share fundamental characteristics that limit their relevance to teaching. Both identify cognitive structures far too broad to be useful for interpreting any specific educational tasks. For instance, the knowledge that basketball relies on "bodily-kinesthetic intelligence" tells a coach nothing about the skills that her players need to learn. Because both general intelligence and MI are theories of ability rather than theories of knowledge or learning, they offer only a static interpretation of children's performance; knowing that a student is high in "musical intelligence" provides no clues about how to enrich his music education; knowing that he is low in musical intelligence provides no clues about how to remedy it. Of course, both general intelligence theorists and MI theorists agree that both education and experience can affect ability (e.g., Neisser et al., 1996), and Gardner has argued for innovative practices, such as expert mentoring in settings outside of school. But learning is not the focus of ability theories, and the positive innovations Gardner advocates derive from other research traditions, such as sociocultural theory, rather than from MI itself (e.g., Gardner, Kornhaber, & Krechevsky, 1993).

Conclusion

In examining the nature of intelligence, Gardner and his colleagues have used a wider set of tools than have traditional psychometric researchers. They have contended compellingly that the arts are as much intellectual activities as are writing, mathematics, and science (Gardner, 1982). MI researchers have drawn educators' attention to an alternative to the theory of general intelligence. And Gardner (1983, p. 297) is admirably willing to consider criticisms of his own framework. However, I contend that MI theory offers a level of analysis neither empirically plausible nor pedagogically useful.

A promising alternative to this kind of research focuses on the knowledge and strategies that children and adults use in carrying out various, specific activities. Such analyses are already being carried out in areas as diverse as drawing (Cox, 1992), argument comprehension (Chambliss, 1995), and volleyball (Allard & Starkes, 1980). Innovative projects have explored the creation of classroom communities in which students collaborate to construct knowledge in areas such as science, mathematics, and interdisciplinary studies (e.g., McGilly, 1994). Such research seems likely to prove more relevant than ability theories in setting curricular goals and interpreting students' learning.

References

Allard,F., & Starkes, J. L. (1980).Perception in sport: Volleyball. *Journal of Sport Psychology, 2*, 22-33.

Allport, D. A. (1980). Patterns and actions: Cognitive mechanisms are content specific. In G. Claxton (Ed.), *Cognitive psychology: New directions* (pp. 26-64). London: Routledge & Kegan Paul.

Armstrong, T. (1994). Multiple intelligences: Seven ways to approach curriculum. *Educational Leadership, 52* (3), 26-28.

Barton, A., Matthews, B., Farmer, E., & Belyavin, A. (1995). Revealing the basic properties of the visuospatial sketchpad: The use of complete spatial arrays. *Acta Psychologica, 89,* 197-216.

Bloom, B.S. (Ed.). (1985). *Developing talent in young people.* New York: Ballantine.

Boss, J. A. (1994). The anatomy of moral intelligence. *Educational Theory, 44,* 399-416.

Brand, C. (1996). *The g factor: General intelligence and its implications.* New York: John Wiley.

Brown, A. L., & Kane, M. J. (1988). Preschool children can learn to transfer: Learning to learn and learning from example. *CognitivePsychology, 20,* 493-523.

Carroll, J. B. (1993). *Human cognitive abilities: A survey of factor-analytic studies.* Cambridge: Cambridge University Press.

Chambliss, M. J. (1995). Text cues and strategies successful readers use to construct the gist of lengthy written arguments. *Reading Research Quarterly, 30,* 778-807.

Chase, W. G., & Simon, H. A. (1973). The mind's eye in chess. In W. G. Chase (Ed.), *Visual information processing* (pp. 215-281). New York: Academic Press.

Cheng, P. W., Holyoak, K. J., Nisbett, R. E., & Oliver, L. M. (1986). Pragmatic versus syntactic approaches to training deductive reasoning. *Cognitive Psychology, 18,* 293-328.

Chi, M. T. H., & Bassok, M. (1989). Learning from examples via self-explanations. In L. B. Resnick (Ed.), *Knowing, learning, and instruction: Essays in honour of Robert Glaser* (pp. 251-282). Hillsdale, NJ: Erlbaum.

Conrad, R. (1964).A coustic confusions in immediate memory. British Journal of Psychology, 55, 75-84.

Covington, M. V. (1992). *Making the grade: A self-worth perspective on motivation and school reform.* Cambridge: Cambridge University Press.

Cox, M. (1992). *Children's drawings.* London: Penguin Books.

de Groot, A. D. (1978). *Thought and choice in chess* (2nd ed.). The Hague: Mouton.

Deluca, L. S. (1993). The arts and equity. *Equity and Excellence in Education, 26*(3), 51-53.

Dweck, C. S., & Leggett, E. L. (1988). A social cognitive approach to motivation and personality. *Psychological Review, 95,* 256-273.

Eisner, E. W. (1994). Commentary: Putting multiple intelligences in context: Some questions and observations. *Teachers College Record, 95,* 555-560.

Elo, A. E. (1978). *The rating of chess players, past and present.* New York: Arco.

Ericsson, K. A., & Charness, N. (1994). Expert performance: Its structure and acquisition. *American Psychologist, 49,* 725-747.

Ericsson, K. A., & Smith, J. (1991). Prospects and limits of the empirical study of expertise: An introduction. In K. A. Ericsson & J. Smith (Eds.), *Toward a general theory of expertise: Prospects and limits* (pp. 1-38). Cambridge: Cambridge University Press.

Feldman, D. H. (1986). *Nature's gambit: Child prodigies and the development of human potential.* New York: Basic Books.

Fodor, J. A. (1983). *The modularity of mind: An essay of faculty psychology.* Cambridge, MA: MIT Press.

Fong, G. T., Krantz, D. H., & Nisbett, R. E. (1986). The effects of statistical training on thinking about everyday problems. *Cognitive Psychology, 18,* 253-292.

Fowler, W. (1986). Early experiences of great men and women mathematicians. In W. Fowler (Ed.), *Early experience and the development of competence* (New Directions for Child Development No. 32, pp. 87-109). San Francisco: Jossey-Bass.

Frith, U. (1989). *Autism: Explaining the enigma.* Oxford: Basil Blackwell.

Gainen, J. (1995). Barriers to success in quantitative gatekeeper courses. *New Directions for Teaching and Learning, 61,* 5-14.

Gardner, H. (1982). *Art, mind, and brain: A cognitive approach to creativity.* New York: Basic Books.

Gardner, H. (1983). *Frames of mind: The theory of multiple intelligences.* New York: Basic Books.

Gardner, H. (1993a). *Creating minds: Ananatomy of creativity as seen through the lives of Freud, Einstein, Picasso, Stravinsky, Eliot, Graham, and Gandhi.* New York: Basic Books.

Gardner, H. (1993b). *Multiple intelligences: The theory in practice.* New York: Basic Books.

Gardner, H. (1994). Intelligences in theory and practice: A response to Elliot W. Eisner, Robert J. Sternberg, and Henry M. Levin. *Teachers College Record, 95,* 576-583.

Gardner, H. (1995, November). Reflections on multiple intelligences: Myths and messages: *Phi Delta Kappan, 77,* 200-203, 206-209.

Gardner, H., & Hatch, T. (1989). Multiple intelligences go to school: Educational implications of the theory of multiple intelligences. *Educational Researcher, 18*(8), 4-9.

Gardner, H., Kornhaber, M., & Krechevsky, M. (1993). Engaging intelligence. In H. Gardner, *Multiple intelligences: The theory in practice* (pp. 231-248). New York: HarperCollins.

Gardner, H., & Krechevsky, M. (1993). The emergence and nurturance of multiple intelligences in early childhood: The Project Spectrum approach. In H. Gardner, *Multiple intelligences: The theory in practice* (pp. 86-111). New York: Basic Books.

Gardner, H., & Walter, J. (1993a). Questions and answers about multiple intelligences theory. In H. Gardner, *Multiple intelligences: The theory in practice* (pp. 35-48). New York: Basic Books.

Gardner, H., & Walters, J. (1993b). A rounded version. In H. Gardner, *Multiple intelligences: The theory in practice* (pp. 13-34). New York: Basic Books.

Griffin, S. A., Case, R., & Siegler, R. S. (1994). Right start: Providing the central conceptual prerequisites for first formal learning of arithmetic to students at risk for failure. In K. McGilly (Ed.), *Classroom lessons: Integrating cognitive theory and classroom practice* (pp. 25-49). Cambridge, MA: MIT Press.

Gustafsson, J. E. (1984). A unifying model for the structure of intellectual abilities. *Intelligence, 8,* 179-203.

Hanson, R. M. (Executive Producer). (1995). *How are kids smart? Multiple intelligences in the classroom: Teachers' Version* [Videotape]. Port Chester, NY: National Professional Resources.

Hearne, D., & Stone, S. (1995). Multiple intelligences and underachievement: Lessons from individuals with learning disabilities. *Journal of Learning Disabilities, 28,* 439-448.

Hoerr, T. R. (1994). How the New City School applies the multiple intelligences. *Educational Leadership, 52*(3), 29-33.

Holding, D. H. (1992). Theories of chess skill. *Psychological Research, 54,* 10-16.

Holding, D. H. (1993). Sharing verbal and visuospatial resources in working memory. *Journal of General Psychology, 120,* 245-256.

Howe, M. J. A. (1990). *The origins of exceptional abilities.* Oxford: Blackwell.

Husserl, E. (1977). *Phenomenological psychology: Lectures, summer semester,* 1925 (J. Scanlon, Trans.). The Hague: Martinus Nijhoff. (Original work published 1962)

Jensen, A. R. (1990). Speed of information processing in a calculating prodigy. *Intelligence, 14,* 259-274.

Levin, H. M. (1994). Commentary: Multiple intelligence theory and everyday practice. *Teachers College Record, 95,* 570-575.

Liu, Y., & Wickens, C. D. (1992). Visual scanning with or without spatial uncertainty and divided and selective attention. *Acta Psychologica, 79,* 131-153.

Logie, R. H., & Baddeley, A. D. (1987). Cognitive processes in counting. *Journal of Experimental Psychology: Learning, Memory, and Cognition, 13,* 310-326.

Logie, R. H., Zucco, G. M., & Baddeley, A. D. (1990). Interference with visual short-term memory. *Acta Psychologica, 75,* 55-74.

Matthews, D. (1988). Gardner's multiple intelligence theory: An evaluation of relevant research literature and a consideration of its application to gifted education. *Roeper Review, 11,* 100-104.

Matthews, N. N., Hunt, E. B., & MacLeod, C. M. (1980). Strategy choice and strategy training in sentence-picture verification. *Journal of Verbal Learning and Verbal Behavior, 19,* 531-548.

McGilly, K. (Ed.). (1994). *Classroom lessons: Integrating cognitive theory and classroom practice.* Cambridge, MA: MIT Press.

McLellan, H. (1994). Virtual reality and multiple intelligences: Potentials for higher education. *Journal of Computing in Higher Education, 5,* 33-66.

Morgan, H. (1992). *An analysis of Gardner's theory of multiple intelligence.* Paper presented at the Annual Meeting of the Eastern Educational Research Association. (ERIC Document Reproduction Service No. ED 360 088)

Mosberg, L., & Johns, D. (1994). Reading and listening comprehension in college students with developmental dyslexia. *Learning Disabilities Research and Practice, 9,* 130-135.

Neisser, U., Boodoo, G., Bouchard, T. J., Jr., Boykin, A. W., Brody, N., Ceci, S. J., Halpern, D. F., Loehlin, J. C., Perloff, R., Sternberg, R. J., & Urbina, S. (1996). Intelligence: Knowns and unknowns. *American Psychologist, 51,* 77-101.

Nelson, K. (1995). Nurturing kids' seven ways of being smart. *Instructor, 105,* 26-30, 34.

Palmquist, M., & Young, R. (1992). The notion of giftedness and student expectations about writing. *Written Communication, 9,* 137-168.

Patterson, K. E., Marshall, J. C., & Coltheart, M. (Eds.). (1985). *Surface dyslexia: Neuropsychological and cognitive studies of phonological reading.* Hillsdale, NJ: Lawrence Erlbaum.

Pechmann, T., & Mohr, G. (1992). Interference in memory for tonal pitch: Implications for a working-memory model. *Memory and Cognition, 20,* 314-320.

Pfau, H. D., & Murphy, M. D. (1988). Role of verbal knowledge in chess skill. *American Journal of Psychology, 101,* 73-86.

Reiff, J. C. (1996). Bridging home and school through multiple intelligences. *Childhood Education, 72* (3), 164-166.

Rosnow, R. L., Skleder, A. A., Jaeger, M. E., & Rind, B. (1994). Intelligence and the epistemics of interpersonal acumen: Testing some implications of Gardner's theory. *Intelligence, 19,* 93-116.

Sloboda, J. A., Hermelin, B., & O'Connor, N. (1985). An exceptional musical memory. *Music Perception, 3,* 155-170.

Smedslund, J. (1979). Between the analytic and the arbitrary: A case study of psychological research. *Scandinavian Journal of Psychology, 20,* 129-140.

Smerechansky-Metzger, J. A. (1995). The quest for multiple intelligences. *Gifted Child Today, 18*(3), 12-15.

Smyth, M. M., & Scholey, K. A. (1994). Interference in immediate spatial memory. *Memory and Cognition, 22,* 1-13.

Snowling, M., & Frith, U. (1986). Comprehension in "hyperlexic" readers. *Journal of Experimental Child Psychology, 42,* 392-415.

Sternberg, R. J. (1983). How much gall is too much gall? A review of *Frames of mind: The theory of multiple intelligences. Contemporary Education Review, 2,* 215-224.

Torgesen, J. K. (1988). Studies of children with learning disabilities who perform poorly on memory span tasks. *Journal of Learning Disabilities, 21,* 605-612.

Wallach, C., & Callahan, S. (1994). The 1st grade plant museum. *Educational Leadership, 52*(3), 32-34.

Wechsler, D. (1974). *Manual for the Wechsler Intelligence Scale for children—Revised.* New York: The Psychological Corporation.

Wiebe, M. J., & Watkins, E. O. (1980). Factor analysis of the McCarthy Scales of Children's Abilities on preschool children. *Journal of School Psychology, 18,* 154-162.

POSTSCRIPT

Can Howard Gardner's Theory of Multiple Intelligences Transform Educational Practice?

It may not be possible to answer the question posed by this issue for several years. In part, this reflects the fact that Gardner's theory of multiple intelligences has been proposed only recently and is still evolving. It also reflects the fact that Gardner's theory, like many other psychological theories, was originally formulated as a description of an important dimension of the human mind and was not intended as a theory of pedagogy. This means that there is considerable theoretical and empirical work to be done before the educational implications of the theory are completely understood. Unfortunately, there is considerable pressure to reform our educational system now. This has led to a number of initiatives that claim to have been inspired by Gardner's theory but that, on careful analysis, have little to do with the theory. Some reformers, for example, have used Gardner's theory to advocate teaching to accommodate a variety of learning styles, including differences between left-and right-brain learners, verbal and visual-spatial learners, and reflective and intuitive learners. See "Multiple Intelligences: Seven Keys to Opening Closed Minds," by Shirley E. Jordan, *NASSP Bulletin* (November 1996). Other reformers have advocated the creation of formal tests for each of the proposed intelligences.

It is also important to recognize that there is not universal support for Gardner's view of intelligence among scholars of the human mind. Many continue to point to the ubiquitous correlations that exist between a wide range of tasks that most of us would agree must tap "intelligence." See "Spearman's *g* and the Problem of Educational Equality," by Arthur R. Jensen, *Oxford Review of Education* (vol. 17, no. 2, 1991).

Readers interested in pursuing Gardner's writings on intelligence are encouraged to read *The Unschooled Mind: How Children Think and How Schools Should Teach* (Basic Books, 1991) and *Multiple Intelligences: The Theory Into Practice* (Basic Books, 1993). An example of an adoption of a multiple intelligences-inspired curriculum can be found in "It's No Fad: Fifteen Years of Implementing Multiple Intelligences," by Thomas R. Hoerr, *Educational Horizons* (Winter 2003). The reader who is interested in alternative conceptions of intelligence should seek out work by Robert Sternberg, including "Ability and Expertise," *American Educator* (vol. 23, no. 1, 1999); *Successful Intelligence* (Plume, 1997); "Raising the Achievement of All Students: Teaching for Successful Intelligence," Educational Psychology Review (December 2002); and "The Theory of Successful Intelligence as a Basis for Gifted Education," coauthored by Elena Grigorenko, *Gifted Child Quarterly* (vol. 46, no. 4, 2002).

ISSUE 11

Will a Push for Standards and Accountability Lead to More Motivated Students?

YES: Lauren B. Resnick, from "From Aptitude to Effort: A New Foundation for Our Schools," *American Educator* (Spring 1999)

NO: Kennon M. Sheldon and Bruce J. Biddle, from "Standards, Accountability, and School Reform: Perils and Pitfalls," *Teachers College Record* (Fall 1998)

ISSUE SUMMARY

YES: Lauren B. Resnick, a professor of psychology at the University of Pittsburgh, presents a plan for reforming American schools. One critical feature of the plan is clear achievement standards set for all students, not just those who are assumed to have the highest academic aptitude. Such standards, Resnick argues, will motivate students to work harder and, thus, increase achievement by all students.

NO: Kennon M. Sheldon and Bruce J. Biddle, both members of the faculty in the department of psychology at the University of Missouri, argue that the mission of schooling must be to create "life-long, self-directed learners"—adults who enjoy learning for its own sake. They argue that an emphasis on standards is inconsistent with this mission because it rewards (and punishes) students and teachers for achieving a narrowly defined set of outcomes.

T he 1990s witnessed ever more frequent calls for the reform of the U.S. educational system. In part, these calls have been sparked by cross-national comparisons of educational achievement. These comparisons have consistently shown that U.S. students are falling behind those in other nations in their mastery of the content in fundamental academic domains, most notably mathematics and science. Many of the plans for reform have included the adoption of a set of standards that would specify the content and skills that students should master, typically on a grade-by-grade basis. In some plans, standards would be set at the level of the individual school district. In other plans, the standards would be common across all districts within a state, or possibly even across all schools within the United States.

Strong proponents of the standards movement argue that much of the failure of U.S. schools can be traced to the fact that teachers and schools have too much freedom over what content to teach and when it is taught. More moderate standards proponents suggest that teachers are overwhelmed by the sheer amount of content that they *could* teach and that they lack a sound, shared basis for making decisions. Less charitable standards proponents suggest that teachers have simply made bad choices—choices motivated by a particular political agenda or ideological stance—that have led them to waste their time teaching content in the social and affective domains at the expense of content in more traditional academic domains, such as science and mathematics. Proponents have also suggested that the freedom provided teachers and schools over the curriculum has resulted in *a priori* decisions about what content falls within the ability of a particular student or group of students. The result is that teachers hold unnecessarily low expectations for certain students or groups of students and, thus, "water down" the curriculum, thereby ensuring that those students will fail to acquire meaningful academic skills.

Proponents of standards point to a number of successes as evidence of the need for even wider adoption of this reform. Mike Schmoker and Robert J. Marzano, for example, in "Realizing the Promise of Standards-Based Education," *Educational Leadership* (March 1999), provide the following examples of the"promise of standards":

1. In Maryland's Frederick County, alignment of the curriculum with standards in the state-wide assessment led to a dramatic increase in assessed performance, with the result being that the district moved to the "highest tier" of Maryland schools.
2. Teachers in Glendale Union High School in Arizona all adopted the same curriculum, which was designed to meet end-of-the-year assessed standards in each subject area. Average student performance improved in nearly every course.

Critics of the standards movement, however, have suggested that short-term gains on outcome measures (typically, standardized tests of achievement) may hide deeper failures. Some argue that the gains in achievement are nothing more than the result of teachers "teaching to the test." Still other critics suggest that the standards proposed have a decidedly "back-to-basics" orientation—an orientation that will lead to drill-and-practice-oriented instruction and student rote memorization rather than true understanding.

In the following selections, another point of disagreement between the supporters and critics of the standards movement is considered. In the first selection, Lauren B. Resnick argues that standards can motivate students to put forth more effort and that such effort can lead to increased aptitude. In the second selection, Kennon M. Sheldon and Bruce J. Biddle argue that standards (or any system of external control) will lead to a decrease in students' motivation to engage in learning for its own sake.

Lauren B. Resnick

 **YES**

From Aptitude to Effort: A New Foundation for Our Schools

Two challenges face American education today: We must raise overall achievement levels, and we must make opportunities for achievement more equitable. The importance of both derives from the same basic condition—our changing economy. Never before has the pool of developed skill and capability mattered more in our prospects for general economic health. And never before have skill and knowledge mattered as much in the economic prospects for individuals. There is no longer a welcoming place in low-skill, high-wage jobs for people who have not cultivated talents appropriate to an information economy. The country, indeed each state and region, must press for a higher overall level of such cultivated talents. Otherwise, we can expect a continuation of the pattern of falling personal incomes and declining public services that has characterized the past twenty years.

The only way to achieve this higher level of skill and ability in the population at large is to make sure that all students, not just a privileged and select few, learn skills that our society requires. Equity and excellence, classically viewed as competing goals, must now be treated as a single aspiration.

To do this will require a profound transformation of our most basic assumptions about the conditions that enable people to learn. What we learn is a function both of our talents—our aptitude for particular kinds of learning—and of how hard we try—our effort. But what is the relationship between aptitude and effort? Are they independent of each other, and, if so, which is more important? Do strengths in one compensate for weaknesses in the other? Or does one help to create the other?

Facing Up to Our Aptitude-Oriented Education System

Historically, American education has wavered between the first and second of these possibilities, the independent and the compensatory. But it has never seriously considered the third possibility—that effort can create ability. Early in this century, we built an education system around the assumption that aptitude is paramount in learning and that it is largely hereditary. The system was oriented toward selection, distinguishing the naturally able from the less able and providing students with programs thought suitable to their talents. In other periods, most notably during the Great Society reforms, we worked on a compensatory principle, arguing that special effort, by an individual or an institution, could make up for low aptitude. The third possibility—that effort actually creates ability, that people can become smart by working hard at the right kinds of learning tasks—has never been taken seriously in America or indeed in any European society, although it is the guiding assumption of education institutions in societies with a Confucian tradition.

Although the compensatory assumption is more recent in the history of American education, many of our tools and standard practices are inherited from the earlier period in which aptitude reigned supreme. As a result, our schools largely function as if we believed that native ability is the primary determinant in learning, that the "bell curve" of intelligence is a natural phenomenon that must necessarily be reproduced in all learning, that effort counts for little. Consider the following examples: (1) IQ tests or their surrogates determine who will have access to the enriched programs for the "gifted and talented." This curriculum is denied to students who are judged less capable. (2) Our so-called achievement tests are normed to compare students with one another rather than with a standard of excellence, making it difficult to see the results of learning, and, in the process, actively discouraging effort: Students stay at about the same relative percentile rank, even if they have learned a lot, so why should they try hard? (3) We group students, sometimes within classrooms, and provide de facto different curricula to different groups. As a result, some students never get the chance to study a high-demand, high-expectation curriculum. (4) College entrance is heavily dependent on tests that have little to do with the curriculum studied and that are designed—like IQ tests—to spread students out on a scale rather than to define what one is supposed to work at learning. (5) Remedial instruction is offered in "pullout" classes, so that students who need extra instruction miss some of the regular learning opportunities. (6) We expect teachers to grade on a curve. If every student gets an A or a B, we assume that standards are too low. We seldom consider the possibility that the students may have worked hard and succeeded in learning what was taught.

These are commonplace, everyday, taken-for-granted features of the American educational landscape. They are institutionalized expressions of a belief in the importance of aptitude. These practices are far more powerful than what we might say about effort and aptitude. Their routine, largely unquestioned use continues to create evidence that confirms aptitude-based thinking. Students do not try to break through the barrier of low expectations because they, like their teachers and parents, accept the judgment that aptitude matters most and that they do not have the right kinds of aptitude. Not surprisingly, their performance remains low. Children who have not been taught a demanding, challenging, thinking curriculum do not do well on tests of reasoning or problem solving, confirming our original suspicions that they did not have the talent for that kind of thinking. The system is a self-sustaining one in which hidden assumptions are continually reinforced by the inevitable results of practices that are based on those assumptions.

Organizing for Effort

It is not necessary to continue this way. Aptitude is not the only possible basis for organizing schools. Educational institutions could be built around the alternative assumption that effort actually creates ability. Our education system could be designed primarily to foster effort. What would such a system look like? How might it work? There are five essential features of an effort-oriented education system: (1) clear expectations for achievement, well understood by everyone, (2) fair and credible evaluations of achievement, (3) celebration and payoff for success, (4) as much time as is necessary to meet learning expectations, and (5) expert instruction. Let us consider each of these features and what the implications may be.

1. Clear expectations.   Achievement standards—publicly announced and meant for everyone—are the essential foundation of an equitable, effort-oriented education system. If students are to work hard, they need to know what they are aiming for. They need not only to try hard, but also to point their efforts in a particular direction. To direct their efforts, students need to know what they are trying to learn, what the criteria of "good" performance are. Artists building a portfolio of work engage in a continuous process of self-evaluation—aided, when they are fortunate, by friendly but critical teachers and peers. If clear standards of achievement existed, elementary and secondary students could work that way, too, building portfolios of work that they continually evaluate, eventually submitting their best work for external "jurying" to see whether it meets the standards they have been working toward.

An equitable standards system must not just make the goals clear but must also set the same expectations for all students. In the absence of publicly defined standards, our inherited assumptions about aptitude lead us to hold out lower expectations for some children than for others. We will go on doing this as long as official standards of achievement do not exist. The best remedy, the equitable solution, is to set clear, public standards that establish very high minimum expectations for everyone, providing a solid foundation for effort by students and teachers alike.

2. Fair and credible evaluations.   If I am to put out serious effort, I need to know that I will be evaluated fairly, and that those evaluations will be honored and respected. But there is more to fairness than the simple absence of bias in tests and examinations: Fair evaluations are also transparent. Students know their content in advance; they can systematically and effectively study for such an evaluation. In America today, students rarely have the experience of studying hard to pass an examination that they know counts in the world and for which they have been systematically prepared by teachers who themselves understand what is to be examined.

Local tests and exams, usually made up by teachers and administered at the end of teaching units or marking periods, may appear to contradict my claim. Students can study for those, and they are clearly related to the taught curriculum. But, especially for students from poor schools, those tests do not really "count." They are not credible to the world at large. It is understood that an A or a B in an inner-city school does not equal the same grade in an upscale suburban or private school.

A credible evaluation system, one that will evoke sustained effort by students and teachers throughout the system, must evaluate students from all kinds of schools against the same criteria. It must include some externally set exams graded by people other than the students' own teachers, along with an external quality control of grades based on class work (as in an audited portfolio grading system, for example). Neither of these is a new idea. Some version of external exams and audited class work is used in virtually every country except ours as the basis for diplomas, university entrance, and employment. Joined with the other elements of an effort-oriented system, this kind of evaluation system constitutes a strategy for optimizing both equity and excellence in our schools.

3. Celebration and the payoff for success.   Hard work and real achievement deserve celebration. And celebration encourages future effort. An education system that actively tries to promote effort will make sure that its schools organize visible, important events highlighting the work students are doing and pointing clearly to achievements that meet the publicly established standards of quality. There are many options for organizing celebrations. School-community nights can become occasions for displaying work, organizing exhibitions, and putting on performances. Local newspapers and radio and television stations can be recruited to publish exemplary student work or otherwise mark achievements. Community organizations can be asked to participate. It is critical that these celebrations include people who matter to the students, and that what is celebrated is work that meets or is clearly en route to meeting the established standards.

For older students, celebration alone may no longer be enough to sustain effort. Adolescents are increasingly concerned with finding their way into adult roles. They will want to see connections between what they are accomplishing in school and the kinds of opportunities that will become available to them when they leave school. This is why many today advocate some kind of high school credential that is based on specific achievements and that is honored for entrance into both college and work. Celebration coupled with payoff will keep the effort flowing; achievement will rise accordingly.

4. Time and results—inverting the relationship.   Schools today provide roughly equal instructional time to all students: a certain number of hours per day, days per year, and years of schooling. As much instruction and learning as can be fitted into that time is offered. Then, at the end of the prescribed period of study, some kind of evaluation takes place. The spread of results confirms the assumptions about aptitude of American schooling.

What if, instead of holding time fixed and allowing results to vary, we did the opposite: set an absolute standard of expectation and allowed time (and the other resources that go with it) to vary? That arrangement would recognize that some students need more time and support than others but would not change expectations according to an initial starting point. Everyone would be held to the same high minimum. Effort could really pay because all students would know that they would have the learning opportunities they need to meet the standards.

Allowing time to vary does not have to mean having young people remain indefinitely in school, repeating the same programs at which they failed the year before. We already know that this kind of additional time produces very little. Instead, schools and associated institutions would need to offer extra learning opportunities early on. For example, pullout instruction could be replaced with enriched, standards-oriented after-school, weekend, and summer programs. Churches, settlement houses, Scouts, 4-H clubs, and other youth service organizations could be asked to join with the schools in providing such programs. A results-oriented system of this kind would bring to all American children the benefits that some now receive in programs organized by their parents and paid for privately.

5. The right to expert instruction.   I have been arguing that we ought to create the right to as much instruction as each child needs. That is what the time-results inversion is about. But an equitable system requires more than that. It requires expert instruction for all children. We are far from providing that. With notable exceptions, the best teachers, and, therefore, the best instruction, gravitate to the schools that teach children with the fewest educational problems. Children who start out with the greatest need for expert instruction are the ones least likely to get it.

That will not do. An effort-oriented system that sets high expectations for all will create a demand—indeed, a right—to expert instruction. To fulfill that demand, it will be necessary to create enhanced instruction expertise up and down the teaching force, so that there is enough expert instruction to go around. This means that new forms of professional development, for teachers now in the force as well as for those preparing to enter the field, are an essential ingredient of the standards and effort revolution.

From Effort to Ability

My proposal is, in some respects, a radical one. The effort-oriented education that I am calling for—a system in which everyone in the schools knows what they are working toward, in which they can see clearly how they are doing, and in which effort is recognized in ways that people value—is based on assumptions about the nature of human ability that are very different from those that predominate today. But in other respects, my proposal is a practical and feasible one. It calls for a return in institutional practice to values that most Americans subscribe to: effort, fair play, the chance to keep trying. Most of the elements of the proposal—standards, exams, celebrations of achievement, extended time for those who want to meet a higher standard, expert instruction, and professional development—already exist somewhere in our educational practice. These elements need to be brought together in a few major demonstrations that show the possibilities of effort-oriented practices.

Just as aptitude-oriented practices have created evidence that confirms our assumptions about aptitude, so a few effort-oriented demonstrations can begin to create evidence of the power of effort to create ability. As evidence accumulates, beliefs will begin to change, and we can, perhaps, look forward to education in America that is equitable in the deepest sense of the word because it creates ability everywhere.

NO

Kennon M. Sheldon
and Bruce J. Biddle

Standards, Accountability, and School Reform: Perils and Pitfalls

Calls for tough, universal academic standards, more use of national tests, and greater accountability, backed by strong "rewards" or "consequences," are frequently heard in current debates about educational reform. Proponents of such actions seem to assume that problems in American schools occur because educators are not sufficiently focused on the bottom-line issue of student performance. To solve such problems, according to this view, we need to set higher standards for students, assess students' performance with standardized tests, and reward or punish students, their teachers, and their schools, depending on whether those standards are met.

Many aspects of this perspective are problematic. One of the most questionable is the use of tangible rewards or punishments to promote better performance by students and their teachers. As we shall show, many perils can arise when politicians try to graft sanctioning systems onto the educational process. Enthusiasm for the use of such systems seems to reflect a top-down view of human enterprise, in which leaders try to maximize productivity by assigning rote tasks to their followers and ensuring their task performance through the provision of rewards or punishments. This hierarchical view was promoted in the first half of the twentieth century by advocates such as F. W. Taylor and Henry Ford and seemed at that time to be a good way to think about the employees who would staff assembly lines.[1] But today's assembly lines are more often staffed by computerized robots, and advanced thinking in the business world now stresses the need for employee flexibility, creativity, and an ability to transcend intraorganizational boundaries.[2]

This does not mean that accountability and incentive systems will disappear completely from the business world. Businesses tend to have a single, easy-to-measure bottom line: economic profit. Given such a goal, explicit reward and punishment systems can sometimes be useful tools for motivating people to perform tedious, difficult, or dangerous (though profitable) tasks, although we would argue that businesses also pay a hidden price when they over-stress such systems. However, education is a different matter: schools are not businesses run for profit, teachers are not assembly-line workers, and students are not commodities to be turned out with specific skills installed and ready to take their place on the assembly lines of America. Rather, schools are complex organizations, with many goals, whose success is

From Kennon M. Sheldon and Bruce J. Biddle, "Standards, Accountability, and School Reform: Perils and Pitfalls," *Teachers College Record*, vol. 100, no. 1(Fall 1998). Copyright © 1998 by Teachers College, Columbia University. Reprinted by permission of Blackwell Publishing Ltd.

often hard to measure. Teachers must cope with a role that is demanding, complex, and moral, and students must be considered as works-in-progress, with multiple interests, unique goals and perspectives,[3] and the enduring potential to construct and reconstruct both themselves and their social worlds—if that potential is not squandered.[4]

Thus, we argue that a key goal of modern education must be to create a population of lifelong, self-directed learners: adults who possess sophisticated interests, an enduring receptivity to new challenges and growth, and a willingness to adapt to the changing needs of the workplace and society-at-large. However, a good deal of research suggests that the practice of bribing or punishing students (and teachers) in order to motivate performance will only thwart this goal. Although such incentives can be used to boost superficial performance in the short run, they are also likely to create an educational climate that alienates teachers from teaching and students from learning. Thus, proposals for educational reform that stress tangible sanctions for performance ... are not merely questionable, they are disasters waiting to happen.

Our task here is to examine this research and to discuss its implications for current debates about educational reform. Most of the studies we review reflect the concepts and ideas of Deci and Ryan's Self-Determination Theory, so we begin with a general overview of the theory.[5] We next describe four examples of research that support the theory. Finally, we consider what these ideas suggest about the probable effects of simple-minded accountability systems and discuss better strategies for educational reform.

Self-Determination Theory

Self-Determination Theory begins with the concept of intrinsic motivation. *Intrinsically-motivated* behaviors are actions carried out because people enjoy doing them. (In contrast, *externally-motivated* behaviors are engaged in to earn a tangible reward or avoid a punishment.) A huge literature now documents the relative advantages of intrinsic motivation. Although externally-motivated persons can demonstrate impressive feats of short-term, rote learning, intrinsically motivated learners retain such rote material longer, demonstrate a stronger understanding of both rote and more complex material, and demonstrate greater creativity and cognitive flexibility.[6] This happens because intrinsically-motivated persons are more wholly engaged and absorbed in their activities, bringing more of their previous knowledge and integrative capacities to bear in their pursuit of new understanding and mastery.[7]

The concept of intrinsic motivation is also integral to a central philosophical position in the life sciences: the organismic perspective. In this view, humans are assumed to be inherently active, with a natural motivation to explore and assimilate their environments. As they do so, they develop new cognitive structures and abilities.[8] This does not mean that their interests cannot be guided. Indeed, those interests can be channelled, expanded, and stimulated by sensitive mentors who are able to respond to the needs of those who learn. It follows that promoting student interests in socially valued topics through such means is one of the key tasks facing education.[9]

However, the literature makes it clear that states of intrinsic motivation are fragile; they are easily undermined by factors such as concrete rewards, surveillance, contingent praise, and punitive sanctions.[10] The common denominator connecting such factors is that they tend to move the "perceived locus of causality" for the activity outside the person's phenomenal self and into the external environment. When this happens, the person feels like a "pawn," rather than an "origin."[11] And once a person begins to feel like a pawn, it is difficult for him or her to reclaim the self-directed initiative and sense of involvement that promote maximal learning, creativity, and performance.

The organismic perspective makes sharply different assumptions than operant theory, in which people are thought to be inherently passive—acting only to relieve biological drives or secondary motives that have been set up through prior conditioning. Ironically, however, the research we discuss below indicates that operant theory's pessimistic assumptions about human nature *can become true* if people are treated in controlling ways. Thus, before endorsing new top-down initiatives for educational reform, it is very important to consider their potential for depriving students and teachers of intrinsic motivation.

Of course, not all of the things that students and teachers must do are "fun" and enjoyable. Almost all students, for example, will find that learning the multiplication table or a foreign-language vocabulary are dull tasks. Students also have their own unique interests and talents, which may not converge with the particular materials a teacher offers in the classroom. Although teachers should try to make materials interesting for most students, it is unlikely that they can meet the unique needs of everyone. When they cannot, they may instead promote a second positive form of motivation specified in Self-Determination Theory—*identified motivation*. A person has identified motivation when he or she willingly chooses to perform a behavior despite the fact that it is not intrinsically interesting. To illustrate, consider the person who goes to the dentist each year for an annual checkup. This behavior is unlikely to be enjoyable, but the person engages in it because it is thought to be important and valuable. As is the case with intrinsically motivated behavior, the perceived locus of causality for identified motivation also resides within the person's phenomenal self. This is because he or she feels "in charge" and that he or she made the decision to engage in the behavior.

It follows that if we want to produce long-term, self-directed learning among students, our schools should not only promote intrinsic motivation for specific topics but should also help to create identified motivation for lifelong learning. This means that students should leave school with the belief that learning is important and valuable, and they should be willing to seek more education without being prodded or forced, even when that education is not intrinsically interesting. From this perspective, a second key task of education is that of helping students to *internalize* the value of learning.

According to Self-Determination Theory, this is often easily accomplished because humans have a natural propensity to take in the values promoted by mentors and authorities. Thus, in their efforts to assimilate and adapt to their environments, students are often willing to be shown which goals and motives are important and may then internalize such ideas. The theory asserts that authorities (i.e., educators) can best facilitate this internalization process by providing support for students' feelings of autonomy.

Three techniques associated with autonomy support have been identified, and all three have been shown to promote increased identification when activities are not intrinsically motivating.[12] Specifically, when asking students to perform such activities, authorities can: (1) acknowledge and validate the person's perspective ("I understand that this may not seem like a lot of fun, and that's O.K."); (2) provide choice whenever possible ("If you'd rather not do it that way, you can choose to do it this way"); and (3) provide a rationale when choice provision is impossible ("It's important to learn these multiplication facts by heart because many of the more interesting things we will do later depend on this knowledge"). When teachers present activities in such ways, students are able to connect their sense of self to the activity and thus are more likely to identify with it. In contrast, when teachers are controlling; that is, dictatorial, coercive, punitive, or uninterested in students' ideas, internalization is forestalled.[13]

The two useful forms of motivation we have discussed (intrinsic and identified) may also be contrasted with two less desirable forms. *Externally motivated* behaviors are those that are done largely or solely to obtain a reward or avoid a punishment. In performing them, the person assigns little value to the activity and feels little or no sense of involvement in doing it. To illustrate: factory workers may perform jobs they consider boring, exhausting, or dangerous, provided they are paid sufficiently. Needless to say, external motivation tends to involve "have to's" and "must's" and is often characterized by cynicism or resignation, where the perceived "locus of causality" lies outside the person.

Finally, *introjected motivation* occurs when persons force themselves to do an activity in order to avoid guilt or anxiety, or, in order to protect or shore up their sense of self-esteem. For example, a person may have a bad case of flu and ought to stay in bed, but decides to attend a scheduled meeting because of an earlier promise that he or she would attend. Introjected motivation involves "should's" and "ought's" and is often characterized by feelings of internal pressure; here, the perceived locus of causality also does not lie fully within the person.

Various studies have shown that external and introjected motivation are common among students when teachers are controlling or when they try to use tangible rewards and punishments.[14] Furthermore, research has indicated that neither of these latter forms of motivation promotes the type of deeper conceptual learning that we desire in students and that neither is likely to generate behavior that persists for long in the absence of external prods and support.[15] What this means, then, is that the use of tangible rewards and punishments tends to defeat the goals of creating student interests in both subject matter and self-directed, lifelong learning. Similarly, when teachers are faced by sanctioning systems that generate only external or introjected motivation, they are likely to experience resentment and loss of morale, to engage in superficial conformity, and (eventually) to quit their jobs as teachers.[16]

Specific Studies Applying These Ideas

These ideas suggest that accountability systems can and often do create negative forces that are inimical to key goals of education. In order to illustrate these ideas more concretely, we describe here the results of four specific studies.

The first study, conducted by Deci, examined the effects of two types of instructional sets upon the performance of teachers asked to teach students about spatial relations puzzles.[17] In one condition, teachers were told, "Your role is to facilitate the student's learning how to work with the puzzles. There are no performance requirements; your job is simply to help the student learn to solve the puzzles." In the other condition teachers were told, "Your role is to ensure that the student learns to solve the puzzles. It is a teacher's responsibility to make sure that students perform up to standards." Thus, the study provided two very different types of instructional set: one in which student understanding was the goal; the other which stressed the need for students to perform "up to standards."

The investigators found sharp differences in the ways in which teachers behaved given these two conditions. Specifically, teachers in the "performance standards" condition talked more and used more controlling strategies (i.e., they issued more "should" statements and made more criticisms of students). Furthermore, they let students solve far fewer puzzles on their own. Although students in this condition completed more puzzles, only in four percent of cases were they allowed to solve the puzzles by themselves. In contrast, students in the "learning only" condition solved 30 percent of completed puzzles by themselves and rated the teacher as promoting greater understanding. Thus, although students with controlling teachers may have appeared to accomplish more, they actually learned less because their teachers were, in essence, doing the puzzles for them. Findings such as these surely challenge the vaunted "advantages" of telling teachers they must make sure their students meet higher performance standards!

Grolnick and Ryan made a related point in a study of reading performance outcomes among fifth-grade children.[18] Specifically, they examined the effects of three types of task-set on students' ability to comprehend the conceptual meaning of a reading passage. Students in the first, *nondirected* condition were told simply, "After you are finished, I'll be asking you some questions." Grading and evaluation were not mentioned. In effect, students were "turned loose" to find their own ways of becoming interested in the material.

Students in a second, *directed* (but noncontrolling) condition were told, "After you're finished, I'm going to ask you some questions about the passage. It won't really be a test, and you won't be graded on it. I'm just interested in what children can remember from reading passages." This manipulation focused students' attention on the goal of learning without emphasizing an ensuing test, thus inviting them to develop identified motivation for the task.

In contrast, students in a third, *controlling* condition were told, "After you are finished, I'm going to test you on it. I'm going to see how much you can remember. You should work as hard as you can because I'll be grading you on the test to see if you're learning well enough." This manipulation was designed, of course, to give students an external locus of causality for their learning. (In effect they were led to believe, "I'm doing this reading largely or solely because of the upcoming test.")

As expected, students given the first, nondirected instructions indicated the most *interest* in the text and felt the least *pressure*. Conversely, students in the third, or controlling, condition felt the most pressure and indicated the least interest. In addition, post-testing showed that students in the controlling condition had the poorest conceptual *understanding* of the material taught, and although they displayed a high level of recall for *rote material* from the reading lesson when tested immediately afterward, they also experienced a large drop in rote recall when retested eight days later. In contrast, nondirected students showed the strongest conceptual understanding of the material they had read and forgot very little of its rote details. In effect, these students had engaged in deeper processing of the information and had integrated that information more fully with their preexisting knowledge.

Interestingly, students in the second, directed (but noncontrolling) condition displayed respectable levels of both understanding and rote recall. This indicates that directive teaching is not necessarily problematic, but it can become a problem when it crosses the line into a controlling mode. And as the first study we reviewed suggests, this threshold is more likely to be crossed when teachers feel pressures from above to ensure that their students perform to high standards.

Of course, teachers do not necessarily become more controlling when performance pressure is imposed from above.[19] Some teachers may have the skills and insights to resist temptations to "bludgeon" their students into learning. There is, however, another way in which top-down performance pressures can generate detrimental effects—when they prompt politicians, education officials, or parents to impose tangible rewards and punishments on students for their performance. Various studies[20] have shown that, when left to their own devices, children will select tasks that are neither too easy nor too hard—tasks just above their current level of skills and understanding. This is consistent with tenets of the organismic perspective, in which humans are assumed to have a natural propensity to seek out optimal challenges as they engage with and assimilate their environments—and when this happens, they tend also to learn at an optimal rate. However, research[21] also shows that this tendency for students to prefer optimal challenges is easily subverted by the introduction of tangible sanctions....

Implications for Reform Proposals That Stress Testing and Sanctioning

With these ideas and findings in mind, let us examine four specific perils which can accompany the testing-and-sanctioning approach to education.

Peril #1: Too much focus on tests can lead teachers to adopt a narrowed curriculum, dampening studen t interest and inhibiting critical thinking.

When strong emphasis is placed on tests and how student performances "stack up," teachers may narrow their curriculum, teach to the test, or encourage students to focus only on knowing how to get the right answers to test-type questions. One problem with such processes is that students' ability to think broadly may be throttled. In addition, they can stultify intrinsic motivation in the subject and thus forestall the self-directed exploration that is crucial to deeper understanding and mastery.

Peril #2: Teacher incentive systems tied to student test scores often cause teachers to become more controlling, thus undermining students' conceptual learning, intrinsic interest in the subject matter, and desire to pursue future education.

Problems associated with too much focus on tests are magnified when those test results are used by central authorities to generate rewards and punishments for teachers. When teachers' livelihoods are tied to test results, they become less willing to let students explore and experiment with subject materials and may instead become more controlling in their presentations. Furthermore, these teachers readily transmit their own externally based motivation to students, quickly eroding whatever intrinsic subject-matter interests students may have had. For example, Wild, Enzle, and Hawkins showed that musically naüve students given a piano lesson reacted very differently if they thought the teacher was motivated by extrinsic concerns rather than intrinsic interest in teaching the lesson. In this study, the teacher was blind to experimental conditions and gave the same lesson to all students. However, students who believed their teacher was intrinsically motivated enjoyed the lesson more, were more interested in further learning, and demonstrated greater exploratory activity during subsequent free play.[22]

Peril #3: Student incentive systems tied to test score scan ruin students' intrinsic interest in subject matter and reduce their willingness to challenge themselves.

Thus far we have discussed how accountability systems may affect teachers. But problems with accountability are worsened when students are given tangible rewards or punishments for their performance. To illustrate, some school districts today punish students who have failing grades by denying them opportunities to participate in extracurricular activities, such as school-sponsored parties or picnics. Such sanctioning systems are likely to cause students to seek the easiest path to better grades rather than to follow their natural (but fragile) propensities to choose optimally challenging tasks.

Peril #4: To the extent that accountability systems are seen as a panacea, they can distract us from dealing with the real problems of education.

More than ever before, students bring problems to the classroom that interfere with their ability to concentrate and learn. Today, many, many American children grow up in poverty, spend their days in miserably funded schools,[23] are surrounded by drugs and violence, receive insufficient attention from parents in dual-career households, and are strongly exposed to the materialistic values and negative role models portrayed in the media. Is it any wonder, then, that they have difficulty with school? Some politicians love to make scapegoats out of teachers and blame them when students do not always succeed in school, but this merely diverts attention from serious social problems those politicians do not want to address. Moreover, those escalating problems mean that the teacher's job today is more difficult than in earlier years. The last thing teachers need is more controlling oversight by politicians and their minions, wielding questionable test scores, focused on narrow domains of academic competence. Instead, the intrinsic motivation that caused teachers to choose this difficult and monetarily unrewarding field in the first place should be nurtured and protected.

Does this mean that teachers will always reject demands for evaluation of their performance? Indeed it does not. Teachers, like other Americans, generally approve of accountability, paying higher wages to persons with outstanding accomplishments, and helping or dismissing those who are incompetent. The problem for teachers, however, is to find legitimate ways to measure their accomplishments in education. Americans set many goals for teaching. Those goals are hard to assess, and teachers who fail to accomplish one or more of them may succeed gloriously in others. Teachers know this: hence, they tend to reject accountability schemes that rely on narrow, simple-minded performance measures. It is possible to imagine an accountability scheme, however, that would assess a wide range of educational goals with sophisticated instruments, and such a scheme might well be embraced by teachers.

In contrast, given the nature of the learning process, accountability schemes that impose sanctions for academic performance on students are almost bound to fail. Learning is best facilitated when students have intrinsic interest in the subject matter, or at least, an identified interest in the task of learning it. But both of these types of motivation are inhibited when student attention is focused on achievement tests and sanctions. Thus, we discover an apparent paradox that applies to student learning. Although maximal student growth may be the goal, if student attention is focused on tests that measure that growth, or on sanctions that reward or punish it, that growth will not be maximized. In contrast, if students are challenged, if their interests in the subject matter are encouraged, if they are given autonomy support, then their intrinsic interests, their motivation for learning, and their test scores will all grow more effectively.

Better Strategies for Reform

The ideas and studies we have reviewed also suggest principles that can be used to guide better reform strategies. For one thing, they suggest that such strategies will be more successful if they are based on trust in students and teachers—if they assume that most students want to learn and most teachers want to teach. Many things can and should be improved in today's classrooms and schools: among them, poor and overcrowded facilities, outdated textbooks, procedures that give too much stress to competition, tracking, lock-step education, and curricula that promote sloth, ignorance, boredom, or prejudice. But these problems are not likely to disappear if we try to force teachers and students to "shape up." Instead, reforms are more likely to succeed if they involve the active and willing participation of teachers and students. This can be done, of course, through encouragement, challenge, and appropriate autonomy-support; that is, through minimizing the salience of external controls and potential sanctions and emphasizing students' and teachers' rights to be taken seriously, to participate in activities they consider interesting, and to understand the educational importance of other activities in which they have little intrinsic interest. The more such processes occur, the more students and teachers will be encouraged to involve themselves in education, and the greater will be students' growth of knowledge and achievement.

Most teachers know that these goals are important; indeed, many have already received explicit training in how to bring them about. What is needed now is to create a political and administrative climate in which all teachers can be given this knowledge and supported in using it. Or, to return to our opening metaphor, instead of being viewed as assembly-line workers who must be forced to do their jobs, teachers should be given the same types of trust and respect we give to other *professionals*.

Can you imagine calls to impose tough, universal standards for performance, the use of narrow, standardized tests to measure that performance, and sanctions, based on those test scores, upon doctors, physicists, the clergy, or Supreme Court justices? The mind boggles. The reason such proposals would be thought absurd is that we assume that the professional roles of doctors, physicists, and the like are complex, that success in them is hard to measure, and that those who perform them are thoroughly trained, highly motivated, and generally competent to do their jobs. This does not mean, of course, that all such professionals are equally competent, and we count on their professional associations (and the law) to detect, review, and ultimately to cashier those who are truly incompetent. But generally we bestow high status, authority, good salaries, and trust on such professionals—and public school teachers should be given the same grace.

Notes

1. Frederick W. Taylor, *The Principles of Scientific Management* (Westport, CT: Greenwood Press, 1911). See also Raymond Callahan, *Education and the Cult of Efficiency* (New York: Free Press, 1962).
2. Barry Jones, *Sleepers Wake: Technology and the Future of Work* (Melbourne: Oxford University Press, 1982); J. Hirsch, "Fordism and Post-Fordism: The Present Social Crisis and its Consequences," in *Post-Fordism and Social Form*, ed. W. Bonefeld and J. Holloway (Basingstoke, England: Macmillan, 1991), pp. 8-32; and Susan L. Robertson, "Restructuring Teachers' Labor: 'Troubling' Post-Fordisms," in *International Handbook of Teachers and Teaching*, ed. B. J. Biddle,

T. L. Good, and I. J. Goodson (Dordrecht, The Netherlands: Kluwer, 1997), pp. 621-70.

3. Kennon M. Sheldon and Tim Kasser, "Coherence and Congruence: Two Aspects of Personality Integration." *Journal of Personality and Social Psychology*, 68 (1995): 531-43.

4. See, among other sources, John Dewey's *Moral Principles in Education* (Boston: Houghton Mifflin, 1909) or *Democracy and Education* (New York: Macmillan, 1916).

5. See Edward L. Deci and Richard M. Ryan, *Intrinsic Motivation and Self-Determination in Human Behavior* (New York: Plenum, 1985); and Edward L. Deci and Richard M. Ryan, "A Motivational Approach to Self: Integration in Personality," in R. Dienstbier, Ed., *Nebraska Symposium on Motivation* (Lincoln, NE: University of Nebraska Press, 1991), pp. 237-88.

6. Kennon M. Sheldon, "Creativity and Self-Determination in Personality," *Creativity Research Journal*, 8 (1995): 61-72.

7. Richard M. Ryan and Jerome Stiller, "The Social Contexts of Internalization: Parent and Teacher Influences on Autonomy, Motivation, and Learning," *Advances in Motivation and Achievement,* 7 (1991): 115-49.

8. John Dewey, *Experience and Education* (New York: Collier, 1938); and Jean Piaget, *Biology and Knowledge* (Chicago: University of Chicago Press, 1971).

9. Russell Ames and Carole Ames, "Motivation and Effective Teaching," in L. Idol & B. F. Hones, Eds., *Educational Values and Cognitive Instruction: Implications for Reform* (Hillsdale, NJ: Lawrence Erlbaum, 1991), pp. 247-71; Carol S. Dweck, "Social Motivation: Goals and Social-Cognitive Processes. A Comment," in J. Juvonen and K. R. Wentzel, Eds., *Social Motivation: Understanding Children's School Adjustment* (New York: Cambridge University Press, 1996), pp. 181-95; and Mark R. Lepper, Sheena Sethi, Dania Dialdin, and Michael Drake, "Intrinsic and Extrinsic Motivation: A Development Perspective" in S. S. Luthar, J. A. Burack, D. Cicchetti, and J. R. Weisz, Eds., *Developmental Psychopathology: Perspectives on Adjustment, Risk, and Disorder* (New York: Cambridge University Press, 1997), pp. 23-50.

10. See Deci & Ryan, "Motivational Approach to Self," for a review of this evidence.

11. Richard deCharms, *Personal Causation: The Internal Affective Determinants of Behavior* (New York: Academic Press, 1968).

12. See Edward L. Deci, Haleh Eghrari, Brian Patrick, and Dean Leone, "Facilitating Internalization: The Self-Determination Theory Perspective," *Journal of Personality,* 62 (1994): 119-42.

13. Christine Chandler and Jim Connell, "Children's Intrinsic, Extrinsic, and Internalized Motivation: A Development Study of Children's Reasons for Liked and Disliked Behavior," *British Journal of Developmental Psychology,* 5 (1987): 357-65.

14. Edward L. Deci, Allan Schwartz, Louise Sheinman, and Richard M. Ryan, "An Instrument to Assess Adult's Orientations Toward Control Versus Autonomy with Children: Reflections on Intrinsic Motivation and Perceived Competence," *Journal of Educational Psychology,* 73 (1981): 642-50.

15. Mark Lepper and David Greene, "Turning Play Into Work: Effects of Adult Surveillance and Extrinsic Rewards on Children's Intrinsic Motivation," *Journal of Personality and Social Psychology,* 31 (1975): 479-86.
16. See Anthony G. Dworkin, *Teacher Burnout in the Public Schools: Structural Causes and Consequences for Children* (Albany: State University of New York Press, 1987); and ibid., "Coping with Reform: The Intermix of Teacher Morale, Teacher Burnout, and Teacher Accountability," in *International Handbook of Teachers and Teaching,* ed. Biddle, Good, and Goodson, pp. 459-98.
17. Edward L. Deci, Nancy H. Spiegel, Richard M. Ryan, Richard Koestner, and M. Christina Kauffman, "The Effects of Performance Standards on Teaching Styles: The Behavior of Controlling Teachers," *Journal of Educational Psychology,* 74 (1982): 852-59.
18. Wendy S. Grolnick and Richard M. Ryan, "Autonomy in Children's Learning: An Experimental and Individual Differences Investigation," *Journal of Personality and Social Psychology,* 52 (1987): 890-898.
19. See Cheryl Flink, Ann K. Boggiano, and Marty Barrett, "Controlling Teaching Strategies: Undermining Children's Self-determination and Performance," *Journal of Personality and Social Psychology,* 42 (1982): 789-97.
20. See Ryan and Stiller, "The Social Contexts of Internalization."
21. Pittman, Emery, and Boggiano, "Intrinsic and Extrinsic Motivational Orientations."
22. See Cameron Wild, Michael Enzle, and Wendy Hawkins, "Effects of Perceived Extrinsic vs. Intrinsic Teacher Motivation on Student Reactions to Skill Acquisition," *Personality and Social Psychology Bulletin,* 1 (1992): 245-51.
23. Bruce J. Biddle, "Foolishness, Dangerous Nonsense, and Real Correlates of State Differences in Achievement," *Phi Delta Kappan,* September 1997, pp. 9-13.

POSTSCRIPT

Will a Push for Standards and Accountability Lead to More Motivated Students?

Sheldon and Biddle offer considerable evidence—most of it from experimental rather than correlational studies—that external rewards or systems of control either decrease students' intrinsic motivation to engage in the controlled activity or leads teachers to alter their behavior in the direction of greater control over the learning process, which in turn limits student motivation. Unfortunately, there are several limitations of the data presented by Sheldon and Biddle that make it impossible to conclude with certainty what effect standards reform will have on student motivation.

Consider two limitations: First, in the research cited by Sheldon and Biddle, the rewards or punishments were grades, prizes, or other relatively minor consequences, and their delivery was contingent on a vague specification of "doing well." Supporters of standards would argue that their plans are very different from the plans embodied in these studies because their plans involve a clearly articulated set of goals associated with far-reaching consequences (e.g., nonpromotion). Second, the studies cited by Sheldon and Biddle were all short-term, involving an assessment of outcomes only a few days or weeks after implementation of the system of external control. It is possible, argue supporters of standards, that the negative effects of an external system of control are transient—a possibility that would require examining student motivation over the course of several semesters or even years.

There are many articles on the issue of standards and accountability. Two papers that focus on the positive elements of standards reform are "Core Knowledge and Standards: A Conversation With E. D. Hirsch, Jr.," by John O'Neill, *Educational Leadership* (March 1999) and "Realizing the Promise of Standards-Based Education," by Mike Schmoker and Robert J. Marzano, *Educational Leadership* (March 1999). Several interesting papers have focused on the establishment of standards in particular content domains, most notably mathematics: "Parrot Math," by Thomas C. O'Brien, *Phi Delta Kappan* (February 1999); "Issues and Options in the Math Wars," by Harold L. Schoen et al., *Phi Delta Kappan* (February 1999); and "A Common Core of Math for All," by Arthur F. Coxford and Christian R. Hirsch, *Educational Leadership* (May 1996). The impact of the push for standards and accountability on multicultural education and the marginalization of students from the nonmajority culture can be found in "Multicultural Education and the Standards Movement: A Report From the Field," by Anita P. Bohn and Christine E. Sleeter, *Phi Delta Kappan* (October 2000).

ISSUE 12

Do Recent Discoveries About the Brain and Its Development Have Implications for Classroom Practice?

YES: **Mariale M. Hardiman**, from "Connecting Brain Research With Dimensions of Learning," *Educational Leadership* (November 2001)

NO: **John T. Bruer**, from "Brain Science, Brain Fiction," *Educational Leadership* (November 1998)

ISSUE SUMMARY

YES: Mariale M. Hardiman, principal of a combined elementary and middle school in Baltimore, Maryland, argues that the pedagogical techniques that are employed in her school are successful because they fit with what is known about how the human brain works.

NO: John T. Bruer, president of the James S. McDonnell Foundation, an organization that provides financial support to researchers investigating basic and applied problems in the behavioral and biomedical sciences, argues that although scientists have recently learned many interesting things about the developing human brain, this research currently has little direct application to education.

Research in the brain sciences has proceeded at a rapid pace since the 1970s, due in large measure to the advent of some amazing new technologies: positron emission tomography (PET), single photon emission computed tomography (SPECT), magnetic resonance imaging (MRI), functional magnetic imaging (fMRI), and high-density event-related potentials (HD-ERP). These technologies provide high-resolution images of the human brain, yielding information about not only structural characteristics but also about how the brain functions "online" as an individual processes perceptual information, solves complex problems, or makes responses as simple as a button press or as complex as a spoken sentence. Some of these techniques require sedation, exposure to radiation, and injections and are thus of limited utility with young children. Other techniques, however, are noninvasive, typically requiring only that the individual whose brain is being "imaged" sit motion-

251

less in a special apparatus while performing the cognitive task being studied, which means that many of these techniques can provide a window into the brains of even very young children.

A few of the findings that have captured the attention of educators (not to mention the news media) in recent years follow:

1. In contrast to what was believed only a few years ago, the structure and function of the human brain is not fixed at birth. It now appears that the brain undergoes dramatic changes in connectedness during infancy. The many neurons (nerve cells) in the baby's brain establish increasing information-exchanging links with each other. The number of connections, or synapses, increases more than 20 times during the first few months of life.

2. The timing of synaptic development varies across different parts of the human brain, which may account in part for the different behavioral capabilities of children at different ages. For example, at 18 to 24 months, a dramatic increase in synaptic density and changes in the metabolic activity of the brain may help to produce the burst in vocabulary learning normally seen at this time.

3. At the same time that synaptic growth is providing the foundation for new skills and capabilities, it is closing off other avenues of learning. For example, there is evidence that early in infancy neurons in the auditory cortex are responsive to a range of speech sounds. As the infant gains exposure to his or her native language, however, neurons become more specialized, responding only to specific, frequently heard sounds, which leaves them "unresponsive" to unfamiliar speech sounds, such as those included in other languages. This seems to occur by 12 months of age.

4. There is evidence that brain regions that are normally responsible for one function can assume other functions depending on the experiences available to the individual. For example, portions of the temporal lobe that are responsive to sound in individuals with normal hearing are sensitive to visual stimuli in congenitally deaf individuals.

5. Chronic traumatic experiences during periods of rapid brain growth can lead to greatly elevated levels of stress hormones, which then flood the brain, altering its structure and function, with serious consequences for subsequent learning and behavior.

Educators have enthusiastically embraced findings emerging from work in the brain sciences. After all, our understanding of the brain informs us about learning; doesn't it follow that our understanding of the brain will inform us about teaching as well? In the first of the following selections, Mariale M. Hardiman argues that current research on brain function does inform educational practice. In the second selection, John T. Bruer argues that research on the brain currently has little direct application to educational practice.

Mariale M. Hardiman

 **YES**

Connecting Brain Research With Dimensions of Learning

In the past 10 years, teachers have been bombarded by education reform initiatives, including standards-based instruction, teaching to students' learning styles, performance-based instruction, multiple intelligences, and, most recently, brain-based learning. In addition, during the 1990s, the Individuals with Disabilities Education Act (IDEA) mandated that students with disabilities have access to the general education curriculum. This mandate has resulted in more students with special needs being taught in general education classrooms (Lombardi & Butera, 1998).

Meeting the needs of diverse learners can be challenging enough for teachers without the charge of determining how to incorporate reform initiatives into practice. Merely superimposing reforms upon existing practices and requirements is generally ineffective. Education initiatives that link current practice with promising new research in neurological and cognitive sciences, however, offer real possibilities for improving teaching and learning, especially for students with diverse learning needs.

Scientists and researchers are making exciting new discoveries related to how the brain processes and stores information (Sousa, 1998). This research has the potential to unlock the mysteries of learning itself. For example, recent research highlights the differences in brain anatomy of students with learning disabilities and attention deficits that can shed light on their performance in the classroom (Semrud-Clikeman et al., 2000). Yet, despite the enormous implications of such research, it is not being effectively disseminated to education practitioners, who, among all professionals, need it most (Sousa, 1998).

How can we familiarize teachers with brain-based learning so that they can apply this latest research to meet the needs of all students, including those with disabilities, in the general education classroom? A basic precept of brain-based research states that learning is best achieved when linked with the learner's previous knowledge, experience, or understanding of a given subject or concept (Perry, 2000). Therefore, we can assume that the use of brain-based research would be most effective when combined with previously established frameworks for teaching and learning (Brandt, 1999).

One such framework that Roland Park Elementary/Middle School has used since 1994 is the Dimensions of Learning model (Marzano, 1992). Roland

Park, a Blue Ribbon School of Excellence in Baltimore, Maryland, has steadily improved the achievement of its 1,350 students during the past six years. Our progress, in part, may be attributed to our use of Dimensions of Learning, which addresses the development of higher-order thinking skills. Robert Marzano describes the five dimensions as "loose metaphors for how the mind works during learning" (1992, p. 2). Linking the five dimensions with the latest brain research suggests a number of best practices for teaching all children—especially students with learning disabilities.

Dimension One: Positive Attitudes

Dimension One explains that a student's attitudes and perceptions serve as filters that enhance or inhibit natural learning. Although educators may have long suspected that attitudes affect learning, brain research clearly supports the link between emotions and cognition. Robert Leamnson (2000) explains that neural pathways connect the limbic system, the brain's emotional center, to the frontal lobes, which play a major role in learning. In addition, hormones alter the chemical makeup of the brain of a person under stress. When the person is threatened, chemicals are released that can impair memory and learning (Jensen, 1998).

Best Practices
- Provide a challenging yet supportive classroom environment by reducing the stress that may come from embarrassment because of academic difficulties or peer rejection. At Roland Park, we make students feel more comfortable by assigning a "peer buddy" as a homework helper, arranging for tutoring in study skills and test-taking strategies, and providing special meetings outside of class time to encourage a trusting teacher-student relationship.
- Teach peer acceptance and social behaviors explicitly. Students with learning disabilities may experience an added fear of rejection from the stigma of special education. Our teachers hold class meetings to encourage social acceptance and interaction, use literature and history to provide instructional materials that demonstrate acceptance of diversity, and model an attitude of acceptance and appreciation for those with different learning styles and needs.
- To cement long-term memory, connect emotions to learning. Techniques such as dramatizations, humor, movement, or arts integration can arouse the emotional systems of the brain and stimulate peak performance. For example, teachers may tell a funny instructional story at the beginning of class to foster a relaxed yet supportive atmosphere.

Dimension Two: Acquiring and Integrating Knowledge

Dimension Two pertains to the acquisition and integration of knowledge. Marzano (1992) proposes that learning new information must occur within the context of what the learner already knows and must be adequately assimilated so that the information can be used easily in new situations.

Much of brain-based research has focused on how the brain acquires, stores, and uses information (Valiant, 1998). Learning occurs through the growth of neural connections, stimulated by the passage of electrical current along nerve cells and enhanced by chemicals discharged into the synapse between neighboring cells. The more often the "trail is blazed," the more automatic a task or memory becomes (Buchel, Coull, & Friston, 1999). Therefore, the more a student repeats a learning task, the greater the connectivity. Researchers also point out that different parts of the brain store particular parts of a memory (Fishback, 1999). For example, one part of the brain might store the lyrics of a song and another part, the melody. Further, Leamnson (2000) explains that the brain must reconstruct a memory each time the person recalls the memory. Learning thus requires both the acquisition of information and the ability to retrieve and reconstruct that information whenever necessary. Evidence from brain-mapping technology indicates that individual differences in learning styles affect this retrieval process. In a study that investigated the differences between normal and disabled readers in visual-perceptual tasks, Richard S. Kruk and Dale M. Willows (2001) found significant processing differences that affected the rate of visual processing for students with reading disabilities. Jean Robertson (2000) suggests that the inability to shift control from the right to the left hemisphere of the brain may cause early reading disorders.

Best Practices

- Present new information within the context of prior knowledge and previously learned content (Perry, 2000). For example, students may better understand the bicameral system of U.S. government by comparing it with their own student government.
- Allow students to repeat learning tasks to cement them in memory (Sprenger, 1998). This is especially important for activities that require an automatic response, such as blending phonemes into words (Shaywitz, 1998) or mastering math facts.
- Use mnemonics, which can significantly increase the memory of content (Carney & Levin, 2000), especially for students with special needs (Lombardi & Butera, 1998). For example, telling students to "write with their FEAT" can remind them to use the transition words "for example" or "according to" to introduce supportive text in their writing.
- Use visually stimulating material and manipulatives to activate the right hemisphere of the brain and text presentation to activate the left hemisphere (Robertson, 2000). The right brain's visual-spatial skills can be activated with features such as a balance scale to help visualize algebraic equations or pictures and graphs to enhance the meaning of text.
- Integrate art, music, and movement into learning activities to activate multiple parts of the brain and enhance learning (Rauscher et al., 1997; Vogel, 2000). For example, students can learn how the earth's tilt and rotation create seasons through body movements—tilting the body toward the center of a circle to simulate spring; turning and tilting away from the center to simulate fall.

Dimension Three: Extending and Refining Knowledge

Extending and refining knowledge requires examining it in a deeper, more analytical way by doing such things as comparing, classifying, inducing, deducing, analyzing errors, constructing support, abstracting, and analyzing perspective (Marzano, 1992). The thinking skills involved in Dimension Three require that the brain use multiple and complex systems of retrieval and integration (Lowery, 1998). Ron Brandt (2000) states that brain research supports thinking-skills programs that have students compare and classify familiar concepts. He explains that

> neurons that often fire at the same time as certain other neurons become more likely to fire whenever those other neurons fire.... We use less brain energy when performing familiar functions than when learning new skills. (p. 75)

Best Practices
- Design tasks that allow students to use prior knowledge to learn new information. For example, students use their prior understanding of photosynthesis to explain the differences between plant and animal cells.
- Offer students an opportunity to compare their performances with model responses and to analyze their error patterns. For example, when asking students to write an essay, provide a model paper that clearly identifies the main idea, supporting details, transition words, and conclusion. Let students use the model to organize their own writing.
- Teach students to identify general patterns that underlie concepts. For example, compare the leadership characteristics of current leaders with those of successful leaders of the past.

Dimension Four: Using Knowledge Meaningfully

Marzano (1992) states that we learn best when we need information to accomplish a goal. Using Dimension Four thinking strategies, students apply information in activities that require them to make decisions, investigate, conduct experiments, and solve real-world problems. Brain research confirms that this type of experiential learning activates the area of the brain responsible for higher-order thinking (Sousa, 1998). Moreover, enriched instruction has been shown to produce significant chemical changes in the brains of students with learning disabilities—changes that indicate less exertion of effort in learning (Richards et al., 2000). A similar study (Bower, 1999) indicated that reinforcement of active learning tasks improves brain efficiency.

Leamnson (2000) warns, however, that merely providing students with hands-on activities does not guarantee learning. Teachers must pair physical activities with problem-solving tasks to connect the "acting modules" of the brain—the motor cortex—with the "thinking modules"—the frontal lobes. Such experiences increase memory and learning, thereby modifying brain structures (Kandel & Squire, 2000).

Best Practices
- Assign students active, hands-on tasks that require them to investigate, analyze, and solve problems using real-world applications (Green, 1999). For example, students can apply the formula for the area of a rectangle by determining how much paint it would take to paint a room given the dimensions of walls, doors, and windows.
- Allow students to use multiple ways to demonstrate learning, such as inventions, experiments, dramatizations, visual displays, music, and oral presentations. For instance, assigning groups of students to write scripts and perform skits to represent each of the 12 labors of Hercules makes this myth come alive.

Dimension Five: Habits of Mind

Dimension Five describes the mental habits that enable students to facilitate their own learning. These habits include monitoring one's own thinking (*metacognitive thinking*), goal setting, maintaining one's own standards of evaluation, self-regulating, and applying one's unique learning style to future learning situations. Understanding and facilitating one's own learning style is especially important for students with learning disabilities. According to Martin Languis (1998), brain-mapping tests reveal individual differences in brain organization and structure that relate to specific differences in learning style. Studies showed that students who were more skilled in spatial-visualization tasks such as visualizing three-dimensional objects demonstrated different brain-processing patterns compared with less-skilled students. Students, however, significantly improved their scores in spatial-visualization assessments after taking courses that taught them specific learning strategies such as the use of imagery, graphic organizers, and puzzles.

Best Practices
- Provide ways for students to engage in metacognitive reflection. Students benefit from the use of think logs, reflective journals, and group discussions within a cooperative learning setting.
- Include reflective discussions of lessons to foster the habit of reflection on learning. Ask students to record one important concept that they learned from the lesson and several important facts.

Putting the Research to Use

Although most researchers agree that our understanding of the human brain is in its infancy, the explosion of research in the field of neurology and cognitive sciences in the past 10 years can and should play an important role in education reform, especially for students who demonstrate differences in their thinking and learning patterns. If teachers combine brain research with a thinking skills framework such as Dimensions of Learning as we have at Roland Park Elementary/Middle School, the research will translate more effectively into practice. Our use of this model has resulted in exciting learning experiences for students as well as increased scores on our state performance assessment every year since 1994. Moreover, the potential of brain research to provide new approaches to teaching students with information-processing difficulties makes its use all the more vital in classrooms today. Students with learning differences, including those with learning disabilities who are in general education classrooms, deserve to have available to them a program of research-based instruction to nurture and enhance both thinking and learning.

References

Bower, B. (1999, March 6). Learning may unify distant brain regions. *Science News* [Online]. Available: www.findarticles.com/cf01/m1200/mag.jhmtl

Brandt, R. (1999). Educators need to know about the human brain. *Phi Delta Kappan, 81,* 235-238.

Brandt, R. (2000). On teaching brains to think: A conversation with Robert Sylwester. *Educational Leadership, 57*(7), 72-75.

Buchel, C., Coull, J. T., & Friston, K. J. (1999). The predictive value of changes in effective connectivity for human learning. *Science, 283,* 1538-1541.

Carney, R. N., & Levin, J. R. (2000). Mnemonic instruction, with a focus on transfer. *Journal of Educational Psychology, 92,* 783-790.

Fishback, S. J. (1999). Learning and the brain. *Adult Learning, 10*(2), 18-22.

Green, F. E. (1999). Brain and learning research: Implications for meeting the needs of diverse learners. *Education, 119,* 682-687.

Jensen, E. (1998). How Julie's brain learns. *Educational Leadership, 56*(3), 41-45.

Kandel, E. R., & Squire, L. R. (2000). Neuroscience: Breaking down scientific barriers to the study of brain and mind. *Science, 290,* 1113-1120.

Kruk, R. S., & Willows, D. M. (2001). Backward pattern masking of familiar and unfamiliar materials in disabled and normal readers. *Cognitive Neuropsychology, 18*(1), 19-37.

Languis, M. (1998). Using knowledge of the brain in educational practice. *NASSP Bulletin, 82*(598), 38-47.

Leamnson, R. (2000). Learning as biological brain change. *Change, 32*(6), 34-40. Available: www.findarticles.com/cf_01/m1254/mag.jhtml

Lombardi, T., & Butera, G. (1998, May). Mnemonics: Strengthening thinking skills of students with special needs. *The Clearing House, 71*(5), 284-286.

Lowery, L. (1998). How new science curriculums reflect brain research. *Educational Leadership, 56*(3), 26-30.

Marzano, R. J. (1992). *A different kind of classroom: Teaching with Dimensions of Learning.* Alexandria, VA: ASCD.

Perry, B. (2000). How the brain learns best. *Instructor, 11*(4), 34-35.

Rauscher, F., Shaw, G., Levine, L., Wright, E., Dennis, W., & Newcomb, R. (1997). Music training causes long-term enhancement of preschool children's spatial-temporal reasoning. *Neurological Research, 19*(1), 2-8.

Richards, T., Corina, D., Serafini, S., Steury, K., Echelard, D. R., Dager, S. R., Marro, K., Abbott, R. D., Maravilla, K. R., & Berninger, V. W. (2000). Effects of a phonologically driven treatment for dyslexia on lactate levels measured by Proton MR spectroscopic imaging. *American Journal of Neuroradiology, 21,* 916-922.

Robertson, J. (2000). Neuropsychological intervention in dyslexia: Two studies on British pupils. *Journal of Learning Disabilities, 33*(2), 137-148.

Semrud-Clikeman, M., Steingard, R. J., Filipeck, P., Biederman, J., Bekken, K., & Renshaw, P. F. (2000). Using MRI to examine brain-behavior relationships in males with attention deficit disorder with hyperactivity. *Journal of the American Academy of Child & Adolescent Psychiatry, 39*(4), 477-484.

Shaywitz, S. E. (1998). Dyslexia. *The New England Journal of Medicine, 338,* 307-312.

Sousa, D. (1998). Brain research can help principals reform secondary schools. *NASSP Bulletin, 82*(598), 21-28.

Sprenger, M. (1998). Memory lane is a two-way street. *Educational Leadership, 56*(3), 65-67.

Valiant, R. (1998). Growing brain connections: A modest proposal. *Schools in the Middle, 7*(4), 24-26.

Vogel, G. (2000). Neuroscience: New brain cells prompt new theory of depression. *Science, 290*(5490), 258-259.

John T. Bruer

Brain Science, Brain Fiction

During the past year, a flood of articles in popular and professional publications have discussed the implications of brain science for education and child development. Although we should consider ideas and research from other fields for our professional practice, we must assess such ideas critically. This is particularly true when we look at how a vast, complex field like brain science might improve classroom instruction.

Three big ideas from brain science figure most centrally in the education literature, and educators should know four things about these ideas to make their own critical appraisals of brain-based education. My own assessment of recent articles about brain research is that well-founded educational applications of brain science may come eventually, but right now, brain science has little to offer education practice or policy (Bruer, 1997, 1998).

Three big ideas arise from brain science: (1) Early in life, neural connections (synapses) form rapidly in the brain; (2) Critical periods occur in development; and (3) Enriched environments have a pronounced effect on brain development during the early years. Neuroscientists have known about all three big ideas for 20 to 30 years. What we need to be critical of is not the ideas themselves, but how they are interpreted for educators and parents.

Early Synapse Formation

Synapses are the connections through which nerve impulses travel from one neuron to another. Since the late 1970s, neuroscientists have known that the number of synapses per unit volume of tissue (the *synaptic density*) in the brain's outer cortical layer changes over the life span of monkeys and humans (Goldman-Rakic, Bourgeois, & Rakic, 1997; Huttenlocher & Dabholkar, 1997; Rakic, Bourgeois, & Goldman-Rakic, 1994). Not surprisingly, human newborns have lower synaptic densities than adults. However, in the months following birth, the infant brain begins to form synapses far in excess of the adult levels. In humans, by age 4, synaptic densities have peaked in all brain areas at levels 50 percent above adult levels. Throughout childhood, synaptic densities remain above adult levels. Around the age of puberty, a pruning process begins to eliminate synapses, reducing synaptic densities to adult, mature levels.

The timing of this process appears to vary among brain areas in humans. In the visual area of the human brain, synaptic densities increase rapidly starting at 2 months of age, peak at 8 to 10 months, and then decline to adult levels at around 10 years. However, in the human frontal cortex—the brain area involved in attention, short-term memory, and planning—this process begins later and lasts longer. In the frontal cortex, synaptic densities do not stabilize at mature levels until around age 16. Thus, we can think of synaptic densities changing over the first two decades of life in an inverted-U pattern: low at birth, highest in childhood, and lower in adulthood.

This much is neuroscientific fact. The question is, What does this inverted-U pattern mean for learning and education? Here, despite what educators might think, the neuroscientists know relatively little. In discussing what the changes in synaptic density mean for behavior and learning, neuroscientists cite a small set of examples based on animal research and then extrapolate these findings to human infants. On the basis of observations of changes in motor, visual, and memory skills, neuroscientists agree that basic movement, vision, and memory skills first appear in their most primitive form when synaptic densities begin their rapid increase. For example, at age 8 months, when synapses begin to increase rapidly in the frontal brain areas, infants first show short-term memory skills for places and objects. Infants' performance on these tasks improves steadily over the next four months. However, performance on these memory tasks does not reach adult levels until puberty, when synaptic densities have decreased to adult levels.

> *Thing to Know No. 1: Neuroscience suggests that there is no simple, direct relationship between synaptic densities and intelligence.*

Increases in synaptic densities are associated with the initial emergence of skills and capacities continue to develop after synaptic densities decrease to adult levels. Although early in infancy we might have the most synapses we will ever have, most learning occurs later, after synaptic densities *decrease* in the brain. Given the existence of the U-shaped pattern and what we observe about our own learning and intelligence over our life spans, we have no reason to believe, as we often read, that the more synapses we have, the smarter we are. Nor do existing neuroscientific studies support the idea that the more learning experiences we have during childhood, the more synapses will be "saved" from pruning and the more intelligent our children will be.

Neuroscientists know very little about how learning, particularly school learning, affects the brain at the synaptic level. We should be skeptical of any claims that suggest they do. For example, we sometimes read that complex learning situations cause increased "neural branching" that offsets neural pruning. As far as we know, such claims are based more on brain fiction than on brain science.

Critical Periods in Development

Research on critical periods has been prominent in developmental neurobiology for more than 30 years. This research has shown that if some motor, sensory, and (in humans) language skills are to develop normally, then the animal must have certain kinds of experience at specific times during its development.

The best-researched example is the existence of critical periods in the development of the visual system. Starting in the 1960s, David Hubel, Torsten Wiesel, and their colleagues showed that if during the early months of life, cats or monkeys had one eyelid surgically closed, the animal would never regain functional use of that eye when it was subsequently reopened (Hubel, Wiesel, & LeVay, 1977). They also showed that closing one eye during this time had demonstrable effects on the structure of the visual area in the animal's brain. However, the same or longer periods of complete visual deprivation in adult cats had no effect on either the animals' ability to use the eye when it was reopened or on its brain structure. Only young animals, during a critical period in their development, were sensitive to this kind of deprivation. They also found that closing *both* eyes during the critical period had no permanent, long-term effects on the animals' vision or brain structure.

Finally, they found that in monkeys, "reverse closure" during the critical period—opening the closed eye and closing the open eye—allowed a young deprived animal to recover the use of the originally deprived eye. If the reverse suturing was done early enough in the critical period, recovery could be almost complete. These last two findings are seldom mentioned in popular and educational interpretations of critical-period research.

Over the past three decades, hundreds of neuroscientists have advanced our understanding of critical periods. We should be aware of three conclusions about critical periods that these scientists generally endorse. First, the different outcomes of closing one eye, both eyes, and reverse suturing suggest that it is *not* the amount of stimulation that matters during a critical period. If only the amount mattered, closing both eyes should have the same effect on each eye as it had when only one eye was closed. Neuroscientists believe that what matters during critical periods in the development of the visual system is the *balance* and *relative timing* of stimulation to the eyes. What does this mean? For one thing, it means that more stimulation during the critical period does not necessarily result in a better-developed visual system.

Second, neuroscientists have learned that critical periods are quite complex and that different critical periods exist for different specific functions (Daw, 1995). For example, within the visual system are different critical periods for visual acuity, binocular function, and depth perception. For humans, even in an early developing system like vision, these periods can last until early childhood. For language, the critical period for learning phonology—learning to speak without an accent—ends in early childhood, but the critical period for learning a language's grammar does not end until around age 16.

Neuroscientists now also think that for each specific function of a sensory system, like vision, there are three distinct phases within the critical period. First, there is a time of rapid change during which a function, like depth perception, quickly matures. During the second phase, sensory deprivation can result in deterioration or loss of that function. After the period of sensitivity to deprivation, there seems to be yet a third phase of the critical period. During this phase, the system retains sufficient plasticity to compensate for deprivation and regains near-normal function if appropriate sensory experience occurs.

Given these complexities, neuroscientists know that it makes little sense to speak of *a* critical period for vision or for any other sensory system, let alone of *a* critical period for brain development. Critical periods are simply windows of learning opportunity that open and then slam shut.

Finally, neuroscientists are beginning to understand why critical periods exist and why critical periods have adaptive value for an organism. They believe that as the result of evolutionary processes, highly sensitive neural systems, like vision, have come to depend on the presence of environmental stimuli to fine-tune their neural circuitry.

Relying on the environment to fine-tune the system results in neural circuits that are more sensitively tuned than they ever could be if they were hardwired by genetic programs at birth. Relying on the presence of certain kinds of stimuli just at the right times would seem to be a highly risky developmental strategy, especially for a system like vision that is fundamental to survival. The reason it is not risky is that the kinds of stimuli needed during critical periods—patterned visual input, the ability to move and manipulate objects, noises, the presence of speech sounds—are ubiquitously and abundantly present in any normal human environment. Nature has made a bet that the stimuli will be present, but nature has placed its money on an almost sure thing. The brain expects certain kinds of stimuli to be present for normal development, and they almost always are, unless a child is abused to the point of being raised in a deprivation chamber. William Greenough and his colleagues (1992) have characterized the kind of brain modification that occurs as a result of critical periods "experience-expectant brain plasticity."

> *Thing to Know No. 2: If critical periods are a result of our evolutionary history and nature's be tonal most sure things occurring in a child's environment, then neuroscientific research on critical periods is likely to have little relevance to formal education.*

From what we know to date about critical periods, they contribute to the development of basic specieswide abilities, like vision, hearing, or language. For this reason, despite what we read, the specifics of home or preschool environments matter little, if at all, to how children's sensory and motor systems develop.

For similar reasons, critical periods say little about formal education. Formal schooling instructs children about the social and cultural particulars, not about evolution-based, specieswide skills and behaviors. Currently, we have no reason to think that there are critical periods for the acquisition of culturally and socially transmitted skills, like reading, mathematics, or music, just to name a few of the favorite examples. As far as we know, people can acquire these skills at any age; can benefit from instruction at any age; and can increase their intelligence and expertise, given the right opportunities, at any age (Greenough, 1997).

The Effects of Enriched Environments

Neuroscientists have been studying the effects of enriched environments on rats' behavior and brain development for nearly 50 years. Some of the best and most current of this work is that of Greenough and his colleagues at the University of Illinois (1992). In this research, neuroscientists study how raising rats in different environments affects their brain structure. Typically, scientists study the effects of two contrasting environments. Some rats are raised alone in small cages with only food and water available. This "isolated environment" is the typical laboratory environment for a rat.

Other rats are raised in large, group cages that also contain novel objects and obstacles. Greenough calls these environments *complex*, rather than enriched. He points out that complex environments are enriched only in comparison with a rat's typical lab cage. Neuroscientists use complex environments to mimic the rats' wild or natural environment. They are not special, accelerated rodent learning environments. One should not think of them as high-quality infant care or Head Start for rats. One should think of them more as attempts to create New York City subway tunnel conditions in the laboratory.

In electron microscopic studies, Greenough and his colleagues found that young rats raised in complex environments have 25 percent more synapses per neuron in the visual areas of their brains than do rats raised in isolation. However, increases in synapses per neuron ratios do not occur to this extent in all brain areas, and some brain areas show no effects of complex rearing at all. On the basis of this research, we can see that it is definitely not the case, as we often read, that complex environments result in a 25 percent increase in brain connectivity.

More important, however, 15 years ago, Greenough and his colleagues established that the brains of *adult* rats also form new synapses in response to complex environments. Other studies in monkeys and humans have definitively established that the adult brain remains highly plastic and capable of extensive neural reorganization throughout life. The brain's ability to reorganize itself in response to new experiences is what makes it possible for us to learn throughout our lives. The ability of the mature brain to change and reorganize, a finding seldom mentioned in the education literature, is a new, exciting finding of brain science (Nelson & Bloom, 1997).

Thing to Know No. 3: Research on complex environments and related findings tells us that the brain can reorganize itself for learning throughout our lifetimes.

This new insight runs counter to our current fixation on early development and critical periods. However, in thinking about how this research relates to educational practice and policy, we must be careful not to confuse *complex* with *enriched*. Neuroscientists use *complex* as a descriptive term for a laboratory simulation of a wild or natural environment. Education writers tend to use *enriched* as a value-laden term. In the popular and education literature, enriched environments tend to be culturally preferred, middle-class environments. These environments tend to include things that the writers value— Mozart, piano lessons, playing chess—and to exclude things that they scorn— video games, MTV, shooting pool. These writers tend to identify enriched environments with Cambridge, Massachusetts, and Palo Alto, California, and deprived environments with Roxbury and East Palo Alto.

As far as neuroscience goes, all these activities and environments are equally complex—and neuroscience says nothing about which are more or less enriched than others. In assessing claims about environments and the brain, we should be aware of how easy it is to slide from describing complexity to prescribing enrichment. We should be careful not to use neuroscience to provide biological pseudo-argument in favor of our culture and our political values and prejudices.

Educators should know one final thing.

> *Thing to Know No. 4: Research on early synapse formation, critical periods, and complex environments has along history. Yet, we have little understanding of what this research might mean for education.*

Our appeals to this research are often naive and superficial. Other brain-related themes popular in the education literature—emotional intelligence, the social brain, the brain in the entire body, the intelligent immune system, downshifting—have a much less reliable grounding in neuroscience. Educators seeking to base practice on the best science might want to assess recommendations stemming from these ideas even more carefully and critically.

References

Bruer, J. T. (1997). Education and the brain: A bridge too far. *Educational Researcher, 26*(8), 4-16.

Bruer, J. T. (1998). Let's put brain science on the back burner. *NASSP Bulletin, 82*(598), 21-28.

Daw, N. W. (1995). *Visual development.* New York: Plenum.

Goldman-Rakic, P. S., Bourgeios, J.-P., & Rakic, P. (1997). Synaptic substrate of cognitive development: Synaptogenes is in the prefrontal cortex of the nonhuman primate. In N. A. Krasnegor, G. R. Lyon, & P. S. Goldman-Rakic (Eds.), *Development of the prefrontal cortex: Evolution, neurobiology, and behavior* (pp. 27-47). Baltimore: Paul H. Brookes.

Greenough, W. T. (1997). We can't focus just on ages zero to three. *APA Monitor, 28,* 19.

Greenough, W. T., Withers, G. S., & Anderson, B. J. (1992). Experience-dependent synaptogenes is as a plausible memory mechanism. In I. Gormezano & E. A. Wasserman (Eds.), *Learning and memory: The behavioral and biological substrates* (pp. 209-299). Hillsdale, NJ: Erlbaum.

Hubel, D. H., Wiesel, T. N., & LeVay, S. (1977). Plasticity of ocular dominance columns in monkey striate cortex. *Philosophical Transactions of the Royal Society of London B., 278,* 307-409.

Huttenlocher, P. R., & Dabholkar, A. S. (1997). Regional differences in synaptogenes is in human cerebral cortex. *Journal of Comparative Neurology, 367,* 167-178.

Nelson, C. A., & Bloom, F. E. (1997). Child development and neuroscience. *Child Development, 68*(5), 970-987.

Rakic, P., Bourgeois, J.-P., & Goldman-Rakic, P. S. (1994). Synaptic development of the cerebral cortex: Implications for learning, memory, and mental illness. In J. van Pelt, M. A. Corner, H. B. M. Uylings, & F. H. Lopes da Silva (Eds.), *Progress in Brain Research 102* (pp. 227-243). Amsterdam: Elsevier Science BV.

POSTSCRIPT

Do Recent Discoveries About the Brain and Its Development Have Implications for Classroom Practice?

Any plausible theory of learning must include the assumption that learning involves the brain. Why, then, is there any controversy about the implications of brain research for educational practice? Doesn't any finding about the brain tell us something useful about how to teach? Unfortunately, it is not always possible to move directly from knowledge about the brain to recommendations for educational practice. This is because learning always involves more than the activity of the brain. Learning results from the interaction of the child (and, of course, his or her brain) with the environment.

Consider, for example, the finding that the "spurt" in children's vocabulary seen at 18 to 24 months of age is associated with a rather dramatic increase in the synaptic density and activity of the brain. This finding is important because it suggests that something may "click" in children's brains at this time that increases their preparedness to learn words. But this finding does not by itself tell us very much about what parents and educators should do during this time to assist children. On the one hand, it may be that children are so prepared at this time that they can pick up words effortlessly from just about any sort of interaction and in any environment. On the other hand, what adults do when children are ready to "spurt" may matter a great deal.

Highly recommended for readers interested in learning more about research on brain sciences is a text by Mark H. Johnson, *Developmental Cognitive Neuroscience,* 2d ed. (Blackwell, 2005). It is an up-to-date, comprehensive, and highly readable (although still fairly technical) summary of much of the current wave of research on the brain-behavior relation. For readers who wish to delve into more technical discussions of research and of the methods used in brain research, there is a wonderful collection of papers in the edited volume by G. Reid Lyon and Judith M. Rumsey, *Neuroimaging: A Window to the Neurological Foundations of Learning and Behavior in Children* (Paul H. Brookes, 1996). Highly recommended is a series of articles on educational applications of brain research in the November 1998 and November 2000 issues of *Educational Leadership.* Particularly noteworthy in these series are "The Brain-Compatible Curriculum," by Anne Westwater and Pat Wolfe, *Educational Leadership* (November 2000) and "Unconscious Emotions, Conscious Feelings," by Robert Sylwester, *Educational Leadership* (November 2000). A critique of Bruer's stance against brain-based education can be found in

"Educators Need to Know About the Human Brain," by Ron Brandt, *Phi Delta Kappan* (November 1999). A book-length treatment of teaching strategies derived from research on neural development and functioning is provided by Eric Jensen in *Teaching With the Brain in Mind* (Association for Supervision and Curriculum Development, 1998). And finally, a recent article on the classroom implications of recent research on neural differences between boys and girls entitled, "With Boys and Girls in Mind," by Michael Guriand and Kathy Stevens, *Educational Leadership* (November 2004), is sure to generate its own controversey.

International Reading Association

The International Reading Association (IRA) supports, conducts, and disseminates research on reading processes and instruction. The IRA accomplishes this through conferences and publications. Issues related to whole language and other instructional approaches have been a frequent concern of the organization and its members.

http://www.reading.org

Pathways to School Improvement

This site of the North Central Regional Educational Laboratory (NCREL) offers extensive information on topics related to improving schools, including assessment, parent and family involvement, goals and standards, and technology.

http://www.ncrel.org/sdrs/

Creating a School Violence Committee

This site shows one state's response to the student violence issue. Produced by the Washington Education Association (WEA), the purpose of this handbook is to provide local association leaders with a systematic approach for dealing with school violence. Included is a guide for development of an association school violence committee and a process for attaining the committee's goals through member and community involvement.

http://www.wa.nea.org/

Calculus, Concepts, Computers, and Cooperative Learning (C4L): The Purdue Calculus Reform Project

This Website contains information on the Calculus, Concepts, Computers, and Cooperative Learning (C4L) program funded by the National Science Foundation and directed by investigators Ed Dubinsky and Keith Schwingendorf of Purdue University. Cooperative learning is an important part of this constructivism-based program.

http://www.math.purdue.edu/~ccc/

PART 3

Effective Teaching and the Evaluation of Learning

*P*edagogical practice is shaped by many factors. The nature of the students being taught and the particular theory of learning adopted by a teacher both help to determine what and how children are taught. But everyday instructional practices are also shaped by other factors. Advances in computer technology, for example, have drastically changed our ability to access information as well as altered the ways we interact with other people. But can and should this technology change how we teach and learn in school? Society has become increasingly violent, and this violence has begun to find its way into our schools with frightening consequences. How should schools react to stem the growing violence within their walls and on their playgrounds? As a society, we have begun to reexamine the skills we value in our citizens and, thus, the outcomes we expect our schools to achieve. But are these the best outcomes? And how should we evaluate the progress that individual students and schools make toward those outcomes? Who should be involved in achieving these outcomes? Should parents have a role? In this section, we consider the controversies that have a risen as our schools and society have tried to define effective teaching and effective evaluation of learning.

- Is the Whole Language Approach to Reading Effective?

- Is Greater Parental Involvement at School Always Beneficial?

- Should Schools Embrace Computers and Technology?

- Will Performance Assessment Lead to Meaningful Education Reform?

- Can a Zero-Tolerance Policy Lead to Safe Schools?

- Should U.S. Schools Be Evaluated Against Schools in Other Countries?

ISSUE 13

Is the Whole Language Approach to Reading Effective?

YES: Steve Zemelman, Harvey Daniels, and Marilyn Bizar, from "Sixty Years of Reading Research—But Who's Listening?" *Phi Delta Kappan* (March 1999)

NO: G. Reid Lyon, from "Why Reading Is Not a Natural Process," *Educational Leadership* (March 1998)

ISSUE SUMMARY

YES: Steve Zemelman, Harvey Daniels, and Marilyn Bizar, faculty in the Center for City Schools at National-Louis University, argue that there is substantial empirical evidence supporting the effectiveness of a whole language approach to teaching reading.

NO: G. Reid Lyon, chief of the Child Development and Behavior Branch of the National Institute of Child Health and Human Development (NICHD), argues that becoming a skilled reader requires explicit, systematic, and direct instruction and practice.

During the late 1980s and into the 1990s there was a change in how reading was taught in U.S. elementary schools—a change that was nothing short of revolutionary. Until that time, instruction in reading emphasized drill-and-practice and "basic skills," particularly those related to learning letter-sound correspondences, or *phonics*. This approach consisted of activities in which students memorized the way particular written symbols, such as c and s, "sounded" in words like *sock, cats*, and *nice*. Students read from basal readers, which emphasized the sound-letter correspondences and rules they were learning: *See Dick run. See Jane run. See Spot run. Run, Spot, run.*

The approach known as *whole language* is very different. With this approach, from kindergarten on, students are engaged in activities that look very much like "real" reading and "real" writing. The whole language approach grew out of the idea that literacy skills are a natural by-product of engaging in *authentic* (i.e., personally meaningful, goal-directed) literacy activities. Proponents of whole language see a parallel between the way in which children learn spoken language and the way in which they learn to read and write. In particular, they argue that children do not learn to speak as the result of explicit instruction. Nor, they argue, do children refrain from participating in real speaking activities (i.e., communication) until they have practiced all the component skills needed to be a fluent speaker. Instead, children learn language naturally and effortlessly by using it to engage in meaningful acts of communication (e.g., to request a desired object or to share joy or distress).

But is the whole language approach effective? Does it lead to the same level of literacy skills as does the more traditional drill-and-practice approach? Critics, who have become more numerous and vocal in recent years, argue that the whole language approach is not effective. States such as California point with frustration to the fact that test scores in reading on the National Assessment of Educational Progress (NAEP) have actually declined during the years in which whole language programs have been popular. These critics suggest that children simply are not being given sufficient practice with phonics and, thus, fail to become efficient at decoding (i.e., at translating print into sound). In the long run, they argue, this limits students' ability to recover meaning from written text.

Supporters of whole language counter that many of the successes of the program have been overlooked. They point to gains in reading scores in New Jersey and Ohio, which have implemented whole language instruction on a wide scale. Supporters also argue that many of the failures highlighted by critics actually are due to systemic factors (e.g., inadequate resources) rather than the nature of the instruction delivered. Supporters of whole language also object that the use of standardized tests of reading achievement may not uncover the very real gains in reading and writing made by students experiencing the whole language approach. They argue for replacing standardized tests, which focus on decontextualized applications of low-level skills, with more authentic assessments, which examine the quality of the actual literacy products generated by students (e.g., journals and reports).

In the first of the following selections, Steve Zemelman, Harvey Daniels, and Marilyn Bizar argue that there is substantial empirical evidence supporting the effectiveness of a whole language approach to teaching reading. Zemelman et al. are critical of what they believe is the selective reporting of results by the proponents of the back-to-basics movement. They argue that the latter are motivated by a negative view of the child as being in need of adult-imposed structure and control—a view that fits well with an emphasis on phonics and other drill-and-practice approaches. In the second selection, G. Reid Lyon argues that *phonemic awareness* (knowledge of the small units of sound that are combined to form words) and the ability to *make meaning* (to link print with previously acquired concepts and experiences) are the keys to successful reading. He also argues that becoming skilled in these areas is not, as whole language advocates contend, a natural process; that is, these skills do not emerge simply as the result of exposure to print and literacy activities. Instead, Lyon contends, these skills depend on explicit, systematic instruction and practice, something that he believes is all too rare in most implementations of the whole language approach.

Steve Zemelman, Harvey Daniels, and Marilyn Bizar

 **YES**

Sixty Years of Reading Research— But Who's Listening?

A reporter calls to get some background for an article about staff development in language arts. Staff development? We are astonished and delighted that any media outlet—even this modest local magazine—actually wants to cover our neglected field. Since our work involves inservice workshops, classroom consulting, and whole-school renewal projects, we're thrilled to talk. We offer quotes, sources, and anecdotes about teacher development efforts around Chicago—our own and others', modest and ambitious, successes and failures. Then, somewhere in the conversation, the term "whole language" comes up.

"Oh," says the young reporter, as if someone has made a rude noise. "That doesn't work." Her tone is flat and certain.

"What do you mean?" we ask.

"You know," she replies impatiently. "There are no scientific studies that show whole language works."

There's a brief pause while we silently bid farewell to cordiality. "Well, actually, there are lots of scientific studies supporting whole language. As a matter of fact, there are a bunch of them sitting right here on the bookshelf."

"But there *aren't* any studies. It's just opinions. There's no research to back it up."

Through gritted teeth: "Are you saying that these shelves are actually empty? That these studies weren't published? We'd be glad to start faxing you some summaries."

"No, no, no." Now she's annoyed. "That can't be *real* research. People have done scientific research and proved that phonics works, not whole language."

Within moments our conversation has foundered on the rocks of educational research. Both parties hang up, peeved and polarized.

If research could actually settle the "great debate" over teaching reading —and over the broader character of education in America—the shouting would have died down long ago. In spite of what our reporter friend thinks, the research overwhelmingly favors holistic, literature-centered approaches to reading. Indeed, the proof is massive and overwhelming.

For six decades, leading researchers and writers have steadily produced summaries and meta-analyses that reiterate the key findings of mainstream, long-term research. For example, Constance Weaver has published research summaries on many aspects of progressive, whole-language teaching, in both book and electronic forms.[1] Margaret Moustafa has pulled together the findings about the role of phonics in teaching reading.[2] For more than 20 years, David Johnson, Roger Johnson, and Edythe Holubec have reviewed the hundreds of studies on the collaborative aspects of the progressive classroom.[3] Michael Tunnell and James Jacobs surveyed the studies on literature-based reading instruction from 1968 to 1988.[4] George Hillocks focused his massive meta-analysis on studies of the teaching of writing.[5] And Richard Thompson looked at 40 studies dating back to 1937.[6]

The most recent volumes of the *Annual Summary of Investigations Related to Reading* include several studies showing statistically significant test score gains in whole-language classrooms and 15 additional studies validating particular strategies within whole language.[7] In our own work, we have tried to connect the research base with the emerging national curriculum standards, as detailed in *Best Practice: New Standards for Teaching and Learning in America's Schools; Methods that Matter: Six Structures for Best Practice Classrooms*; and articles such as "Whole Language Works: Sixty Years of Research."[8] Just this past year, Jeff McQuillan's book *The Literacy Crisis: False Claims, Real Solutions* has offered yet another powerful review of the research on reading instruction, debunking faddish phonics claims and pointing to the strong evidence favoring holistic approaches.[9]

Of course, we need to learn still more about the detailed mechanics of reading and other thinking processes. We can argue over the degree to which competent readers use letter/sound relationships as they read, as opposed to sampling larger chunks of information and fitting it into a context. No thoughtful progressive teacher would say that readers don't need phonics knowledge. And no thoughtful student of phonics can deny that a reader must consult the wider context of a passage to make meaning. But the large and clear outlines are there: whole language works.

Yet 60 years of research and thousands of studies that resoundingly validate progressive approaches to literacy learning still haven't produced the strong consensus we might expect. In fact, many school people—even progressive teachers themselves—act as though this information didn't exist at all or were somehow unreliable, inconclusive, or tainted. We witness this phenomenon every time the promoters of the latest "breakthrough study" seek to overturn decades of solid, workmanlike research with a faddish, mechanistic gimmick such as "decodable text." Curiously cowed by such dubious "evidence," many educators stand mute even as the preponderance of scientific proof shouts just the contrary. So what's up? Clearly, if a shortage of convincing research is not the main reason that progressive methods have failed to be widely acknowledged or supported, then some large and troubling questions are before us:

- Why haven't whole-language teachers and leaders shared their research base more effectively?
- Why does it often seem that back-to-basics proponents have cornered the market on "scientific proof"?
- How is it that one brand-new study can sometimes overturn our confidence in decades of research?

- Why is there so much antagonism toward whole language and other progressive teaching methods these days—especially when they have been so strongly endorsed by the many national standards projects released in recent years?

There are many ways in which research that confirms good practice comes to be misunderstood, ignored, or subverted. Let's start with some of the factors nearest the surface and work toward the deeper ones. First, there's the fact that the teachers who use these practices haven't spoken up very strongly about the research supporting them. One simple reason for this is that many educators simply don't know their own research heritage. When confronted by the authoritative-sounding claims of citation-spewing opponents, they lack ready access to the huge body of knowledge that supports their own practice. In fact, most teachers, whatever their philosophies, select their actions toward children based not on research but on what they see each day in the classroom and on the beliefs they've acquired through their own culture and education.

This is really no different from parents (no doubt including those who challenge the research on whole language), who don't usually make parenting decisions about bedtime or curfews by consulting academic research. Good teachers chose to teach because of their interest in children, not because they encountered some statistically significant experimental finding. The research is valuable in that it may confirm particular practices or call them into question, but culturally, research is a relative newcomer to the calculus of human decision making.

Further, many teachers, both progressive and traditional, look on social science research with broad and well-merited skepticism. They've seen claims and absolute "proofs" come and go over the years. They're wise to the often tortuous attempts of educational, psychological, and cognitive researchers to cloak themselves in the sometimes ill-fitting garb of "science." They worry that, if researchers don't understand the realities of the classroom, their experiments will not reflect those realities. And they know that, even in the best experimental studies, it's impossible to control all the variables associated with dozens or hundreds of human beings in multiple locations over any appreciable span of time. Instead, many thoughtful teachers have learned to pay more attention to qualitative studies that provide a "thicker," more detailed picture of the classroom. They recognize that there are multiple ways of measuring and evaluating a teaching strategy besides conducting statistical studies with large numbers of children that provide only a very sketchy picture of what any given child actually experienced.

With regard to teachers' lack of outspokenness, whether for good or ill, teachers are not usually very political creatures. They focus on the intense and immediate needs of the students in their classrooms and on the concerns of the parents, and they have little time or energy left over to mount campaigns to inform a broader public. Attacks on progressive education, on the other hand, tend to come from policy gurus like William Bennett, Diane Ravitch, and E. D. Hirsch, Jr., whose time is fully devoted to the public forum.

Some of these pundits work directly to discredit educational research, and "cultural literacy" guru Hirsch is perhaps the leading debunker. In his latest book, *The Schools We Need and Why We Don't Have Them*, Hirsch introduces himself as a middle-of-the-roader, a peacemaker, an old lion sadly creaking toward retirement in an era of regrettable polarization. He inveighs against the "selective use of research," decrying the "deplorable development" that "research is being cited as a rhetorical weapon to sustain a sectarian position." Then he goes on to describe progressive education as a cancer that has "metastasized" throughout the schools, a vast "conspiracy" to keep American children stupid and to spawn "chaos." Virtually all American educators, he explains, live in an evil "thought world," where phony research undermines knowledge, repels facts, "quashes" debate, and prevents children from becoming literate. Hirsch repudiates the hundreds of studies cited in the reviews we listed earlier, including all the current national standards projects that were, of course, based on that research. He concludes: "No studies of children's learning in mainstream science support these generalizations.... The consensus in research is that [these] recommendations are worst practice, not 'best practice.' "[10]

In Hirsch's idiosyncratic thought world, "mainstream research" is from *outside* the mainstream. The only acceptable studies are from outside education, specifically from the fields of neurophysiology, psychometrics, and cognitive psychology. (By Hirsch's logic, "mainstream medical research" would exclude all studies conducted by medical doctors.) Hirsch approvingly cites the research (and lots of opinions) from the interlocking directorate of the right-wing back-to-basics movement: John Saxon, Chester Finn, William Bennett, Diane Ravitch, Jeanne Chall, Charles Sykes. He spends hundreds of pages denigrating "tragic," "harmful," "time-wasting" teaching methods, such as collaborative learning, thematic units, and assessment portfolios, but offers little alternative. Hirsch's own recommended pedagogy is surprisingly thin: "The class period can be formed into a little drama," he suggests, "with a beginning, middle and an end...."[11]

Hirsch is not the dispassionate, grandfatherly observer of education that he claims, but an aggressive vendor, who sells millions of dollars' worth of books (*A Dictionary of Cultural Literacy, What Every First-Grader Should Know, What Every Second-Grader Should Know*, and so on) to the schools he vilifies and to the parents whom he encourages to distrust their children's teachers.

The news media are no help, either. Hand-wringing stories about falling test scores provide good headlines. So do politicians' and administrators' declarations that they're going to get tough, crack knuckles, and raise standards. A detailed story about the 20 ways a good teacher makes learning happen in a progressive classroom and how those methods have been statistically validated just might make the feature page—but only if it includes a sensational twist, like the principal spending the day on the roof if all the kids get 100% on their spelling tests. David Berliner and Gerald Bracey have made a helpful if quixotic hobby out of identifying misinformation in news reports and then campaigning (with little success) to get errors corrected and to see more balanced reporting in the first place.[12] When test scores go up, there's a mild ripple, a squib on page 12 with a tone of "Well, maybe, but there are still plenty of problems." When they go down, it's a front-page story.

Whatever the difficulty with delivery of the news, however, we must also reflect on why so many people are indisposed to hear anything positive about schools, and particularly about progressive classrooms. Again, let's start with the simplest cause. Progressive innovations usually change the classroom into something considerably different from what parents remember from their own school days. They worry: Is my child getting what she needs from this stuff? Will I be able to help with the homework? They think: I wasn't taught this way, and I turned out okay! It's not news that people resist change.

Of course, the issues go deeper. Recently, a *New York Times* editorial writer argued that education has become an ideological battleground because we've lost the comfortable old arena of communism versus capitalism.[13] People looking for something wrong need somewhere to duke it out. When politicians seek a "hot" issue, public education usually fits the bill. With education's implications for our children and our property values, most Americans can quickly go round the bend about the quality, or lack of it, of our schools.

Actually, the opposition between conservative and progressive views of education has existed for a long time. Conservatives see children as primarily in need of discipline, while progressives see them as creatures seeking opportunities for expression and initiative. Conservatives look to education mainly to supply basic skills for a competent labor force—skills taught one at a time and tested by standardized, impersonal instruments—while progressives want school mainly to nurture active citizens and creative individuals. Conservatives think of education as socializing students to the status quo, while progressives view it as an opportunity to teach students to critique and question the world they've inherited. Many conservatives doubt that public education is even an appropriate domain for government, while progressives see it as the seedbed of democracy.

While it's obvious which side we are on in this debate, we will not try to plumb all the depths or lay out our most cherished arguments here. Rather, we just want to remind people that, when research is touted or when one study is suddenly elevated over decades of previous inquiry, this old, ongoing debate is probably the subtext, and research is not really going to settle it. If people are talking about differing purposes—and thus differing characteristics—of education, then each side will find the other's research irrelevant.

The latest stir over tests comparing the performance of U.S. students in math and science with that of students from 20 other countries offers a perfect illustration. Conservative critics immediately cry out for tougher standards. Progressives ask why American technology remains so dominant if our schooling is so poor and propose that one reason is the freedom our students experience. Young people in the other countries are good at tests, Larry Cuban asserts, but it's the American scientists who excel in research and invention.[14] Gerald Bracey shows that international comparisons are often not even valid, sometimes matching other countries' 22-year-olds against U.S. high-schoolers.[15]

Perhaps there's an even deeper reason that people don't want to hear good news about progressive classrooms. The late education writer James Moffett theorized that some parents are unconsciously terrified of their children's dawning independence, as symbolized by their learning to read and write.[16] A strong phonics program appeals to these parents because it is the only approach to reading that takes meaning out of the bargain. As long as a child spends most of her time enunciating t's and d's and decoding only synthetic, denatured texts, she will never encounter troubling or dangerous ideas, or begin to think and read for herself. This parallels some parents' preference for grammar drills over writing workshops. If children only do exercises and never write original texts, then they can never utter dangerous ideas on paper. Though Moffett would never have said it so inelegantly, people who want to replace whole, balanced reading programs with phonics-only curricula may unconsciously be holding children back, stunting their growth, and keeping them ignorant.

Looked at through Moffett's lens, the "great debate" isn't a clash over phonics or educational research at all, but rather a symbolic skirmish in the broader culture wars between two opposing camps on matters of teaching and learning, of child development, and of human nature. In a sense, research studies and journal articles are beside the point; this is a religious controversy. After all, if you believe that children are intrinsically flawed beings who need to be tightly controlled and amply punished, you will design a very different kind of classroom from the one you would design for people who were seen as basically good, worthy of love and respect, and capable of self-actualization. If you believe that books—especially religious scriptures—have only one correct meaning that is inherent in the text, you are not going to be very friendly to schools that teach children to explore a wide range of books and ideas, to write and discuss their own responses, to make critical evaluations of what they read, and to develop strong and independent voices as authors.

People may say that this is an oversimplified picture, that each side in the debate actually values some of what the other side advocates, and that good teachers choose approaches to create a balance that works for them. All of this is true, of course. We acknowledge that most good teachers take a "balanced" approach, combining activities that give students voice and choice—individually and in small and large groups—with more information and direct instruction on valuable skills and strategies. In fact, many of the studies cited in the research reviews involved classrooms in which the teachers used progressive student-centered strategies along with more traditional teacher-centered instruction.

One of the most frustrating aspects of the debate is that whole language is mischaracterized as merely turning children loose to do their own thing, with no support or guidance from the teacher. In the good whole-language classrooms we've observed, nothing could be further from the truth. Whole language is, in fact, a balanced and mainstream approach to teaching and learning.

Good teachers who "balance" instruction know that one of the most important aspects of teaching is to be a good "kid watcher." Whether in an affluent suburb, a rural community, or the heart of the inner city, good teachers focus on the learner and what she brings to school. Sweeping statements about "the right way" to teach all beginning readers just don't make good sense. If children already have the ability to segment phonemes, why teach it? If, on the other hand, children are unable to hear sounds in words, it is urgent that we help them acquire this necessary skill. If we concentrated on learning, rather than just on teaching, and designed instruction to meet students' needs, we wouldn't be in the predicament that one downstate Illinois teacher reported to us. Her district has mandated direct instruction in "intensive phonics" in all primary grades. This third-grade teacher, under extreme duress, is forced to teach one full hour of phonics a day to children who already can and do read.

We also see some powerful and disturbing crosscurrents as we move away from the simplified picture. Some educators working in troubled urban schools advocate a highly restrictive skill-and-drill approach because they believe that this is the only thing that will work for minority children or in a school culture that has been extremely resistant to change. Yet whole language advocates observe again and again in strong and well-run whole-language classrooms that these approaches work wonderfully with inner-city students. These students, the whole-language teachers say, need more of what works in privileged, high-achieving schools, not less. Both groups say they want more of the population to enter the mainstream of American social and economic life, and yet they profoundly disagree about how to achieve this goal. It's a challenge to acknowledge cultural differences in social and learning styles and yet not pigeonhole or restrict children as we take account of those differences when we teach.

In spite of these complexities, however, there are clear distinctions between conservative and progressive approaches to education. A classroom in which children are working in small groups on various projects they've chosen looks and feels far different from one in which students are sitting in rows listening to a lecture or filling in worksheets. We've watched children from all backgrounds excel when given lots of opportunities to choose their own reading, writing, and inquiry topics and when classrooms are structured so that the teacher can provide lots of individual attention that's well-tuned to students' personal needs. Students at the Best Practice High School, a small Chicago public high school we helped found in 1996, prove to us every day that progressive ideas can be brought to life in the inner city. And on the other side of the equation, we've observed the failure of punitive approaches, of approaches that assume that young people bring to school no relevant knowledge or abilities of their own, and of lockstep scripts that prevent teachers from using their own judgment to provide what students need at a given moment.

In the latest chapter of the "great debate," the National Research Council brought together a panel of reading experts that included some of the most outspoken researchers and educators on both sides, plus some who occupy the middle ground. In their report, this diverse group not only appealed for an end to the squabbling but endorsed the value of teaching both letter/sound relationships and a range of whole-language strategies, including the extensive use of good literature, a focus on comprehension, and the use of developmental spelling for beginning writers. The real challenge, the panel asserts, is to provide much more training to increase prekindergarten and elementary teachers' knowledge of reading research and effective teaching strategies.

Nevertheless, as many of us try once again to get people to pay attention to and be guided by the research on progressive literacy education, let's remember that the debate is not likely to resolve itself anytime soon. Many of the differences do represent real disagreements about the nature of childhood, the human psyche, government, and society. And parents' anxieties about their children will find expression and, like air squeezed from one side of a balloon, will simply well up somewhere else nearby. Meanwhile, schools and teachers, always lacking the resources to push far enough in any direction, will continue to struggle, sometimes to react politically, and most often to do the best they can with the funds and the knowledge that they have.

Notes

1. Constance L. Weaver, Lorraine Gillmeister-Krause, and Grace Vento-Zogby, *Creating Support for Effective Literacy Education* (Portsmouth, N.H.: Heinemann, 1996); and Constance Weaver, bibliographies at www.heinemann.com.
2. Margaret Moustafa, *Beyond Traditional Phonics: Research Discoveries and Reading Instruction* (Portsmouth, N.H.: Heinemann, 1996).
3. David W. Johnson, Roger T. Johnson, and Edythe Johnson Holubec, *Cooperation in the Classroom* (Edina, Minn.: Interaction Book Co., 1991).
4. Michael O. Tunnell and James S. Jacobs, "Using 'Real' Books: Research Findings on Literature-Based Reading Instruction," *Reading Teacher*, vol. 42, 1989, pp. 470-77.
5. George Hillocks, *Research on Written Composition: New Directions for Teaching* (Urbana, Ill.: National Conference on Research in English and ERIC Clearinghouse on Reading and Communication Skills, 1986).
6. Richard A. Thompson, *Summarizing Research Pertaining to Individualized Reading* (Arlington, Va.: ERIC Document Reproducing Service, 1971).
7. Sam Weintraub, ed., *Annual Summary of Investigations Related to Reading* (Newark, Del.: International Reading Association, 1992-97).
8. Steven Zemelman, Harvey Daniels, and Arthur Hyde, *Best Practice: New Standards for Teaching and Learning in America's Schools,* 2nd ed. (Portsmouth, N.H.: Heinemann, 1998); Harvey Daniels and Marilyn Bizar, *Methods That Matter: Six Structures for Best Practice Classrooms* (York, Me.: Stenhouse, 1998); and Harvey Daniels, Steven Zemelman, and Marilyn Bizar, "Whole Language Works: Sixty Years of Research," Educational Leadership, in press.
9. Jeff McQuillan, *The Literacy Crisis: False Claims, Real Solutions* (Portsmouth, N.H.: Heinemann, 1998).
10. E.D.Hirsch, Jr., *The Schools We Need and Why We Don't Have Them* (New York: Doubleday, 1996), p. 173.
11. Ibid., p. 174.
12. David C. Berliner, *The Manufactured Crisis: Myths, Fraud, and the Attack on America's Public Schools* (Reading, Mass.: Addison-Wesley, 1995); and periodic reports by Gerald W. Bracey, such as "A Nation

of Learners: Nostalgia and Amnesia," *Educational Leadership,* February 1997, pp. 53-57.

13. Jacques Steinberg, "Clashing Over Education's One True Faith," *New York Times,* 14 December 1997, sec. 4, pp. 1, 14.

14. Larry Cuban, quoted in Ethan Bronner, "Freedom in Math Class May Outweigh Tests," *New York Times*, 2 March 1998, pp. A-1, A-14.

15. Bracey, op. cit.

16. James Moffett, *Harmonic Learning: Keynoting School Reform* (Portsmouth, N.H.: Heinemann, 1992).

NO

G. Reid Lyon

Why Reading Is Not a Natural Process

I am frequently asked why the National Institute of Child Health and Human Development (NICHD) conducts and supports research in reading, given that the NICHD is part of the National Institutes of Health, a federal agency that emphasizes basic biomedical science and health-related research. A primary answer is that learning to read is critical to a child's overall well-being. If a youngster does not learn to read in our literacy-driven society, hope for a fulfilling, productive life diminishes. In short, difficulties learning to read are not only an educational problem; they constitute a serious public health concern.

The NICHD has been studying normal reading development and reading difficulties for 35 years. NICHD-supported researchers have studied more than 10,000 children, published more than 2,500 articles, and written more than 50 books that present the results of 10 large-scale longitudinal studies and more than 1,500 smaller scale experimental and cross-sectional studies. Many of the longitudinal research sites initiated studies in the early 1980s with kindergarten children before they began their reading instruction and have studied the children over time. Researchers have studied some children for 15 years, with several sites following the youngsters for at least 5 years. Additional research sites have joined within the past 3 years to investigate the effects of different reading instructional programs with kindergarten and 1st grade children. At most research sites, multidisciplinary research teams study cognitive, linguistic, neurobiological, genetic, and instructional factors related to early reading development and reading difficulties.[1]

Reading Research and Scientific Tradition

The NICHD reading research has centered on three basic questions: (1) How do children learn to read English (and other languages)? What are the critical skills, abilities, environments, and instructional interactions that foster the fluent reading of text? (2) What skill deficits and environmental factors impede reading development? (3) For which children are which instructional approaches most beneficial, at which stages of reading development? Before summarizing findings related to these questions, I would like to explain the NICHD research process.

First, the NICHD reading research program is rooted in scientific tradition and the scientific method. The program rests on systematic, longitudinal,

From G. Reid Lyon, "Why Reading Is Not a Natural Process," *Educational Leadership*, vol. 55, no. 6 (March 1998). Copyright © 1998 by The Association for Supervision and Curriculum Development. Reprinted by permission of The Association for Supervision and Curriculum Development.

field-based investigations, cross-sectional studies, and laboratory-based experiments that are publicly verifiable and replicable. Second, the research integrates quantitative and qualitative methods to increase the richness, impact, and ecological validity of the data. However, using qualitative research methods requires the same scientific rigor employed in quantitative studies. Third, the NICHD reading research program is only one of many programs dedicated to understanding reading development and difficulties. The U.S. Department of Education's Office of Research and Improvement, the Office of Special Education Programs, and the Canadian Research Council have supported many outstanding reading researchers (see Adams 1990 for a research review).

The cumulative work of federally and privately funded researchers illuminates how children develop reading skills, why some children struggle to learn to read, and what can be done to help all readers reach proficiency. Although much remains to be learned, many findings have survived scrutiny, replication, and extension.

The Critical Role of Phonemic Awareness

How do children learn to read English? Reading is the product of decoding and comprehension (Gough et al. 1993). Although this sounds simple, learning to read is much tougher than people think. To learn to decode and read printed English, children must be aware that spoken words are composed of individual sound parts termed phonemes. This is what is meant by *phoneme awareness.*

Phoneme awareness and phonics are not the same. When educators assess phoneme awareness skills, they ask children to demonstrate knowledge of the sound structure of words *without any letters or written words present.* For example, "What word would be left if the /k/ sound were taken away from *cat?*" "What sounds do you hear in the word *big?*" To assess phonics skills, they ask children to link sounds (phonemes) *with letters.* Thus, the development of phonics skills depends on the development of phoneme awareness.

Why is phoneme awareness critical in beginning reading, and why is it difficult for some children? Because to read an alphabetic language like English, children must know that written spellings systematically represent spoken sounds. When youngsters figure this out, either on their own or with direct instruction, they have acquired the alphabetic principle. However, if beginning readers have difficulty perceiving the sounds in spoken words—for example, if they cannot "hear" the /at/ sound in *fat* and *cat* and perceive that the difference lies in the first sound—they will have difficulty decoding or sounding out new words. In turn, developing reading fluency will be difficult, resulting in poor comprehension, limited learning, and little enjoyment.

We are beginning to understand why many children have difficulty developing phoneme awareness. When we speak to one another, the individual sounds (phonemes) within the words are not consciously heard by the listener. Thus, no one ever receives any "natural" practice understanding that words are composed of smaller, abstract sound units.

For example, when one utters the word *bag*, the ear hears only one sound, not three (as in /b/-/a/-/g/). This is because when *bag* is spoken, the /a/

and /g/ phonemes are folded into the initial /b/ sound. Thus, the acoustic information presented to the ears reflects an overlapping bundle of sound, not three discrete sounds. This process ensures rapid, efficient communication. Consider the time it would take to have a conversation if each of the words we uttered were segmented into their underlying sound structure.

However, nature has provided a conundrum here: What is good for the listener is not so good for the beginning reader. Although spoken language is seamless, the beginning reader must detect the seams in speech, unglue the sounds from one another, and learn which sounds (phonemes) go with which letters. We now understand that specific systems in the brain recover sounds from spoken words, and just as in learning any skill, children understand phoneme awareness with different aptitudes and experiences.

Developing Automaticity and Understanding

In the initial stages of reading development, learning phoneme awareness and phonics skills *and* practicing these skills with texts is critical. Children must also acquire fluency and automaticity in decoding and word recognition. Consider that a reader has only so much attention and memory capacity. If beginning readers read the words in a laborious, inefficient manner, they cannot remember what they read, much less relate the ideas to their background knowledge. Thus, the ultimate goal of reading instruction—for children to understand and enjoy what they read—will not be achieved.

Reading research by NICHD and others reveals that "making meaning" requires more than phoneme awareness, phonics, and reading fluency, although these are necessary skills. Good comprehenders link the ideas presented in print to their own experiences. They have also developed the necessary vocabulary to make sense of the content being read. Good comprehenders have a knack for summarizing, predicting, and clarifying what they have read, and many are adept at asking themselves guide questions to enhance understanding.

Linguistic Gymnastics

Programmatic research over the past 35 years *has not* supported the view that reading development reflects a *natural process*—that children learn to read as they learn to speak, through natural exposure to a literate environment. Indeed, researchers have established that certain aspects of learning to read are highly unnatural. Consider the linguistic gymnastics involved in recovering phonemes from speech and applying them to letters and letter patterns. Unlike learning to speak, beginning readers must appreciate consciously what the symbols stand for in the writing system they learn (Liberman 1992).

Unfortunately for beginning readers, written alphabetic symbols are arbitrary and are created differently in different languages to represent spoken language elements that are themselves abstract. If learning to read were natural, there would not exist the substantial number of cultures that have yet to develop a written language, despite having a rich oral language. And, if learning to read unfolds naturally, why does our literate society have so many youngsters and adults who are illiterate?

Despite strong evidence to the contrary, many educators and researchers maintain the perspective that reading is an almost instinctive, natural process. They believe that explicit instruction in phoneme awareness, phonics, structural analysis, and reading comprehension strategies is unnecessary because oral language skills provide the reader with a meaning-based structure for the decoding and recognition of unfamiliar words (Edelsky et al. 1991, Goodman 1996). Scientific research, however, simply does not support the claim that context and authentic text are a proxy for decoding skills. To guess the pronunciation of words from context, the context must predict the words. But content words—the most important words for text comprehension—can be predicted from surrounding context only 10 to 20 percent of the time (Gough et al. 1981). Instead, the choice strategy for beginning readers is to decode letters to sounds in an increasingly complete and accurate manner (Adams 1990, Foorman et al. 1998).

Moreover, the view some whole language advocates hold that skilled readers gloss over the text, sampling only parts of words, and examining several lines of print to decode unfamiliar words, is not consistent with available data. Just and Carpenter (1987), among others, have demonstrated consistently that good readers rarely skip over words, and readers gaze directly at most content words. Indeed, in contrast to conventional wisdom, less-skilled readers depend on context for word-recognition. The word recognition processes of skilled readers are so automatic that they do not need to rely on context (Stanovich et al. 1981). Good readers employ context to aid overall comprehension, but not as in aid in the recognition of unfamiliar words. Whether we like it or not, an alphabetic cipher must be deciphered, and this requires robust decoding skills.

The scientific evidence that refutes the idea that learning to read is a *natural process* is of such magnitude that Stanovich (1994) wrote:

> That direct instruction in alphabetic coding facilitates early reading acquisition is one of the most well established conclusions in all of behavioral science.... The idea that learning to read is just like learning to speak is accepted by no responsible linguist, psychologist, or cognitive scientist in the research community (pp. 285-286).

Why Some Children Have Difficulties Learning to Read

Good readers are phonemically aware, understand the alphabetic principle, apply these skills in a rapid and fluent manner, posses strong vocabularies and syntactical and grammatical skills, and relate reading to their own experiences. Difficulties in any of these areas can impede reading development. Further, learning to read begins far before children enter formal schooling. Children who have stimulating literacy experiences from birth onward have an edge in vocabulary development, understanding the goals of reading, and developing an awareness of print and literacy concepts.

Conversely, the children who are most at risk for reading failure enter kindergarten and the elementary grades without these early experiences. Frequently, many poor readers have not consistently engaged in the language play that develops an awareness of sound structure and language patterns. They have limited exposure to bedtime and lap time reading. In short, children raised in poverty, those with limited proficiency in English, those from homes where the parents' reading levels and practices are low, and those with speech, language, and hearing handicaps are at increased risk of reading failure.

However, many children with robust oral language experience, average to above average intelligence, and frequent early interactions with literacy activities also have difficulties learning to read. Why? Programmatic longitudinal research, including research supported by NICHD, clearly indicates that deficits in the development of phoneme awareness skills not only predict difficulties learning to read, but they also have a negative effect on reading acquisition. Whereas phoneme awareness is necessary for adequate reading development, it is not sufficient. Children must also develop phonics concepts and apply these skills fluently in text. Although substantial research supports the importance of phoneme awareness, phonics, and the development of speed and automaticity in reading, we know less about how children develop reading comprehension strategies and semantic and syntactic knowledge. Given that some children with well developed decoding and word-recognition abilities have difficulties understanding what they read, more research in reading comprehension is crucial.

From Research to Practice

Scientific research can inform beginning reading instruction. We know from research that reading is a language-based activity. Reading does not develop naturally, and for many children, specific decoding, word-recognition, and reading comprehension skills must be taught directly and systematically. We have also learned that preschool children benefit significantly from being read to. The evidence suggests strongly that educators can foster reading development by providing kindergarten children with instruction that develops print concepts, familiarity with the purposes of reading and writing, age-appropriate vocabulary and language comprehension skills, and familiarity with the language structure.

Substantial evidence shows that many children in the 1st and 2nd grades and beyond will require explicit instruction to develop the necessary phoneme awareness, phonics, spelling, and reading comprehension skills. But for these children, this will not be sufficient. For youngsters having difficulties learning to read, each of these foundational skills should be taught and integrated into textual reading formats to ensure sufficient levels of fluency, automaticity, and understanding.

Moving Beyond Assumptions

One hopes that scientific research informs beginning reading instruction, but it is not always so. Unfortunately, many teachers and administrators who could benefit from research to guide reading instructional practices do not yet trust the idea that research can inform their teaching. There are many reasons for this lack of faith. As Mary Kennedy (1997) has pointed out, it is difficult for teachers to apply research information when it is of poor quality, lacks authority, is not easily accessible, is communicated in an incomprehensible manner, and is not practical. Moreover, the lack of agreement about reading development and instruction among education leaders does not bode favorably for increasing trust. The burden to produce compelling and practical information lies with reading researchers.

Most great scientific discoveries have come from a willingness and an ability to be wrong. Researchers and teachers could serve our children much better if they had the courage to set aside assumptions when they are not working. What if the assumption that reading is a natural activity, as appealing as it may be, were wrong and not working to help our children read? The fundamental purpose of science is to test our beliefs and intuitions and to tell us where the truth lies. Indeed, the education of our children is too important to be determined by anything but the strongest of objective scientific evidence. Our children deserve nothing less.

Note

1. See Fletcher and Lyon (in press) and Lyon and Moats (1997) for reviews of NICHD reading research findings. Contact the author for a complete set of references of published research from all NICHD reading research sites since 1963.

References

Adams, M. J. (1990). *Beginning to Read: Thinking and Learning about Print.* Cambridge, Mass.: MIT Press.

Edelsky, C., B. Altwerger, and B. Flores. (1991). *Whole Language: What's the Difference?* Portsmouth, N.H.: Heinemann.

Fletcher, J. M. and G. R. Lyon. (in press). *Reading: A Research-Based Approach.* Palo Alto, Calif.: Hoover-Institute.

Foorman, B. R., D. J. Francis, J. M. Fletcher, C. Schatschneider, and P. Mehta. (1998). "The Role of Instruction in Learning to Read: Preventing Reading Failure in At-risk Children." *Journal of Educational Psychology* 90, 1-15.

Goodman, K. S. (1996). *Ken Goodman on Reading: A Common Sense Look at the Nature of Language and the Science of Reading.* Portsmouth, N.H.: Heinemann.

Gough, P. B., J. A. Alford, and P. Holley-Wilcox. (1981). "Words and Contexts." In *Perception of Print: Reading Research in Experimental Psychology,* edited by O. J. Tzeng and H. Singer. Hillsdale, N.J.: Erlbaum.

Gough, P. B., C. Juel, and P. Griffith. (1992). "Reading, Spelling, and the Orthographic Cipher." In *Reading Acquisition,* edited by P. B. Gough, L. C. Ehri, and R. Trieman. Hillsdale, N.J.: Erlbaum.

Just, C., and P. A. Carpenter. (1980). "A Theory of Reading: From Eye Fixations to Comprehension." *Psychological Review* 87, 329-354.

Kennedy, M. M. (1997). "The Connection Between Research and Practice." *Educational Researcher* 26, 4-12.

Liberman, A. M. (1992). "The Relation of Speech to Reading and Writing." In *Orthography, Phonology, Morphology and Meaning,* edited by R. Frost and L. Katz. Amsterdam: Elsevier Science Publishers B.V.

Lyon, G. R., and L. C. Moats. (1997). "Critical Conceptual and Methodological Considerations in Reading Intervention Research." *Journal of Learning Disabilities* 30, 578-588.

Stanovich, K. E. (1994). "Romance and Reality." *The Reading Teacher* 47, 280-291.

Stanovich, K. E., R. F. West, and D. J. Freeman (1981). "A Longitudinal Study of Sentence Context Effects in Second grade Children: Tests of an Interactive-Compensatory Model." *Journal of Experimental Child Psychology* 32, 402-433.

POSTSCRIPT

Is the Whole Language Approach to Reading Effective?

Can empirical research be relied on to determine whether or not whole language is more effective (or at least no less effective) than a basic skills (e.g., phonics) approach to reading instruction? The answer to this question is yes. Unfortunately, however, the current data are not complete enough to allow judgment on whole language to be passed with certainty. Take, for example, the contention of whole language supporters that gains in reading achievement have been observed in many states that have adopted whole language instruction. Although these gains may have been caused by the shift to whole language, it is also possible that the gains had nothing to do with whole language but instead resulted from other factors, such as an increase or redirecting of resources to literacy instruction or a renewed commitment to tackling literacy problems on the part of teachers and administrators. What is needed to provide unequivocal proof that whole language has caused any gains in reading achievement are *experimental* studies, in which students are assigned randomly to various instructional conditions, such as whole language versus phonics/drill-and-practice.

Critics of whole language have been able to bolster their arguments with an impressive array of studies, many of which have, in fact, involved an experimental design. These studies have clearly shown that skilled reading depends on the acquisition and automatization of basic knowledge and skills, including phonics—skills that typically receive little systematic instruction within the context of the whole language approach. Critics also have amassed considerable empirical data demonstrating that many children who have difficulty learning to read (e.g., those with a learning disability) fail precisely because they lack basic knowledge in phonics and other decoding skills.

But does the whole language approach have any advantages over a basic skills approach? Supporters of whole language argue that students who experience a whole language approach will find literacy activities to be inherently more interesting than will children who experience a basic skills approach. Presumably, this difference will lead these students to read and write more, which, in turn, will sharpen their literacy skills over time. Supporters might also argue that the whole language approach assists children in incorporating reading and writing into their other academic pursuits, such as science and social studies, which will lead to greater gains in these latter domains compared to the basic skills approach to literacy. Unfortunately, such assertions have yet to be evaluated fully, largely because most studies in this area, whether correlational or experimental, have included only a narrow set of outcome measures (i.e., measures focused only on reading and writing rather than on other academic domains) or have not charted student progress over a period sufficient to address long-term achievement. Although it is too early to tell, these data may eventually indicate that some combination of whole language and the basic skills approach is most effective in producing the widest gains for the most children.

The controversy surrounding the relative merits of whole language and phonics shows no signs of resolution. Indeed, the report of the National Reading Panel in 1999, which was first used to tout the advantages of phonics, has recently come under fierce attack. A particularly careful, empirically based version of this attack can be found in "Beyond the Smoke and Mirrors: A Critique of the National Reading Report on Phonics," by Elaine Garan, *Phi Delta Kappan* (March 2001). Readers interested in reading more about whole language should turn to "The Whole Truth About Hole Language—Whoops! I Mean the Hole Truth About Whole Language—Can You Dig It!" by Mimi B. Chenfield, *Early Childhood Education Journal* (vol. 23, no. 3, 1996); "I Didn't Found Whole Language; Whole Language Found Me," by Kenneth S. Goodman, *Education Digest* (October 1993); and "Back to the Basics of Whole Language," by Reggie Routman, *Educational Leadership* (February 1997). Critiques of whole language are numerous and include "Where's the Phonics? Making a Case for Its Direct and Systematic Instruction," by Patrick Groff, *The Reading Teacher* (vol. 52, no. 2, 1998) and "Teaching Decoding," by Louisa C. Moats, *American Educator* (Spring/Summer 1998). The latter article provides an excellent discussion of research on decoding, as well as some concrete pedagogical suggestions. There are also articles in which the authors outline ways in which the whole language and basic skills approaches can be profitably combined: "Every Child a Reader," by Marie Carbo, *American School Board Journal* (February 1997); "Whole Language vs. Phonics: The Great Debate," by Marie Carbo, *Principal* (January 1996); and "Whole-to-Parts Phonics Instruction: Building on What Children Know to Help Them Know More," by Margaret Moustafa and Elba Maldonado-Colon, *The Reading Teacher* (February 1999). For an interesting analysis of the political side of the whole language controversy, see "Politics and the Pendulum: An Alternative Understanding of the Case of Whole Language as Educational Innovation," by Paula Wolfe and Leslie Poynor, *Educational Researcher* (January–February 2001). An interesting pair of articles in the October 2002 issue of *Phi Delta Kappan* address the political debate surrounding reading instruction in California: Richard G. Innis, "There's More Than Mythology to California's Reading Decline," and Stephen Kashen, "Speculation and Conjecture." Finally, an eclectic collection of strategies for teaching reading can be found in *Guide to Human Development for Future Educators* by Leonard Abbeduto and Stephen N. Elliott (McGraw-Hill, 1998); *Straight Talk About Reading: How Parents Can Make a Difference During the Early Years* by Susan L. Hall and Louisa C. Moats (Contemporary Books, 1999); and *Best Practices in Literacy Instruction* edited by Lesley Mandel Morrow et al. (Guilford Press, 2003).

ISSUE 14

Is Greater Parental Involvement at School always Beneficial?

YES: Laura Van Zandt Allen and Eleanor T. Migliore, from "Supporting Students and Parents Through a School-University Partnership," *Middle School Journal* (January 2005)

NO: Rodney T. Ogawa, from "Organizing Parent-Teacher Relations Around the Work of Teaching," *Peabody Journal of Education* (1998)

ISSUE SUMMARY

YES: Laura Van Zandt Allen and Eleanor T. Migliore point to evidence that parental involvement in children's schooling is associated with improvements in children's academic performance and social-emotional development. Van Zandt Allen and Migliore also describe a program to help teachers solicit and use parental input, something the authors argue few teachers are normally prepared to do.

NO: Although Rodney T. Ogawa acknowledges that there is evidence that parental involvement has a positive impact on student outcomes, he questions the assumption that if some parental involvement is good, more must be even better. Ogawa argues, instead, that schools must build "buffers" as well as bridges between themselves and parents.

Parents may be more involved in the schooling of their children today than at any time in the history of public education in the United States. But does parental involvement matter? Does it translate into improvements in children's academic achievement and their increased investment in school? In fact, there is considerable empirical evidence to suggest that parental involvement in schooling does have positive effects. First, it has been found that parent participation in activities at school (e.g., classroom volunteering, attending parent-teach conferences) is related to student grades, with more parental participation being correlated with higher grades. Second, the extent of parental involvement in school-related activities at home (e.g., assisting with or monitoring homework) is positively correlated with children's scores on standardized achievement tests. It is important to recognize, however, that high levels of parental involvement do not just happen. Instead, they result from the effort and interest not only of parents but also of teachers and school administrators who solicit and provide avenues for parental participation.

Bolstered at least in part by research on the positive effects of parental involvement on children's academic progress, politicians and educational reformers have often made parents the focal point of their plans. Such was the case in Chicago in the late 1980s. Chicago's schools were generally rated as among the most wasteful and least effective in the nation. In an attempt to turn the schools around, massive restructuring of the administrative structure and curriculum were mandated. Schools were decentralized, and parents were placed in charge of their neighborhood schools. Parents could hire and fire staff, including principals. Parents controlled a considerable portion of the budget. Parents even worked with teachers to determine the curriculum and the nature of the instruction that occurred in the classroom. In the 10 years following the decentralization, Chicago schools improved dramatically and that positive trend continues today. Many in the media, politics, and education have given much of the credit for positive change to increased parental involvement.

But is parental involvement always helpful? Is it always a positive force for change? There is often considerable variability among parents in how they wish to deal with controversial issues, such as inclusion of students with special needs in regular classrooms, the effectiveness of whole language instruction, and how to discipline disruptive students. In light of the passionate ways in which parents can express their views on these issues, it is difficult to see how all of them can have a hand in shaping curricular policy. As any principal or administrator will tell you, there are also frequent instances of a parent requesting changes in this or that aspect of the curriculum to better suit his or her child's inclination. Here, too, one wonders if it would be feasible for each and every such parental request to be honored. Can parents be completely shut out of such decisions? On the other hand, should the voices of all parents be heard?

Educators and scholars have also recently begun to question the roles that parents should play in the schooling of their children. Is the involvement of parents always beneficial? In the following selection, Laura Van Zandt Allen and Eleanor T. Migliore enthusiastically support parental involvement, although they do note that often there is considerable work to be done to ensure that parents and school personnel are collaborators rather than adversaries. In the second selection, Rodney T. Ogawa suggests that although schools should build bridges to support parent involvement, schools also need to buffer themselves against unwanted parental influence to ensure that the basic requirements of teaching and learning occur.

**Laura Van Zandt Allen
and Eleanor T. Migliore**

 **YES**

Supporting Students and Parents Through a School-University Partnership

For many of us, memories of elementary school include not only teachers and classmates but also our parents. A plethora of opportunities existed for their involvement such as homeroom parent, PTO/PTA, Halloween carnivals, Christmas pageants, and monthly "Muffins with Mom" or "Donuts with Dad" gatherings. As we entered middle school, however, the context changed. Multiple teachers, complex subject matter, the importance of peer relationships, and a need for autonomy came to the fore, while the level of parental involvement decreased and, for some, was almost nonexistent by high school.

The evidence is compelling: Parent involvement at school and with schoolwork positively affects a number of student outcomes including achievement, attendance, self-esteem, behavior, and attitudes toward school and learning (Mapp, 1997; National Association of School Psychologists, 1999). Using data from the National Education Longitudinal Study, two reports (Keith, Keith, Quirk, Cohen-Rosenthal, & Franzese, 1996; Singh et al, 1995) found that parental involvement with eighth graders had a significant effect on achievement, especially in math and social studies. In an analysis of 66 studies targeting parent involvement in schooling, Henderson and Berla (1994) concluded that the most accurate predictor of a student's achievement in school is not income or social status, but the extent to which that student's family is able to:

1. Create a home environment that encourages learning
2. Express high (but not unrealistic) expectations for their children's achievement and future careers
3. Become involved in their children's education at school and in the community

Unfortunately, parent involvement declines at the very time young adolescents may need it most (Brough, 1997; Eccles & Harold, 1993; 1996; Epstein & Dauber, 1991). In one study, 39% of parents of children in grades three to five classified themselves as "highly-involved" in their child's school while only 24% of parents with children in grades six to eight did so (U.S. Department of Health and Human Services, 1998). Another report found that three-fourths of parents of eight-, nine-, and ten-year-olds said they were either moderately or highly involved with their children's schooling, while by the time children were 16, only half of parents stated this level of involvement (Carnegie Council on Adolescent Development, 1995). Conversely, 72% of student sages 10 to 13 said they would like to talk more with their parents about schoolwork (Nationals Commission on Children, 1991). Given the array of developmental changes occurring during the middle grades years, there is perhaps no more important time for educators to harness the power of parent involvement.

Ironically, preparation on parent involvement has been referred to as one of the "missing elements" in most teacher education programs (Hiatt-Michael, 2001). While the past decade has witnessed an increase in standards addressing families, parents, and community (e.g., National Board for Professional Teaching Standards; National Middle School Association/National Council for the Accreditation of Teacher Education), preservice teachers spend little time studying the experiencing a variety of effective methods for parent involvement (Gray, 2001; Greene & Tichenor; 2001). Studies have found that teacher education prepares future teachers for holding parent conferences but not for initiating and implementing other types of programs such as home-school partnerships, class newsletters, or interactive homework (Epstein, 2001; Hiatt-Michael, 2001). As a result, teachers often enter the profession possessing minimal knowledge and skills for working with parents.

Similar issues are apparent in the education of school psychologists. Viewing the student as part of a system and working with parents and teachers using an ecological paradigm requires a shift in thinking for many in the field who may be more comfortable with a more traditional focus on individual assessments. ... Although collaborating with teachers and parents is an essential component of the school psychologist's role, nearly 30% of those entering the profession believe that they received "insufficient training ... in a range of basic teaming skills" (Guest, 2000, p. 243).

The Parent Support Program

To address these issues, educators at Trinity University and Jackson Middle School in San Antonio (North East Independent School District) designed a program to increase parent involvement while providing authentic experiences for preservice teachers and school psychology students. The Parent Support Program (PSP) began with a teacher at Jackson Middle School who realized the need for a structured support program for students and families. The principal also endorsed preventive, proactive collaboratives that kept students out of in-school and off-campus disciplinary settings and buoyed their success in middle school.

The PSP provides free support sessions one evening a week to students and their families with school-related problems during the fall semester. Issues range from using inappropriate language and completing homework on time to developing better communication skills with parents and social adjustment. Support sessions are led by the PSP director (a Jackson teacher with a master's degree in marriage and family counseling) and pairs of school psychology students in Trinity University's graduate school psychology program.

Referrals, parent contacts, student background information, and follow-up reports are the responsibility of graduate interns in the Middle Grades Master of Arts in Teaching (MAT) program at Trinity. Together, this school-university collaborative addresses four goals centered around parent involvement at the middle level.

1. *The overriding goal of the PSP is to assist parents and teachers in making middle school a positive experience for students.*
Brough and Irvin (2001) noted that elementary schools provide concrete roles for parents to play that become less defined as students move into middle school. As a result, parents need leadership and guidance from the school regarding opportunities and expectations for involvement. Epstein and Dauber (1991) found that the strongest and most consistent predictors of parental engagement at school and at home are the specific school programs and teacher practices that encourage and guide parent involvement.

The PSP provides guidance for parents in two ways. First, it identifies a potential problem. While parents may request participation in the PSP, they are more often notified of a recurring problem their child is having at school as a result of a teacher-initiated referral to the program. Young adolescents often share less information with parents as the importance of peer confidences increases; thus, making parents aware of issues that may need to be addressed is key, especially if the issue is not directly related to a specific class or subject (ie., dress code). Since there are no limiting criteria for participation in the PSP, students who may not qualify for special services have access to a resource often unavailable to the "average" student.

Second, the PSP provides families a means for addressing the problem in a proactive setting. The support sessions help parents and students problem solve; they do not offer counseling. For example, Rachel was referred to the program by a teacher who noticed a discrepancy between her ability and her grades. ... Rachel, a sixth grade student, lived with her grandmother who often felt overwhelmed with schoolwork dilemmas. The problem was narrowed down to a lack of organization and not turning in homework. Interventions included use of an agenda book for writing down assignments that Rachel and her grandmother went over each evening; setting aside structured homework time daily; checking with teachers each week regarding progress; and suggesting specific homework hints such as reading the assigned questions before the chapter. Breaking the problem down into manageable steps helped Rachel and her grandmother deal with it effectively. ...

Crystal was referred to the PSP for dress code violations. During the sessions, communication, setting boundaries, and identifying roles surfaced as primary issues between 12-year-old Crystal and her mother. For example, the mother regularly answered questions for her daughter; conversely, Crystal was afraid to voice her true feelings. For the mother, the roles of friend and parent had become entangled resulting in an inability to set limits in many areas. Neither trusted the other, but both genuinely desired to be closer. To address this, the PSP sessions focused on communication and getting to know one another as individuals. This included enacting scenarios, providing specific questions to ask one another, describing the other from one's own perspective, and assigning the pair to spend 30 minutes together each week doing something fun, alternating who chose the activity. As a result, mother and daughter were able to discuss important topics, reach some agreements, and set reasonable limits. Crystal also began dressing more appropriately for school....

Organization, responsibility, communication, boundaries, and roles are issues common to many young adolescents and their parents. Helping families find constructive ways to address these if they become problematic is the key to success at home and at school.

2. Another goal of the PSP is for preservice teachers to experience diverse methods of parent involvement in an authentic context.
Teaching preservice teachers to envision possibilities for home-school connections and then placing them in field experiences that exemplify only traditional methods of parent involvement is counterproductive. To substantively impact students' beliefs and practice, forward-thinking models of parental involvement must be in place, with preservice teachers taking an active role in the implementation and evaluation of the program. Greene and Tichenor (2001) described a four-tiered model for infusing parent involvement curricula in teacher preparation programs. To effect change, such attempts must be intentional, field-based, and move beyond the study of issues into the application of home-school involvement in the field.

Graduate students completing yearlong internships at Jackson Middle School in the Middle Grades MAT program play active and essential roles in the PSP. From day one, interns are instructed to begin mentally gathering potential referrals as they work with students on their team. By week two, interns are given a complete orientation to the program, which includes responsibilities and benefits to their development as teachers. The first step is the collection of two student referrals and the completion of initial phone interviews for each by the beginning of the second six weeks. While interns are enthusiastic about teaching, this requirement is often received with a mixture of hesitation and alarm. "How will I know who needs to be referred?" "School has barely started, and we're already looking for problems?" "I have to call parents? I thought my mentor did that." "I don't know what to say. What if the parent gets upset?" To assist interns with these tasks, specific forms are provided that detail each step of the process including a sample paragraph for introducing the program to parents by phone. Preservice teachers are also reassured that as they journal about their internship experiences, numerous candidates for the PSP will surface and be pointed out by their professor. Referrals, in fact, may come from myriad sources including teams, counselors, administrators, special education teachers, and even parents. By the time referrals are due, interns' attitude toward the process has changed dramatically. One intern wrote, "I made my first parent phone call today. I had been dragging my feet about doing it for days. The student is a painfully bright little boy who is doing poorly and causing behavior problems. He is difficult but completely likable. The conversation with his mother was pleasant. I was telling her nothing she didn't already know. ... I guess what I'm saying is that it was a thousand times easier than I had expected. I think the PSP sessions will really help this family."

The objectives of this stage are twofold. First, gathering referrals helps interns distinguish between students and issues that respond to standard interventions (i.e., meeting with the student; parent conference) and those that may require additional support from school and home. Next, it forces contact with parents early in the year in a safe, highly structured format

With referrals and parental consent secured, interns begin work on student case studies. In the fall, this initially involves collecting student background information. To do so, interns learn data collection techniques that help them shadow students for a day, interview teams, talk with counselors, and review records as participant observers (i.e., observation, interviewing, gathering artifacts). Information is then compiled and shared with school psychology students working with specific families prior to the first PSP session. Once sessions begin, interns serve as liaisons between teachers and the PSP, providing critical feedback on student progress. For example, an intern and pair of psychology students may communicate bi-weekly via e-mail to assess the effectiveness of a suggested intervention (e.g., checking agenda book) or meet after school at Jackson prior to scheduled evening sessions.

In January, school psychology students debrief with interns regarding outcomes of the support sessions. Afterwards, interns repeat the same process of data collection used in the fall to assess the potential impact of the PSP for specific students. They also contact parents for feedback on the PSP. Complete case studies are then compiled and shared with the PSP director, school psychology students, and university professors.

The case study addresses two additional objectives. First, it forces interaction and collaboration between teacher interns and school psychologists. Too often, these key stakeholders of student success work in isolation during preservice and inservice experiences. This model requires focused collaboration to ensure no student "falls through the cracks" in the system.

Second, it teaches interns to be proactive. Beginning teachers typically enter the profession full of idealism, only to have this image shattered by the reality of day-to-day teaching. When this occurs, a feeling of powerlessness emerges, and interns shift into survival mode (Kagan, 1992). Working intimately with the PSP provides a way for interns to "do something" about student issues that have yet to be resolved. It is a model for problem solving instead of problem dependence that will, hopefully, set a precedent for the rest of their careers.

   3. *A third goal of the PSP is to provide school psychology students the experience of working with parents and teachers in a school setting solving real-life problems.*
... When dealing with a student or family problem, school psychologists are expected to consider the research findings related to the case and determine approaches that would be most effective. Although this is a positive first step, as Sheridan and Gutkin (2000) have pointed out, it is not likely to be sufficient. Indeed, these authors urge school psychologists to focus on learning a process for approaching the problem rather than the specific interventions. Since no two cases are the same, school psychologists must be aware that the research literature studied in class is useful but cannot be transported in its entirety to

real-life situations (Phillips, 1999). This expanded scientist-practitioner model involving gathering relevant data, developing hypotheses, generating and implementing intervention plans, and continuing to collect data which then influence new interventions is the approach used by the school psychology students in the PSP (Stoner & Green, 1992). School psychology students are given the opportunity to deal with unique situations that cannot be hypothetically created through textbooks and addressed with "cookbook" solutions. Families arrive with problems needing immediate and flexible approaches. As one school psychology student stated, "Working with our family was different from what you read about in books. You have to go with the flow since they don't present with a perfect sequence of steps." Another commented, "The program gave us the opportunity to enter the student's world, understand family roles and hierarchies, and put theory into practice."

After the briefing by teacher interns, school psychology students meet with families for several hour-long sessions. These collaborative meetings take place in the evening to accommodate busy family schedules. In addition to working with scheduling needs, students learn to meet other individual family preferences (e.g., based on gender, ethnicity, and language). Siblings are welcome, if appropriate, and their presence may add an important dimension while providing helpful information.

To illustrate, Jorge was referred to the PSP because of disrespectful behaviors in several classes. Teachers reported that he did not follow their directions in the classroom and sometimes used profanities. When the PSP director interviewed the parents initially, she noted that they would be more comfortable with Spanish speaking male and female school psychology partners. In addition, Jorge's two siblings also wanted to attend. The PSP was able to meet these requests with positive results

During the first meeting, students observed that the father was hesitant to set any limits with all three children, while the two boys often ignored their parents' requests for compliance. In addition, both Jorge and his brother spent a great deal of the session competing for attention with their verbalizations or through their physical activities. Their younger sister always sat quite close to either her father or mother. The school psychology students felt that the two boys were jealous of their younger sister who appeared to receive a great deal of attention from both parents. When the father was encouraged to schedule some special after school and weekend time with his sons and establish more appropriate limits with their behaviors, the boys' expressions of anger in the meetings began to lessen. Their language became more appropriate and their physical activity somewhat calmer. All the problems in this case were not resolved, and the parents were still somewhat inconsistent in their limit setting at the end of the sessions; however, the PSP experience was so positive that the family expressed an interest in continuing with a community counselor to which they were referred.

The PSP allows school psychology students to apply or "practice" learning in context. Meeting at the middle school, working with preservice teachers, and problem-solving with families provides essential experience for school psychologists. Perhaps more important, however, is the model of professional collaboration of which they become a part now and, hopefully, in the future.

4. A fourth goal of the PSP is to extend collaboration between the Professional Development School and the university to include family and community.

Professional Development Schools (PDS) address several comprehensive goals. "They bring together university and school-based faculty to share responsibility for the clinical preparation of new teachers, the professional development of experienced faculty, the support of research directed at improving practice, and enhanced student learning" (Levine, 1997, p. 1). Such traditional school-university partnerships center on educational reform and school improvement. Lawson and associates (1995) argued, however, that this is only the beginning and that few partnerships go far enough in regard to making substantive differences in the lives of students. To do so, they advocate school-university-family-community partnerships where the child and family are at the core. In these expanded partnerships, families move from the role of client to that of partner.

> Expanded partnerships cultivate support and empowerment networks for children and families. ... The agenda that began with school reform is thus expanded to include organizational restructuring, cross-system collaboration, family support, and community development. The intended result is the transformation of the organizations and systems that serve families. (Lawson et al, 1995, 213)

The PSP is a direct effort to include families as partners in their child's middle school experience. The program forces stakeholders to ask new questions, explore different issues, and take bolder risks. It also involves invention, ambiguity, and revision. ...

Conclusion

The success of the PSP is due to four factors. First, the program was developed to meet an existing need; it was not created from abstract ideas and superimposed on a school setting. While this seems obvious, universities must take care not to project their own agendas on partner schools. Second, all partners were strongly committed to supporting students and families. The PSP director volunteered her time in the evenings; the university provided start-up grant funds for summer program development; professors restructured courses and supervised graduate students; administrators endorsed the school-university-family collaborative; and parents supported the school's efforts to help their children and the learning of beginning teachers and school psychologists. Third, as with any program, the PSP requires extra time and effort. Collaborations among partners resulted in shared responsibilities for program development, implementation, and evaluation. With the sizable demands already placed on educators at all levels, no one group had the necessary resources to establish and sustain this type of program alone. Finally, the program created a "win-win" situation for all stakeholders. Middle school students, parents, teachers, interns, school psychology students, professors, and administrators all benefit in different ways, making the school a true learning community.

Without doubt, the power of parent involvement can be witnessed through the PSP. Hopefully, its impact will provide a model not only for those entering the profession but also for collaborative partnerships between schools, universities, and families.

References

Brough, J. A. (1997). Home-school partnerships: A critical link. In]. Irvin (Ed.). *What research says to the middle level practitioner.* Columbus, OH: National Middle School Association.

Brough J. A., & Irvin, J. L. (2001). Parental involvement supports academic improvement among middle schoolers. *Middle School Journal, 32*(5), 56-61.

Carnegie Council on Adolescent Development. (1995). *Great transitions: Preparing adolescents for a new century.* Concluding Report. New York: Carnegie Corporation.

Eccles, J. S., & Harold, R. H. (1993). Parent-school involvement during the early adolescent years. *Teachers College Record, 94*(3), 568-587.

Eccles, J. S., & Harold, R. H. (1996). Family involvement in children's and adolescents' schooling. In A. Booth & J. F. Dunn (Eds.), *Family-school links: How do they affect educational outcomes?* (pp. 3-34). Mahwah, NJ: Lawrence Erlbaum Associates.

Epstein, J. L. (2001). *School, family, and community partnerships: Preparing educators and improving schools.* Boulder, CO: Westview Press.

Epstein, J. L., & Dauber, S. L. (1991). School programs and teacher practices of parent involvement in inner-city elementary and middle schools. *Elementary School Journal, 91*(3), 289-305.

Gray, S. F. (2001). *A compilation of state mandates for home school partnership education in pre-service teacher training programs.* Unpublished manuscript. Culver City, CA: Pepperdine University.

Greene, P. K., & Tichenor, M. S. (2001). Parent involvement strategies in teacher education programs: Applying a four-tier model. *Teacher Education and Practice, 14*(3), 96-118.

Guest, K. E. (2000). Career development of school psychologists. *Journal of School Psychology, 38*(3), 237-257.

Henderson, A., & Berla, N. (Eds.). (1994). *A new generation of evidence: The family is critical to student achievement.* Washington, DC: National Committee for Citizens in Education, Center for Law and Education.

Hiatt-Michael, D. (2001). *Preparing teachers to work with parents.* Washington, DC: ERIC Clearinghouse on Teaching and Teacher Education (ERIC Document Reproduction Service No. 460123)

Kagan, D. (1992). Professional growth among preservice and beginning teachers. *Review of Educational Research, 62*, 129-169.

Keith, T. Z., Keith, P. B., Quirk, K. J., Cohen-Rosenthal, E., Franzese, B. (1996). Effects of parental involvement on achievement for students who attend school in rural America. *Journal of Research in Rural Education, 12*(2), 55-67.

Lawson, H., Flora, R., Lloyd, S., Briar, K., Ziegler, J., &. Kettlewell, J. (1995). Building links with families and communities. In R. Osguthorpe, R. Harris, M. Harris,

& S. Black (Eds.). *Partner schools: Centers for educational renewal.* (pp. 205-227). San Francisco: Jossey-Bass Publishers.

Levine, M. (1997). Introduction. In M. Levine &. R. Trachtman (Eds.), *Making professional development schools work: Politics, practice, and policy.* (pp. 1-11). New York: Teachers College Press.

Mapp, K (1997). Making the connection between families and schools. *The Harvard Education Letter, 13*(5), 1-3.

National Association of School Psychologists (1999). *Position statement on home-school collaboration: Establishing partnerships to enhance educational outcomes.* Bethesda, MD: Author.

National Commission on Children. (1991). *Speaking of kids: A national survey of children and parents.* Washington, DC: Author.

Phillips, B. N. (1999). Strengthening the links between science and practice: Reading, evaluating, and applying research in school psychology. In C. R. Reynolds &. T. B. Gutkin (Eds.), *The handbook of school psychology* (3rd ed., pp. 56-77). New York: Wiley.

Sheridan, S. M., &. Gutkin, T. B. (2000). The ecology of school psychology: Examining and changing our paradigm for the 21st century. *School Psychology Review, 29*(4), 485-502.

Singh, K., Bickley, P. G., Trivette, P., Keith, T. Z., Keith, P. B., &. Anderson, E. (1995). The effects of four components of parental involvement on eighth-grade student achievement: Structural analysis of NELS:88 data. *School Psychology Review, 24*(2), 299-317.

Stoner, G., &. Green, S. K. (1992). Reconsidering the scientist-practitioner model for school psychology practice. *School Psychology Review, 21*(1), 155-166.

U.S. Department of Health and Human Services, Office of the Assistant Secretary for Planning and Evaluation. (1998). *Trends in the well-being of America's children and youth 1998.* Washington, DC: Author.

NO

Rodney T. Ogawa

Organizing Parent—Teacher Relations Around the Work of Teaching

For as long as most educators can remember, public education in the United States has been undergoing reform. In just the 14 years that have passed since the publication of the highly critical report, *A Nation at Risk* (U.S. Department of Education, 1983), three "waves" of reform are reported to have washed over public schools.

The use of waves as a metaphor for recent educational reform efforts is fitting. After all, from the perspective of most people, waves rise at sea, toss ships and wash ashore, but generally do not significantly disrupt the lives of sailors and seaside dwellers. Like waves, educational reform has originated largely in the external environment of schools, drawn attention and resources, but, in the end, hardly affected the core of the educational enterprise, namely teaching and learning.

The impetus for reform in public education has come largely from the nation's institutional environment, an environment shaped by government and the professions (Ogawa, 1994; Scott, 1987). Political leaders at all levels of government have undertaken administrative initiatives and enacted legislation to set "Goals 2000," to press schools to restructure and, otherwise, to generally improve the nation's public schools. Every leading professional organization—representing teachers, school principals, district superintendents, and others—has forged and advanced an educational reform agenda.

Although successive waves of reform have buffeted schools, they seldom have centered on teaching (Murphy, 1991). On those occasions when reformers have focused directly on teachers, they generally have sought not to capitalize on or facilitate existing practices, but to alter what teachers do (Elmore, 1990). This extends beyond curriculum and pedagogy to include teachers' relationships with administrators, colleagues, and parents.

The second wave of reform, in particular, sought to involve teachers in decision making and to expand their responsibilities to include mentoring novice teachers, developing curriculum and the like, and reaching out to engage parents and the community. Curiously, these efforts to enhance the context and practice of teaching often have not taken teaching, itself, as their starting point. This is no where more true than in the campaign to increase parent involvement in schools.

From Rodney T. Ogawa, "Organizing Parent-Teacher Relations Around the Work of Teaching," *Peabody Journal of Education*, vol. 73, no. 1 (1998). Copyright © 1998 by Lawrence Erlbaum Associates, Inc. Reprinted by permission. References omitted.

Parent Involvement:
An Assumption That More Is Always Better

In the search for factors that affect the academic performance of students, educational research has provided few clear-cut answers. One, however, that echoes across a considerable body of research is the family. Families, most notably parents, exert a crucial influence on important student outcomes, including grades and standardized achievement test scores. Consequently, parents, policy makers, and educators have moved to adopt and implement programs aimed at bolstering the involvement of parents in schools, whereas researchers continue to study the relation between parent involvement and student achievement.

Research on family–school relations clearly has made important advances. Researchers, however, typically have adopted a rather narrow view. They tend to approach parent involvement as if it were an unmixed blessing: more always being better. This assumption is apparent in the issues on which researchers have concentrated. For example, Epstein (1995) identified six types of parent involvement, the practices that schools presently employ to encourage each type of involvement, and the challenges posed by each type of involvement. She then redefined each type of involvement with an eye to broadening the scope of parent participation in schools. Her focus is clearly on enhancing and even expanding parent involvement.

It is surprising that the assumption that more parent involvement of all types is always better has gone largely unexamined and unchallenged. After all, this is true of few things in life. Even excessive amounts of oxygen or water can be toxic. Moreover, anyone who has spent much time in schools knows that not all teachers, administrators, or staff members share this view.

The limitations of this view are revealed by a theoretical perspective drawn from organization theory. This perspective suggests that effective organizations create both bridges and buffers between their core technologies and external environments. If teaching is assumed to constitute the core technology of schools, and if parents are assumed to be a crucial and immediate element of the external environment of schools, then schools would be expected to enhance their effectiveness by building bridges to parents under some conditions and buffers against them in others.

Adopting this theoretical orientation provides at least two advantages. First, it treats teaching as the hub around which parent involvement turns. Second, it focuses attention on the organization characteristics of schools, a dimension that is largely ignored by research on family–school relations (Corwin & Wagenaar 1976).

Bridging and Buffering the Core Technology of Schools

Recently, scholars in the field of educational administration have encouraged the adoption of theoretical perspectives that emphasize the symbolic or interpretive dimension of organizations (Deal & Peterson, 1990; Sergiovanni, 1994). In embracing perspectives that highlight culture, community, and institution, many scholars have ignored and even criticized perspectives that emphasize organizations' technical cores as the bases for developing structure. However, pronouncements of the technical perspective's demise may be premature, because it continues to shed conceptual light on important educational issues.

Briefly, the technical perspective contends that organizations develop formal structures to enhance the effectiveness and efficiency of core technologies, especially where technologies are relatively routinized. This includes developing structures to manage organizations' relations with the technical dimension of their external environment (Aldrich, 1979; Thompson, 1967). Organizations manage their relations with the technical environment in two basic ways: They bridge between their core technologies and the environment and they buffer their core technologies from the environment.

Organizations bridge when they depend on their environments for resources to fuel their core technologies (Scott, 1992; Thompson, 1967). Three conditions increase the dependency of organizations on their environments. First, organizations are more dependent when resources are scarce. Second, organizations are more dependent when resources are concentrated, or available from a limited number of sources. Third, organizations are more dependent when the sources of inputs are coordinated.

When confronted by these conditions, typically in some combination, organizations employ several bridging strategies to manage relations with sources of inputs. They include bargaining, contracting, and co-opting.

Organizations buffer to protect their core technologies from uncertainty that the environment can introduce (Thompson, 1967). Uncertainty undermines the rationality and thus the effectiveness and efficiency of core technologies by compromising the certitude and uniformity with which organizations yield products. Environmental uncertainty can result from several conditions, including heterogeneity and instability (Scott, 1992). To manage uncertainty, organizations develop many buffering strategies, including simply blocking or limiting access and coding. Coding involves the classification of inputs prior to their introduction to the technical core.

What Does the Research Say?

Is there evidence that this framework applies to schools? Do schools face the environmental conditions that lead organizations to build bridges and buffers? If so, do schools employ bridging and buffering strategies? The answer to all of these questions is a tentative "yes." Research indicates that the conditions of interdependence and uncertainty exist in schools' environments and that schools employ both bridging and buffering strategies in response. However, the evidence is indirect because researchers have not explicitly focused on bridging and buffering in school organizations.

The Core Technology of Schools

Previous studies, although not guided by the theoretical framework outlined in this [selection], have produced findings that are consistent with many of the framework's elements. Since Cohen, March, and Olsen (1972) coined the concept of *organized anarchy*, it has become axiomatic among scholars of educational administration that school organizations do not have clear technologies.

However, research suggests that school organizations do possess a core technology that is characterized by a degree of routineness, or certainty. For example, Rowan, Raudenbush, and Cheong (1993) reported that some teachers perceive their work to be fairly routinized.

Two related studies conducted nearly 2 decades apart offer a broader sense of how teachers view their work. Lortie's (1975) groundbreaking study in which "teachers describe their world" (p. ix) and Cohn and Kottkamp's (1993) partial replication reveal that social interaction lies at the very center of teaching. Lortie noted that teachers emphasize the interpersonal dimension over interest in subject matter. Cohn and Kottkamp reported that teachers identify three general categories of skills that members of their profession must possess to be successful. The first includes skills that teachers employ to develop basic and direct relations with students. The second involves skills that teachers use to organize students, individually or in groups, for instruction. The third consists of skills to engage students in the subject matter being taught or in the instructional process itself (Ogawa, 1996).

Research suggests, then, that teaching is characterized by a measure of routineness, or clarity. Moreover, there is evidence that such clarity lies in teaching's social technology. Thus, schools would be expected to employ bridges and buffers to manage relations between the social technology of teaching and the external environment, including the parents of students.

The Use of Bridging Strategies

The findings of research on parent involvement in schools reflect the use of bridging strategies by schools to manage relations with parents. It is clear that schools confront conditions that give rise to the use of bridging. Schools are dependent on parents to provide resources that affect the academic performance of students. For example, research indicates that parent involvement in school activities is associated with grades received by students in school; other research demonstrates that parent involvement in education-related activities at home is a predictor of students' performance on standardized achievement tests (Schneider & Coleman, 1993).

Given this dependency, we would expect to find that schools regularly construct bridges to parents. In fact, research documents the use of several types of bridging strategies by educators (Becker & Epstein, 1982; Epstein, 1990, 1995). In some cases, these strategies take the form of organized programs in districts and schools that seek to enhance communications between schools and families, involve parents on school-based management councils, provide parent effectiveness workshops, and dispense health and social services. However, in many instances individual teachers employ bridging strategies to encourage parents to read to their children, discuss school with their children, monitor their children's completion of homework assignments, and engage in education-related activities (e.g., visiting the local public library).

The Use of Buffering Strategies

Research on family–school relations does not directly address whether or how schools buffer their core technology from uncertainties that parents may introduce. However, research on a variety of other educational topics is a bit more instructive. Research suggests that families are, indeed, a source of uncertainty for school organizations. The uncertainly takes two general forms. First, there is the uncertainty that can be introduced when parents directly interfere with the professional discretion of teachers and principals. Studies suggest that well-educated, middle-class parents are sometimes perceived by educational professionals as intruding into their domain by insisting on or questioning particular practices or programs (Chavkin & Williams, 1987; Davies, 1987; Epstein & Becker, 1982). Second, families can present schools with uncertainties in the form of both heterogeneity and instability. For example, research documents the increasing ethnic and linguistic diversity of families served by schools in many sections of the United States (Coleman, 1987). Other studies record the high mobility rates of families served by many of the nation's schools and the changing composition of families (Hoffer & Coleman, 1990). Faced with increasing uncertainty, schools would be expected to buffer their core technology.

Although research has not focused on the use of buffering strategies, some evidence exists. For example, research consistently demonstrates that teachers expect principals to shield them from undue parental influence and that principals do perform this function. We are all familiar with the sign placed on the front of every public school, directing all visitors, including parents, to check in at the school office. Moreover, a large body of research documents the use of grouping strategies by schools and teachers, which bear a striking resemblance to coding as an approach to buffering. Although such groupings are usually and arguably based on student ability or interest, they also reflect differences in family background. For example, research shows that, beginning as early as kindergarten, teachers place students in groups that correspond closely to the students' socioeconomic backgrounds (Rist, 1970). Research also demonstrates that educational tracks correlate with social class and that curriculum content varies across tracks, and, thus across class (Oakes, 1985). In addition, programs that provide students with breakfast and health care and their families with social services are aimed at buffering schools from conditions that can undermine their efforts to instruct students by minimizing uncertainties posed by such hinders as poor health and dysfunctional family situations.

Conclusions

Existing research documents that school organizations, indeed, confront environmental conditions to which bridging and buffering are appropriate responses. Moreover, it reveals that school organizations implement programs and individual educators employ practices that correspond to bridging and buffering. Thus, research seems to demonstrate that the dominant conceptualization of family—school relations, which treats parent involvement as an unmixed blessing, is conceptually blind to half of the picture.

The theoretical perspective advanced in this [selection] holds the promise of extending the study of parent involvement by providing a more balanced and, thus, complete view. The proposed approach would build on existing research, which highlights positive forms of parent involvement by adding research that examines the ways in which schools buffer their core technology from disruptive forms of parent involvement. Ultimately, the framework leads to considering how a combination, or balance, of bridging and buffering contributes to the effectiveness of school organizations and, hence to the academic performance of students.

However, the research cited is merely suggestive, not confirmatory. The evidence is largely indirect; that is, it arose from studies that were not intended to examine bridging and buffering in school organizations. As a consequence, the research did not address several potentially important issues. For instance, research has neither done the basic work of describing strategies that school organizations use to buffer uncertainties introduced by parents, nor has it addressed the issue noted in the previous paragraph: assessing the impact of various combinations of buffering and bridging on the instructional effectiveness of schools.

More complex conceptual issues also remain. For example, existing evidence on the use of bridging and buffering by educators suggests that the theoretical framework does not adequately depict the structure of these practices in school organizations. Theory emphasizes the role of managers in controlling the relations between organizations and environments. However, research on schools suggests that administrators alone do not bridge and buffer. Rather, teachers, staff members, as well as principals buffer and bridge through both formal and informal means, some of which are not reflected in existing theoretical treatments.

The theoretical framework also does not adequately explain relations between bridging and buffering. The examples cited in this [selection] suggest that the line distinguishing bridging from buffering may not be all that clear. For example, increasing numbers of schools are working with public health and social service agencies to provide assistance to families of students. The bridging and buffering involved in these programs is complex and occurs at several levels. The schools must bridge with the agencies on which they must depend for services that they, themselves, do not provide. They must also build bridges to parents in order to gain their participation. However, all of this is done in order to buffer schools from uncertainties that can be introduced by parents who do not provide their children with adequate health care or stable home environments. These and other issues await the attention of scholars. Although the applicability of the concepts of bridging and buffering has not been established empirically, they can bring attention to previously unacknowledged theoretical and empirical issues, which is promising in and of itself.

POSTSCRIPT

Is Greater Parental Involvement at School always Beneficial?

Can we answer this question with empirical data? The answer is yes, but a cautious yes. One reason for caution is that it is likely to be the case that the only way to collect such empirical data would be within the context of a correlational study, which is often associated with some ambiguity regarding its findings. Consider the case of the Chicago public schools, which we described in the introduction to this issue. At first glance, the interpretation seems clear: the Chicago schools were decentralized so that parents had greater involvement, and then student achievement improved. The cause of the improvement must be increased parental involvement. What else could it be? In fact, a more careful analysis brings to light several other, equally plausible, explanations for the improvement in student achievement. Perhaps the increased scrutiny in the media brought about increased effort by teachers and principals, either because of fear for their jobs or because they were reinvigorated by the knowledge that the city cared about education. Or perhaps the changes in curriculum and disciplinary prac- tices-changes were responsible, changes that could have been implemented without increased parental involvement. Or maybe the schools received increased financial resources for direct instruction because the administrative budget was trimmed? Any or all of these factors could have been involved in producing the gains in student achievement in addition to, or even instead of, increased parental involvement.

Caution is also in order because the answer to the question ultimately may be dictated as much by a political or ideological agenda as by empirical evidence regard- ing the effects of parental involvement. That is, parental involvement in children's schooling may be viewed by some people to be a parent's right or even a parent's obli- gation. From this point of view, the question of whether parental involvement leads to higher achievement or other tangible outcomes for students is not important. What is important, it could be argued, is that schools must create multiple routes by which parents can have input into their children's education.

Readers interested in the various ways in which schools could involve, or have involved, parents in their children's schooling will find the following articles useful: "School-Family-Community Partnerships: Caring for the Children We Share," by J. L. Epstein, *Phi Delta Kappan* (1995); "Parental Involvement in the Reform of Mathemat- ics Education," by Dominic Peressini, *The mathematics Teacher* (September 1997); "Parental Involvement supports academic Improvement Among Middle Schoolers," by J. A. Brough and J. L. Irvin, *Middle School Journal* (2001); "Parent Involvement Strat- egies in teacher Education Programs: Applying a Four-Tier Model," by P. K. Greener and M. S. Tichenor, *Teacher Education and Practice* (2001); and "A Transition Program Based on Identified Student and Parent Concerns," by Angela Koppang, *Middle School Journal* (September 2004). See also *The Parent Project: A Workshop Approach to Parent Involvement* (Stenhouse Publishing, 1994).

ISSUE 15

Should Schools Embrace Computers and Technology?

YES: Marcia C. Linn and James D. Slotta, from "WISE Science," *Educational Leadership* (October 2000)

NO: R. W. Burniske, from "The Shadow Play: How the Integration of Technology Annihilates Debate in Our Schools," *Phi Delta Kappan* (October 1998)

ISSUE SUMMARY

YES: Marcia C. Linn, a professor of cognition and development, and James D. Slotta, director of the Web-based Integrated Science Environment (WISE) project library at the University of California, Berkeley, present an overview of the WISE project, which is designed to teach science and technological literacy through Web-based activities. They contend that this project will make teachers more effective and increase their flexibility in the classroom.

NO: R. W. Burniske, of the Computer Writing and Research Lab at the University of Texas, Austin, argues that schools have been too uncritical in their acceptance of technology and that computer-based education, in many instances, may actually contribute to the very problems it is intended to correct.

Computers and related technologies have become intertwined with every facet of our daily lives. They can be found in nearly every place of business, from Wall Street to the neighborhood auto shop. In the United States desktop computers can be found in millions of homes.

Computers are also becoming increasingly commonplace in schools. More than 6 million computers were in U.S. schools by the mid-1990s, and this number is likely to continue growing as government support for technology increases. Not only are computers increasing in number in schools, but so are the educational devices they power and the educational functions they perform. Educational devices include CD-ROMs, digital cameras, laser disc players, overhead projector panels, and scanners. Educational functions include computer-assisted instruction, word processing, desktop publishing, e-mail, Internet searching, and distance education. Many of these devices and functions have been organized into networked systems for presenting the entire curriculum in a subject area to students across multiple classrooms and schools.

Many educators and policymakers have embraced computer-based technologies. In large measure, this is because these technologies appear to be consistent with constructivist theory, which now holds sway among most educational researchers and practitioners. According to this theory, we construct new knowledge when the results of our physical and mental actions on the world challenge our current ways of knowing. This implies that schooling should provide students with opportunities to act on the material to be mastered and to "figure things out for themselves," rather than transmit ready-made knowledge to them through an all-knowing teacher. Moreover, because different students will come to the material to be learned with different "ways of knowing," they may require different experiences and different amounts of time to achieve mastery. Computer-based instruction is appealing because students are actively involved in the learning process, they can work at their own pace, and presumably they can receive lessons that are well suited to their current ways of knowing.

Critics, however, argue that much of the interest in these technologies reflects a rather naive desire to use whatever is new with little attention to its appropriateness for the educational goal in question. As a result, critics argue, sophisticated technologies are often put to rather trivial uses, uses for which other, less-expensive approaches are available. Perhaps more important, critics suggest that there may be features of the current technologies that are antithetical to the goals that most educators hope to achieve. For instance, they suggest that activities such as surfing the Internet may encourage a superficial, unsystematic approach to studying rather than one that is focused, goal-directed, and self-reflective. Others argue that the technology makes learning an individual, isolated activity rather than the cultural activity that they believe best facilitates learning. Finally, some critics raise the possibility that because computer-mediated instruction depends critically on a student's ability to monitor his or her own progress, such technology may increase the gap between the more- and the less-capable students; that is, highly motivated students with good self-monitoring skills will flourish, while those who are less motivated or less self-reflective will flounder without the benefit of a human teacher to support them.

In the first of the following selections, Marcia C. Linn and James D. Slotta describe their Web-based library of science projects, each of which is designed to be adaptable to the needs and interests of teachers and students from elementary school to high school. Linn and Slotta argue that the projects facilitate debate among students and make technology available to all students. In the second selection, R. W. Burniske suggests that technology is often adopted blindly, without any consideration of whether it is necessary or even helpful for achieving the intended educational objectives. Moreover, he suggests that technology frequently precludes the critical discussion of ideas, which he believes is the foundation of a meaningful educational experience.

Marcia C. Linn and
James D. Slotta

 **YES**

WISE Science

How can we bridge the barrier between research innovations and their adoption in science classrooms? Too often, educational research demonstrates exciting learning gains for local students but never reaches schools outside the initial research partnership.

A partnership of classroom teachers, technologists, natural scientists, and pedagogical researchers has designed a flexible learning environment that makes teachers more effective in their classrooms and enables them to respond creatively to state standards, prior student experiences, time commitments, and available resources. New groups of teachers and schools can bridge the gap between educational research and classroom practice by using the Web-based Integrated Science Environment (WISE) project library.

Partnerships supported by the National Science Foundation and others have created a library of WISE projects. These partners have designed pilot projects, observed their use in science classrooms, and refined the projects on the basis of their observations. WISE projects can be improved by teachers, tailored to their course topics, and connected to local conditions and to state and national standards.

Schools and individual teachers can join WISE by going to the Web site (http://wise.berkeley.edu) and selecting activities for their classes from the project library. Classes—using only a Web browser and an Internet connection—can register to use WISE at school or at home. A video of teachers using WISE and a book called *Computers, Teachers, Peers* (Linn & Hsi, 2000) are also available.

The Design Framework

The WISE learning environment implements design principles to promote lifelong science learning along with language and technology literacy (Linn & Hsi, 2000). These principles reflect the scaffolded knowledge integration framework, as well as cognitive apprenticeship (Collins, Brown, & Holum, 1991), intentional learning (Scardamalia & Bereiter, 1991), and the traditions of constructivist psychology. The design framework—developed from 15 years of classroom research—helps students connect, refine, and revisit all their science ideas rather than isolate and forget the science that they have studied in school. We organize the design framework around four design strategies.

Make science accessible.   WISE design partnerships seek an appropriate level of analysis for the scientific content of a project so that students can restructure, rethink, compare, critique, and develop more cohesive ideas. The WISE curriculum uses scientific models that students can easily grasp and connects these models to personally relevant problems. The WISE learning environment represents the scientific inquiry process through an inquiry map, which leads students though inquiry steps, providing cognitive and procedural guidance along the way.

Make thinking visible.   WISE partnerships make scientific arguments more visible by carefully designing interactive simulations, model-building environments, and argument-representation tools. WISE projects use embedded assessments to make student thinking visible and to engage students as designers (diSessa, 2000).

Help students learn from one another.   WISE projects use collaborative tools—such as online discussions, peer review, and debate—to help students take advantage of classmates' ideas. Online tools enable all students to participate in the deliberations of science, allowing equitable access to the discourse and rhetoric of science (Hoadley & Linn, in press; Hsi, 1997).

Foster lifelong learning.   To help students become lifelong science learners, students critique Web sites, design arguments, or debate science controversies, such as the reasons for the observed decline in amphibian populations. Students reflect on scientific materials including Web sites (Davis & Linn, in press).

Design Studies

WISE classroom research combines the features of Japanese lesson studies (Lewis & Tsuchida, 1997; Linn, Tsuchida, Lewis, & Songer, 2000) and design experiments (Brown, 1992; Collins, 1999; diSessa, 2000) in what we call *design studies* (Linn, in press). The effectiveness of a curriculum project can increase by as much as 400 percent using this approach (Linn & ilsi, 2000).

In our customization research, teachers have made WISE curriculum projects locally relevant to students in diverse geographical or demographic areas, have made projects more successful on the basis of classroom trials, and have tailored instruction to personal practices.

Houses in the Desert

In the Houses in the Desert project, students collaborate with a partner in designing a house that is comfortable for living in the desert. The project, created by physical-science experts, teachers, and educational researchers, is targeted to the middle school level. Students create a preliminary design and then critique several Internet sites advocating varied energy-efficient house designs. Next, they analyze alternate materials for designing walls, roofs, and windows, and they specialize in one housing component. Students revise their preliminary designs, perform a heat-flow analysis, and submit their design for peer review.

After reviewing peer comments, they finalize and publish their desert-house designs on a secure class Website. In the course of this project, students gain science and language literacy by critiquing Web sites, collaborating in design, and contributing to peer review. They gain technology literacy by searching for relevant materials on the Web and using design tools.

To make thinking visible, the project uses animated representations of heat flow through building materials, such as wood or glass, which enables students to distinguish insulators and conductors. The project also illustrates the interaction between air and ground temperature during day and night in the desert. To make the science accessible, the project connects to real-life experiences; for example, students use the heat-flow model to compare designs for picnic coolers and to discuss how to keep a drink cold in their lunch box. To promote lifelong learning, the project helps students critique Web sites, formulate critical questions, and develop arguments to support design decisions. Finally, to help students learn from one another, the project orchestrates peer review of designs, helping students develop a set of shared criteria for evaluating house designs.

To help teachers make the project relevant to their students, the partners included a Web site where students could compare climate data in a desert to the climate in any specified location, including their own school. Students reflect on how their climate is different from that of the desert. Teachers also add Web sites that feature local house designs—for example, students in some classes explored a solar house in Maine—making the project more relevant and engaging.

Plants in Space

In the Plants in Space project, students construct a small hydroponic garden in their classroom, analyze factors responsible for plant growth (such as light, water, and soil), compare the growth of earth plants and Wisconsin Fast Plants (referred to as NASA space plants), and analyze what factors are important for plant growth in a space-station environment. NASA scientists, research biologists, teachers, educational researchers, and technology specialists designed the project. Web-based materials bring the space station to life and raise questions that are relevant to elementary students: Can we grow plants without dirt?

To make science accessible, students explore a personally relevant problem and investigate their ideas about plant growth. Students asked, Do plants eat dirt? To help make thinking visible, students represent plant growth through online graphing. To promote lifelong learning, students reflect on the Web evidence, record observations about the plants in their own minigardens, and report on their recommendations. To help students learn from one another and from experts, the project includes online discussions with NASA scientists about the challenges of growing plants in space.

Teachers can customize the hints, prompts, discussions, and even the focus of the project—for example, they can choose whether to emphasize plant growth factors or conditions aboard the space station. After first using the Plants in Space project, one 5th grade teacher added Internet materials about photosynthesis, enhanced online discussions about light and energy, and revised the hints and prompts. The students using the second version developed a more coherent understanding of plant growth as a result (Williams, 2000).

Cycles of Malaria

In the Cycles of Malaria project, students debate three different perspectives on how to control malaria worldwide: developing an effective pesticide that targets the anopheles mosquito; developing a vaccine against the disease; and creating social programs that reduce exposure to mosquitoes, such as distributing mosquito nets or having community cleanups. Students explore evidence related to each control method and debate alternate approaches. The project is targeted at upper-middle and high school biology students and has been customized by advanced-placement biology teachers.

To make thinking visible, the project includes animations and videos of the mosquito and parasite life cycles, as well as maps showing the worldwide incidence of malaria. To make the project accessible to students, teachers draw connections to diseases in North America, such as HIV or sickle-cell anemia. The project promotes lifelong learning by helping students understand scientific viewpoints, evaluation of evidence, and policy trade-offs. To learn from others, students participate in asynchronous electronic discussions with peers and engage in class debates.

Cycles of Malaria has been customized by teachers working in a wide range of grade levels and topic areas and with diverse teaching approaches. These teachers added activities and varied their patterns of interaction with students. Middle school biology teachers included field trips to local ponds or puddles to collect mosquito larvae. Another teacher added a short story about the struggles of the family of Kofi, a young African villager with malaria. Norwegian teachers connected the material to international policies for DDT use. A high school chemistry teacher focused on the chemical compounds within the DDT pesticide and how they affect the environment.

To determine whether WISE is robust enough to support these diverse customizations while retaining the instructional framework, we contrasted the adaptations of Cycles of Malaria by three different teachers in a middle school that has implemented WISE in every science class. We found that teachers varied greatly in the frequency and duration of their interactions with students during the project. One teacher spent considerable time talking in depth with each student group, visiting groups once, at most, during a class period. Another teacher interacted for very short periods of time but visited each group several times.

Although WISE strives to enable teachers to interact deeply with their students, we were gratified that WISE accommodated even these major differences in teaching practice. Students were challenged to reflect and make connections to rich problem contexts. For example, in the post-assessment for the Cycles of Malaria project, teachers measured the improvement in students' understanding of disease vectors, vaccines, life cycles, and medical research. Students connected applications to personally relevant situations (such as traveling to a foreign country) and transferred ideas to novel situations (such as advising a small country on a pending law to clean up standing water around all rural villages). Students in all three classes showed identical, substantial learning gains. The assessments were sensitive to teaching styles as well. For example, students who had longer interactions with their teacher gave more coherent answers to complex questions. This research helps us understand how diverse teaching approaches influence outcomes and how curriculum designs can meet the needs of diverse teachers.

Three Literacies

WISE promotes lifelong learning by addressing three mutually reinforcing literacies: technology, science, and language.

Technology literacy.   We base our definition of technology literacy on the National Academy of Sciences report on what everyone should know about information technology (Snyder et al., 1999). The WISE curriculum interweaves technology with science instruction, targeting three complementary aspects of technology literacy. First, students learn to use technology in complex, sustained problem solving—identifying unanticipated consequences, searching for relevant information, communicating, collaborating, and critiquing. Second, students learn contemporary skills, such as using e-mail, the Internet, word processing, and spreadsheets. Third, students learn the concepts of technology, such as modeling, simulations, and the societal impacts of technology.

WISE helps students develop technology literacy in school instead of relying on inequitable home access (American Association of University Women, 2000). More students are developing fluency with information technology at home. They join chat rooms, play networked versions of games, do homework on word processors, and use graphics and drawing tools. These experiences prepare many students to use technology in the classroom, but they also divide students along economic lines.

WISE remedies these inequalities by incorporating technologies for tomorrow's workforce in the classroom. In many schools, students come with a good understanding of digital media, only to find that their teachers employ an old-fashioned, low-tech presentation of science and other topics. Schools often relegate computers to a lab space where they are used for "skills training" or extracurricular project work rather than for universal technology literacy. This disconnect between technology in the home and technology in the classroom contributes to the increasing sense of irrelevance and disinterest that students feel about science instruction.

Science literacy.   Science literacy requires reconsidering scientific ideas and seeking a more coherent understanding of them. To respond to rapid increases in science knowledge, frequent job changes, and consequential policy debates, citizens must constantly update their science knowledge. Nutritional decisions (Is butter or margarine more healthy?), environmental decisions (Should I choose paper or plastic?), and political or economic issues require citizens to revisit their ideas as well as critique contradictory, persuasive messages in the popular press and on the Internet. Schools can no longer cover all the science topics that students will use in their lives, so we must motivate students to continue to learn. WISE projects connect to relevant issues—such as space exploration, environmental stewardship, and wilderness survival—to set students on a path toward lifelong learning.

Language literacy.   Lifelong science learning depends on a critical reading of science material, effective communication about science issues, and clear writing about science topics (Heath, 1983). In WISE, students communicate about scientific topics, evaluate scientific texts, ask questions about science policies, participate in debates about contemporary controversies, and create and critique arguments.

WISE Conclusions

Students need opportunities to independently explore complex problems, to flounder, to learn from their peers, to reflect on their experiences, and to become responsible stewards of their own learning. This linked, coherent learning only arises when science instruction presents students with theories and principles that they can connect to personal experiences, interests, and past instruction.

The process of thinking about science, reorganizing ideas, incorporating new information, and remaining skeptical of evidence is both difficult and exhilarating. If we convert the science curriculum to a lifelong learning enterprise, we can capture that exhilaration. This approach can amplify the rewards that teachers feel when they teach students about science and can also increase the opportunities for researchers to make science instruction effective and successful.

References

American Association of University Women (AAUW). (2000). *Tech-savvy: Educating girls in the new computer age.* Washington, DC: Author.

Brown, A. L (1992). Design experiments: Theoretical and methodological challenges in creating complex interventions in classroom settings. *Journal of the Learning Sciences, 2*(2), 141-178.

Collins, A. (1999). Design issues of learning environments. In *Psychological and educational foundations of technology-based education.* New York: Springer-Verlag.

Collins, A., Brown, J. S., & Holum, A. (1991). Cognitive apprenticeship: Making thinking visible. *American Educator, 15*(3), 6-11, 38-39.

Davis, E. K, & Linn, M. C. (in press). Scaffolding students' knowledge integration: Prompts for reflection in KIE. *International Journal of Science Education, Special Issue, 22*(8), 819-837.

diSessa, A. A. (2000). *Changing minds: Computers, learning, and literacy.* Cambridge, MA: MIT Press.

Heath, S. B. (1983). *Ways with words: Language, life, and work in communities and classrooms.* New York: Cambridge University Press.

Hoadley, C., & Linn, M. C. (in press). Teaching science through on-line peer discussions: Speak Easy in the knowledge integration environment. *International Journal of Science Education,* Special Issue, *22*(8), 839-857.

Hsi, S. (1997 *Facilitating knowledge integration in science through electronic discussion: The multimedia forum kiosk.* Unpublished doctoral dissertation, University of California, Berkeley.

Lewis, C., & Tsuchida, I. (1997). Planned educational change in Japan: The case of elementary science instruction. *Journal of Educational Policy, 12*(5), 303-331.

Linn, M. C. (in press). Designing the knowledge integration environment: The partnership inquiry process. International *Journal of Science Education,* Special Issue, *22*(8), 781-796.

Linn, M. C., & Hsi, S. (2000). *Computers, teachers, peers: Science learning partners.* Mahwah, NJ: Lawrence Erlbaum Associates.

Linn, M. C., Tsuchida, I., Lewis, C., & Songer, N. B. (2000). Beyond fourth grade science: Why do U.S. and Japanese students diverge? *Educational Researcher, 29*(3) 4-14.

Scardamalia, M., & Bereiter, C. (1991). Higher levels of agency for children in knowledge building: A challenge for the design of new knowledge media. *Journal of the Learning Sciences 1*(1), 37-68.

Snyder, L., Aho, A. V., Linn, M. C., Packer, A., Tucker, A., Ullinan, J., & Van Dam, (1999). Be FIT! Being fluent with information technology. Washington, DC: National Academy Press.

Williams, L. M. (2000). *Exploring how a web-based integrated science environment and hands-on science can promote knowledge integration.* Paper presented at the annual meeting of the American Education Research Association, New Orleans, LA.

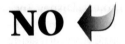

R. W. Burniske

The Shadow Play

The greatest threat to education is the death of dialectics. Without dialectics, the pursuit of truth through argumentation, we offer students sterile information or pernicious propaganda. I've learned this lesson many times during the past 16 years while teaching at four different schools in as many countries and continents. I've witnessed the repressed discourse of schools in Egypt, Ecuador, Malaysia, and the U.S., where traditional hierarchies and administrative hegemonies preserve the status quo.

One cannot fault the schools entirely, however, for we must consider the societies that breed them. In Malaysia, where I taught at an international school from 1992 to 1996, government censorship thwarted debate; in America, corporate brainwashing achieves much the same result. What's troubling in both instances, however, is the public's acquiescence. The latest example is America's zealous embrace of computer technology and the absence of public debate over its adoption. Upon repatriation a year ago, after nearly a decade as an expatriate educator, this situation puzzled me. I wonder if it's possible to revive the moribund dialectics in this country, particularly as they relate to technology's role in education, and so consider how best to prepare teachers for dramatic changes in their classrooms. Sometimes it's necessary to step back from our local scene, viewing it from a distance and comparing it with foreign situations, in order to comprehend our circumstances more fully.

Consider, then, one of the defining cultural metaphors of Malaysia: the "shadow play." To understand Malay politics, one needs to be familiar with this form of entertainment, but one needs to study the audience rather than the performance. People in front of the screen are mesmerized by the shadows playing upon it; those on the periphery, however, are less susceptible to the illusion. They see the shadows and hear the music and the narrative, but they also observe the puppet master behind the screen, deftly manipulating both the puppets *and the audience.*

Now, let's step from the Malay shadow puppets to the theater of American politics, which exploits a national obsession with television to mesmerize its audience. In both instances, infatuation with shadows playing upon a screen distracts people from the substance and motives of the puppet master.

I learned a great deal about this phenomenon while coordinating a global telecomputing project called "The Media Matter," which I created to allow students in different countries to discuss with one another the role of the media in shaping public perceptions. In the midst of that project, Disney, Inc., purchased the ABC television network. My students in Malaysia were surprised to find their counterparts in Iowa—the ones self-righteously attacking the "evils" of government censorship—apathetic about this "business merger." My students at the International School of Kuala Lumpur asked how journalistic integrity could possibly be maintained if Disney CEO Michael Eisner should be interviewed for an ABC news program, such as "Nightline" or "20/20." Amazingly, this issue didn't cause much of a stir among the students in Des Moines.

Three years later, how many American viewers of the "ABC Evening News" realize that it is owned and operated by the people responsible for the Magic Kingdom? How many would even see a problem with that? It's ironic that people shrug at corporate-controlled media yet rail against state-controlled media. Don't both lead to the censorship of opposing viewpoints? How can a society teach its young the value of "Truth" if it tolerates the daily deceptions practiced by its government or its media? It is this inability to subject media to a "critical" reading that has prompted Neil Postman and others to fret over "the end of education."[1]

Developing genuine, dialectical discourse, whether face-to-face or in cyberspace, is no simple matter. The classroom environment suffers when the surrounding community fails to nurture healthy discursive practices.

Consider the present generation of students, weaned on the "boob tube," imbibing a crass ideology that says, "Don't think. Consume!" Our children didn't invent this ideology, but they quickly absorb it. A few years ago a national brewing company had the temerity to sell its product with the flippant query "Why ask why?" Implicit in that advertising campaign and in many others like it was a dismissal of critical thinking. Imagine the impact of that dismissal on young people. Then consider the plight of a teacher attempting to use the Socratic method in a classroom by asking, "Are there any questions?" Adolescents lack the skills necessary for dialectical discourse, and little in popular culture encourages them to cultivate those skills. That's the way the advertising agencies want it, but it doesn't bode well for democracy. Modern rhetoricians remind us of this disturbing reality:

> Persuasion is concerned primarily with influencing the way people think or act, whereas argument is concerned with discovering and conveying our best judgments about the truth of things through an appeal to reason. All arguments involve persuasion, but all persuasive acts do not involve argument.[2]

Rather than pursue truth through dialectical discourse, we too often settle for "persuasive acts" that exert their influence by exciting our passions and overwhelming our reason. Will the Internet and educational telecomputing help us overcome the seductive power of persuasion? Not if they simply encourage more channel surfing, a definite possibility with the advent of Web TV. Unfortunately, the initial hype and hysteria surrounding the "Information Superhighway" have distracted us from more substantial debates, ones that we must revive. We are barraged with these persuasive acts, most of them exploiting our fundamental anxieties, but seldom do we hear rational argument. How else can we explain the change of stance of politicians—the ones who squeezed public education in the 1980s with the claim that we "can't fix what's wrong with education by throwing money at it"—who now giddily promote on-ramps to the Information Superhighway in every classroom? In both instances, rather than sound argument, they have given us emotional appeals that prey on our concerns about children, job opportunities, and national interests.

As an educator I'd like to ask those elected officials why they prefer investing in machines rather than investing in people. Do they realize that they've mistaken job training for education? I doubt it.

But what I'm certain they do know is that the "boxes and wires" of telecomputing are manufactured by "Big Business." And Big Business fills those campaign coffers we keep hearing about. So if we keep Big Business happy by investing in its gadgetry, then Big Business will keep the politicians happy by spreading largesse—and occasionally donating hardware and software to schools and libraries. This, in turn, will get youngsters "hooked" early, thereby oiling the machine that paves the Information Superhighway.

Unfortunately, there's one significant casualty along the way: public debate. As government of the people, by the people, and for the people succumbs to government of the corporation, by the corporation, and for the corporation, the dialectics of democracy yield to the spreadsheets of plutocracy. Perhaps this explains my sensitivity to the rhetoric of ... would-be Education President [Bill Clinton]. Consider the following excerpt from his second inaugural address:

> Now, for the third time, a new century is upon us, and another time to choose. We began the 19th century with a choice, to spread our nation from coast to coast. We began the 20th century with a choice, to harness the Industrial Revolution to our values of free enterprise, conservation, and human decency. Those choices made all the difference. At the dawn of the 21st century a free people must now choose to shape the forces of the Information Age and the global society, to unleash the limitless potential of all our people, and, yes, to form a more perfect union.

As I understand it, implicit in the idea of "choice" is that we have at least two options from which to select. And yet the President made no mention of alternatives to these choices. Note, too, the businesslike detachment of the statement "Those choices made all the difference." Yes, Mr. President, they most certainly did. But could we stop to consider whether the differences they made were positive or negative? Could we hear a rational argument, instead of emotional rhetoric, about how this current "choice" will help us "form a more perfect union"? What these statements reveal is how little "choice" the common person actually had at the start of each new century. What are the chances of creating "a more perfect union" when the leader of it declares that "a free people must now choose to shape the forces of the Information Age?"

If we're told what we must choose, then how free are we? If there is no alternative, no opposing view, where's the dialectical tension necessary to discover Truth?

Access to the Internet will not solve the problem of this paucity of debate. Nor will it necessarily reinvigorate "public discourse in the age of show business."[3] It is unrealistic to expect children who spend 35 hours a week in front of television screens that shower them with persuasive acts to suddenly develop critical thinking skills and engage in healthy on-line discourse the moment they log on.

Rather than wring our hands, however, we should look upon the outrageous expenditures for wiring schools as a challenge. It's no longer a question of whether we should introduce computer technology into our classrooms. I'm afraid that "choice" has already been made for us. The question now is how we should make use of this technology for educational purposes. How can we use it to help young students acquire a literacy that's more hospitable to dialectical discourse?

We might, as we so often do, blame the schools for these problems— even as we demand that they save us from them. If we're genuinely concerned, however, then we must provide more and better professional development opportunities for teachers. In February 1997 the National Center for Education Statistics published a report indicating that Internet access in K-12 schools in the U.S. had increased from 35% in 1994 to 65% in 1996, while only 14% of the schools surveyed had provided mandatory "teacher training" in that time span.[4] Teachers, it would seem, are left to train themselves and are marginalized when it comes to debates over education reform.

Meanwhile, politicians who saw no problem squeezing public education funding in the 1980s now rhapsodize over technology in the classroom. Does anyone else have a problem with this? I think a number of people do, but to articulate one's reservations is to invite the mockery of powerful opponents who ridicule thoughtful objections and attach the "Luddite" label to those who raise them. The consequence of this is the stifling of essential debates and the repression of significant questions, such as: At what age should we introduce children to computers? What impact will computers have on the social, emotional, and psychological development of our children? And how will computers alter the dynamics of a classroom and school?

Instead of these inquiries, we hear the more utilitarian question, one carrying the assumption that computers are *ipso facto* a good addition: *How can we get more computers into the classrooms?* This isn't a recipe for successful schools, nor is it healthy for democracy in this country. As Samuel Sava, head of the National Association of Elementary School Principals, observed before the start of the 1997-98 school year:

> I have not the slightest doubt about the value of computers in our society. But I question whether we have learned to apply this technology to K-8 instruction. ... If computers make a difference, it has yet to show up in achievement. We must have the courage to resist the public enthusiasm for sexy hardware and argue for the funds necessary to train our teachers. We

cannot send them into the computer room with nothing but a user's manual. If you've ever read one of those things, ... they give new meaning to the phrase "English as a second language."[5]

I'd like to challenge every parent in this country, as well as every student, faculty member, and administrator, to think critically about computers in the classroom. Let's revive the dialectical discourse that is absent from so many discussions of the issue. If there's one thing I've learned while teaching nearly 1,500 students from the Middle East to North America and from Southeast Asia to South America, it is this: *schools will never be good places for students until they are good places for teachers.* Given current trends, I'd say our schools are in danger of becoming good places for machines.

So let's argue about this one a little, shall we? It's time for free people to choose wisely, demanding more options than technology affords and more substance than shadows provide.

Notes

1. Neil Postman, *The End of Education: Redefining the Value of School* (New York: Knopf, 1995).
2. John D. Ramage and John C. Bean, *Writing Arguments: A Rhetoric with Readings*, 3rd ed. (Boston: Allyn and Bacon, 1995), p. 3.
3. Neil Postman, *Amusing Ourselves to Death: Public Discourse in the Age of Show Business* (New York: Penguin, 1985).
4. Sheila Heaviside, Toija Riggins, and Elizabeth Farris, *Advanced Telecommunications in U. S. Public Elementary and Secondary Schools, Fall 1996* (Washington, D.C.: National Center for Education Statistics, 1997), available on-line at http://www.ed.gov/NCES/pubs/97944.html.
5. Quoted in Tamara Henry, "Questioning Computers," *USA Today,* 25 July 1997, p. 4-D.

POSTSCRIPT

Should Schools Embrace Computers and Technology?

Can we rely on empirical research to decide whether computers and related information technologies are superior to other instructional methods? The answer is a cautious yes. In principle, it should be possible, for example, to compare a computer-based approach to teaching American history to a more traditional, teacher-centered approach. Of course, the curricula covered by the two approaches would have to be identical so that any observed differences in student achievement could be attributed to the instructional approach rather than to the curriculum. The results of such a study should be interpreted cautiously, however, for at least five reasons. First, results obtained from a study based on teaching American history might not match results obtained for a study on teaching algebra, language arts, physics, etc. Perhaps American history lends itself more (or less) readily to computer-based instruction than other subjects do. A second consideration is the age or grade level of the students participating in the study. Although the computer-based approach might be highly effective in teaching high school-level American history, it might not be the best option for teaching an elementary school version of this same subject. Third, this study would not be a test of computer technology in general but rather of one particular software package, hardware configuration, and set of activities. Fourth, there would remain the question of whether or not any advantages found for the computer-based approach really have anything at all to do with technology. It is possible, for example, that benefits associated with a computer-based approach derived from the fact that the students were actively involved with the material to be learned rather than passively listening to the teacher present the information. Finally, how would researchers know they had observed students for a sufficient length of time to know the full effects of computer-based approach to instruction?

Comprehensive reviews of research on the impact of computers on academic achievement and cognitive development can be found in "Technology's Promises and Dangers in a Psychological and Educational Context," by Gavriel Salomon, *Theory Into Practice* (vol. 37, no. 1, 1998) and "Educational Psychology and Technology: A Matter of Reciprocal Relations," by Gavriel Salomon and Tamar Almog, *Teachers College Record* (Winter 1998). Also see "The I-Generation—From Toddlers to Teenagers: A Conversation With Jane M. Healy," by Carol Tell, *Educational Leadership* (October 2000) and "Mad Rushes Into the Future: The Overselling of Educational Technology," by Douglas Noble, *Educational Leadership* (November 1996). For examples of educational programs based on computer technologies, see "Attacking Literacy With Technology in an Urban Setting," by Michael R. Blasewitz and Rosemarye T. Taylor, *Middle School Journal* (January 1999); "From Compliance to Commitment: Technology as a Catalyst for Communities of Learning," by Mary Burns, *Phi Delta Kappan* (December 2002); and "Integrating Technologies Throughout Our Schools," by Richard L. Schwab and Lin J. Foa, *Phi Delta Kappan* (April 2001). For a book-length critique of technology in the schools, see *Oversold and Underused: Computers in the Classroom* by Larry Cuban (Harvard University Press, 2001).

ISSUE 16

Will Performance Assessment Lead to Meaningful Education Reform?

YES: D. Monty Neill, from "Transforming Student Assessment," *Phi Delta Kappan* (September 1997)

NO: Edward H. Haertel, from "Performance Assessment and Education Reform," *Phi Delta Kappan* (May 1999)

ISSUE SUMMARY

YES: D. Monty Neill, executive director of the National Center for Fair and Open Testing, argues that performance assessment is consistent with the emphasis on standards and accountability of the high-stakes testing reform movement but avoids many of the pitfalls of traditional approaches to testing.

NO: Edward H. Haertel, a professor in the School of Education at Stanford University, argues against the philosophy of "high-stakes testing and accountability" and contends that performance assessment does not make this philosophy any more palatable or successful than does the use of traditional standardized tests.

Calls for a massive overhaul of the U.S. educational system grew louder throughout the 1990s. These calls have been prompted largely by comparisons between the academic achievement of today's students with that of students in the past and between students in the United States and those in other industrialized countries. At the heart of these comparisons have been standardized tests, such as the ACT, the SAT, the National Assessment of Educational Progress, and the International Assessment of Education, which typically involve a multiple-choice format and always involve consistency in terms of administration, content, and scoring. Such tests have generally demonstrated that in the United States today's students score more poorly than yesterday's and more poorly than students in a host of other nations. Proposals for educational reform have likewise been tied in important ways to standardized tests. Most notable here are plans that have been dubbed *high-stakes testing* by critics.

High-stakes testing refers to proposals in which all the "players" in the educational process (i.e., students, teachers, school personnel, district administrators, etc.) are to be held accountable for achieving certain standards, often set by state legislatures and typically codified by a minimum acceptable score on one or more standardized tests. Such proposals are "high-stakes" because of the seriousness of the consequences that follow from failure to achieve acceptable scores. In the state of Wisconsin, for example, plans are now in the works to link entrance into and graduation from high school to passing standardized tests administered on a statewide basis. Students who fail to achieve the acceptable minimum score will be held back, with no exceptions for extenuating circumstances. In other districts and states around the country, similar plans for the evaluation of teachers, schools, and whole school districts are being developed. In some of these plans, teachers whose students fail to achieve a minimum score will be required to seek additional training; they may receive smaller pay raises or even be dismissed. Funding decisions within and across school districts also may be tied to student performance on standardized tests.

Many in the educational community have opposed high-stakes testing. Much of this criticism has focused on the limitations of standardized tests. The purported limitations include the following:

1. Standardized tests focus on decontextualized facts and skills and not on the kinds of deeper knowledge that will enable students to solve real-life problems in domains such as mathematics and science.
2. Standardized tests largely indicate only which problems a student has answered correctly or incorrectly, and they provide few insights into the strategies or knowledge that the student has brought to bear on the problems. Consequently, such tests cannot serve as a guide for determining whether or not a student is ready for promotion.

Some critics of standardized tests, however, have suggested that high-stakes testing can be made to work if standardized tests are replaced with *performance assessments.* In performance assessment, teachers rely on "authentic" student-generated products—products that emerge naturally from the material to be learned and that provide a basis for planning the next step in the student's learning. Performance assessments can include teacher observations, collections of a student's writing, extended projects, exhibitions, mini-plays, and even short-answer testing. In principle, performance assessment allows students to demonstrate their progress through a variety of products and performances that allow for in-depth qualitative analyses.

But can performance assessment really ensure the success of this latest wave of educational reform? In the following selection, D. Monty Neill argues that performance assessment can make high-stakes testing work. In the second selection, Edward H. Haertel argues that performance assessment—when it is embedded in the high-stakes testing and accountability philosophy—will be saddled with many of the same limitations of traditional standardized tests.

D. Monty Neill

 **YES**

Transforming Student Assessment

Imagine an assessment system in which teachers had a wide repertoire of classroom-based, culturally sensitive assessment practices and tools to use in helping each and every child learn to high standards; in which educators collaboratively used assessment information to continuously improve schools; in which important decisions about a student, such as readiness to graduate from high school, were based on the work done over the years by the student; in which schools in networks held one another accountable for student learning; and in which public evidence of student achievement consisted primarily of samples from students' actual schoolwork rather than just reports of results from one-shot examinations.

Many would probably dismiss this vision as the product of an overactive imagination. However, these ideas are at the core of *Principles and Indicators for Student Assessment Systems*, developed by the National Forum on Assessment and signed by more than 80 national and local education and civil rights organizations.[1] The widespread support for this document indicates a deep desire for a radical reconstruction of assessment practices, with student learning made central to assessment reform. In this article I draw on *Principles* to outline what a new assessment system could look like and to suggest some actions that can be taken to further assessment reform.

1. The seven principles endorsed by the Forum are:
2. The primary purpose of assessment is to improve student learning.
3. Assessment for other purposes supports student learning.
4. Assessment systems are fair to all students.
5. Professional collaboration and development support assessment.
6. The broad community participates in assessment development.
7. Communication about assessment is regular and clear.
8. Assessment systems are regularly reviewed and improved.

Classroom Assessment

Assessment for the primary purpose of improving student learning must rest on what the Forum calls "foundations" of high-quality schooling: an understanding of how student learning takes place, clear statements of desired learning (goals or standards) for all students, adequate learning resources

Adapted from D. Monty Neill, "Transforming Student Assessment," *Phi Delta Kappan* (September 1997). Copyright © 1997 by *Phi Delta Kappan*. Reprinted by permission of Phi Delta Kappa International and the author. Some notes omitted. The complete article is available on the Internet at http://www.fairtest.org/MNKappan.html.

(particularly high-quality teachers), and school structures and practices that support the learning needs of all students.

Assessment to enhance student learning must be integrated with, not separate from, curriculum and instruction.[2] Thus assessment reform is necessarily integrated with reform in other areas of schooling. In particular, schools need to ensure the development of "authentic instruction," which involves modes of teaching that foster understanding of rich content and encourage students' positive engagement with the world.

Both individual and societal interests come together in classroom instruction and assessment. Assessment works on a continuum. Helping the student with his or her individual interests and ways of thinking lies at one end. At the other are the more standard ways of knowing and doing things that society has deemed important. In the middle are individualized ways of learning, understanding, and expressing socially important things. There are, for example, many ways for a student to present an understanding of the causes of the U.S. Civil War.

For all these purposes, teachers must gather information. Teachers must keep track of student learning, check up on what students have learned, and find out what's going on with them. Keeping track means observing and documenting what students do. Checking up involves various kinds of testing and quizzing. Finding out is the heart of classroom assessment: What does the child mean? What did the child get from the experience? Why did the child do what he or she did? To find out, teachers must ask questions for which they do not already know the answers.[3]

To gather all this information, teachers can rely on a range of assessment activities. These include structured and spur-of-the-moment observations that are recorded and filed; formal and informal interviews; collections of work samples; use of extended projects, performances, and exhibitions; performance exams; and various forms of short-answer testing. In this context, teachers could use multiple-choice questions, but, as the Forum recommends, they would have a very limited role.

The evidence of learning can be kept in portfolios, which in turn can be used by students and teachers to reflect on, summarize, and evaluate student progress. Documentation systems, such as the *Primary Language Record,* the *Primary Learning Record,* the *California Learning Record,* and the *Work Sampling System,* can be used to organize assessment information and to guide evaluation of student learning.[4]

Following the continuum from individual to societal interests, evaluation should be both "self-referenced" and "standards-referenced."[5] The former evaluates the learner in light of her own goals, desires, and previous attainments and thus helps the student understand and further her own learning. In this way standards for the student's learning emerge from her work, not just from external sources. Standards-referenced evaluation is by now commonly understood. For example, students can be evaluated against the *Curriculum and Evaluation Standards for School Mathematics* of the National Council of Teachers of Mathematics.[6] Standards-based assessment has been mandated in the new federal Title I legislation. Whether standards are established by the school, district, or state, the Forum recommends wide participation in the standards-setting process. However, as the slogan "standards without standardization" suggests, excellence can take many forms. Thus, according to the ideals of *Principles*, "Assessment systems allow students multiple ways to demonstrate their learning."

When students are allowed multiple ways to show what they have learned and can do, evaluation becomes more complex. It becomes essential for educators to define "high quality" in a lucid way and to let students, parents, and the community know what variations on such quality look like. Clear scoring guides and examples of student work of varying kinds and degrees of quality are needed.

An additional objective of classroom performance assessment, supportive of both self-referenced and standards-referenced evaluation, is that students learn to reflect on and evaluate their own work. After all, an important goal of school is for students to be able to learn without relying on teachers. As students become engaged in developing scoring guides and evaluating work, they learn more deeply what good work looks like, and they more clearly understand their own learning processes.

The process of assessment, however, is not just focused on evaluating student accomplishment. Rather, the heart of assessment is a continuing flow in which the teacher (in collaboration with the student) uses information to guide the next steps in learning. The educator must ask, What should I do to help the student progress? This can be a very immediate issue (How can I help him get past a misunderstanding in multiplying fractions?) and thus should be an integrated part of the daily process of instruction. The question can be asked after any significant moment of assessment, such as completion of a project. It can also be asked periodically during the year and at the end of the year, at moments designed for summing up and planning.

The assessment practices outlined above are not common, even though these kinds of approaches are now widely promoted in the professional literature. Substantial professional development for teachers and restructuring of school practices are needed if this kind of assessment is to flourish....

Implications for Equity

A powerful concern for equity should underlie all efforts to reform assessment. Traditional tests have presumed that assessing all students in the same format creates a fair situation. However, the process of test construction, the determination of content, and the use of only one method—usually multiple-choice—all build in cultural and educational biases that favor some ways of understanding and demonstrating knowledge over others.[7] Testing's power has, in turn, helped shaped curriculum, instruction, and classroom assessment to advantage certain groups. Thus the uniformity and formal equity of the tests contribute to real-world educational inequity.

The solution is to allow diversity to flourish and to do so in ways that neither unfairly privilege some methods of demonstrating knowledge nor excuse some students from learning what society has deemed important. Too often, however, "different" has meant "lesser." For example, to meet the supposed needs of students in vocational education, the curriculum may be watered down. Students of color and those from low-income backgrounds have been most damaged by low expectations and low-level curricula. With regard to assessment, as Norman Frederiksen noted over a decade ago, the "real test bias" is that "multiple-choice tests tend not to measure the more complex cognitive abilities,"[8] which in turn are not taught, especially to low-income students.[9] This double bias must be overcome.

Students come from many cultures and languages. Instruction and assessment should connect to the local and the culturally particular and not presume uniformity of experience, culture, language, and ways of knowing.

In the context of classroom assessment, perhaps the thorniest issue is whether teachers will be able to assess all their students fairly, accurately, and comprehensively. Such evaluation requires more than that teachers be unbiased; they must also understand their students. Classroom performance assessments can provide a powerful vehicle for getting to know students. For example, the learning records noted above all ask teachers to interview students and their parents at the start of the year, to inquire about the child's learning experiences and interests. Classroom performance assessment requires thinking about the child and about the contexts in which the child is or is not successfully learning. Teachers who do not know their students cannot do self-referenced evaluation.

The hope is that, as teachers make use of instructional and assessment practices that give them more powerful insights into each student's learning processes and styles, they will be more likely to hold high expectations and provide strong support for learning for all their students. At least some evidence is beginning to show that this can happen. The use of clear, strong standards should be flexible enough to accommodate student diversity. For example, a standard stating that students should understand various interpretations of the separation of powers spelled out in the U.S. Constitution could be met in a variety of ways, such as an essay, an exhibition, a performance by a group of students, or a short story.

Teachers must also help all their students learn the ins and outs of the assessment methods being used. For example, when students select materials for a portfolio, teachers must ensure that all students know what the portfolio is used for, how to construct it, and how it will be evaluated. Students may need help in thinking about choosing work for projects or portfolios so that they will be able to select activities that best show their accomplishments.

Finally, equity requires meeting the needs of all students, including those who are learning English and those with disabilities or other special needs. Teachers must be able to assess their students in ways that allow them to demonstrate their learning and that provide the information teachers need to guide their future learning. Assessors need to know how to make accommodations and adaptations that are congruent with classroom instructional practices.

Back to Basics?

Some critics have argued that, while performance assessments are useful for assessing more advanced learning, multiple-choice tests are fine for the "basics." Others have even maintained that using performance assessment will undermine teaching of the "basics."[10] These misconceptions are dangerous.

What is meant by the "basics"? Presumably, the term encompasses reading well across a range of subject areas, writing fluently for a variety of purposes, and knowing and understanding math well enough to use it as needed in common educational, social, and employment settings. Rather than opposing such basics, it was largely because so many students were not attaining them that many educators became advocates of performance assessment.

Effective writing, for example, requires feedback on one's actual writing— that is, performance assessment. Writing assessment cannot be reduced to multiple-choice tests. But writing a few paragraphs on a topic about which students may know little and care less provides only minimally useful information. Good writing involves using knowledge and understanding and takes time for reflection and revision. High-quality performance assessment encourages just such practices and is therefore a needed element of learning the "basic" of clear writing.

Another troublesome notion is that first one learns the "basics"—usually defined as being able to do sufficiently well on a low-level multiple-choice test— and then, almost as a reward, one gets to read something interesting or apply math to a real problem. However, denying many students the opportunity to engage in real thinking while they learn some impoverished version of the "basics" only guarantees that the "later" for thinking will never arrive for them.

A somewhat more subtle variant of this idea is that first one learns content and then one learns to apply it. This approach, though discredited by cognitive psychology,[11] now appears to be making a comeback. It is wrong for several reasons. First, humans learn by thinking and doing. The content one thinks about and the thinking itself can and should get more complex as one learns, but one does not learn without thinking.[12] Schooling, however, can narrow and dull the range and intensity of thought by a focus on drill and repetition with decontextualized bits of information or skills. Such narrowed schooling is inflicted most often on children from low-income backgrounds and on students of color. It also reduces the likelihood of connecting schoolwork to the local and cultural contexts of the students.

In the "first know, then do" approach, it could be argued that math has a content knowledge that can be "learned" and then "applied." However, if one does not know how to go about solving the problem (application), knowing the math procedures does not help. More fundamentally, "the distinction between acquiring knowledge and applying it is inappropriate for education."[13] Separating knowing from doing for testing purposes reinforces instruction that isolates these elements, usually with the result that students don't grasp deep structures of knowledge and can't use the procedures and information they supposedly know.[14]

This separation of knowing and doing is used to justify calls, by test publishers and others, for multiple measures—using multiple-choice tests for basic facts and performance assessments for the ability to use knowledge. While it may be true that teachers can separately and efficiently test for declarative knowledge using multiple-choice or short-answer questions, it is critical that educators not allow the occasional use of such tools to reinforce an artificial separation that has had substantially harmful effects on schooling.

These separations also lead to complete confusion in some subjects. For example, multiple-choice reading tests are not described and used as measuring a few limited aspects of "reading skills"; they are erroneously described as measuring "reading."[15] The pervasiveness of these tests makes separating the test from its use a misleading exercise that only serves to disguise the difficulty of using these dangerous products safely.

This version of "basics first" also implies that whether one is excited about or engaged in learning has nothing to do with the results of learning. But if students don't get engaged, they won't think very much or very seriously about their schoolwork, and their learning will suffer.[16] A curriculum organized on "drill and kill" to raise test scores is no way to foster a desire to learn.

This does not mean that attention to particular bits (e.g., phonics) or that repetition in instruction is never acceptable. However, these practices must be subordinate elements of curriculum and instruction, to be used as needed and appropriate for a particular student or group. To determine need, a teacher must understand the particular student or group—which is to say, the teacher must assess students' actual strengths and learning needs, which requires classroom-based performance assessment.

Outside the Classroom

Assessment is, of course, used outside the classroom. Indeed, tests made for such purposes as comparing students to national norms, certifying their accomplishments (or lack thereof), and providing public accountability have come to dominate both public conceptions of assessment and classroom assessment practices. Teachers do use a range of methods, though not often enough and not well enough, but the underlying conceptions of what it means to assess and how to do it are dominated by the model of the external, multiple-choice, norm-referenced test. This domination tends to reduce curriculum and instruction to endless drill on decontextualized bits modeled on multiple-choice questions.[17] Thus assessment beyond the classroom must be changed for two fundamental reasons: to provide richer and fairer means of assessment for these purposes and to remove the control the tests exert over classroom instruction and assessment.

School improvement.   If classroom-based assessment is essential for student learning, it is equally essential for school improvement. If teachers talk with one another about student learning, then they will reflect on how to help particular children learn and how to improve the school as a whole.

The Prospect School in Vermont pioneered the use of such a collaborative process. Teachers met regularly to discuss student work.[18] A similar process has been adopted at the Bronx New School, an elementary school in New York City.[19]...

As ... a growing body of work on professional development show[s],[20] talking with one another helps teachers improve their practice and simultaneously work on improving their schools. As with individuals, knowing what works and what does not, figuring out why, and then deciding how to make improvements are essential parts of school progress.

Certification and making decisions.   *Principles and Indicators* states that decisions about individuals and schools should be made "on the basis of cumulative evidence of learning, using a variety of assessment information, not on the basis of any single assessment." Neither important individual decisions, such as high school graduation or special placement, nor collective sanctions or rewards for a school should be made on the basis of a test used as a single, required hurdle. The work students actually do should be used to make these decisions.

In many ways this approach is the same one that was used historically: if a student passed his or her courses, that student graduated, perhaps with honors if he or she did well. The problem was that this approach became divorced from high expectations and serious standards, so that some students could graduate knowing very little. The solution often imposed has been the high school exit test, which appears to be enjoying an unfortunate comeback after a decline in the first half of the 1990s. High-stakes exit tests are now used in 17 states,[21] with still more states planning to adopt them. The use of such tests means that some deserving students do not obtain diplomas, in some instances the dropout rates increase, and often schooling is ever more intensively reduced to a test-coaching program.

There is a better way: hold schools, in collaboration with the community, responsible for establishing clear and public criteria for graduation. That way, the community knows what students who graduate actually must know and be able to do. Such requirements can be flexible, with student strengths in one area allowed to balance weaknesses in another.

In this better way, each student compiles a record of achievement through portfolios, culminating projects or exhibitions, or simply doing a good job in a serious course. The record becomes the evidence used for determining readiness for graduation. Independent evaluations of the graduation requirements and of the work students are actually doing can be used to determine the quality of student accomplishments.

It is simply unconscionable—and even violates the quite conservative *Standards for Educational and Psychological Testing*[22]—to allow major decisions to be made on the basis of one-time exams. The testing profession should unite with reformers to educate and pressure policy makers to stop this practice.

Accountability.   Key areas of school accountability include student achievement, equity, the proper use of funds, and whether the school provides a supportive environment for its children. My focus here is on student achievement.

Students, their parents or guardians, and their teachers need to know how individual students are doing in terms of the school's curriculum, relevant standards, and the student's previous achievement and interests. This individualized accountability information comes mostly from in-school work: various forms of performance assessment provide substantial information for reporting, through conferences and report cards, on individual student learning.

How should information about schools and districts—evidence of accountability for learning by groups of students—be obtained and presented? Usually, this is done with standardized test results from commercial norm-referenced tests or statewide criterion-referenced tests.[23] Most items on both types are multiple-choice questions. Individual scores are aggregated to provide school and district scores. Unfortunately, aggregation can produce results that are misleading or simply wrong.[24] Extensive evidence also shows that these tests often do not measure much of the curriculum, and scores on them are apt to be inflated by teaching to the tests, thereby invalidating the results.[25] This combination of limited measures and coaching has truly damaging effects on the curriculum. Thus the effort to attain accountability effectively undermines the quality of education. This perverse result needs to be changed.

Principles and Indicators suggests that, for evidence of accountability, states and districts rely on a combination of sampling from classroom-based assessment information (e.g., portfolios or learning records) and from performance exams. In essence, the process could work along the following lines.

Each teacher, using scoring guides or rubrics, indicates where on a developmental scale or a performance standard each student should be placed and attaches evidence (records and portfolio material) to back up the decision. A random sample of the portfolios or learning records is selected from each classroom. Independent readers (educators from other schools, members of the community, and so on) review the records as evidence of student learning and place students on the scale. The scores of teachers and readers are then compared to see whether the judgments correspond. If they do not, various actions, beginning with another independent reading, can be used to identify the discrepancy. A larger sample from the classroom can be rescored. In addition, several procedures can be used to adjust the scores to account for teacher variation in scoring ("moderation"). Initial agreement among readers is usually low to moderate, but it can rise quickly if 1) the readers are well-trained and 2) the guides to what is in the records and how to score them are very clear.[26] Professional development can be targeted to help teachers improve their scoring.

This procedure validates teacher judgments and makes teachers central to the accountability process. It enables independent reviews of teachers' evaluations to check for equitable treatment of the students.

Another advantage of this approach is that it is not necessary to ask all students to enter the same kinds of work. Substantial diversity can be allowed in the records and portfolios, provided that they demonstrate student learning in the domain.

Such models have been used fairly extensively in Britain (and were proposed as the basis for a national assessment system there) and in pilot projects in the U.S.[27] ...

Using classroom-based information for accountability involves selecting from a wide range of data rather than trying to generalize from a narrow set of information, as is done in most testing programs. There may be a danger that, in trying to choose from wide data, the requirements for selection of material come to dominate instructional practice. However, allowing diversity in the components of the record or portfolio and rescoring only a sample might prevent such a harmful consequence. In any event, this concern must be considered in any effort to use a valuable classroom assessment for accountability purposes.

As an additional means of checking on the overall accuracy of the portfolio process, the Forum suggests that primarily performance exams can be administered. Using a matrix sample, as is done by the National Assessment of Educational Progress (NAEP), every student in a sample of students is administered one part of the entire exam. The parts are then assembled to provide district or state scores. The results of the exam can be compared at the school level to scores on the sample of portfolios. If a discrepancy exists, further work can be done to find the cause of the difference.

Time and money constraints limit what can be administered in one or a few performance exam sittings, making it difficult to include enough tasks to be able to generalize about student learning in the area being tested. Through sampling, much more can be assessed for the same cost than if every student took an entire test.

Performance exams are often used by states to direct and then measure reforms in curriculum and instruction. These efforts seem to have had mixed results. However, on-demand assessments are limited in their classroom utility, even as a model for classroom assessment practices, because they do not help teachers learn to do continuous classroom assessment. That is, most assessment reform at the state level has involved attempting to find formative, classroom uses for summative, on-demand exams. It is a nearly impossible task, though exam items can be the basis for interesting classroom projects if adapted to involve formative aspects of assessment as well. The on-demand exam approach to overcoming the limitations and dangers of traditional multiple-choice tests will probably prove to be a limited success. These exams make much more sense when used on a sampling basis for assessing achievement at the school or district level and as a complement to classroom-based information. In time, they may prove to be unnecessary.

Beyond scores. A new approach to accountability should involve more than changing the measures of student learning. It should involve alternative ways of using information both to improve schools and to inform the public.

For example, groups of schools in New York City are beginning to form networks in which they share the development of standards for student learning and of means to assess students and faculty.[28] In this way, they work together to improve the schools and to hold one another accountable for, among other things, enhanced student learning. Evidence of learning exists at the school level through portfolios, exhibitions, and other presentations of student work, and one purpose of the networks is to help schools refine these assessment processes....

These processes are based on the understanding that improvement and accountability should not be separated, any more than instruction and assessment should be. This approach also proposes to move accountability largely to the communities served by the school. It accepts that real accountability is a human and social process and therefore asks for human engagement in looking at schools and striving to make them better.

Accountability reform can thus take several complementary approaches. One is to revise how assessment is done, shifting from testing every student with a simplistic exam to using a combination of classroom-based information and on-demand performance exams. Both methods should use sampling procedures to report on student achievement in light of agreed-upon standards. This can be done at district or state levels. The second approach is to ask schools to work together in networks to hold one another accountable and to bring the community back into the process of evaluating the schools and networks. These complementary processes can help improve school practices and ultimately improve student learning.

However, parents, the public, and other social institutions have become conditioned to seeing test scores. Indeed, test scores have become nearly synonymous with accountability. But in order to avoid paying the price of forever narrowing schooling to what can be easily and cheaply measured, parents will have to exchange these narrow statistics for richer local information. They can rely on school-based data about their child's performance in light of standards and then use school-level information, also in relation to standards, to compare schools and districts. Through this procedure, parents can determine how well their child is learning.

What Next?

We are in reactionary times. While far more states include some form of performance testing today than at the start of the decade and more have such assessments in the planning or development stage, California and Arizona have dropped performance exams, and such exams are under attack in Kentucky and elsewhere. A right-wing ideological offensive has been mounted against performance assessment in many locales.[29] The calls for "basics" are often trumpeted together with calls for "basic skills tests." In a "get tough" environment in which we are seeing an increase in the use of graduation and even grade-promotion tests, more testing seems to be on the agenda. This includes President Clinton's proposed mostly multiple-choice exam in reading and math.

Yet the problems with traditional testing have not gone away. Those tests offer no solution to the educational needs of our children. Assessment is thus at a crisis point: the old model is incapable of meeting real needs, and a new approach is not yet clear. In this situation, most states have done little more than tinker at the edge of reform, adding some constructed-response items to mostly multiple-choice tests.[30] Whatever forms of exams are eventually used, they cannot provide much help for teachers in learning to integrate assessment with instruction in a continuous flow—and that is the heart of assessment in the service of learning.

... [R]eform advocates, educators, and researchers must continuously point out the limits of and the harm done by traditional testing. Comparing multiple-choice items to real work in portfolios or even to performance exam tasks and asking parents or community members which option represents the kind of work children should be doing is one powerful educational tool. When shown the alternatives, parents typically prefer performance tasks to multiple-choice items.[31] If parents could consistently get the richer information provided by such assessments, they might be willing to give up their desire for simplistic test scores. We should also expose the limitations of the tests. Few parents, not even many teachers, understand the underpinnings and structures of norm-referenced, multiple-choice standardized tests and therefore understand how narrow and biased they are. In 1994 a slight majority of the public thought that essays would be preferable to multiple-choice tests.[32] This indicates a solid base on which to build public understanding of the need to transform assessment.

Notes

1. National Forum on Assessment, *Principles and Indicators for Student Assessment Systems* (Cambridge, Mass.: FairTest, 1995). Principle scan be purchased for $10 from FairTest, 342 Broadway, Cambridge, MA 02139. ...
2. ... D. Monty Neill et al., *Implementing Performance Assessment: A Guide to Classroom, School, and System Reform* (Cambridge, Mass.: FairTest, 1995). See also National Forum on Assessment, op. cit.; and *Selected Annotated Bibliography on Performance Assessment*, 2nd ed. (Cambridge, Mass.: Fair Test, 1995).
3. Edward Chittenden, "Authentic Assessment: Evaluation and Documentation of Student Performance," in Vito Perrone, ed., *Expanding Student Assessment* (Alexandria, Va.: Association for Supervision and Curriculum Development, 1991), pp. 22-31.
4. Myra Barrs et al., *Primary Language Record* (Portsmouth, N.H.: Heinemann, 1988); Hillary Hester, *Guide to the Primary Learning Record* (London: Centre for Language in Primary Education, 1993); Mary Barr, *California Learning Record* (El Cajon, Calif.: Center for Language in Learning, 1994); and Samuel J. Meisels et al., "The Work Sampling System: Reliability and Validity of a Performance Assessment for Young Children," *Early Childhood Research Quarterly*, vol. 10, 1995, pp. 277-96.
5. Peter H. Johnston, *Constructive Evaluation of Literate Activity* (New York: Longman, 1992); and Patricia F. Carini, "Dear Sister Bess: An Essay on Standards, Judgment, and Writing," *Assessing Writing*, vol. 1, 1994, pp. 29-65.
6. *Curriculum and Evaluation Standards for School Mathematics* (Reston, Va.: National Council of Teachers of Mathematics, 1989).
7. D. Monty Neill and Noe J. Medina, "Standardized Testing: Harmful to Educational Health," *Phi Delta Kappan*, May 1989, pp. 688-97.

8. Norman Frederiksen, "The Real Test Bias: Influence of Testing on Teaching and Learning," *American Psychologist,* March 1984, p. 193.

9. George F. Madaus et al., *The Influence of Testing on Teaching Math and Science in Grades 4-12* (Chestnut Hill, Mass.: Center for the Study of Testing, Evaluation, and Educational Policy, Boston College, 1992).

10. "KERA: What Works What Doesn't," *Daily Report Card,* 22 May 1996 (on-line); and Fran Spielman, "Schools Try New Tests, Curriculum," *Chicago Sun-Times,* 22 September 1995.

11. Lauren B. Resnick, *Education and Learning to Think* (Washington, D.C.: National Academy Press, 1987); and Lauren B. Resnick and Daniel P. Resnick, "Assessing the Thinking Curriculum: New Tools for Educational Reform," in Bernard R. Gifford and Mary C. O'Connor, eds., *Further Assessments: Changing Views of Aptitude Achievement, and Instruction* (Boston: Kluwer, 1992), pp. 37-76.

12. James Hiebert et al., "Problem Solving as a Basis for Reform in Curriculum and Instruction: The Case of Mathematics," *Educational Researcher,* May 1996, pp. 12- 21; and Scott G. Paris et al., "The Development of Strategic Readers," in P. David Pearson, ed., *Handbook of Reading Research,* Vol. 2 (New York: Longman, 1991), pp. 609-40.

13. Hiebert et al., p. 14.

14. Howard Gardner, *The Unschooled Mind* (New York: Basic Books, 1991); and Resnick and Resnick, op. cit.

15. Deborah Meier, "Why the Reading Tests Don't Measure Reading," *Dissent,* Winter 1982-83, pp. 457-66.

16. John Raven, "A Model of Competence, Motivation, and Behavior and a Paradigm for Assessment," in Harold Berlak et al., eds., *Toward a New Science of Educational Testing and Assessment* (Albany: State University of New York Press, 1992), pp. 85- 116; and Thomas Kellaghan, George F. Madaus, and Anastasia Raczek, *The Use of External Examinations to Improve Student Motivation* (Washington, D.C.: American Educational Research Association, 1996).

17. Joan L. Herman and Shari Golan, "The Effects of Standardized Testing on Teaching and Schools," *Educational Measurement: Issues and Practice,* Winter 1993, pp. 20-25, 41; George F. Madaus, "The Influence of Testing on the Curriculum," in Laura N. Tanner, ed., *Critical Issues in the Curriculum: 87th NSSE Yearbook, Part I* (Chicago: National Society for the Study of Education, University of Chicago Press, 1998), pp. 83-121; Thomas A. Romberg et al., "Curriculum and Test Alignment," in Thomas A. Romberg, ed., *Mathematics Assessment and Evaluation* (Albany: State University of New York Press, 1992), pp. 61-74; and Mary Lee Smith, "Put to the Test: The Effects of External Testing on Teachers," *Educational Researcher,* June/July 1991, pp. 8-11.

18. Walter Haney, "Making Tests More Educational," *Educational Leadership,* October 1985, pp. 4-13.

19. Linda Darling-Hammond, Jacqueline Ancess, and Beverly Falk, *Authentic Assessmentin Action: Studies of Schools and Students at Work* (New York: Teachers College Press, 1995).

20. See especially Judith Warren Little, "Teachers' Professional Development in a Climate of Educational Reform," *Educational Evaluation and Policy Analysis,* Summer 1993, pp. 129-51.

21. Linda Ann Bond et al., *State Student Assessment Programs Database, School Year 1994-1995* (Washington, D.C., and Oak Brook, Ill.: Council of Chief State School Officers and North Central Regional Educational Laboratory, 1996).

22. American Educational Research Association, American Psychological Association, and National Council on Measurement in Education, *Standards for Educational and Psychological Testing* (Washington, D.C.: American Psychological Association, 1985).

23. Bond et al., op. cit.

24. Walter Haney and Anastasia Raczek, "Surmounting Outcomes Accountability in Education," in *Issues in Educational Accountability* (Washington, D.C.: Office of Technology Assessment, 1994).

25. Thomas M. Haladyna, Susan Bobbit Nolen, and Nancy S. Haas, "Raising Standardized Achievement Test Scores and the Origins of Test Score Pollution," *Educational Researchers,* June/July 1991, pp. 2-7; Robert M. Linn, M. Elizabeth Graue, and Nancy M. Sanders, "Comparing State and District Results to National Norms: The Validity of the Claims That 'Everyone Is Above Average,' " *Educational Measurement: Issues and Practice,* Fall 1990, pp. 5-14; and Lorrie A. Shepard, "Inflated Test Score Gains: Is the Problem Old Norms or Teaching the Test?," *Educational Measurement: Issues and Practice,* Fall 1990, pp. 15-22.

26. Suzanne Lane at al., "Generalizability and Validity of Mathematics Performance Assessment," *Journal of Educational Measurement,* Spring 1996, pp. 71-92; Robert Linn, "Educational Assessment: Expanded Expectations and Challenges," *Educational Evaluation and Policy Analysis,* Spring 1993, pp. 1-16; William Thomas et al., *The CLAS Portfolio Assessment Research and Development Project Final Report* (Princeton, N.J.: Educational Testing Service, 1996); and "Using Language Records (PLR/CLR) as Large-Scale Assessments," *FairTest Examiner,* Summer 1995, pp. 8-9.

27. Myra Barrs, "The Road Not Taken," *Forum,* vol. 36, 1994, pp. 36-39.

28. Deborah Meier and Jacqueline Ancess, "Accountability by Bloated Bureaucracy and Regulation: Is There an Alternative?," interactive symposium at the annual meeting of the American Educational Research Association, New York, April 1996.

29. "Right Wing Attacks Performance Assessment," *FairTest Examiner,* Summer 1994, pp. 1, 10-11.

30. D. Monty Neill, *State of State Assessment Systems* (Cambridge, Mass.: FairTest, 1997).

31. Lorrie A. Shepard and Carribeth L. Bliem, *Parent Opinions About Standardized Tests, Teacher's Information, and Performance Assessments* (Los Angeles: Center for Research on Evaluation, Standards, and Student Testing, CSE Technical Report 367, 1993); and John Poggio, "The Politics of Test Validity: Performance Assessment as a State-Sponsored Educational Reform," interactive symposium at the annual meeting of the American Educational Research Association, New York, April 1996.

32. Jean Johnson and John Immerwahr, *First Things First: What Americans Expect from the Public Schools* (New York: Public Agenda Foundation, 1994).

NO

Edward H. Haertel

Performance Assessment and Education Reform

Beginning with the publication in 1983 of A Nationat Risk, a stream of reports and pronouncements has fueled the popular perception that the U.S. education system is in crisis.[1] Real and imagined declines over time in performance on tests such as the SAT and the National Assessment of Educational Progress (NAEP); cross-national comparisons on tests including the International Assessment of Educational Progress and, more recently, the Third International Mathematics and Science Study; and comparisons to benchmarks such as the NAEP achievement levels established by the National Assessment Governing Board have been publicized as evidence that our educational problems continue unabated. The use of test scores to index educational success or failure is almost never questioned. Low scores are bad news; high scores are good news. In the rhetoric of education reform, it often sounds as if improving the education system is synonymous with improving test scores.

In such a climate, the logic of high-stakes testing seems compelling. Test students and see what they can do. Hold them or their schools accountable if they fail to make the grade. Rather than micro-manage schools, policy makers can dictate that content standards and performance standards be created to codify expected learning outcomes and then let teachers and school administrators determine how best to attain those outcomes.

It sounds like a rational management plan. If there are clear expectations, teachers will know what they are supposed to teach, students will see how hard they must work to make the grade, and taxpayers will know whether their schools are measuring up. If the standards are appropriate, if students and teachers are prepared to accept the challenge of meeting them, if the phase-in period for accountability is realistic, if reliable and valid tests are available to ascertain the extent of students' mastery, if teachers have the requisite knowledge and training to help students meet the challenge of new standards, if schools are not hobbled by extraneous demands and requirements, if necessary instructional materials and resources are available, if out-of-school factors are given appropriate consideration ... then a measurement-driven accountability system ought to show just which students are working and which ones are slacking off, which teachers and schools should be rewarded and which ones should be punished.

It is not hard to understand why accountability testing is popular with policy makers. Testing enjoys broad popular support.[2] Calling for more or higher-stakes testing is a visible, dramatic response to public concerns about education. Moreover, the idea that demanding higher test scores will improve schooling carries with it the not-too-subtle implication that students, teachers, and administrators just aren't trying hard enough. If efforts are redoubled, scores will rise. Proposing a new testing plan diverts attention from the problems alluded to by all those "ifs," including conflicting curricular expectations, inadequate teacher preparation, inadequate teaching materials and facilities, and the changing demography of the student population.[3] Attacking those other problems is likely to take a lot of time and money, but calling for another new test costs next to nothing. Moreover, a new test can be implemented quickly, before the terms of current officeholders expire. Scores on an unfamiliar test are likely to be poor at the beginning and then to rise in years two and three. As Robert Linn observes, "The resulting overly rosy picture that is painted by short-term gains observed in most new testing programs gives the impression of improvement right on schedule for the next election."[4]

If only it weren't for all those "ifs." The high-stakes testing approach to education reform has been tried repeatedly, with generally sorry results.[5] With each new wave of reform, hope springs anew that this time past mistakes will be avoided, there will be dramatic improvements in student learning outcomes, and score gains will generalize beyond the specific tests used to hold teachers and students accountable. Over the past decade, one identified "past mistake" has been reliance on multiple-choice tests. One identified solution has been reliance, instead, on performance assessments. Performance assessment has been a centerpiece of state and national education reform initiatives in the 1990s.

I will argue here that, although there is some validity of the charges against the use of multiple-choice and other selected-response item formats, the fundamental deficiency of high-stakes testing as an education policy tool lies in the logic of the reform strategy itself, not in the reliance on one format of test item versus another. As educators and policy makers come to see that high-stakes performance assessment may have been oversold as a tool of education reform, there are two lessons to be learned.

First, there is no solution to be found in a return to the mistakes of the past—simply replacing performance assessments in their turn with multiple-choice tests—or in a move to some other new type of item. Instead, the accountability-testing argument itself must be examined and reconsidered.

Second, the failure of high-stakes performance assessment to effect sweeping education reform should not detract from the real value of performance assessments used for instructional purposes. The hoped-for benefits of assessing students using complex, integrative, hands-on tasks that blur the lines between testing and teaching can in fact be realized when teachers themselves make skillful use of sound performance assessments in their own classrooms.

The Logic of Measurement-Driven Reform

The rationales being advanced for measurement-driven reform often begin with a critique of earlier high-stakes testing programs.[6] It is said that multiple-choice tests came into wide use largely because they were inexpensive to create, administer, and score. The information they provided met psychometric criteria for reliability and criterion-related validity—predicting grades in college, for example. Once the effects of test unreliability were accounted for, high correlations were generally found between multiple-choice tests and less objective examinations. These correlations meant that even if multiple-choice tests and more expensive alternatives didn't really measure the same thing, they rank-ordered examinees in much the same way, and so the multiple-choice tests provided essentially the same information as could be obtained using more costly and time-consuming testing procedures.

All would have been well, the story goes, if selected-response tests had in fact served merely as indicators of educational performance. But when rewards and sanctions were attached to these tests, getting high scores became an end in itself, and distortions of classroom instruction inevitably followed. When newspapers ranked schools according to their average test scores, school administrators urged teachers to devote more time and effort to test preparation. The best way to get high scores on multiple-choice tests was to touch on as many isolated bits of information as possible, in the hope of covering the ones appearing on the examination. Thus high-stakes external tests drove classroom instruction in the direction of using worksheets consisting of pages and pages of fill-in-the-blank and selected-response exercises. Inevitably, classroom assessment came to resemble external assessment, to the detriment of higher-order thinking, real-world problem solving, and other more worthy educational goals.

The corollary to this story is captured in the aphorism "What you test is what you get." If multiple-choice tests could drive instruction in the wrong direction, then why not use some better sort of test to drive instruction in the right direction? There were calls for tests that we would want teachers to teach to.[7] If the high-stakes tests were authentic, engaged students in real-world problem solving, and called for higher-order thinking that multiple-choice items could not measure, then instruction would soon become aligned to more worthy educational goals.

Policy makers were not the only ones to embrace performance assessment as a tool for education reform. Advocates for various curriculum reforms saw performance assessment as a vehicle to communicate and popularize new visions of school learning. These new forms of assessment would promote active engagement both in learning and in demonstrating what had been learned. They would serve as models of sound instructional activities. Expectations would rise as teachers saw concrete evidence that students could solve more complex problems than they had thought possible, even problems requiring several days or more to work through. Parents would come to value the kinds of learning that resulted when groups of children worked together to design an experiment or investigate some topic they actually cared about.

As the line between teaching and testing blurred, classroom time would be better employed. Students would show better motivation, and teachers would spontaneously adopt enlightened instructional strategies.

There were also hopes that, with performance assessments, average scores would be more nearly equal between students from rich communities and those from poor communities and between white and non-Hispanic students and black and Hispanic students. Despite decades of research on item bias and test bias, suspicion lingers that the content or form at of multiple-choice tests unfairly favors students from traditionally higher-scoring groups. It was hoped that, given a chance to demonstrate directly what they really knew and could do, traditionally lower-scoring student groups would perform as well as any others.

Note that, according to this straightforward account, external assessment leads, and classroom practice follows. In fact, the story is more complicated. Externally mandated high-stakes tests do exert some influence on curriculum and instruction, but their power in that regard has been overstated.[8] There are competing explanations for the classroom use of worksheets, the teaching of decontextualized skills, and an overemphasis on factual recall at the expense of more complex problem solving and application. High-stakes multiple-choice testing played a role, but there were independent justifications for introducing component skills in isolation and for deferring more complex reasoning until basic skills were mastered.

As Lauren Resnick and Daniel Resnick explain, multiple-choice testing comported well with the behaviorist educational psychology that held sway into the early 1970s.[9] Two tenets of much educational psychology at that time were "decomposability" and "decontextualization." Curriculum designers drawing on behaviorist principles sought to build up complex performances from more basic constituents. It was believed that the key to helping all children master the complexities of reading, writing, mathematics, and other school subjects was to teach (and test) each component skill in the proper sequence. Skills learned in isolation (out of context) could later be assembled and applied to accomplish meaningful tasks. Learning objectives were defined in terms of observable behaviors, and mastery of prerequisites was to be demonstrated before more complex skills were introduced. Multiple-choice and fill-in-the-blank questions seemed well suited to testing component skills as they were taught. Learning objectives were written in terms of observable behaviors, and they often read like test specifications.

The reasons that worksheets, objective test item formats, and so forth became so entrenched in American classrooms had less to do with high-stakes external tests than with the design of instructional materials and of teacher pre-service and in-service training. Educational researchers and curriculum specialists consciously fostered such practices. A generation of teachers was schooled in the theory and methods of criterion-referenced testing. Changing curriculum and instruction has always required more than just introducing some new variety of high-stakes test.

Behaviorism waned, and criterion-referenced testing became less popular as an instructional management strategy. Today, there is less emphasis on the teaching and testing of isolated component skills and greater recognition that skills learned in one context may be inaccessible in another. Even if adults can readily see how the morning's drill and practice should support the afternoon's reading or problem solving, young learners have an amazing capacity for not making such connections. Indeed, during the highly publicized test score decline of the 1970s and early 1980s, multiple-choice test scores at the early elementary level were actually rising at the same time as older students' performance on more complex tasks declined.

As disillusionment grew with the idea that component skills, once learned, would somehow be spontaneously assembled into skillful performances, there was a shift away from the implicit model of tests as indicators of component skills toward a model of tests as direct samples of desired criterion performances. Performance assessments were seen not as better tools for measuring the same constructs, or even primarily as tools for measuring more important constructs. Rather, they were conceived as demonstrations or accomplishments to be valued for their own sakes.[10]

That shift has important implications for the logic of making inferences from test scores to broader task domains.[11] If test items are designed to be indicators of underlying dimensions of developed proficiency (constructs), then, other things being equal, test scores should predict performance on any other tasks that depend on the same constructs. If instead assessment tasks are chosen for their intrinsic value, then it is harder to say just what the scores should predict. There is no clear rationale for expecting such test scores to predict anything except performance on other tasks that are in some vague sense similar to the test itself.

Samuel Messick has drawn a helpful distinction in this regard, referring to construct-driven versus task-driven performance assessments. The difference is one of degree; there is always some interest in measuring constructs. Nonetheless, the shift in focus from measuring constructs to demonstrating valued performances has significant implications for large-scale performance assessment. Messick observes that "the task-centered approach to performance assessment is in danger of tailoring scoring criteria and rubrics to properties of the task and of representing any educed constructs in task-dependent ways that might limit generalizability."[12] In fact, the limited generalizability of performance assessments is well documented.[13]

This shift from construct-driven selected-response testing to task-driven performance assessment is most clearly seen in portfolio-based assessment systems. With construct-driven assessment, it is assumed that the items given are a sample from some larger domain of items that could have been chosen instead. This assumption warrants the statistical inference from an examinee's performance on the test to predicted performance across the hypothetical item domain the test represents. With portfolios, however, students participate in selecting the work samples presented. Each portfolio entry may be a worthy demonstration of proficiency, but any statistical inference to a larger domain of potential portfolio entries is problematic.

In summary, multiple-choice and other objective, selected-response tests are clearly inadequate as the sole indicators of intended schooling outcomes.

Performance assessments can measure some important kinds of outcomes that multiple-choice tests cannot, but they have also brought a shift in measurement perspective that has the potential to limit generalizability.

External Versus Classroom Performance Assessments

Even if accountability tests had greater power to shape curriculum and instruction, and even if the generalizability of performance assessments were of no concern, serious objections would remain to the high-stakes performance assessment reform strategy. Any test perceived as "high stakes" has the potential to narrow the curriculum and bend classroom instruction toward demonstrating knowledge in the particular forms the test calls for. As teachers teach to even the best of tests, the meaning of test scores can change, and validity can erode. Thus a tremendous weight is placed on the assumptions that external performance assessments do, in fact, represent comprehensive, valid, and robust indicators of desired learning outcomes.[14] But there is serious reason to question whether external performance assessments can fulfill those assumptions.

The multiple-choice testing format is easy to describe. A multiple-choice question looks much the same whether it appears on a test mandated by a state or a district or on a worksheet created by a teacher. With the external multiple-choice test, the psychometric properties of the items are likely to be better documented; responses may be indicated by darkening circles on a separate answer sheet; and there may be more formality in reading the instructions, responding to student questions, and timing the administration. Nonetheless, a multiple-choice item is much the same in either context.

It is more difficult to describe a performance assessment. The term covers many different kinds of tasks and scoring procedures.[15] In particular, performance tasks in external as opposed to classroom assessments are often radically different—so much so that high-stakes external performance assessments may serve as poor models for classroom instruction and may in fact undermine communication about the goals of curricular reform.[16] External tasks may not engage children's interest and may fail to show what children really know and can do, particularly children from traditionally underserved groups. They may fall far short of exemplifying tests we would want teachers to teach to.

The most obvious differences between classroom performance assessments and external performance assessments stem from the practical constraints placed on external high-stakes testing programs. Although some external tests, particularly in writing and language arts, may be administered over several days, most are limited to a brief examination period. With the exception of basic materials and supplies available in every school, whatever equipment is needed must be brought to the testing site. Because scoring is done at some centralized location, the scorable record is largely limited to responses students can write in a brief period of time. Speeches, skits, projects, and extended papers are likely to be infeasible. The resulting heavy writing demands may be especially problematical for learners lacking proficiency in English and for those lacking motivation.

There have been some attempts, in Vermont and in Kentucky for example, to circumvent these limitations by having students assemble portfolios of their writing or mathematics problem solving that are then collected and evaluated. Teachers generally report modest positive effects on instructional practices as a result of such assessments, but portfolio scores have shown poor psychometric properties.[17] Furthermore, it has been questioned whether high-stakes portfolios truly represent students' own work.[18]

Beyond matters of format, time, and scoring, there are more significant distinctions between external and classroom assessment contexts. The performance assessment a teacher creates or selects is grounded in the preceding instruction. It may require some application of skills or ideas in new contexts, but it is appropriately referenced to material that the students have had an opportunity to learn. The external performance assessment is appropriately referenced not to the instruction that has been provided but rather to the curriculum framework that defines the intended goals of instruction. A classroom test that included material not taught would be considered unfair, even if that material were specified in some curriculum framework. An external test that omitted material from the framework because it was untaught would be considered invalid for most purposes.

Because the classroom assessment can build on the preceding instruction, it can draw on component skills, special vocabulary, scoring rubrics, and content knowledge the teacher and students have built up over time. Any demonstration of reasoning (or "higher-order thinking") depends on some previous base of knowledge; reasoning must be about something. If one science class had studied the ecology of a pond and another the ecology of a meadow, students in either class might be able to construct a food chain or reason about the consequences of introducing some exotic species, but the particular questions required to elicit those understandings would differ. If two English classes studied different novels, students in either class might be able to demonstrate their ability to analyze character development or recognize irony, but again, the particular questions needed to elicit those understandings would differ.

In posing questions, the classroom teacher can use terms and concepts introduced earlier. In addition, if students have had an opportunity to practice answering similar questions, they are likely to understand what is called for by way of a response. An external performance assessment might include a scenario describing an ecosystem or a brief passage for students to read and analyze, but these stimuli would probably be impoverished relative to material students would have available from their own classwork. In posing questions on an external assessment and explaining how students are to respond, very little can be assumed by way of common background. As a result, external performance assessments may lean toward measurement of cleverness, test-wiseness, or reading speed rather than of reasoning and reflection.

Scores from external assessments must be comparable across schools and over time. It follows that the scores assigned must not depend on the identity of the scorer and must not be influenced by contextual factors.[19] As a consequence, scoring rubrics for external assessments tend to focus on specific, well-defined features of responses to particular assessment tasks. Such rubrics help to ensure objectivity but may fail to capture the essence of the performance.[20] Task-specific rubrics make it difficult for students and teachers to reach sound generalizations about the criteria for excellence on the next task encountered. In contrast, scores on classroom assessments need only reflect teachers' judgments of the quality of work in one classroom, on one occasion. Students' performances can be evaluated relative to more global criteria. Fairness dictates that the work of different students must be evaluated according to the same standards, but the teacher is a privileged observer, able to interpret and respond to students' work in the context of collateral information.[21]

Finally, the conflict between accountability and the goals of instruction interferes with the value of external assessments for the improvement of classroom instruction.[22] In the classroom, the teacher can offer assistance, ideally providing multiple opportunities for students to master the tasks set for them. That function is at odds with the role of test administrator. Classroom performance assessments are likely to be announced in advance, with ample time to study and prepare. The external performance assessment is likely to be kept a secret, often taking both the students and the teacher by surprise. In completing a classroom performance assessment, students often present their work to an audience of their peers, their teachers, and even their parents. They are motivated to show what they can do, and they can expect to receive individual scores and feedback. With external assessments, the audience is anonymous, and, in most cases, students cannot expect to receive any information about their individual performances.

Taken together, the differences between classroom and external performance assessments in format, context, relation to antecedent instruction, scoring, and purpose are so large as to render external assessments unpromising models for classroom instruction or assessment activities.

Conclusions

School improvement strategies that rely on high-stakes testing rest on a number of unfounded assumptions. Multiple-choice tests do have serious limitations, but those limitations do not explain the failure of past efforts at measurement-driven reform.

The power of high-stakes testing to influence classroom instruction has been oversold. Selected-response testing became prevalent in classrooms because it was part of a complex web of beliefs and practices; its favored status was not just a reaction to the stakes attached to external multiple-choice examinations. Changing the formats of high-stakes tests will effect some changes, but these will be limited.

The shift from multiple-choice testing to performance assessment, especially portfolio-based assessment, has brought with it a subtle but important shift in measurement philosophy. The selection of assessment tasks on the basis of their inherent value complicates inferences from test scores to nontest situations, especially if students and teachers participate in that selection, as with portfolios. As construct interpretations become less salient and assessment tasks come to be viewed as demonstrations valued in their own right, the traditional warrants for interpreting and generalizing from test scores are weakened. The limited generalizability of performance assessments is well documented. If scoring rubrics become too task-specific, substantive generalizations about the meaning of high scores, as well as statistical generalizations to other tasks, are threatened.

Finally, the term "performance assessment" itself is slippery. The inherent requirements of high-stakes testing programs have led to the creation of a kind of performance task that bears little resemblance to the high-quality performance assessments that teachers are able to use in their day-to-day instruction. Thus, psychometric concerns aside, it must be questioned whether external performance assessments can even serve as models of worthwhile instructional activities.

There is much to applaud in the shift from nearly exclusive reliance on selected-response tests toward a mix of methods including performance assessments. There is no guarantee, however, that the potential benefits of performance assessment will be realized. Regardless of the value of performance assessments in the classroom, a measurement-driven reform strategy that relies on performance assessments to drive curriculum and instruction seems bound to fail.

Notes

1. David C. Berliner and Bruce J. Biddle, *The Manufactured Crisis* (Reading, Mass.: Addison-Wesley, 1995).
2. Lowell C. Rose and Alec M. Gallup, "The 30th Annual Phi Delta Kappa/Gallup Poll of the Public's Attitudes Toward the Public Schools," *Phi Delta Kappan*, September 1998, p. 51; and Lowell C. Rose, Alec M. Gallup, and Stanley M. Elam, "The 29th Annual Phi Delta Kappa/Gallup Poll of the Public's Attitudes Toward the Public Schools," *Phi Delta Kappan*, September 1997, pp. 43-44.
3. Edward H. Haertel, "Student Achievement Tests as Tools of Educational Policy: Practices and Consequences," in Bernard R. Gifford, ed., *Test Policy and Test Performance: Education, Language, and Culture* (Boston: Kluwer Academic Publishers, 1989), pp. 35-63.
4. Robert L. Linn, "Assessment and Accountability," paper presented at the annual meeting of the American Educational Research Association, April 1998, San Diego, p. 2.
5. Linda Darling-Hammond, "National Standards and Assessments: Will They Improve Education?," *American Journal of Education*, August 1994, pp. 478-510; Gene V. Glass, "Matthew Arnold and Minimal Competence," *Educational Forum*, January 1978, pp. 139-44; Daniel M. Koretz, George F. Madaus, Edward H. Haertel, and Albert E. Beaton, *National Educational Standards and Testing: A Response to the Recommendations of the National Council on Education Standards and Testing* (Santa Monica, Calif.: RAND Corporation, 1992); Linn, op. cit.; George F. Madaus, "The Influence of Testing on the Curriculum," in Laurel N. Tanner, ed., *Critical Issues in Curriculum: 87th NSSE Yearbook* (Chicago: National Society for the Study of Education, University of

Chicago Press, 1988), pp. 83-121; and Milbrey W. McLaughlin and Lorrie A. Shepard with Jennifer A. O'Day, *Improving Education Through Standards-Based Reform: A Report by the National Academy of Education Panel on Standards-Based Education Reform* (Stanford, Calif.: National Academy of Education, 1995).

6. Joan L. Herman, *Large-Scale Assessmentin Support of School Reform: Lessons in the Search for Alternative Measures* (Los Angeles: Center for the Study of Evaluation, University of California, 1997).

7. Lauren B. Resnick and Daniel P. Resnick, "Assessing the Thinking Curriculum: New Tools for Educational Reform," in Bernard R. Gifford and Mary C. O'Connor, eds., *Changing Assessments: Alternative Views of Aptitude, Achievement, and Instruction* (Boston: Kluwer Academic Publishers, 1992), pp. 37-75; and Grant Wiggins, "Creating Tests Worth Taking," *Educational Leadership*, May 1992, pp. 26-33.

8. Lorrie A. Shepard, *Insights Gained from a Classroom-Based Assessment Project* (Los Angeles: Center for the Study of Evaluation, University of California, 1997); Mary L. Smith, Reforming Schools by *Reforming Assessment: Consequences of the Arizona Student Assessment Program (ASAP): Equity and Teacher Capacity Building* (Los Angeles: Center for the Study of Evaluation, University of California, 1997).

9. Resnick and Resnick, pp. 41-44.

10. Wiggins, op. cit.

11. Edward H. Haertel, "Construct Validity and Criterion-Referenced Testing," *Review of Educational Research,* vol. 55, 1985, pp. 23-46.

12. Samuel Messick, "Validity of Performance Assessments," in Gary W. Phillips, ed., *Technical Issues in Large-Scale Performance Assessment* (Washington, D.C.: National Center for Education Statistics, 1996), pp. 1-18.

13. Eva L. Baker, Harold F. O'Neil, and Robert L. Linn, "Policy and Validity Prospects for Performance-Based Assessment," *American Psychologist,* December 1993, pp. 1210-18; Stephen B. Dunbar, Daniel M. Koretz, and H. D. Hoover, "Quality Control in the Development and Use of Performance Assessments," *Applied Measurement in Education,* vol. 4, 1991, pp. 289-303; Robert L. Linn, "Educational Assessment: Expanded Expectations and Challenges," *Educational Evaluation and Policy Analysis,* vol. 15, 1993, pp. 1-16; Linn, "Assessment and Accountability"; and Richard J. Shavelson, Gail P. Baxter, and Jerry Pine, "Performance Assessments; Political Rhetoric and Measurement Reality," *Educational Researcher,* May 1992, pp. 22-27.

14. Madaus, op. cit.

15. Edward H. Haertel and Robert L. Linn, "Comparability," in Phillips, pp. 59-78.

16. Smith, op. cit.

17. Daniel Koretz et al., "The Vermont Portfolio Assessment Program: Findings and Implications," *Educational Measurement: Issues and Practice,* Fall 1994, pp. 5-16; Smith, op. cit.; and Brian M. Stecher et al., *The Effects of Standards-Based Assessment on Classroom Practices: Results of the 1996-97 RAND Survey of Kentucky Teachers of Mathematics and Writing* (Los Angeles: Center for the Study of Evaluation, University of California, 1998).

18. Herman, p. 25.

19. Haertel and Linn, op. cit.
20. Messick, op. cit.; and W. James Popham, "What's Wrong—and What's Right—with Rubrics," *Educational Leadership*, October 1997, pp. 72-75.
21. Pamela A. Moss et al., "Portfolios, Accountability, and an Interpretive Approach to Validity," *Educational Measurement: Issues and Practice,* Fall 1992, pp. 12-21.
22. Smith, op. cit.

POSTSCRIPT

Will Performance Assessment Lead to Meaningful Education Reform?

Performance assessment is a promising alternative to traditional standardized tests, if for no other reason than its potential to yield a richer picture of what a student knows (and does not know) and thereby what he or she needs to be taught next. But does this mean that we should rush to incorporate it into high-stakes testing or any other plan for educational reform? There are at least three reasons to exercise caution.

First, performance assessment is a new method. In the past, new methods of assessment have been introduced with enthusiastic claims about the potential of the method to "transform education." In "Unintended Consequences of Performance Assessment: Issues of Bias and Fairness," *Educational Measurement: Issues and Practice* (Winter 1995), Lloyd Bond reminds us that few of these methods have lived up to their early claims and that some have had unintended negative consequences. It may be unwise to rely too heavily on performance assessment until the consequences of its use are fully understood.

Second, there is some preliminary evidence that performance assessment may not be free of all the limitations of traditional standardized tests. Some research indicates that individuals from ethnic minority backgrounds are evaluated less positively on at least some performance assessments than are individuals from a majority culture background. There may be bias in scoring such assessments that advantage students from the majority culture.

And finally, what if high-stakes testing does not lead to the hoped-for gains in student achievement? If performance assessment is closely linked to a failed reform in the public mind, it may be abandoned before its power as an educational tool is fully realized.

Readers interested in other articles about performance assessment are encouraged to read D. Monty Neill et al.'s *Implementing Performance Assessment: A Guide to Classroom, School, and System Reform* (FairTest, 1995). There are many critiques of high-stakes testing, including "The Misuse of Tests in Retention," by Karen Hartke, *Thrust for Educational Leadership* (January/February 1999) and "Why Standardized Tests Don't Measure Education and Quality," by W. James Popham, *Educational Leadership* (March 1999). Interesting articles on the link between assessment and learning are "Working Inside the Black Box: Assessment for Learning in the Classroom," by Paul Black, Christine Harrison, Clara Lee, Bethan Marshall, and Dylan Wiliam, *Phi Delta Kappan* (September 2004) and "New Assessment Beliefs for a New School Mission," by Rick Stiggins (September 2004). Also, an interesting and highly readable series of articles on the high-stakes testing movement and performance assessment appears in the May 1999 issue of *Phi Delta Kappan*.

ISSUE 17

Can a Zero-Tolerance Policy Lead to Safe Schools?

YES: Albert Shanker, from "Restoring the Connection Between Behavior and Consequences," *Vital Speeches of the Day* (May 15, 1995)

NO: Russ Skiba and Reece Peterson, from "The Dark Side of Zero Tolerance: Can Punishment Lead to Safe Schools?" *Phi Delta Kappan* (January 1999)

ISSUE SUMMARY

YES: The late Albert Shanker, long-time president of the American Federation of Teachers (AFT), advocates a policy of zero tolerance for violence and other disruptive behavior in school. He argues that such a policy is necessary because disruptive and violent behavior denies equal access to educational opportunities for the nonoffending students in a class or school.

NO: Russ Skiba, director of the Institute for Child Study at Indiana University, and Reece Peterson, a member of the faculty in the Department of Special Education at the University of Nebraska, argue that despite several recent, highly publicized incidents of violence, there are no data to support the contention that there has been an increase in school-based violence, nor are there data demonstrating the effectiveness of zero-tolerance policies in deterring violence and crime.

$\mathbf{A}$s violence has become more commonplace in society, many people—particularly parents—have taken solace in the assumption that at least the children are safe at school. This seemed guaranteed by the fact that schools are populated only by teachers, who always have the best interests of the children at heart, and students, who, because of their tender ages, are all but incapable of acts of violence or criminality. Unfortunately, this sentimental image of school as a safe haven has been shattered—repeatedly—in recent years. The turn of the century brought horrific scenes of death and destruction in schools in Arkansas, Colorado, Kentucky, and California, all of which were perpetrated by children, some as young as 10 years old. For teachers and other school personnel, these acts of brutality are only examples of the extreme of a continuum. It has become all too commonplace for students to bring weapons to school, to get into fist fights, to sexually harass classmates, and to use or sell illegal drugs. Less dramatic, although perhaps no less disruptive of teaching and learning in the classroom, are the unruly students who curse, act out, threaten, or simply refuse to follow basic rules of classroom decorum and conduct. In short, neither safety nor unfettered access to educational opportunities are guaranteed for students in U.S. schools today, and the causes are the students themselves— at least some of them.

Schools have implemented a variety of strategies to deal with problem students. Some strategies involve providing counseling, therapy, or special educational services. Other strategies focus on controlling the more serious problem behaviors by instituting various security measures, such as police officers patrolling the corridors, metal detectors at school entrances, locker searches for drugs and weapons, and random urine testing for illegal drug use. Critics have questioned the effectiveness—and the ethics or legality—of nearly all of these strategies.

Arguably, however, the most controversial of all of these strategies has been the so-called *zero-tolerance* policies. These policies generally specify a list of "unacceptable" behaviors and a set of explicit consequences for students found to be engaging in such behaviors. Invariably, more serious behaviors (e.g., bringing a weapon to school) or repeat offenses (e.g., being disciplined for frequent fighting) earn a suspension or even expulsion. The cornerstone of this policy is the idea that consequences are immediate and applied without regard for extenuating circumstances. Supporters argue that zero tolerance not only removes problem students, thereby increasing the safety and access to instruction for the remaining students, but that it also acts as a deterrent, making students think twice before violating the school's behavior code. Critics of zero tolerance, however, have characterized it as an ineffective overreaction to a real but exaggerated problem.

In the first of the following selections, Albert Shanker argues that a zero-tolerance policy is necessary because disruptive and violent behavior denies equal access to educational opportunities for nonoffending students. Moreover, he condemns programs that devote special attention to the offenders (e.g., programs targeting self-esteem) as ineffective, as diverting resources from the education of deserving students, and as perhaps reinforcing the offending behavior. He also argues that concerns about the rights of nonoffending students to a quality education must take precedence over the rights of offenders. In the second selection, Russ Skiba and Reece Peterson question the need for zero-tolerance policies based on their contention that—contrary to media reports—there are no data to support the assertion that there has been an increase in school-based violence. They also argue that there are no data demonstrating the effectiveness of zero tolerance in deterring violence and crime. Finally, Skiba and Peterson suggest that the application of zero-tolerance policies is discriminatory, affecting more African American students than majority background students.

Albert Shanker

 **YES**

Restoring the Connection Between Behavior and Consequences

I can't think of a more important topic.... [T]here have been and will be a number of conferences on this issue. I can assure you, all of the other conferences resemble each other, and this one will be very different. It will have a very different point of view.

We have had, over the last decade or more, a national debate on the issue of school quality. And there is a national consensus that we need to do a lot better. We are probably doing better than we used to, but we're not doing as well as other industrial countries. And in order to do well, we are going to have to do some of the things that those other countries are doing, such as develop high standards, assessments related to those standards, and a system of consequences so that teachers and youngsters and parents know that school counts. School makes a difference, whether it's getting a job or getting into a college or getting into a training program.

We're well on the way. It's going to take time, but we're on the way to bringing about the improvement that we need. But you can have a wonderful curriculum and terrific assessments and you can state that there are consequences out there but none of this is going to do much good in terms of providing youngsters with an education if we don't meet certain basic obvious conditions. And those conditions are simply that you have to have schools that are safe and classrooms where there is sufficient order so that the curriculum means something. Without that, all of this stuff is nonsense. You can deliver a terrific curriculum, but if youngsters are throwing things, cursing and yelling and punching each other, then the curriculum doesn't mean anything in that classroom. The agenda is quite different.

And so we have a very interesting phenomenon. We have members of Congress and governors and state legislators talking about choice and vouchers and charter schools, and you know what the big incentive is for those issues. Parents are not really pushing for these things, except in conditions where their children seem to be unsafe or in conditions where they can't learn. And then they say, well, look, if you can't straighten things out here, then give me a chance to take my youngster somewhere else. And so we're about to put in place a ridiculous situation. We're going to create a system of choice and vouchers, so that 98 percent of the kids who behave can go some-place and be safe. And we're going to leave the two percent who are violent and disruptive to take over the schools. Now, isn't it ridiculous to move 98 percent of the kids, when all you have to do is move two or three percent of them and the other 98 percent would be absolutely fine?

Now this is a problem which has a number of aspects and I want to talk about them. First, there is, of course, the problem of extreme danger, where we are dealing with violence or guns or drugs within the school. And, as we look to the schools, what we find is that the schools seem to be unable to han-dle this. We had headlines here in DC ... saying that the mayor and school offi-cials say they don't know what else to do. In other words, they've done everything that they can, and the guns, and the knives, and the drugs are still there. So, it just happens that they have actually said it, but that is, in fact, how many school administrators and school boards across the country behave. They treat violence as a fact of life, that's what society is like, and they just go through a couple of ritual efforts to try to show that they're doing something. But, basically they give up.

What we have is what amounts to a very high level of tolerance of this type of activity. Now, of course, the violence and the guns and the drugs have to be distinguished from another type of activity. This other type isn't deadly in the sense that you are going to read tomorrow morning that some young-ster was stabbed or shot. And that's the whole question of just plain out-and-out disruption: the youngster who is constantly yelling, cursing, jumping, fighting, doing all sorts of things, so that most of the time the other students in the class and the teacher is devoted, not to the academic mission of the schools, but to figuring out how to contain this individual. And in this area, we have an even higher tolerance than we do in the area of violence, where occasionally youngsters are suspended or removed for periods of time....

Last year when Congress was debating the Goals 2000 education pro-gram, there were an awful lot of people who said, you know, in addition to having different kinds of content standards—what you should learn—and performance standards—how good is good enough—you ought to have opportunity-to-learn standards. It's not fair to hold kids to these standards unless they've had certain advantages. It's not fair, if one kid has had early childhood education and one hasn't, to hold them to the same standard. It's not fair, if at this school they don't have any textbooks or the textbooks are 15 years old, and in that school they have the most modern books. It's not fair, if in this school they've got computers, and in that school kids have never seen a computer.

Well, I submit to you that if you want to talk about opportunity-to-learn standards, there are a lot of kids who've made it without the most up-to-date textbooks. It's better if you have them. There are a lot of kids who've made it without early childhood education. It's a lot better if you've got it, and we're for that. Throughout history, people have learned without computers, but it's bet-ter if you've got them. But nobody has ever learned if they were in a classroom with one or two kids who took up 90 percent of the time through disruption, violence, or threats of violence. You deprive children of an opportunity to learn if you do not first provide an orderly situation within the classroom and within the school. That comes ahead of all of these other things.

Now, I said that this conference was going to be different from every conference that I've been to and every conference that I've read about. I have a report here that was sent to me by John Cole [President of the Texas Federation of Teachers], who went to The Scholastic Annual Summit on Youth Violence on October 17 [1994]. I'm not going to read the whole thing, but I'll just read enough that you get the flavor of what these other conferences are like:

> "So start with the concept that the real victims of violence are those unfortunate individuals who have been led into lives of crime by the failure of society to provide them with hope for a meaningful life. Following that logic, one must conclude that society has not done enough for these children and that we must find ways to salvage their lives. Schools must work patiently with these individuals offering them different avenues out of this situation. As an institution charged with responsibility for education, schools must have programs to identify those who are embarking on a life of crime and violence and lift them out of the snares into which they have fallen. Society, meanwhile, should be more forgiving of the sins of these poor creatures, who through no real fault of their own are the victims of racism and economic injustice.
>
> "Again and again and again, panelists pointed out that the young people we are talking about, to paraphrase Rodney Dangerfield, 'don't get no respect.' The experts assured us that young people take up weapons, commit acts of violence, and abuse drugs because this enables them to obtain respect from their peers. I found myself thinking that we aid and abet this behavior when we bend over backwards to accommodate those young people who have bought into this philosophy. By lavishing attention on them, we may even encourage a spread of that behavior. Many of these programs are well meaning but counterproductive.
>
> "I don't want to condemn this conference as a waste of time. Obviously, we do need programs to work with these young people, and we should try to salvage as many as we can. However, we must somehow come to grips with the idea that individuals have responsibility for their own actions. If we assume that society is to blame for all of the problems these young people have, may we then assume that society must develop solutions that take care of these young people's problems? We take away from each individual the responsibility for his or her own life. Once the individual assumes that he or she has lost control of his own destiny, that individual has no difficulty in justifying any act because he or she feels no responsibility for the consequences."

Now with that philosophy, the idea is not that we want to be punitive or nasty, but essentially schools must teach not only English and mathematics and reading and writing and history, but also teach that there are ways of behaving in society that are unacceptable. And when we sit back and tolerate certain types of behavior, we are teaching youngsters that certain types of behavior are acceptable, which eventually will end up with their being in jail or in poverty for the rest of their lives. We are not doing our jobs as teachers.

And the system is not doing its job, if we send youngsters the message that this is tolerable behavior within society. ...

All we ask of our schools is that they behave in the same way that a caring and intelligent parent would behave with respect to their own children. I doubt very much, if you had a youngster who was a fire bug or a youngster who used weapons, whether you would say, well, I owe it to this youngster to trust him with my other children to show him that I'm not separating him out or treating him differently. Or I'm going to raise his self-esteem by allowing him to do these things. All of these nutty things that we talk about in school, we would not do. So the starting point of this conference, which is different from all of the others, is that I hope that you people join withme in a sense of outrage that we have a system that is willing to sacrifice the overwhelming majority of children for a handful. And not do any good for that handful either. And we need to start with that outrage, because without that we're not going to change this system.

That outrage is there among parents. That outrage was partly expressed in the recent election as people's anger at the way government was working. Why can't government do things in some sort of common sense way? And this is one of the issues that's out there. Now, what are some of the things that enter into this? Well, part of it is that some people think of schools as sort of custodial institutions. Where are we going to put the kids? Put them here. Or they think the school's job is mostly socialization. Eventually troubled kids will grow up or grow out of this, and they're better off with other youngsters than they are separated. Of course, people who take that point of view are totally ignoring the fact that the central role of schools, the one that we will be held accountable for, is student academic achievement.We know the test scores are bad. And we know that our students are not learning as much as youngsters in other countries. So we can't just say we know we are way behind, but, boy, are we good custodians. Look at how socialized these youngsters are.

People are paying for education and they want youngsters who are going to be able to be employed and get decent jobs. We want youngsters who are going to be as well off or in better shape than we are, just as most of us are with respect to our parents and grandparents. And the academic function is the one that's neglected. The academic function is the one that's destroyed in this notion that our job is mainly custodial.

So our central position is that we have to be tough on these issues, and we have to be tough because basically we are defending the right of children to an education. And those who insist on allowing violence and disruptive behavior in the school are destroying the right to an education for the overwhelming majority of youngsters within our schools.

Two years ago or three years ago, I was in Texas at a convention of the Texas Federation of Teachers. I didn't know this was going to happen, but either just before I got there or while I was there, there was a press conference on a position the convention adopted, and they used the phrase "zero tolerance." They said that with respect to certain types of dangerous activities in schools, there would be zero tolerance. These things are not acceptable and there are going to be consequences. There might be suspension, there might be expulsion, or there might be something else, but nevertheless, consequences will be clear. Well, that got picked up by radio, television, legislators. I was listening to a governor the other night at the National Governors Association, who stood up and came out for zero tolerance. It is a phrase which has caught on and is sweeping the country.

I hope it is one that all of you will bring back to your communities and your states, that there are certain types of activities that we will not tolerate. We will not teach youngsters bad lessons, and we're going to start very early. When a youngster does something that is terribly wrong, and all of the other youngsters are sure that something is going to happen to him because he did something wrong, we had better make sure that we fulfill the expectations of all those other youngsters that something's going to happen. And they're all going to say, "Thank God, I didn't do a terrible thing like that or I would be out there, and something would be happening to me." That is the beginning of a sense of doing something right, as against doing wrong.

And we have to deal with this notion that society is responsible, social conditions are responsible. The AFT does not take second place to anybody in fighting for decent conditions for adults and for youngsters and for minorities and for groups that have been oppressed. We're not in a state of denial; we're not saying that things have been wonderful. But when your kids come home and say "I'm doing these terrible things because of these conditions," if you're a good parent, you'll say, "That's no excuse." You are going to do things right, because you don't want your youngster to end up as a criminal or in some sort of horrible position....

Now what should schools do? Schools should have codes of conduct. These codes can be developed through collective bargaining or they can be mandated in legislation. I don't think it would be a bad idea to have state legislation that every school system needs to have a code of discipline that is very clear, not a fuzzy sort of thing, something that says these things are not to be done and if this happens, these are the consequences. A very clear connection between behavior and consequences. And it might even say that, if there is a legitimate complaint from a group of parents or a group of teachers or a group of students that clearly shows the school district doesn't have such a code or isn't enforcing it, there would be some sort of financial penalty against the district for failing to provide a decent education by allowing this type of violence and disruption to continue.

Taxpayers are sending money into the district so that the kids can have an education, and if that district then destroys the education by allowing one or two youngsters to wipe out all of the effects that money is supposed to produce, what the hell is the point of sending the money? If you allow these youngsters to so disrupt that education, you might as well save the money. So there's a reason for states to do this. And, by the way, I think that you'll find a receptive audience, because the notion of individuals taking responsibility for their actions is one of the things fueling the political anger in this country—that we have a lot of laws which help people to become irresponsible or encourage them not to take responsibility for their own actions.

Now, enforcement is very important. For every crime, so to speak, there ought to be a punishment. I don't like very much judgment to be used, because once you allow judgment to be used, punishments will be more severe for some kids than for others and you will get unfairness. You will get prejudice. The way to make sure that this is done fairly and is not done in a prejudiced way is to say, look, we don't care if you're white or Hispanic or African-American or whether you're a recent immigrant or this or that, for this infraction, this is what happens. We don't have a different sanction depending upon whether we like you a little more or a little less. That's how fairness would be ensured, and I think it's very important that we insist on that....

One of the big problems is school administrators. School administrators are concerned that, if there are a large number of reports of disruptions and violence in their schools, their reputations will suffer. They like to say they have none of those problems in their schools. Now, how do you prove that you have none of these problems in your school? Very simple. Just tell the teachers that if they report it, it's because they are ineffective teachers. If you tell that to one or two teachers, you will certainly have a school that has very little disruption or violence reported. You may have plenty of disruption and violence. So, in many places we have this gag rule. It's not written, but it's very well understood.

As a teacher, I myself faced this. Each time I reported something like this, I was told that if I knew how to motivate the students properly, this wouldn't happen. It's pretty universal. It wasn't just one district or just my principal. It's almost all of them. Therefore, I think that we ought to seek laws that require a full and honest reporting of incidents of violence and extreme disruption. And that would mean that, if an administrator goes around telling you to shut up or threatening you so that you're not free to report, I think that there ought to be penalties. Unless we know the extent of this problem, we're never going to deal with it adequately.

Of course, parents know what the extent of it is. What is the number one problem? It's the problem of violence and order in the schools. They know it. The second big problem and obstacle we face is, what's going to happen if you put the kid out on the streets? It reminds me of a big campaign in New York City to get crime off the streets, and pretty soon they were very successful. They had lots of policemen on the streets, and they drove the criminals away. The criminals went into the subways. Then they had a campaign about crime in the subways, and they drove them back up into the streets. So the business community, parents, and others will say, you can't just throw a kid out and put them on the streets. That's no good. But you could place some conditions on it. To return to school, students would have to bring with them a parent or some other grown-up or relative responsible for them. There is a list of ways in which we might handle it. But we can't say that we're going to wait until we build new schools, or build new classrooms, or have new facilities. The first thing you do is separate out the youngster who is a danger to the other youngsters.

Now, let me give an example. And I think it's one that's pretty close. We know that, when we arrest adults who have committed crimes and we jail them, jail will most likely not help those who are jailed. I don't think it does, and I don't think most people do. However, most of us are pretty glad when someone who has ommitted a pretty bad crime is jailed. Not because it's going to do that person any good, but because that person won't be around to do the same thing for the next ten or fifteen years. And for the separation of youngsters who are destroying the education of others, the justification is the same. I'm not sure that we can devise programs that will reach those youngsters that will help them. We should try. But our first obligation is to never destroy the education of the twenty or twenty-five or thirty because you have an obligation to one. Especially when there's no evidence that you're doing anything for that one by keeping him there.

Now, another big obstacle is legal problems. These are expensive and time consuming. If a youngster gets a lawyer and goes to court, the principal or some other figure of authority from the school, usually has to go to court. They might sit a whole day and by the end of the first day, they decide not to hear it. And they come a second day, and maybe it's held over again. It might take three or four days for each youngster. So if you've got a decent-sized school, even if you're dealing with only two or three percent of the youngsters, you could spend your full time in court, instead of being in school. Well, I wouldn't want to do that if I were the principal of the school. And then what does the court do when you're all finished? The court says, well, we don't have any better place to put him, so send him right back. So, that's why a lot of teachers wouldn't report it, because nothing happens anyway. You go through all of this, you spend all of that time and money, and when you're all finished, you're right back where you started. So we need to change what happens with respect to the court, and we have two ideas that we're going to explore that have not been done before.

One of the things we need to do is see whether we can get parents, teachers, and even perhaps high school students to intervene in these cases and say, we want to come before the judge to present evidence about what the consequences are for the other children. When you go to court now, you have the lawyer for the board of education, the lawyer for the youngster, and the youngster. And the youngster, well, he's just a kid and his lawyer says, "This poor child has all of these problems," and the judge is looking down at this poor youngster. You know who is not there? The other 25 youngsters to say, this guy beats me up every day. If I do my homework, I get beat up on the way to school because he doesn't want me to do my homework. So instead of first having this one child standing there saying, "Poor me, let me back in school, they have kicked me out, they have done terrible things to me," you also have some of the victims there saying, "Hey, what about us?" You'll get a much fairer consideration if the judge is able to look at both sides, instead of just hearing the bureaucrat from the board of education. None of these board of education lawyers that I've met talk about the other students. They talk about the right of the board of education under the law to do thus, and so what you have is a humane judge who's thinking of the bureaucrat talking about the rights of the board of education as against the child. I think we need to balance that.

Now, there's a second thing we are going to explore. We are all familiar with the fact that most of our labor contracts have a provision for grievance procedures. And part of that grievance procedure is arbitration. Now, you can take an arbitration award to court and try to appeal it, but it's very, very difficult to get a court to overthrow an arbitrator's award. Why? Because the court says, look, you had your day, you went to the arbitrator and you presented all your arguments, the other side presented all their arguments. In order for me to look into that arbitration and turn it over, you're going to have to prove to me that something in this arbitration was so terrible that we have to prove that the arbitrator was absolutely partial or that he broke the law. You've got to prove something outrageous. Otherwise, the judge is going to say, "You've had your day in court."

Now, why can't school districts establish a fair, inexpensive, due-process arbitration procedure for youngsters who are violent or disruptive? So that when the youngster goes to court, they can say, "Hey, we've had this procedure. We've had witnesses on both sides, and here was the determination. And, really, you shouldn't get into this stuff unless you can show that these people are terribly prejudiced or totally incompetent or something else." In other words, we don't have to use the court. We could create a separate school judicial system that had expertise and knowledge about what the impact is on students and teachers and the whole system of these kinds of decisions. Arbitration is a much cheaper, much faster system, especially if you have an expedited arbitration system. There is a system in the American Arbitration Association of expedited arbitration that says how many briefs you're allowed to write and how much time each side can take, and all of that. So we have a legal team and we're going to explore the notion of getting this stuff out of the courts and creating a system that is inexpensive and fair to the youngster and fair to the other youngsters in the school.

Now, let me point out that a lot of the tolerance for bad behavior is about to change, because we are about to have stakes attached to student academic outcomes. In other words, in the near future, we are going to have a situation where, if you don't make it up to this point, then you can't be admitted into college. Or if you don't make it here, then you will not get certified for a certain type of employment. But in Chapter I schools, this is going to start very soon. There is a provision in the new Chapter One, now called Title I, and very soon, if Title I schools do not show a substantial progress for students, the school's going to be punished. And one of the punishments is reconstitution of the school. The school will be closed down, teachers will go elsewhere, students will go elsewhere, and the school will open up with a new student body, slowly rebuild. That's one of the punishments. There are other punishments as well. So if you've got a bunch of these disruptive youngsters that prevent you from teaching and the other students from learning, it won't be like yesterday, where nobody seems to care, the kids are all going to get promoted anyway and they can all go to college, because there are no standards. There are no stakes.

Now, for the first time, there will be stakes. The teachers will know. The parents will know, hey, this school's going to close. I'm going to have to find a way of getting my kid to some other school because of the lack of learning that comes from this disruption. Teachers are going to say, hey, I'm not going to have my job in this school a couple of years from now because they're going to shut it down. I don't know what the rules are, what happens to these teachers, whether other schools have to take them or not. But we are entering a period where there will be consequences and parents and teachers are going to be a lot more concerned about achievement.

Now, one of the other issues that has stood in the way of doing something here is a very difficult one to talk about in our society, and that's the issue of race. And whenever the topic of suspension or expulsion comes up, there's always the question of race. Cincinnati is a good example. The union there negotiated a good discipline code as part of a desegregation suit. And the question was raised, "Well, is there a disparate impact, with more minority kids being suspended than others?" And who are the teachers who are suspending them? Do you have more white teachers suspending African-American kids?

Our position on that is very clear. In any given school, you may have more white kids with infractions or you may have more African-American kids, or you may have more Hispanic kids. We don't know. I don't think anybody knows. But we handle that by saying, "Whatever your crime is and whoever you are, you're going to get exactly the same punishment." If we do that, I'm sure that the number who will be punished will end up being very, very small. Because, as a young kid, if you see that there is a consequence, you will change your behavior. ...

Now we have another very big problem, and we're going to try to deal with this in legislation. Under legislation that deals with disabled youngsters, we have two different standards. Namely, if a youngster in this class is not disabled and commits an infraction, you can do whatever is in that discipline code for that youngster. But if the youngster is disabled and is in that same class (for instance, the youngster might have a speech defect), you can't suspend that youngster while all of the proceedings are going on because that's a change in placement. It might take you a year-and-a-half in court, and meanwhile that youngster who is engaged in some threatening or dangerous behavior has to stay there. This makes no sense. We have a lot of support in the Congress on this, and we think we have a good chance of changing this....

Well, that's the whole picture. And to return to the theme at the beginning, we have a cry for choice, a cry for vouchers, a cry for charters. It's not really a cry for these things. People really want their own schools, and they want their kids to go to those schools, and they want those schools to be safe and orderly for their youngsters.

It is insane to set up a system where we move 98 percent of our kids away from the two percent who are dangerous, instead of moving the two percent away from the 98 percent who are OK. We need to have discipline codes, we need to have a new legal system, we need to have one standard for all students. We need to have a system where we don't have to wait for a year or a year-and-a-half after a student has perpetrated some terrible and atrocious crime before that student is removed for the safety of the other students. How are we going to do this? We are going to do this, first of all, by talking to our colleagues within the schools. Our polls show that the overwhelming majority accepts these views.

The support of African-American parents for the removal of violent youngsters and disruptive students is higher than any other group within our society. Now very often when youngsters are removed, it's because some parents group or some committee starts shouting and making noise, and the school system can't resist that. Now I think that it's time for us to turn to business groups, it's time for us to turn to parents' groups. When youngsters commit such acts, and when they've had a fair due-process within the system, we need to have a system of public support, just as we have in the community when someone commits a terrible crime. People say, send that person to jail, don't send him back to us. We need to have a lot of decent people within our communities, when you have youngsters who are destroying the education of all the others, who will stand up and say, "Look, we don't want to punish this kid, but for the sake of our children, you're going to have to keep that one away, until that one is ready to come back and live in a decent way in society with all of the other youngsters."

I'm sure that if we take this back to our communities, and if we work on it, the appeal will be obvious. It's common sense. And we will save our schools and we will do something which will give us the basis for providing a decent education for all of our children.

NO

Russ Skiba and
Reece Peterson

The Dark Side of Zero Tolerance

The 1997-98 school year was a shocking and frightening one, filled with reports of seemingly random violence in communities heretofore immune to such incidents. In the wake of these tragedies, we can expect to hear renewed calls for increasingly severe penalties for any kind of school disruption, a stance that has led to the widespread adoption of so-called zero tolerance discipline policies.

Already many districts have decreed that making any sort of threat will result in automatic expulsion. Some have gone as far as to suggest that principals be armed in order to deter—or perhaps outshoot—students who bring firearms to school. Such an approach is extreme, to say the least, and is unlikely to be implemented. Yet it is simply the far end of a continuum of responses to what has become the largely unquestioned assumption that school violence is accelerating at an alarming rate and that increasingly draconian disciplinary measures are not only justified but necessary to guarantee school safety.

Before we continue down a path that may well turn school principals into town marshals and cafeterias into free-fire zones, however, we would do well to examine more closely the track record of zero tolerance. What is "zero tolerance"? What is the nature of the school violence that has brought us to this point? How well does the approach address the serious issues of school safety toward which it has been aimed?

The Origins of Zero Tolerance

The term "zero tolerance"—referring to policies that punish all offenses severely, no matter how minor—grew out of state and federal drug enforcement policies in the 1980s. The first use of the term recorded in the Lexis-Nexis national newspaper database was in 1983, when the Navy reassigned 40 submarine crew members for suspected drug abuse. In 1986 zero tolerance was picked up and used by a U.S. attorney in San Diego as the title of a program developed to impound seacraft carrying any amount of drugs. By February 1988 the program had received national attention, and U.S. Attorney General Edwin Meese authorized customs officials to seize the boats, automobiles, and passports of anyone crossing the border with even trace amounts of drugs and to charge those individuals in federal court. Zero tolerance took hold quickly and within months was being applied to issues as diverse as environmental pollution, trespassing, skate-boarding, racial intolerance, homelessness, sexual harassment, and boom boxes.

From the outset, the harsh punishments meted out under zero tolerance drug policies engendered considerable controversy. Private citizens whose cars, boats, and even bicycles were impounded for sometimes minute amounts of drugs complained bitterly, and the American Civil Liberties Union considered filing suit against the program. By 1990 the U.S. Customs Service quietly discontinued its initial zero tolerance program after strict applications of the rule resulted in the seizure of two research vessels on which a small amount of marijuana was found.

Yet just as the early zero tolerance drug programs in the community were being phased out, the concept was beginning to catch on in the public schools. In late 1989 school districts in Orange County, California, and Louisville, Kentucky, promulgated zero tolerance policies that called for expulsion for possession of drugs or participation in gang-related activity. In New York, Donald Batista, superintendent of the Yonkers public schools, proposed a sweeping zero tolerance program as a way of taking action against students who caused school disruption. With its restricted school access, ban on hats, immediate suspension for any school disruption, and increased use of law enforcement, the program contained many of the elements that have come to characterize zero tolerance approaches in the past decade.

By 1993 zero tolerance policies were being adopted by school boards across the country, often broadened to include not only drugs and weapons but also tobacco-related offenses and school disruption. In 1994 the federal government stepped in to mandate the policy nationally when President Clinton signed the Gun-Free Schools Act into law.[1] This law mandates an expulsion of one calendar year for possession of a weapon and referral of students who violate the law to the criminal or juvenile justice system. It also provides that the one-year expulsions may be modified by the "chief administrative officer" of each local school district on a case-by-case basis.

School Violence: Reality and Perception

Last year's string of school shootings has left all educators shaken and nervous about the potential for violence in their own schools. The fear that drugs and violence are spreading in our nation's schools provided the initial motivation for adopting zero tolerance disciplinary policies and may well motivate still another round of tough disciplinary measures. But what is the reality of school violence and drug use? How bad is it, and is it getting worse?

It is hard to say that we are overreacting when the incidents we have witnessed on a regular basis are so horrific. Yet some data on the topic suggest that we are doing just that. In a report titled *Violence and Discipline Problems in U. S. Public Schools, 1996-1997*, the National Center for Education Statistics (NCES) surveyed a nationally representative sample of 1,234 school principals or disciplinarians at the elementary, middle, and high school levels.[2] When these principals were asked to list what they considered serious or moderate problems in their schools, the most frequently cited problems at all levels were the less violent behaviors such as tardiness (40%), absenteeism (25%), and physical conflicts between students (21%). The critical incidents that are typically the focus of school safety debates were reported to be at least "a moderate problem" only relatively infrequently: drug use (9%), gangs (5%), possession of weapons (2%), and physical abuse of teachers (2%). The NCES report found that violent crimes occurred at an annual rate of only 53 per 100,000 students.

When we watch the evening news or walk through the edgy and noisy corridors of urban middle schools, it is difficult to believe that school behavior is not worsening. But again, the evidence seems to contradict our gut feelings. Comparisons of the current NCES survey data with results from an earlier survey of public school principals conducted in 1991 show virtually no changes across either minor misbehavior or more serious infractions. Noted school violence researcher Irwin Hyman tracked a number of indicators of school violence over the past 20 years and concluded, "As was the case 20 years ago, despite public perceptions to the contrary, the current data do not support the claim that there has been a dramatic, overall increase in school-based violence in recent years."[3]

It seems almost inconceivable that there are so few incidents of truly dangerous behavior and that things are not necessarily getting worse. Perhaps there are some behaviors that just shake us up, whatever their absolute frequency. School shootings involving multiple victims are still extremely rare from a statistical standpoint. However, statistics are hardly reassuring as long as the possibility exists that it could happen in *our* school, to *our* children. It is probably healthier that a single shooting on school grounds be viewed as one too many than that we become inured to violence.

Yet this fear of random violence is clearly the prime motivator for the adoption of zero tolerance approaches to school discipline. From that first boat's impoundment in San Diego harbor, zero tolerance has cast a broad net, by its very definition treating both minor and major incidents with equal severity in order to "send a message" to potential violators.

Indeed, infractions that fall under the rubric of zero tolerance seem to multiply as the definition of what will not be tolerated expands. Test cases of school district zero tolerance policies reported in the media from 1988 to 1993 did involve difficult judgments about the severity of the punishment, but they were also clearly concerned with weapons and drugs: a high school senior in Chicago was expelled from school when police found marijuana in the trunk of his car during the lunch hour; an honor student in Los Angeles was expelled when he pulled out a knife to scare away peers who had been harassing him because of his Filipino-Mexican heritage.[4]

Over time, however, increasingly broad interpretations of zero tolerance have resulted in a near epidemic of suspensions and expulsions for seemingly trivial events. ...

The reaction to these cases has created sharp divisions in schools and communities. In a number of these incidents, parents have filed lawsuits against the school districts, for the most part unsuccessfully.[5] A number of states have amended their zero tolerance policies to allow more flexibility for individual cases,[6] while the Office for Civil Rights in the U.S. Department of Education began advocating a less comprehensive interpretation of sexual harassment after the suspension of 6-year-old Jonathan Prevette for kissing a classmate made national headlines.[7] Yet in many cases school administrators and school boards have not backed down even in the face of public clamor. They claim that their hands are tied by federal or state law (despite language in the federal law that allows local review on a case-by-case basis), or they assert that continued application of zero tolerance is necessary to send a message to disruptive students.

Who Gets Suspended and Expelled?

If the NCES data on school violence are correct, it is not surprising that the broad net of zero tolerance will catch a host of minor misbehaviors. Since there are few incidents of serious violence and many incidents of minor disruption, policies that set harsh consequences indiscriminately will capture a few incidents of serious violence and many incidents of minor disruption.

In fact, data on suspension and expulsion suggest that the incidents brought to national attention by the media are not all that inaccurate in describing the types of behavior that lead to exclusion from school. Data on suspension consistently show that, as the NCES has reported, referrals for drugs, weapons, and gang-related behaviors constitute but a small minority of office referrals leading to suspension. Fighting among students is the single most frequent reason for suspension, but the majority of school suspensions occur in response to relatively minor incidents that do not threaten school safety.[8] At the middle school level, disrespect and disobedience are among the most common reasons for suspension, and a significant proportion of suspensions are for tardiness and truancy. In one of the few reported studies of school expulsion in American education, Gale Morrison and Barbara D'Incau reported that the majority of offenses in the sample they investigated were committed by students who would not generally be considered dangerous to the school environment.[9] In their study, as in many that have explored suspension and expulsion, poor academic skill was a strong predictor of school exclusion.

One of the more troubling characteristics of the zero tolerance approach to discipline is that a disproportionate number of those at risk for a range of school punishments are poor and African American. In 1975 the Children's Defense Fund, studying data on school discipline from the Office for Civil Rights (OCR), found high rates of suspension for black students. Of the nearly 3,000 school districts represented in the OCR data, more than two-thirds showed rates of black suspension that exceeded rates for white students.[10]

Since then, researchers have consistently found disproportionate minority representation among students on the receiving end of exclusionary and punitive discipline practices. African American students are overrepresented in the use of corporal punishment and expulsion, and they are underrepresented in the use of milder disciplinary alternatives.[11] This overrepresentation of minorities in the application of harsh discipline appears to be related to the overall use of school exclusion: schools that rely most heavily on suspension and expulsion are also those that show the highest rates of minority overrepresentation in school disciplinary consequences.

Of course, there are hypotheses other than racial bias that might be called upon to explain minority overrepresentation in school discipline. First, the unfortunate correlation of race and poverty in our society suggests that inequitable racial treatment in discipline may be a socioeconomic issue rather than a racial one. Yet multivariate studies have continued to find evidence of black overrepresentation in suspension—even after controlling for socioeconomic background—suggesting that racial disproportionality in suspension involves more than just poverty.[12]

A second hypothesis suggests that racial differences in punishment are the result of differences in school behavior: higher rates of suspension for African American students would not be bias if those students misbehaved more frequently. Yet when rates of behavior for African American and other students are taken into account, the differences are minor at best, and behavior makes a weak contribution to explaining the discrepancy in the suspension rates of blacks and whites.[13] While there are doubtless complex factors involving defiance, fighting, and school authority that determine who is suspended or expelled in any given situation, it is clear that the burden of suspension and expulsion falls most heavily on poor black males.

How Effective Is Zero Tolerance?

It has been almost a decade since school districts first began to adopt zero tolerance policies. And it has been four years since the policy was institutionalized nationally in the Gun-Free Schools Act. How well has it worked?

The short answer is that we don't really know. Unlike the domain of academic achievement, in which constant calls for accountability have led to state and national standards and tests, there has been no concomitant pressure to test the efficacy of interventions that target school behavior. Perhaps as a result, there are almost no studies that evaluate the effectiveness of zero tolerance strategies.

Of course, the media have reported claims by school districts that zero tolerance approaches have curtailed guns, gangs, or fighting in their schools. The most comprehensive and controlled study of zero tolerance policies, however, appears once again to be the NCES study of school violence. The NCES survey asked principals to identify which of a number of possible components of a zero tolerance strategy (e.g., expulsions, locker searches, the use of metal detectors, school uniforms) were employed at their school. Of the responding principals, 79% reported having a zero tolerance policy for violence. Schools with no reported crime were less likely to have a zero tolerance policy (74%) than schools that reported incidents of serious crime (85%). From one perspective, the relationship is unsurprising, since unsafe schools might well be expected to try more extreme measures. Yet after four years of implementation, the NCES found that schools that use zero tolerance policies are still less safe than those without such policies.

As time has allowed all of us to gain some perspective on the school shootings of last year, the media have begun to report data showing that the rate of school violence has remained fairly level since the early 1990s. One overlooked implication of these figures is their evaluative significance for the Gun-Free Schools Act. In an era of accountability, it is unfair to expect that a national policy implemented consistently, one might even say aggressively, over a four-year period should demonstrate some measurable effect on its target: school disruption and violence? Virtually no data suggest that zero tolerance policies reduce school violence, and some data suggest that certain strategies, such as strip searches or undercover agents in school, may create emotional harm or encourage students to drop out.[14] When the lives of schoolchildren and staff members continue to be claimed in random shootings after extensive implementation of the most extreme measures in our schools, is it wise to push these strategies harder?

Our concerns about the long-term effects of zero tolerance multiply when we look more closely at one of its central components: school exclusion. In the 1980s, national concern over children termed "at risk" led to extensive investigations of the causes and correlates of dropping out. Consistently, school suspension was found to be a moderate to strong predictor of a student's dropping out of school. More than 30% of sophomores who dropped out of school had been suspended, a rate three times that of peers who stayed in school.[15]

Indeed, the relationship between suspension and dropping out may not be accidental. In ethnographic studies, school disciplinarians report that suspension is sometimes used as a tool to "push out" particular students, to encourage "troublemakers" or those perceived as unlikely to succeed in school to leave.[16]

Recent advances in developmental psychopathology suggest other explanations for the relationship between suspension and dropping out. In the elementary school years, students at risk for developing conduct disorders exhibit disruptive behavior, below-average achievement, and poor social skills. Together, these deficits cause them to become increasingly alienated from teachers and peers.[17] As they reach middle school, these youngsters become less interested in school and seek the company of other antisocial peers, perhaps even gangs. At the same time, their families often fail to monitor their whereabouts, allowing more unsupervised time on the streets. In such a context, it seems unlikely that suspension will positively influence the behavior of the student being suspended. Rather, suspension may simply accelerate the course of delinquency by giving a troubled youth with little parental supervision a few extra days to "hang" with deviant peers. One student interviewed while in detention expresses this aptly.

> When they suspend you, you get in more trouble, 'cause you're out in the street. ... And that's what happened to me once. I got into trouble one day 'cause there was a party, and they arrested everybody in that party.... I got in trouble more than I get in trouble at school, because I got arrested and everything.[18]

Whether and how to provide services to students who are suspended and expelled may be our next pressing national discussion. Without such services, school personnel may simply be dumping problem students out on the streets, only to find them later causing increased violence and disruption in the community. In sum, we lack solid evidence to support the effectiveness of harsh policies in improving school safety, and we face serious questions about the long-term negative effects of one of the cornerstones of zero tolerance, school exclusion.

Indeed, the popularity of zero tolerance may have less to do with its actual effects than with the image it portrays. Writing in the *Harvard Educational Review*, Pedro Noguera argues that the primary function of harsh punishment is not to change the behavior of the recipient, but to reassert the power of authority.[19] Seemingly random violence poses a profound threat to schools and to the authority of those who administer those schools. In the face of an apparent inability to influence the course of violence in schools, harsh measures are intended to send a message that the administration is still in charge. Whether the message is effectively received or actually changes student behavior may be less important than the reassurance that sending it provides to administrators, teachers, and parents.

In his recent book, *The Triumph of Meanness*, Nicholas Mills argues that a culture of meanness has come to characterize many aspects of our nation's social policies, from "bum-proof" park benches to sweeping social welfare reform. According to Mills, "Meanness today is a state of mind, the product of a culture of spite and cruelty that has had an enormous impact on us."[20] The zeal with which punitive policies are sometimes implemented suggests that zero tolerance discipline may be yet another example of what Mills is referring to. Whether such policies work or how they affect the lives of students may be less important than providing harsh punishment for offenders as a form of generalized retribution for a generalized evil.

What Else Should We Do?

In any institution, the preservation of order demands that boundaries be set and enforced. Children whose families set no limits for them soon become uncontrolled and uncontrollable. In the same way, schools and classrooms in which aggressive, dangerous, or seriously disruptive behaviors are tolerated will almost inevitably descend into chaos.

Yet the indiscriminate use of force without regard for its effects is the hallmark of authoritarianism, incompatible with the functioning of a democracy, and certainly incompatible with the transmission of democratic values to children. If we rely solely, or even primarily, on zero tolerance strategies to preserve the safety of our schools, we are accepting a model of schooling that implicitly teaches students that the preservation of order demands the suspension of individual rights and liberties. As we exclude ever-higher proportions of children whose behavior does not meet increasingly tough standards, we will inevitably meet many of those disruptive youths on the streets. In choosing control and exclusion as our preferred methods of dealing with school disruption, even as we refrain from positive interventions, we increase the likelihood that the correctional system will become the primary agency responsible for troubled youths. Ultimately, as we commit ourselves to increasingly draconian policies of school discipline, we may also need to resign ourselves to increasingly joyless schools, increasingly unsafe streets, and dramatically increasing expenditures for detention centers and prisons.

Seriousness of purpose in seeking to avert the tragedy of school violence does not necessarily demand rigid adherence to harsh and extreme measures. There *are* alternatives to politically facile get-tough strategies, alternatives that rely on a comprehensive program of prevention and planning. However, prevention is not a politically popular approach to solving problems of crime and violence in America. A recent task force on prevention research, commissioned by the National Institutes of Mental Health [NIMH], found wide gaps in our knowledge, noting that "virtually no preventive services research of any kind was found under NIMH sponsorship."[21]

Yet if we are to break the cycle of violence in American society, we must begin to look beyond a program of stiffer consequences. We must begin with long-term planning aimed at fostering nonviolent school communities. First, programmatic prevention efforts—such as conflict resolution and schoolwide behavior management—can help establish a climate free of violence. Conflict resolution has been shown to have a moderate effect on the level of student aggression in schools,[22] but more important, it teaches students to consider and use alternatives to violence in solving conflicts. Schoolwide discipline plans and the planning process required to develop and implement them help ensure that school staff members have both the consistent philosophy and the consistent procedures that are so critical to effective behavior management.[23]

Second, screening and early identification of troubled young people appear to be critical in preventing the eruption of violence. In a number of the multiple-victim shooting incidents that occurred last year, the shooter left warning signs, cries for help that went unheeded.[24] There is at least one widely available and well-researched measure designed to screen for troubled students, whether the primary concern is acting-out behavior or social withdrawal.[25] With such screening and with knowledge of the early warning signs listed in the President's guide for preventing violence,[26] we are beginning to have the capability of identifying students with serious problems while they can still be helped.

Finally, schools with effective discipline have plans and procedures in place to deal with the disruptive behaviors that inevitably occur. School safety teams or behavior support teams—composed of regular and special education teachers, personnel from related services, administrators, and parents—ensure a consistent and individualized response to disruptive students.[27] ... In short, effective interventions emphasize building positive prosocial behaviors rather than merely punishing inappropriate behaviors. Whether at the level of the school or at the level of the individual, effective intervention requires a wide spectrum of options that extend significantly beyond a narrow focus on punishment and exclusion.

There are doubtless those with little patience for the complex and careful planning that such a program demands, those who prefer the quick fix that zero tolerance purports to be. But the problems that have brought us to the current precarious situation in our nation's schools are highly complex and will not abide simplistic solutions. Zero tolerance strategies have begun to turn our schools into supplemental law enforcement agencies, but they have demonstrated little return despite a decade of hype. In contrast, long-term, comprehensive planning and prevention can build safe and responsive schools over time by emphasizing what American education has always done best: teaching.

Notes

1. The original definition of "firearm" as contained in the Gun-Free Schools Act did not include weapons other than firearms. Later amendments and state policies have since expanded the definition to include any instrument intended to be used as a weapon.
2. *Violence and Discipline Problems in U.S. Public Schools: 1996-1997* (Washington, D.C.: National Center for Education Statistics, NCES 98-030, 1998).
3. Irwin A. Hyman and Donna C. Perone, "The Other Side of School Violence: Educator Policies and Practices That May Contribute to Student Misbehavior," *Journal of School Psychology,* vol. 30, 1998, p. 9.
4. Tom McNamee, "Student's Expulsion Tests Zero Tolerance," *Chicago Sun-Times,* 4 April 1993, p. 5; and Bert Eljera, "Schools Get Dead Serious: No Weapons," *Los Angeles Times,* 7 March 1993, p. B-1.
5. Perry A. Zirkel, "The Right Stuff," *Phi Delta Kappan,* February 1998, pp. 475-76.
6. Chris Pipho, "Living with Zero Tolerance," *Phi Delta Kappan,* June 1998, pp. 725-26.
7. Jessica Portner, "Suspensions Spur Debate over Discipline Codes," *Education Week on the Web,* 23 October 1996 (http// www.edweek.org.ew/vol16/08react.h16).
8. For a more complete review, see Russell J. Skiba, Reece L. Peterson, and Tara Williams, "Office Referrals and Suspension: Disciplinary Intervention in Middle Schools," *Education and Treatment of Children,* vol. 20, 1997, pp. 295-315.
9. Gale M. Morrison, and Barbara D'Incau, "The Web of Zero Tolerance: Characteristics of Students Who Are Recommended for Expulsion from School," *Education and Treatment of Children,* vol. 20, 1997, pp. 316-35.

10. Children's Defense Fund, *School Suspensions: Are They Helping Children?* (Cambridge, Mass.: Washington Research Project, 1975).

11. See Skiba, Peterson, and Williams, op. cit.

12. Shi-Chang C. Wu et al., "Student Suspension: A Critical Reappraisal," *Urban Review,* vol. 14, 1982, pp. 245-303.

13. Ibid.; and John D. McCarthy and Dean R. Hoge, "The Social Construction of School Punishment: Racial Disadvantage out of Universalistic Process," *Social Forces,* vol. 65, 1987, pp. 1101-20.

14. Hyman and Perone, op. cit.

15. Ruth B. Ekstrom et al., "Who Drops Out of High School and Why? Findings from a National Study," *Teachers College Record,* Spring 1986, pp. 356-73.

16. Christine Bowditch, "Getting Rid of Troublemakers: High School Disciplinary Procedures and the Production of Dropouts," *Social Problems,* vol. 40, 1993, pp. 493-507; and Michelle Fine, "Why Urban Adolescents Drop into and out of Public High School," *Teachers College Record,* Spring 1986, pp. 393-409.

17. Gerald R. Patterson, "Developmental Changes in Antisocial Behavior," in Ray D. Peters, Robert J. McMahon, and Vernon L. Quinsey, eds., *Aggression and Violence Throughout the Life Span* (Newbury Park, Calif.: Sage, 1992), pp. 52-82.

18. Sue Thorson, "The Missing Link: Students Discuss School Discipline," *Focus on Exceptional Children,* vol. 29, 1996, p. 9.

19. Pedro A. Noguera, "Preventing and Producing Violence: A Critical Analysis of Responses to School Violence," *Harvard Educational Review,* Summer 1995, pp. 189-212.

20. Nicholas Mills, *The Triumph of Meanness: America's War Against Its Better Self* (Boston: Houghton Mifflin, 1997), p. 2.

21. National Institutes of Mental Health, *Priorities for Prevention Research at NIMH: A Report by the National Advisory Mental Health Council Workshop on Mental Disorders Prevention Research* (Washington, D.C.: National Institutes of Health, 1998).

22. Richard J. Bodine, Donna K. Crawford, and Fred Schrumpf, *Creating the Peaceable School: A Comprehensive Program for Teaching Conflict Resolution* (Champaign, Ill.: Research Press, 1995).

23. Denise C. Gottfredson, Gary D. Gottfredson, and Lois G. Hybl, "Managing Adolescent Behavior: A Multiyear, Multischool Study," *American Educational Research Journal,* vol. 30, 1993, pp. 179-215; J. David Hawkins, Howard J. Doueck, and Denise M. Lishner, "Changing Teaching Practices in Mainstream Classrooms to Improve Bonding and Behavior of Low Achievers," *American Educational Research Journal,* vol. 25, 1988, pp. 31-50; and Geoff Colvin, Edward J. Kameenui, and George Sugai, "Reconceptualizing Behavior Management and Schoolwide Discipline in General Education," *Education and Treatment of Children,* vol. 16, 1993, pp. 361-81.

24. T. Egan, "Where Rampages Begin: A Special Report: From Adolescent Angst to Shooting Up Schools," *New York Times,* 14 June 1998, p. 1.

25. Hill M. Walker and Herbert H. Severson, *Systematic Screening for Behavior Disorders (SSBD): User's Guide and Administration Manual,* 2nd ed. (Longmont, Calif.: Sopris West, 1992).

26. Kevin Dwyer, David Osher, and Cynthia Warger, *Early Warning, Timely Response: A Guide to Safe Schools* (Washington, D.C.: U.S. Department of Education, 1998).
27. Barbara Ries Wager, "No More Suspensions: Creating a Shared Ethical Culture," *Educational Leadership,* December 1992/January 1993, pp. 34-37.

POSTSCRIPT

Can a Zero-Tolerance Policy Lead to Safe Schools?

Skiba and Peterson are correct in asserting that there are no data available to allow us to evaluate whether or not a zero-tolerance policy leads to safer schools. What do we need to do to find such data? Ideally, we would like to rely on data from experimental studies of a sufficient number of schools, some adopting a zero-tolerance policy and others not. Experimental rather than correlational data would be preferred because the random assignment of schools to conditions that would be entailed by an experiment would ensure that the schools with and without a zero-tolerance policy were similar on important variables, such as the racial, ethnic, and socioeconomic make-up of the student body. Unfortunately, correlational studies often involve comparisons of very different types of schools; for example, zero-tolerance programs are more likely to be implemented in urban schools than rural schools, in schools serving poorer neighborhoods than affluent neighbor-hoods, etc. It really is not sufficient simply to compare what happens at a school before and after the implementation of a zero-tolerance policy. Often such programs are implemented after a highly publicized incident (e.g., a shooting). As a result, before and after differences *may* be due to the zero-tol-erance policy *or* differences may be due to increased parental awareness of the need to monitor their children, to increased caution on the part of stu-dents about being caught, to a greater police presence in and near the school, or even to a change of demographics in the schools (e.g., with more affluent parents opting to send their children to private schools).

But with what should a zero-tolerance policy be compared? Should schools with such a policy be compared to schools with no program of any kind for deal-ing with violence and unruly behavior? Probably not. It is not particularly com-pelling to conclude that zero tolerance is better than doing nothing. Instead, it would be more reasonable to compare the effectiveness of a zero-tolerance pol-icy with another, very different type of program for dealing with unacceptable behavior. Reasonable candidates would include programs that focus on keeping offending students in school and improving their behavior through counseling, self-esteem enhancement, and the like, as well as programs that focus on improv-ing school climate and the conflict resolution skills of all students. As Shanker points out, it is these programs that are seen as the approach of choice by many educators, so it is important to know which of the two options—zero tolerance or offender-focused intervention—is more effective.

On what variables or dimensions should we compare these programs to determine their relative effectiveness? What should we expect to change as a result of these programs? Certainly, we would want data on the rates of violence and other deviations from acceptable behavior. However, we might also want information about what happens to the students who offend. Are they "saved" by the policy, or do they engage in other problem behaviors? Do they drop out of school? Do they go on to commit more serious crimes out of school? Answers to these questions are relevant because if a school program can decrease all sorts of unacceptable behaviors, including criminal behaviors, it has to be considered a success for the society as a whole. In addition, we might also want to learn about the impact of the various programs on *nonoffending* students. Recall Shanker's statement that the zero-tolerance policy is motivated, in part, by the contention that disruptive students prevent their classmates from gaining full access to a high-quality education. This suggests that a successful program should lead to increases in the amount of actual instructional time that nonoffending students receive and, perhaps, to increases in their achievement. If zero tolerance does not lead to improvements for nonoffending students, is it really worth implementing in light of the ethical problems accompanying it?

There are many articles on both sides of the zero-tolerance issue, as well as many articles on alternatives to zero tolerance. Highly recommended articles on these alternatives are "Setting Limits in the Classroom," by Robert J. Mackenzie, *American Educator* (Fall 1997); "Making Violence Unacceptable," by Carole Remboldt, *Educational Leadership* (September 1998); "Waging Peace in Our Schools: Beginning With the Children," by Linda Lantieri, *Phi Delta Kappan* (January 1995); "Zero Tolerance for Zero Tolerance," by Richard L. Curwin and Allen N. Mendler, *Phi Delta Kappan* (October 1999); "Creating Peaceful Classrooms: Judicious Discipline and Class Meetings," by Mary Anne Raywid and Libby Oshiyama, *Phi Delta Kappan* (February 2000); "Feeling Scared," by Thomas J. Cottle, *Educational Horizons* (Fall 2004); and "Safety from the Inside Out: Rethinking Traditional Approaches," by Alfie Kohn, *Educational Horizons* (Fall 2004). An interesting comparison of several popular violence prevention programs is provided in "Evaluating the Effectiveness of School-Based Violence Prevention: Developmental Approaches," by Christopher Henrich, Joshua Brown, and J. Lawrence Aber, *Social Policy Report* (vol. 13, no. 3, 1999), published by the Society for Research in Child Development. Finally, a brief discussion of some of the evidence on the effectiveness of zero-tolerance policies can be found in "The Dilemma of Zero Tolerance," by John H. Holloway, *Educational Leadership* (December 2001/ January 2002).

ISSUE 18

Should U.S. Schools Be Evaluated Against Schools in Other Countries?

YES: Richard M. Haynes and Donald M. Chalker, from "World-Class Schools," *The American School Board Journal* (May 1997)

NO: Ernest G. Noack, from "Comparing U.S. and German Education: Like Apples and Sauerkraut," *Phi Delta Kappan* (June 1999)

ISSUE SUMMARY

YES: Richard M. Haynes and Donald M. Chalker, professors of administration, curriculum, and instruction, summarize the results of their analysis of the educational systems in 10 countries, including the United States and several countries considered by many to have successful, or "world-class," schools. They identify eight dimensions of difference between U.S. and world-class educational systems— dimensions that they feel explain the relative lack of success of U.S. schooling.

NO: Ernest G. Noack, a faculty member in education, argues that comparisons between the U.S. educational system and the educational systems of other countries are not useful because schooling serves a role in the United States that is different from that in other countries.

Much has been written about the declining achievement of students attending U.S. schools and about the superior performance of students from other industrialized nations, especially in Europe and Asia. The data on achievement in subjects such as mathematics and science are clear: No matter how one measures achievement, American students fare quite poorly in nearly every published cross-national comparison. Consider the following facts:

1. In a cross-national comparison involving 16 countries conducted by the Educational Testing Service in the early 1990s, U.S. fourth- to eighth-graders ranked 13th in science achievement and 15th in mathematics achievement.

2. In a comparison of mathematics achievement in 120 classrooms from Taiwan, Japan, and the United States, Harold W. Stevenson, James W. Stigler, and their colleagues found that more than 50 percent of the lowest-scoring first graders and 67 percent of the lowest-scoring fifth graders were from the United States. They also found that the highest-achieving U.S. classroom still scored lower on average than did the lowest-scoring classroom from Japan and nearly all of the classrooms from Taiwan.
3. In a comparison of first- and fifth-grade classrooms from Chicago and Beijing, China, Stevenson and Stigler found that nearly 98 percent of the Chinese students scored above the average of the U.S. students on a test of mathematical computation ability.

Early critics of such findings often responded that the superior achievement of Asian students was either (a) "superficial"—reflecting an emphasis on rote memorization in Asian schools—and would not translate into superiority on "meaningful" problems or (b) came at a high cost, a cost that included the sacrificing of the playful preschool years for a too-early emphasis on academics and the constant stress of too much schooling. There is little support for these early criticisms, however.

New concerns about the validity of cross-national comparisons of student achievement have arisen, however—concerns that are largely free of stereotypes, more thoughtful, and perhaps more difficult to resolve. These concerns emanate from the belief that the roles of schools and schooling differ in important respects in the United States compared to many other countries. It is suggested, for example, that U.S. schools are designed to meet not only the academic needs of students but many social and emotional needs as well, such as understanding of and respect for ethnic diversity. This is an important function of schooling, critics of cross-national comparisons argue, because the social problems that children face (e.g., violence, drugs, homelessness) have grown in number and complexity while families have become increasingly less able to deal with those issues because of factors such as divorce, the need for both parents to work full-time outside the home, etc. Critics of cross-national comparisons also point to the fact that schools in the United States educate a more diverse population of students—including students with minimal proficiency in English, students with special educational needs (e.g., cognitive disabilities), and students from economically disadvantaged backgrounds—than many other countries do.

The following selections offer two perspectives on the validity and utility of cross-national comparisons. In the first selection, Richard M. Haynes and Donald M. Chalker argue that such comparison is useful and valid. In the second selection, Ernest G. Noack concludes that cross-national comparisons of student achievement are not valid because schools play a unique social role in the United States. Although Noack's analysis focuses on comparisons between schools in the United States and in Germany, his arguments can be extended to comparisons between the United States and other European and Asian countries as well.

**Richard M. Haynes and
Donald M. Chalker**

 **YES**

World-Class Schools

French middle school students giggle when they hear that U.S. students either do no homework or do homework while watching television. Israeli students call multiple-choice tests "American tests"—a derogatory reference to how easy U.S. tests are, compared to Israeli essay tests. Many foreign high school exchange students find their native countries do not accept U.S. high school credits.

It is disturbing that U.S. schools are held in such low regard, especially when the United States has become a world leader largely because of its educated citizenry. Everyone, from the parents in your district to the President of the United States, wants world-class schools.... But what, exactly, are the characteristics of a world-class school?

In research for our two books, *World Class Schools: New Standards for Education and World Class Elementary Schools: An Agenda for Action*, we studied the education systems in Canada, France, Germany, Great Britain, Israel, Japan, New Zealand, South Korea, Taiwan, and the United States. We chose these countries for different reasons—France has the most widely copied school system, for instance, and Germany has the most productive European workforce—and we wanted to study the characteristics of their school systems. We reviewed literature, visited schools around the world, interviewed embassy personnel, and talked with students from each of the countries in our study. The result: data comparing the school systems on 35 variables (such as the amount of money spent on schools and the amount of time students spend on homework). We used that data to compile averages that we defined as "world-class standards" in education.

As we sorted through our findings, two truths became apparent: First, we realized that just because an education practice is world class doesn't mean Americans will want it. A powerful national education ministry is world class, but do most Americans want one?

Second, just because something is a U.S. practice doesn't mean it isn't world class. We need to remind ourselves: Which country has produced the most Nobel laureates in the 20th century? Today's U.S. schools also deal with diversity better than schools in any other country. And universal education is a noble American concept that several other countries have tried to emulate.

We've found Americans often have a distorted perception of schools and students in other countries. U.S. educators like to say, for instance, that Japanese students are under such terrific pressure that they commit suicide at alarming rates. The truth is that the Japanese suicide rate among school-aged students is roughly one-half that of the United States. In the primary grades, Japanese students typically spend 45 minutes concentrating on work, then take a 15-minute break to run and play. Japanese students commonly think of U.S. schools as "sweatshops" where students work constantly with no break.

Let's straighten out the misunderstandings—and define what we found are world-class standards in education:

World-class schools have a national curriculum and national testing.

Of the 10 countries we studied, only the United States and Canada have no national curriculum. Other countries have a rigorous national curriculum. The Eastern Pacific Rim countries of Japan, South Korea, and Taiwan offer top academic students the chance to excel at academic high schools where they take two science courses and two math courses per year during three years of high school. Singapore's students, who scored highest on the 1996 Third International Mathematics and Science Study (TIMSS) tests administered by the International Association for Evaluation of Educational Achievement (IEA), attend academic high schools where they take three math courses and three science courses per year.

In contrast, nearly 40 percent of the typical U.S. curriculum is dedicated to nonacademic subjects such as driver education and AIDS education, according to *Japan and United States Education Compared*, a 1992 Phi Delta Kappa publication. Otherwise, course titles vary only slightly among the 10 countries—with one notable exception: The United States is alone in not regularly offering some form of moral, religious, or values education. The emerging character education movement—definitely a world-class idea—might bring the United States in line with other countries.

Many Americans continue to resist a national curriculum—and expect individual states to come up with world-class schools. This doesn't make sense to us, especially when most standardized tests are nationally normed and textbooks are nationally marketed. If textbook manufacturers could design books for a single curriculum, the books could surely be cheaper and better. (In Japan, a high school science or math textbook costs about as much as a U.S. workbook.) A national curriculum would also level the playing field on national tests like the American College Testing program and the Scholastic Assessment Test.

And a national curriculum would certainly help children in our mobile society. One out of every six students attends three different schools by the third grade, and these are the children most likely to be left behind in math and reading skills. With a national curriculum, kids could use the same textbook and follow the same course of study as they move from school to school.

The dawning of the information age has brought a further argument for a national curriculum: Children browsing the web need the same skills and information whether they live in Cullowhee, N.C., or Fairbanks, Alaska.

The United States spends close to the world-class average on education.

The amount of gross national product (GNP) that is spent on education is an important measure of a nation's commitment to education. In 1995, the percentage of GNP spent on elementary and secondary education in the countries we studied ranged from a low of 2.4 percent in Germany to a high of 4.62 percent in Canada, according to the United Nations Educational, Scientific, and Cultural Organization (UNESCO). That same year, the United States spent 4.02 percent of its GNP on elementary and secondary education, according to UNESCO. The world-class average was 3.9 percent.

The U.S. per-pupil expenditure for K-12 education—which averaged $6,098 in the 1995-96 school year—is among the most generous in the world, but it includes more funds for transportation, food, custodians, and other services than other countries spend. Asian students, for example, walk or use public transportation, and German schools generally do not include cafeterias. In some countries, teachers and students clean their own classrooms rather than rely on janitors. The United States also spends more on special education and extracurricular activities, such as marching bands and football teams.

When you strip away the extras, it's almost impossible to figure accurately how much the United States spends on education, but it's safe to guess that we are in the mid-range of what other countries spend. It's not unreasonable for a rich country to provide these extras, but communities should know what they're paying for and resist comparing U.S. education costs to those in other countries that don't provide the extras.

U.S. students spend less time in school and on school work than students in other countries.

The U.S. school year of 180 days is considerably below the world-class average of approximately 201 days. This means that, over 13 years of school, the United States provides more than one full year less schooling than the world-class average.

Some U.S. educators seem to consider 180 a sacred number that can never be changed. But we should look to France, where the school year was recently lengthened, and Japan, where it was shortened. Other countries are examining each other's school systems and copying what works.

Students in other countries often spend more than 13 years on their basic education. There is a clear international trend toward providing more early childhood education. New Zealand reports half of all 2-year-olds are in preschool. In France, almost 100 percent of 3-year-olds are enrolled in preschool.

In Eastern Pacific Rim countries, students continue their studies after regular school hours by enrolling in private "cram schools," where elementary school students receive instruction in the arts while older students receive additional preparation for competitive high school entrance exams.

World-class schools have larger class sizes than U.S. schools.

Very large classes are the norm in many countries. Korea—whose students placed second on the 1996 TIMSS math test—reports 93 percent of its eighth-graders are in classes of 41 students or more. In first-place Singapore, 18 percent were in such large classes; 72 percent were in classes of 31 to 40.

At the middle-school level, U.S. educators generally consider 30 students the borderline between large and small classes. Sixteen percent of U.S. eighth-grade math teachers have classes with more than 30 students, according to the IEA. In the other countries we studied, an average of 27 percent reported such large classes.

As any teacher can tell you, tolerable class size depends on student behavior. The countries with large classes generally have students who are well-behaved and motivated. The presence of lazy or misbehaving students in U.S. classrooms partially explains the need for smaller classes. If, by some miracle, better behaved and more serious students started showing up in U.S. classrooms, larger classes might be possible (though not necessarily desirable).

World-class students turn off television and turn on to homework.

World-class schools use homework—which is free—to increase learning time. Many U.S. teachers lack formal training in the use of homework, and many U.S. parents rebel at the idea that students should do homework consistently. In 1996, U.S. eighth-graders averaged 2.3 hours per day on homework, slightly less than the international average of 2.4 hours, according to IEA. Singapore students spent a whopping 4.6 hours hitting the books.

In 1996, U.S. eighth-graders spent an average of 2.6 hours a day watching television. French students averaged the least amount of time—1.5 hours—in front of the set, and Israeli students spent the most time, averaging 3.3 hours a day.

World-class school governance includes strategic planning and site-based management.

World-class schools receive direction from national agencies, but parents elect school governors to make decisions in individual schools. In our visits abroad, we have been impressed with how well these local governors, or trustees, know their teachers, parents, and children. They work on school improvement, provide feedback, and sometimes even make hiring and firing decisions.

The schools are usually led by "heads"—teachers chosen because of their outstanding performance in the classroom—and many continue to teach while they handle administrative tasks. (One Canadian head told us he would quit if he had to be "nothing but a paper-pusher" and couldn't teach at least two hours a day.) This sends a powerful message about the importance of teaching and learning.

The heads usually receive no training in school management until after they assume their administrative position—which means they come to the job with little or no knowledge of school finance, law, special education, or management issues. The United States clearly does a better job, in our opinion, of preparing teachers to become school administrators.

Teachers in other countries receive more respect than they do in the United States.

In Japan, it is considered a status symbol to have a teacher live in your neighborhood, and the government offers teachers low or no-interest mortgages on their homes. In Taiwan, teachers don't pay income tax, and Confucius' birthday is celebrated as Teachers Day, a national holiday on Sept. 29.

Instead of respect, U.S. teachers—who undergo longer training than teachers in most other countries—find a morass of state certification laws that makes moving across state lines and getting a job difficult. A national system of teacher licensure would help U.S. teachers—who are nearly as mobile as U.S. students— find positions when they move.

An education ethic permeates other countries, encouraging students to try hard and do well in school.

In every country that delivers a world-class education, communities and parents exhibit a high regard for education, a healthy respect for teachers, and a holy regard for learning—all key ingredients in an "education ethic" that creates positive expectations for student learning. Unfortunately, the United States lags badly in this area.

In world-class schools, the students are motivated and ready to learn. In the United States and Canada, too many students ignore educational opportunities and work instead at disrupting other students. These disruptive students must be removed, for safety's sake, and often are placed in alternative schools. Many other countries avoid this expense and distraction by having a strong education ethic that encourages students to try hard and do well in school.

This education ethic begins with parents. The difference in attitude is probably most evident when parents are called in to discuss a problem at school. When Japanese school officials call parents to school because a child is disruptive, the parents typically ask, "What's wrong with my child?" In the United States, the parent often asks, "What's wrong with this school?"

Historically, mothers in Japan and Taiwan have been intensely involved in their children's learning environment. Many Japanese mothers, for instance, attend their child's school and take notes when the child is ill. Both parents are expected to come to school to observe a child's work habits.

Recent research shows the benefits of parental involvement in American schools. In their research for *Running in Place: How American Families are Faring in a Changing Economy and an Individualistic Society,* Nicholas Zill and Christine Nord asked parents in all 50 states if they attended parent meetings, school events, or volunteer activities. Their study defined "high-involvement" parents as those who participated in all three activities. "Moderate-involvement" parents participated in two of the three categories, and "low involvement" parents participated in one activity or none at all. Their findings:

Students from low-involvement families were twice as likely to be in the lower half of their class as students from high-involvement families. Students from low-involvement families also experienced more discipline problems.

These results don't surprise anyone who's spent time in a school. But they do explain, at least partially, why many American students lack motivation to do well in school. The United States has more splintered families than any other country we studied. In 1990, the U.S. divorce rate was about double the average of other countries in our study. (Indeed, some countries reported a divorce rate as low as 1 percent.) Single parents might do an outstanding job of preparing children for school, but two parents can devote twice as much time to supporting education.

The education ethic of the parents is probably the key difference between a world-class school and one that's so-so. A University of Michigan study looked at Indo-Chinese refugee children who arrived with no knowledge of the language or culture in the 1980s. The children were scattered in different schools throughout the United States, and two years later, the children were earning world-class scores in science and mathematics and were on grade level in language. How could refugee students, who had so much catching up to do, score higher than other students at the same U.S. schools?

The difference, of course, was in their education ethic. The refugee students worked harder, and their parents supported them, believing that education would lead to success in life. U.S. schools can—and do—deliver a world-class education, but students have to be willing to work at it.

We understand that schools can't change cultural mores—and schools shouldn't be blamed for the inevitable results of dysfunctional parents and communities. But school leaders can try to instill an education ethic in new parents. You might start with programs that improve parenting skills, maybe by bringing the parents of preschool youngsters to school and teaching them how to prepare their preschoolers for the years ahead.

It will not be easy to create world-class schools—or communities with a commitment to an education ethic—but it is gratifying that the United States is finally turning its attention to this need. Just as good teachers are adept at borrowing and using the best ideas of other teachers, school leaders should borrow and use the best ideas in the world. Our children deserve no less.

NO

Ernest G. Noack

Comparing U.S. and German Education

How often do we hear or read disparaging remarks about American students' performances on standardized achievement tests, especially in comparison with their Asian or European peers? Yet those comparisons are as useful as comparing apples with sauerkraut, or as misleading as using gas mileage to compare a compact car with a full-sized sedan, family van, ¾-ton truck, or motor home. If all one wants is a vehicle with the best gas mileage, then the compact or subcompact car may indeed be the best choice. But what if, along with good gas mileage, one also wants increased safety, comfort, or load-carrying ability—then which vehicle is best? Similarly, which education system is best should depend on which educational features and outcomes are most important to us. To use only standardized academic tests to evaluate the comprehensive American public education is like using only gas mileage to evaluate sedans, trucks, and motor homes. Academics is a very important component, but not the whole of American education. In Europe, however, academics is the whole of education. The German system provides a good example.

From Firsthand Experience

I recently lived in Germany for one school year. This situation enabled me to visit a few of the country's public schools repeatedly and to study its education system through official channels. My ailing mother, whom I was visiting in the Black Forest in southwest Germany, coincidentally lived not far from the two high schools in Tuttlingen, with which my school district near Seattle had maintained a thriving GAPP (German American Partnership Program) student and teacher exchange for more than 10 years. As a high school principal and district curriculum director, I had formed strong professional ties with the Tuttlingen teachers. Consequently, they invited me into their schools not as an outsider but as a trusted colleague. I visited their classrooms, sat in on faculty meetings, and attended special events.

The public education campus in urban Tuttlingen consists of two adjoining grade 5-13 high schools (one is somewhat college-prep oriented, the other more standard), one grade K-4 primary school (two others lie at the city's periphery), and one grade 10-12 vocational/technical school. One gorgeous special education school (for students aged 3 to 21) is also located in the city; its principal and I have shared a lifelong friendship, dating back to our fathers' friendship in East Prussia in the 1930s. In addition, I became quite familiar with the regular primary, middle, and high schools in Koenigsfeld, a quaint town in the Black Forest in which my parents resettled in 1970. My dad had served the small community as its music director, and through him I had ready access to their schools as well.

I also have firsthand knowledge of the education system in the former Communist East Germany, having attended school there until fourth grade, when my family escaped to West Germany. Ultimately, in 1956, we settled in Chicago, where I resumed my education without knowing a word of English (we had been taught Russian, not English, in East Germany). No ESL [English as a second language] program existed in Chicago, nor was any teacher or student willing to teach me English. So I had to learn English on my own to survive—to reduce the number of times I was beaten up by classmates and openly ridiculed by teachers for being a "Nazi" (which was still synonymous with "German" back then). I also have some limited knowledge of education in Nazi Germany through my brothers, who are 11 and 13 years my senior. One was a product of the Nazis' vocational apprenticeship program and the other of their college-prep program.

Furthermore, I keep up with current education in Germany and the European Union through subscriptions to official education publications.[1] And my ongoing correspondence with several German teachers and former exchange students keeps me informed about how government policy translates into daily operation.

As a result of all my sources, I consider the German education system to be quite representative of Continental Europe. In comparison with the American education system, however, the German system is quite different. Let us examine those differences.

Historical Foundations and Purpose

Initially the purposes for public schools in America were to teach children to read and write and to enable them as adults to participate knowledgeably in our democracy and to work productively on an assembly line. Since then our schools have taken on many other functions beyond the teaching of the three R's, such as melting-pot socialization (the blending of diverse ethnicities, races, creeds, and cultures); recreation and avocation (extracurricular clubs and sports); vocational education (small classes and often expensive equipment); special-interest classes (art, music, theater); special education (including institutional-type care with extremely small staff/student ratios); health and safety education (from AIDS and drug education to drivers' education); and food service and student transportation. None of these programs or services are provided in Germany or elsewhere in Europe. Most of these additional functions in the American public schools are extremely costly and draw on the same human and fiscal resources that also support the academic mission of the American schools.

By comparison, public education in Germany has pursued a much narrower mission all along. Initially reading and writing were taught to prepare the population to read the Bible, and during this century academic skills have been taught to prepare students for careers (whether blue or white collar). Only in the last 15 to 20 years have the German public schools taken on the responsibility for special education (which until then was the responsibility of medical and state institutions or the home) and the responsibility for socialization (to assimilate a growing 12% Turkish, Muslim, non-Western student population). Extracurricular activities—from music to sports—remain exclusively the responsibility of the communities, churches, and amateur athletic associations. Vocational training continues to be primarily the responsibility of business and industry. Students must rely on private or public transportation and food services. And health and safety issues are the responsibility of HMOs, government, churches, private institutions, and the home.

School Structures

Kindergarten—although a German invention—is voluntary, and some students may not start school until age 7. But primary education in German schools appears very similar to that in the U.S.: neighborhood-based and self-contained. However, starting in fifth grade, students and parents may select the school of their choice. The school-type options are the main school, the intermediate school, the college-prep school, and the new comprehensive school. The program of studies in grades 5 and 6 is similar in all of them. But in seventh grade students may start to specialize in career-prep programs according to their interests and abilities, an approach that is more similar to colleges than to public schools in America.

The main school (*Hauptschule*) was once the choice of half of the students, but now only one-third choose it. From grades 5 to 9 or 10, students in the main school fulfill the state's minimum education requirements and prepare to enter a vocational/trades apprenticeship program. During their on-the-job apprenticeships (which will be described later), students continue to receive about 10 hours of relevant language and math training weekly. The main school's curriculum adequately prepares students to become apprentice auto-body repairers, bakers, butchers, carpenters, fast-food cooks and servers, flower arrangers, hair stylists, or janitors or to take any other jobs that require only minimal language and math skills.

Or students may enroll in an intermediate school (*Realschule*), which once was the choice of one-third of the students and is today the choice of one-fourth. From grades 5 to 10 students can fulfill the state's minimum education requirements and prepare to enter any two- or three-year apprenticeship program. The intermediate school curriculum is somewhat more comprehensive and more difficult than that of the main school, including more math and science and four to six years of one foreign language. It prepares students for career apprenticeships that require relatively more language or math skills—for example, apprenticeships as auto mechanics, bank tellers, electricians, health-care attendants, repair/service technicians, sales clerks, secretaries, and workers in any jobs that use computers.

Or students may select a college-prep school (*Gymnasium*)—once the choice of only a fifth of the students, now the choice of one-third, and soon to be the choice of half, according to the trend. (An interesting side note: the designation *Gymnasium* is derived from the Greek school, which equally emphasized the development of both the mind and the body. Whereas in America the term "gymnasium" came to represent exclusively the development of the physical body, in Germany *Gymnasium* came to represent exclusively the development of the mind.) From grades 5 to 12 or 13, students can study in various college-prep and white-collar-career-prep programs. Most of the *Gymnasiums* offer specialized programs, such as math and physical sciences, natural sciences, social sciences and languages, health and physical education, and visual and performing arts. Students select the most appropriate *Gymnasium* based on their career interest—for example, architecture, business, education, engineering, law, medicine, or science.

Also, in many large cities a comprehensive school (*Gesamtschule*) has been jump-started but currently accounts for fewer than 10% of the students. Like the comprehensive American school, which serves as its model, this school represents the government's hope for the future of Germany: an amalgamation of Germans and non-European foreigners, particularly in some metropolitan areas where Turkish Muslims exceed 50% of the population.

Finally, there is the special school (*Sonderschule*) for all handicapped students who could not succeed without special assistance in any of the schools above. Unlike some special education schools in the U.S. 20 years ago, these schools are first-class operations. Strong parent lobbies keep these programs from being integrated into the regular schools.

Common Foundations

Four generalizations can be made about the German system of school specialization.

1. German teachers are totally committed to grouping students by interest and ability, first by school and then again by curriculum program (similar to American higher education). The concept of teaching heterogeneous groups does not fit into their learning theory. Consequently, their profession vehemently resists the government's attempt to introduce the American-style comprehensive school and heterogeneous grouping.

2. The concept of specialized schools and easy student access to them is thoroughly feasible in Germany. Open enrollment (on a first-come, first-served basis) anywhere within a state is possible in Germany and Europe because of the close proximity of towns and because of efficient public transportation between them. Even the most remote hamlet is located only a few miles from the nearest city and is connected by well-scheduled feeder buses and trains. Passes provide students free or reduced-rate fares. Also, schools are situated inside the cities and close to stores, rather than in remote suburbs. Hence, even the youngest students can easily and safely commute to the most specialized school in 30 minutes or less.

3. The transfer of students from one school or program to another is quite flexible. Although students are taught to be career-oriented as early as grade 7, a student may change his or her pre-career major at any grade level. However, the later the student does so, the more he or she will bear a cost in extra time needed to make up any deficient prerequisites—just as would be the case in an American college. Yet "all roads lead to Rome"; some are just more direct. Upon graduation from any intermediate high school or college-prep school, a student can enroll in any specialized college. (Incidentally, all higher education is tuition-free in Germany.) Higher education schools (*Hochschulen*) are as specialized as the public schools and are geared to virtually any profession. There are teachers' colleges, law colleges, dental and medical and veterinary colleges, performing and visual arts colleges, religious colleges, and technical colleges (for architects, builders, computer programmers, engineers, and so on). They grant only master's degrees, as they prepare the "master" professional—the highest level of the three-tier system: apprentice, journeyman, and master. This tier applies to all blue-collar trades as well as white-collar professions. The comprehensive *Universitaet* is another option open to all, but it is rooted exclusively in doctoral programs for research and teaching in the liberal arts, mathematics, and sciences.

4. Classes are spread over 12 months and six days of the week. The class schedule repeats by the week, not by the day. For instance, a student may not have a first-period class on Mondays or afternoon classes on Wednesdays but may have morning classes on Saturdays. A flexible schedule consists of classes varying from 30 minutes to two hours (e.g., a lab). Although school is in session for 12 months (save for a short summer vacation and several more holidays and mini-vacations than we have in the U.S.), in terms of class time the German school year is equivalent to our 180 days. All the German curricula are continuously sequential (e.g., grade 5 "math" to grade 12 "math" and grade 5 "science" to grade 12 "science") rather than sequenced in parts as in the U.S. (e.g., algebra/geometry/calculus, biology/chemistry/physics). Written and verbal comprehensive final exams—similar to those given for graduate degrees in the U.S.—determine a student's graduation from high school.

Student Responsibilities

As stated before, from grade 5 on, German students experience education that is closer to an American college than to K-12 education. What they do during the hours when they have no class is up to them. The school has never assumed its role to be in loco parent is. It is only for student safety that some restrictions on off-campus student mobility are now being implemented in schools that are located in the largest metropolitan areas. To have access to resources, a student must go to a public library; the school does not duplicate the community library. Heavy homework is expected of and done by students daily, outside of school. In most ways German students assume much greater responsibility for independent study than do their U.S. peers.

To still their hunger or thirst during breaks, German students frequent a nearby grocery store, fast-food place, bakery, restaurant, or butcher shop serving delicious sandwiches, hot or cold. (Remember that schools are located inside cities, close to stores.) Students either bike to school or take public buses or trains. Students' use of automobiles is extremely rare because 1) the cost of operating a car in Europe is outrageous, in comparison to the U.S.; 2) the minuscule school parking lots barely serve the staff's needs; and 3) students may not earn a driver's license until age 18. Hence, student parking lots are filled with bicycles, not cars.

Teacher Responsibilities

The public teaching profession in Germany also has more in common with higher education than with K-12 education in the U.S. On a part-time basis master teachers assume total responsibility for the training of teacher candidates and novice teachers, for the evaluation of teachers regarding contract renewal (tenure) and promotion, for curriculum development and the selection of instructional materials, and for campus administration. By law even teachers in these leadership positions must continue to teach at least 25% to 50% of the time; they remain teachers foremost. The concept of full-time administrators or coordinators is alien to Germans. Each cohort of students (a class of 20 to 25) elects one of its teachers as its class advisor and liaison to the rest of the faculty. There are no separate positions for counselor, librarian, or "vice" principal. Only the most serious and criminal-like student infractions are referred to the part-time principal (called director, leader, or rector), who may in turn summon the police.

Teachers in Germany are relatively better paid and respected than their American colleagues. A recent poll ranked teachers second behind judges on the "most-respected" list of professionals. Teachers earn that respect and salary. Although by contract teachers are not required to be in school except when they are teaching classes, most maintain long hours. Those who serve as class advisors make themselves available to their advisees at almost any time of day.

The teaching profession adheres to its own professional hierarchy, which is similar to that of the professional guilds (apprentice, journeyman, and master) and that of higher education in the U.S. (assistant professor, associate professor, and full professor). Upon graduation from a teachers college, successful completion of student teaching, and passage of the state's certification test, a novice teacher is employed for two years as an apprentice teacher under the continuous tutelage of a master teacher. The apprentice teacher may earn passage to the second tier of independent teaching and tenure as a civil servant (equivalent to journeyman or associate rank) once he or she has received advanced training at a teachers college, on-site staff development, a recommendation from the mentor teacher, and successful evaluations from outside master teachers and has passed the second state certification exam. Many teachers stay at this level for the remainder of their careers.

However, a multi-pronged career ladder awaits those who seek higher responsibilities. After several more years of teaching, three-day observations by two outside master teachers, passage of a third state certification exam, and nominations from in-building master teachers, the journeyman teacher may qualify to become a master teacher. (At the *Gymnasium* level most teachers who aspire to this highest rank will also have earned a doctorate along the way.) This highest rank qualifies a teacher to serve part time in regional or statewide leadership capacities in curriculum development, selection of instructional materials, professional growth and development, teacher evaluation, or campus administration.

State Responsibilities

Each of Germany's 16 states assumes exclusive responsibility for the education within it. Although each state is divided into regional education administrative units, these are not independent or intermediate school districts as we know them in the U.S. Each state is fully responsible for the salaries of its teachers, who are civil servants in the state. A committee of subject-matter master teachers develops curriculum by subject matter and grade level for the entire state. (This is an example of the lure to achieve master teacher status.) The office of the state minister of education provides coordination, communication, and consultation. Likewise, the promotion of teachers to the independent journeyman or master ranks is conducted exclusively by master teachers (who are never from the school of the teacher being evaluated). Teachers who serve as part-time campus administrators report to area administrators, who work under the state minister of education. The lay public plays no role at all in German public education—again similar to American higher education.

Community Responsibilities

A community's responsibility, in turn, is to provide and maintain the educational facilities and to supply the operating costs, including those for instructional materials (which the faculty selects from a state-approved list). The schools are a function of the local government—no different from the police department, fire department, or parks and recreation department. It is also the community organizations, not the schools, that fill the a vocational needs (from athletics to music and theater) of all residents—children and adults. It is quite common for a town band, orchestra, chorus, or theater group to include people of all ages, from young children to senior citizens. Facilities such as an auditorium, a gym, a track, and even the library are used by both the school and the community, but make no mistake about it: these facilities are owned and operated by and for the entire community. Don't look for any "school" athletic teams or cheerleaders; they don't exist. Only the classroom building per se constitutes "the school."

Business and Industry Responsibilities

By far the greatest cost saving to German public education is the comprehensive responsibility that industry and business assume for vocational education in Germany. The public schools educate children in pre-career skills such as reading, writing, computing, thinking, and responsible work habits. Thereafter, the craft guilds and business and industry take over the responsibility for on-site vocational training. A few vocational/technical schools exist primarily to prepare students for technical college.

Most important, by law one cannot apply for a job without job certification—not even at a fast-food place, not even part-time! The implication of this law for schools is virtually a 0% dropout rate. A student must be enrolled in either an apprenticeship program or a college to learn a trade. Those who select professions that require formal education past high school will also serve apprenticeships or internships in their professions after graduation from college.

The school/employer/apprenticeship relation is quite symbiotic in nature. The initial matching of a high school student's choice of trade/vocation and an employer's needs for apprenticeship candidates is coordinated through the public school. The school ranks the students on each career/trade interest list according to their past performance in school (including academics, attendance, and attitude). Prospective employers then interview the top students from the list to select their apprentices. This process provides motivation for students to do well in school, regardless of their trade/career interests. The employer gets to hire part-time apprentices at below minimum wage. The apprentice in turn is trained on the most up-to-date equipment by up-to-date journeymen or masters—something no public or vocational school could match. The apprentice also earns some wages while studying and is almost always guaranteed permanent employment as a journeyman, once he or she completes the apprenticeship satisfactorily and passes the on-site state certification tests. Apprentices continue to spend an average of 10 hours a week in school (any combination of evenings and Saturdays) to learn more language and math, but all in the context of the job—i.e., the language and math skills they need for a particular trade.

Conclusion

From this brief look at the German education system, it should be clear that there is little point in comparing the performances of German and American students on any standardized achievement test, because public education in Germany fulfills a vastly different role from public education in America. This can probably be said of any other country's public education as well. An evaluation of any education system is meaningful only if it relates its students' performances to its own mission and goals.

Note

1. *Bildung und Wissenschaft/Education and Science* (Inter Nationes e.V.), issues 1-4, 1998.

POSTSCRIPT

Should U.S. Schools Be Evaluated Against Schools in Other Countries?

Scholars on both sides of this issue generally do not dispute the fact that students in U.S. schools do more poorly on measures of academic achievement than do students attending schools in many other nations, such as Japan, China, and Germany. Instead, they disagree on whether or not it is fair to expect similar achievement in subjects such as science and mathematics because U.S. schools have a much broader agenda than do the educational systems in other countries. Opponents of cross-national comparisons argue that the U.S. educational agenda includes a more diverse set of goals for any individual student (i.e., the need to educate the "whole" child) and that the United States aims to educate a more diverse student population than other nations.

Implicit in Noack's argument is the notion that shortcomings in the achievement of U.S. students cannot be attributed simply to the *quality* of the instruction they receive in school. But is there any empirical evidence to support this notion? Is there evidence that factors besides instructional quality account for the lower achievement seen in U.S. students? In fact, there is such evidence in the area of mathematics. First, children in the United States begin school with less knowledge about mathematics than do students in China. Second, parents in the United States are more likely than parents in many other countries to believe that mathematics achievement is determined by innate ability rather than by experience. These findings raise the possibility that U.S. students receive far less support for their mathematics learning at home and, thus, are less prepared for and less invested in the mathematics instruction they receive at school than are their peers in Europe and Asia.

Can the achievement gap be explained entirely by such factors? Or is there room for improvement in the instruction that students in the United States receive in mathematics, science, and other traditional academic domains? In fact, there is evidence that instruction, at least in the domain of mathematics, could be improved by adopting some of the procedures and attitudes characteristic of schooling in Japan. James W. Stigler and his colleagues, for example, have found that teachers in the United States emphasize discrete skills rather than "deep" understanding; they assume that mathematics will be uninteresting to most students; they present skills incrementally, a little piece at a time; they assign problems that ensure success quickly and with little error; and they demonstrate how to solve problems before allowing students to solve them on their own. In contrast, Stigler found that teachers in Japan assume mathematics is inherently interesting; they present difficult problems that ensure that students will struggle; they seldom demonstrate solutions for students; and they encourage group discussion of the relative advantages and disadvantages of different approaches to the problems. Stigler argues that adoption of such pedagogical practices by U.S. teachers would help to close the achievement gap, even in the face of other systemic barriers to high levels of mathematics achievement.

Readers interested in cross-national comparisons of academic achievement can turn to *World-Class Elementary Schools: An Agenda for Action* by Richard M. Haynes and Donald M. Chalker (Rowman & Littlefield, 1997) and *The Learning Gap: Why Our Schools Are Failing and What We Can Learn From Japanese and Chinese Education* by Harold W. Stevenson and James W. Stigler (Simon & Schuster, 1992). There are also several interesting and highly readable articles that provide insight into the pedagogical practices of other countries, including "Cooperative Education: Lessons From Japan," by Marcia Baris-Sanders, *Phi Delta Kappan* (April 1997); "Teaching Is a Cultural Activity," by James W. Stigler and James Hiebert, *American Educator* (Winter 1998); "Comparative Research and Public Policy: From Authoritarianism to Democracy," by José Joaquín Brunner, *Peabody Journal of Education* (Issue 1, 2005); and "Integrated Curriculum in the Context of Challenges to Middle Schooling: An Australian Perspective," by Kay Whitehead, *Middle School Journal* (March 2005). A paper that continues the theme of the selection by Noack is "A Closer Examination of American Education," by David Aviel, *Childhood Education* (Spring 1997). Readers interested in the barriers that U.S. educators face can turn to "Mathematics Achievement of Chinese, Japanese, and American Children: Ten Years Later," by Harold W. Stevenson, C. Chen, and S. Y. Lee, *Science* (January 1, 1993) and "Even Before Formal Instruction, Chinese Children Outperform American Children in Mental Addition," by D. C. Geary et al., *Cognitive Development* (vol. 8, 1993), pp. 517-529.

Contributors to This Volume

EDITORS

LEONARD ABBEDUTO, a developmental psychologist, is a professor of educational psychology at the University of Wisconsin–Madison. He is also associate director for behavioral sciences of the Waisman Center on Mental Retardation and Human Development at the university. He has authored more than 65 articles, chapters, and reviews, and he has written two books, including *Guide to Human Development for Future Educators,* with Stephen N. Elliott (McGraw-Hill, 1998), which is a text designed to demonstrate how research and theory in developmental psychology can be applied in the classroom. Professor Abbeduto is well known for his research on language development, families, and developmental disabilities and mental retardation, which has been supported by several grants from the National Institutes of Health. He has served on the editorial boards of the *American Journal on Mental Retardation* and the *Journal of Speech and Hearing Research.* For more than a decade, he has directed an NIH-funded program designed to train future researchers interested in the behavioral aspects of developmental disabilities. In 1996, he was recognized with the Emil A. Steiger Award for distinguished teaching at the University of Wisconsin-Madison. Professor Abbeduto earned his Ph.D. from the University of Illinois at Chicago in 1982. He has two sons, Jackson and Mack, who are in high school. He credits his sons with teaching him about the importance of the controversies in educational psychology for the lives of America's children.

STAFF

Larry Loeppke   Managing Editor
Jill Peter   Senior Developmental Editor
Nichole Altman   Developmental Editor
Lori Church   Permissions Coordinator
Beth Kundert   Production Manager
Jane Mohr   Project Manager
Kari Voss   Lead Typesetter
Luke David   eContent Coordinator

AUTHORS

LAURA VAN ZANDT ALLEN is on the faculty in the department of education at Trinity University in San Antonio, Texas. She is the author of many articles on the middle school curriculum and the education of adolescents.

JOSEPHINE ARCE is an assistant professor in the Department of Elementary Education at San Francisco State University in San Francisco, California.

JANICE M. BAKER is assistant professor of special education and clinical services at Indiana University of Pennsylvania. Her professional interests focus on services for students with learning disabilities.

KEITH BAKER is an education consultant living in Heber City, Utah. He is coauthor, with Christine H. Rossell, of *Bilingual Education in Massachusetts: The Emperor Has No Clothes* (Pioneer Institute for Public Policy Research, 1996).

BRUCE J. BIDDLE is a professor of social psychology and director of the Center for Research in Social Behavior at the University of Missouri in Columbia, Missouri. He is also editor of the journal *Social Psychology of Education.*

MARILYN BIZAR holds a doctorate in reading and language education, and she serves on the graduate faculty of National-Louis University in Chicago, Illinois. She is coauthor of several books, including *Methods That Matter: Six Structures for Best Practice Classrooms,* with Harvey Daniels (Stenhouse, 1998).

JOHN T. BRUER is president of the James S. McDonnell Foundation in St. Louis, Missouri. He is the author of *The Myth of the First Three Years: A New Understanding of Early Brain Development and Lifelong Learning* (Free Press, 1999).

R. W. BURNISKE is an assistant instructor in the Computer Writing and Research Lab in the Division of Rhetoric and Composition at the University of Texas in Austin, Texas. He is the author of *Literacy in the Cyberage: Composing Ourselves Online* (SkyLight Professional Development, 2000) and coauthor, with Lowell Monke, of *Breaking Down the Digital Walls: Learning to Teach in a Post-Modern World* (State University of New York Press, 2000).

CAROL CORBETT BURRIS is the principal of South Side High School in Rockville Centre, New York. She has written articles for *Education Week, Phi Delta Kappan,* and other periodicals.

DONALD M. CHALKER is head of administration, curriculum, and instruction at Western Carolina University in Cullowhee, North Carolina. He is coauthor, with Richard M. *Haynes, of World Class Elementary Schools: An Agenda for Action* (Technomic, 1997).

HARVEY DANIELS is a senior faculty member in the Center for City Schools at National-Louis University in Chicago, Illinois. His books include *Best Practice: New Standards for Teaching and Learning in America's Schools,* coauthored with Steven Zemelman and Arthur A. Hyde (Heinemann,

1998) and *Literature Circles: Voice and Choice in the Student-Centered Classroom* (Stenhouse, 1994).

TASHAWNA K. DUNCAN is a licensed psychologist, a licensed school psychologist, and a nationally certified school psychologist with more than 10 years of experience working with children, adolescents, and families in clinical and educational settings. She holds masters degrees in elementary education and school psychology from the University of Florida, where she received her doctoral training.

CAROL S. DWECK is a professor of psychology at Columbia University. Her research has focused on self-esteem, motivation, and academic achievement, and she is the author of *Self-Theories: Their Role in Motivation, Personality, and Development* (Psychology Press, 1999).

HOWARD GARDNER is a professor of education and codirector of Project Zero at the Harvard Graduate School of Education and an adjunct professor of neurology at the Boston University School of Medicine. A prolific author, his publications include *The Disciplined Mind: What All Students Should Understand* (Simon & Schuster, 1999) and *Extraordinary Minds* (Basic Books, 1998).

EDWARD H. HAERTEL is a professor of education at Stanford University in Stanford, California. He is coeditor, with Thomas James and Henry M. Levin, of *Comparing Public and Private Schools, Vol. 2: School Achievement* (Taylor & Francis, 1987).

MARIALE M. HARDIMAN is the principal of Roland Park Elementary/Middle School in Baltimore, Maryland. She is the author of *Connecting Brain Research With Effective Teaching: The Brain-Targeted Teaching Model* (Scarecrow Press, 2003).

RICHARD M. HAYNES is an associate professor and director of student teaching in the Department of Educational Leadership and Foundations at Western Carolina University in Cullowhee, North Carolina, where he teaches courses in supervision and comparative education. He earned his Ph.D. in educational administration and supervision from Duke University.

E. D. HIRSCH, JR., is a professor at the University of Virginia, Charlottesville, and president and founder of the Core Knowledge Foundation. He is the author or coauthor of numerous publications, including *The Schools We Need: And Why We Don't Have Them* (Doubleday, 1999) and, with John Holdren, *What Your First Grader Needs to Know: Fundamentals of a Good First-Grade Education,* rev. ed. (Dell, 1998).

KRISTEN N. KEMPLE is an associate professor in the School of Teaching and Learning at the University of Florida. She has taught young children in a wide variety of early childhood programs, including Head Start, a parent cooperative, and a teen parenting center. She holds a Ph.D. from the University of Texas at Austin.

PERRY D. KLEIN is on the faculty at the University of Western Ontario.

ALFIE KOHN writes and lectures widely on education and human behavior. His books include *Punished by Rewards* (Houghton Mifflin, 1993) and *Beyond Discipline: From Compliance to Community* (Association for Supervision and Curriculum Development, 1996).

THOMAS LICKONA, a developmental psychologist, is a professor of education at the State University of New York College at Cortland and director of the Center for the Fourth and Fifth Rs (Respect and Responsibility). He is a member of the board of directors of the Character Education Partnership, a national coalition working to promote character development in schools and communities. He is a frequent consultant to schools across the United States, and he has also lectured in Canada, Japan, Switzerland, Ireland, and Latin America on teaching moral values in the school and at home.

MARCIA C. LINN is a professor of cognition and education at the University of California, Berkeley. She earned her Ph.D. in educational psychology from Stanford University in 1970. Her publications include *Computers, Teachers, Peers: Science Learning Partners,* coauthored with Sherry Hsi (Lawrence Erlbaum, 1999).

G. REID LYON is chief of the Child Development and Behavior Branch of the National Institute of Child Health and Human Development, National Institutes of Health and Human Services, in Bethesda, Maryland. He is coeditor, with Judith M. Rumsey, of *Neuroimaging: A Window to the Neurological Foundations of Learning and Behavior in Children* (Paul H. Brookes, 1996).

WILLIAM J. MATHIS is superintendent of Rutland Southeast Supervisory Union, a school district in Vermont.

ELEANOR T. MIGLIORE is an associate professor in the department of education and director of school psychology at Trinity University.

D. MONTY NEILL is executive director of the National Center for Fair and Open Testing (FairTest) in Cambridge, Massachusetts.

SARAH COTTON NELSON was director of grants and research at the Dallas Women's Foundations in 2004, which is an organization designed to support community programs focused on creating opportunities for women and girls.

ERNEST G. NOACK is an assistant professor of education at Western New Mexico University in Silver City, New Mexico. He has also been a public school educator in Washington State.

JEANNIE OAKES is a professor in the Graduate School of Education and Information Studies at the University of California, Los Angeles. She is the author of *Becoming Good American Schools: The Struggle for Civic Virtue in Education Reform* (Jossey-Bass, 1999) and coeditor, with Karen H. Quartz, of *Creating New Educational Communities* (University of Chicago Press, 1995).

RODNEY T. OGAWA is a professor in the School of Education at the University of California, Santa Cruz. Dr. Ogawa is well-known for his research on the organization of schools and the connections between schools and communities.

REECE PETERSON is an associate professor of special education at the University of Nebraska in Lincoln, Nebraska, and vice president of the Council for Children with Behavioral Disorders (CCBD).

SALLY M. REIS is a professor of educational psychology in the School of Education at the University of Connecticut in Storrs, Connecticut. She is the author of *Work Left Undone: Choices and Compromises of Talented Women* (Creative Learning Press, 1998) and coauthor, with Joseph S. Rezulli, of *The Schoolwide Enrichment Model: A How-to Guide for Educational Excellence* (Creative Learning Press, 1997).

LAUREN B. RESNICK is director of the Learning Research and Development Center and a professor of psychology at the University of Pittsburgh. Her many publications include *Discourse, Tools, and Reasoning: Essays on Situated Cognition* (Springer-Verlag, 1998), coedited with Clotilde Pontecorvo and Roger Saljo.

JO SANDERS is a gender equity consultant and director of the Center for Gender Equity Studies. Her articles have appeared in numerous educational periodicals, including published articles on gender equity in *Educational Leadership* and *Phi Delta Kappan.*

MARA SAPON-SHEVIN is a professor of education at Syracuse University and the author of Playing Favorites: Gifted Education and the Disruption of Community (State University of New York Press, 1994).

ALBERT SHANKER (1928–1997) is president of the American Federation of Teachers in Washington, D.C., an organization that works with teachers and other educational employees at the state and local levels in organizing, collective bargaining, research, educational issues, and public relations. A leader in the educational reform movement, he is recognized as the first labor leader elected to the National Academy of Education. He is the author of the Sunday *New York Times* column "Where We Stand."

KENNON M. SHELDON is an assistant professor in the Department of Psychology at the University of Missouri–Columbia.

RUSS SKIBA is director of the Institute for Child Study and an associate professor in the Department of Counseling and Psychology at Indiana University in Bloomington, Indiana.

JAMES D. SLOTTA is the research cognitive science director of the Web-based Integrated Science Environment (WISE) project library in the Graduate School of Education at the University of California, Berkeley. He also codirected the Knowledge Integration Environment (KIE) project at the university. His current research focuses on the design of inquiry activities, online community supports, and teacher professional development approaches. He earned his M.S. in psychology from the University of Massachusetts in 1989 and his Ph.D. in psychology from the University of Pittsburgh in 1996.

TINA M. SMITH is an assistant professor in the Department of Educational Psychology at the University of Florida. Her research interests include temperament and behavioral adjustment of high-risk preschoolers, development of children with prenatal exposure to drugs and alcohol, and school psychology. She holds a Ph.D. from the University of North Carolina, Chapel Hill.

JANICE STREITMATTER is a professor of educational psychology at the University of Arizona in Tucson, Arizona.

ROBERT SYLWESTER is an emeritus professor of education at the University of Oregon. His research focuses on the educational implications of new developments in science and technology, and he is the author of *A Biological Brain in a Cultural Classroom: Applying Biological Research to Classroom Management* (Corwin Press, 2000) and *Emotion and Attention: How Our Brain Determines What's Important* (Zephyr Press, 1998).

AMY STUART WELLS is an associate professor in the Graduate School of Education and Information Studies at the University of California, Los Angeles. She is the author of *Stepping Over the Color Line: African-American Students in White Suburban Schools* (Yale University Press, 1999).

KEVIN G. WELNER is an associate professor of education at the University of Colorado at Boulder. He has written extensively about educational policy and legislative issues that affect education. He is the author of *Legal Rights, Local Wrongs: When Community Control Collides with Educational Equity* (SUNY Press, 2001).

MARK WINDSCHITL is an assistant professor of curriculum and instruction in the College of Education at the University of Washington in Seattle, Washington. He is coauthor of *Cultures of Curriculum* (Lawrence Erlbaum, 1999).

CHARLES H. WOLFGANG is a professor of early childhood education at Florida State University. His research interests include cognitive process, discipline models, early childhood education, and teacher education. He holds a Ph.D. from the University of Pittsburgh.

STEVE ZEMELMAN directs the Center for City Schools at National-Louis University in Chicago, Illinois. He has coauthored several books on language and education, including *A Community of Writers* (Heinemann, 1987) and *Best Practice: New Standards for Teaching in America's Schools* (Heinemann, 1998).

NAOMI ZIGMOND is a professor in and chair of the Department of Instruction and Learning at the University of Pittsburgh, where she has been teaching since 1970. She is a former editor of *Exceptional Children,* and her research won her the Research Award from the Council for Exceptional Children in 1997. She has written a number of articles for such journals as *Phi Delta Kappan* and *Journal of Special Education.*

Index

poverty's impact on test scores, 96
praise, 107–15, 171, 186–87
press coverage. *See* media coverage
prevention of violence, 370–71
Principles and Indicators for Student Assessment Systems, 326
procedural learning, 174–75
prodigies, multiple intelligence view of, 219
Professional Development Schools, 298
Proposition 63 (California), 48
Proposition 227 (California), 40, 45
Prospect School, 332
Prozac, 105
prudence, 122
public transportation, impact on school choice in Germany, 387
pullout programs, 72–73, 81
punishments: to enforce standards, 239–46; in zero-tolerance policies, 353–62, 363–71

racial minorities. *See* minorities
Ramirez, J. David, 37–38
reading, whole language approach debated, 272–79, 281–86
Realschule, 386
reform. *See* educational reform
Regents diplomas, 88–89, 90–91
Regents exams, 88, 89, 90
Regular Education Initiative, 73
reinforcement: effectiveness debated, 182–92, 195–200; to enforce standards, 239–46
Reis, Sally M., on ability grouping, 28–31
religious values, 123, 277
remediation, 73, 74
Resnick, Lauren B., on standards, 233–38
resource room model, 71, 72
rewards: in character education, 130; to enforce standards, 239–46; use in early childhood education, 185–88
Right Start program, 221
risk taking, in mixed- versus single-gender classes, 9, 10–11
Rockville Centre School District, 88–91
Roland Park Elementary/Middle School, 253–54, 257
Rosenshine-Stevens studies, 168
Roxbury Latin School, 132
Ryan, Kevin, 132

Sanders, Jo, on gender equity, 15–19
Sapon-Shevin, Mara, on full inclusion, 61–70
savants, multiple intelligence view of, 220–21
scaffolding, 154
school psychologists, 293, 296–98
school shootings, 365, 368, 370
schools of education, character education strategies for, 125–26

science education, 15–19, 310–15
science literacy, 314–15
screening for troubled students, 370
seatwork, 173
segregation: of ability groups, 23–24; of students with disabilities, 64–65
self-confidence: girls' demonstrated lack, 5; praise and, 186–87; single-gender class effects on, 11–13
self-control, 132–33
self-determination theory, 240–42
self-esteem, 102–6, 107–15
self-referenced evaluation, 327
serotonin, 103, 104–6
shadow plays, 317
Shanker, Al: as inclusion critic, 68, 69; on zero-tolerance policies, 353–62
Sheldon, Kennon M., on standards, 239–47
single-gender classes, 4–13
skepticism, 134–35
Skiba, Russ, on zero-tolerance policies, 363–71
Slotta, James D., on technology in schools, 310–15
small group instruction, 78–79
Smith, Tina M., on reinforcement, 182–92
social atmosphere, 171
social hierarchies, 103–6
social reinforcers, 186–87, 191, 199
Sonderschule, 387
spatial intelligence, 220
special education: early childhood, 183–84; in Europe, 386, 387; full inclusion debated, 61–70, 71–82
spiritual intelligence, 209
Stallings studies, 166–67
standardized testing: impact on motivation and instruction, 243–47; performance assessment alternatives, 331–35. *See also* tests
Standardized Testing and Reporting (STAR) examination, 56
standards: effects on motivation debated, 233–38, 239–47; reconciling constructivist approach with, 155–56
standards-referenced evaluation, 327–28
stories, 175
Streitmatter, Janice, on single-gender classes, 4–13
Structured English Immersion, 37–43
students with disabilities: discipline policies for, 361; European programs for, 386, 387; full inclusion debated, 61–70, 71–82; pressure on teaching practices, 183
subordinate class, 46
success, celebrating, 236
successful examples, as fallacies, 95
suicide rates, 379
suspensions, 366–67, 368–69
Sylwester, Robert, on self-esteem and aggression, 102–6
synapse formation, 260–61